MW01621010

Ruth Fine
with contributions by
Mary Lee Corlett,
Nnamdi Elleh,
Jacqueline Francis,
Abdul Goler,
and Sarah Kennel

National Gallery of Art,
Washington,
in association with
Harry N. Abrams, Inc.,
Publishers

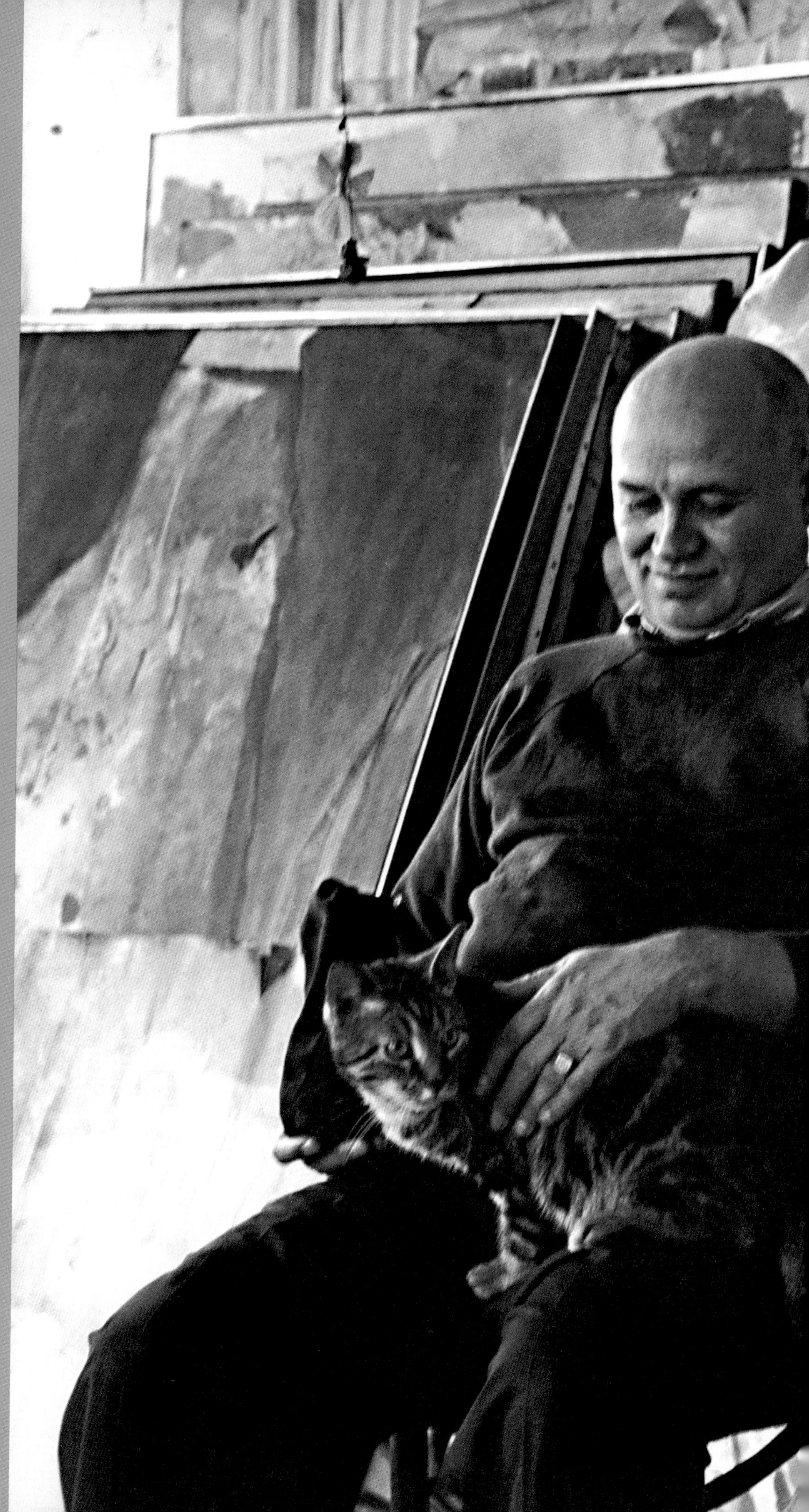

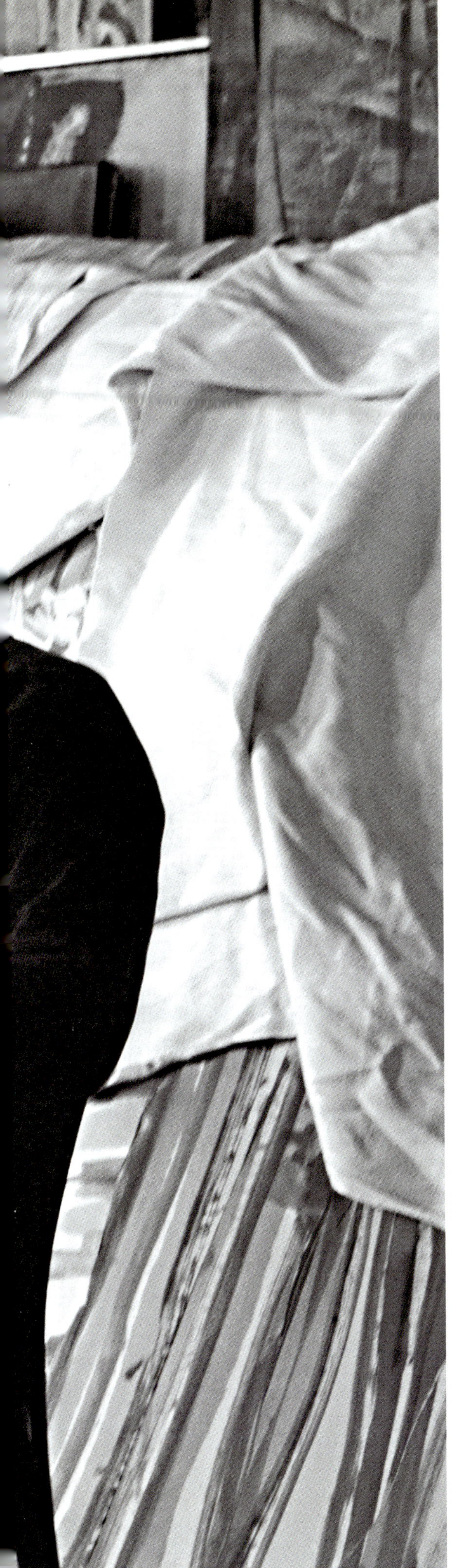

THE ART OF

Romare Bearden

The exhibition is made possible with generous support from AT&T

This exhibition was organized by the National Gallery of Art, Washington

EXHIBITION DATES

National Gallery of Art,
September 14, 2003–January 4, 2004

San Francisco Museum of Modern Art,
February 7–May 16, 2004

Dallas Museum of Art,
June 20–September 12, 2004

Whitney Museum of American Art, New York,
October 14, 2004–January 9, 2005

High Museum of Art, Atlanta,
January 29–April 24, 2005

Produced by the Publishing Office, National Gallery of Art, Washington

Editor in Chief Judy Metro

Senior Editor Karen Sagstetter

Designer Wendy Schleicher Smith

Production Manager Chris Vogel

Editorial Assistant Amanda Mister Sparrow

Typeset in Scala and Scala Sans by Duke & Company, Devon, Pennsylvania, and printed on DacoStern, 150 gsm by Grafisches Zentrum Drucktechnik, Ditzingen-Heimerdingen, Germany

Library of Congress Cataloging-in-Publication Data

Bearden, Romare, 1911–1988.
The art of Romare Bearden / Ruth Fine with contributions by Mary Lee Corlett ... [et al.].

p. cm.

"Exhibition dates: National Gallery of Art, September 14, 2003–January 4, 2004 and other venues."
Includes bibliographical references and index.

ISBN 0-89468-302-0 (pbk. : alk. paper)—
ISBN 0-8109-4640-8 (hardcover : alk. paper)

1. Bearden, Romare, 1911–1988—Exhibitions. I. Fine, Ruth, 1941– II. Corlett, Mary Lee. III. National Gallery of Art (U.S.) IV. Title.

N6537.B4A4 2003
709'.2—dc21 2003011001

The hardcover edition is published by the National Gallery of Art, Washington in association with Harry N. Abrams, Incorporated, New York.

Harry N. Abrams, Incorporated, New York
100 Fifth Avenue
New York, N.Y. 10011
www.abramsbooks.com
Abrams is a subsidiary of
La Martinière Groupe

10 9 8 7 6 5 4 3 2 1

Front: Romare Bearden, *Profile/Part II, The Thirties: Artist with Painting and Model,* 1981, detail (no. 141). Glen and Lynn Tobias

Back: Romare Bearden in New York, mid-1970s. Estate of Romare Bearden, courtesy of the Romare Bearden Foundation, New York. Photograph by Nancy Crampton

Back flap: Romare Bearden, *Untitled (Girl in a Pond),* 1972 (no. 99). Judy and Patrick Diamond

Title page: Romare Bearden, Canal Street, New York, 1966. Estate of Romare Bearden, courtesy of the Romare Bearden Foundation, New York. Photograph by Paul Waters

page vi: Romare and Nanette Bearden in front of the Hispanic Society of America, New York, 1958. Estate of Romare Bearden, courtesy of the Romare Bearden Foundation, New York

pages 2–3: Nanette and Romare Bearden in his studio, New York, 1966. Estate of Romare Bearden, courtesy of the Romare Bearden Foundation, New York

pages 138–139: Romare Bearden working on a version of *Conversation II* in his Long Island City Studio, early 1980s

pages 156–157: Romare Bearden at the Izaka Zango Gallery, New York, late 1970s

pages 172–173: Romare Bearden, Canal Street, New York, 1976. Estate of Romare Bearden, courtesy of the Romare Bearden Foundation, New York

pages 190–191: Romare Bearden at the Art Garden Gallery, Venice, California, early 1980s

pages 212–213: Romare Bearden in St. Martin, 1980

CONTENTS

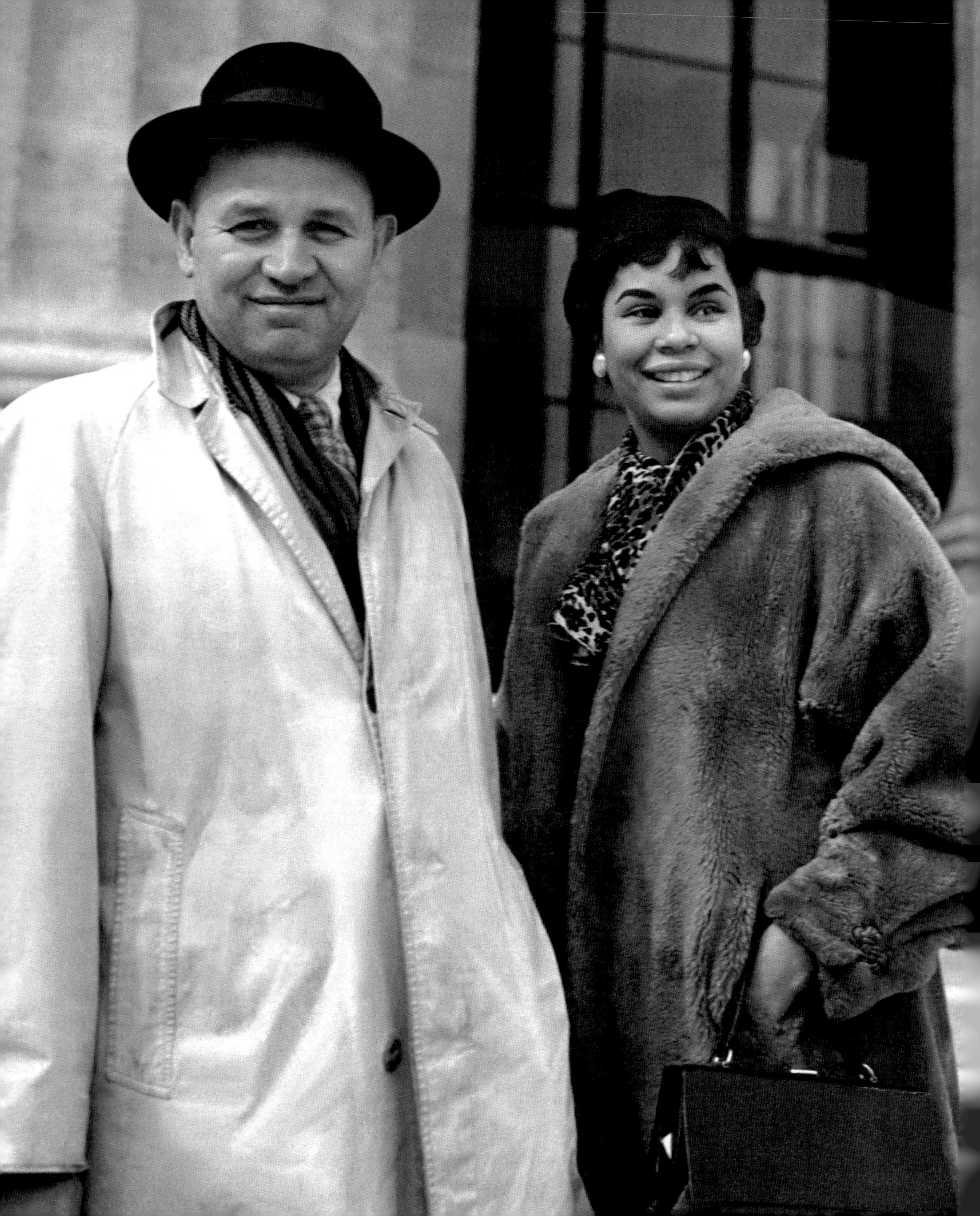

The Art of Romare Bearden celebrates one of the most fascinating and challenging accomplishments of late twentieth-century American art. Best known for his collages, Bearden was an artist of extraordinary invention in many media. This survey of his achievements over almost half a century includes many selections that reveal the experimental evolution of his collages, but also examples of his paintings in oil and gouache; watercolors and drawings; photographs, monotypes, and edition prints; designs for record album covers, book illustrations, and the ballet; and the artist's only known sculpture.

Bearden's probing curiosity and the depth of his humanistic concerns are reflected in the subjects of his art, from quotidian experiences in the northern and southern United States and the Caribbean, to classic biblical and literary motifs. While reflecting the African-American community into which he was born, the universality of Bearden's visual concerns offers a complex world-overview, fraught with contradictions and problems yet filled with beauty and hope.

Shortly after Bearden's death in 1988, the artist's wife, Nanette, visited the National Gallery of Art, seeking advice on the care and preservation of her husband's work. Mrs. Bearden met with Ruth Fine, the Gallery's curator of special projects in modern art, whose in-depth study of Bearden's art began at that time, sowing the seeds for this exhibition. In planning *The Art of Romare Bearden* Ruth Fine especially sought works from private collections. As a result, we are pleased to offer our visitors the unusual privilege of seeing many special treasures that have rarely if ever been on public view. With slight variations, viewers of the show at its subsequent venues, the San Francisco Museum of Modern Art, the Dallas Museum of Art, the Whitney Museum of American Art, New York, and the High Museum of Art, Atlanta, will likewise enjoy this exceptional opportunity, and it is our pleasure to share the exhibition with them.

We are extremely grateful for the early and generous support of AT&T that facilitated the research, organization, and national tour of *The Art of Romare Bearden*.

In addition we acknowledge the gracious assistance of the Board of Directors of the Romare Bearden Foundation: Marie Rohan, chairperson, and Tallal ELBoushi, co-chair; Diedra Harris-Kelley, secretary; Dorothy Rohan Dow, treasurer; Joseph Gumbs; Ron Jackson; Priscilla Johnson; Robert O'Meally; and E.T. Williams, as well as the Foundation's former executive director, Joan Sandler.

We also thank Derek Walcott for his gracious permission to include his poem, "To Romare Bearden," in this volume.

Most important to the success of any exhibition are the lenders. Listed elsewhere in this volume, they have graciously parted with their beloved works by Romare Bearden for a lengthy period of time. We thank them heartily for their enthusiastic interest in our exhibition. Many lenders were personal friends of the artist, and their memories have greatly enhanced the history recounted in this book. For those contributions, too, we are extremely grateful.

Earl A. Powell III
Director

FOREWORD

I am most grateful to Earl A. Powell III, director of the National Gallery of Art, for his constant and enthusiastic support for *The Art of Romare Bearden* from its inception. I echo the appreciation expressed in his Foreword to our lenders and to AT&T, whose generosity has made the exhibition possible. Alan Shestack, the Gallery's deputy director and chief curator; D. Dodge Thompson, chief of exhibitions; Mark Leithauser, chief of design and installation; and Jeffrey Weiss, curator and head of the department of modern and contemporary art, have offered wise counsel.

All of the contributors to the catalogue are indebted to the directors of the Romare Bearden Foundation acknowledged in the director's Foreword, but especially to Diedra Harris-Kelley, who located both art and documents for which we were searching; and Sheila Rohan, who responded to our many inquiries.

Previous Bearden scholarship has been essential to our undertaking as is apparent in this volume's endnotes. We are especially grateful to Mary Schmidt Campbell, David C. Driskell, Sharon F. Patton, Richard Powell, and Lowery Stokes Sims. Authors Carroll J. Greene, Jr., Myron Schwartzman, and M. Bunch Washington were exceedingly generous in sharing various materials in their possession. Indeed, virtually everyone contacted for assistance during our research has been extraordinarily gracious. For providing access to their extensive files on the artist we thank Jane and Raphael Bernstein, Ann and Nicolas Ekstrom, Linda and Walter O. Evans, Bernice and Jack Fein, Russell L. Goings, Jr., June Kelly, Mary and Jerald Melberg, Albert Murray, and Phyllis Ross.

We also are indebted to Billie Allen, Peg Alston, Emma Amos, Will Barnet, Avis Berman, the late Robert Blackburn, Luca Bonetti, Kathy Caraccio, James Craig, Allan Edmunds, Akosua Barthwell Evans, Garth Fagan, Reginald Gammon, Sam Gilliam, Laura Grosch and Herb Jackson, Harry Henderson, Earle Hyman, Paul R. Jones, Alitash Kebede, Paul and Laura Keene, Timothy Keny, Mohammad O. Khalil, Samella Lewis, Richard A. Long, Richard Maschal, Wynton Marsalis, Richard Mayhew, Mary Anne Rose (especially for the recorded interview she conducted on our behalf in Sweden with her husband Herbert Gentry), Alex Rosenberg, Michael Rosenfeld and halley k harrisburg, Peter Selz, Merton Simpson, Ed Spriggs, Barrie Stavis, Frank Stewart, Lou Stovall, Barbara Wallace, Marga and Sidney Wallach, John Walker, Joan Washburn, Jesse Washington, and Carl Worth.

We are grateful to colleagues who have facilitated our loan requests. At public institutions— African American Museum in Philadelphia: Harry Harrison, Beverly Kendall, Judith Mueller, and Richard Watson; City of Berkeley: Mary Anne Merker; Bryn Mawr College, Pennsylvania: Carol W. Campbell; Carnegie Museum of Art, Pittsburgh: Richard Armstrong, Ellen Baxter, Elizabeth Hansen, Elizabeth Thomas; Cleveland Museum of Art: Katharine Lee Reid, Kenneth Bé, Tom Hinson; Van Every/Smith Galleries, Davidson College, North Carolina: Brad Thomas; Hammonds House Galleries, Atlanta: Cathy Watson; High Museum of Art, Atlanta: Michael Shapiro, Carrie Przybilla, Amy Simon; Hirshhorn Museum and Sculpture Garden, Smithsonian Institution, Washington, D.C.: Ned Rifkin, Phyllis Rosenzweig, Judith Zilczer; Honolulu Academy of Arts: Stephen Little, Jennifer Saville; Hood Museum of Art, Dartmouth College: Derrick Cartwright, Bart Thurber; Milwaukee Art Museum: David Gordon; Mint Museum of Art, Charlotte: Philip E. Kline, Charles Mo; Museum of Art, Rhode Island School of Design: Lora Urbanelli; Museum of Fine Arts, Boston: Malcolm Rogers, Stephanie Stepanek; Smithsonian American Art Museum: Elizabeth Broun, Joann Moser, Denise D. Wamaling; Spelman College Museum of Fine Art, Atlanta: Andrea Barnwell, Kara Lyn Anderson; The Studio Museum in Harlem: Lowery Stokes Sims, Thelma Golden, Anne Kovach; Tougaloo College Art Collections, Mississippi: Beverly Wade Hogan, Susan McClintock, Bruce O'Hara, Ronald Schnell; University of Michigan, Clements Library: John C. Dann, Brian Leigh Dunnigan, John Harriman; Yale University Art Gallery: Jock Reynolds.

With regard to the coordination of loans from private collectors we thank: for Fanny Ellison, John Silberman Associates, New York; for Donald Byrd, Belena S. Chapp, Director of Museums, University of Delaware; for Robert and Faye Davidson, Dennis Powell; for Garth Fagan, Deborah Ronnen Fine Arts; for Stéphane Janssen, Ann Sanchez; for Robert L. Johnson Art Acquisitions, Naomi Duckenfield and Linda C. Simmons; for the Estate of Reginald F. Lewis, Bimal Amin; for Wynton Marsalis, Genevieve Stewart, Jazz at Lincoln Center; for the Manoogian Collection, Jonathan Bose; for Eileen Harris Norton and Peter Norton, Kelley Barry, Susan Cahan, and Gwen Hill.

Jean Frye, whom I met at the Charlotte/ Mecklenburg County Public Library, volunteered to assist us, and she has been a gracious and invaluable ally. In addition, for various assistance we thank ACA Galleries: Doreen and Jeffrey Bergen; Albany Museum of Art: Joanne Lue; Albright-Knox Art Gallery: Claire Schneider; American Academy of Arts and Letters: Kathy Kienholz, archivist; Art Students League: Stephanie Cassidy, archivist; Brooklyn Museum library and archives staff; Charlotte/Mecklenburg County Public Library: Chris Bates and Shelia Baumgarner; Adger W. Cowans; Richard L. Feigen & Co.; Essie Green Galleries: Sherman Edmiston and

ACKNOWLEDGMENTS

Dejáy Byrd; Hatch-Billops Archive, Inc.: Camille Billops; New York University, Boobst Library, Division of Student Life Publications; the staff at the Schomburg Center for Research in Black Culture, New York Public Library, especially Tammi Lawson; Shaw Family Archives staff, especially Meta and Edith Shaw; Wendell Street Gallery, Cambridge, Massachusetts: Constance Brown and Jane Shapiro; Whitney Museum of American Art library and archives staff.

At the National Gallery, my research associate, Mary Lee Corlett, has made invaluable contributions to the exhibition and book at every stage. I am also indebted to Jacqueline Francis, Department of the History of Art, University of Michigan, for her consistently helpful counsel. Dr. Francis' participation and that of other contributors to this volume began with their tenure at the National Gallery either as predoctoral fellows at the Center for Advanced Studies in the Visual Arts, or as interns; we have worked together as a team, with their assistance continuing after they moved on to other positions: Rocío Aranda-Alvarado, associate curator, Jersey City Museum of Art; Nnamdi Elleh, College of Design, Architecture, Art, and Planning, University of Cincinnati; Abdul Goler, independent researcher; Carmenita Higginbotham, University of Michigan and Center for Advanced Studies in the Visual Arts; Sarah Kennel, Department of Photographs, National Gallery of Art. I also thank intern Felicity Colman for her early assistance.

Other Gallery staff essential to the exhibition and catalogue are Jennifer Cipriano, Jennifer Overton, and Alicia Thomas in the exhibitions office as well as Susan Arensberg, Carroll Moore, Lynn Matheny, and Michelle Wilkinson in the Department of Exhibition Programs. Sally Freitag Michelle Fondas, and Melissa Stegeman oversaw registrarial concerns. From the conservation division, Jay Krueger (paintings), Julia Burke (textiles), Shelley Fletcher, Yoonjoo Strumfels and Judith Walsh (paper), Connie McCabe (photographs), Mervin Richard, Bethann Heinbaugh, Hugh Phibbs, Virginia Ritchie, and Steve Wilcox (exhibitions) were invaluable as always. Lynn Russell, Faya Causey, Barbara Moore, and Heidi Hinish have coordinated a wide range of related education programs. We are indebted to Deborah Ziska, chief press officer, who on a daily basis has shared my enthusiasm for this exhibition, and her staff, whose efforts have brought Bearden and the Gallery to a wider audience. Christine Myers, her predecessor Sandy Masur, and the staff of the corporate relations office secured funding that made the show possible. We are grateful to Elizabeth Croog, the Gallery's secretary-general counsel and her staff, especially Nancy Breuer and Lara Levinson; Genevra Higginson, assistant to the director for special events, who has provided much assistance and support, and her staff; Dean Beasom and Bob Grove and their staffs in photographic and digital services; and Carol W. Kelley in the director's office.

We thank Carlotta Owens, involved with the exhibition during its early stages, as were Ava Lambert and Charles Ritchie, all in modern prints and drawings. Thanks also is due our associates in special projects in modern art, Renée Maurer and Laili Nasr, who have brought to our attention materials related to Bearden they noted in the course of their work on Mark Rothko. A special thank you goes to our colleagues in the library whose extraordinary assistance under pressure facilitated this volume's bibliography: Neal Turtell, Ted Dalziel, Lamia Doumato, Roberta Geier, Frances Lederer, Thomas McGill, and Maria Sampang.

The handsome installation of *The Art of Romare Bearden* was coordinated by Gordon Anson, William Bowser, Mari Forsell, Barbara Keyes, and Lisa Farrell. It is the book, however, that becomes the lasting record of an exhibition, and for their contributions we thank Judy Metro, editor in chief; Karen Sagstetter, senior editor, for her thoughtful coordination of a complex project; Ira Bartfield, Sara Sanders-Buell, and Mariah Shay. In particular we are grateful to Wendy Schleicher Smith for her handsome and sympathetic design.

Larry Day remains my intellectual guide and the extensive library he formed shares uncanny parallels with that assembled by Romare Bearden. It was of immense importance to this project.

No single exhibition can include all of the important works made by an artist so masterful and prolific as Bearden. In addition to those mentioned above, I visited many institutional and private collections and dealers too numerous to cite individually. I am, however, grateful to everyone whose hospitality aided our research and to the many people who contacted us regarding works by Bearden that the limitations of our exhibition schedule prevented me from viewing.

Despite this plethora of assistance, data about Bearden's life and work remain rife with discrepancies and gaps. Thus we end this project with questions more numerous than those with which we began. We hope, however, that our work will encourage others to probe further into Romare Bearden's life and the extraordinary body of work he created during the middle years of the twentieth century.

Ruth Fine
Curator of Special Projects in Modern Art

Mr. and Mrs. Louis K. Adler

African American Museum in Philadelphia

Billie Allen

Allen Memorial Art Museum, Oberlin College, Oberlin, Ohio

Peg Alston

John P. Axelrod

Harvey and Phyllis Baumann

Merrill C. Berman

Jane and Raphael Bernstein

Juliette Bethea

Evelyn N. Boulware

Frederick L. Brown

Bryn Mawr College, Bryn Mawr, Pennsylvania

Donald Byrd

Carnegie Museum of Art, Pittsburgh

City of Berkeley, California

Clements Library, University of Michigan, Ann Arbor

The Cleveland Museum of Art

Dr. and Mrs. Mark Couture

Robert & Faye Davidson, Los Angeles, California

Judy and Patrick Diamond

Professor and Mrs. David C. Driskell

Mr. and Mrs. Nicolas H. Ekstrom

Ekstrom & Ekstrom, Inc., New York

Fanny Ellison

Estate of Reginald F. Lewis

Estate of Romare Bearden

Dr. and Mrs. Walter O. Evans

The Walter O. Evans Foundation for Art and Literature

Garth Fagan

James D. Fishel and Barbara L. Micale

Herbert Gentry and Mary Anne Rose

Priscilla T. Grace

Laura Grosch and Herb Jackson

David A. Hagelstein

Hammonds House Galleries, Atlanta

halley k harrisburg and Michael Rosenfeld

James R. Haynes

Harry Henderson

High Museum of Art, Atlanta

Grant Hill

Hirshhorn Museum and Sculpture Garden, Smithsonian Institution, Washington

Melvin Holmes

Honolulu Academy of Arts, Hawaii

Hood Museum of Art, Dartmouth College

Mr. and Mrs. Douglas Houchens

LENDERS TO THE EXHIBITION

Earle Hyman

Paul and Karen Izenberg

Stéphane Janssen

Marian B. Javits

Robert L. Johnson

Harmon and Harriet Kelley

Rowan Khaleel

Jack Krumholz

Elisabeth M. and William M. Landes

Stan and Marguerite Lathan

Keith Lee and Lori Andochick

Richard A. Long

Manoogian Collection

Wynton Marsalis

Yvonne and Richard McCracken

Raymond J. McGuire

Michael Rosenfeld Gallery

Milwaukee Art Museum

Mint Museum of Art, Charlotte, North Carolina

David H. Moore

Albert Murray

Museum of Art, Rhode Island School of Design

Museum of Fine Arts, Boston

National Gallery of Art, Washington

Eileen Harris Norton

Peter Norton

Private collections

Philip J. and Suzanne Schiller

Smithsonian American Art Museum, Washington

Ann and Harold Sorgenti

Spelman College Museum of Fine Art, Atlanta

Frank Stewart

The Studio Museum in Harlem

Stephen and Francine Taylor

Thelma Harris Galleries

John and Norma Thompson

Glen and Lynn Tobias

Tougaloo College Art Collections, Tougaloo, Mississippi

Van Every/Smith Galleries, Davidson College, Davidson, North Carolina

George and Joyce Wein

Yale University Art Gallery, New Haven

Beverly Zimmerman

To Romare Bearden

DEREK WALCOTT

How you have gotten it! It's all here, all right.
The lean, long black hand of the night
has swirled the cut throat of the cockerel
of daybreak, and the flecks of its blood splatter
the hills and the sacred ground
where the chalk-circles and the spiked diagrams
are drawn on the Loa's ground.
Dawn bleeds without a sound.
In all religions sacrifices matter,
but to these rituals we ascribe malign reasons,
and primitive dreams, but as was the lamb
to Isaac, the ram to Abraham, all tribes have laid
on the threshold of heaven, cocks, ewes, horned rams
to the force that has made the fountain of the blood
in which we are born, and the harvest of our mortal seasons,
for a shadow comes towards us all, with its clean blade.

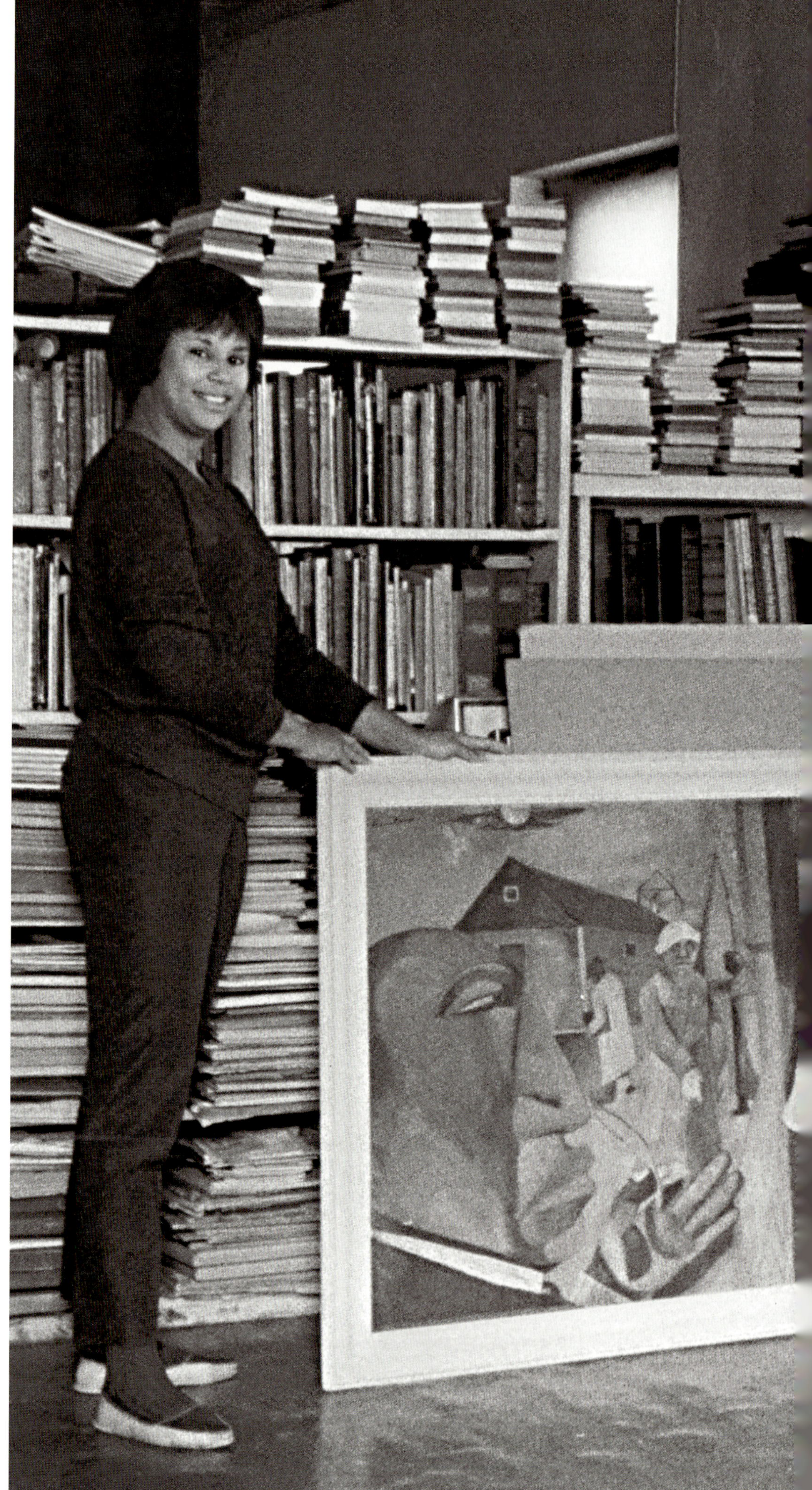

Romare Bearden: The Spaces Between

RUTH FINE

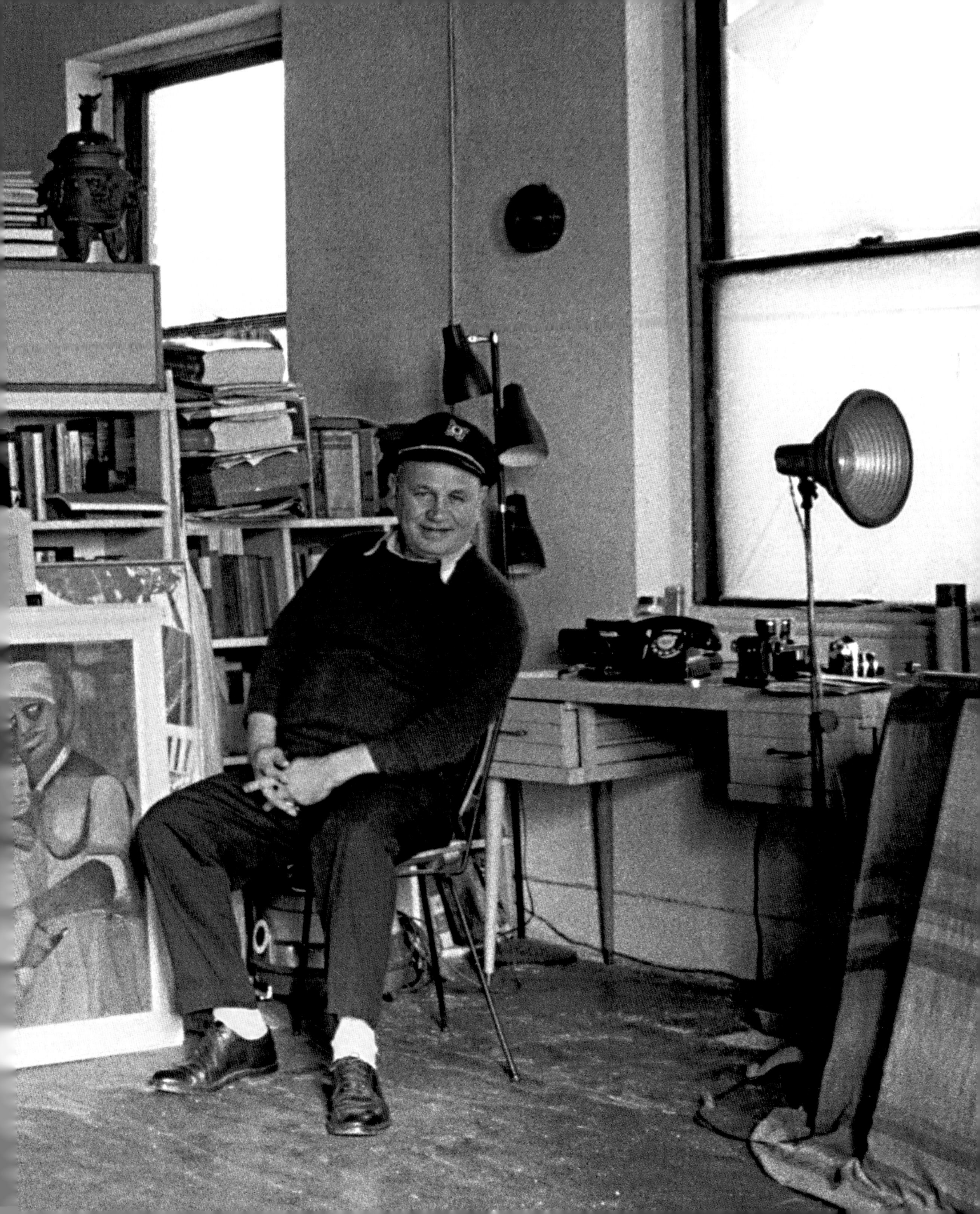

Romare Bearden's large and diverse oeuvre, numbering thousands of objects in many media, reveals the artist's remarkable curiosity and intelligence as well as his fervent desire to defy the limits of artistic and cultural categorization. An African American by birth who enjoyed considerable professional success, Bearden nonetheless encountered the prejudices of a fearful world. Facing head-on the demands that situation presented, he responded by creating a powerful body of work set within his own cultural context that is fully attentive to his understanding of universal motifs. One great legacy of Bearden's art is its insight that what we share as a global community is equal in both interest and importance to what makes each of us unique. He achieved this by embracing themes and practices from diverse times and places and imbuing them with an imaginative character and physical presence that is distinctively his own. In the materiality of his expansive expression, method and message become one.[1]

Romare Bearden was born to (Richard) Howard and Bessye Johnson Bearden, in Charlotte, North Carolina, the seat of Mecklenburg County. About that there has been no controversy. The question of when this blessed event took place, however, has engendered conflicting answers for many years. Throughout much of his lifetime Bearden's birthdate was most often given as 2 September 1914, but occasionally as the same day in 1912.[2] Since his death scholars have published accounts of a baptismal record in the registry of the Episcopal Church of St. Michael's and All Angels in Charlotte dated to 19 November 1911 (fig. 1) and a Mecklenburg County certificate of birth dated to 2 September 1912. Both documents exist.[3] However, the birth certificate is actually a "Delayed Certificate of Birth Registration," filed in Charlotte on 19 March 1949. At that time it was certified that no prior birth certificate for Bearden had been located. The 1912 date on the certificate filed almost forty years after the fact was based on an insurance record from 16 July 1927, an army enlistment certificate of 7 May 1942, and an affidavit from Bearden's father, the earliest of these dating from more than a decade later than the baptism.[4] We are unlikely to learn why a 1912 birthdate was established, but the probability that the church would have been more concerned than the state with the birth of a son in the Bearden family in either 1911 or 1912 suggests the 1911 baptismal record as the most reasonable documentation of Fred Romare Harry/Howard's birth.[5]

Bearden's paternal family was among the African-American middle class that had established itself following the Civil War in the growing commercial city of Charlotte, where the railroad and cotton industries were thriving.[6] His grandfather had died before Bearden was born, but he was close to his grandmother, Cattie, and her parents Henry B. and Rosa Kennedy. After moving north with his parents, Bearden spent many vacations in Charlotte until about 1925; by that time his great-grandparents had died and Cattie had remarried, moving with her Methodist minister husband, Charles Cummings, to Lutherville, Maryland, a small town near Baltimore to which Bearden also paid occasional childhood visits.[7] The Kennedys, whose photograph was a fixture in Bearden's studio (fig. 2), were property owners not only of their own home and general store, but also of two adjacent houses in which they accommodated renters (fig. 3). Among a small group of citizens listed in a 1915 publication, *Colored Charlotte,* H. B. and Mrs. Kennedy were described as "former servants of Dr. Joseph Wilson the father of President Woodrow Wilson.... Mr. Kennedy... in the United States Mail Service... resigned some years ago and is now doing business in the city.[8] Bearden's maternal grandmother and step-grandfather, Carrie and George T. Banks, were additional influential forces in his life. They too were propertied, their boardinghouse serving

1

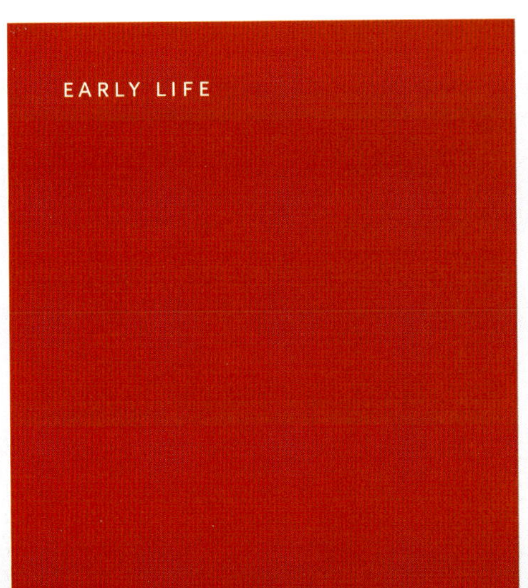

figure 1
Baptismal Registry, dated 19 November 1911, Episcopal Church of St. Michael's and All Angels, showing Bearden's date of birth as 2 September 1911. Mrs. Anna Alston, Wm. H. Perry, and A. Myron Cochran are listed as witnesses.

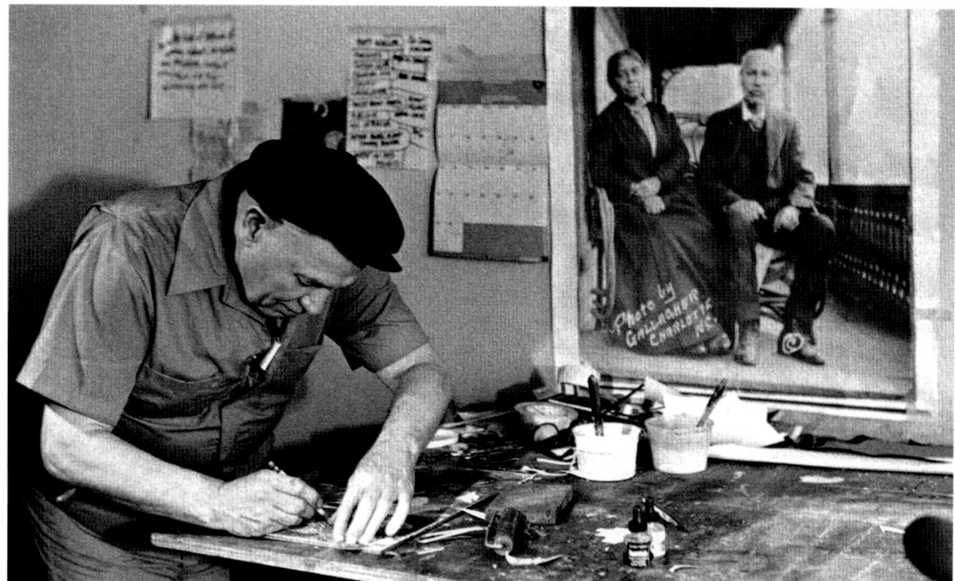

2

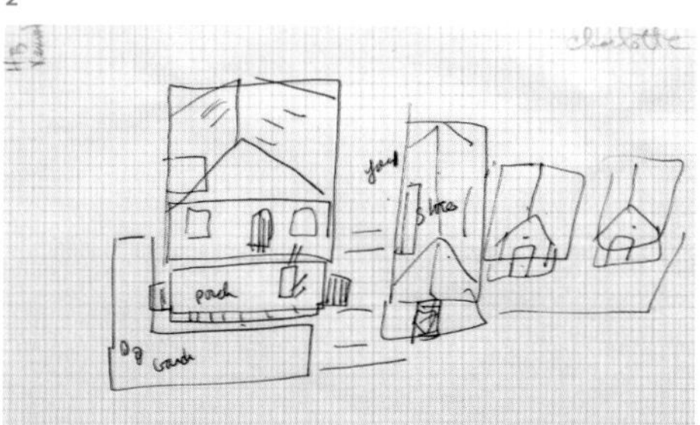

3

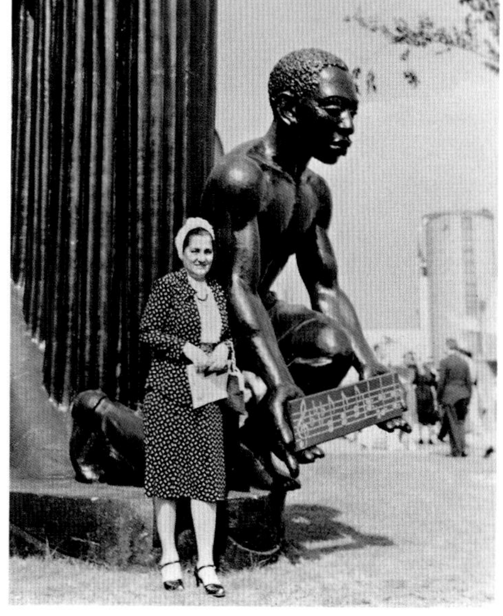

4

as a Pittsburgh, Pennsylvania, haven for migrant steel mill workers from the south.

Both of Bearden's parents had attended college: Bessye (fig. 4) started at Hartshorn Memorial College in Richmond, Virginia, and graduated from the Virginia Normal and Industrial Institute in Petersburg; Howard attended Bennett College in Greensboro, North Carolina (which became a women's college in the 1920s). By the time of Bearden's birth, however, menacing Jim Crow laws were causing life to be increasingly difficult for Charlotte's African-American families, even successful ones such as his. Around 1914, Howard, Bessye, and Romare participated in the Great Migration north, moving to New York City, which remained Bearden's base for the rest of his life.[9] After an unsettled period during the teens, the Beardens became prominent members of the Harlem community. Bessye, a social and political activist, was the New York correspondent for the *Chicago Defender,* a major African-American newspaper of the period (for which Langston Hughes later wrote extensively).[10] Howard, a less visible figure about whom few details are known, worked as a sanitation inspector for the New York Health Department, played the piano in his off-hours, and, according to Bearden's close friend, writer Ralph Ellison, "was a teller of tales," an ability he passed on to his son.[11]

In the Beardens' apartment at 154 West 131 Street family life was centered in the intellectual, artistic, and political mainstream of the Harlem Renaissance. Their circle included writers Hughes, Countee Cullen, and George Schuyler; musicians Duke Ellington, Thomas Wright "Fats" Waller, and his lyricist Andy Razaf; actor, activist, and athlete Paul Robeson; William Edward Burghardt Du Bois, the first African American to receive

figure 2
Romare Bearden in his Long Island City Studio with a photograph of his Kennedy great-grandparents, c. 1980

figure 3
Romare Bearden, *H. B. Kennedy's House and Yard in Charlotte* [with his store and rental houses], 1985, ink on graph paper. Mint Museum of Art, Charlotte, North Carolina; gift of Myron Schwartzman 2002.63

figure 4
Bessye Bearden at the 1940 World's Fair in front of Augusta Savage's sculpture *Harp,* also called *Lift Ev'ry Voice and Sing.* Bessye Bearden Portrait Collection, Schomburg Center for Research in Black Culture, New York Public Library, Astor, Lenox, and Tilden Foundation

figure 5
Romare Bearden, Cover, *Opportunity: A Journal of Negro Life,* March, 1932. Reprinted by permission of the National Urban League

a Ph.D. from Harvard University, a founder of the National Association for the Advancement of Colored People (NAACP), and the editor of the organization's magazine *The Crisis* for more than two decades; Mary McLeod Bethune, the founder-president of the National Council of Negro Women and vice president of the NAACP; and Dr. Aubré de L. Maynard, the first African-American surgical intern at Harlem Hospital.

Attending public institutions, Bearden spent his primary school years in New York (possibly attending fourth grade in Pittsburgh) and his high school years in both New York and Pittsburgh where he lived with his grandparents in their boardinghouse. His lifelong friend Harry Henderson recalled that Bearden had told him he preferred Pittsburgh to New York during those years, that in New York you needed to engage in the politics of teenage gangs. The young man also liked being part of after-dinner sessions on the Pittsburgh boardinghouse steps where recently arrived mill workers would sit and "tell stories about down-home in the South" that Bearden so loved.[12]

With the United States entering the Great Depression Bearden started college at Lincoln University in suburban Philadelphia, taking courses in Greek, Spanish, biology, rhetoric, and trigonometry. His course of study changed radically when he transferred to Boston University (BU) after the academic year of 1929–30. Bearden's autobiographical notes throughout his life omit any record of formal art education except for classes with George Grosz at the Art Students League after his college years. As it turns out, however, the four semesters he spent at BU (1930–1932) followed by five at New York University (NYU, 1932–1935) were dominated by courses in art, not mathematics, which he generally cited as his major. According to BU records, Bearden was enrolled in the School of Education Art Department, where his courses included Painting, Design, and Color as well as Cast Drawing, Perspective, Drawing of Ornament, Freehand Drawing, and Art History. At NYU, he also registered for an art education major; his studies included Figure Drawing, Water Color Painting, Linoleum Block Printing (listed as a Craft), Mechanical Drawing, Lettering, Appreciation of Art, several literature courses, and a number directed to education, including Teaching of Art and Observation of Teaching in High Schools. He received a degree in education in 1935.[13] Bearden had an interest in mathematics that he sustained throughout his life, and at his mother's behest he undoubtedly gave consideration to a career in medicine, as suggested by his courses at Lincoln University. Indeed, given Bessye Bearden's strong desires for her son's future, it seems possible that his clandestine pursuit and later refusal to acknowledge his extensive formal art training initially were precipitated by his desire to avoid either hurting her or incurring her wrath, or both.

Bearden was a cartoonist for university journals in both Boston and New York. During 1934 he was art editor for NYU's monthly *The Medley*, and his extensive student research on the history of the cartoon as a form of ridicule is documented in an untitled essay written about 1933–34.[14] His survey begins with the ancient Egyptians, Greeks, and Romans, then touches on figures on facades of Gothic and Romanesque cathedrals and from the era of Martin Luther, crediting the origination of the cartoon's modern form to English artist William Hogarth, who "revived the art of caricature after its long decline during the middle ages." Thomas Rowlandson, George Cruikshank, and especially James Gillray were among other Englishmen whom Bearden considered influential for American cartoonists, with Honoré Daumier singled out to represent France. Bearden named Benjamin Franklin father of the art in the United States, where cartoonists "were not at all creative [until Thomas Nast], the first really great cartoonist of America [whose] cartoons are not just cartoons, but they stand the test as being first class works of art." This judgment shows Bearden already rejecting thought patterns calling for tight compartmentalization. Contemporary American practice followed the historical patterns he wrote about, involving the role of syndication, salaries, and the capacity of mass-media cartoons to sway popular opinion and function as instruments of social change. Overall, his essay asserts the young artist's intellectual prowess and commitment to understanding historical precedent, something he would maintain as central to his artistic endeavors.

Bearden published the first of many journal covers during his university years and the first of numerous texts he would write on social and artistic issues. Both appeared in *Opportunity: A Journal of Negro Life* sponsored by the National Urban League. The cover (fig. 5) was on the March 1932 issue, when Bearden was just twenty years

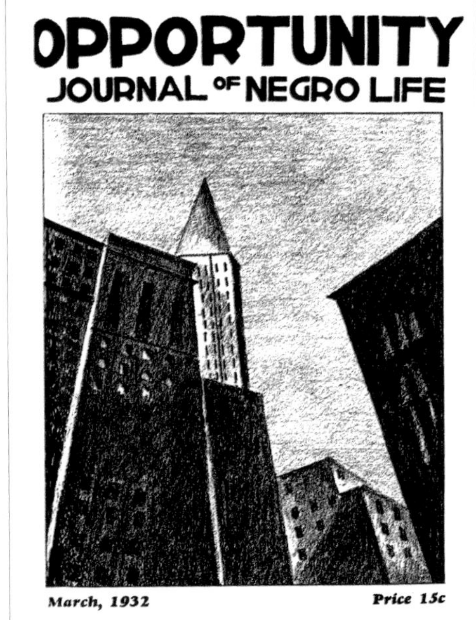

5

old; and the article, "The Negro Artist and Modern Art," was in the December 1934 issue (371–72). The cover design shows H. R. Bearden, as he was named on the contents page, concerned with the architectural density of lower Manhattan, a popular motif among painters and photographers of the period. Inspired by the Harmon Foundation's exhibitions in 1928 through 1931 and 1933, Bearden observed in the article that the heightened pace of modern life called for a break from earlier and outmoded academic practice and attacked the foundation for what he viewed as a philanthropic, patronizing attitude and lack of critical artistic standards.[15]

Following graduation and employed by the New York City Department of Social Services, which provided insight on the effects of the Depression, Bearden satisfied his growing desire to be an artist by drawing and painting at night and on weekends. His initial interest in art is generally dated to the mid-1920s and associated with Eugene Bailey, a sickly and handicapped Pittsburgh lad who lived near the Banks' boardinghouse. In 1979, however, Bearden remembered his interest as originating with a group of teenagers (including Norman Lewis who likewise matured to become a painter) that spent time with Augusta Savage, "a flesh and blood artist with a studio which we were welcome to use as a workshop, or even just to hang out in. She was open, free, resisted the usual conventions of the time, and lived for her art, thinking of success only in terms of how well her sculptures turned out."[16] These memories of Savage's studio either pre-date or are approximately parallel in time to Bearden's encounter with Bailey and suggest an even more powerful source (albeit a less colorful story) for his introduction to art.

As to Bailey, Bearden described his own first drawings as copies of his friend's depictions of people observed through the floorboards in Sadie's brothel where he lived with his mother. They included images of the house with its facade removed to reveal the adult activities inside, a format that would later reverberate in Bearden's collages *The Block* (reproduced Schwartzman, 1990, 52–53; see note 3) and *The Block II* (see no. 63). Carrie Banks, horrified to discover in her grandson's artwork the nature of Bailey's home environment, brought him to live at her boardinghouse; sadly he died shortly thereafter. Bearden commemorated their youthful friendship more than five decades later, however, in *Profile/Part I, The Twenties: Pittsburgh Memories, Farewell Eugene,* 1978 (see no. 115); and in an undated poem, an excerpt from which reads:

Nothing like this was necessary
        Eugene
I stand here among these tombs,
        holding this flower
which will fall endlessly into this
        open earth
that rejects nothing.[17]

Bearden's poignant *Profile/Part I* encompasses memories of Mecklenburg County and Pittsburgh during the 1920s, a decade in which much of his time actually was spent in Harlem. Recollections of sites and experiences in all three places, one agrarian, one urban working class, one emergent bourgeoisie, had long before become essential fodder for Bearden's artistic enterprise.[18] Less frequently acknowledged is that several places associated with the history of the blues and of jazz were also important to Bearden's visual world although he is not known ever to have visited them—Chicago, Kansas City, New Orleans, and the Louisiana bayou.

Bearden's student interest in cartooning led to professional work. Several monthly issues of *The Crisis* from April 1934 through January 1936 included his images. And from September 1935 through May 1937, his drawings were published weekly on the editorial page of Baltimore's *Afro-American*, a major mass-circulation weekly that vied for importance with the *Chicago Defender*, the *New York Amsterdam News*, and the *Pittsburgh Courier*.[19] These trenchant visuals commented on numerous demanding subjects: the Italian-Ethiopian conflict; the Scottsboro boys' trial; the Ku Klux Klan; anti-lynching legislation; Depression-era soup lines and inequitable job opportunities; relationships between student and labor protesters; the rise of Adolf Hitler; imminent war and memories of how few gains were made by the colored boys [Bearden's language] who fought for democracy and their country in the last Great War; the relationship of war and human greed; the Methodist Episcopal Church Conference and church support for segregation; colored athletes and the 1936 Olympics; Supreme Court decisions as a barrier to racial equality; and the defection of colored voters from the Republican Party with consequent support for Franklin Delano Roosevelt. It is both astonishing and heartbreaking to realize how many of Bearden's concerns remain timely today. In their dramatic use of space and scale Bearden's powerful editorial drawings appear to take inspiration from social comment pervasive in etchings by the nineteenth-century Spaniard, Francisco de Goya, and from the Mexican muralists whose politically charged imagery had an enormous impact in the United States during the 1930s: José Clemente Orozco, Diego Rivera, and David Alfaro Siqueiros, the first two of whom Bearden mentioned in his 1934 *Opportunity* article.[20]

Both political cartoonist Elmer Simms Campbell and Charles "Spinky" Alston, Bearden's cousin by marriage whom he cited as teaching him much about painting, are credited with suggesting he take night classes at the Art Students League with German-born artist George Grosz. Grosz fled Hitler's tyrannical regime in 1932, settling in the United States the following year. Bearden took a class in August 1933; for September 1935 he is recorded as taking life class, presumably under Grosz's tutelage, drawing from the model nightly from 7:00 to 10:00 PM. He remembered the experience with great enthusiasm: "I couldn't wait for the evenings to get there because I felt I had a lot to learn."[21] It would appear that after Grosz appointed him as a class monitor his presence was on an informal basis. The school archives show no record of Bearden registered for classes beyond the single months in 1933 and 1935.[22]

Painter James Rosenquist, who attended classes at the League in the 1950s, has recalled that even then, two decades after Bearden took classes, Grosz was not fully comfortable conversing in English, that his teaching primarily consisted of technical demonstrations and showing students a range of art-historical reproductions.[23] This reinforces the notion that Grosz's important contribution to Bearden's art (in addition to helping him develop drawing skills) was an introduction to the art of Duccio di Buoninsegna, Giotto di Bondone, Albrecht Dürer, Hieronymus Bosch, Pieter Brueghel, Pieter De Hooch, Jean-Auguste-Dominique Ingres, Jean-Louis Forain, and Käthe Kollwitz among others, vastly expanding the field of artistic precedents set down in Bearden's history of cartooning.[24]

Grosz had been one of the signers of the 1919 manifesto *Dadisten Gegen Weimar/Dadaism Against Weimar,* along with Hans Arp, Tristan Tzara, and others. It seems reasonable to assume that the highly political drawings and collages associated with the German Dada group, Grosz's own, e.g., *Untitled (Panorama),* 1919 (fig. 6), and those of others such as Max Ernst, John Heartfield, and Hannah Höch would have been among works to which Grosz introduced his students. They offer excellent precedents for the politically charged collages Bearden was to make a quarter century later.[25] It is likewise fascinating to examine Grosz's art from the time of Bearden's studies, watercolors such as *Street in Harlem* (fig. 7), a subject that later would become closely associated with Bearden. Grosz's loose and expressive painterly style in such scenes may have remained among Bearden's memories, emerging in the 1980s in his own dynamic watercolors and collages, such as the glowing view of New York at night, *City Lites,* and the dense Caribbean landscape, *Birds in Paradise* (see nos. 120, 127).

Grosz was one of many downtown (below 110th Street) forces to expand Bearden's artistic purview. During the late 1930s he formed a long-term intellectual and artistic friendship with painter Walter Quirt who was among the first artists he met outside of Harlem. And after the

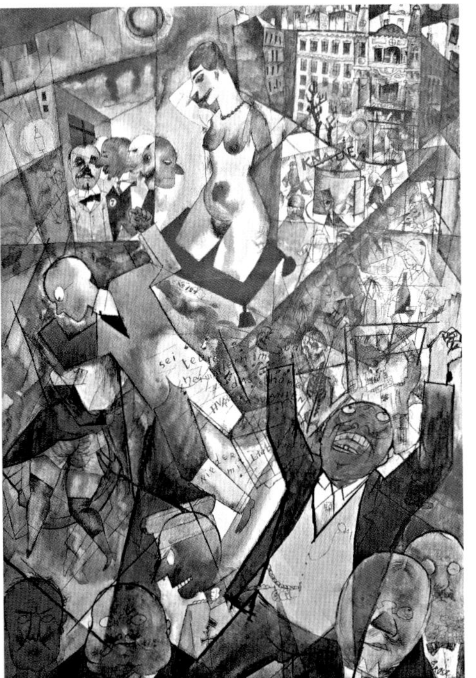

6

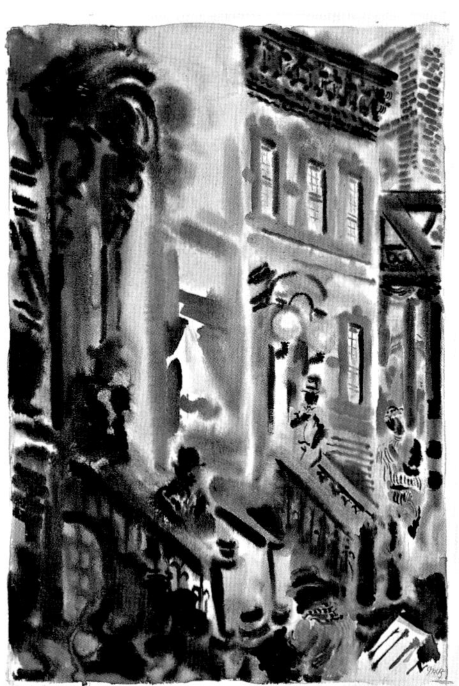

7

figure 6
George Grosz, *Untitled (Panorama),* 1919, watercolor on paper. Courtesy Richard L. Feigen & Co.

figure 7
George Grosz, *Street in Harlem,* c. 1935, watercolor on paper. The Phillips Collection, Washington

war, Carl Holty and Stuart Davis also became close friends. Bearden often mentioned discussions with Davis about interval in the music of jazz pianist Earl "Fatha" Hines. He also acknowledged Davis' advice to "always remember about color that in a painting it has a position and a place, and it makes space. And thinking of color this way, not as a separate entity but color also as form, as space, and not as decoration, taught me a great deal."[26] Painters William Baziotes and John Graham were important too, the former for introducing him to "certain ideas of feeling through painting" and the latter for his book *System and Dialectics of Art,* which Bearden, likewise of a theoretical bent, found fascinating.[27] In the late 1940s and early 1950s Bearden attended Friday night drawing sessions Graham conducted, in which the use of form as metaphor was a prime topic.[28] Bearden and Graham would also have shared an interest in African art, of which Graham was a knowledgeable collector.[29]

An influential figure uptown during the 1930s was "Professor" Charles Seifert, who generously shared his knowledge of African and African-American art, as well as his extensive African art collection and related library. Bearden was one of many young artists who were grateful for this bounty, noting many years later events such as Professor Seifert's guided tour of the Museum of Modern Art's (MoMA) 1935 *African Negro Art* exhibition. Bearden was involved with activities of the Harlem Artists Guild, the 137th Street YMCA, the Harlem Community Art Center, and the Harlem Art Workshop in the New York Public Library's 135th Street branch (now the Schomburg Center for Research in Black Culture). The last two, Depression-era undertakings, were sponsored by the Works Progress Administration/Federal Art Project (WPA/FAP). Although Bearden's family support made him ineligible to participate formally in these programs, he was closely allied with many who did, and he later commented upon the loyalty in the community during these years and the encouragement artists gave each other. The collective most important to his early career was the informal group of painters and sculptors, writers, dancers, and musicians that assembled at 306 West 141st Street, generally called "306" or "the studio," which was a gathering place on the first floor of a three-story former stable.[30]

Alston along with sculptor Henry (Mike) Bannarn, at first, and then Addison (Ad) Bates, a dancer, cabinet maker, and artists' model at the Art Students League and elsewhere, lived and worked for various periods in the second-floor space. All three men were central figures in the 306 group, which at one time or other included William Attaway, Robert Blackburn, Ernest Crichlow, Aaron Douglas, musicians from bands, including Duke Ellington's, Ellison, Hughes, Jacob Lawrence, Lewis, Claude McKay, William Saroyan, and the Steig brothers, Arthur and William, among others.[31] A third-floor apartment housed various individuals as well, including Ad Bates' younger brother, Leonard, and his wife, Myrtle, and Ellison and his first wife, Rose. The intellectual stimulation at 306 enabled these creative artists, working in a wide variety of media often in contradictory styles, to interact productively across generations.

Bearden's place within the 306 studio and the Art Students League, essential to his artistic development, also established a social pattern he was to follow for the rest of his life—active involvement in the communities above and below 110th Street, with considerable commitment and activism in both arenas. This may be seen as an aspect of the double-consciousness W. E. B. Du Bois set out as early as 1897 in his speech, "The Conservation of Races." Whatever conflicts this may have presented to daily living, Bearden's art manages to control and bond this two-ness to create a world view far richer than just one aspect of his identity would have permitted.[32]

When the 1930s came to a close Bearden was thoroughly engaged with painting. Surviving works from this decade (or works known from reproductions and catalogue listings) include genre scenes of the social realist bent typical of many Depression-era artists both uptown and downtown. A painting Bearden retained throughout his life, *Soup Kitchen* (fig. 8), was in his first solo show, organized by Ad Bates at 306 for a week in May 1940. Twenty-four works made between 1937 and 1940 were presented: seven oils, six gouaches, five watercolors, and six drawings (medium not specified), including four studies of the nude. In a statement Bearden wrote for the exhibition pamphlet, his intention is vivid:

> I believe the function of the artist is to find ways of communicating, in sensible, sensuous terms, those experiences which do not find adequate expression in the daily round of living and for which, therefore, no ready made means of communication exists.... [two things essential to "good" painting are]: that there be a communion of belief and desire between artist and spectator; that the artist be able to see and say something that enriches the fund of communicable feeling and the medium to express it.[33]

The same year as the show Bearden rented a studio for $8 per month (including electricity) at 33 West 125th Street where Attaway, Lawrence, and McKay also worked.[34] Likewise in 1940 he traveled to North Carolina for the first time in the fifteen years since his great-grandparents' deaths, stopping in Charlotte and Greensboro to see family. He then went on to Atlanta, Georgia, where he visited artist Hale Woodruff who was teaching at Atlanta University (now Clark Atlanta University) and Spelman College. Years later, articles about Bearden reported the trip had been "for the purpose of painting scenes in North Carolina and other Southern states."[35] No sketches or paintings are documented to the journey but it appears to have sparked childhood memories of the region that caused a profound change in Bearden's imagery. He also committed to a paint medium and substrate at that time, and over the next few years completed approximately twenty paintings in gouache on brown paper, including *The Visitation*, *The Family*, *They That Are Delivered from the Noise of the Archers*, and *Presage* (nos. 1, 2, 3, 4). Many were painted in a second studio at 243 West 125th Street in the Apollo Theater building to which Bearden moved in 1941.

Bearden's ambition was grand. These gouaches are heroic in scale (measuring as large as 48 x 32 inches). In this respect, and in expressive presence, they reflect Bearden's kinship with social realists such as Jacob Lawrence and Ben Shahn.[36] Perhaps more important was his continued admiration for the Mexican muralists. Orozco painted his multiwall fresco mural, *American Civilization*, in the library at Dartmouth College in Hanover, New Hampshire, in 1932; Rivera had a retrospective at New York's MoMA that year and worked on his ill-fated Rockefeller Center mural, *Man at the Crossroads*.[37] Siqueiros, in New York in 1936 and 1937, participated in the first American Artists' Congress and established the Siqueiros Experimental Workshop, which attracted many young WPA/FAP artists. There he encouraged experimentation with synthetic paints, photography, and film, all of which would have undoubtedly appealed to Bearden, and it seems likely their paths would have crossed. Bearden also admired Rufino Tamayo, evident from the several reproductions of his work among Bearden's papers. Tamayo had moved to New York permanently in 1936 and exhibited through the early 1940s at the Valentine Gallery on 57th Street where Bearden could readily have seen his paintings. The Mexican artist's amalgam of heroic figures defined by interlocking flat color areas and linear contours bears similarities to Bearden's art during the 1940s.

Christian iconography, which plays a role throughout Bearden's oeuvre, often covertly, is evident from the start. *The Visitation* if otherwise titled could be viewed as a genre scene, two women in conversation; *The Family*, suggesting the Holy Family, likewise may be understood as a quotidian situation. In both, hand gestures are mannered and pronounced, a characteristic of figural details in Bearden's work from this point on. The gouaches are carefully painted, with

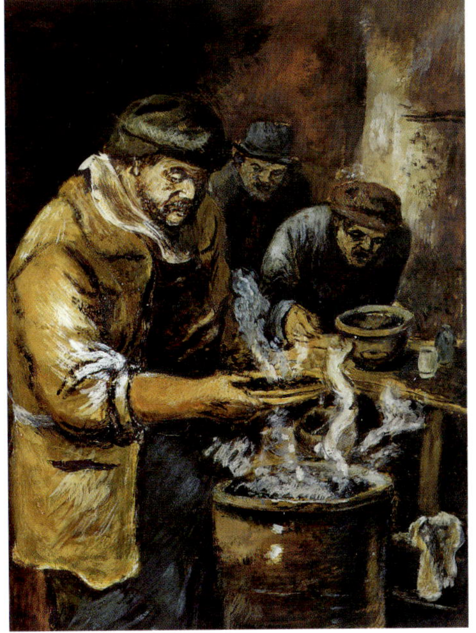

8

figure 8
Romare Bearden, *Soup Kitchen*, 1937, oil on paper. Estate of Romare Bearden, courtesy of Romare Bearden Foundation, New York

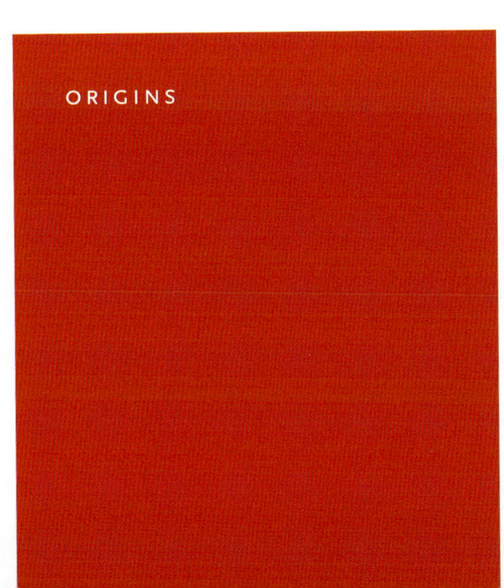

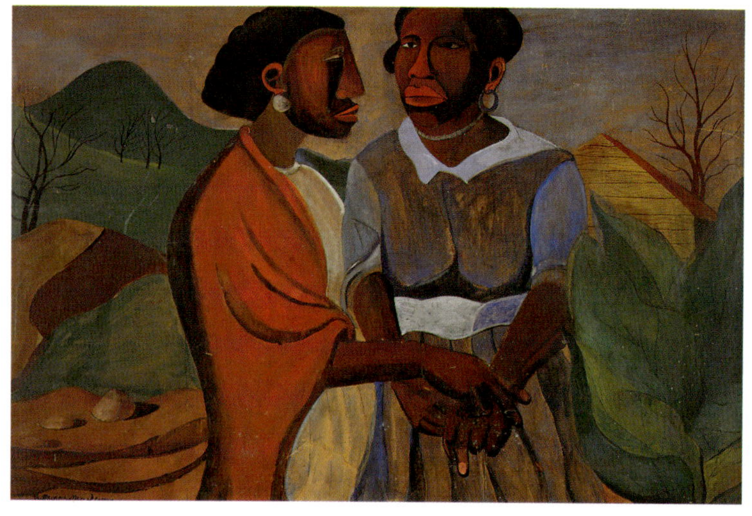

1

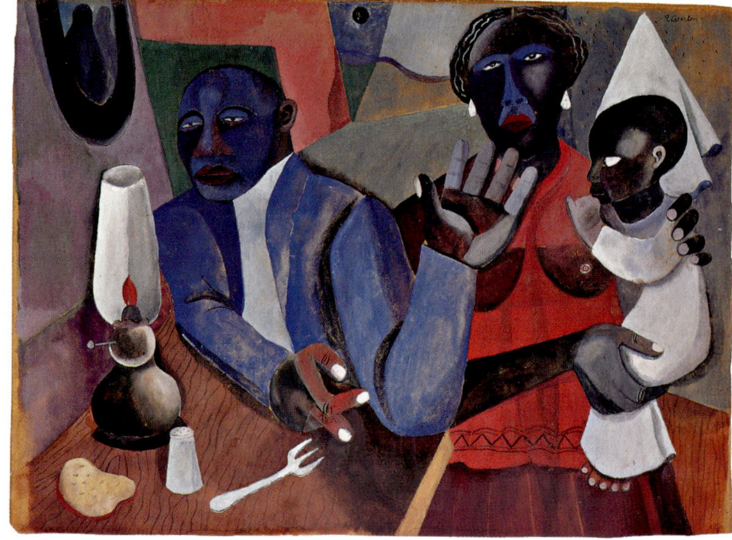

2

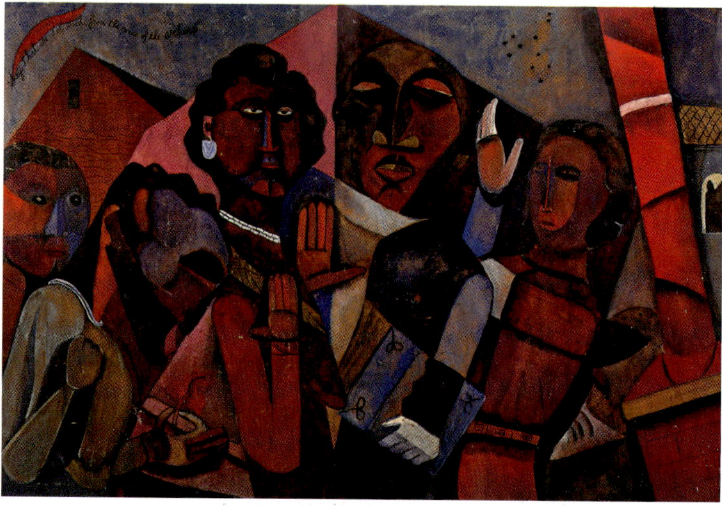

3

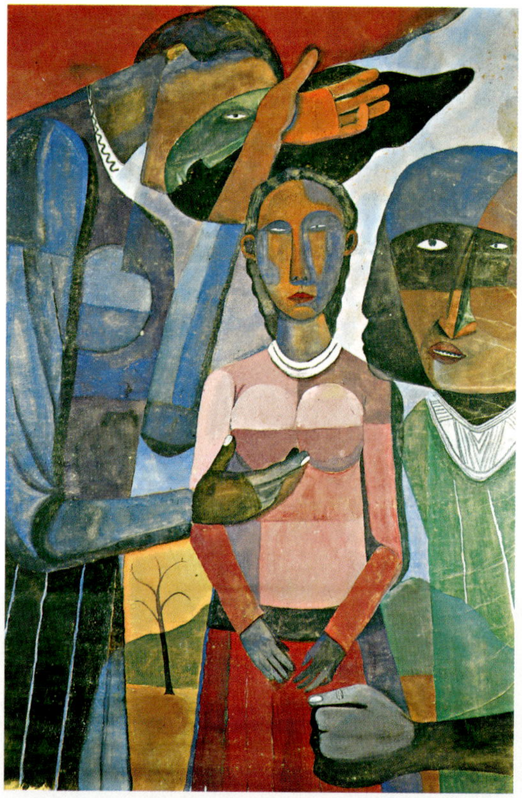

4

modeled form essential to building space; and they initiate Bearden's experimental engagement with the materials of his art, his immense concern for both visual and tactile aspects of his painted (and later collaged) surfaces. In *The Family* this may be seen throughout the father's jacket, in which opaque paint application contrasts with pigment diluted by water to achieve translucency. Multiple blues add richness, and black shadows (thin lines and wide swaths) adjacent to thread-like areas of visible paper enhance the luminosity of the jacket and painting. Throughout the composition Bearden achieved subtle hues by layering contrasting colors, most visible in the pale, opaque violet along the left, covering a dark green that may be seen at the far edge. Overall, however, the colors in *The Family, The Visitation,* and the other gouaches of the early 1940s are earthy, eschewing those made from metallic pigments such as titanium, the cadmiums, cobalt, and chromium, the use of which by artists was prohibited during the war in support of defense priorities.[38]

Roughened surfaces throughout *The Family* reveal that after applying paint Bearden rubbed some areas of the sheet with a rag, paper towel, or possibly his hand. This kind of activation throughout the father's head, for example, is emphasized by the smoothly painted green shape enframing it, possibly signifying a door into another room. Drawn lines—in black ink, and opaque white or translucent gray paints—activate the field, adding specificity to the mother's hair, the pattern along the bottom of her blouse, the figures' facial features and hand gestures, and objects on the table: kerosene lamp, fork, salt or pepper shaker, and hoecake. Painted lines simulate wood grain on the table and on the floor at right behind the mother. These "wood" panels compress the composition and create a space very different from the more literal conception of *The Visitation.*

Two motifs of special interest in *The Family* are a double portrait photograph in an oval frame on the wall at left, presumably a source of great family pride,[39] and a suggestion of landscape seen through a window at top center, marked by a black sun/moon high in the sky. This heavenly body will remain a common, if often ambiguous, signifier in Bearden's art, just as landscapes will appear through the windows of his interiors into the 1980s, and family photographs will decorate their walls.[40] Indeed, in theme, pictorial detail, and methodology, as art historian Sharon F. Patton has pointed out, these gouaches from the early 1940s appear in retrospect as the origins of Bearden's artistic persona as we know it.[41] But much was to happen en route.

By sometime in 1942 Bearden was fully engaged with the dialectical tension between abstraction and representation that was to be a focus throughout his career. Pablo Picasso and African sculpture were early guides, with Picasso's embrace and transformation of African art as important to Bearden as his own roots in the African diaspora. It seems possible as well that cubism, which Bearden continued to embrace for decades, held special interest for him *because* of its roots in African art. He noted with apparent pride in "The Negro Artist and Modern Art" that "modern art has borrowed heavily from Negro sculpture." It may be equally apt to consider Bearden's ever increasing sophistication of surface and distortion of form in light of this article:

> Artists have been amazed at the fine surface qualities of the sculpture, the vitality of the work, and the unsurpasssed ability of the artists to create such significant forms. Of great importance has been the fact that the African would distort his figures, if by so doing he could achieve a more expressive form. This is one of the cardinal principles of the modern artist.

The article ends by suggesting that political subject matter is not so much called for but such subjects are apt to engender passion. "An intense, eager devotion to present day life, to study it, to help relieve it, this is the calling of the Negro artist."[42]

They That Are Delivered from the Noise of the Archers and *Presage* suggest the changes that ensued as Bearden moved further from the modeled forms in deep space of *The Visitation* through the transitions in *The Family* toward flat iconic shapes in shallow composition. Forms are more fractured in these two slightly later gouaches, and masks implied within faces in the earlier works are here fully developed in compositions that are more dense and abstract overall, imbued with a new pictorial energy.

Bearden's work in the studio came to an abrupt halt in 1942 when he entered the army and was assigned to several posts within the United States through 1945. Another immense disruption to his life occurred in 1943, when Bessye Bearden suddenly died of pneumonia. Although he retained his studio during this period, it seems unlikely he would have accomplished much, if any, painting.[43]

About that time, Bearden's art was introduced into the American mainstream when, through artist William H. Johnson, he met the dynamic Caresse Crosby, cofounder (with her

1
***The Visitation*, 1941, gouache with ink and graphite on brown paper, 77.8 x 117.5 (30 5/8 x 46 1/4). Estate of Romare Bearden, courtesy of Romare Bearden Foundation, New York**

2
***The Family*, c. 1941, gouache with ink and graphite on brown paper, 74 x 104.8 (29 1/8 x 41 1/4). Collection of Earle Hyman**

3
***They That Are Delivered from the Noise of the Archers*, 1942, gouache with ink and graphite on brown paper, 80 x 116.8 (31 1/2 x 46). Lent by the Grant Hill Collection**

4
***Presage*, c. 1942, gouache with ink and graphite on brown paper, 121.9 x 81.3 (48 x 32). The Walter O. Evans Collection of African American Art**

second husband Harry) of the Black Sun Press in Paris that had in the 1920s published Hart Crane, James Joyce, and D.H. Lawrence. The introduction led to Bearden's first solo exhibition outside Harlem, *Ten Hierographic Paintings by Sgt. Romare Bearden,* sponsored by Crosby and her business associate, David Porter, at their forward looking G Place Gallery in Washington, D.C., from mid-February through early March 1944.[44] Within a year Bearden was singled out in an *Art News* review of *The Negro Artist Comes of Age,* an exhibition at the Albany Institute of History and Art, with a reproduction of *Factory Workers* (Minneapolis Institute of Arts), which was on view. The painting had previously illustrated a June 1942 *Fortune* magazine article "The Negro's War," (fig. 9) and was described in *Art News* as "typical of the formal style of this well-known Negro artist."[45] Despite such successes, after the war Bearden returned to his job with the New York City Department of Social Services where his assignments were with the gypsy community. He was particularly sympathetic to the disintegration of the group's social networks and "attracted to the ritualistic magic of their fortune tellers, and their carnivals and circuses."[46] Writing in July 1945 to Walter Quirt, who was teaching in Milwaukee, Wisconsin, Bearden explained that he considered returning to cartooning to make a living but found that making the cartoons hurt his painting. "If by any chance a worldly success comes—well and good, but to seek it yourself under this system, you have to be a combination of business man, press agent, and phoney—all not appealing to me."[47] Worldly success did come, but for two more decades Bearden would work at his art after full days with the welfare department and on weekends.

Shifting from gouache to watercolor for his second Washington show, in June 1945, Bearden's motifs were based on the gospels of Saints Matthew and Mark and other biblical events and titled as a group *The Passion of Christ,* a subject he might have explored for many reasons, one of them his enormous admiration for Henry Ossawa Tanner's biblical paintings.[48] About the time of this show Crosby introduced Bearden's art to Samuel M. Kootz who had recently opened a Manhattan gallery at 15 East 57th Street, between Madison and Fifth Avenues. Kootz responded enthusiastically, and in an exhibition that autumn introduced Bearden's Passion watercolors, augmented by related oils, to New York's downtown art audience. Bearden's above-mentioned letter to Quirt, sent between the Washington and New York showings, includes comments about nine sketches he concurrently had mailed to provide his friend with an overview of current work:

> I showed [Alston] the drawings I did for you and told him I did them in an hour or so. This, he claimed was physically impossible, and if you can do things that easily you'd better watch yourself.... these guys remain on such safe, conservative, petty levels—I'm tired of "can not," "you shouldn't," "you ought," "reflect," "not so fast," "that's impossible"—what is painting but to dare, but to try and control your madness.

Four of these *Untitled* drawings are included here: *(Untitled) En Route to Calvary, (Untitled) Crucifixion, (Untitled) He Is Arisen,* and *(Untitled) The Resurrection* (nos. 5, 6, 7, 8; the others are figs. 10–14).[49] As a group they reveal Bearden's practice from the start of his career to work in series, and they suggest the freedom with which he moved further into abstraction.

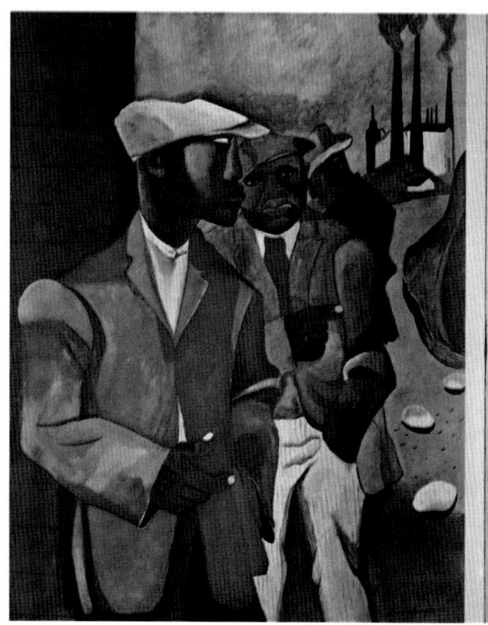

THE NEGRO'S WAR

One-tenth of the U.S. population still has not a full share in America's greatest undertaking. Nine-tenths may have to pay the costs of wasteful discrimination.

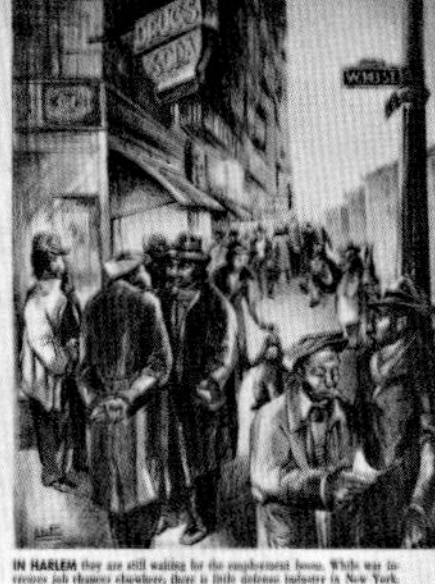

9

figure 9
Romare Bearden, *Factory Workers* in "The Negro's War," *Fortune* magazine, June 1942, with additional illustrations by Charles Alston. Courtesy Sheldon Ross Fine Arts LLC

5
***Untitled (En Route to Calvary)*, 1945, watercolor and ink on paper, 30.5 x 22.9 (12 x 9). Mr. Keith Lee and Dr. Lori Andochick**

6
***Untitled (Crucifixion)*, 1945, watercolor and ink on paper, 30.5 x 22.9 (12 x 9). Mr. Keith Lee and Dr. Lori Andochick**

7
***Untitled (He Is Arisen)*, 1945, watercolor and ink on paper, 30.5 x 22.9 (12 x 9). Mr. Keith Lee and Dr. Lori Andochick**

8
***Untitled (The Resurrection)*, 1945, watercolor and ink on paper, 30.5 x 22.9 (12 x 9). Mr. Keith Lee and Dr. Lori Andochick**

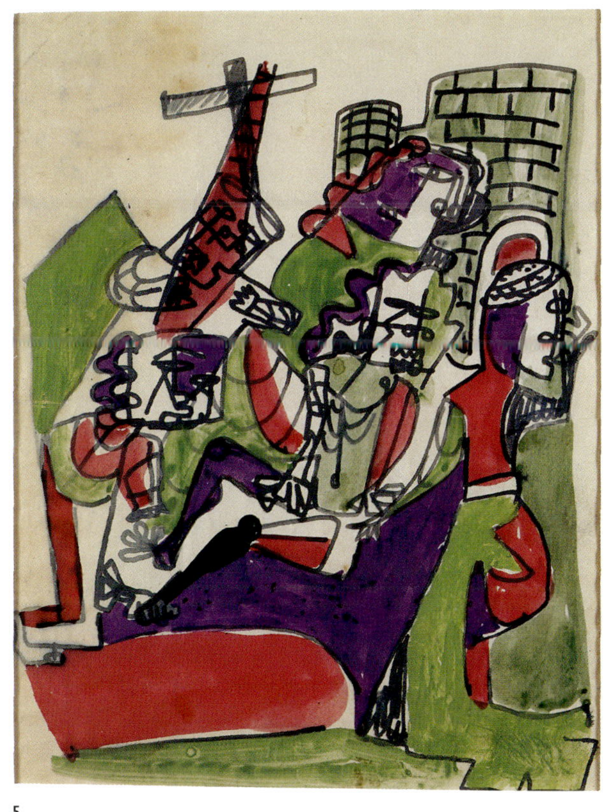
5

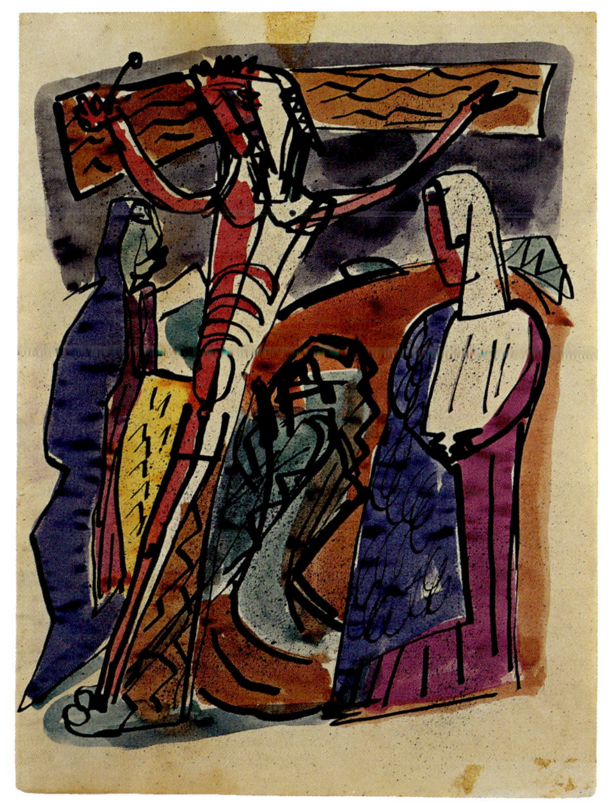
6

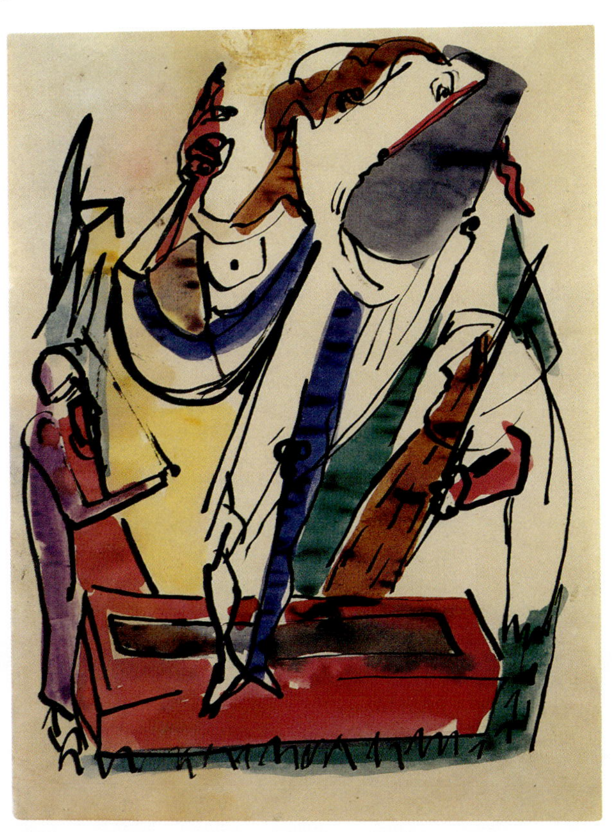
8

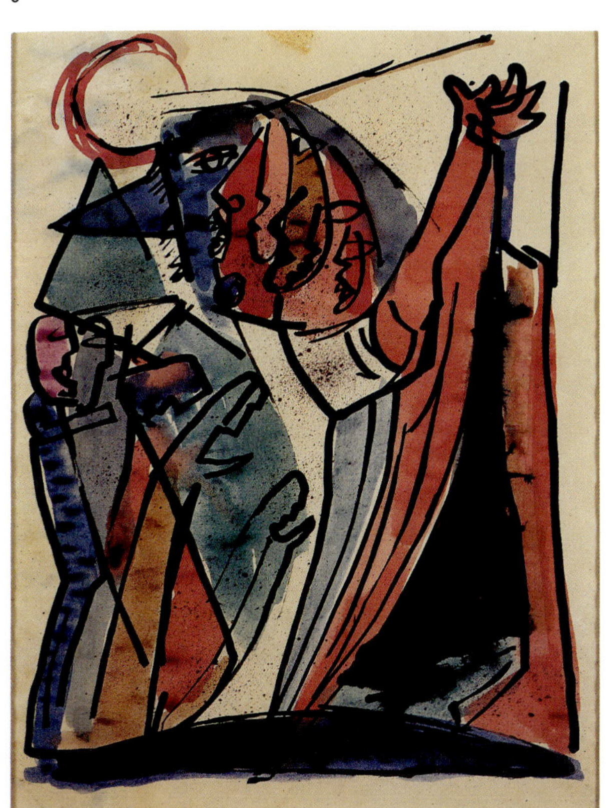
7

11

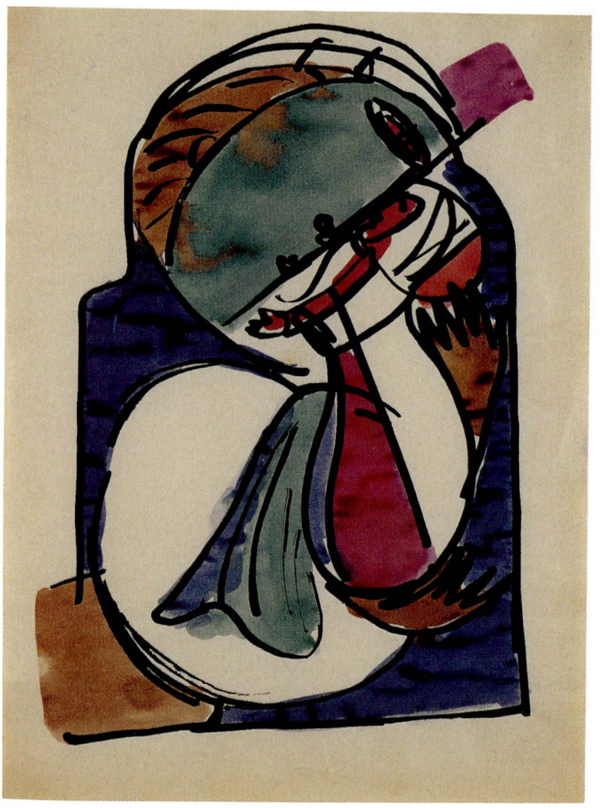

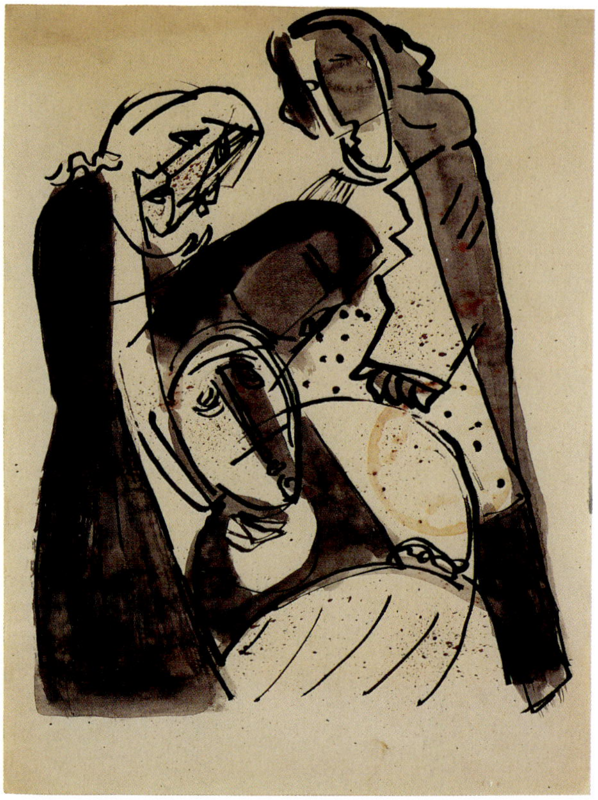

10

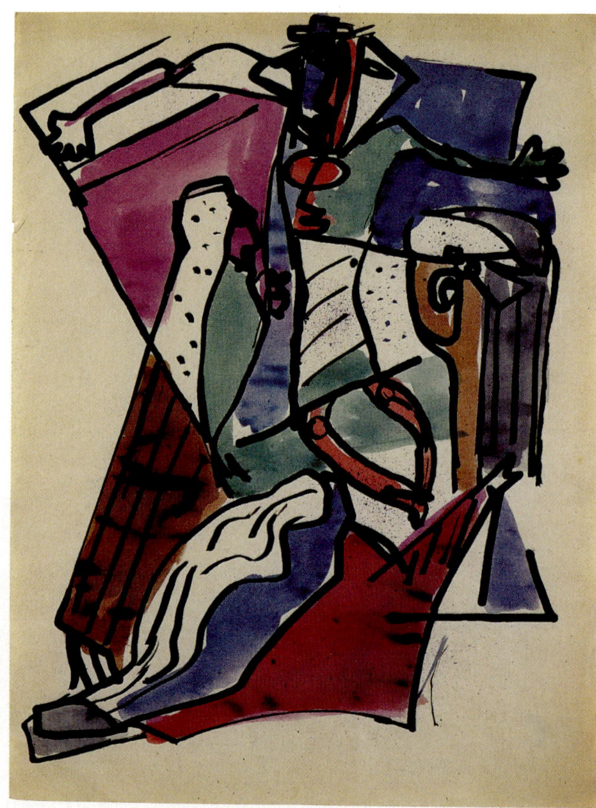

12

figure 10
Romare Bearden, *Untitled (Madonna and Child)*, 1945, watercolor and ink on paper. Mr. Keith Lee and Dr. Lori Andochick

figure 11
Romare Bearden, *Untitled (Pietà)*, 1945, watercolor and ink on paper. Mr. Keith Lee and Dr. Lori Andochick

figure 12
Romare Bearden, *Untitled (The Deposition)*, 1945, watercolor and ink on paper. Mr. Keith Lee and Dr. Lori Andochick

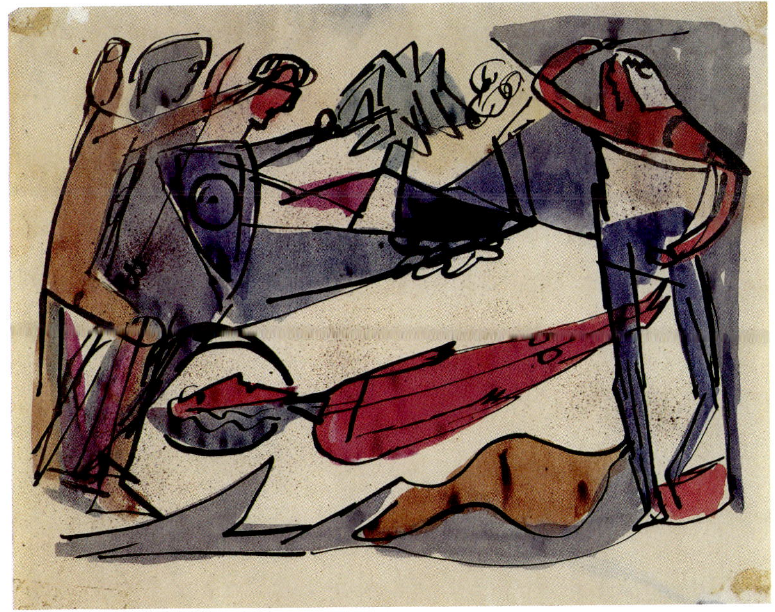

13

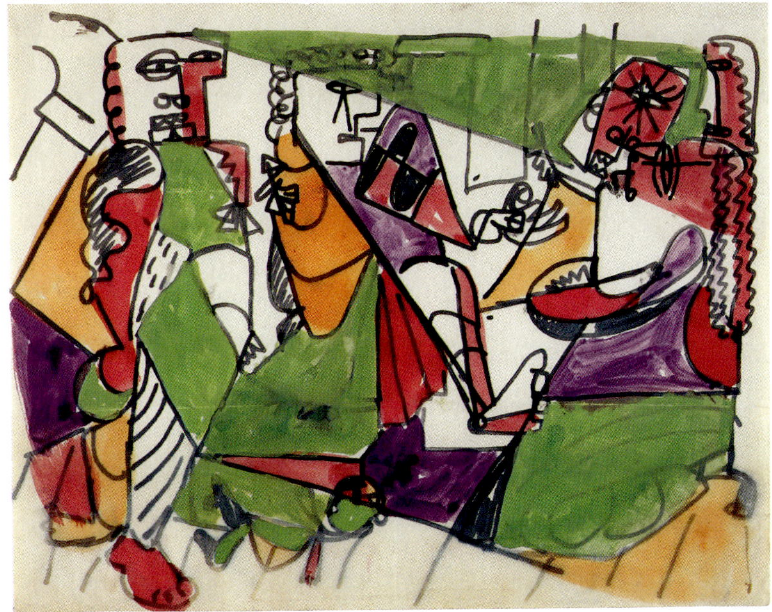

14

figure 13
Romare Bearden, *Untitled (Roman Soldiers Beating Christ)*, 1945, watercolor and ink on paper. Mr. Keith Lee and Dr. Lori Andochick

figure 14
Romare Bearden, *Untitled (Adoration of the Wise Men?)*, 1945, watercolor and ink on paper. Mr. Keith Lee and Dr. Lori Andochick

To convert his Passion images to oils for the Kootz showing, Bearden began by tracing photostatic enlargements of the full-scale watercolors (not these sketches) onto gessoed panels, an early example of his use of photographic and transfer processes. He then diluted oil paint with a solvent, probably turpentine, permitting it to mimic the fluidity and transparency of watercolor.

The Passion watercolors and oils sharply separate from Bearden's pre-war work. Transparent inks or watercolors, and thinly applied oils had supplanted the opacity of gouache; for the watercolors and some oils a single application of paint replaced the layering of diverse hues; color shifted from earth tones to a high-keyed palette; forms became more geometric in character and compositions more interlocking. Bearden also employed bold black lines throughout his pictorial field, an emphatic force enclosing color segments and suggesting another artistic model—the great twentieth-century French religious painter, Georges Rouault, whose work was given a retrospective at MoMA in April 1945, just as Bearden was embarking in his new direction.[50] Indeed, according to Patton, Carl Van Vechten referred to Bearden as "the Negro Rouault."[51]

These general characteristics would hold true for Bearden's three subsequent narratives, all based on powerful literary themes by a roster of major international writers: Spanish poet/playwright Federico García Lorca's 1935 poem, "Lament for a Bullfighter (Llanto por Ignacio Sánchez Mejías)," 1946; French humanist François Rabelais' sixteenth-century political satire, *Gargantua and Pantagruel,* 1947; and Homer's eighth-century BC epic Greek poem *The Iliad,* an early example of literary invention recounting events leading to and during the Trojan War,

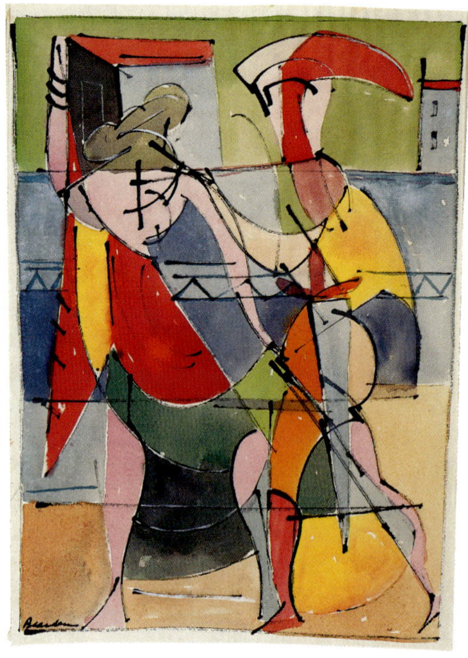

15

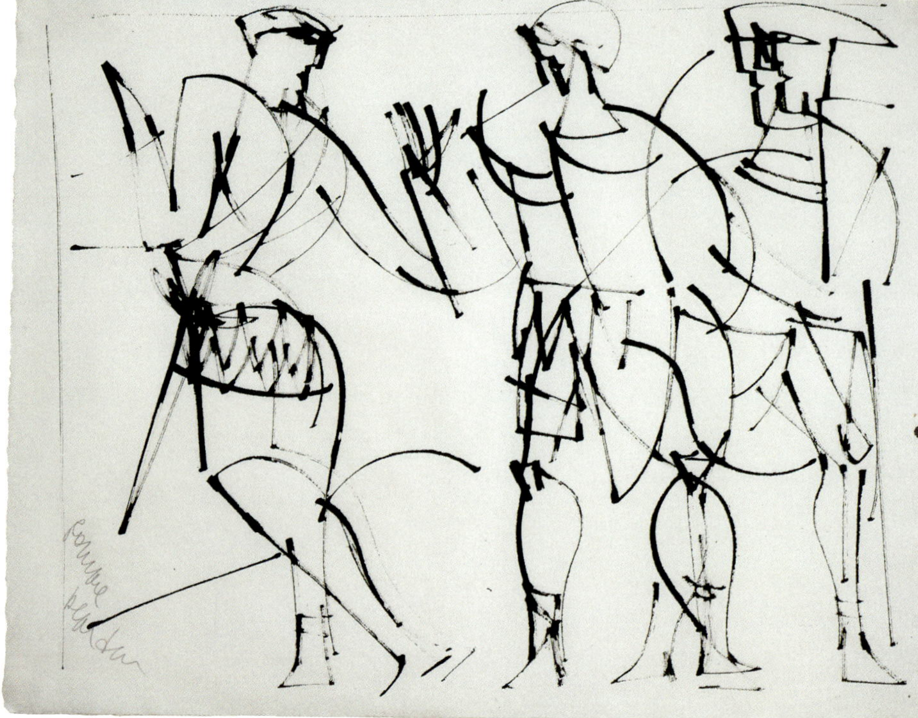

16

c. 1948 (fig. 15). As art historian Lowery S. Sims has pointed out, these heroic narratives share (in some measure) the themes of violence, suffering, death, and resurrection, coupled with that of "the searcher, the wandering individual seeking a noble goal."[52]

Like the Passion, Bearden's next two series included watercolors and oils, the last, solely watercolors, although with many related ink drawings on the warrior theme such as the highly gestural *Untitled (Three Figures)*, c. 1947 (fig. 16). The drawings employ the black calligraphic line that appears in the watercolors but lack the facets of color.[53] Close connections between Bearden's watercolors and oils in the Lorca series may be seen by comparing *Now the Dove and the Leopard Wrestle*, 1946, with the parallel composition in watercolor (nos. 9, 10).[54] Characteristic of many works in the series is a red spatter across the field, presumably symbolizing blood. It prefigures Bearden's extensive use of spray paint on collages starting in the late 1960s. The Lorca was one of Bearden's most far-reaching series. Although only twenty-one works were included in the Kootz exhibition, Bearden may have completed some hundred pieces inspired by the theme.

In general, the Lorca and Pantagruel oils are more thickly painted than those in the Passion, exploring further the tactile and visual properties of oil paint rather than trying to imitate watercolor. The Rabelais exhibition was accompanied by a brochure, the text for which was written by Bearden's friend Barrie Stavis.[55] That series and the Iliad embraced a more extensive and subtle palette than the earlier two. Also, Bearden's lines became more colorful in them, employing not only black but also red and white, a move he credited in his conversations with Myron Schwartzman (see note 3) to a suggestion from Holty.

figure 15
Romare Bearden, *Untitled (from the Iliad Series)*, c. 1948, watercolor and ink on paper. Collection of June Kelly

figure 16
Romare Bearden, *Untitled (Three Figures)*, c. 1947, pen and ink on paper. Collection of Dr. Akosua Barthwell Evans

9
***Now the Dove and the Leopard Wrestle*, 1946, oil on canvas, 59.7 x 74.3 (23½ x 29¼). Clements Library, University of Michigan, Ann Arbor**

10
***Untitled (Lorca Series)*, c. 1946, watercolor and ink on paper, 50.2 x 64.8 (19¾ x 25½). Mr. and Mrs. Louis K. Adler, Houston, Texas**

Lorca, whom Bearden met personally, was in the United States from June 1929 through March 1930. For part of these months he was enrolled at Columbia University but appears to have spent much time using the city rather than formal institutions as his classroom, a model Bearden would follow during his first visit to Paris twenty years later. Lorca's admiration for the Harlem atmosphere has often been described, recently by biographer Leslie Stainton:

> Nearly everywhere he went in New York, Lorca encountered greed, poverty, and filth. Only one place seemed free of depravity—Harlem. . . . [which he considered] a sanctuary of art and beauty and carnality. . . . an oasis of freedom.[56]

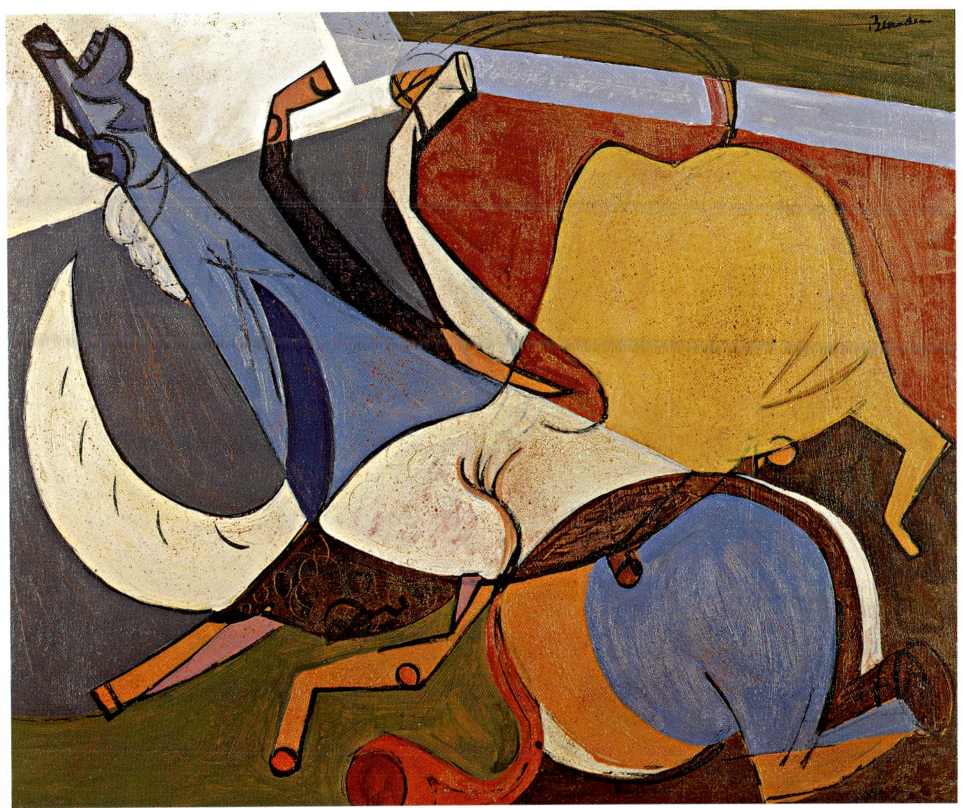

9

Bearden also could have met the bullfighter, Ignacio Sanchez Mejias, when he and guitarist Andrés Segovia visited Lorca in late 1929, a possible reason for the artist's choice of this particular poem.

Throughout his career Bearden left many works undated, and it is difficult to establish a finely-tuned chronology for his oeuvre, especially for works from the mid- and late-1940s, a period of considerable transition. The fact that he revisited subjects over decades eliminates motif as a practical aid to dating his work and, although over time he changed the materials and methods he used, he also continued to use processes associated with earlier periods. During the late 1940s in addition to the literary-based series most often discussed in accounts of his work, Bearden's production included other oils, and numerous watercolors and drawings. Individual works are distinctive in ways not readily associated with any others. One such is a fascinating gouache on

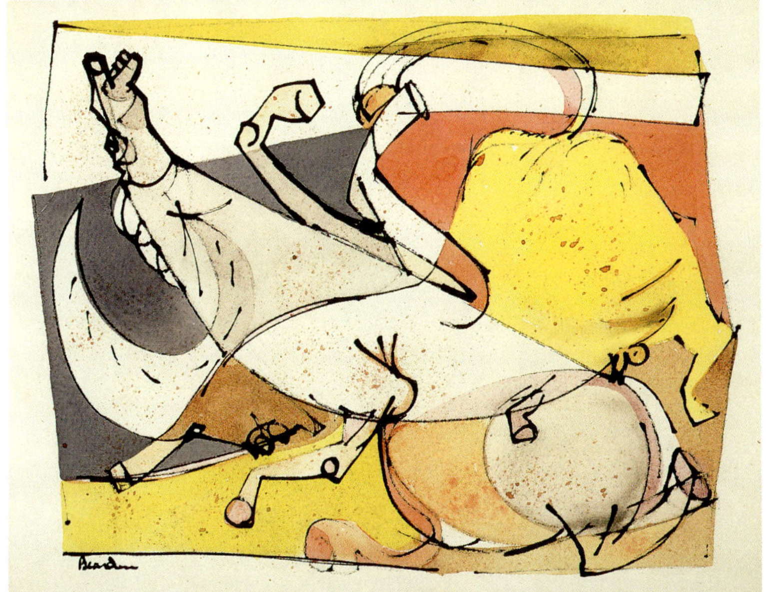

10

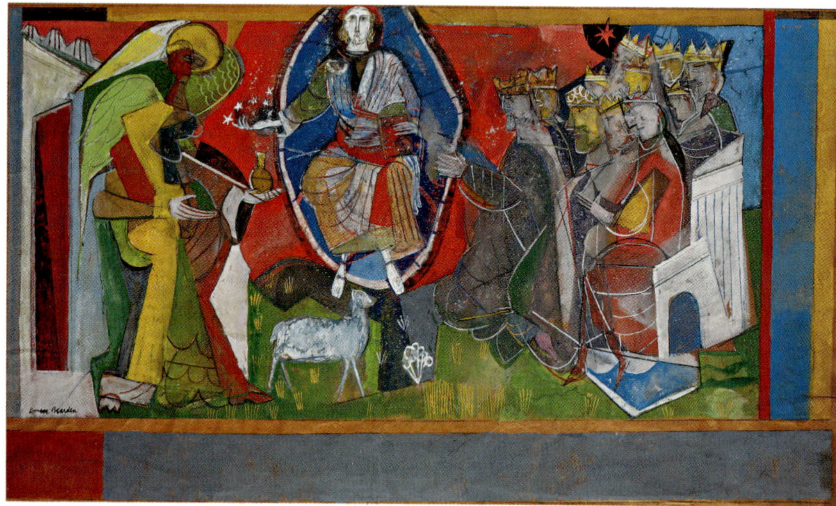

11

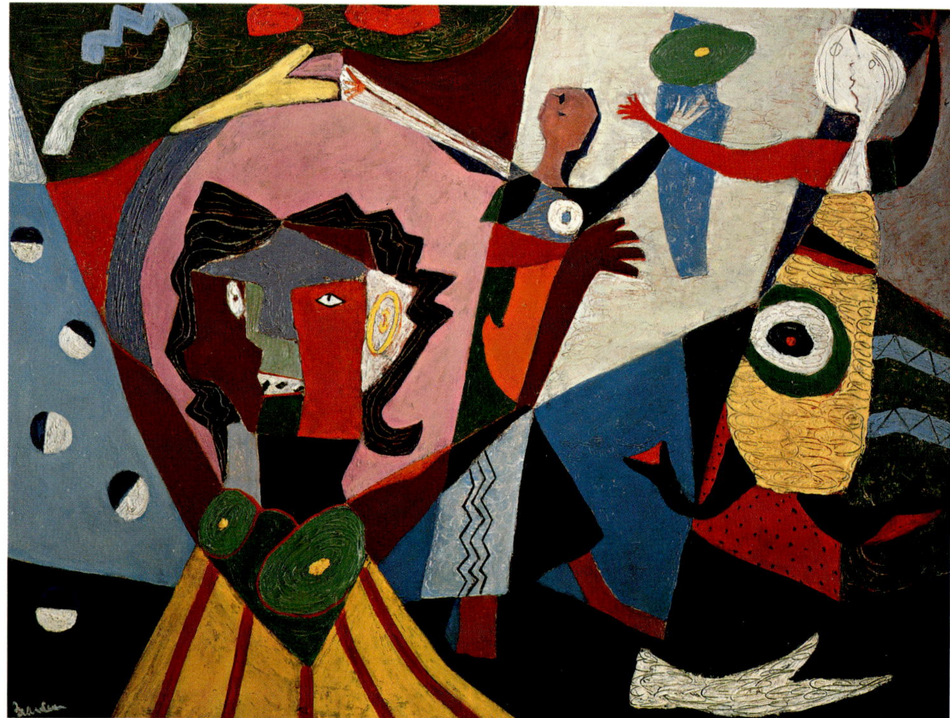

12

brown paper, *The Ascension of Christ in Glory,* 1945/46 (no. 11). As with many of Bearden's images, works by earlier masters probably served as inspiration for the angel at left, Ascension at center, and the kings at right. There is coherence within the gouache's color structure, but each motif is approached in a somewhat different style permitting us to track a moment of artistic transition.

Also unusual is *Two Figures,* which has been dated to c. 1946 (no. 12), but may date from c. 1947, the year Bearden met Joan Miró. The American's appreciation for the Spaniard's playful biomorphic forms is suggested, for example, by elements such as the swirling circles throughout the composition. Given Bearden's receptivity to new ideas about abstraction at this time it makes sense that Miró's world would have had impact on him.[57] Bearden's own essential interest in surface properties is also evident, particularly in his use here of a provocative variety of painterly means. Within some color fields he incorporated sand or another grit, a common characteristic of many of his oils; other areas are extensively enriched with sgraffito incisions that are both more numerous and more varied than in other paintings of this period.

For approximately two years at the close of the 1940s Bearden concentrated primarily on studies from the masters, an attempt to compensate for what he stated as insufficient formal training. Depictions primarily of biblical motifs and genre scenes, they derive from Italian primitive, Northern Renaissance, and Dutch seventeenth-century painting, and, on occasion, from nineteenth- and twentieth-century works by, for example, Edgar Degas and Henri Matisse. In engaging with these precedents and later in revisiting his own imagery, Bearden placed

11
The Ascension of Christ in Glory, **c. 1945/1946, gouache with ink and graphite on brown paper, 48.3 x 81.3 (19 x 32). Anonymous lender**

12
Two Figures, **c. 1946, oil on fiberboard, 55.9 x 76.2 (22 x 30). Estate of Reginald F. Lewis**

13
Madonna and Child, **1945, oil on canvas, 95.9 x 76.2 (38 x 30). Bryn Mawr College Collections, Pennsylvania, Roy R. Neuberger Collection**

himself at the center of modernist practice as detailed by Fred Orton in writing about Jasper Johns: "Modern artists cannot exclude art history from their project, and many choose consciously to carry their own art history with them, continually making reflexive paintings: paintings of their studios"[58] (see Kennel in this volume, no. 141).

Bearden's 1945 Kootz Gallery exhibition had been a great success. A watercolor, *He Is Arisen,* was acquired by MoMA, and an oil, *Madonna and Child* (no. 13), by the important private collectors Marie and Roy R. Neuberger. (This oil was not in the *Passion* exhibition according to the catalogue, which lists only a watercolor with this title.) Seriously committed to the art of their contemporaries, the Neubergers believed they were:

> living in a period when the art of our own America is flourishing in a strong and healthy development—outstripping that of Europe, long the seat of such activity. We see in this country a variety of subject-matter and treatment which reflects the social, political, the Ivory Tower—every imaginable aspect and corner of our national life.[59]

Bearden was called Kootz Gallery's "new find" in a 1945 review encouraging shoppers to seek Christmas gifts in art galleries. His "memorable" watercolors *Betrayal of Christ* and *Calvary* were priced at $75 each, and because his spring show had sold out in the first two weeks, gallery-goers were urged to purchase quickly.[60] Despite extensive sales and enthusiastic reviews, Bearden's association with Kootz ended in 1948 when the dealer briefly closed his gallery. *The Iliad: 16 Variations by Romare Bearden* was exhibited in Manhattan the following year (November 1948 for one week) in his single show at Niveau Gallery.[61] Shortly before this exhibition Bearden's dual career as social worker and painter was discussed in a *New York World-Telegram* article. Having sold forty paintings, one for $500, Bearden still needed:

> to keep on working as a social investigator in order to live. A tube of cadmium yellow...costs about $3. Frames cost from $24 to $30 for a medium-sized painting. A fine camel's hair brush costs $10. Good linen canvas costs $40 a roll for five yards and yields only four pictures...."There is a richness in this social work," muses the 36 year old Bearden, "a storehouse of things seen that I draw upon in my painting. But, being an abstractionist painter, I only show—I never depict.... The function of the artist is to organize the facets of life according to his imagination."[62]

This embrace of social work as a contribution to his artistic enterprise soon was abandoned when Bearden curtailed work in painting for several years. Among factors that would have contributed to this hiatus, when Kootz reopened in 1949 his focus was on abstract expressionism, and he excluded three artists from the stable: Bearden, Holty, and [George] Byron Browne.[63] Although Bearden's Iliad watercolors already had been exhibited elsewhere, the withdrawal of support from so highly esteemed a dealer as Samuel M. Kootz must have been a serious blow, causing him to rethink priorities and his situation as a painter.[64] These complicated considerations would have been made more so by his ties in both the African-American and mainstream art communities

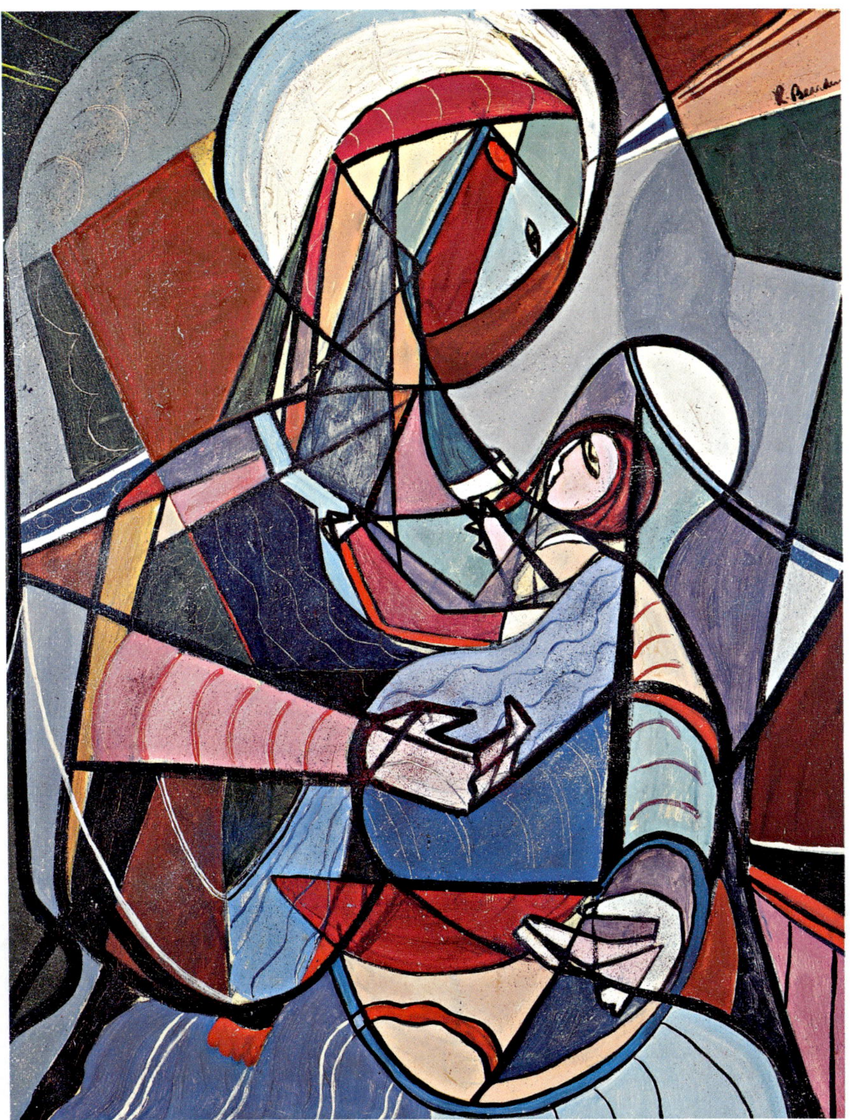

13

that enabled, perhaps required, Bearden to negotiate ideas with a wide range of artistic colleagues. Through the late 1940s he was navigating between social realism (the primary mode in Harlem) and abstraction (the ascendant mode in the New York avant-garde). In reflecting upon his own artistic project one imagines philosophical conflicts would have arisen that in turn were both intellectually stimulating and emotionally draining, constantly calling upon Du Bois' double-consciousness or two-ness. As cultural historian James Hall said about African-American antimodernism and the American sixties: "The character of African-American intellectual life at midcentury was marked by an increasingly disruptive ambivalence, a liminality, a 'betwixt-and-between-ness.'"[65]

These issues are vividly reinforced in Bearden's 1946 essay, "The Negro Artist's Dilemma," in which he essentially moved in the opposite direction from ideas he had stated a dozen years earlier in "The Negro Artist and Modern Art." Rejecting his 1934 notion that there was a particular calling rooted in the realities of everyday life that was specific to the Negro artist, by 1946 he believed "The Negro artist must come to think of himself not primarily as a Negro artist, but as an artist."[66] One can only imagine the conflicts that provoked both of these essays in the first place, and then, in addition, the conflicts engendered by the thought process that would have led from one point of view to the other.

Accepting Keith Morrison's statement that formalism as a "driving force in the evolution of modern art... has been far less of a preoccupation among African Americans than among whites" Bearden stands as an exception to the rule.[67] There were others, of course, for example, his childhood friend Norman Lewis who fully committed to abstraction. That Bearden's concern with formal properties of picture making equaled his commitment to narrative was stated in his letters of the 1940s to Quirt and the 1950s to Holty, and in his 1969 publications, "Rectangular Structure in My Montage Paintings" in the journal *Leonardo,* and the text he coauthored with Holty, *The Painter's Mind: A Study of the Relations of Structure and Space in Painting.*[68] An abstract of the *Leonardo* essay suggests that one aim of the piece was to describe similarities and differences regarding cubism in Bearden's style "with the hope that the structural content of his work will be understood and even more valued than its social message." There can be no doubt, however, that Bearden maintained the social, intellectual, and cultural commitments he had so strongly conveyed in his editorial cartoons of the mid-1930s. This is evident in the way he constructed his life and in his work, in his efforts to bring the work of African-American artists into the mainstream and in the power of his art to bridge diverse cultural experience.

Evidence of this may be found in the personal art history he created in which images were populated by figures with African roots. In 1953 Bearden suggested to Holty that he make photographic reversals of a painting by Poussin; he may have been making positive/negative reversals himself by that time, using the photostat process to turn "positive" into "negative" images, white faces into black faces, referencing artistic interests such as seventeenth-century Dutch painting and Japanese woodblock prints (figs. 17, 18).[69] This was Bearden's "museum without walls" as designated by André Malraux's book of that title which Bearden greatly admired.[70] Malraux's museum,

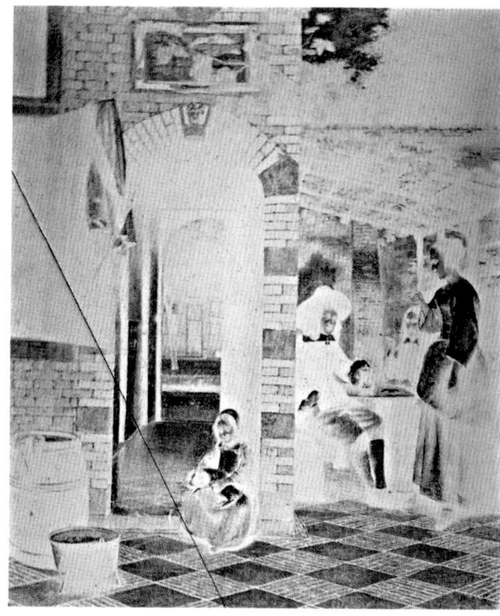
17

like Bearden's, featured art of diverse origin, including Ivory Coast masks, Byzantine mosaics, Romanesque frescoes, stained glass from Chartres Cathedral, paintings by Bosch, Frans Hals, Eugène Delacroix, and Rouault, and a drawing by a madman (listed on the book's contents page as "Lunatic Art"). Within this context, the balance of narrative and formalist issues Bearden sought in his work depended upon the structure and form he understood as essential to aspects of African art as articulated in his *Leonardo* article: "I do not burden myself with the need for complete abstraction or absolute formal purity but I do want my language to be strict and classical, in the manner of the great Benin heads."[71] More than three decades earlier, MoMA curator James Johnson Sweeney had likewise responded to this classicism in a 1935 catalogue essay praising:

figure 17
Negative photostat image of Pieter de Hooch's *Figures Drinking in a Courtyard,* date of photostat unknown. Estate of Romare Bearden, courtesy of Romare Bearden Foundation, New York

figure 18
Negative photostat image of Toshusai Sharaku's portrait of actor Morita Kanya, date of photostat unknown. Estate of Romare Bearden, courtesy of Romare Bearden Foundation, New York

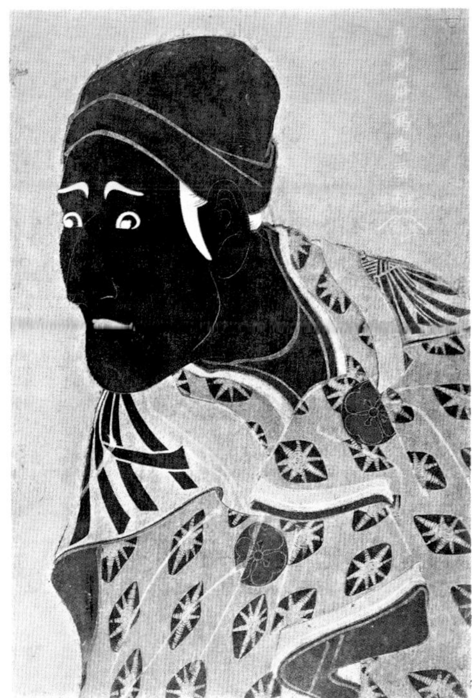

18

> simplification without impoverishment, the unerring emphasis on the essential, the consistent three-dimensional organization of structural planes in architectonic sequences, the uncompromising truth to material with a seemingly intuitive adaptation of it, and the tension achieved between the idea or emotion to be expressed through representation and the abstract principles of sculpture.[72]

Change the closing word "sculpture" to "art" and this could be a description of Bearden's oeuvre.

From 1949 through 1963 Bearden's artistic production was erratic and is difficult to track.[73] He was in France for approximately seven months in 1950, and like many veterans of World War II he enrolled in classes financed by the G.I. Bill of Rights.[74] Bearden most often reported studying French at the Institut Britannique and philosophy with Gaston Bachelard at the Sorbonne. Many years after the fact in an undated letter, he wrote to his friend Jack Fein that his teachers had also included Jean Wahl and Maurice Merleau-Ponty. Bearden's trip to Europe may also have been a response to that double-consciousness of African-Americans' lives—called there as part of the decades' old journey of visual artists to Paris, which was still viewed as the art capital of the world; and as part of the post–World War II migration of African-American intellectuals and artists not only to Paris, but also to Rome, Stockholm, and Amsterdam, where they sought a more hospitable environment than could be found in the United States.

At 5 rue des Feuillantines in the fifth arrondissement, Bearden lived in a skylit studio, with three meals per day for about $40 a month.[75] The pension also served as a home for Sidney Wallach, a young American reporter for the *Herald Tribune;* the two had met crossing the Atlantic on the S.S. *America.* Wallach reported that on at least one occasion Bearden showed friends a stack of watercolors he had brought from New York, perhaps hoping to find representation in a Paris gallery.[76] Bearden alleged that he did no painting during this European sojourn, but in an undated letter to Holty from rue des Feuillantines he wrote that he "came home late and drew with charcoal, something I've never heretofore been able to do—and I drew very well, with rich tones and nice passages felt all over the paper. I'll be able to work in Paris from now on." None of these drawings has been identified.

In that same letter Bearden tells of going to "the Louvre, the Cluny, the Museum of Oriental art, the Bibliotheque National [*sic*] with Rembrant [*sic*] drawings, the Museum of Man (with the African sculpture)." In another undated letter to Holty from the same address Bearden discussed his travel by train to Italy, including Genoa, Milan, Florence, Pisa, Sienna, Orvieto, Rome, Orezzo, Livorgno, and back to Paris:

> Certainly the whole trip would have been more than justified by only having seen the frescoes of Michael Angelo in the Sistine Chapel. Now I really understand why they call him the "Divine Michael Angelo." The scope; problems of scale; the use of even the overlapping cracks of the plaster where the work was done day by day, to carry movements, is simply astonishing.

Particularly fascinating is Bearden's observation of Michelangelo's use of the fresco process. Likewise he was concerned about his "beloved mosaics at St. Maria Maggiore in Rome.... They are under open windows so that rain and soot are gradually demolishing what is left." When a priest who became aware of his distress asked if Bearden wanted confession, he reported to Holty that he had said, "No, Father, but I must confess I don't like the treatment given those mosaics," again expressing concern for the physicality of works of art in all of their aspects.

Bearden frequented Paris' many cafés and visited studios of artists he met, notably Brancusi.[77] Writer Albert Murray and he initiated their lifelong friendship during this Paris period, and Murray remembers accompanying the artist during his last day there, as he purchased an assortment of papers, including oriental and special colored sheets, for use in New York—artistic practice must have been on his mind. Often recounted is the strong impression left on Bearden by the sight of the elderly Henri Matisse being applauded by waiters and customers in a sidewalk café as the older artist walked by, a display of recognition and reverence impossible to imagine an artist receiving in the United States.

Back home Bearden lived in Harlem with his father. He must have applied for a Fulbright fellowship before leaving for Paris, or during his stay abroad, based on an August letter he wrote to Howard Backus in the Fulbright Division of the Department of State, requesting a review of his application which, he had been told, had netted him a position as an alternate. Apparently it was inferred that his age, thirty-seven, may have mitigated against his receipt of a grant. Objecting that the application form made no mention of an age limit, Bearden went on to suggest that "considerations should be given those persons who had long tenures of service in the Armed Forces" noting that "the development of any artist is a slow process, so that in France a painter is considered as a 'young painter' until he is about 45 years of age.... Far from any idea of special pleading for veterans"; however, he went on to cite personal factors in his career that he considered special qualifications. These included his extensive exhibition record, including shows in Paris, and "a wide knowledge of French culture, especially of Gothic stained-glass and Romanesque frescoes, such as those in the churches of St. Savin and St. Tavant ...an adequate reading and speaking knowledge of French" and his courses at the Sorbonne.[78]

Apparently Bearden's plea was not successful, and during the early 1950s much of his artistic concentration was devoted to writing songs with the intention still of earning return passage back to Paris.[79] His accomplishments include lyrics for "Seabreeze," popularized by Billy Eckstine and others; "Missus Santa Claus" and "My Candy Apple," recorded by Leslie Uggams (see Francis in this volume, figs. 15, 16); and pieces for Billie Holiday, who worked as a receptionist in the Apollo Theater building. The urge to paint kept resurfacing, however, and contrary to much that has been published, there is evidence that he did some work, perhaps mainly on paper, during these difficult years (see fig. 20).[80] In addition encouragement from Nanette Rohan, whom Bearden married in 1954, and from his friends Heinrich Blücher and Hannah Arendt, was important to his serious return to the visual arts by the mid-1950s.

An exhibition of new paintings went on view in autumn 1955 at the Barone Gallery, including watercolors and oils that were "more-or-less abstract."[81] The watercolors, especially, were "notable for the handling of space problems and for their suggestiveness of season and mood," qualities that would remain essential to Bearden's art as it underwent other radical changes.[82] A conflation of figurative and abstract forms dominant in paintings of the late 1940s, although of a different nature, may also be seen, for example, in *A Walk in Paradise Gardens,* 1955 (no. 14). By the end of the decade, however, Bearden was privileging abstraction with only occasional coded references to landscape if to anything representational. Henderson speaks of Bearden's elation at New York's displacement of Paris as the world's art capital, his excitement over "an art movement that pushed Picasso out of the picture." A new mentor with whom he studied was a Mr. Wu, a Chinese

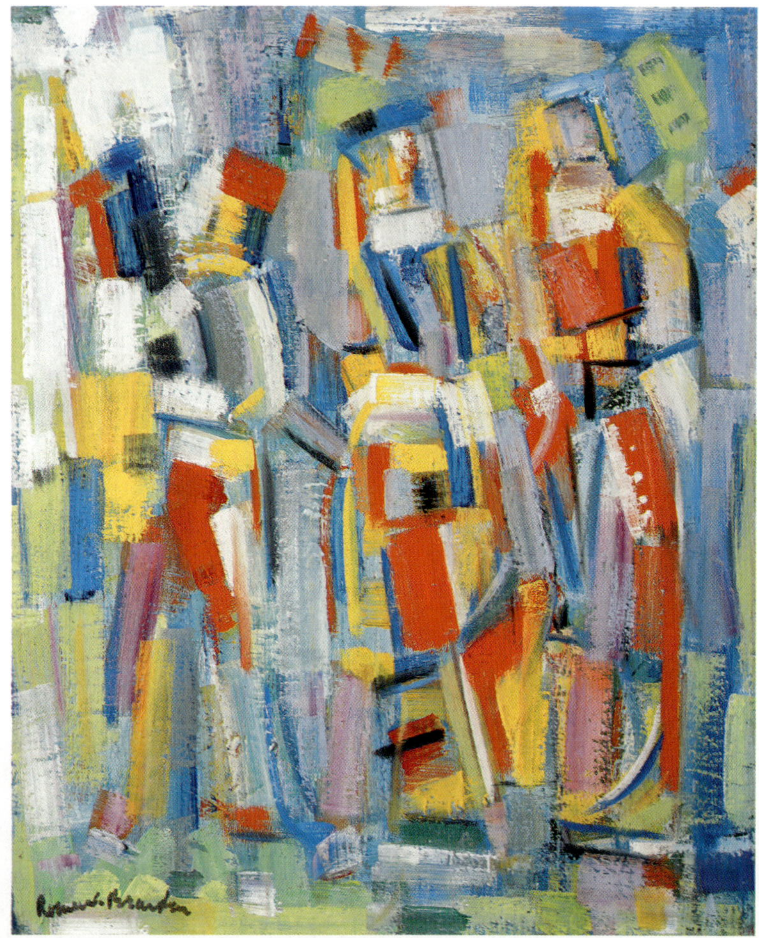

14

calligrapher who provided Bearden's introduction to Chinese landscape painting, which he added to his roster of interests. He attributed to his study of Chinese landscape the concept of a path of entry: "the device of the open corner to allow the observer a starting point in encompassing the entire painting."[83]

Sometime in the 1950s (or possibly the late 1940s) Bearden became interested in Zen Buddhism, a subject of considerable discussion within the international art world. Among the Americans engaged by Zen was Ad Reinhardt, whom Bearden would have known through Carl Holty, and whose cartoons including "How to Look at Space," "How to Look at Things," and "How to Look at an Artist," are among Bearden's papers.[84] Bearden appears to have maintained this interest on some level for the rest of his life based on references to Zen that appear throughout his notebooks, once on a page dated 1970. It is an unusual point of reference for Bearden whose notebooks generally are undated throughout. Never comfortable with the "action painting" aspect of abstract expressionism, according to Henderson, Bearden found in Zen a quieter road to abstraction, one in which the canvas itself played an important role, "its character and how you applied the paint and you lifted [the canvas] and let [the paint] roll. The artist's role, in the end, was to select and retain forms that emerged and say 'that's a painting.'"

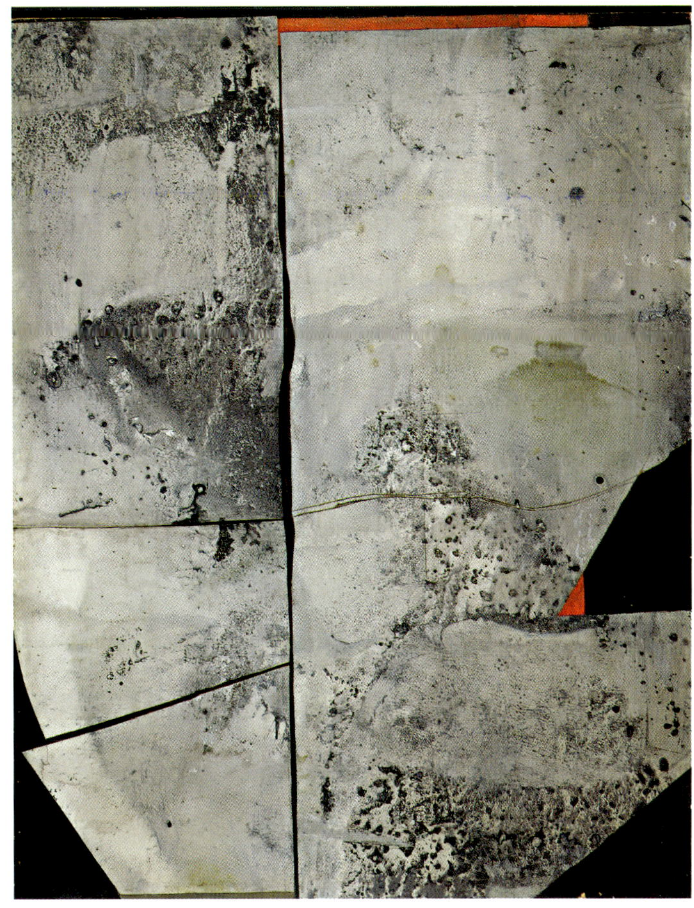

15

Bearden's conscious activation of painterly surfaces grew stronger, a concern shared by other postwar abstract artists in the United States and abroad. From France, for example, Jean Dubuffet's paintings and collages, which Bearden greatly admired, present splendid reference points for this, just as Jackson Pollock's canvases similarly do for the New York milieu.[85] In an undated letter to Holty Bearden called Dubuffet "the strongest painter to have come out of France since the war." The coordination of elements from classical Chinese painting with others from contemporary international modernism provided Bearden's abstract expressionism with a beauty and energy that was distinctly its own. His color world during these years was quite varied as he moved from the thickly worked surfaces of *A Walk in Paradise Gardens,* with its vestiges of figural form to splashes and veils of thinly applied paint that left the canvas itself to play an active role, and eventually to canvas-collages such as *North of the River* (no. 15). These two paintings elegantly convey the poles of Bearden's painterly abstraction and the rich facture he employed as a prime expressive element.

14
A Walk in Paradise Gardens, **1955, oil on fiberboard, 61 x 50.8 (24 x 20). Robert L. Johnson from The Barnett-Aden Collection, Washington, D.C.**

15
North of the River, **1962, canvas collage with oil, watercolor, ink, and graphite on canvas, 132.1 x 106.7 (52 x 42). Collection of The Studio Museum in Harlem, New York, Museum Purchase 1993**

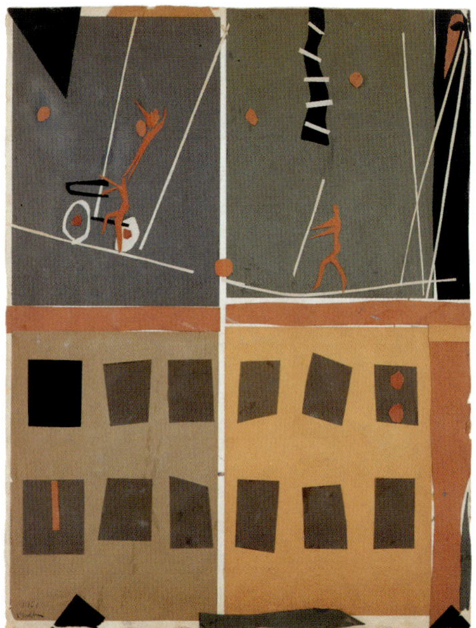

19

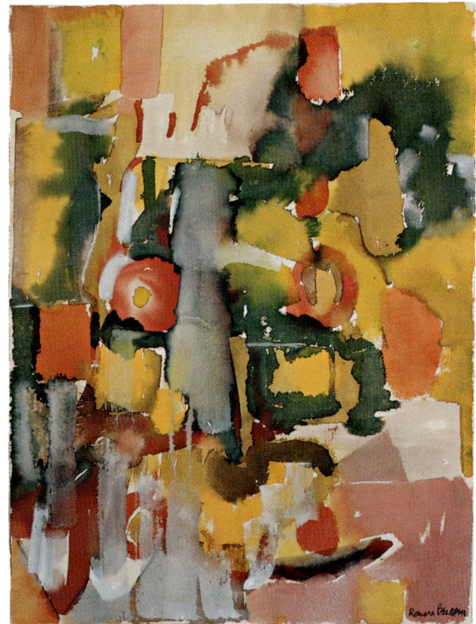

20

Between the 1955 Barone Gallery exhibition and 1960, Bearden had no solo shows. This withdrawal from public view may have been necessary to permit him time for quiet renewal following an emotional breakdown in 1956.[86] One can think of many causes of such an occurrence in addition to specific concerns about his own artistic practice. Among them were the lack of a strong community of African-American artists during this period; the seeming impossibility of true unity between the uptown and downtown artists; and the threatening atmosphere of McCarthyism that had already taken its toll on friends including Paul Robeson.[87] In any case, Bearden "blew a fuse" and he later discussed this in the context of:

the things that an artist may have had to go through to reach these things that he ought to be able to paint. All of painting is a kind of talking about life or society, but it doesn't need to be overtly so. Often we don't know how to read it. *Alice in Wonderland* talked about a lot of these things, about English morals and customs of the Victorian era, but we thought it was a children's fairy tale.[88]

After living in the Harlem apartment with Howard Bearden for the first two years of their marriage, Romare and Nanette moved downtown to a walk-up building at 357 Canal Street in 1956, likely in response to the breakdown as well as an ongoing need for privacy. They lived there for the rest of their lives, on the fifth floor at first, later adding another apartment on the second level. Bearden obviously got back to work, and in the winter of 1960 had a solo exhibition at the Michel Warren Gallery from which MoMA purchased *Silent Valley of the Sunrise,* a 1959 oil. The following year, with the gallery renamed Daniel Cordier & Michel Warren Inc., Bearden showed works with less metaphysical titles such as *Circus (Circus: The Artist's Center Ring)* (fig. 19), suggesting he was en route back to representation. He was. For the rest of his life, however, he periodically returned to a lyrical abstraction, similar to that of the watercolor *Blue Ridge,* c. 1952 (fig. 20).

figure 19
Romare Bearden, *Circus (Circus: The Artist's Center Ring)*, 1961, collage of various papers on paper. Estate of Romare Bearden, courtesy of Romare Bearden Foundation, New York

figure 20
Romare Bearden, *Blue Ridge,* c. 1952, watercolor on paper. Collection of June Kelly

In 1963–64, during a period of extraordinary political ferment in the United States, indeed in the world, Bearden, at age fifty-one, simultaneously made the two most dramatic changes to his work of his career. He returned to figuration (at a small size that was likewise a break from his relatively large abstractions), and he shifted from a painting-based art to a collage-based practice. It seems reasonable to speculate that viewing old master paintings in France, Italy, and Switzerland during a 1961 trip with Nanette may have inspired Bearden to reconsider working figuratively. His move toward collage is less readily pinpointed.[89]

In the 1940s collage had been explored by many New York artists, including Willem de Kooning and Robert Motherwell; the latter was in the Kootz Gallery stable with Bearden. Moreover, in 1951 Motherwell edited *The Dada Painters and Poets: An Anthology,* which highlights collage and which Bearden likely would have known.[90] Also of note, in October 1961, just two years before Bearden began his landmark work in collage, MoMA mounted *The Art of Assemblage,* an exhibition of 252 pieces including Dubuffet's *Portrait of a Man,* 1957, made of butterfly wings and watercolor, collages by Grosz and Höch that incorporate magazine advertisements and halftone illustrations respectively, Motherwell's *In Grey with Parasol,* dating to the Kootz Gallery years, and thirty-five works by Kurt Schwitters. The show would not have gone unnoticed by Bearden.[91]

Bearden was working in collage by the time this exhibition took place, however, so its function would have been a supportive rather an inspirational one. Assuming *Harlequin* (no. 16) is accurately dated to about 1956 (which seems likely based on formal relationships to *A Walk in Paradise Gardens*), it is the earliest of his collages we have seen.[92] A dynamic and colorful image that subtly suggests the title figure, *Harlequin* is composed of an array of papers: fragments from one of Bearden's watercolors or drawings from the late 1940s, identifiable by the webs of black calligraphic lines; colored construction paper of the sort children still use in art classes (and which was employed by many abstract painters, including Pollock and Mark Rothko); and a medium-weight, relatively smooth, creamy-white sheet. To this paper substructure Bearden added details in paint, ink, and graphite. *Harlequin*'s vigorous facture is consistent with contemporaneous abstract expressionist methods and its motif reminiscent both of Picasso's paintings from the early part of the century and of circus pictures by American artists as diverse as Walt Kuhn and John Marin. Indeed Bearden's own attention to the subject may be tracked back to *Mad Carousel* dating to 1946 (see Chronology, 1946), the year Samuel M. Kootz mounted an exhibition entitled *The Big Top.*

Distinctive in its combination of subject and process within Bearden's oeuvre, *Harlequin* beautifully conflates his multiple concerns at this pivotal moment. Other circus-inspired collages dated to 1961, such as *Circus (Circus: The Artist's*

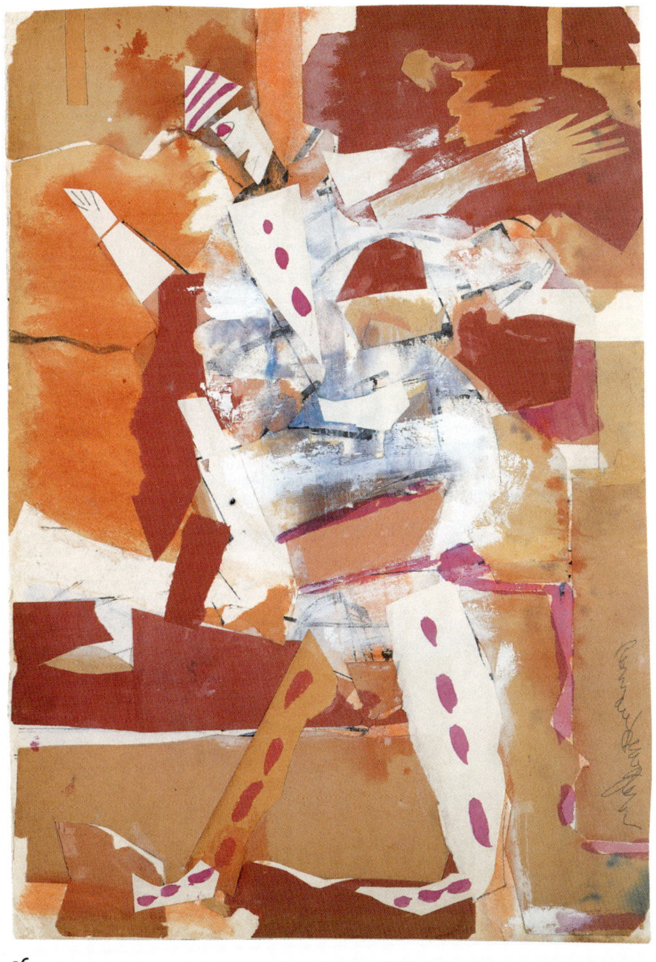

16

16
***Harlequin,* c. 1956, collage of various papers with paint, ink, and graphite on paper, 62.6 x 44.5 (24⅝ x 17½). Collection of Frank Stewart**

1964

Center Ring) presumably were part of or related to Bearden's Cordier & Warren exhibition of that year. Very different in facture from *Harlequin,* their spare compositions lack painterly expressionism and suggest Bearden's admiration for Matisse's radical "cut-outs" (as his collages dating from the 1930s through the early 1950s are called), as well as the glorious 1947 pochoir book, *Jazz,* which subject undoubtedly would have attracted the younger artist.[93] Whether or not the circa 1956 date is accurate for *Harlequin,* firmly dated works such as *Circus: The Artist's Center Ring* and *Number 9* (see fig. 26), both dated to 1961, and *North of the River* of the following year inform us without question that collage played a role in Bearden's art before his revolutionary works of 1963–64.

In early July 1963, the month before Martin Luther King led two hundred fifty thousand Americans on the historic march on Washington, several African-American painters met in Bearden's Canal Street studio to form an alliance that came to be named Spiral.[94] The designation stemmed from senior member Hale Woodruff's proposal that the Archimedian spiral representing expansive positive energy be the group's symbol: "from a starting point, [it] moves outward embracing all directions, yet constantly upward."[95] Spiral meetings were held in various studios until the artists rented a space downtown at 147 Christopher Street. In addition to Bearden and Woodruff, early Spiral participants included Alston, Lewis (the group's first president), and Merton Simpson, all of whom had shared in the psychic support generated by the Harlem Artists Guild and the 306 community during the 1930s. Younger artists including Emma Amos, Reginald Gammon, and Richard Mayhew joined later.[96] Spiral's purpose was to discuss "what should be their attitudes and commitments as Negro artists in the present struggle for Civil Rights" and to explore ways they might make a unique contribution to that struggle.[97] Mayhew remembers Spiral as a "think tank," a term in keeping with the spirit of Bearden's 1966 response to a query from journalist Jeanne Siegel: "Why Spiral?" Bearden believed:

> Western society, and particularly that of America, is gravely ill and a major symptom is the American treatment of the Negro. The artistic expression of this culture concentrates on themes and "absurdity" and "anti-art" which provide further evidence of its ill health. It is the right of everyone now to re-examine history to see if Western culture offers the only solutions to man's purpose on this earth.[98]

Lewis wanted the group to "point to a broader purpose and never be led down an alley of frustration. Political and social aspects should not be the primary concern; esthetic ideas should have preference." He then framed the question "Is there a Negro Image?" to which Felrath Hines responded, "There is no Negro Image in the twentieth century—in the 1960s. There are only prevailing ideas that influence everyone all over the world, to which the Negro has been, and is, contributing. Each person paints out of the life he lives."[99]

According to Bearden someone proposed the group "work together on some project, and [he] suggested that we take magazines and clip and just start pasting."[100] Memories of the details vary: from Bearden bringing to a meeting a bag of snippets from newspapers and magazines for use in a communal collage in support of civil rights; to Bearden showing collages he already had made hoping to inspire the group in using the method. This last is confirmed by Bearden's report to Henri Ghent that he "worked on one or two [collages] alone just to try to get the idea myself to show the other artists."[101] In any case a group collage did not materialize, but Bearden's own use of the process thrived. Other Spiral members worked toward their goals individually as well, meeting weekly (or biweekly or monthly depending on the speaker or writer) through 1965 when their lease on the Christopher Street space was lost.

In addition to functioning as a forum for discussion, Spiral aimed to generate exhibition opportunities for members. One context for their concern was provided by MoMA's *Americans 1963* exhibition from May through August, at the very moment Spiral's meetings began. In her foreword to the catalogue, organizer and curator Dorothy C. Miller explains the exhibition as the latest in a series of group shows, the first of which, *Paintings by Nineteen Living Americans,* had opened (as did the museum) in 1929. Among other shows in the series were *Americans 1942: Eighteen Artists from Nine States; Fourteen Americans,* 1946; *Twelve Americans,* 1956; and *Sixteen Americans,* 1959. *Americans 1963* included fifteen artists, four women and eleven men, divided fairly equally (for the first time) between painting and sculpture. Paintings included Richard Anuszkiewicz's optical investigations; the pop-oriented representation of Robert Indiana and Rosenquist (for whom collage played and plays an important role); Sally Hazelet Drummond's pointillist abstractions; and Reinhardt's "purist, abstract, non-objective object[s]."[102] Sculpture included Gabriel Kohn's laminated wood pieces; Lee Bontecou's welded steel, canvas, and wire constructions; Marisol Escobar's collagelike figurative structures of wood, plaster, and other materials; and Claes Thure Oldenburg's painted plaster foodstuffs and clothing. The artists were of several generations, their birth dates ranging from 1901 to 1933.[103] None was African American. None of the artists in the earlier "Americans" exhibitions had been either. Discouragement, even rage, is readily understood from the point of view of the Spiral artists, as is their need to generate exhibition opportunities.

Spiral's one group show was held at the Christopher Street space from 14 May to 5 June 1965: *First Group Showing: Works in Black and White.*[104] Represented were Alston, Amos, Bearden, Calvin Douglass, Perry Ferguson, Gammon, Hines, Alvin Hollingsworth, Lewis, William Majors, Mayhew, Earl Miller, Simpson, Woodruff, and James Yeargans. The catalogue foreword situated their joining together because:

> we, as Negroes, could not fail to be touched by the outrage of segregation, or fail to relate to the self-reliance, hope, and courage of those persons who were marching in the interest of man's dignity.... If possible, in these times, we hoped with our art to justify life.... [choosing] to use only black and white and eschew other coloration. This consideration, or limitation, was conceived from technical concerns; although deeper motivations may have been involved.... What is most important now, and what has great portent for the future, is that Negro artists, of divergent backgrounds and interests, have come together on terms of mutual respect. It is to their credit that they were able to fashion art works lit by beauty, and of such diversity.[105]

Bearden's contribution to the exhibition was *Conjur Woman* (The Studio Museum in Harlem), a photostatic enlargement, possibly made by Joe Walchecko, from a collage/photomontage, a genre of picture-making that may be tracked back to the late nineteenth century, historically more popular in Europe than America.[106] Bearden called the photostatic enlargements of his collages *Projections,* a term suggested by Arne Ekstrom. It served as the title of the October 1964 exhibition at Cordier & Ekstrom, Inc., where twenty-one of them were first shown.[107] Like *Conjur Woman* in the Spiral show, all twenty-one were enlargements of small collages that had developed from Bearden's efforts to generate the Spiral collaboration. This suggests a date of mid-1963 for the earliest of the small collages. None, to our knowledge, has been dated to that year, but perhaps all were dated to the year they initially left the studio for exhibition. May 1964 appears to be the first time this happened: *Evening Meal of Prophet Peterson* (no. 17) was in a benefit show on behalf of the Congress of Racial Equality (CORE), at the American Federation of Arts Gallery, New York.

As evident from the works in the *Americans 1963* exhibition, the early 1960s (and back into the 1950s) was a period in which many American artists were concerned with collage concepts and assemblage techniques. Given Bearden's intrepid curiosity he would have been reading every sort of art publication and viewing as many exhibitions uptown and downtown as possible, and his personal and cultural commitments would have continued to engage mainstream currents as well as those specific to an African-American milieu. Building on these experiences and his amalgam of talent and imagination, Bearden created collages

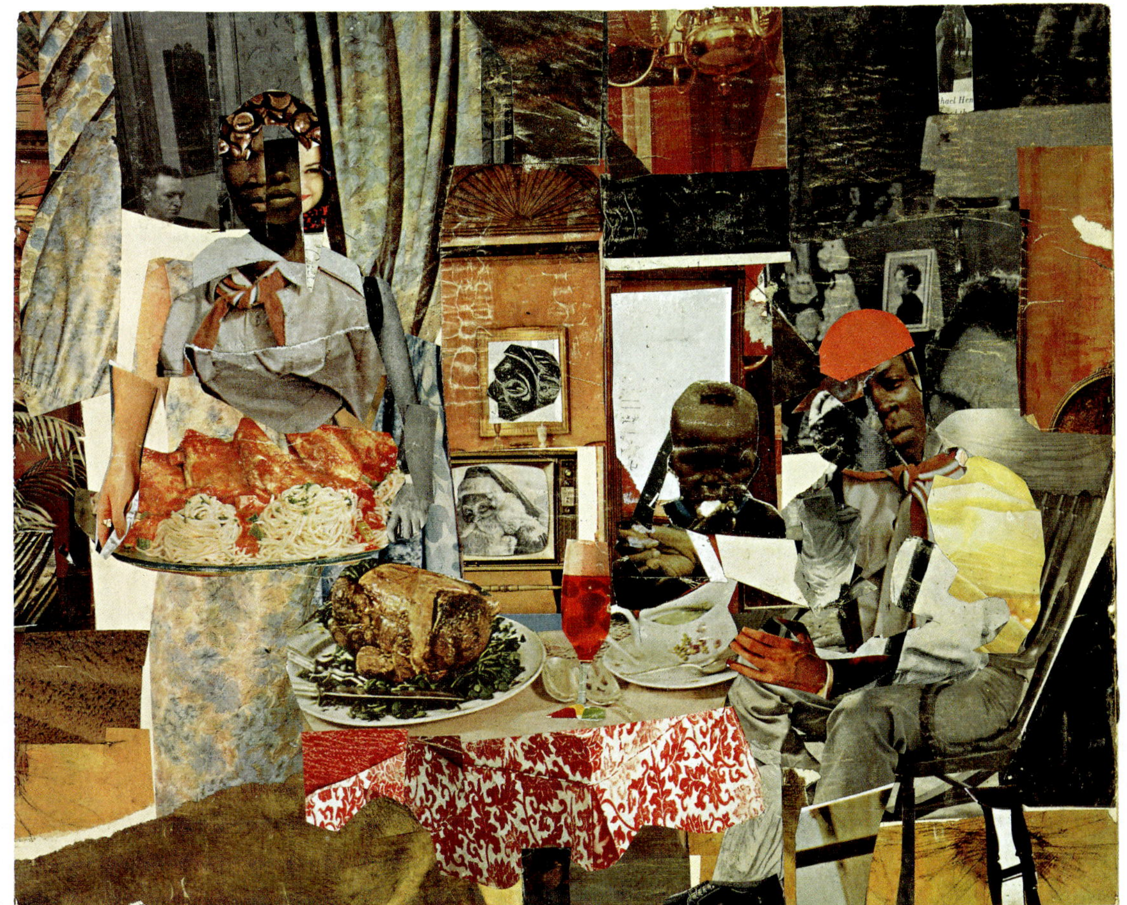

17

17
Evening Meal of Prophet Peterson, **1964, collage of various papers with graphite on cardboard, 30.5 x 38.7 (12 x 15¼). Elisabeth M. and William M. Landes, Chicago, Illinois**

and photostatic Projections that take their place on the artistic cutting edge in two very different ways. Unfortunately, despite radical differences in size, methodology, and relationships to other art, the jewellike collages and the powerful journalistic Projections, directly corresponding as they do to each other in image and title, are frequently discussed interchangeably, the distinctive qualities of each thereby diminished.[108]

In concept, method, and size, Bearden's circa 1964 collages may be allied with a painterly practice rooted in cubism and passing through that aspect of Dada marked by the delicately beautiful collages of Schwitters and Höch. They also associate themselves with aspects of African-American cultural history including the patchwork quilts coded with information that aided escaped slaves traveling the underground railroad, and collages fieldworkers made on the walls of their cabins in the southern region of the United States.[109] These collages could equally accurately be termed photomontages, as most are made entirely of snippets of photographs from magazines and newspapers. Bearden, however, consistently referred to his works as paintings or collage paintings rather than collages, and to shift from his conceptual painterly emphasis to the term photomontage would counter the artist's apparent intentions. In addition few of his later works come so purely under a photomontage umbrella, engaged as they are with a wide array of nonphotographic materials.

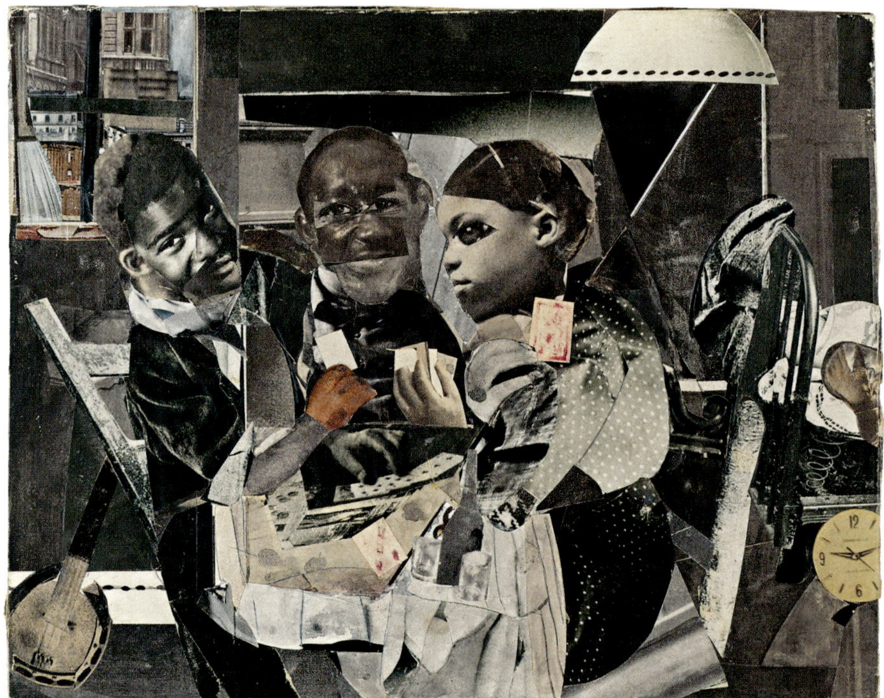

18

Henderson recalled that Bearden particularly wanted his Projections to have the flat, matte finish the photostat method would produce. Less commonly used now than in the 1960s due to the digital revolution in photographic practice, photostats were made using a special camera loaded with rolls of photographic paper rather than film. Either a positive or negative image could be produced, depending upon the type of paper and processing chemicals used. Flat objects such as drawings or photographs and three-dimensional objects, could all be copied with a photostat camera, and subjects could be enlarged or reduced in size, making the process perfect for meeting Bearden's needs. It was also fairly uncomplicated so long as he had access to proper equipment.[110] Bearden's photostat Projections align themselves with that aspect of Dada associated with the photomontages of Heartfield and Höch, but they more fully associate with direct photographic practice—still photography, cinema, and television, which by 1963–64 had emerged as a new and persuasive cultural force.[111] With their strong journalistic overtones the Projections are more radical than the collages and are prescient of large-scale photographic work undertaken by growing numbers of artists in recent years.[112]

From mid-1963 through 1965, working on a diminutive format (from approximately 5 x 10 to 13 x 19 inches), Bearden completed approximately two dozen collages (later enlarged as Projections). Their images include genre, as in *Evening, 9:10, 461 Lenox Avenue* (no. 18); motifs from literature, as in, *Expulsion from Paradise* (no. 19; the photostat based on it is no. 20); and rituals such as *The Burial, Ritual,* and *Baptism* (nos. 21, 22, 23), all in a narrow vertical format to which Bearden

18
Evening, 9:10, 461 Lenox Avenue, **1964, collage of various papers with paint, ink, and graphite on cardboard, 21.3 x 27.9 (8⅜ x 11). Van Every/Smith Galleries, Davidson College, Davidson, North Carolina**

19
Expulsion from Paradise, **1964, collage of various papers with paint, ink, and graphite on cardboard, 34.1 x 44.5 (13 7/16 x 17½). Anonymous lender**

20
Expulsion from Paradise, **1964, photostat on fiberboard, Edition 1/6, 71.8 x 95.3 (28¼ x 37½). Estate of Romare Bearden, courtesy of Romare Bearden Foundation, New York**

periodically returned (see *Untitled [Girl in a Pond]*, no. 99). Laden with mystery, these small, complex works reveal the dense body of artistic and cultural knowledge Bearden had been accumulating for three decades, and they should be considered monuments in both Bearden's oeuvre and in American art of the early 1960s.[113] Allusion is basic to them, and as with Bearden's later works, grasping references and possible meanings requires lengthy engagement. Gracefully intertwined are allusions to pre-twentieth century Western art, African art, literature and music of many cultures, the political and artistic anarchy of Dada, and a multitude of other twentieth-century "isms" that led from an explosive pictorial space to the flatness central to later modernist concerns. Cubism, futurism, surrealism, expressionism, and the fluctuation between abstraction and representation were essential to them all. It is a

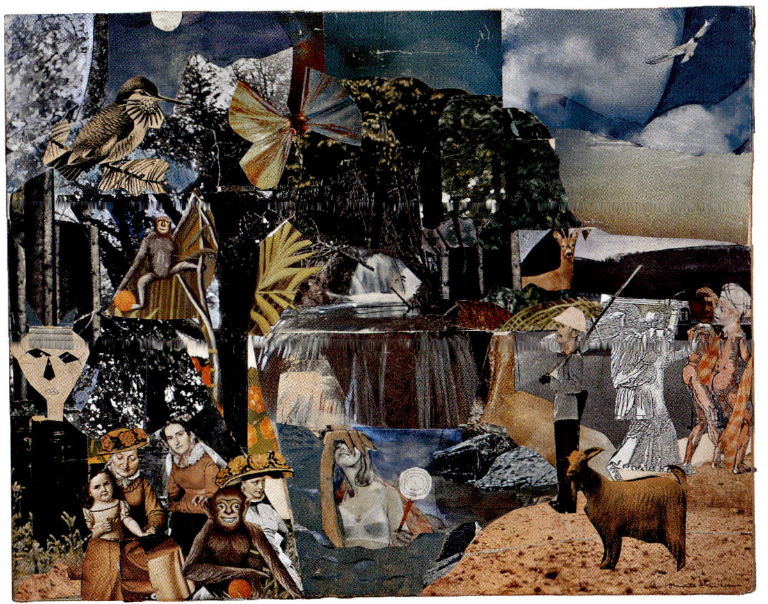

19

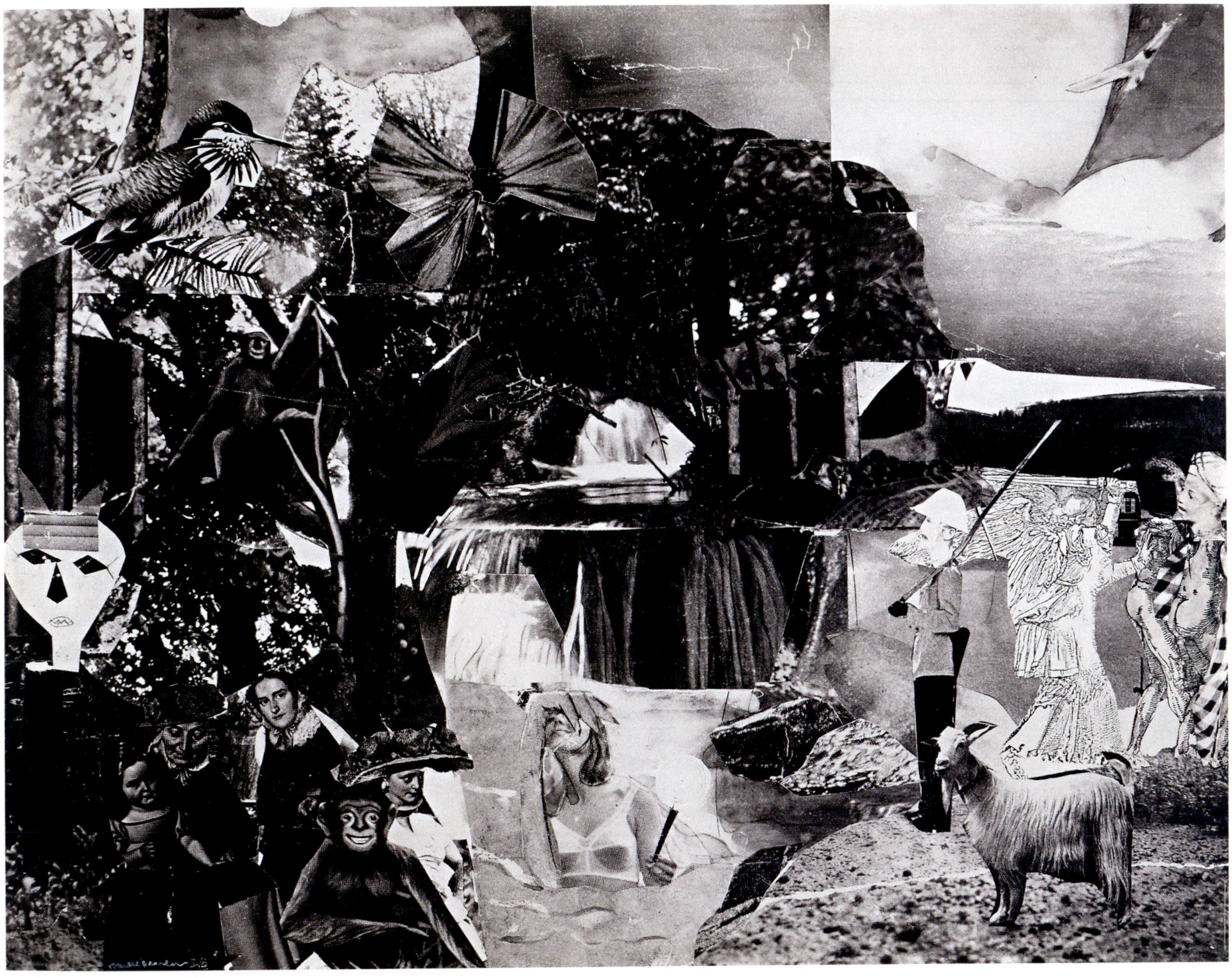

20

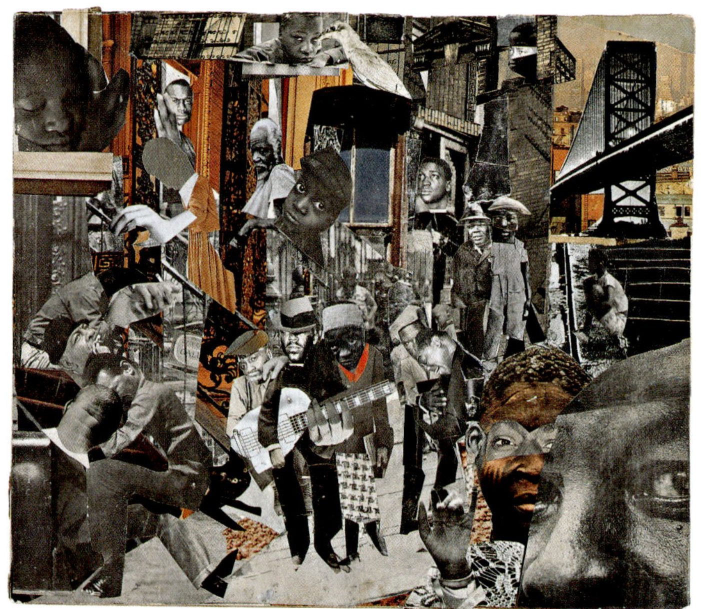

32

his making of a work to determine subsequent actions. Likewise, the jazz practice "call and recall" is embedded in his repetition of motifs, always with variation of one sort or another. This may take the form of radical changes, as seen when comparing the relatively calm *Prevalence of Ritual: Conjur Woman* from 1964 with *Conjur Woman* from 1975 (see no. 97), who seems both menacing and emblematic of evil spirits, brilliantly enhanced in this regard by Bearden's use of color. This spirit-figure, who reappears frequently in Bearden's work, is critical to southern African-American culture—called on to prepare love potions, cure illnesses, and assist with personal problems. "Much of her knowledge had been passed on through the generations from an African past, although a great deal was learned from the American Indians. A conjur woman was greatly feared and it was believed that she could

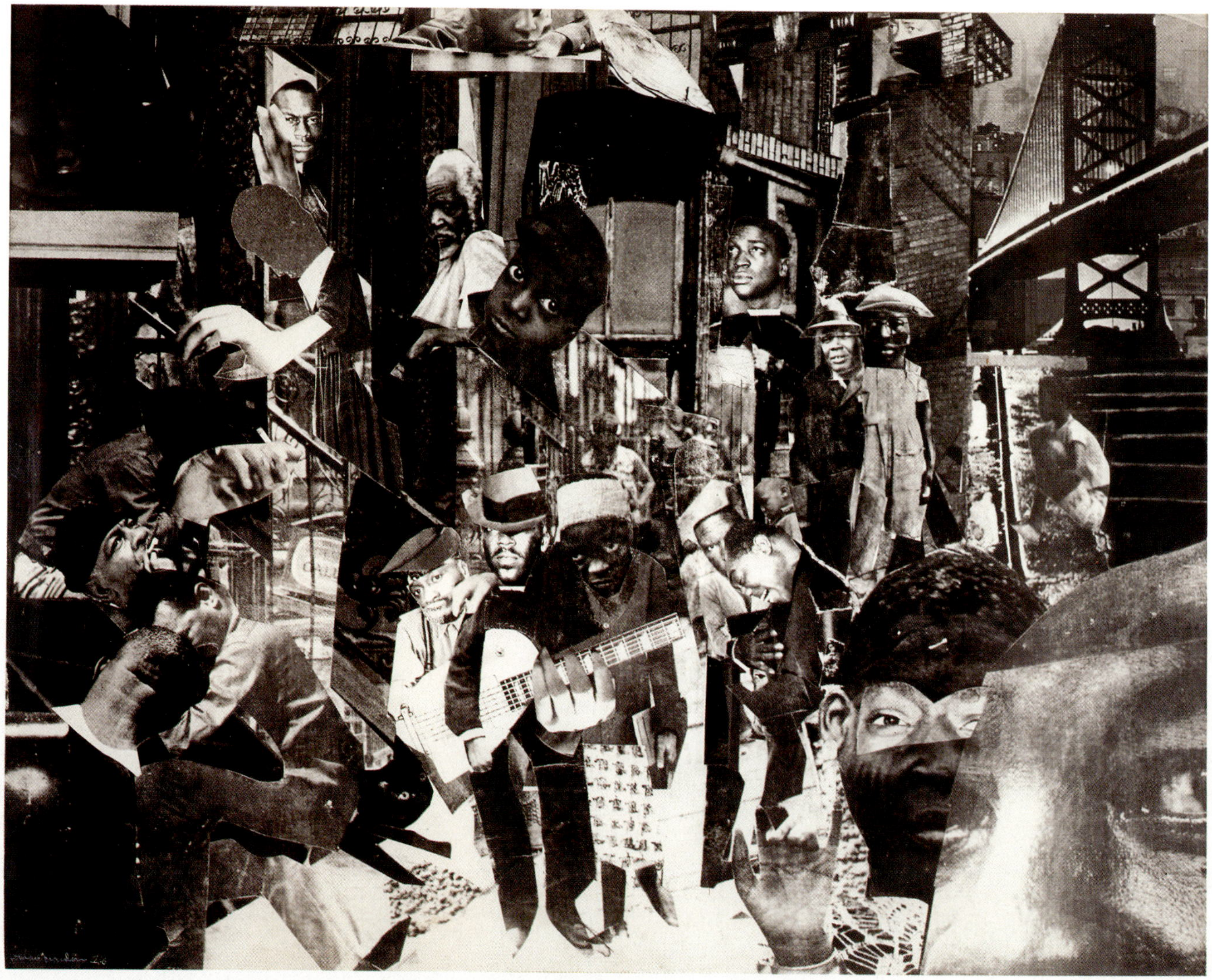

33

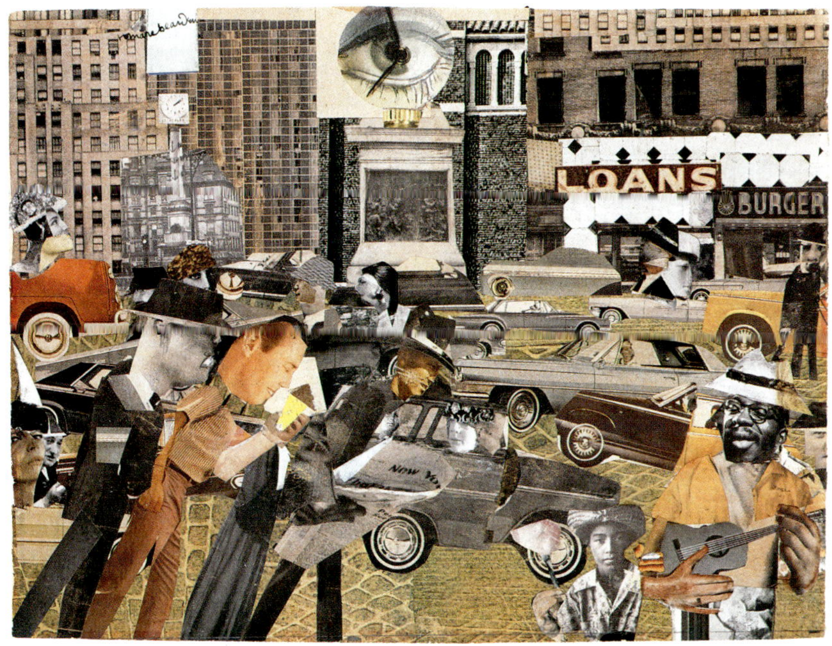

34

change her appearance."[116] Campbell placed the conjure woman at the center of what she referred to as Bearden's "magic woman in nature," a concept that is beautifully matched to his varied approaches to images of women.[117]

Collages with closely related images may have very different titles and suggested meanings, such as *Early Morning*, c. 1964, and *Sun and Candle*, 1971 (nos. 35, 36). Also of note, Bearden explored similar images in various media as exemplified by *Prevalence of Ritual: Tidings* (itself a restatement of *The Visitation*, 1941), in 1964 collage and photostatic versions, and a watercolor from the early 1970s, *The Visitor* (nos. 37–39) as well as a monoprint collagraph, *Annunciation #1*, c. 1976 (fig. 21).

Bearden's circa 1964 collages are composed primarily of magazine images *cut* rather than torn from their sources, and they employ a relatively thin cardboard substrate. Particularly fascinating

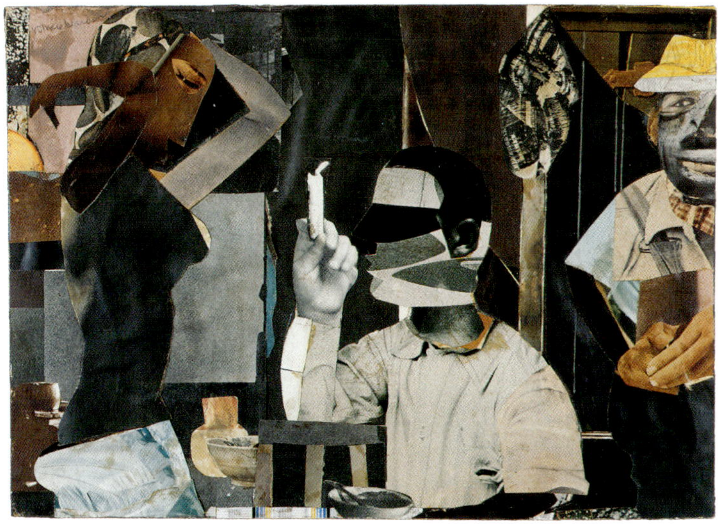

35

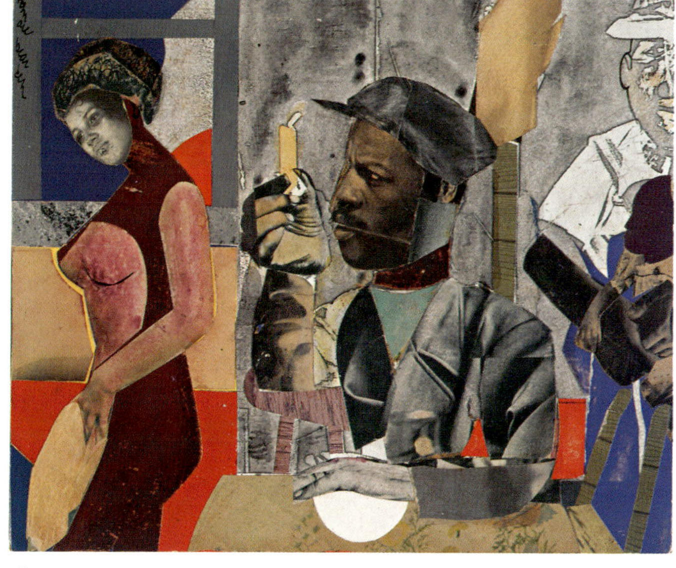

36

32
The Street, 1964, collage of various papers on cardboard, 24.5 x 28.9 (9⅝ x 11⅜). Milwaukee Art Museum, gift of Friends of Art and the African American Art Acquisition Fund

33
The Street, 1964, photostat on fiberboard, Edition 1/6, 78.7 x 101.6 (31 x 40). Estate of Romare Bearden, courtesy of Romare Bearden Foundation, New York

34
Childhood Memories, 1965/1966, collage of various papers with paint and ink on cardboard, 29.5 x 38.4 (11⅝ x 15⅛). Collection Merrill C. Berman

35
Early Morning, c. 1964, collage of various papers with paint and graphite on cardboard, 24.8 x 35.6 (9¾ x 14). Spelman College Museum of Fine Art, Atlanta, Georgia, gift of Mr. and Mrs. Chauncey Waddell

36
Sun and Candle, 1971, collage of various papers with paint, ink, graphite, and surface abrasion on fiberboard, 26.7 x 32.7 (10½ x 12⅞). Tougaloo College Art Collections, Mississippi

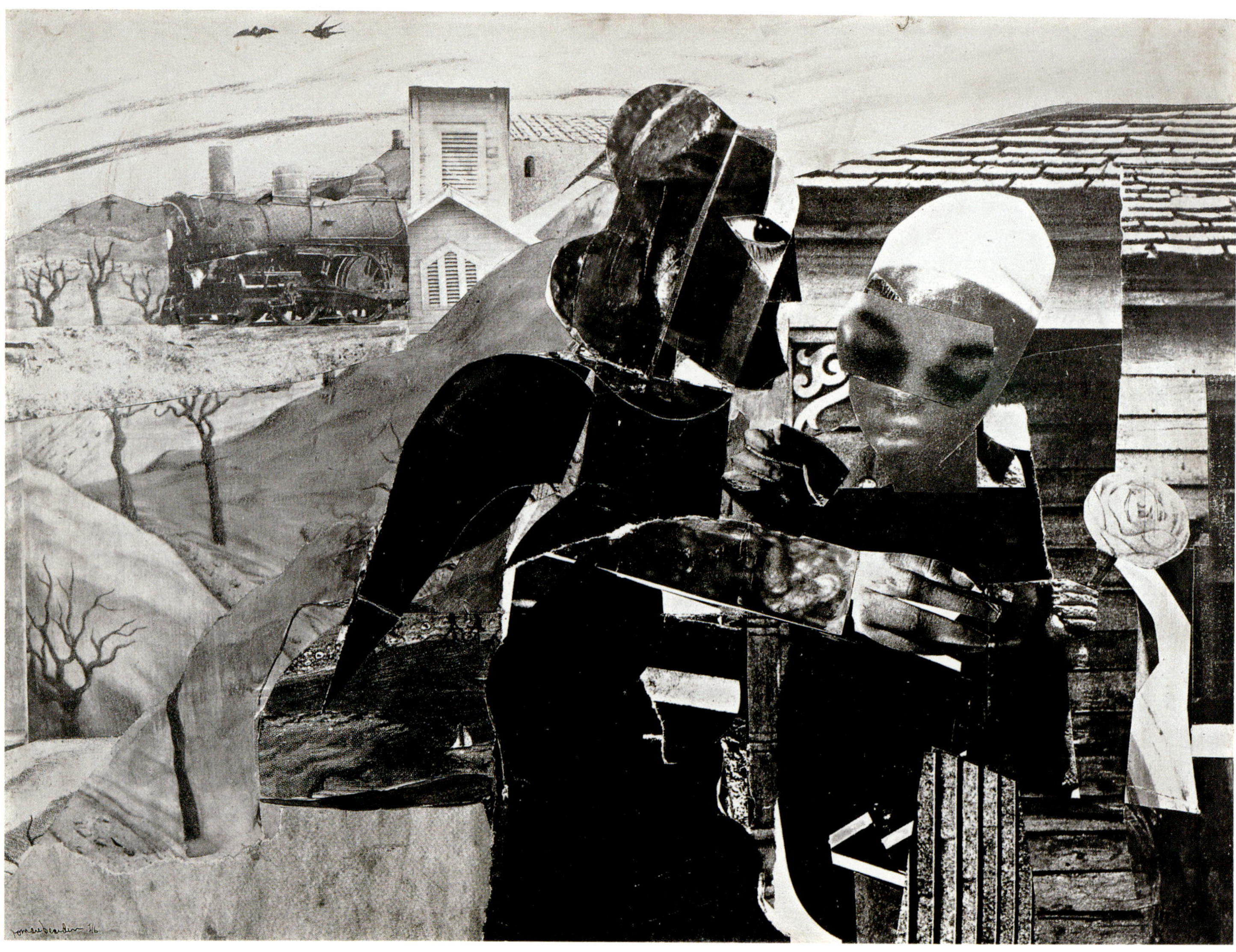

37

37
Prevalence of Ritual: Tidings, 1964, photostat on fiberboard, Edition 1/6, 69.2 x 95.3 (27¼ x 37½). Estate of Romare Bearden, courtesy of Romare Bearden Foundation, New York

38
Prevalence of Ritual: Tidings, 1964, collage of various papers with graphite on cardboard, 19.7 x 26.7 (7¾ x 10½). Stéphane Janssen, Arizona

39
The Visitor, 1970/1974, watercolor and gouache with ink and graphite on paper, 19.1 x 25.4 (7½ x 10). Herbert Gentry and Mary Anne Rose

figure 21
Romare Bearden, *Annunciation #1,* c. 1976, monoprint collagraph. Courtesy Jerald Melberg Gallery

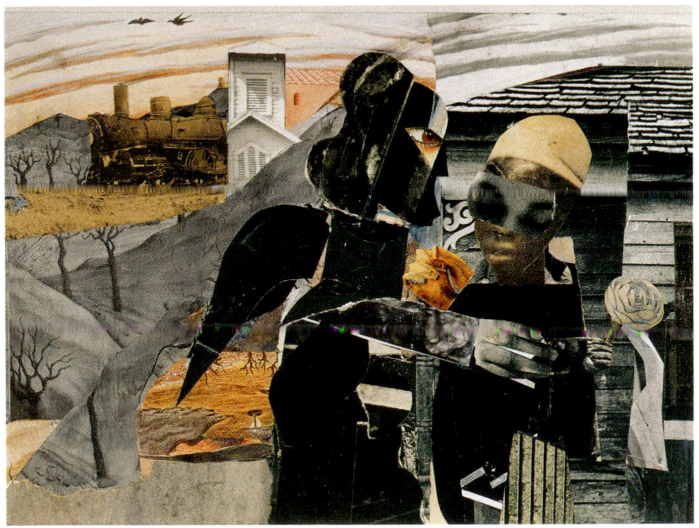

38

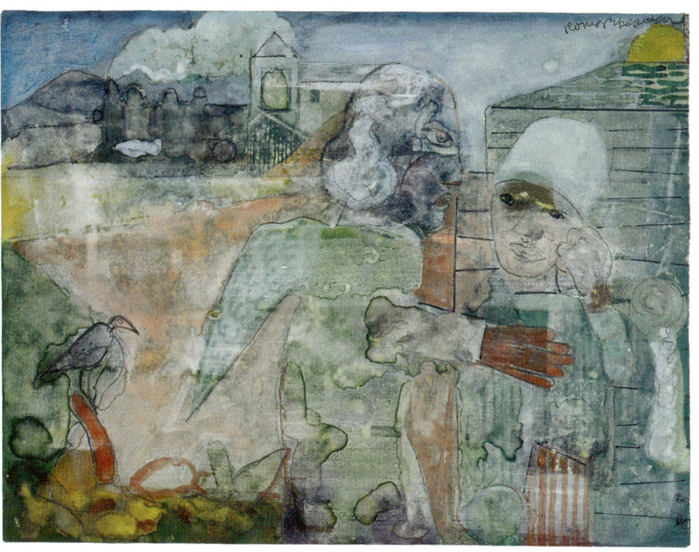

39

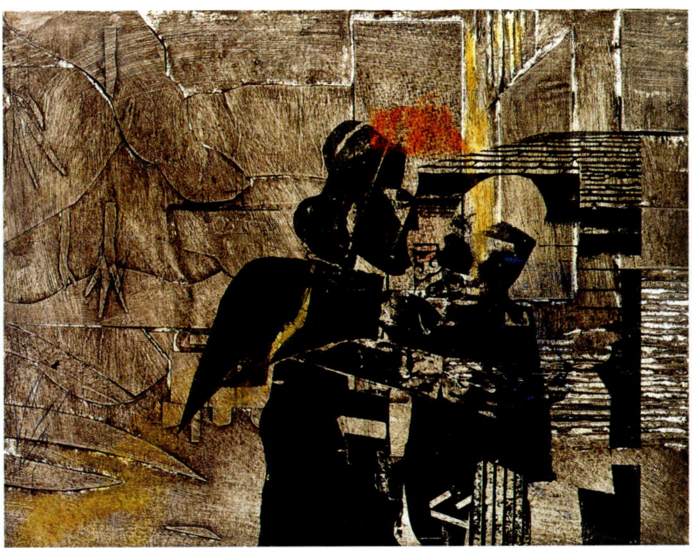

21

in terms of actually seeing his process is *Untitled* (no. 40a,b), visible both recto and verso, showing how Bearden collaged the back as well as the front in order to keep the board's surface flat and in equal tension. Details of imagery often are enhanced in graphite or pen and ink, demonstrating the continued importance to Bearden of the delineation incorporated in gouaches and watercolors from the 1940s.[118] Some collage papers appear crushed, suggesting Bearden did this to achieve textural effects, or that he selected similarly worn papers to enhance the expression of his ideas, or that the papers' condition was inconsequential to him, or, and this seems most likely, that sometimes one of these options was active and sometimes another. Fragments from reproductions of old master and modern paintings occasionally appear as well. The most vivid use of a contemporary work we have identified is in *Prevalence of Ritual: Conjur Woman as an Angel* (no. 41) for which Bearden appropriated an ox from Bill Brandt's landscape photograph *Loch Slapin, Isle of Skye,* 1947 (fig. 22).[119] It is unusual. In most other collages Bearden so severely fractured the photographic elements as to make them unrecognizable. In so doing he developed multiple forms of representation in a single work, specifically within individual figures, but beyond that as a premise of his compositional structures as a whole. This quality remained essential to his approach and has contributed to Bearden's continuing importance. His collages are considered to be some of the first works "to pointedly engage black popular cultural practices in contemporary visual production [contributing to his position as] the main interpreter of a complex view of black subjectivity in his time."[120] In addition, as others continue to probe his expansive

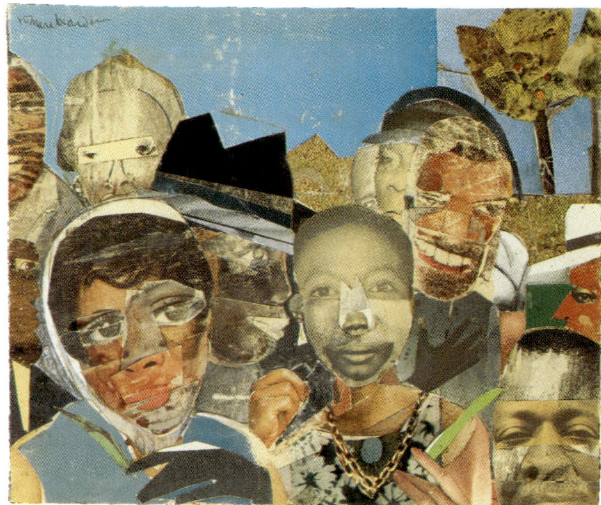

40a

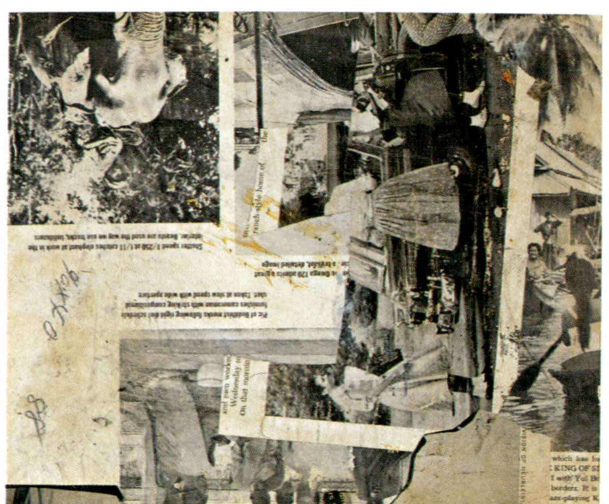

40b

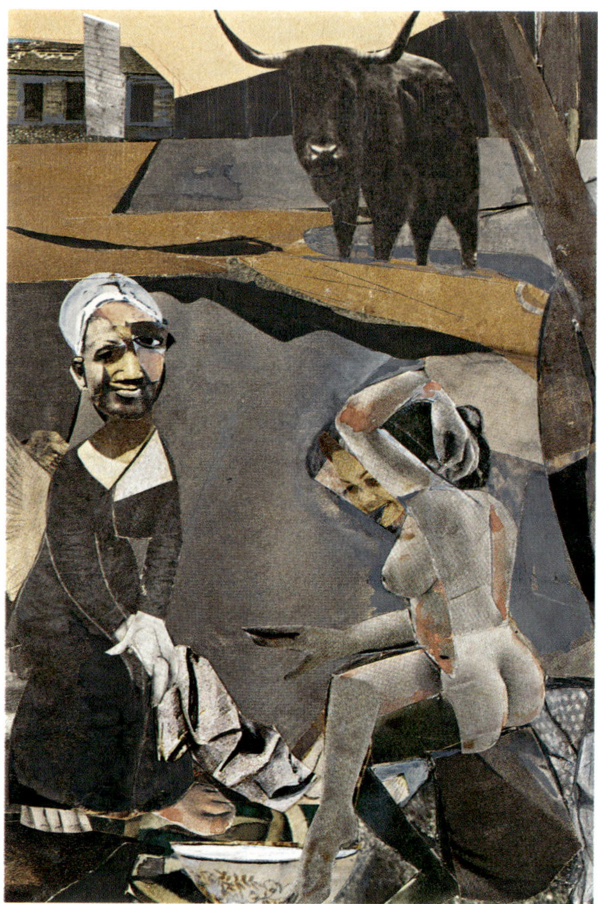

41

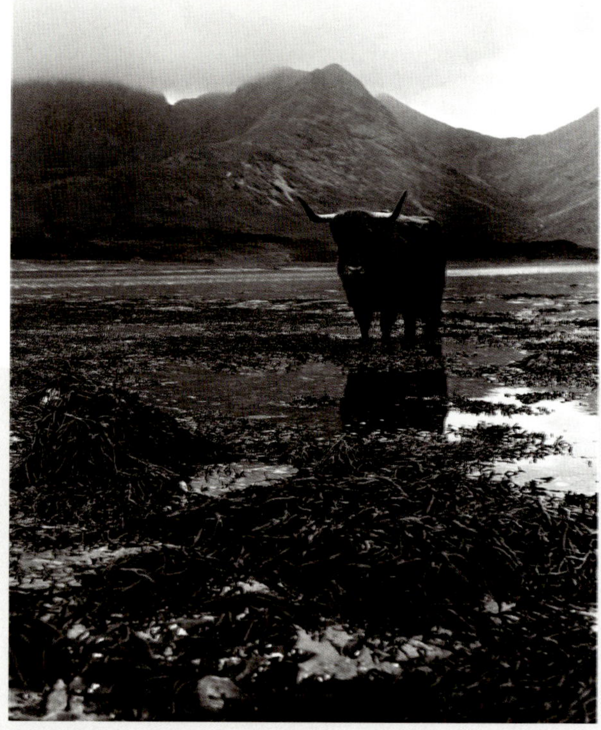

22

approach to representation, Bearden's collages remain a model for postmodern figuration in the broadest of contexts.

In evolving his methods and forms, collages by Picasso, Georges Braque, and Juan Gris made their mark on Bearden's imagination, reinforcing the lessons of Grosz. He would have been aware of fragmentation in other media as well, for example in the sculpture of Auguste Rodin.[121] Collage methodology, fracturing space and form, was a brilliant choice for an artist wishing to convey his responses to a society increasingly aware of the possibilities of nuclear war, of the growing controversy that preceded and accompanied the United States' engagement in Southeast Asia, and on a daily basis for African Americans, of the ongoing bestiality imposed by the Jim Crow laws, which both limited opportunities in every aspect of life and maintained the splintered existence of an illegal de facto segregation. Bearden's 1964 *Projections* exhibition featured the journalistic enlargements of the small collages, thereby indirectly introducing the collages to the public. So far as we can determine, no collages were formally included in the show, although they may have been at the gallery and available for private viewing.[122] Bearden's early use of photographic processes—for transforming motifs from one medium to another, for providing study images of old master paintings, and for the creation of a dark-skinned art history—while critical to his artistic development, was of an essentially private nature. The *Projection* photostats gave a public presence to his use of such techniques.

Bearden apparently made his first Projections early in 1964 and set them aside until Arne Ekstrom spied them on a visit to the Canal Street studio in May.[123] Fascinated by their visual power, he suggested Bearden make more, enough to form an entire show. Ekstrom's enthusiasm as well as numerous details about the project may be gleaned from his letter to Darthea Speyer in an effort to arrange a European showing:

> Romare Bearden has done a series of twenty-one collages which have been photographed in quite large format some 2 x 3′ and some larger. I am showing these as an edition of six, each signed and numbered, mounted on board and put on strainers and framed by Kulicke Frames in narrow silver frames. They are really extraordinary and constitute a sort of re-living and re-telling of his memories as a Negro. The subjects range from burials and cotton fields to jam sessions, Harlem streets, Conjur women, etc. In these days of civil rights strife they are, on the sociological side, a unique statement of pride in tradition, dramatic in many instances but never a form of protest or agitation. Artistically they are most remarkable.... I have in mind the possibility of having these shown by U.S.I.A. or UNESCO as I think that it would be very important to have them be seen in Europe for all the reasons I have set forth above.[124]

The show never did take place, perhaps because Speyer had left the exhibition program of the United States Information Agency.[125]

Four Projections are included here: in addition to *Prevalence of Ritual: Tidings,* already mentioned, there are *Expulsion from Paradise, The Street,* and *City of Brass* (see nos. 20, 33, 42); all are placed with the collages from which they were enlarged. *City of Brass* is enhanced by color additions both with paint and with printed papers to more closely mirror the collage, *Village of Yo* (no. 43). Other Projections were printed on blue, green, and red papers.[126] Bearden's numbering on the three with no color (1/6) confirms that the images were to be produced in editions of six.[127]

The Projections received considerable acclaim for their scale and daring use of photographic techniques. A critic for the *New York Herald Tribune* described several as having "the shock and impact of a swift cinematic passage. Easily one of the best shows in town."[128] Over time admiration for the small collages has surpassed that given the Projections, although the latter's acclaimed kinship with cinema and photojournalism provides them with an independent importance. Critic Dore Ashton commented on this in 1964, and in 1971, photography historian Van Deren Coke more firmly positioned Bearden's work in this context, appreciating:

> a level of tangibility that, while formally broken up in a somewhat Cubist fashion, read like a collection of short film clips taken at varying distances from his subjects. ...[achieving] a graphic technique that is both original and effectively full of life—a life that is tender and tragic....[His Projections] retain the immediacy of newsphotos and, through his use of optical shifts and arrangements similar to jigsaw puzzles, cover much more ground factually and metaphorically than a group of photographs presented in a conventional fashion.[129]

In 1965 Bearden's first solo museum exhibition at the Corcoran Gallery of Art, Washington, D.C., included Projections from the previous year plus an additional one, *Other Mysteries,* and five of the prototype collages: *Spring Way; Pittsburgh Memory; Evening, 9:10, Lenox Avenue* [*sic*]; *Expulsion from Paradise;* and *Tidings* [*sic*].[130] The exhibition was enthusiastically reviewed, if only partially understood. It is astonishing to read *Washington Star* critic Frank Getlein virtually dismissing Bearden's relationship to Schwitters:

40a, b
***Untitled,* 1964, recto: collage of various papers with paint, graphite, and surface abrasion on cardboard; verso: newspaper collage on cardboard; 22.2 x 27.3 (8¾ x 10¾), John P. Axelrod, Boston, Massachusetts**

41
***Prevalence of Ritual: Conjur Woman as an Angel,* 1964, collage of various papers with paint and ink on cardboard, 23.3 x 16.4 (9³⁄₁₆ x 6⁷⁄₁₆). John P. Axelrod, Boston, Massachusetts**

figure 22
Bill Brandt, *Loch Slapin, Isle of Skye,* 1947. Bill Brandt Archive Ltd.

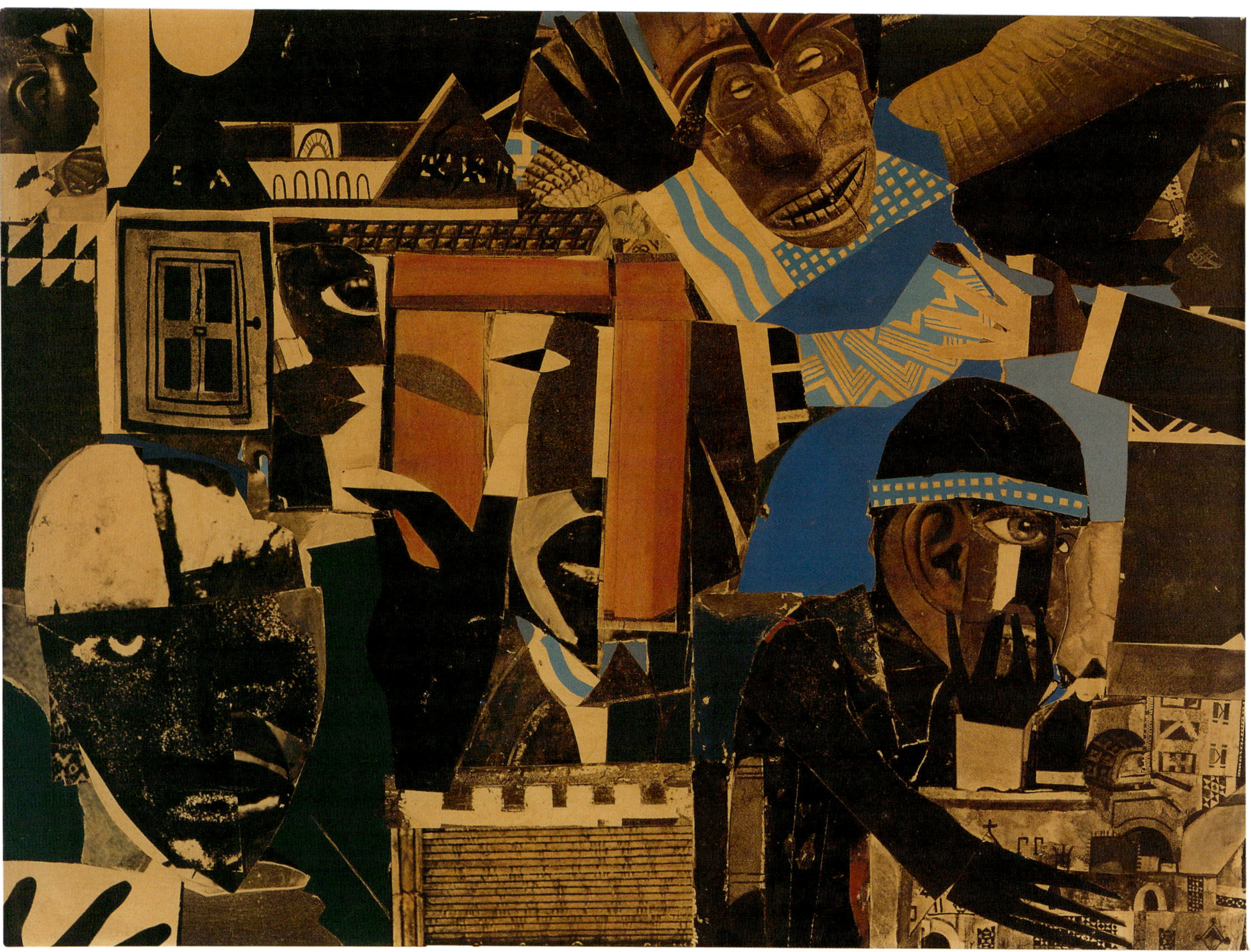

42

42
City of Brass, c. 1965, photostat with paper collage and gouache on wood, 73 x 101.6 (28¾ x 40). Collection Fanny Ellison

43
Village of Yo, c. 1964, collage of various papers with ink on cardboard, 22.9 x 31.1 (9 x 12¼). Yale University Art Gallery, New Haven, Leonard C. Hanna, Jr., B.A. 1913, Fund

44
Family, 1970, collage of various papers with paint, ink, and graphite on wood, 22.9 x 30.5 (9 x 12). Harry Henderson

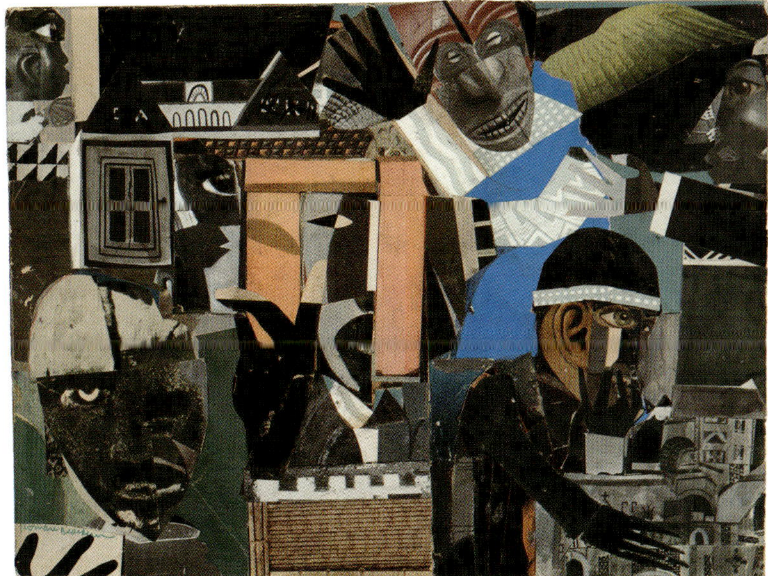

43

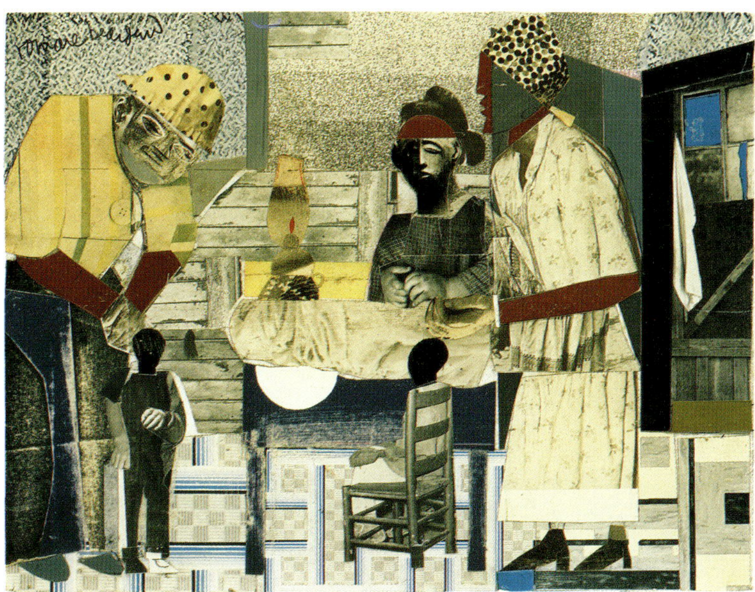

44

> There is some small social comment in the Schwitters-isch sweepings together of street debris, old cigarette wrappers, ticket stubs, transfers and the rest, but you pretty well have to read it into it. . . . Schwitters relates more closely to Braque than to his fellow Germans. . . . Bearden doesn't relate to either one, although both collage and cubism are dimly in the background. The relationship is quite direct to the anguish of the American Negro. That anguish is what is projected. The only related art that comes easily to mind is some of the Mexican mural work during the social revolutionary period of that art, most notably Siquieros [*sic*].[131]

Twenty years earlier, relating Bearden's art to that of the Mexican muralists made sense; by 1965, except for the notion of protest, this was a strange connection, and certainly less useful than one to the European collage tradition would have been. Getlein's comments make clear the difficulty Bearden faced in having his art measured in terms legitimate to both his concepts and his aspirations. As James Hall has stated succinctly: "The set of artistic practices (mode of reflection and mechanical procedures to make visual images) [Bearden] perfects in the early sixties allows him to display his commitment to African-American community, capture the character of contemporary American life, and develop a unique artistic vocabulary that has remarkable cross-disciplinary and cross-cultural resonance," —what Ralph Ellison earlier had described as his and Bearden's shared concern "with the relationship between our racial identity, our identity as Americans, and our mission as writer and artist."[132]

Bearden continued throughout his life to make collages at the small scale associated with the 1963–65 pieces, for example, *Family*, 1970, and *Conversation II*, 1981 (nos. 44, 60). The

23

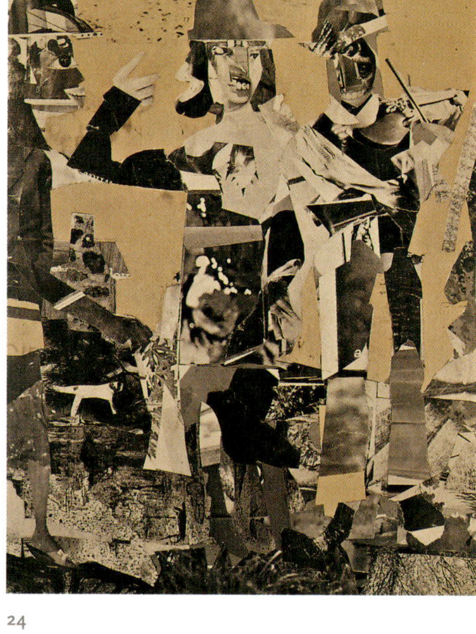

24

photostat Projections, by contrast, were a singular effort, although Bearden incorporated photostat fragments in his collages as part of the array of printed papers he came to use. A variety of photographic and other methods for replicating images, both as positives and as negatives, also remained essential to his practice. It is noteworthy that in the later 1960s Bearden experimented with photographic-screenprint to extend the Projections idea into another realm. The single example we have seen printed onto canvas, *The Fiddler* (fig. 23), is based on a photostat of the same size (fig. 24).

A drawback of the screenprint, like that of the Projections methodology, is that in the end both are prints and thus capable of existing as multiple originals even if they are made as unique works. Despite size and intrinsic visual power, the potential for multiplicity meant that the Projections would be valued both financially and, unfortunately, aesthetically, at a lower level than singular pieces, possibly a contributing factor to their elimination from Bearden's practice.

Some of Bearden's 1963–1964 collages suggest particular sites, but others are marked more by a dynamic sense of event or activity than place. Starting in 1965–66 specific kinds of locations more consistently define his pictorial direction. Even in *Pittsburgh, Farm Couple,* and *Southern Recall,* all around 1965 (nos. 45–47), works of similar small size as the 1964 collages, these changes may be seen. Bearden's methodology changed also. Constructed spaces that read as places began to rely less on photographic images and incorporated instead snippets of the flat-color and other papers that would remain essential to his palette. Next, from 1966 to 1969, Bearden made expansive unique works equal to or greater in size than the Projections; he completed more than two dozen of them along with many smaller pieces, one of which, *La Primavera* in a private collection (reproduced Schwartzman 1990, 118) shows that for some collages Bearden continued solely to employ magazine snippets.

With few exceptions other than murals, tapestries, and stage sets, Bearden's largest collages date to this period. Their motifs allude primarily to Mecklenburg County: people with friends and family, as in *Three Men, Three Folk Musicians, Tomorrow I May Be Far Away, Old Couple,* and the large *La Primavera* (nos. 48–52),[133] and Mecklenburg scenes conflated with literary references, such as *Return of the Prodigal Son* (Albright-Knox Art Gallery). According to Bearden:

> From far off some people that I have seen and remembered have come into the landscape.... Sometimes the mind relives things very clearly for us. Often you have no choice in dealing with this kind of sensation, things are just there.... There are roads out of the secret places within us along which we all must move as we go to touch others.[134]

figure 23
Romare Bearden, *The Fiddler,* c. 1965, screenprint on canvas mounted on fiberboard. National Gallery of Art, gift of James Halpin in memory of Dorothy Rees Halpin

figure 24
Romare Bearden, *The Fiddler,* 1965, photostat. Collection of Nicola Wallach

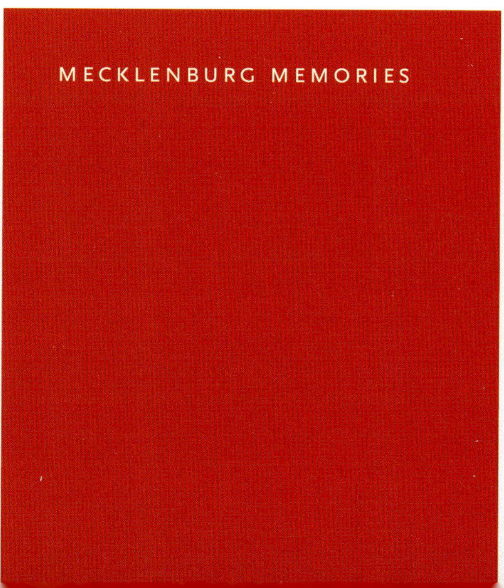

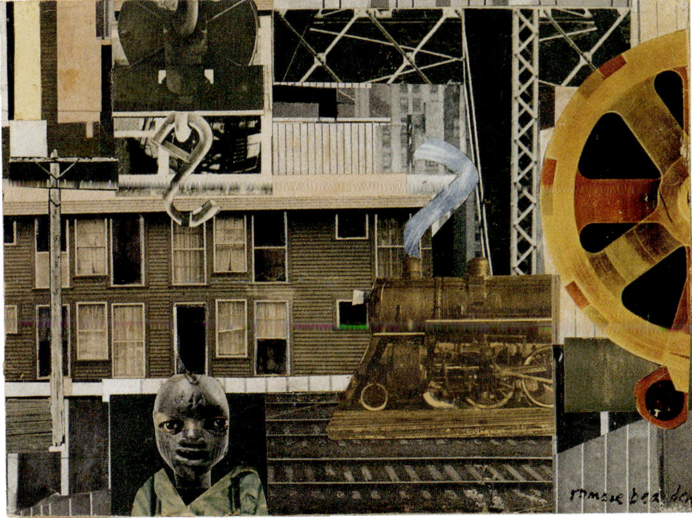

45

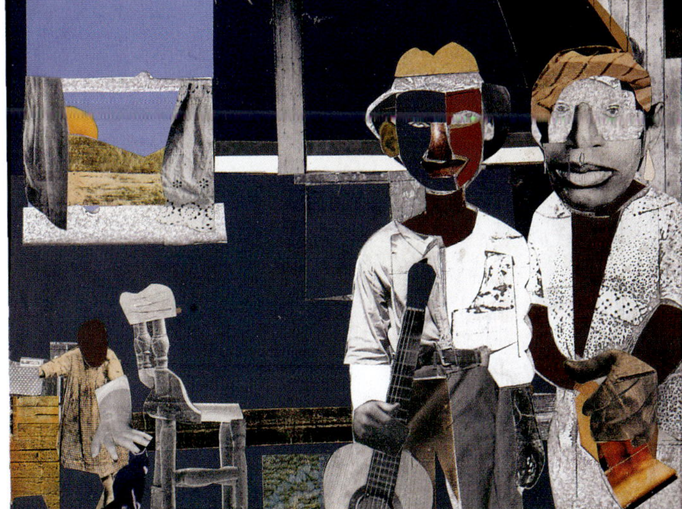

46

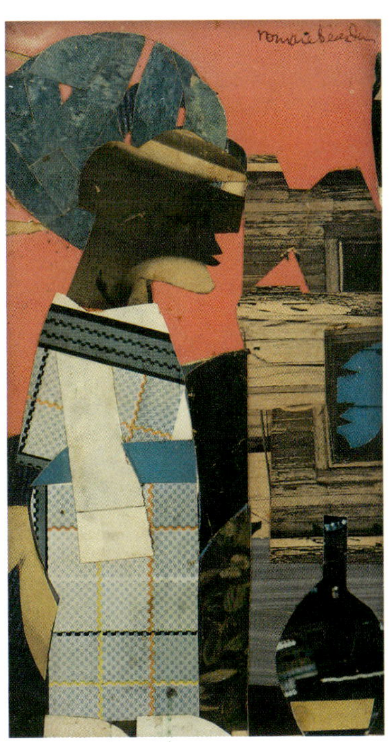

47

45
Pittsburgh, 1965, collage of various papers with ink on cardboard, 15.9 x 22.2 (6¼ x 8¾). Harry Henderson

46
Farm Couple, c. 1965, collage of various papers with paint, ink, and graphite on cardboard, 23.2 x 29.9 (9⅛ x 11¾). Anonymous lender

47
Southern Recall, 1965, collage of various papers with ink and graphite on cardboard, 20 x 11.4 (7⅞ x 4½). Thelma Harris Galleries

In an undated notebook, possibly from the mid-1960s, Bearden wrote the following:

What did Charlotte Offer? South
A Moral Landscape

He followed these lines with references to the Lake District for Wordsworth, Wessex for Hardy, Innisfree for Yeats, as places that offered "value experience-sense of identity."

Bearden's invention, extraordinary at small scale, was yet more emphatic in these masterful larger collages that are infused with a sense of delight in the making of art. African masks again reference Picasso referencing African masks as Bearden continued to embrace a multiplicity of themes from earlier art. *Sunday Morning Breakfast* (no. 53), for example, refers to a 1943 work by African-American artist Horace Pippin. *Backyard* and *Monday Morning* (nos. 54, 55) recall courtyards in the seventeenth-century Dutch paintings that held special appeal, alluding to both Haarlem and Harlem. Citing Rembrandt, Delacroix, and Mondrian among his conceptual guides, in 1968 Bearden described his collage practice:

I first put down several rectangles of color some of which...are in the same ratio as...the rectangle that I'm working on. [Then] I might paste a photograph, say, anything just to get me started, maybe a head, at certain —a few—places in the canvas....I try to move up and across the canvas, always moving up and across. If I tear anything I tear it up and across. What I'm trying to do then is establish a vertical and a horizontal control of the canvas. I don't like to get into too many slanting movements. When I do...I try to find something that compensates right away for a slant or a tilt or a diagonal movement on the canvas. I like the language of what

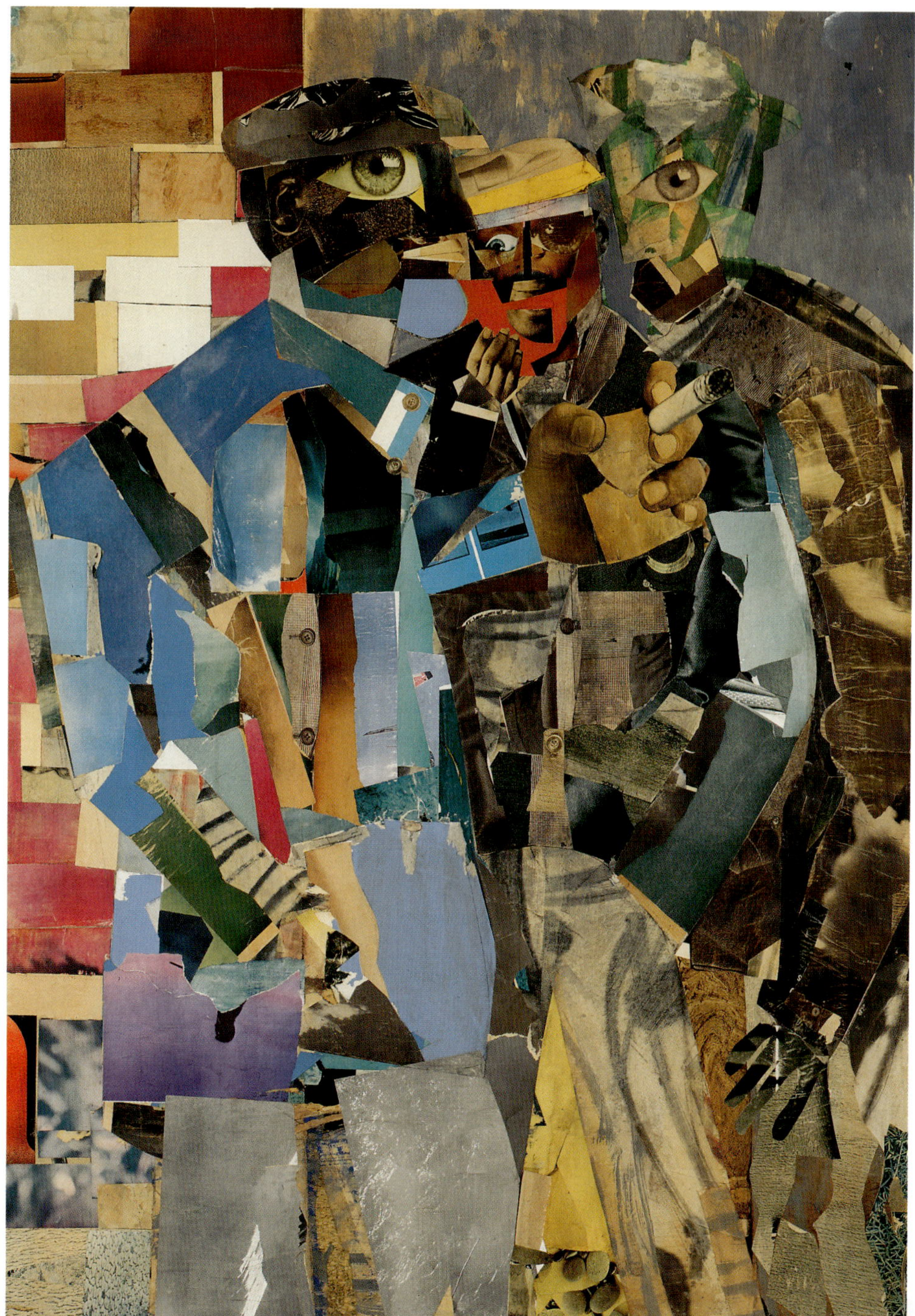

48

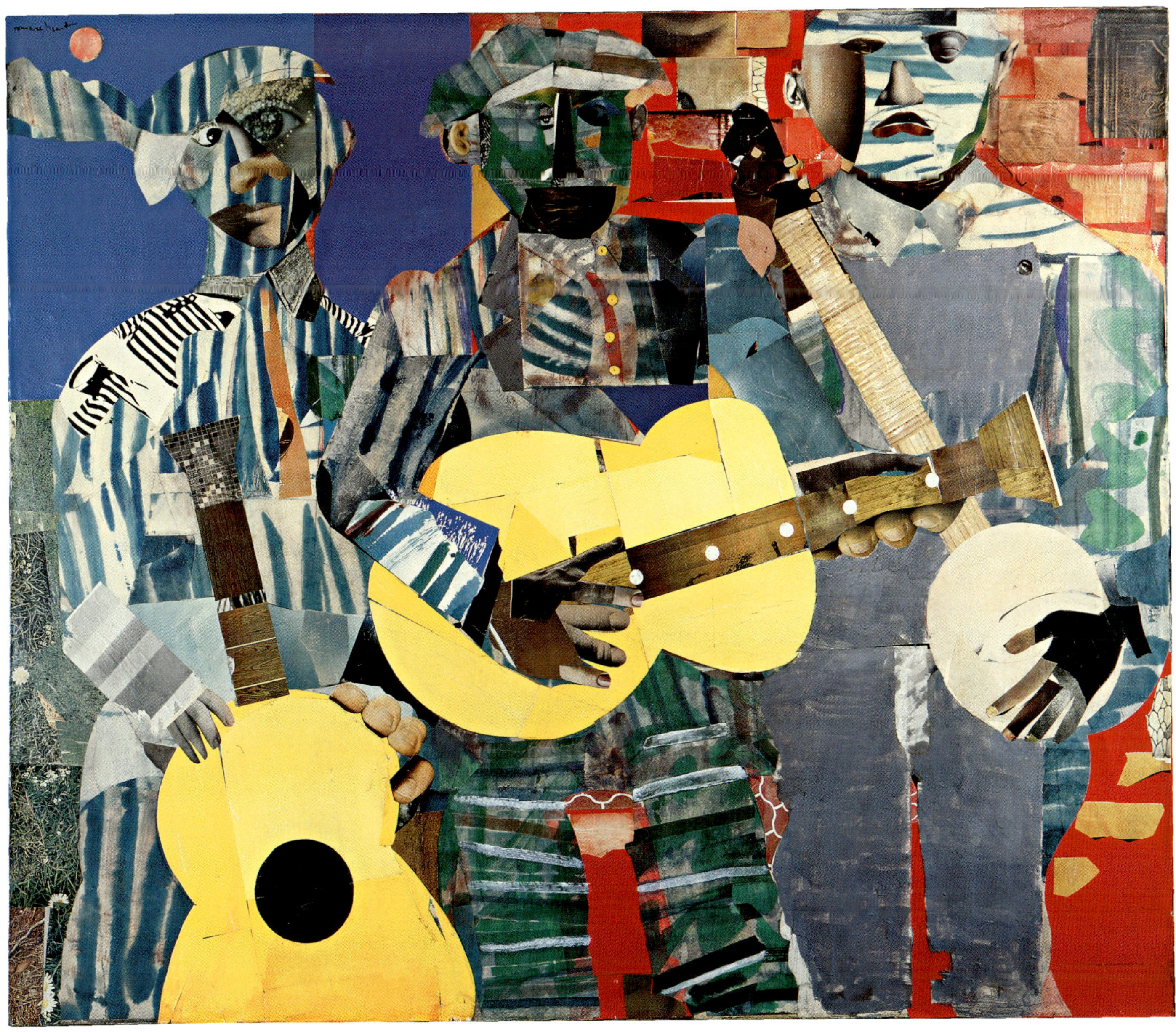

49

48
Three Men, 1966–1967, collage of various papers on canvas, 147.3 x 106.7 (58 x 42). Manoogian Collection

49
Three Folk Musicians, 1967, collage of various papers with paint and graphite on canvas, 127.3 x 152.4 (50⅛ x 60). Anonymous lender

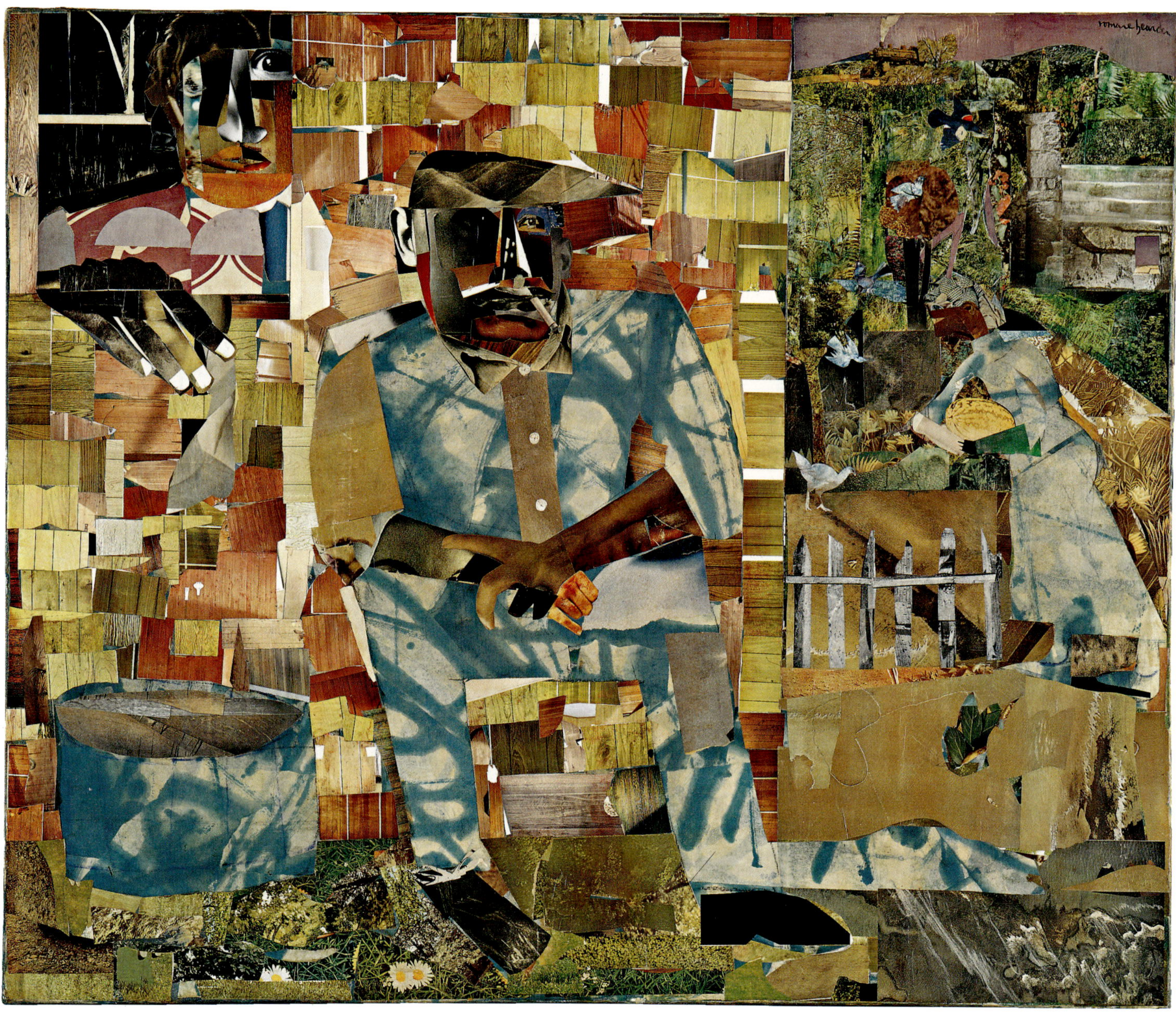

50

50
Tomorrow I May Be Far Away, 1966/1967, collage of various papers with charcoal and graphite on canvas, 116.8 x 142.2 (46 x 56). National Gallery of Art, Washington, Paul Mellon Fund

51
Old Couple, 1967, collage of various papers with paint, charcoal, and graphite on canvas, 112.7 x 143.5 (44 3/8 x 56 1/2). Collection of Jane & Raphael Bernstein

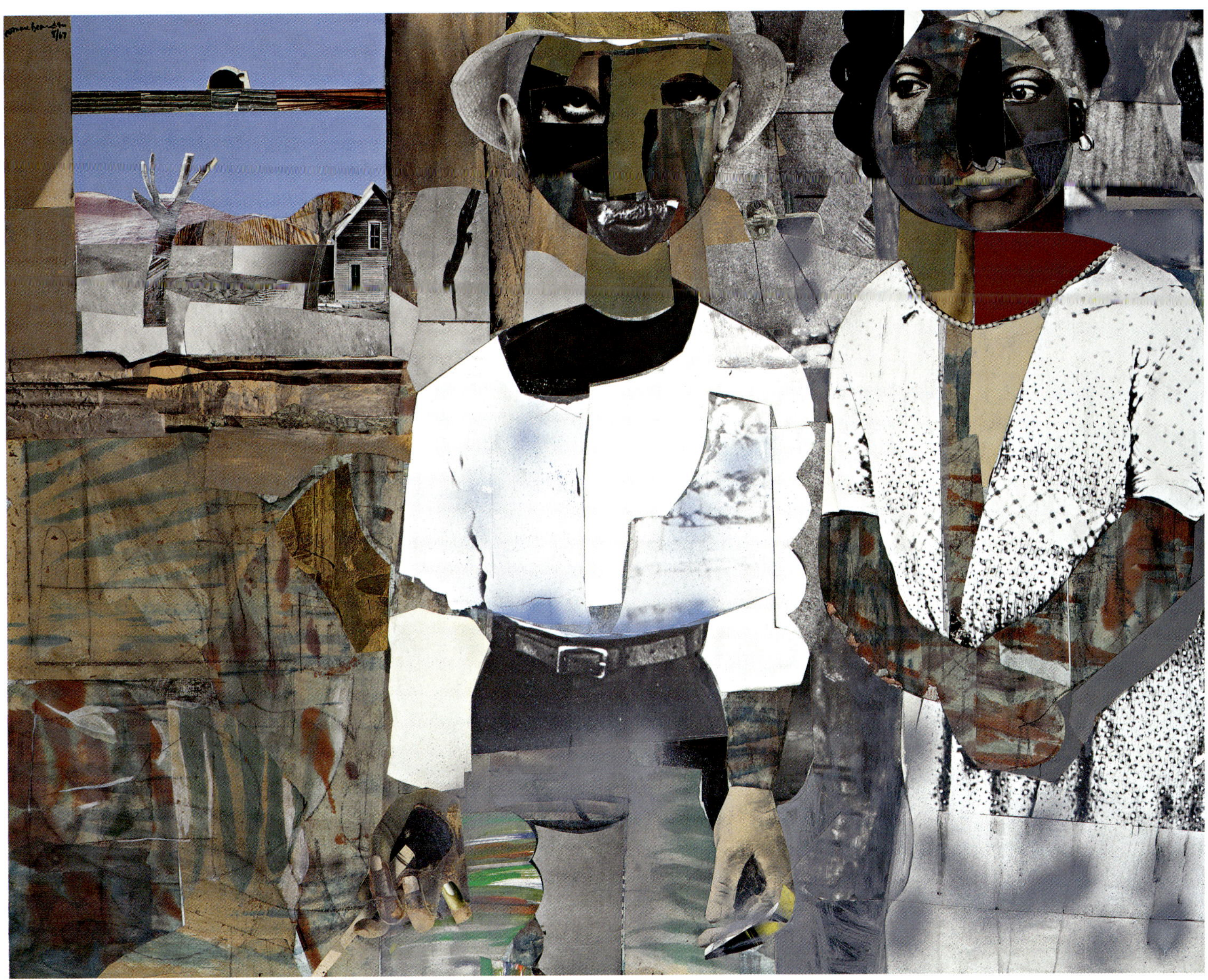

51

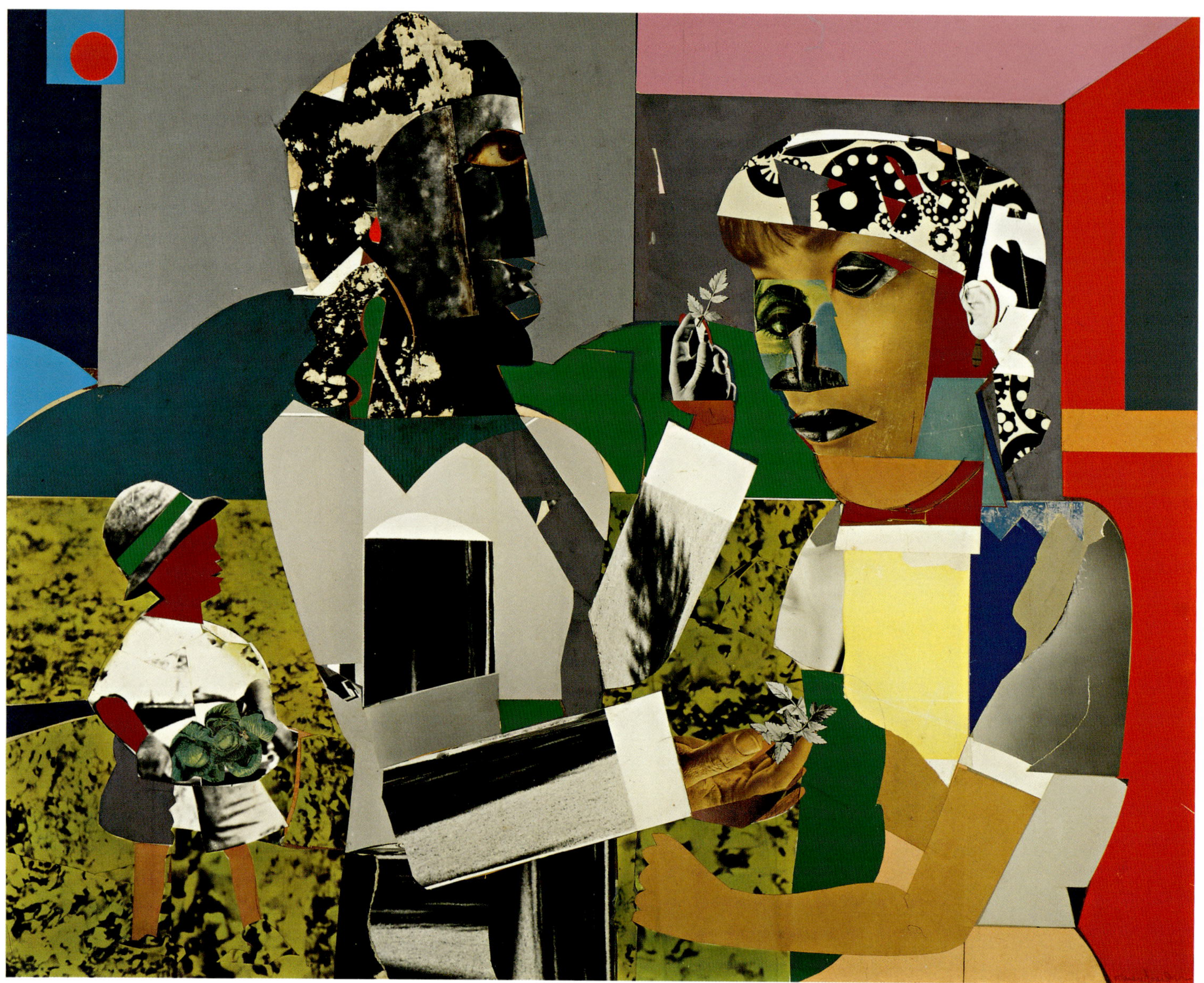

52

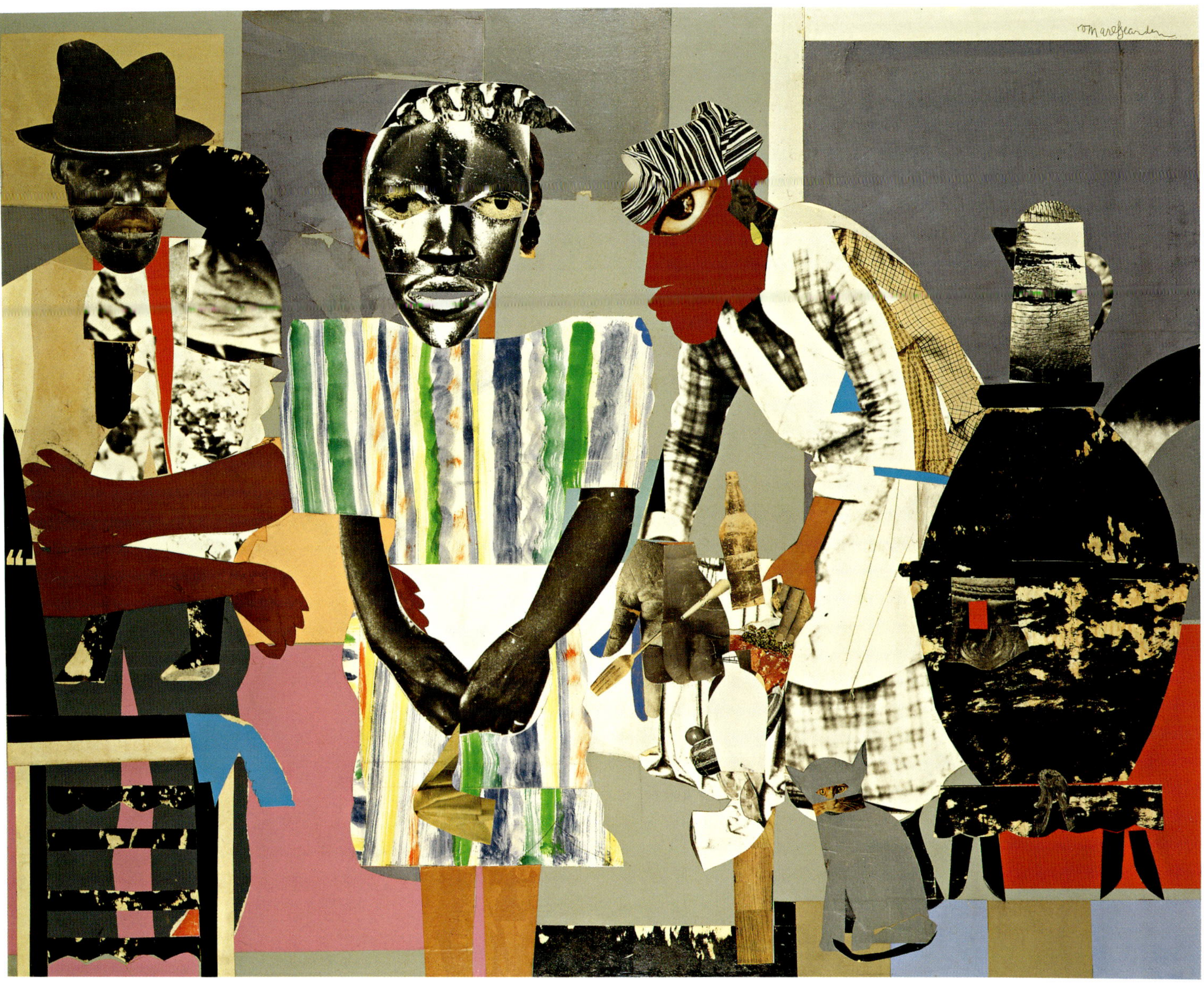

53

52
La Primavera, 1967, collage of various papers with fabric, paint, ink, and graphite on fiberboard, 111.8 x 142.2 (44 x 56). The Collection of Philip J. and Suzanne Schiller, American Social Commentary Art 1930–1970

53
Sunday Morning Breakfast, 1967, collage of various papers with paint, ink, and graphite on fiberboard, 111.8 x 142.2 (44 x 56). Collection of halley k harrisburg and Michael Rosenfeld, New York

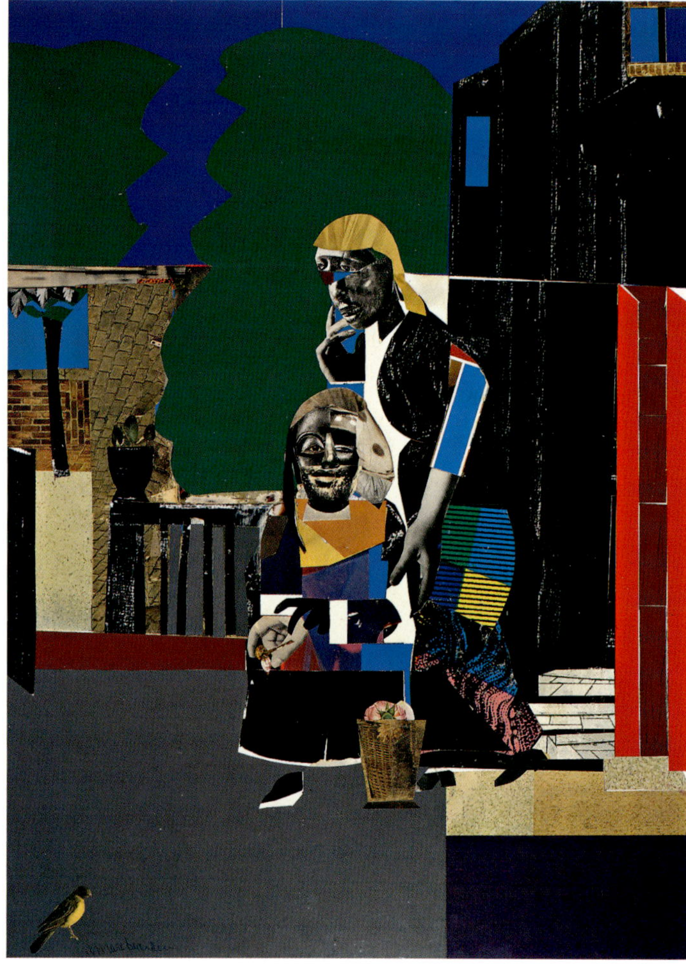

54

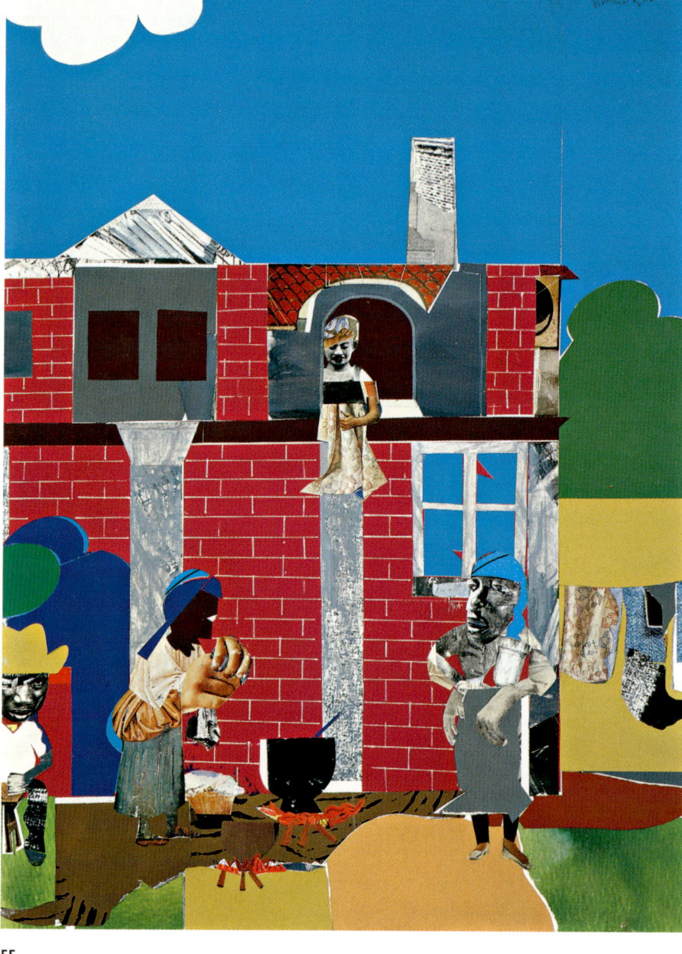

55

54
Backyard, 1967, collage of various papers with graphite on fiberboard, 101.6 x 76.2 (40 x 30). Marian B. Javits

55
Monday Morning, 1967, collage of various papers with paint and graphite on fiberboard, 100.3 x 74.9 (39½ x 29½). Private collection

figure 25
X-radiograph of *Three Folk Musicians* (no. 49), showing wooden stretcher bar support, mends in the canvas (the white areas), and a suggestion of an abstract expressionist painting beneath the collage

figure 26
Romare Bearden, *Number 9,* 1961, collage of painted papers mounted on canvas. The Grant Hill Collection

I'm trying to do to be as classical as possible but I don't want complete reductionism like a Malevich or white on white where you end up with an empty canvas.... Moreover I try to incorporate some of the techniques of documentary film or the camera eye into the art of painting....Also involved is the interplay between the photograph and the actual painting and I constantly find myself adjusting my color to the gray of the photograph so that there won't be too much disparity in color between them.[135]

Bearden's statement discusses structural complexity but in no way describes his complicated technique in the application of layers in these splendid works. Several, including *Three Men, Tomorrow I May Be Far Away, Old Couple,* and *Three Folk Musicians,* were made on canvases previously used for abstract expressionist paintings (fig. 25). Traces of the canvas substrate may be seen throughout all of them in small areas left uncovered by collage.[136] They also have in common a visible layer of Japanese paper (perhaps one of those that Murray remembered Bearden buying in Paris) bearing painted gestural markings, mainly in blues and greens—in the seated man's clothing in *Tomorrow I May Be Far Away,* on the wall to the left and behind the figures in *Old Couple,* and in the clothing and faces in *Three Folk Musicians,* most vividly in the left and right figures. This painted paper also is a primary element in *Number 9,* 1961 (fig. 26), an abstraction on canvas, and its presence there suggests that some or all of the figurative canvases employing it may have had two lives previous to their current form—first as abstract expressionist paintings, then as abstract collages. This impulse toward layering that eventually led Bearden to collage may be traced back to his thickly painted canvases of the

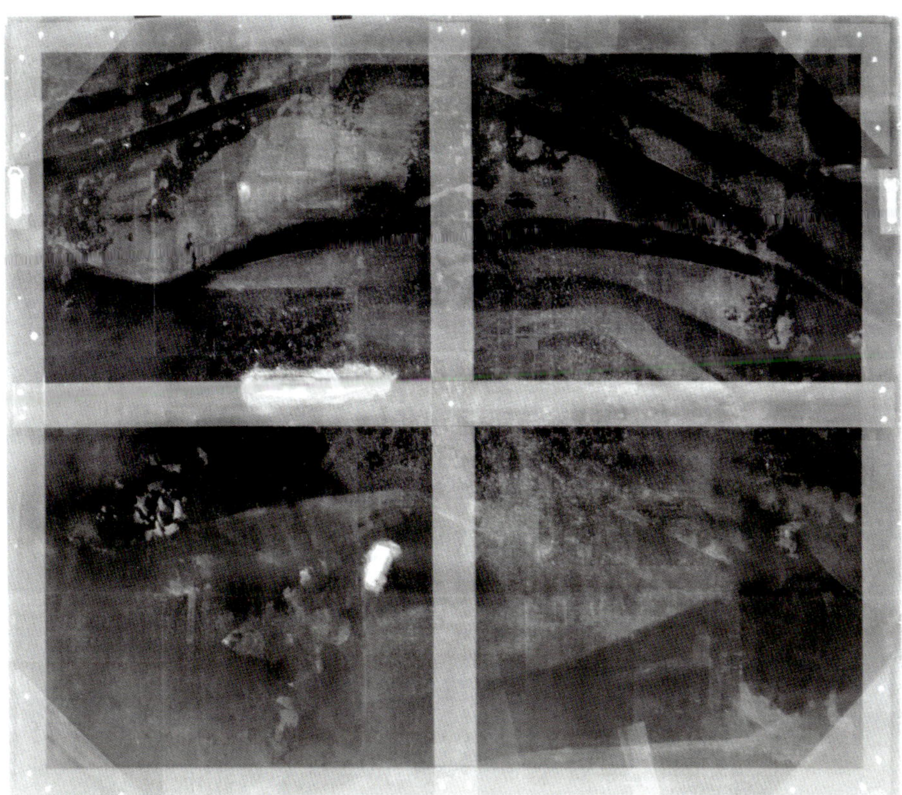

25

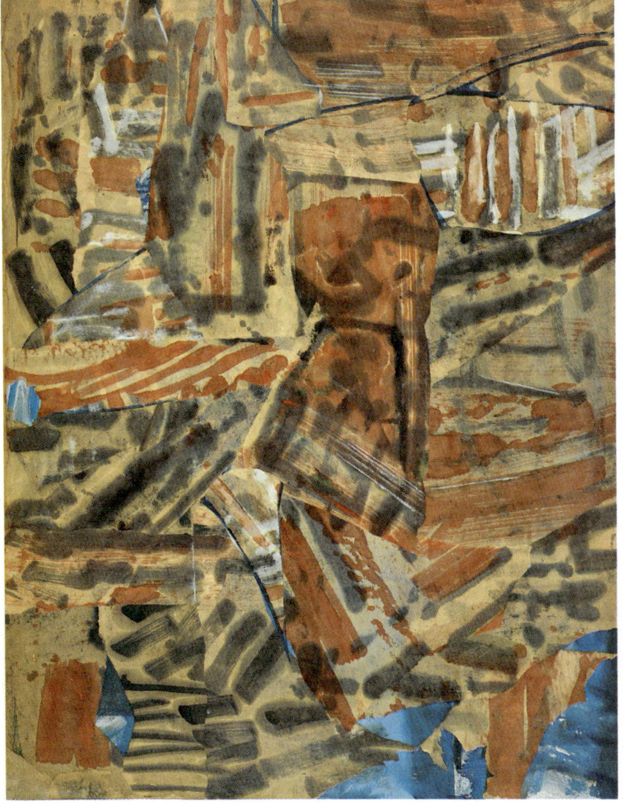

26

mid-1950s. When not able to afford canvas in the quantities necessary to his investigations, it was his practice to overpaint unsatisfactory works. Simpson recalled that Bearden's abstractions had as many as ten layers of paint beneath what became the final versions.[137]

Many of Bearden's titles have their origins in literature and music. *Tomorrow I May Be Far Away* can be tracked to lyrics recorded by Edith Johnson in 1929, in the first verse of her "Good Chib Blues":

Aah, tomorrow I may be far away
Oh, tomorrow I may be far away
Don't try to jive me, sweet talk can't make me stay.

Of the collages on canvas, this one is closest to those from 1963–64 in three respects: its use, almost entirely, of magazine cuttings as collage elements; the elements' relatively small size overall; and the lack of drawn or painted additions except for occasional charcoal and graphite lines. Because of these affinities, it seems possible this landscape with cabin and figures might date to 1966 rather than its generally documented date of 1967, close in time to *Three Men,* which is one of few collages associated with the earlier year.[138] Close observation of *Tomorrow I May Be Far Away,* lush in its descriptions of nature (including at right a snippet from a reproduction of Henri Rousseau's *The Sleeping Gypsy* [Museum of Modern Art]) reveals birds in flight, a second cabin situated midfield, a woman harvesting the land, and the ever-present train, here speeding across the right horizon. The train, in fact, is the most prevalent symbol in Bearden's work, calling up his own travels between north and south as a child. It also holds historical importance in African-American history, not only in regard to the Great Migration but also the Underground Railroad, the proximity of train tracks to many black communities, and its role in the sound of jazz music.[139]

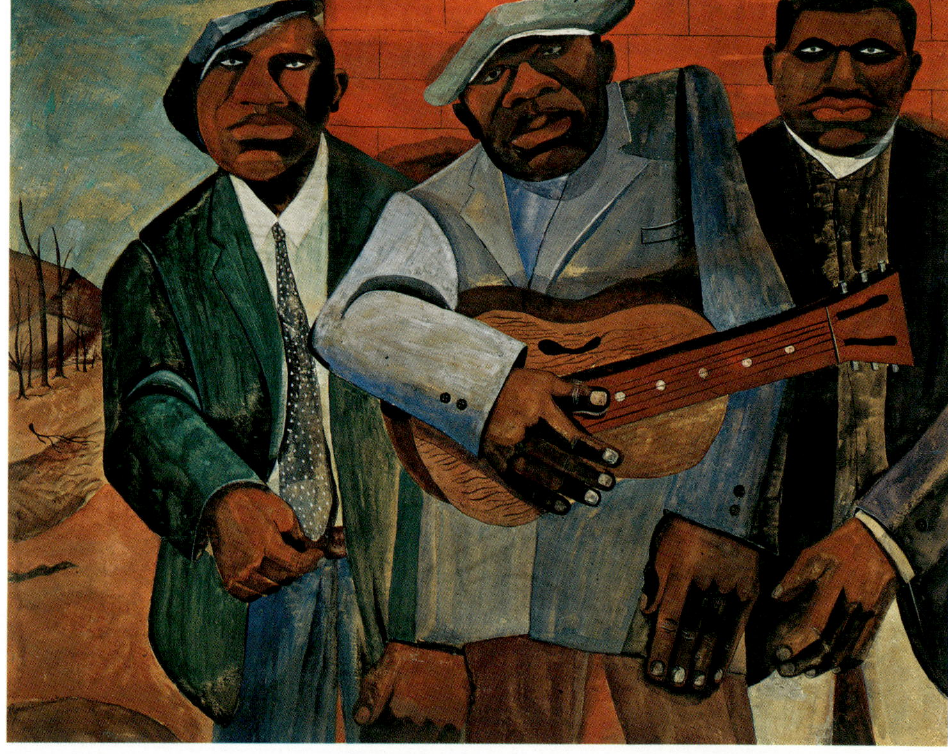

27

Moving away from the homogeneity of *Tomorrow I May Be Far Away,* other collages on canvas employ elements of diverse sizes cut from a varied palette that includes fragments of posters, wallpaper, and printed color papers, some of which are of a brilliance that presents striking shifts from the quieter hues of the magazine cuttings, and photostats. They also are extensively worked with drawing and/or painting. In *Old Couple,* dated at the upper left to August 1967 ("8/67"), appear a man and woman similar in circumstance to the figures in *Tomorrow I May Be Far Away.* The "old couple" is in an interior setting with a window view out to a barren landscape that represents a radical change in both form and mood from the other work. The faces in *Old Couple* are as poignant as any in Bearden's collages, with gazes riveting in their mournful intensity. From a technical standpoint, the collage incorporates one of Bearden's earliest uses of spray paint, probably Krylon. The ways in which the paint alters the surface vary from the woman's skirt with its heavy roundish areas of gray—just as they would have landed on the field in a series of rapid spurts, the paint can held relatively close to the surface—to the lighter sprays of blue resulting both from the paint being held at a greater distance and a lighter touch on the spray; to areas of paint Bearden manipulated with a brush after spraying the surface, as in the upper right corner. Both *Old Couple* and *Three Folk Musicians,* a Picassoesque subject Bearden had earlier approached in a 1942 gouache (fig. 27), show numerous, yet subtle, linear elements, some in graphite, some in ink, some in a soft, friable charcoal. In addition to using spray paint, so important to *Old Couple,* for *Three Folk Musicians* Bearden also painted traditionally, with a brush.

Also from the late 1960s but more homogeneous in their use of collage than the works on canvas are *Illusionist at 4 P.M.* and *Palm Sunday Procession* (nos. 56, 57). Both are on fiberboard, the substrate that essentially replaced canvas at the end of the 1960s and remained Bearden's primary collage surface. The subtle colors and flat matte fields of *Illusionist at 4 P.M.*, an interior scene that could be any place, and the celebratory hues of *Palm Sunday Procession,* a religious ritual, when added to the Mecklenburg County collages on canvas suggest the range of Bearden's subject, palette, and methods. In subsequent years, within any given time frame and often bracketed by exhibitions, he engaged many additional variations as his materials and process became increasingly complex and diverse, his experimental approach expanding his pictorial possibilities.

A particularly important work in this regard is *Strange Morning, Interior* (no. 58), a composition of three women and a man that to our knowledge is not repeated in Bearden's oeuvre. Primarily photostats and printed color papers, their surfaces have been extensively and heavily abraded, bringing areas back almost to the white of the original paper before either photograph or color was applied. The abrasion, probably from sandpaper used with gestures in all directions, establishes an overall field unconfined by specific forms and of a particularly open and painterly disposition. It is one of Bearden's early uses of a working method he will employ extensively through the 1970s, generally with more specific relationships between form and abrasion. Here the openness of the gestures establishes a moody and dreamlike aura, a "strange morning" indeed.

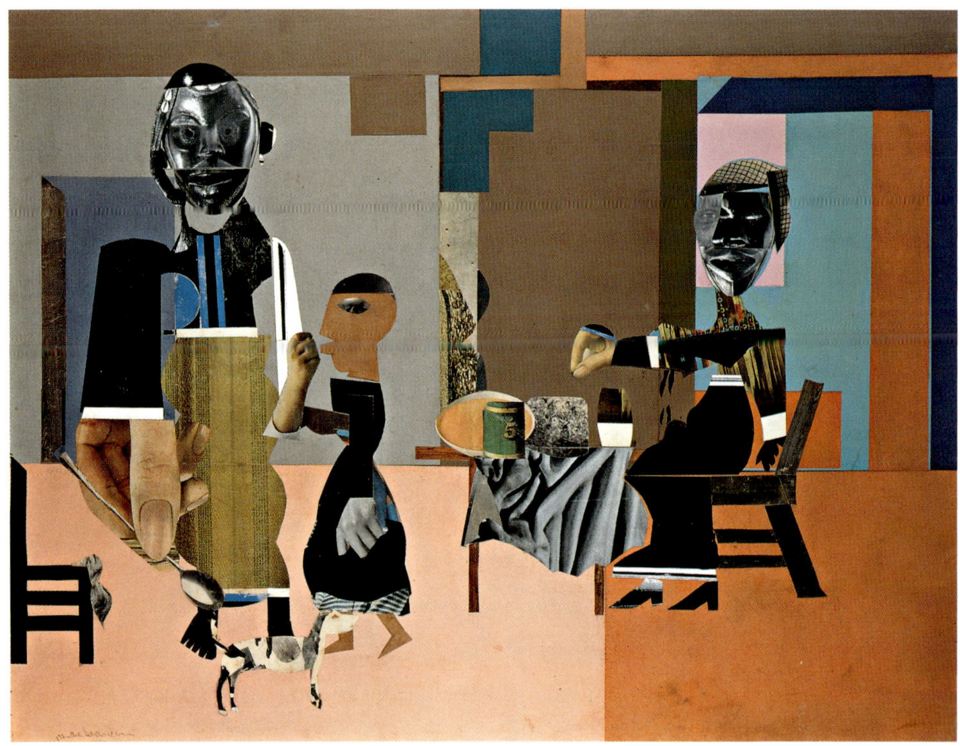

56

At the start of the 1970s Bearden did a few Mecklenburg scenes in outsized stitched fabric collage that were sewn by Nanette, moving as close to the quilt tradition as he would come in regard to materials. Among them is *Conjunction* (no. 59). Like many collages from the 1960s and 1970s, it served as a model both for later work in collage, *Conversation II* (no. 60), and print, in this case a 1979 lithograph, *Conjunction (Island Paradise)*. The extreme size difference between the two collages reveals Bearden's distinct ability to shift from one set of scale relationships to another.

Collage remained Bearden's method of choice for the rest of his life. He worked primarily on fiberboard, or another hardboard, a more logical carrier for applying layered papers and other materials with pressure than was the thin cardboard of the early 1960s or the canvas that followed. Bearden further enhanced his palette with fabrics, foils, and miscellaneous found materials as well as papers he painted and printed himself. From the late 1960s through the mid-1970s, in particular, he manipulated his papers with sanding and other abrasive methods. He also expanded his use of brushing, spraying, puddling, and otherwise

figure 27
Romare Bearden, *Folk Musicians,* 1942, gouache with ink and graphite on brown paper. Courtesy of Curtis Galleries

56
***Illusionist at 4 P.M.*, 1967, collage of various papers with ink and graphite on fiberboard, 74.9 x 101.6 (29½ x 40). Courtesy of Michael Rosenfeld Gallery, New York, N.Y.**

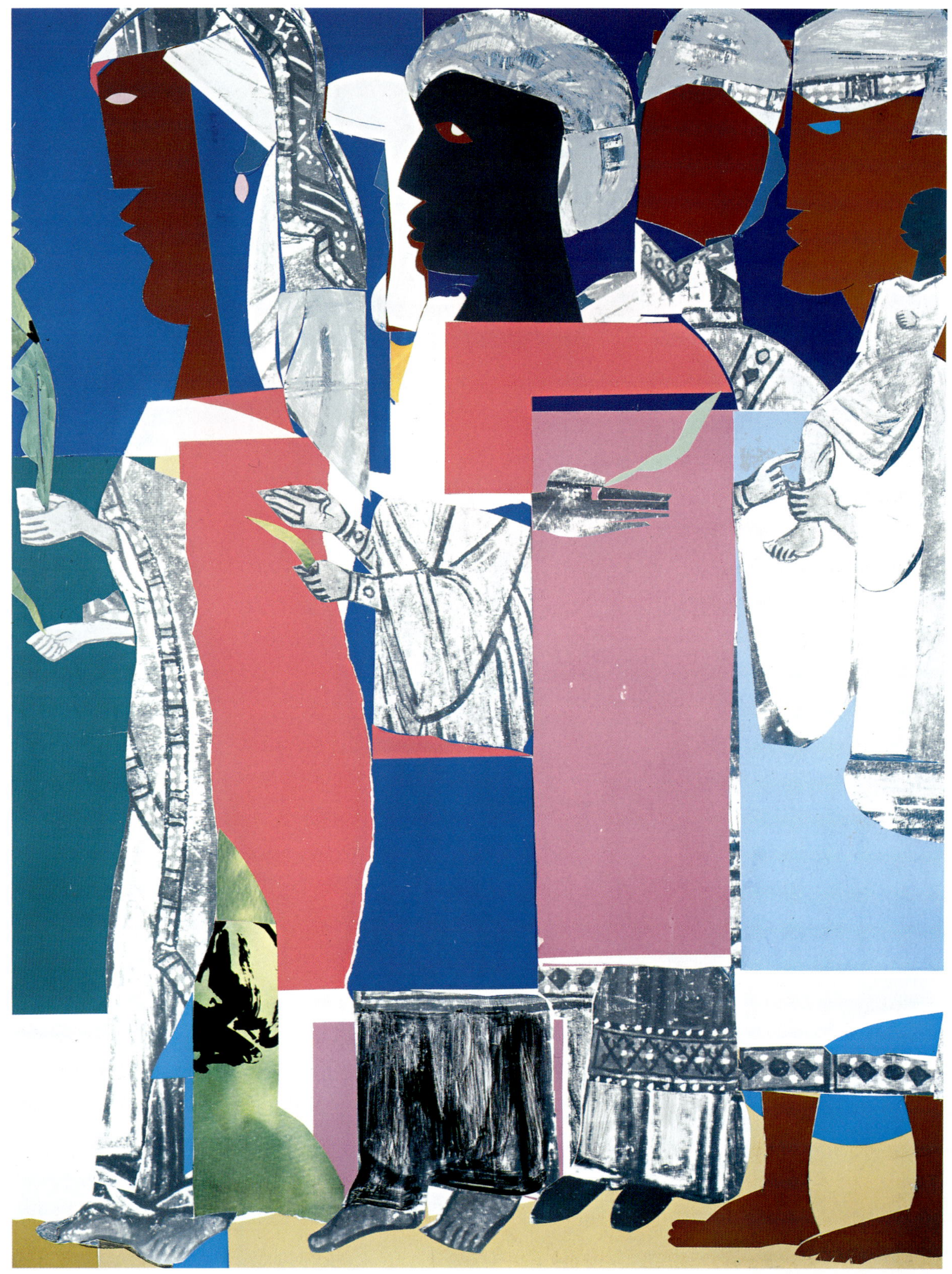

57

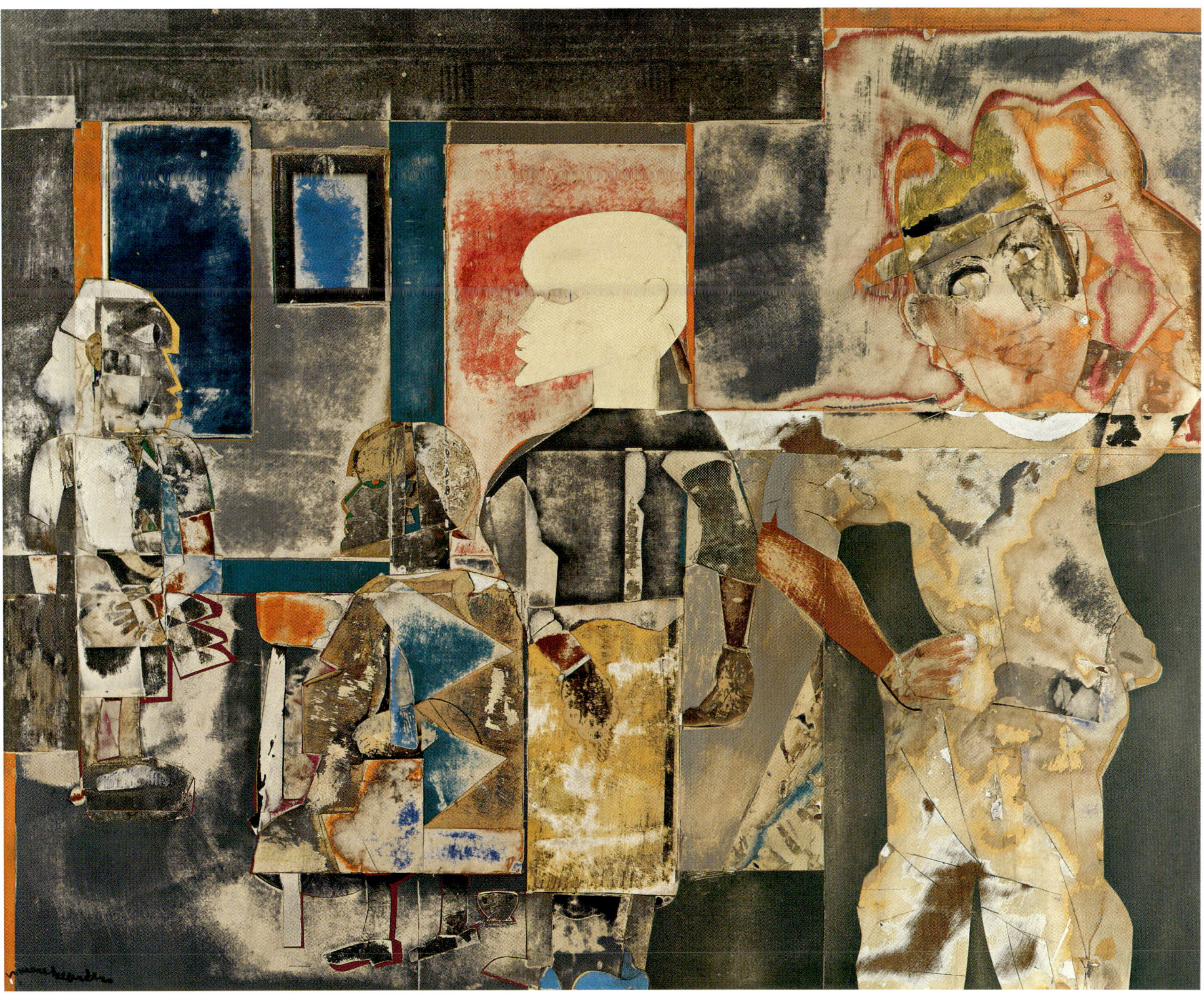

58

57
Palm Sunday Procession, 1967–1968, collage of various papers with paint on fiberboard, 142.2 x 111.8 (56 x 44). Hood Museum of Art, Dartmouth College, Hanover, New Hampshire; gift of Jane and Raphael Bernstein

58
Strange Morning, Interior, 1968, collage of various papers with paint, ink, charcoal, graphite, and surface abrasion on fiberboard, 110.5 x 141.6 (43½ x 55¾). Collection Fanny Ellison

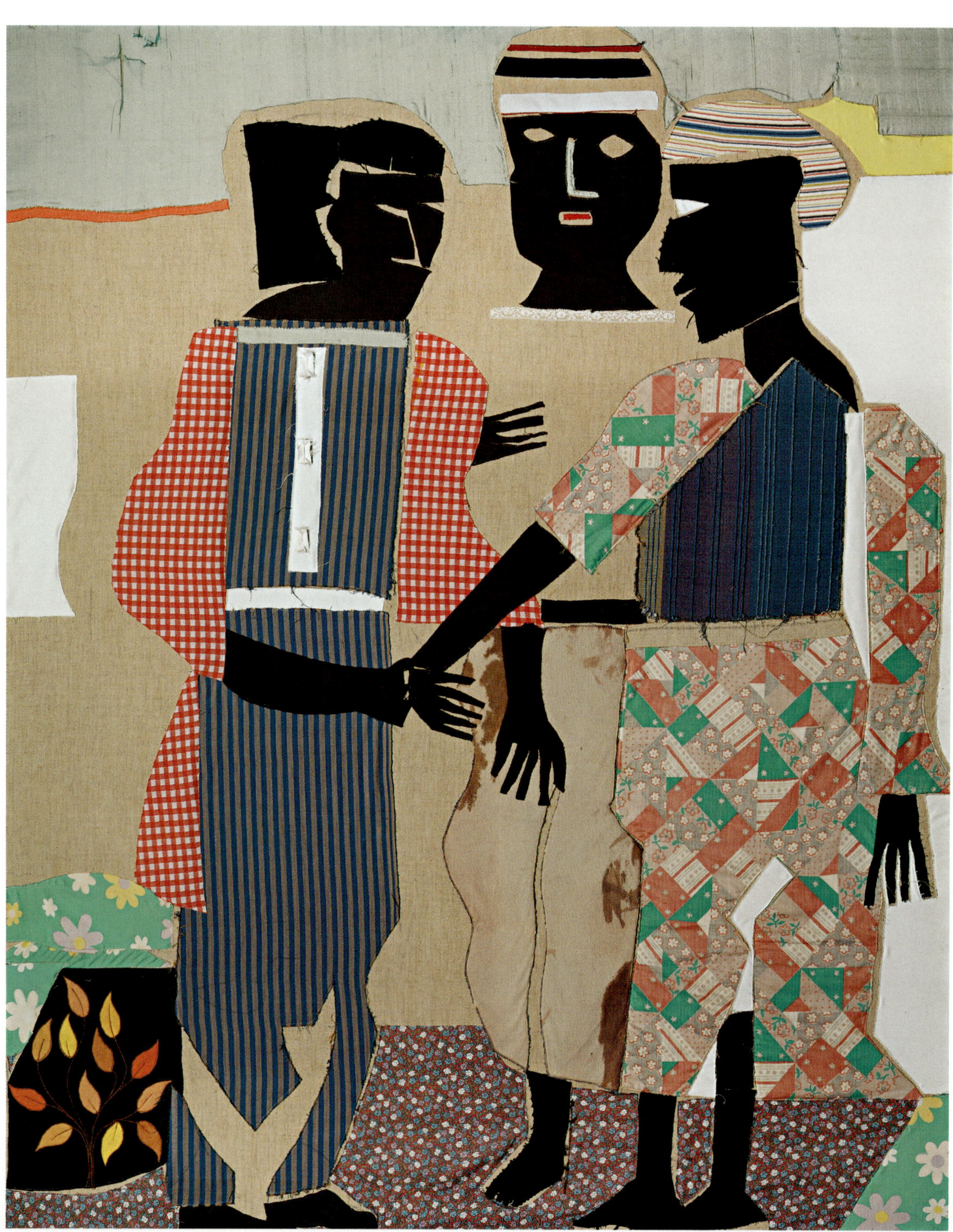

59

59
Conjunction, 1971, collage of various fabrics with crayon and charcoal on canvas, 175.3 x 144.1 (69 x 56¾). Tougaloo College Art Collections, Mississippi

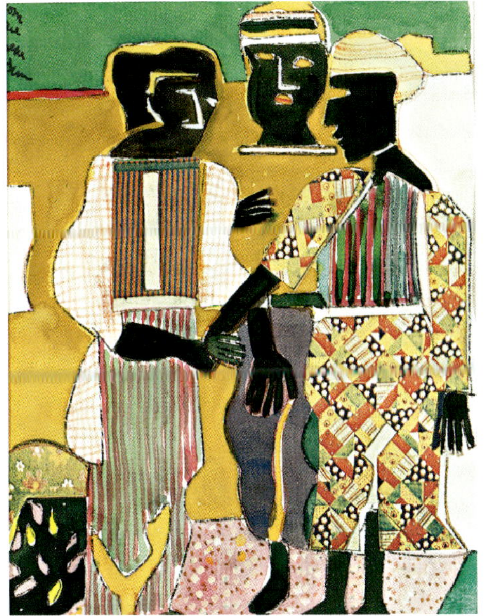

60

applying and sometimes partially removing the paints and inks that eventually became as diverse as the papers. He continued to draw details in graphite, colored pencil, and ink, and the skill with which he wielded his scissors transformed that implement into a refined drawing tool.

In the late 1960s while maintaining work space on Canal Street, Bearden also rented a studio in Long Island City from John Schindler, a designer of signs and displays. Henderson recalled that Schindler had a large space and the ability and equipment to produce the photostats Bearden required, making for a particularly good working situation. In 1986 Bearden discussed with Schwartzman another asset of Schindler's studio: the various technical pointers he learned there. These included how best to mount papers on masonite, which may have influenced his move away from the canvas substrate; the use of adhesives called Sobo, which he diluted with water, and "Glue-fast" which he did not (we have not further identified the latter, reportedly developed during World War II by the Navy for use with paper); and the use of a pressure spray-gun to "lacquer" his collage surfaces. Many collages, in fact, are marked by a glossy glue residue and by the matte varnishes applied as part of their finish.[140] At some point, probably in the mid-1970s, certainly not before his completion of two large collage murals, Bearden moved to the first of two much smaller studios in a building at 23-03 45th Road, in Long Island City, where he worked for the rest of his life.

Details about the materials of his work were of considerable interest to Bearden, both in terms of their visual properties (the transparency of watercolor as distinct from the opacity of gouache) and their soundness with respect to conservation. His conversations with Schwartzman reveal that he was fully aware of the problems of discoloration caused to paper by certain glues. He described how he used unnamed "lacquers" to protect his collages from light damage (not an effective approach); he did not use such coatings for the purpose of enhancing the color in his work, believing our understanding of Rembrandt's color, for example, is greatly diminished because of varnishes applied to his canvases.[141]

Bearden's serious engagement with printmaking likewise began in the late 1960s, although there were earlier experiments. He never reported doing so but we now know he took a class in linoleum block printing in his 1933–34 year at NYU. This knowledge makes all the more interesting two recently discovered impressions of linoleum cuts, one a cityscape printed in black, the other a landscape with figure, in black with details in color.[142] His next work in printmaking so far as we know was in approximately 1964, when Spiral member William Majors introduced Bearden to intaglio processes. At that time he produced a few city scenes related to collages.[143] According to Blackburn, Majors' equipment was quite primitive—a wringer from a clotheswashing machine functioning as a press, perhaps the reason Bearden printed very few impressions from these experimental plates.[144]

Starting about 1960 it became common for artists whose primary engagement was painting or sculpture, or in Bearden's case collage, to produce edition prints with specially trained printers, some of them artists themselves like Blackburn (fig. 28), Kathy Caraccio, Mohammad O. Khalil, and Joseph Kleineman. This permitted artists to undertake the complex methods of printmaking without personally mastering all the techniques, and without taking the necessary time, often many dozens of hours, to print the editions. Bearden's published

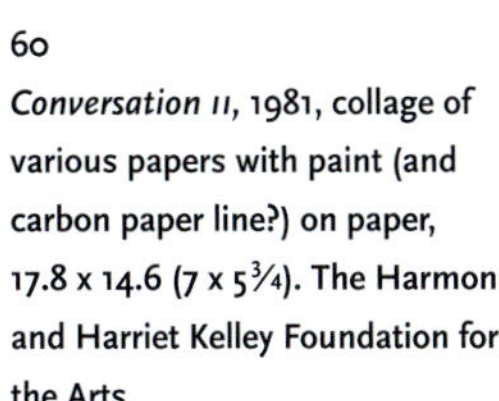

60
***Conversation II*, 1981, collage of various papers with paint (and carbon paper line?) on paper, 17.8 x 14.6 (7 x 5¾). The Harmon and Harriet Kelley Foundation for the Arts**

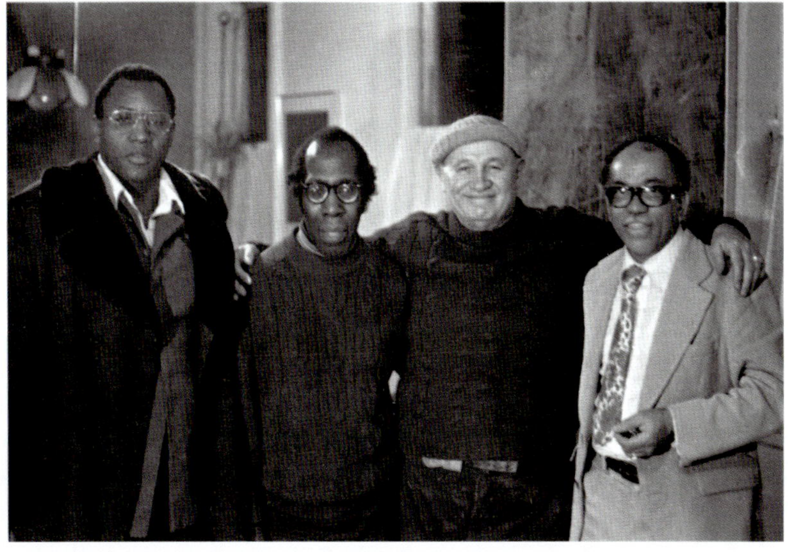

28

figure 28
Al Hinton, Robert Blackburn, Bearden, and Reginald Gammon in Bearden's Canal Street studio, 1978

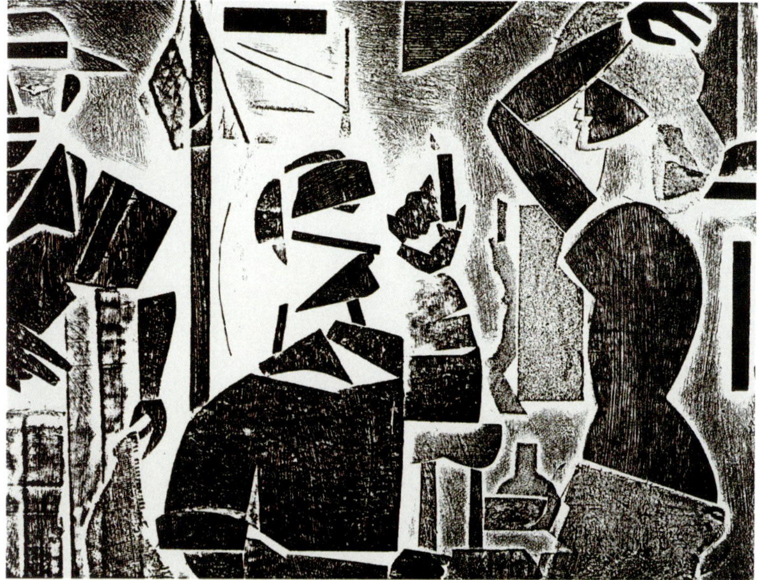

29

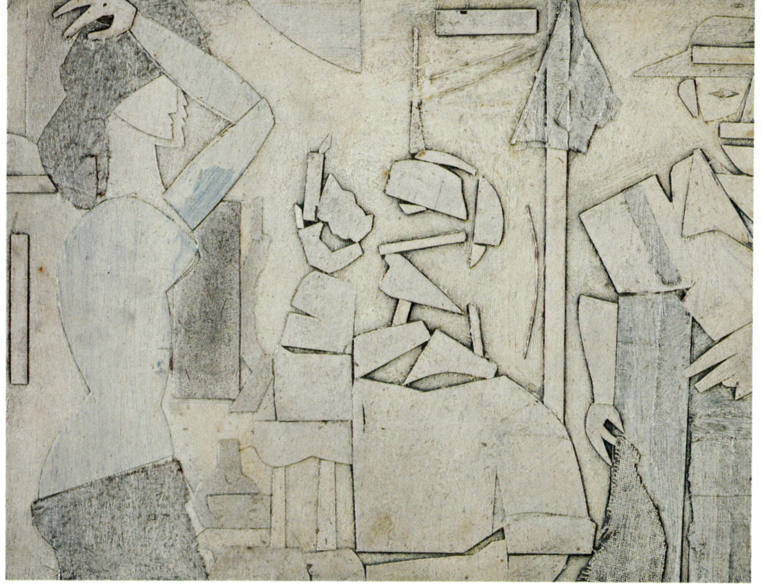

30

editions number approximately 110, primarily in lithography, screenprint, and intaglio photographically derived from collages and monotypes. In the late 1960s and early 1970s, however, he made approximately ten collagraphs in unique impressions or small editions, printed from collage matrices made especially for this purpose. According to Khalil, who was working with Blackburn at the time, Blackburn suggested this process to Bearden and introduced him to the various methods involved.

The Bearden-Blackburn association dated back to shared experiences at the Harlem Community Art Center, in the 306 studio, and at 33 West 125th Street where both young artists had studios. Blackburn's Printmaking Workshop was a presence in Manhattan starting in 1948, and in 1957 he became the first lithography printer at Tatyana Grosman's Long Island workshop, Universal Limited Art Editions, where he was an important force in what is often referred to as a printmaking renaissance. Over the years Blackburn, like Bearden, earned a reputation as being among the most influential and generous artists in New York.[145] From 1971 when the Printmaking Workshop was incorporated as a nonprofit space until his death, Bearden served on its board. He would have understood that edition prints could introduce his (and other artists') imagery to a wider public than unique works and that they enabled people of limited means to own an original work, something that his friends recall as being exceedingly important to Bearden.

The collagraph process grows directly from collage, the reason Blackburn saw it as a useful approach for Bearden. The name suggests the method: "collage prints." Bearden's were printed from three types of matrices: (1) collages made

figure 29
Romare Bearden, *Untitled (Sun and Candle)*, c. 1969, collagraph on paper. Courtesy Mohammad O. Khalil

figure 30
Romare Bearden, *Untitled (Sun and Candle)*, collagraph printing matrix, c. 1969, cardboard, various papers, and fabric, with a synthetic polymer coating. Courtesy Mohammad O. Khalil

from layered drawing papers, cardboard, sandpaper, and fabric such as burlap, and coated with a synthetic that would resist absorption of the printing ink, as with *Untitled (Sun and Candle)* (figs. 29, 30); (2) cardboard drawn onto with Elmer's Glue squeezed from the bottle to create globules that hardened as they dried, likewise coated for printing; and (3) a combination of these two methods, as in *Prelude to Troy* derived from Lucas Cranach's *The Judgment of Paris* (see Kennel in this volume, no. 140; fig. 16). According to Khalil, this was Bearden's first collagraph.[146] Plates made these ways may be printed either relief (ink rolled on the surface), as was *Untitled (Sun and Candle)*, or intaglio (ink pressed into the crevasses of the coating and removed from the top surface). They may be printed from one plate either in a single or multiple colors, like *Iliad* (fig. 31); or printed from multiple plates. They are among Bearden's most distinctive and important prints.

Bearden's lithographs and screenprints are based on photographically transferred collage and monotype images. However several multicolor etchings, like the collagraphs, engaged experimental variations on the collage process. The first was *The Train*, a photoengraving using cut-out plates assembled like a jig-saw puzzle for printing.[147] Next came *The Family* (no. 61) using multiple collage-based photographic transfers to achieve an incredibly sophisticated result. According to Blackburn, Herb Wheeler, a commercial photoengraver, was essential to this collaboration. Starting with a photograph of a collage, also titled *The Family*, Wheeler replicated its intermediary negative five times, each using a different photographic screen to create printing surfaces with five different patterns: including a line plate, dotscreens, and a mezzotint-like texture. Bearden then cut apart the negatives for use in a new collage in which all five photographic surfaces played a distinct visual role. That collage was then rephotographed and transferred to a copper plate for etching with acid. This became the key plate for the image, and proofs were printed in relief and intaglio (figs. 32, 33). Additional plates were prepared for the color fields. Comparing the proofs of the key plate with the edition print makes clear that Bearden again reworked his plate, removing texture throughout, and adding details such as the two children's faces. Other dramatic and successful color photo-etchings followed, but none attempted to push the combination of photography, collage, and etching beyond what was accomplished in *The Family*.

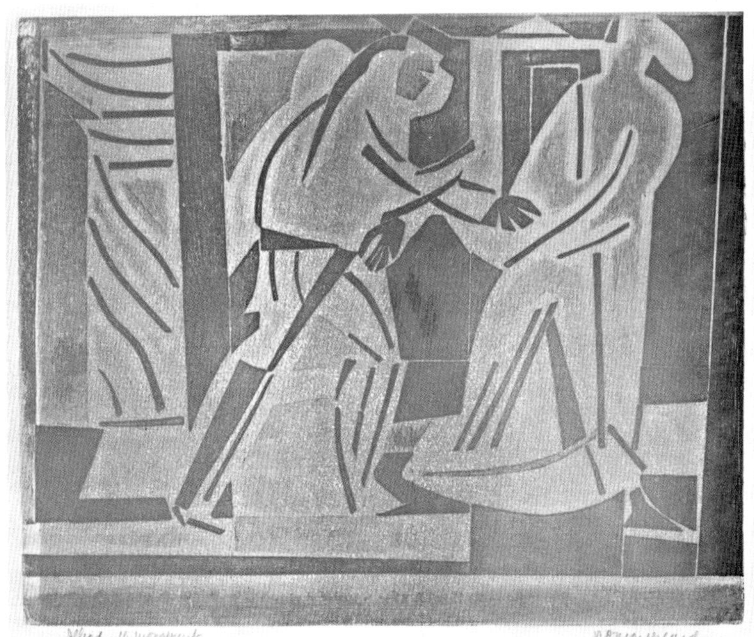

31

figure 31
Romare Bearden, *Iliad*, c. 1970, multicolor collagraph. National Gallery of Art, gift of the Collectors Committee

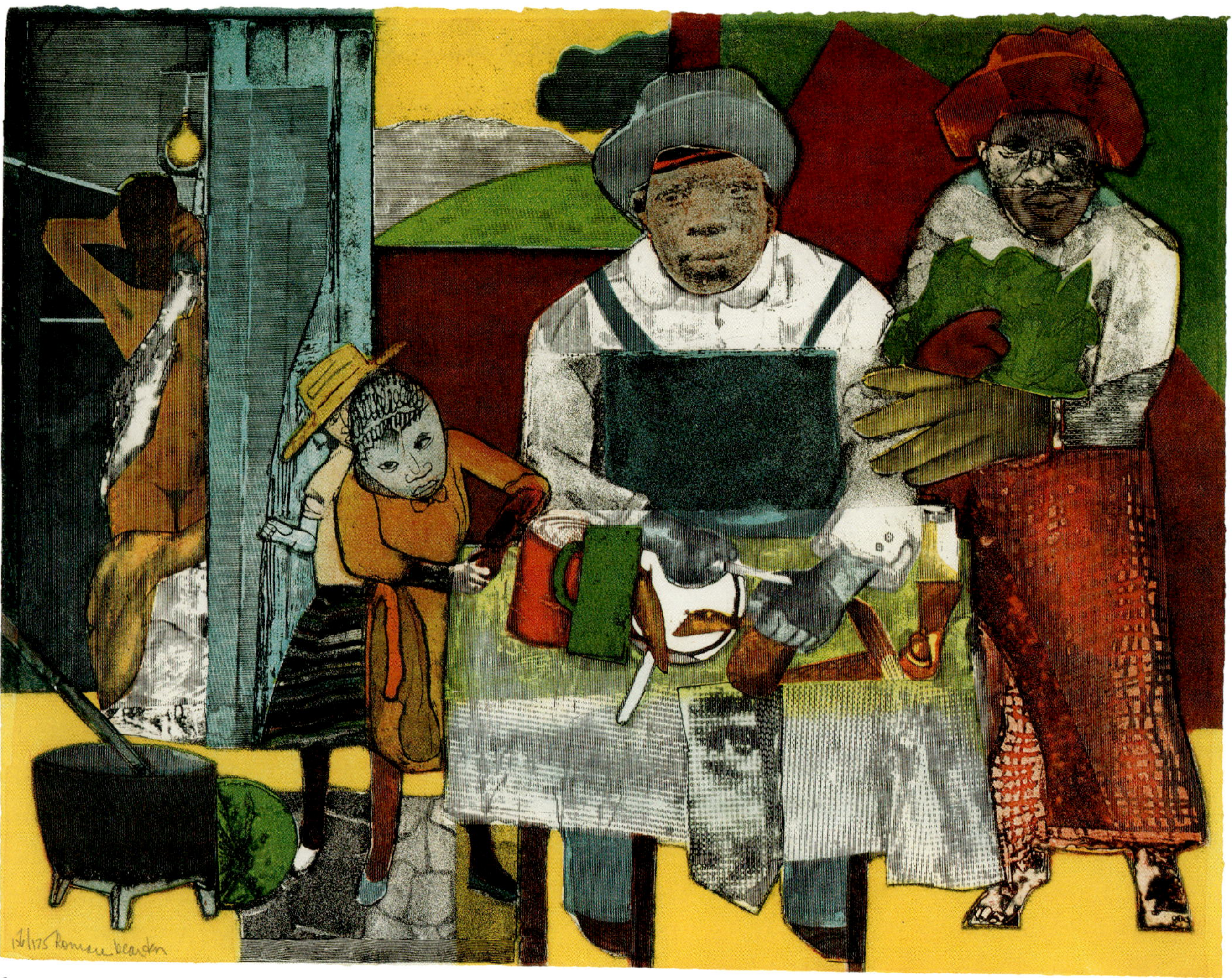

61

61
The Family, 1975, photoetching and aquatint, Edition 156/175, 50.2 x 66 (19¾ x 26). Juliette Bethea

figure 32
Romare Bearden, *The Family*, 1975, proof impression of key plate, printed relief. Courtesy Kathy Caraccio

figure 33
Romare Bearden, *The Family*, 1975, proof impression of key plate, printed intaglio. Courtesy Mohammad O. Khalil

32

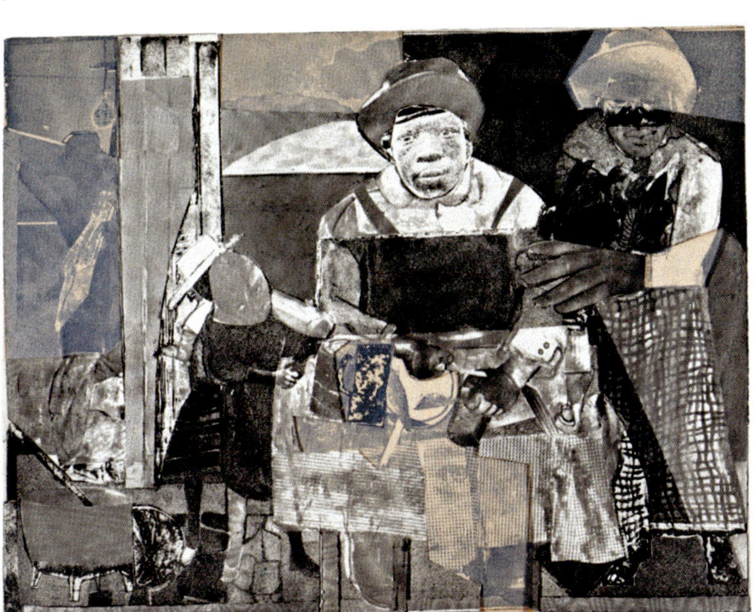

33

As Bearden's artistic practice developed, apart from his breaks for the army, to travel, and for health reasons, he had continued his work with the gypsy community.[148] In the late 1960s financial success through his association with Cordier & Ekstrom finally permitted him to leave the city's employ to work at his art uninterruptedly. It was, however, a period of considerable activism in Bearden's life, of time and attention given to the needs of African-American painters less successful than himself. He coorganized two exhibitions, *Art of the American Negro,* 1966, and *The Evolution of Afro-American Artists: 1800–1950* the following year. The latter was jointly sponsored by the City University of New York where the exhibition was held, the New York Urban League, and the Harlem Cultural Council (founded in 1964) of which Bearden was art director; his co-curator was art historian Carroll J. Greene, Jr., the author a few years later of a catalogue essay for Bearden's MoMA retrospective. The challenge of organizing the 1967 show, and a lecture he was asked to deliver at MoMA, led to Bearden's comprehensive study of art by African Americans, an understudied subject in American art history. His friend Harry Henderson was involved in this research also from the start, but given both men's multiple undertakings (for Bearden both in and outside of his studio) it turned out to be a very extended project resulting in the text *A History of African-American Artists: From 1792 to the Present.* In the end Henderson shepherded the book alone, and it was published after Bearden's death.[149]

Among other projects outside the studio, in 1968 Bearden and Norman Lewis, on behalf of the Harlem Cultural Council, expressed dissatisfaction with plans for the Met's (Metropolitan Museum of Art) multimedia exhibition *Harlem on My Mind:*

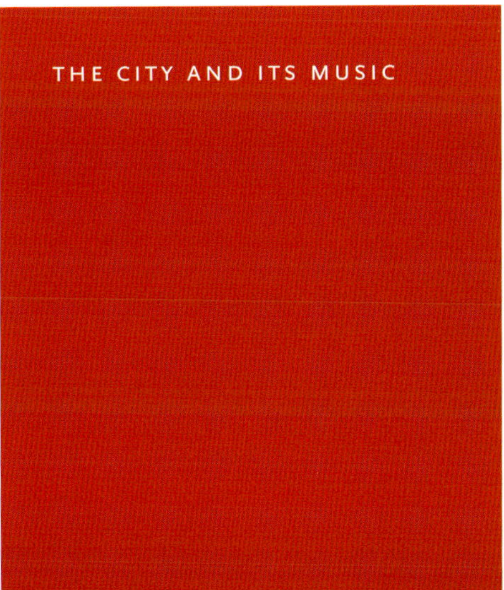

Cultural Capital of Black America 1900–1968. This protest effort was expanded in 1969 by artist Benny Andrews and the Black Emergency Cultural Coalition formed expressly for this purpose.[150] The lack of attention paid to the opinions of the Harlem artistic community by organizers of *Harlem on My Mind* and the exhibition's focus on documentary data, rather than accomplishments of artists, led to demonstrations on behalf of African-American artists at other New York art museums as well as at the Met. We are not apt to learn the extent to which Bearden's 1971 MoMA exhibition was a response to demonstrators' demands that included a retrospective for him, but it seems likely they played a role.

Also important to an understanding of Bearden's commitment to African-American artists is Cinque Gallery, named for Joseph Cinque, the leader of a mutiny on the slave ship *Amistad* in 1839. Initiated by Crichlow, Lewis, and Bearden in 1969, the year of *Harlem on My Mind,* the gallery continues today as a place for young artists to show their work. In 1972 Bearden expressed his support for the enterprise:

> Until they are about thirty years old, [young artists] find the art world very difficult. They can't get into galleries and show their work. They decide to drop out and do something else. A lot of the minority artists are a little reluctant to go around and ask to show their work at the Galleries. So Cinque Gallery was opened to provide a showcase for young minority artists, thirty years of age and under. We pay all the expenses for the ads and the catalogues and opening. The only expense that the artist has is bringing his work there. If he or she sells anything, the artist gets 100 percent of the sales price.[151]

By this time Bearden himself was experiencing considerable success. Building on a consistent program of exhibitions and sales through Cordier & Ekstrom, *Romare Bearden: The Prevalence of Ritual* opened at MoMA in 1971. The show included fifty-six works dating from 1941 through 1971. Those that appear here from that group are *The Visitation; They That Are Delivered from the Noise of the Archers;* three of the 1964 *Prevalence of Ritual* collages: *Baptism, Conjur Woman as an Angel,* and *Tidings; Childhood Memories; Backyard; La Primavera; Old Couple; Three Folk Musicians; Palm Sunday Procession; Strange Morning, Interior; Susannah at the Bath; Carolina Interior;* and *Ritual Bayou.* Bearden's exhibition was held concurrently with a solo show of work by Chicago-based African-American sculptor Richard Hunt. But Bearden and Hunt had more in common than race. Hunt, twenty-four years younger than Bearden, explored (and explores) assemblage techniques rooted in the work of Picasso, conflated his concerns with figuration and abstraction, made reference to classical literature, and exhibited at MoMA works in many media—graphite drawings and lithographs as well as sculpture.[152]

Bearden's show (not Hunt's) traveled from New York to Washington, D.C.; Pasadena and Berkeley, California; Atlanta, Georgia; and Raleigh, North Carolina, receiving enthusiastic reviews. A particularly apt one came from Berkeley:

> The quality that struck me the strongest [in this exhibition] is a seriousness. [Bearden] is not playing games. With a gentle sympathy, he explores his culture and our culture with the delicate sensuality of a good physician feeling for broken bones. All the faces in his work are serious. The laughing part he leaves for someone else. The work is not unhappy or solemn, only quietly serious. Even the rich lushness of some of his latest work, like "Ritual Bayou" of 1970 [see no. 98], has a calm quietness about it. He is not trying to kncok [*sic*] your head off, only open your eyes a little.[153]

The most recently completed work in the retrospective, *The Block* (Met), was a cityscape installation on six fiberboard panels horizontally joined to measure four by eighteen feet and accompanied by recorded sounds (street noises, news broadcasts, and church music according to *New York Times* critic Grace Glueck in her 24 March 1971 review). A view from Albert Murray's apartment where the initial sketches were made (figs. 34–38), *The Block* portrays vendors, children playing, families walking, a funeral, and life behind the walls, including sleepers, lovers, and faces peering out to the street, all reminiscent of Eugene Bailey's drawings of Pittsburgh houses with their facades removed.[154]

By creating a mural-size cityscape that specifically echoed the *Harlem on My Mind* exhibition with its accompanying recorded "block" sounds, *The Block* may have been Bearden's presentation of what was lacking in that 1969 show, a non-photographic depiction of Harlem by an African-American artist who had lived there.[155] The multi-panel conception of *The Block* inspired a major mural project for Berkeley, California, entitled *Berkeley—The City and Its People* (no. 62), and two additional New York scenes, *The Block II* (no. 63) and a collage mural *Cityscape,* 1976, now on view at Bellevue Hospital, New York.[156]

figures 34–38
Studies for *The Block,* c. 1971, color inks. Collection Albert Murray

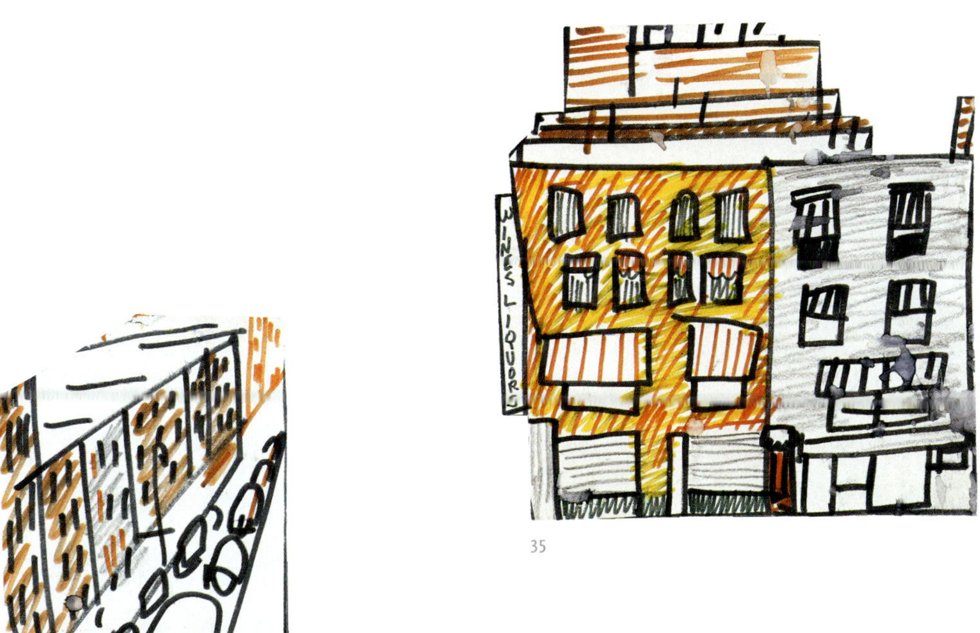

35

34

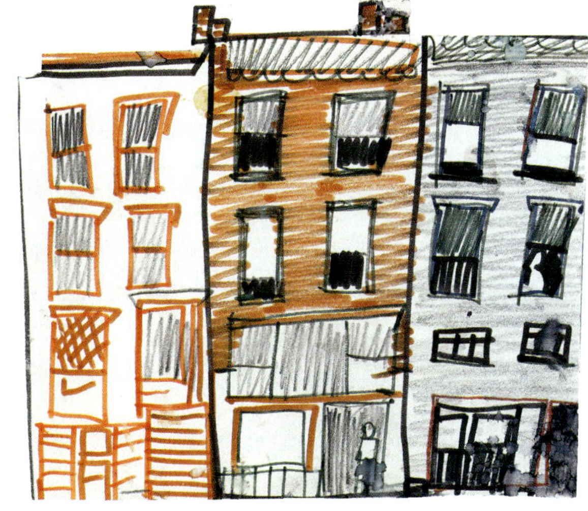

36

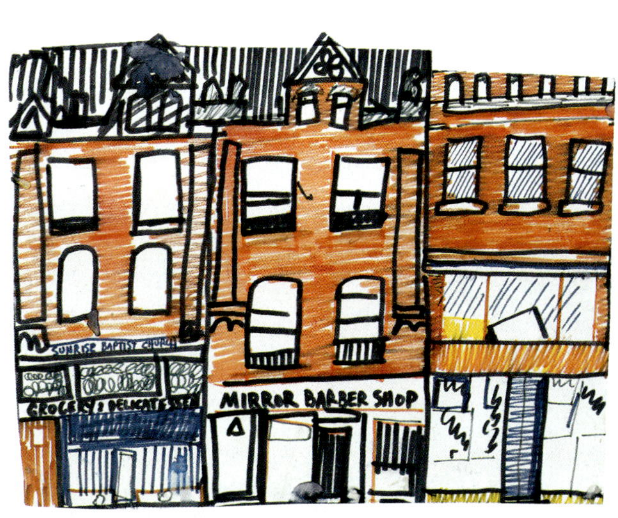

38

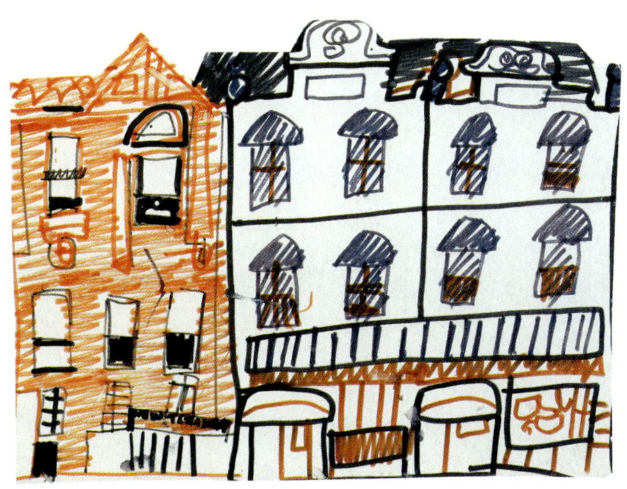

37

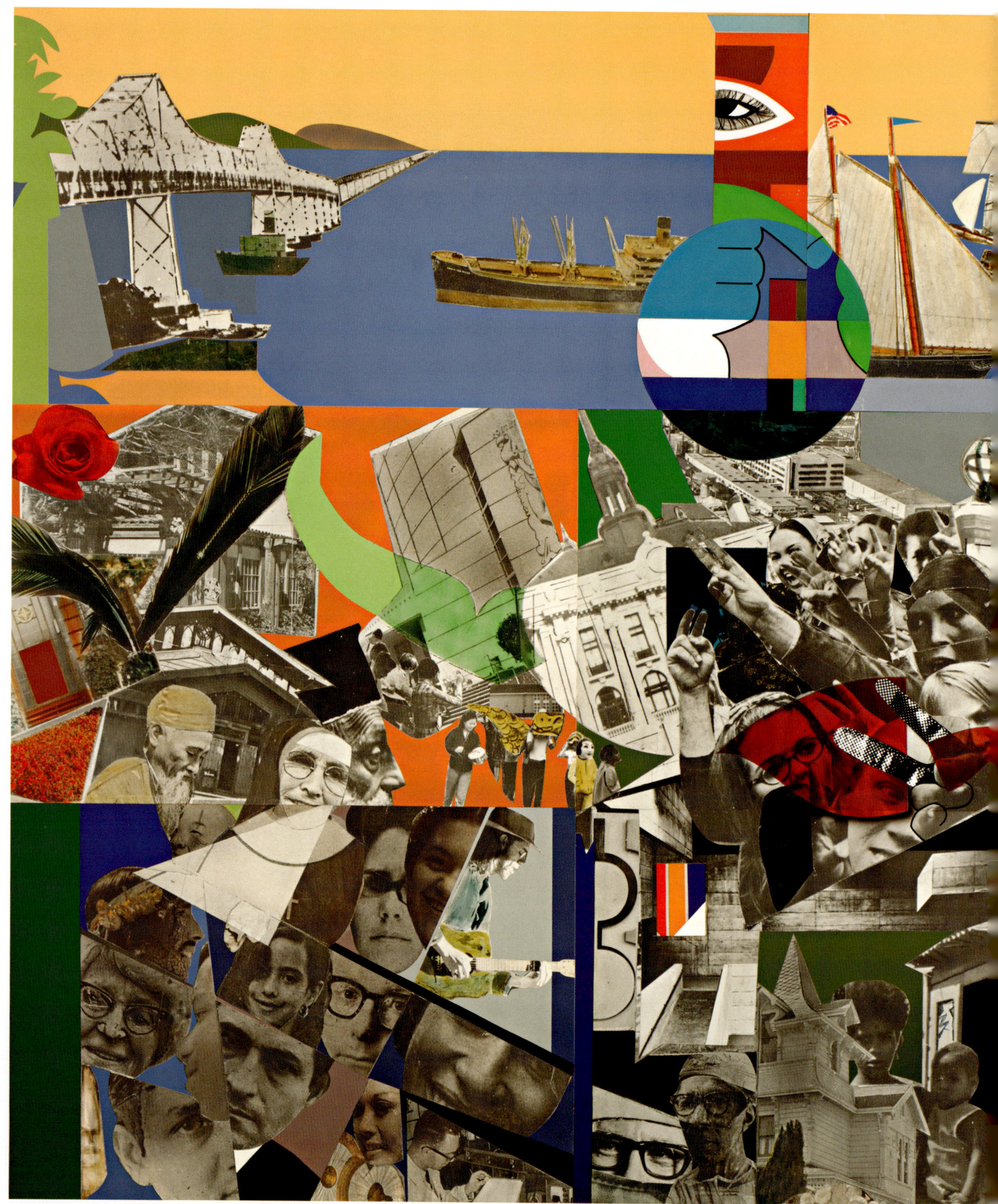

62

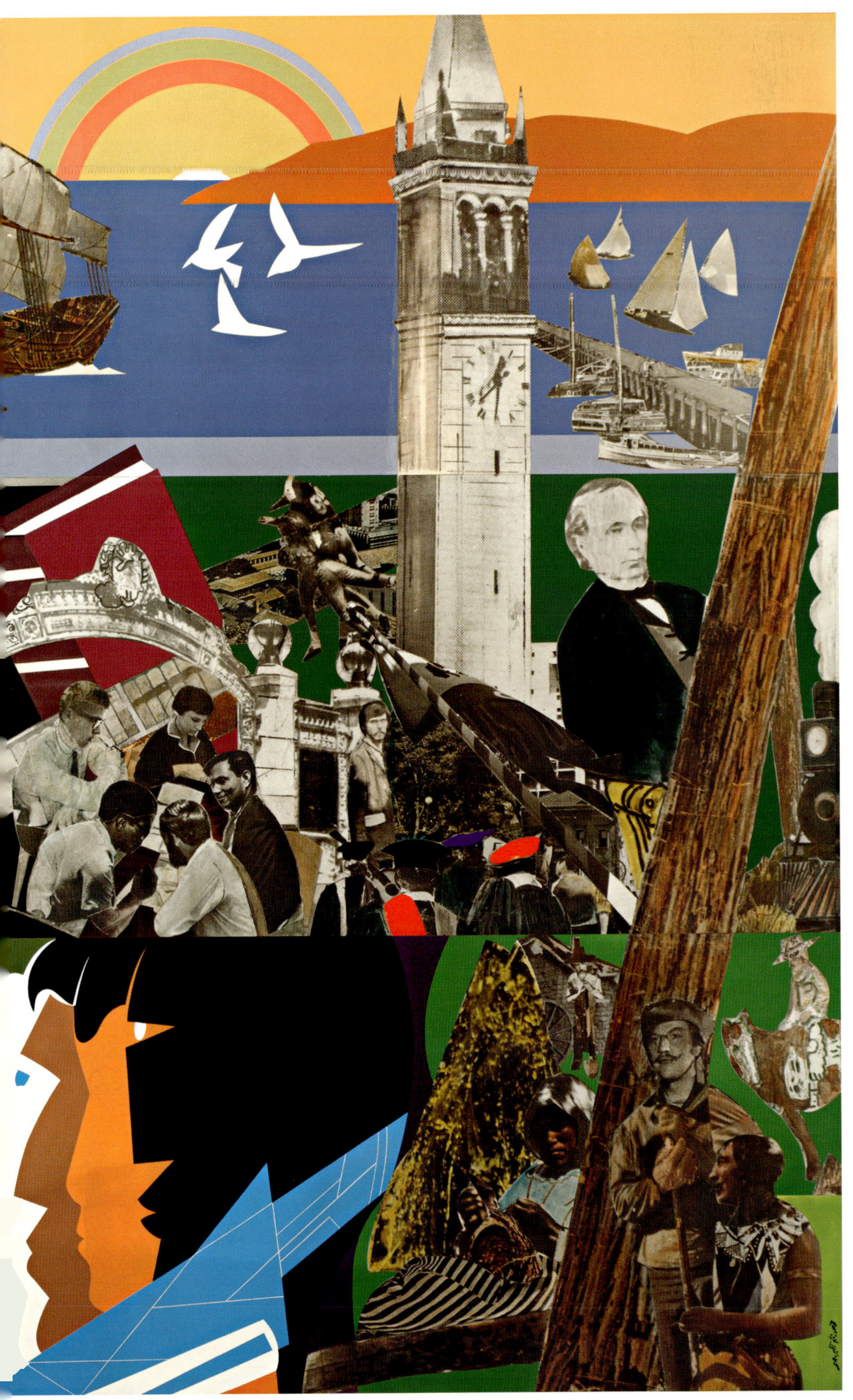

Berkeley—The City and Its People, installed in January 1974 in the city council chambers of what was then the City Hall, is an extraordinary blend of photographs and colored papers on seven panels that together measure ten by sixteen feet. Bearden's largest known work of paper, it vividly demonstrates the artist's flexibility to engage this material at its outer limits. This was one of Bearden's rare undertakings not rooted in autobiographical experiences in Mecklenburg County, Pittsburgh, or New York, yet he managed quickly to grasp the essence of his temporarily adopted university community.[157] His presence there has been credited to artists Russell T. Gordon and Raymond Saunders as well as to Peter Selz, director at the Museum of Art, University of California, Berkeley, who mounted Bearden's MoMA retrospective there, the artist's first major exhibition on the West Coast.[158] This was at a time when the renovation of the city council chambers was under discussion including the possibility of a mural project. *The Block,* therefore, generated particular attention. The following year, with the commission by Bearden for the city council chambers mural in discussion, Gordon and Saunders invited him to spend a week as a visiting artist at California State University, Hayward, where they taught. Bearden then traveled throughout Berkeley for several days compiling photographic data (and memories) for a mural. Traveling with Bearden and Nanette was a family friend, Ellsworth Mitchell, who did the documentary photography for the project. The commission was given strong support both by Selz and by Carl Worth, director of the Berkeley Art Center and secretary of the Civic Art Commission which coordinated the city council chambers project.

62
***Berkeley—The City and Its People,* 1973, collage of various papers with paint, ink, and graphite on seven fiberboard panels, 320 x 487.7 (126 x 192). City of Berkeley, California, Public Art Collection**

Architectural details, political rallies on Telegraph Avenue, Buddhist worship services, sailing vessels—both outdated and contemporary—on San Francisco Bay, Native Americans and early white historical figures, all specific to the region, are brought together into a collage that is singularly Bearden's in its use of materials, shifts in scale, profile heads, and other telling narrative details—not the least of which is the ever-present train that edges in at the right. An amazing response to a community spirit, *Berkeley—The City and Its People* embodied the diverse factions in that complex city. The group of four heads in the lower right quadrant, representing the racial diversity of the community, has since become Berkeley's city logo.

Smaller but structurally more complicated than the Berkeley mural, both *The Block II* and *Cityscape* (which echoes *The Block II* composition but with two segments added at the far left) are bas-reliefs in which some panels are inset and others built out, the only such examples we have identified in Bearden's work. To achieve this *The Block II* is composed of eighteen fiberboard and wood panels, more than in the larger *Cityscape,* which is similarly structured. In addition to the segments added to the latter there are other differences in detail throughout *The Block II* and *Cityscape,* for example, in parallel figures. The compactness of the smaller version allows an immediate grasp of the composition's totality and generates a greater psychic intensity than either the larger mural version of this image or the earlier *The Block.*

Unlike the cordial relations leading to the Berkeley mural, with all aspects of the community working together to accomplish a goal, *The Block II* in its *Cityscape* form was fraught with

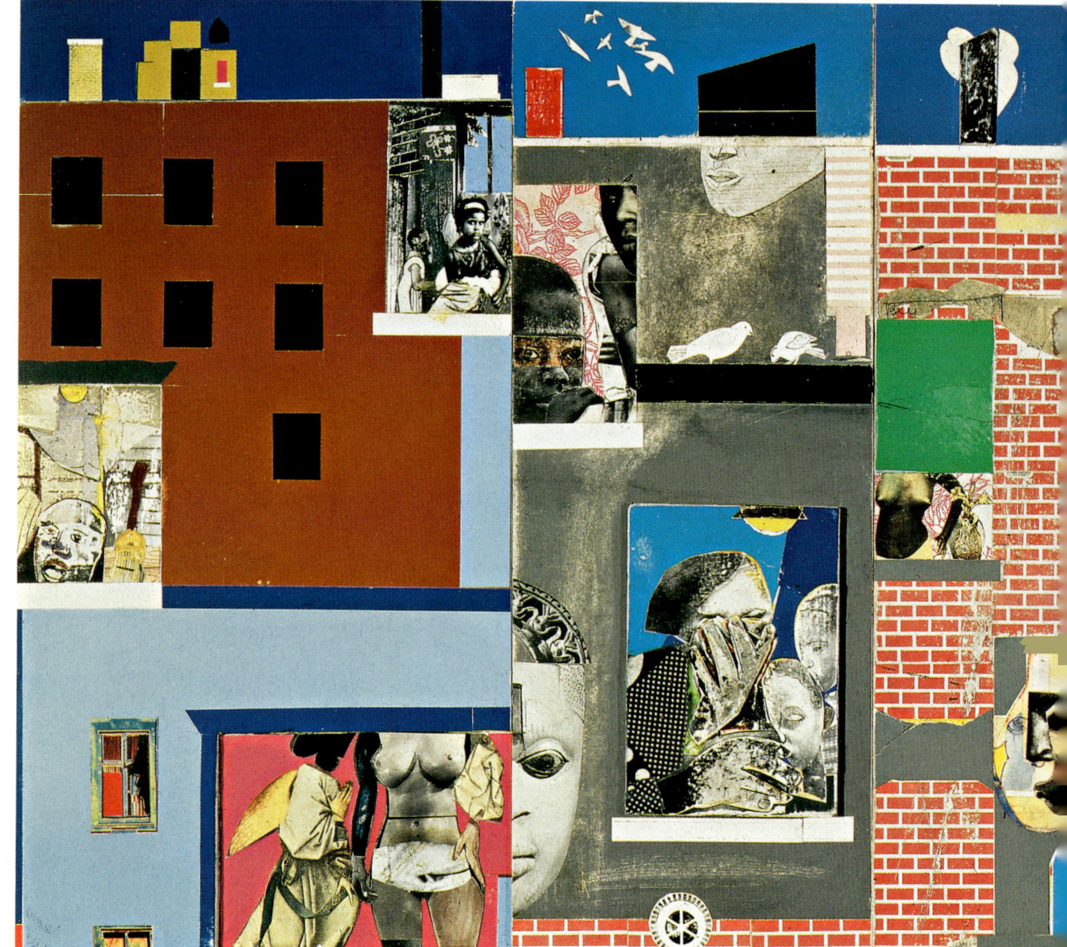

63

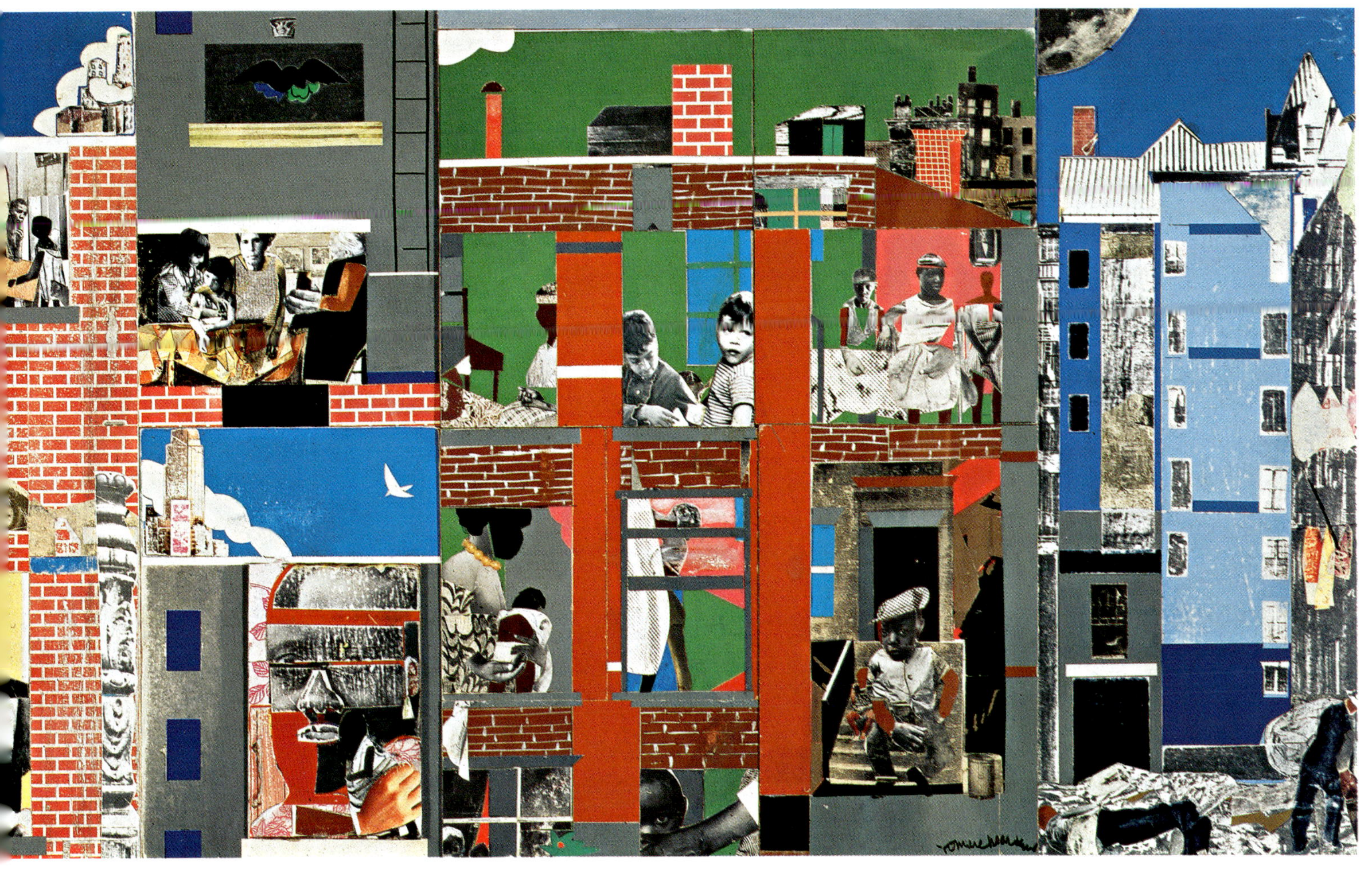

63
The Block II, 1972, collage of various papers with foil, paint, ink, graphite, and surface abrasion on eighteen fiberboard and plywood panels including two applied in relief and one recessed, 64.8 x 188 (25 1/2 x 74). The Walter O. Evans Collection of African American Art

controversy. Commissioned in 1974 for the new Lincoln Medical and Mental Health Center in the Bronx, it was completed two years later but within months was wasting away in a warehouse, thought to be "too obscene and not relevant enough... a piece of junk that is not worth anything... done without any community involvement. We wanted to discuss ideas and concept, but no, they would not listen to us," language that sounds frightfully close to that used in the *Harlem on My Mind* controversy.[159] Despite outrage at the mural languishing in storage, it remained there until its 1983 installation in the first of several Bellevue Hospital locations (currently in a second-floor passageway near the chapel).

Paper was an unlikely material for mural projects such as *Berkeley—The City and Its People* and *Cityscape,* and all but one of Bearden's subsequent murals employed more permanent materials and were executed in their final form by commercial companies specific to each material, such as Crovatto Mosaics Inc., based on Bearden's preliminary collage studies.[160] Among those accomplished in this material are *Quilting Time,* 1986, at the Detroit Institute of Arts and *Before Dawn,* based on a 1985 collage, but completed posthumously for the Charlotte/Mecklenburg County Public Library.[161]

Because Bearden's working methods were so varied and complicated, close observations by knowledgeable professionals are essential to any study of his practice. A report prepared by Manhattan-based paintings conservator Luca Bonetti when he cleaned and restored *Cityscape* in 1998–99 describes "collaged paper and photographs on oil-painted masonite panels. Pencil, oil colors, markers." A detailed discussion of the mural's fourth panel which is "quite representative [of the work as a whole] and interesting as far as technique and painterly execution" suggests the technical contradictions with which Bearden's art is laden:

> The black stain-like area visible at center and at bottom left appeared at first sight to be mold damage.... Yet the stains were clearly 'artist intent' and were created by pouring thinned black paint over the surface. The abrasions present on many of the red collaged bricks and on the green field at left center are also 'artist intent' rather than accidental. Similarly, the peelings visible on the B/W [black and white] collaged photographs near the bottom right corner were intentional 'defects' that Bearden intended to leave or even to purposely create.[162]

These effects are evident throughout Bearden's work of the 1970s. The abrasions are variations on the surfaces of a sort Bearden developed as early as 1968 in *Strange Morning, Interior.* In many works circular markings (fig. 39), possibly made with an electric eraser, create a distinctive texture.[163] Starting about 1974, Bearden sprayed brilliantly colored paint onto his abraded layered papers using a freer hand than previously, masking areas to create sharp edges and to keep some places free of spray as in *The Blues* (see no. 64; fig. 40). This further enriched his increasingly colorful and highly textured compositions.

Several New York City scenes, including *Departure from Planet Earth* and *The Street* (nos. 65, 66), are marked by these high-key colors and painterly surfaces. *The Street* restates at larger format and with different collage materials the 1964 collage of the same title. Its densely layered figures, heads, details of buildings and such city and landscape furniture as bridges, fire hydrants, and street signs, all in conflicting scale relationships, are invested with the sense of heightened abandon that Bearden's new technical approach allowed. The title of *Departure from Planet Earth* (filled with similar pictorial elements as *The Street*) suggests additional physical and metaphysical readings in regard to the contemporary environment, referencing the exploration of space internationally during this period, and also a pervasive drug culture that presented other kinds of alternatives to earthbound experience.

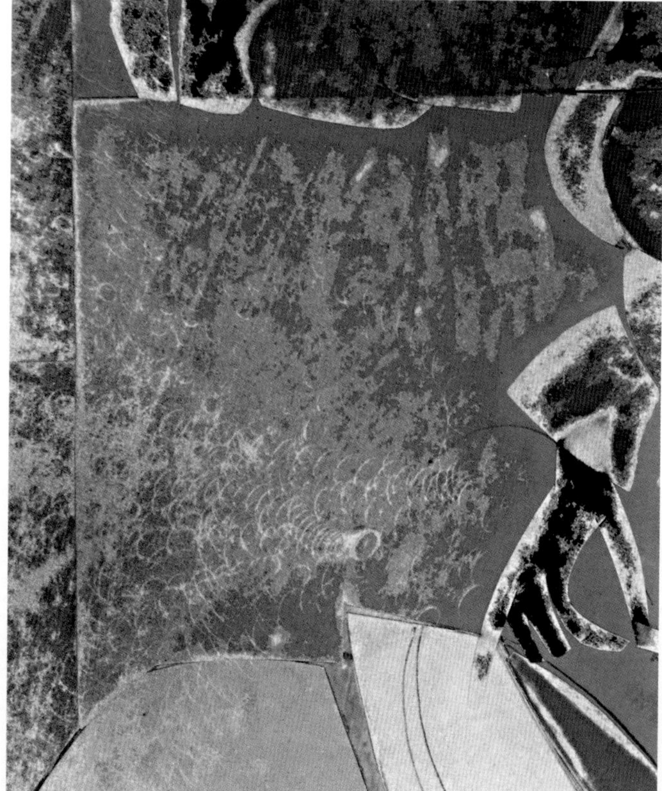

39

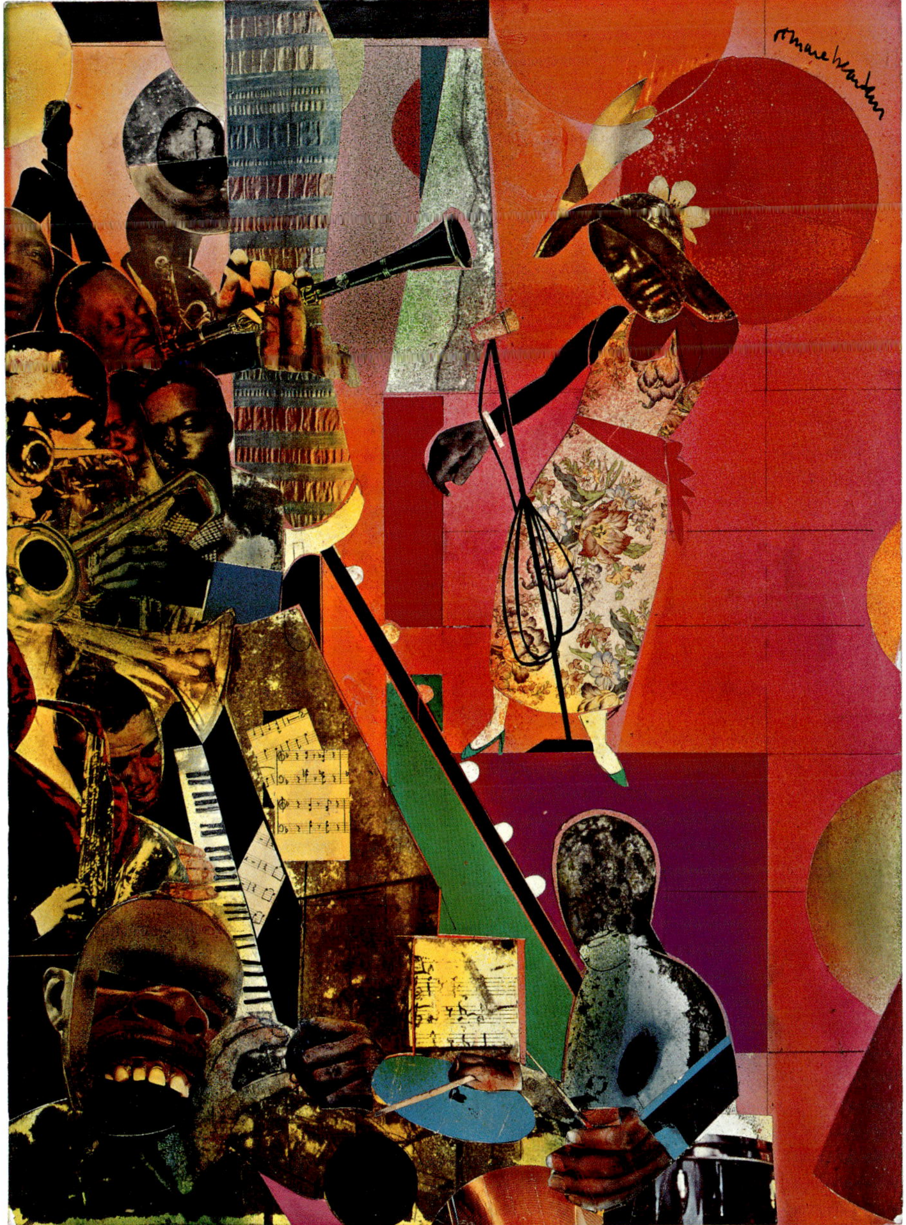

64

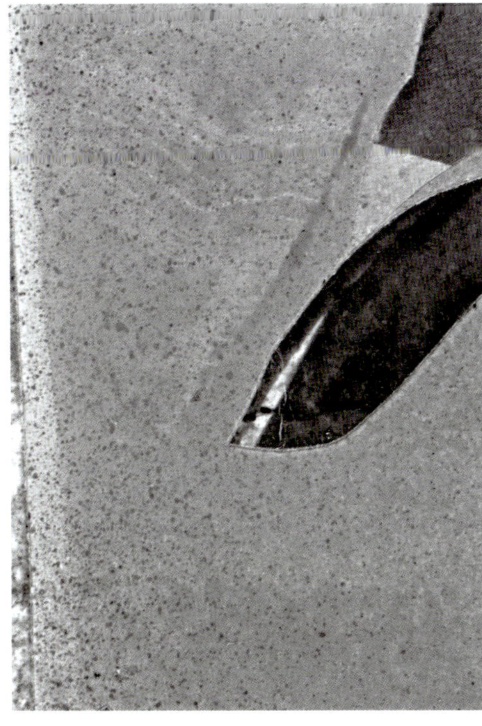

40

figure 39
Detail of *Delilah* (no. 79), showing circular markings from abrasive tool

64
***The Blues,* 1975, collage of various papers with paint, ink, and graphite on fiberboard, 61 x 45.7 (24 x 18). Honolulu Academy of Arts/gift of Geraldine P. Clark, 1977 (4451.1)**

figure 40
Detail of *The Blues* (no. 64), showing spray paint with sharp edge defined by mask

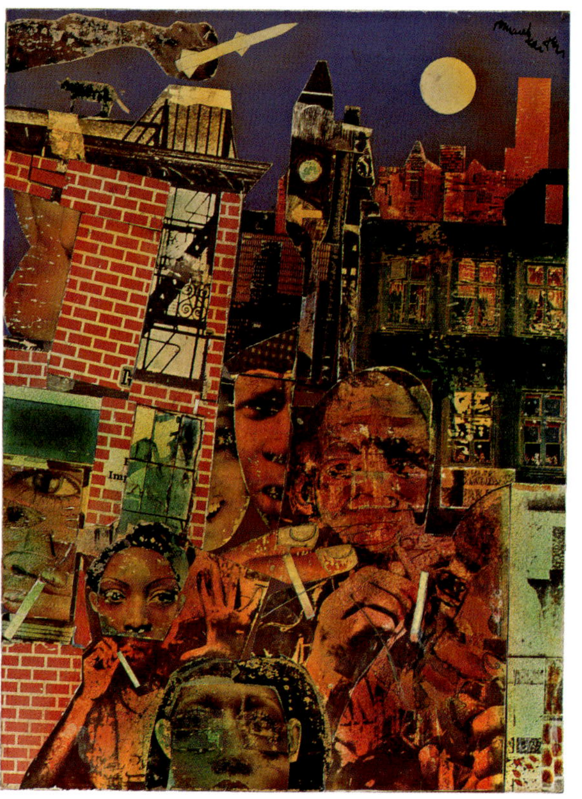

65

Another work entitled *The Street (Composition for Richard Wright)* (no. 67) echoes a different but related image originating in 1964, *The Dove* (Museum of Modern Art). An ink drawing, it was reproduced in the *New York Times,* 8 April 1977, to accompany "What Sets Storms to Rolling in His Soul," excerpted from Wright's then forthcoming *American Hunger.* Large "finished" drawings such as this are few in number. Mainly Bearden made small sketches like the untitled ones on an unfolded envelope, drawn during a conversation between him and a friend (fig. 41a, b), and his letters and notebooks are filled with images to expand what is stated in words.

Bearden's New York images convey the vast complexity of the city, from the packed particulars of *The Block II, Departure from Planet Earth,* and *The Street,* to the more abstract celebratory aura of *City Lights* (no. 68), its small size and bright hues virtually bursting with energy. A most unusual city scene is the poignant *Untitled* (no. 69). Composed of multiple vantage points, the essential one suggests the artist looking down rather than up or out, observing pools of water, perhaps left by rain (suggested by an atmospheric grayness), perhaps

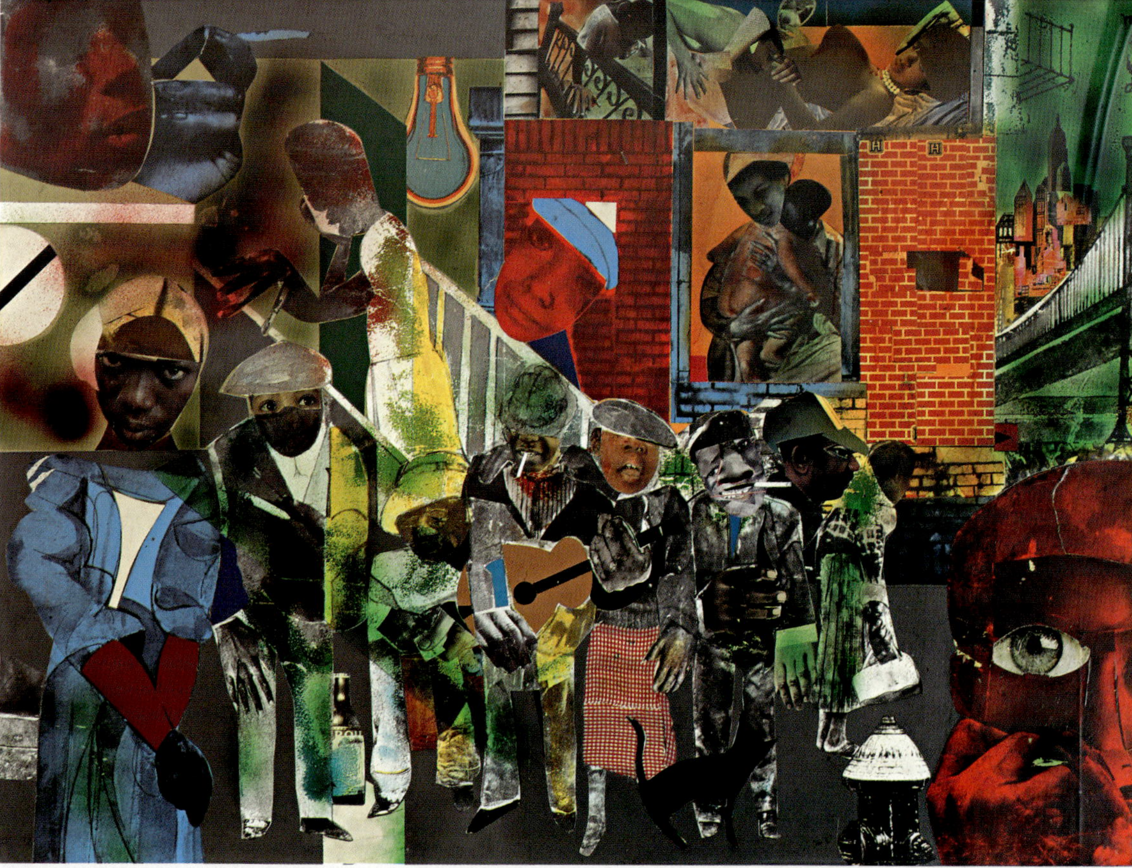

66

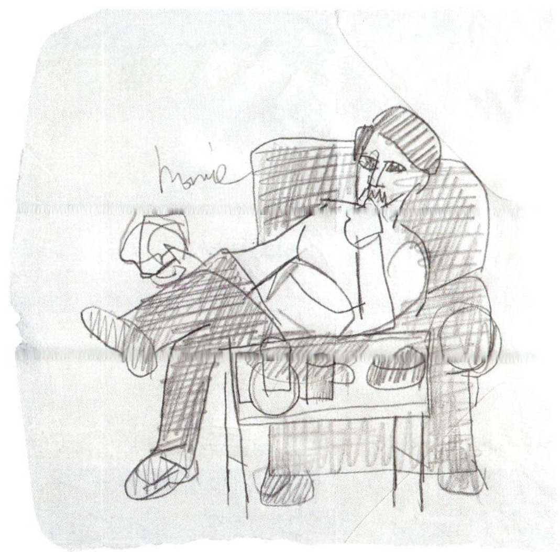

41 a

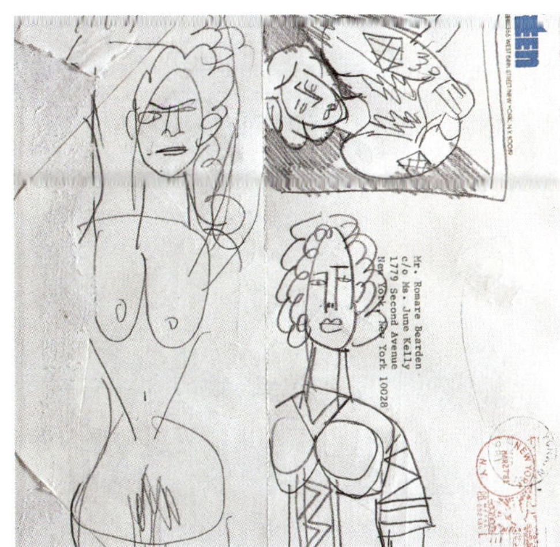

41 b

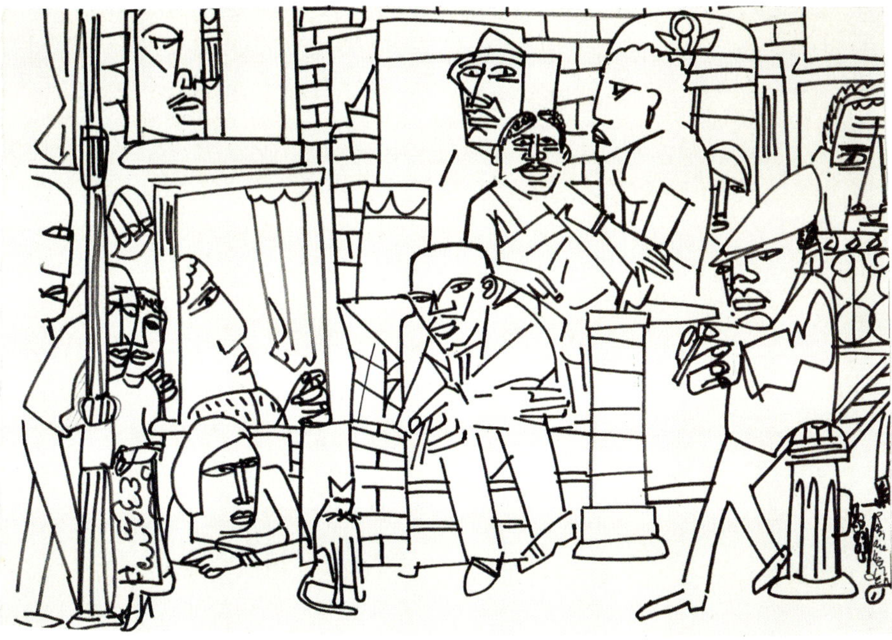

67

65
Departure from Planet Earth, **1975, collage of various papers with paint, ink, and surface abrasion on fiberboard, 61 x 45.7 (24 x 18). David A. Hagelstein, Bloomfield Hills, Michigan**

66
The Street, **1975, collage of various papers with fabric, paint, and ink on fiberboard, 94 x 128.3 (37 x 50 1/2). Lent in memory of Elaine Lebenbom**

67
The Street (Composition for Richard Wright), **c. 1977, ink on paper, 48.4 x 70.7 (19 1/16 x 27 13/16). National Gallery of Art, Washington, gift of Werner H. and Sarah-Ann Kramarsky and Collectors Committee Fund**

figure 41a, b
Romare Bearden, *Untitled* (recto and verso), 1981, graphite on unfolded envelope. Collection of Charles Storer

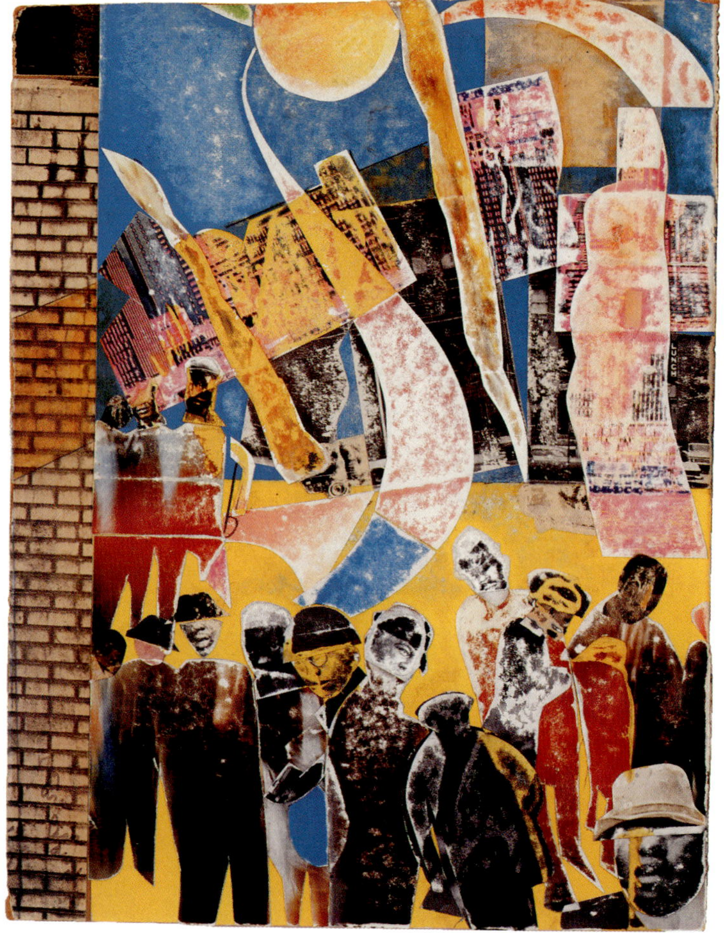

68

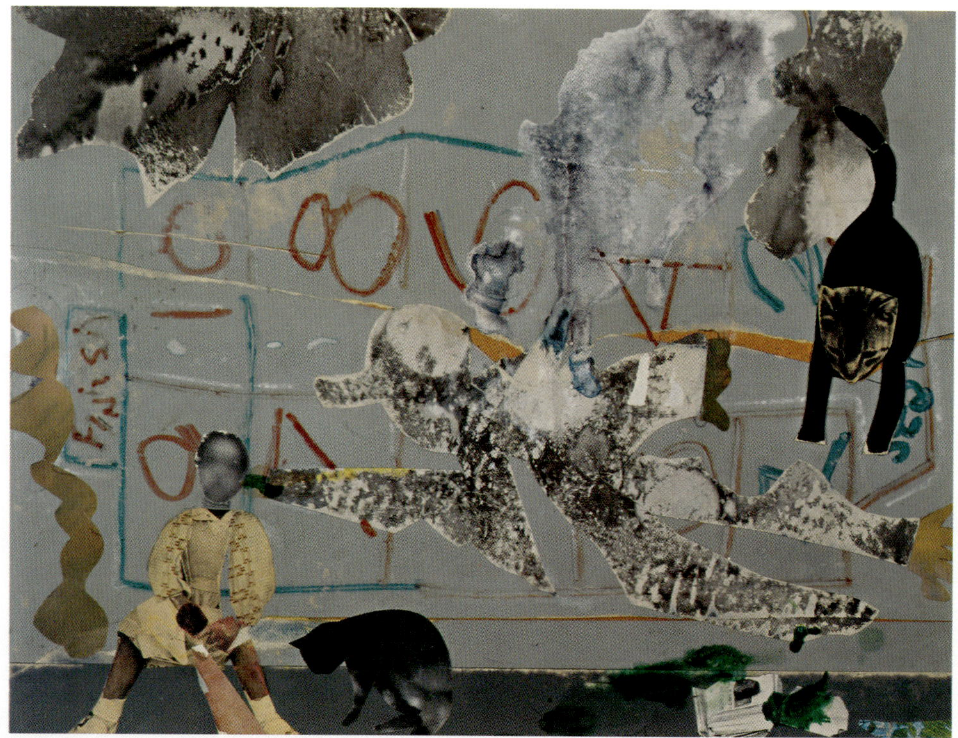

69

by an opened fire hydrant. Numbers of a gridded hopscotch game chalked on the street are interrupted by a shadowlike figure hopping midair. A young girl seated on the curb and two cats add to the tender nature of this lovely and unusual image. Fascinating is the almost featureless head of the child in relation to the specificity of the cat's face, upper right. Childless himself, Bearden has been described as exceedingly warm toward the young people who entered his realm (fig. 42), and his cat Gypo is an essential component in the lore of his life.

Music culture was a critical aspect of Bearden's New York. Ellison recounted shared experiences with the artist in the 1930s: "the days of swinging big bands.... when we danced the Lindy at the Savoy Ballroom, and nights when new stars were initiated on the stage of the Apollo Theatre."[164] The subject has also been discussed extensively in various places by Murray, including his essay "The Visual Equivalent of the Blues."[165] Several collages that feature music palaces are imbued even more than the cityscapes with that magical richness Bearden created throughout the 1970s. His 1975 exhibition at Cordier & Ekstrom, entitled *Of the Blues*, joined New York club scenes with images rooted in Mecklenburg blues memories. Among works in that show included here (all of which have at the start of their titles the phrase *Of the Blues:*) are *At the Savoy; Wrapping It Up at the Lafayette; Mecklenburg County, Saturday Night;* and *Carolina Shout* (nos. 70–73). The last of these titles corresponds to a well-known piano work by James P. Johnson, linking the gestures to "the dance hall, the juke joint, the honkey tonk and the barrelhouse [and at the same time suggesting] an ecstatic high point in a downhome church service," an extraordinary conflation of

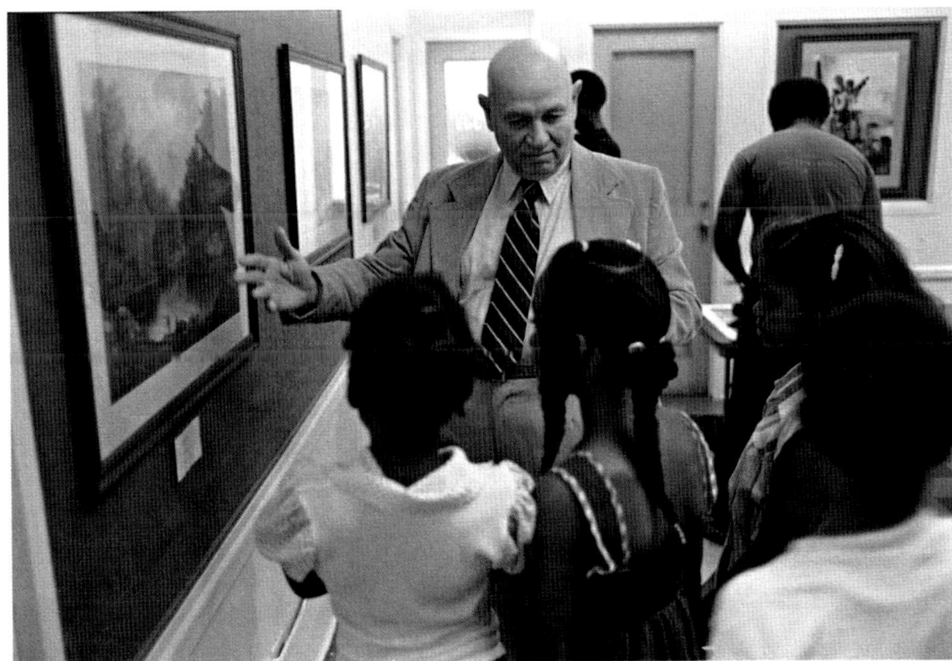

42

the profane with the sacred.[166] As a group these collages offer a glimpse into Bearden's densely layered interaction with music's visual realm. The Savoy Ballroom, "a big square room... that held about five or six hundred people" where "everybody was jammed tight and doing a number," and the Lafayette Theater, possibly the first in New York to desegregate (in 1913), were at the heart of Harlem. Six nights a week (closed Mondays) the clubs were in full swing from 9 or 10 P.M. till three or four in the morning.[167] Hot sounds and movements generated by musicians, vocalists, and dancers who frequented them can almost be heard and felt while looking at Bearden's

68
***City Lights*, c. 1970, collage of various papers with ink, graphite, and surface abrasion on fiberboard, 34.3 x 26.7 (13½ x 10½). Beverly Zimmerman Private Collection**

69
***Untitled*, c. 1971, collage of various papers with ink on fiberboard, 29.2 x 39.7 (11½ x 15⅝). Rowan Khaleel**

figure 42
Romare Bearden speaking to children at an exhibition on the Yale University campus, 1979

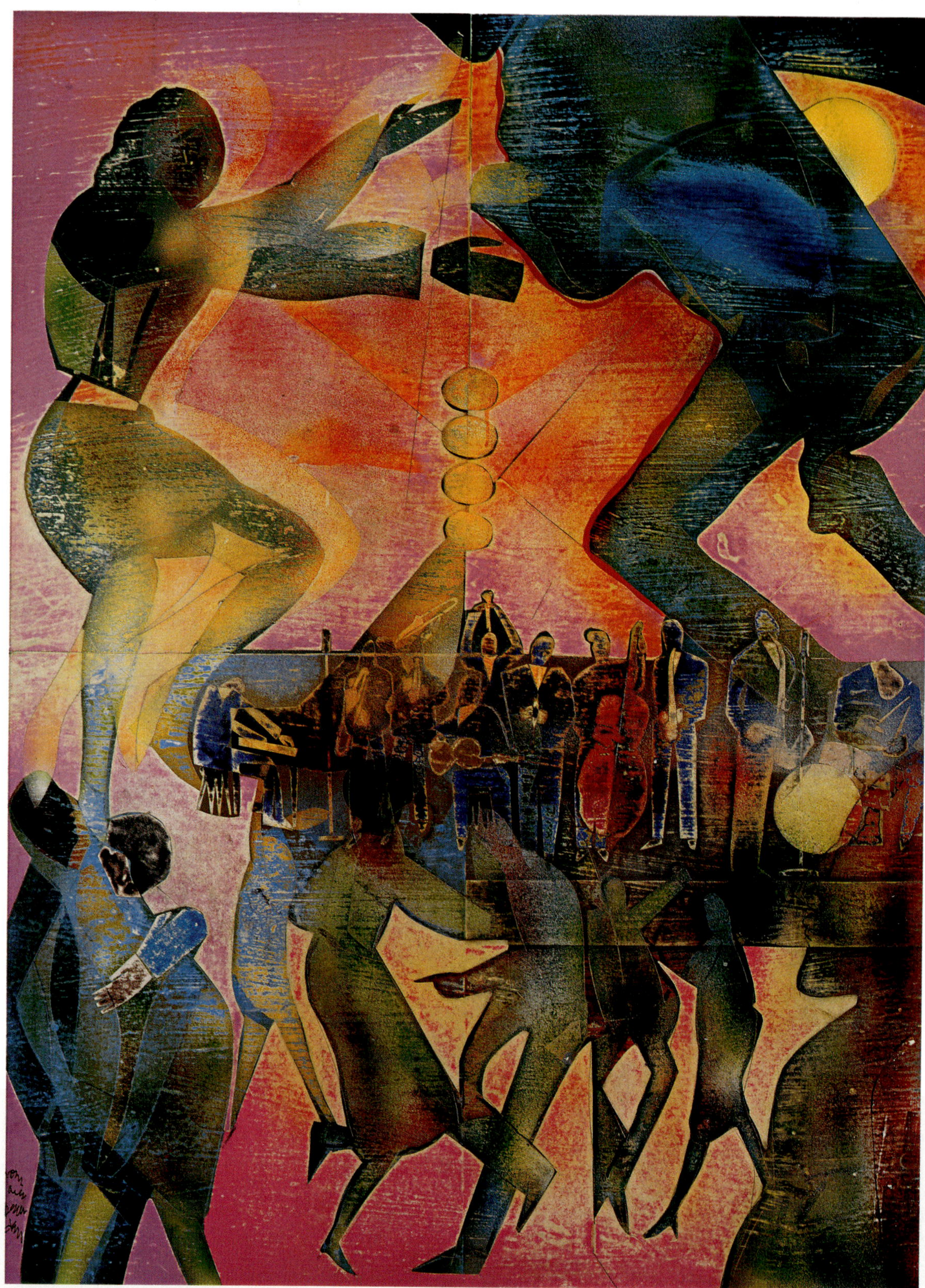

70

70
Of the Blues: At the Savoy, 1974, collage of various papers with paint on fiberboard, 121.9 x 91.4 (48 x 36). From the Collection of Raymond J. McGuire

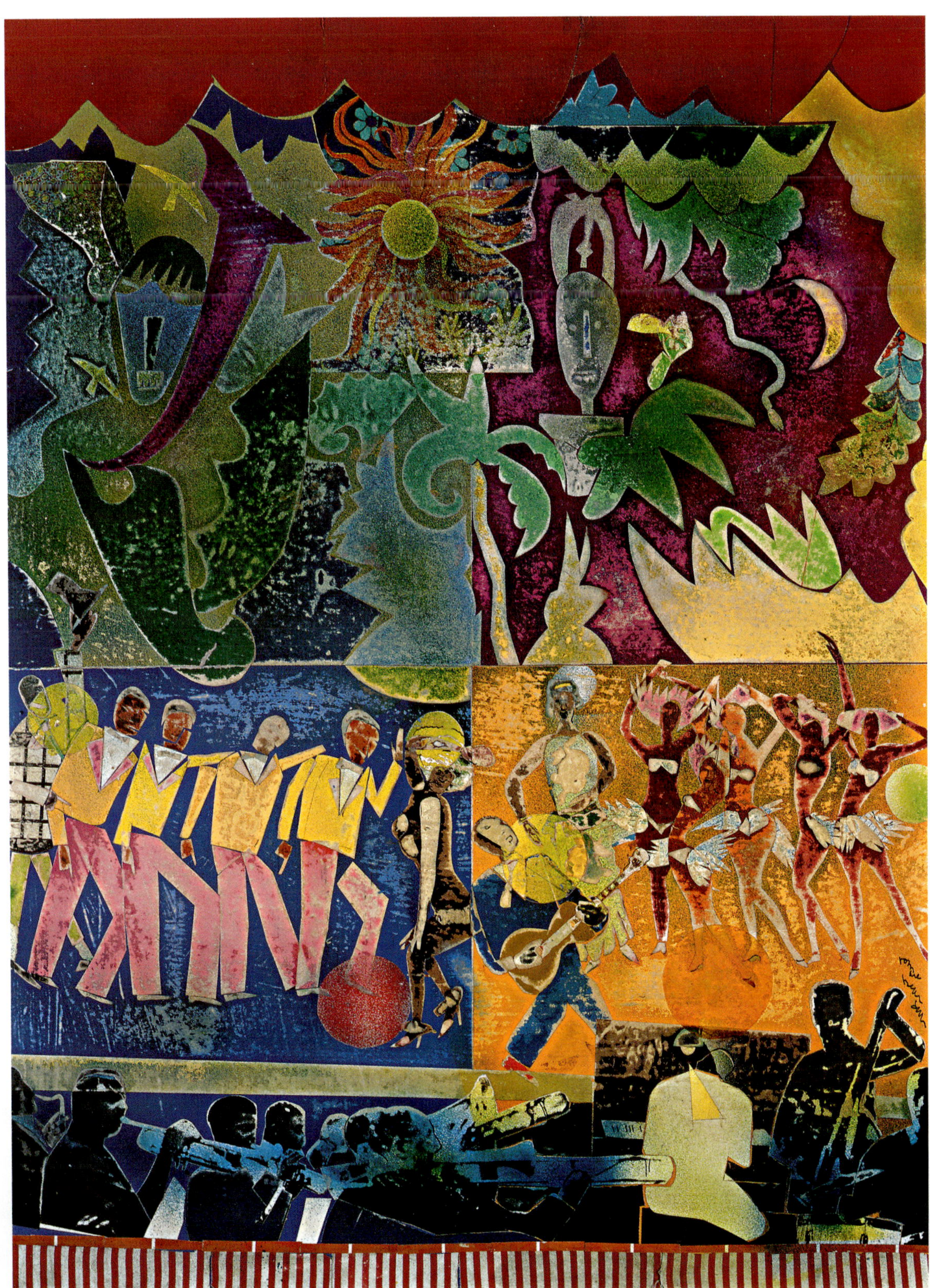

71

71
Of the Blues: Wrapping It Up at the Lafayette, 1974, collage of various papers with fabric, paint, ink, and surface abrasion on fiberboard, 121.9 x 91.4 (48 x 36). The Cleveland Museum of Art, Mr. and Mrs. William H. Marlatt Fund 1985.41

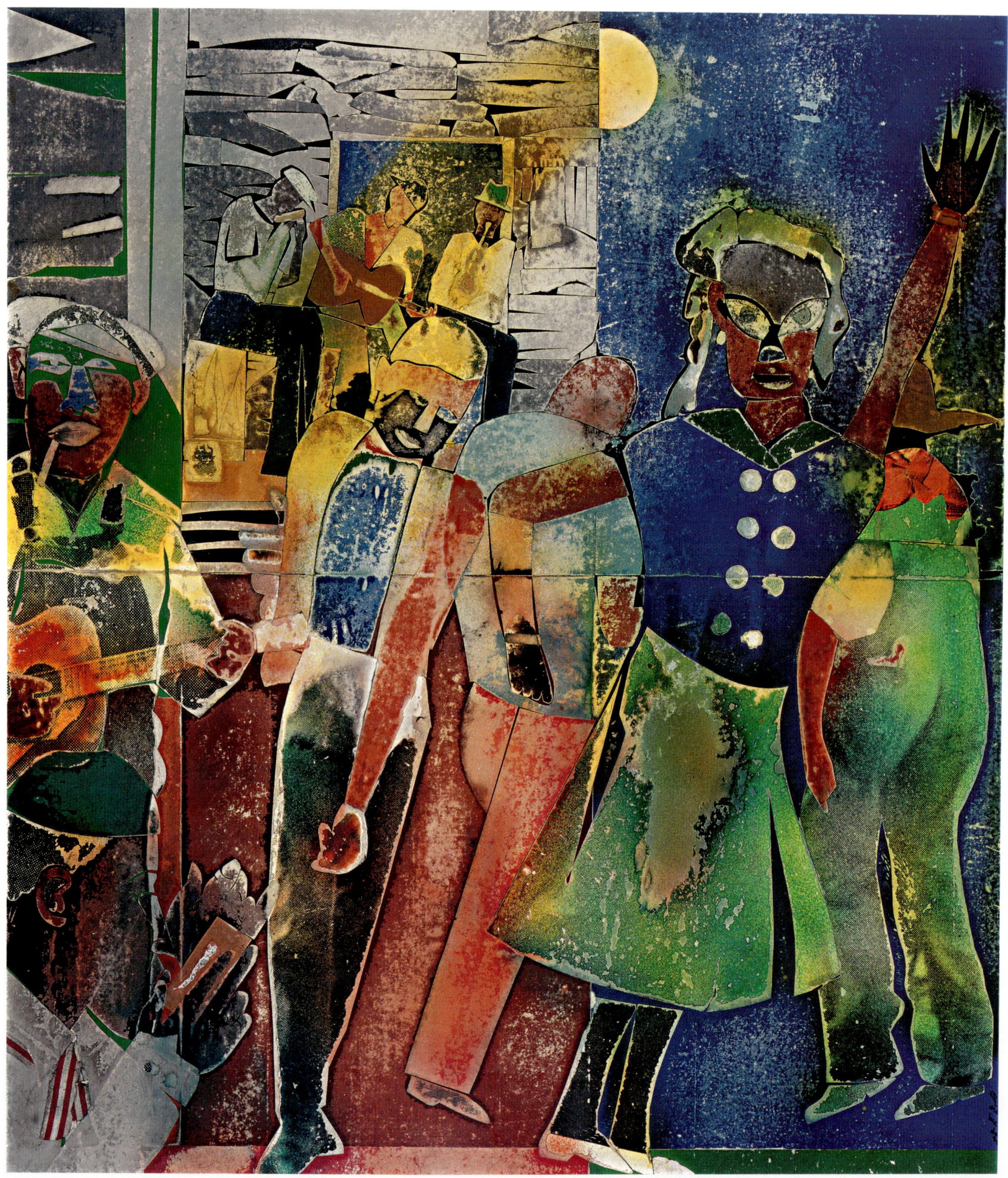

72

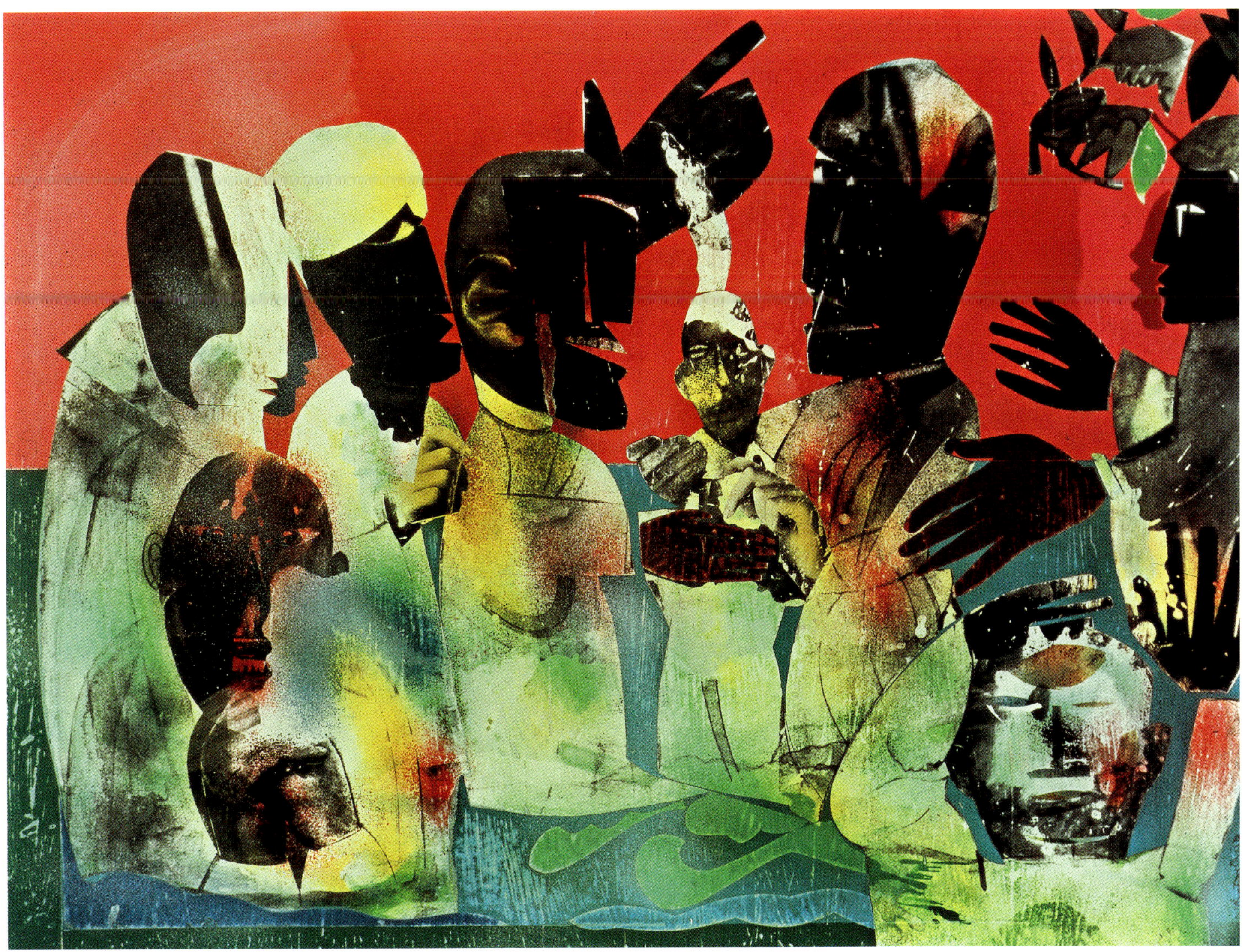

73

72
Of the Blues: Mecklenburg County, Saturday Night, 1974, collage of various papers with paint, ink, graphite, and surface abrasion on fiberboard, 128.3 x 112.4 (50½ x 44¼). Mr. and Mrs. Douglas Houchens

73
Of the Blues: Carolina Shout, 1974, collage of various papers with paint and surface abrasion on fiberboard, 95.3 x 129.5 (37½ x 51). Mint Museum of Art, Charlotte, North Carolina, Museum Purchase: National Endowment for the Arts Matching Fund and the Charlotte Debutante Club Fund

evocations of these places. Other cities are evoked, too, as in *Of the Blues: Kansas City 4/4* (no. 74). Starting in conversations with Davis in the 1940s, and continuing with Murray among others, Bearden often discussed relationships between his work and jazz music. The subjects of freedom and improvisation dominated this discourse during a 1984 interview in which he pointed out that artists turning to Africa for inspiration were, in fact, turning to:

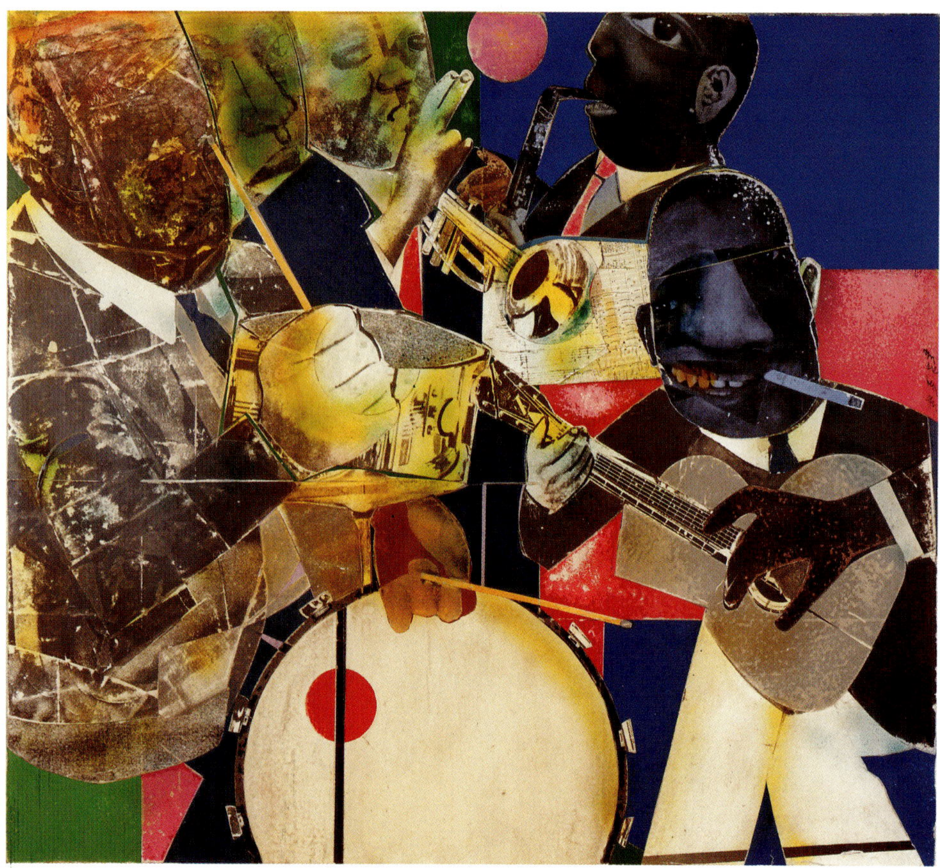

74

> a most structured kind of society and life [where people] lived under hundreds of taboos or regulations. They were not free. And the same applies to jazz: its basic element is spiritual, but at its best it is as highly structured as Mozart.... And while I don't necessarily make a drawing and then realize it in my work, I am nonetheless thinking about how things are going together and have a feeling about how the work is going to grow.[168]

Bearden went on to discuss his most constant jazz topic, interval, as in the piano music of Earl Hines, equating the silences between the notes of the music with the lines of leading between the color shapes in Gothic stained-glass windows.

The clarity of form and brilliant color of Bearden's jazz world is vastly different from what others have variously recorded, in word, on film, in paint. Musician Donald Byrd and his wife Yourna, described the clubs as dark gray "smokey, smokey places; everything was seen through smoke; like fog...from one of those fog machines. ...they had lights with red, green, blue [cellophane] shields, but you couldn't see hardly anything...that's what the night club was supposed to be: alcohol, smoke, dancing. Everything was about dancing.... There was more electricity in the air there and all of this sound...with no amplification and the band blowing your brains

74
Of the Blues: Kansas City 4/4, 1974, collage of various papers with paint and ink on fiberboard, 111.8 x 132.1 (44 x 52). Courtesy of Michael Rosenfeld Gallery, New York, N.Y.

75
Thank You...For F.U.M.L. (Funking Up My Life), 1978, collage of various papers with ink and graphite on fiberboard, 38.1 x 46.7 (15 x 18 3/8). Donald Byrd

76
J Mood, c. 1985, collage of various papers with ink on fiberboard, 64.1 x 53.3 (25 1/4 x 21). Courtesy of Wynton Marsalis

out."[169] That these places were devoid of the high-key color with which Bearden invested them suggests the degree to which that sparkle, the sense of style and showmanship that permeated the clubs, made its impact on the artist's eye.

This is portrayed in the cover Bearden designed for one of Byrd's albums, *Thank You... For F.U.M.L. (Funking Up My Life)* (no. 75). The following decade he did one for a disc by Wynton Marsalis, *J Mood* (no. 76). These album covers for Jazz by musicians Bearden knew personally suggest how closely his "commercial" work paralleled his "fine" art. The Byrd album of 1978, depicting the trumpeter and his quartet, is composed essentially of flat forms cut from vibrant colored papers and set down in a spare manner related to the Odysseus collages of the previous year. The Marsalis album, by contrast, is more gestural and painterly, in keeping with Bearden's direction in the mid-1980s when he met Marsalis through Murray. This connection comes together in *Celebrations: Trumpet Spot, Wynton,* c. 1983 (see no. 107), a monotype in Murray's collection.

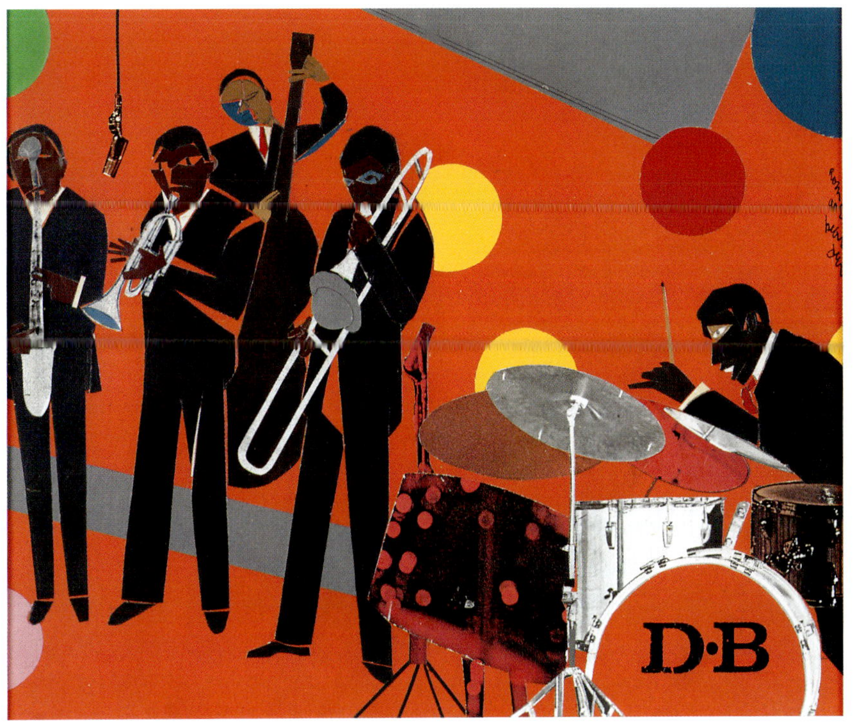

75

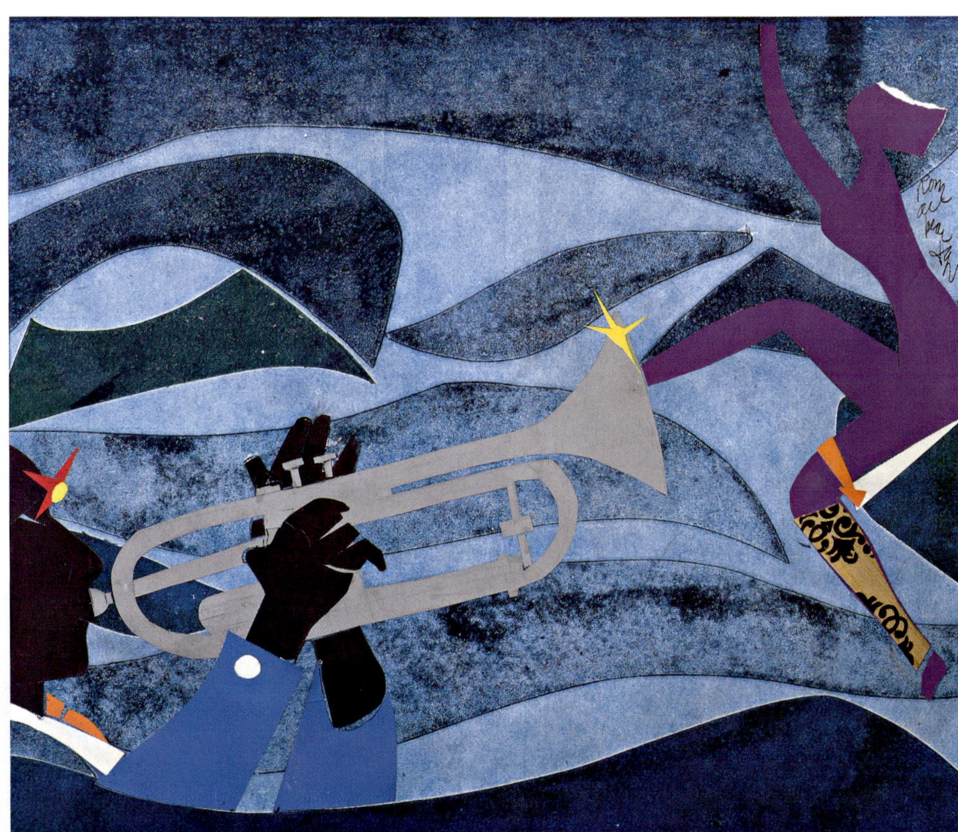

76

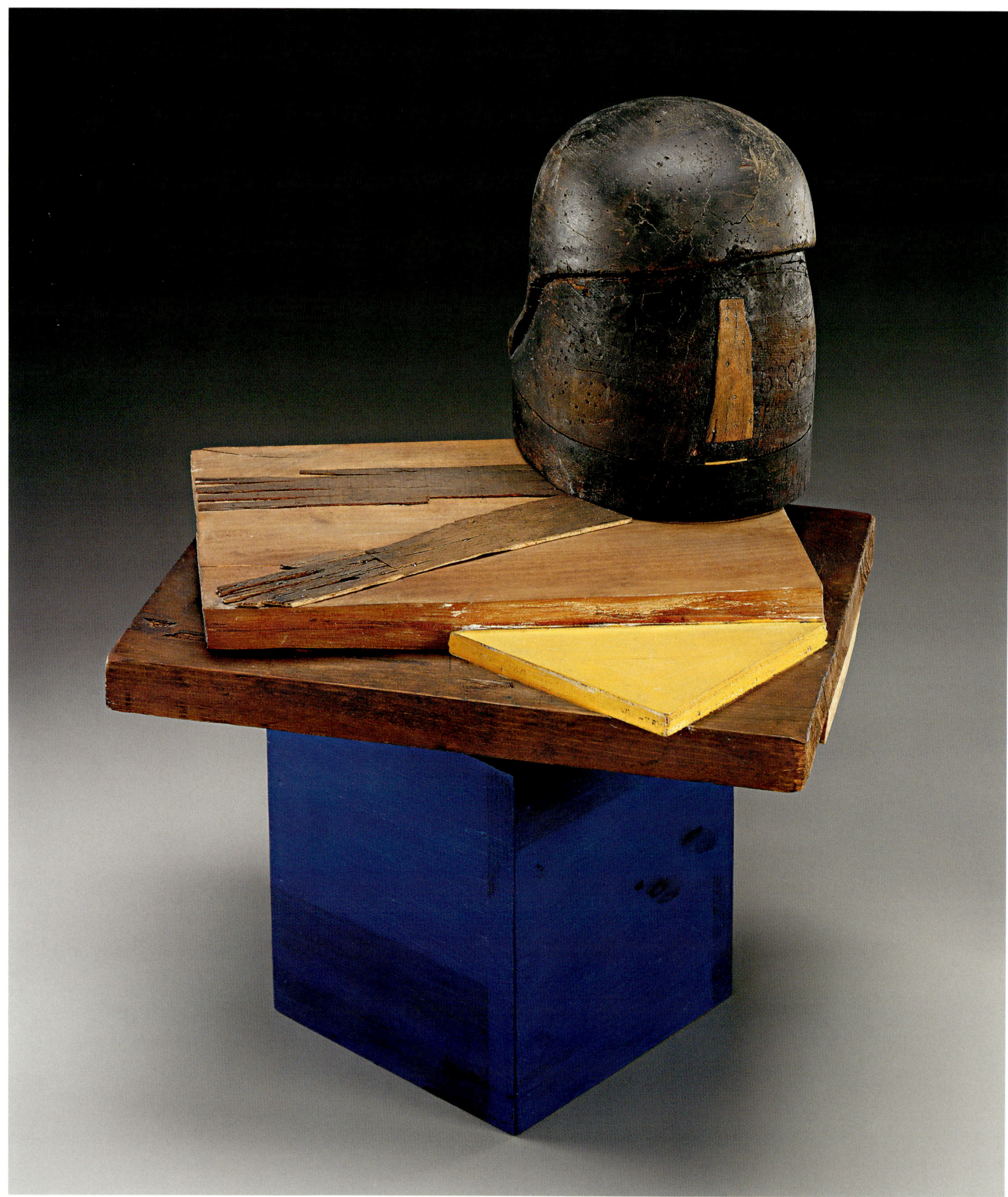

77

To Malraux's writings must be added those of Joseph Campbell as essential to Bearden's thinking: *Hero with a Thousand Faces* published in 1949; *The Flight of the Wild Gander,* in 1951; and *The Masks of God,* a four-volume history of mythological forms, in 1959. Bearden's concern with myth, history, and narrative would have been nourished by such texts, enhancing his imaginative meanderings on a range of motifs.

In addition to one-person exhibitions, Arne Ekstrom on occasion would install thematic group shows, one of which was *Blocked Metaphors* in 1969. Included was Bearden's sculpture *Mauritius* (no. 77), alluding to a martyred Roman soldier, (?–c. A.D. 286), an African recruited from Upper Egypt, who is said to have been executed by Maximilian after refusing to offer sacrifices to Roman gods.

The artists who participated in *Blocked Metaphors* were given a hatmaker's block with which to start their work. Ekstrom had obtained them from Alfonso Ossorio, a member of his gallery stable who also participated in the show, as did Nancy Grossman, Jasper Johns, Man Ray, and Andy Warhol. Bearden's only construction of wood elements, some painted, some not, indeed his only work of sculpture so far as we know, remained close to his collage practice, just as the subject of *Mauritius* is in keeping with his attention to history.

Specific to African-American history is Bearden's *Captivity and Resistance* (no. 78), a dramatic textile collage commissioned to mark the 1976 opening of the African American Museum in Philadelphia, the year corresponding to bicentennial celebrations throughout the United States.[170] Bearden's major theme is the 1839 Mende rebellion aboard the sailing ship *Amistad.* At the far left a dramatic brown figure holds a scale on which a black man, alone and wearing little clothing, equally balances a white man, helmeted and booted, and accompanied by luggage and a plant, thus suggesting an unequal balance if the figures were equally appointed, the black man the more weighty of the two.

Included as well are images of the continent of Africa; a wood sculpture; a writhing figure in chains; slave ships with voyagers below deck and at battle on deck; and Prince Cinque, the hero of the battle and a handsome and gentle figure at the mural's center, who holds a staff against a landscape with the sun/moon rising/setting. At the far right is the ominous apparatus for a lynching, presumably that of John Brown whose bearded spirit shadow in gray hangs over two figures that reference Frederick Douglass and Harriet Tubman, a rifle on end between them. Also depicted is a regiment of African-American Civil War soldiers in the gray uniform of the Confederate side, although accompanying them on horseback is what may be a blue-jacketed Union officer.

The subtlety of color central to Bearden's collages is here in full force in the use of multiple versions of hues, several greens and browns, the three different grays used for Tubman's attire, and the shifts within the water, particularly Matissean in the curves of the waves that move from blue to green. Some of the stitching blends into the flat shapes because their colors match; in other places the stitching establishes a linear contrast, highlighted in the facial features, particularly the eyes and nose, of the Douglass figure. The assembled fields of color are varied in their physical surfaces, employing felted, woven, and knitted fabrics of disparate weights and, probably, fibers—both linen and cotton, at least, appear to have been used. The collage overall was machine-sewn, presumably by a professional, but details are applied by hand, for example, the hair and eyes of the central head.[171] A powerful, highly political object, *Captivity and Resistance* makes clear that the concerns Bearden had addressed in the Baltimore *Afro-American* forty years earlier were still very much on his mind.[172]

Bearden's Prevalence of Ritual narrative also remained on his mind and had taken on renewed prominence in the early 1970s in slices from stories well known: *Delilah; Noah, Third Day* (nos. 79, 80); and in less specific subjects such as *Untitled (Prevalence of Ritual)* (no. 81), highlighting a palm leaf which, like the train, is one of Bearden's oft-repeated symbols. The first two were included in Bearden's spring 1973 Cordier & Ekstrom exhibition, which included twelve Prevalence of Ritual works. At the time the High Museum of Art purchased *Noah, Third Day,* Bearden wrote to the museum's director about the collage:

> "Noah Third Day" represents my continuing interest in the prevalence of ritual. That is, as a young boy in the Baptist Church, I'd hear many sermons around such Biblical happenings as—Noah's Ark. And what I've tried to do is show the continuing relationship of these myths throughout the years.[173]

In addition to Prevalence of Ritual subjects Bearden's 1973 show featured two other topics: Martinique (four works) and The Rain Forest (eight works), signaling a new motif in Bearden's work—landscape. It was to be given increasing importance during the last fifteen years of his life. In 1973 the Beardens had a house built on the Caribbean Island of St. Martin, Nanette's ancestral

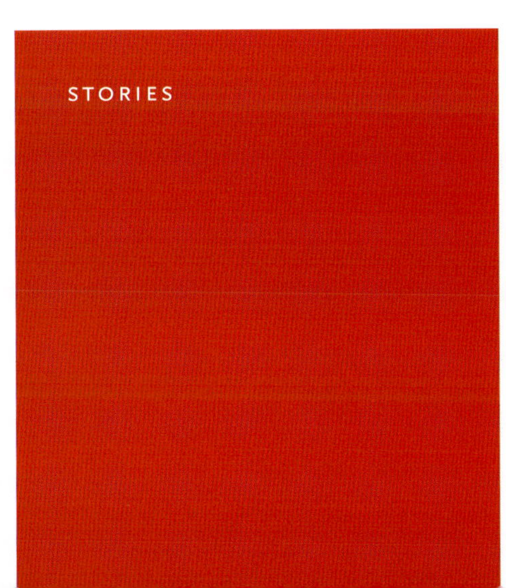

77
***Mauritius,* 1969, various woods, paint, stain, nails, screws, and staples, 49.4 x 45.7 x 45.7 (19 7/16 x 18 x 18). Courtesy of Ekstrom & Ekstrom, Inc., New York**

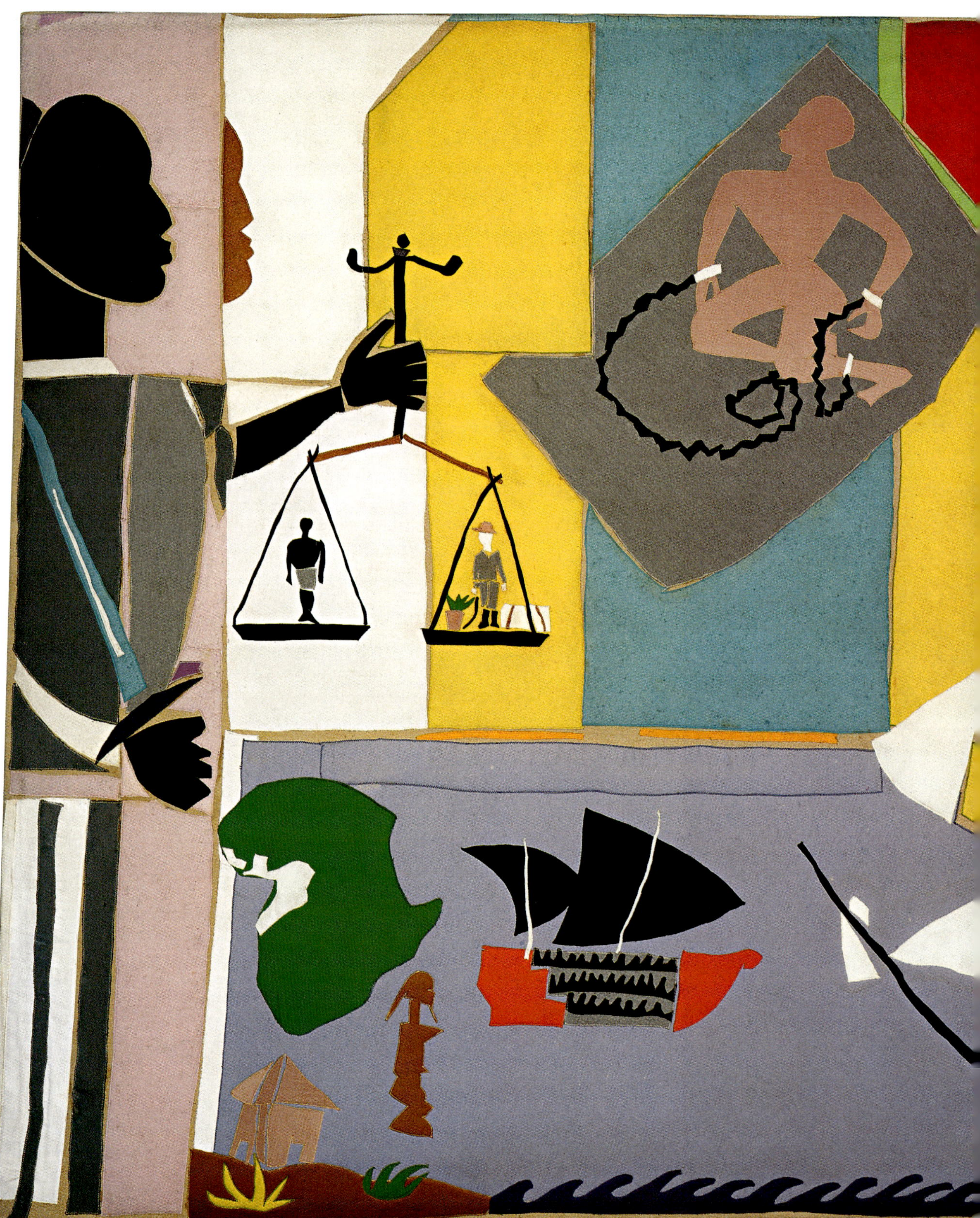

78

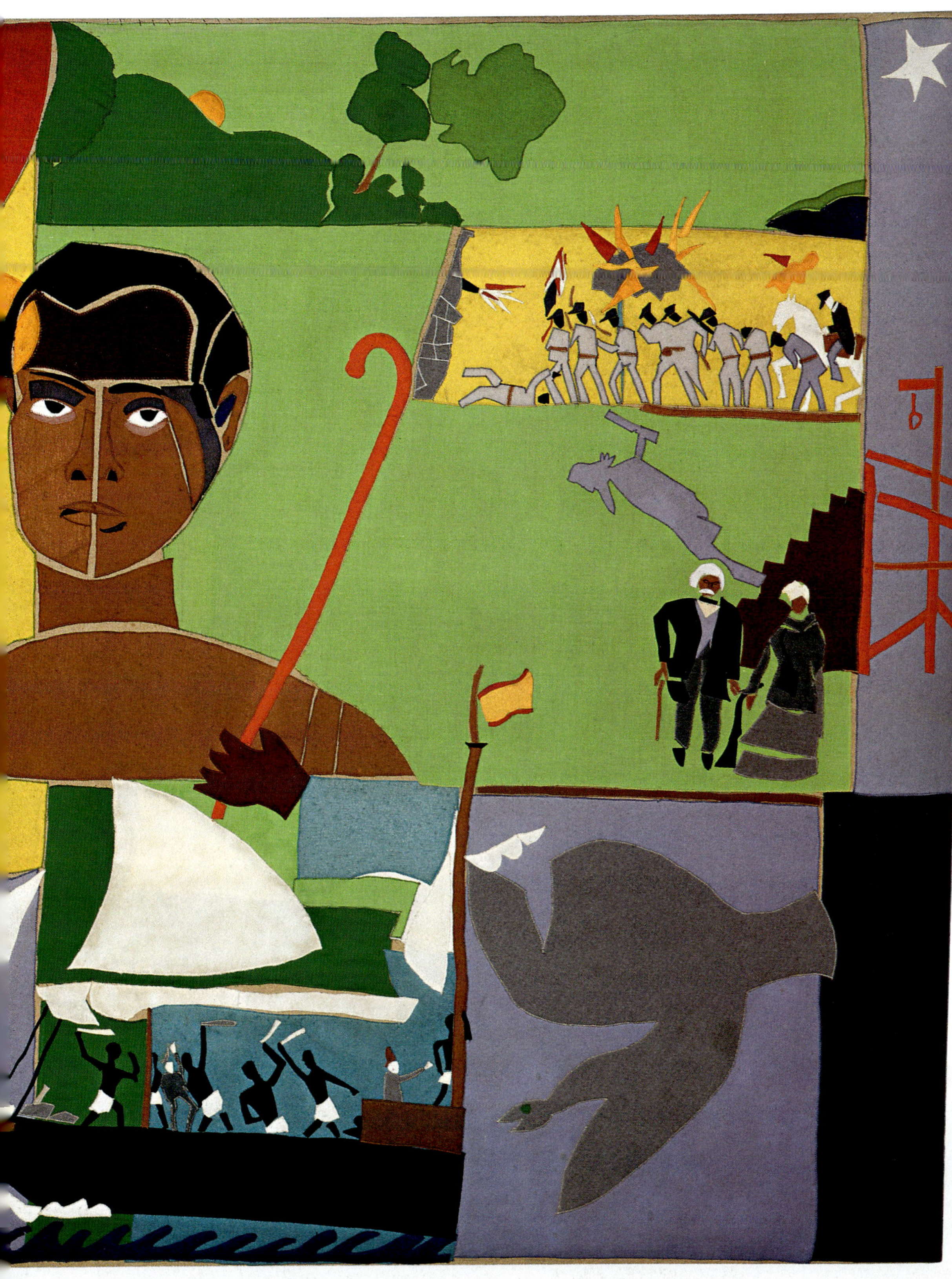

78
Captivity and Resistance, 1976, collage of various fabrics on canvas, 199.4 x 318.8 (78½ x 125½). African American Museum in Philadelphia

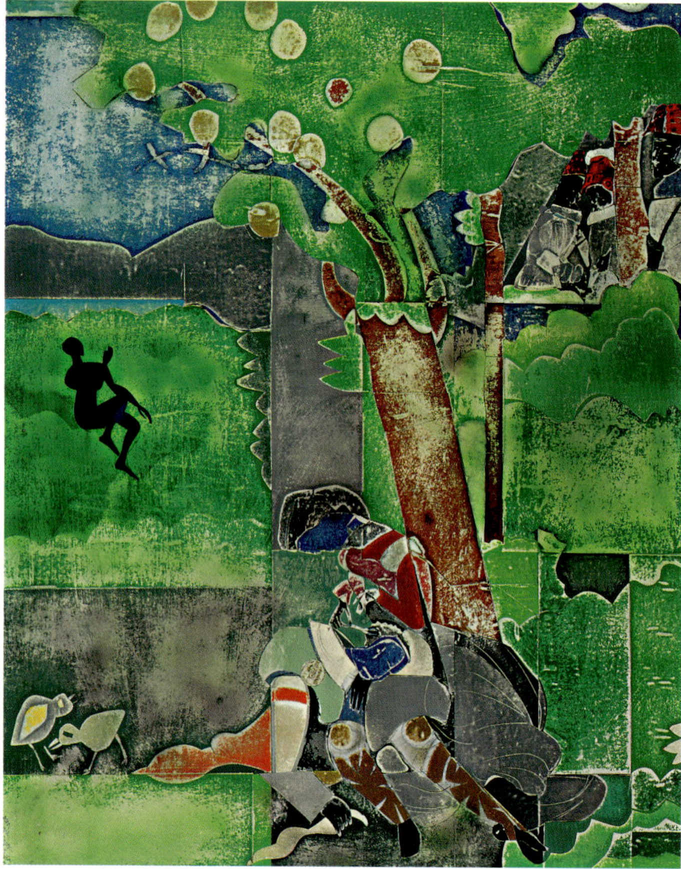

79

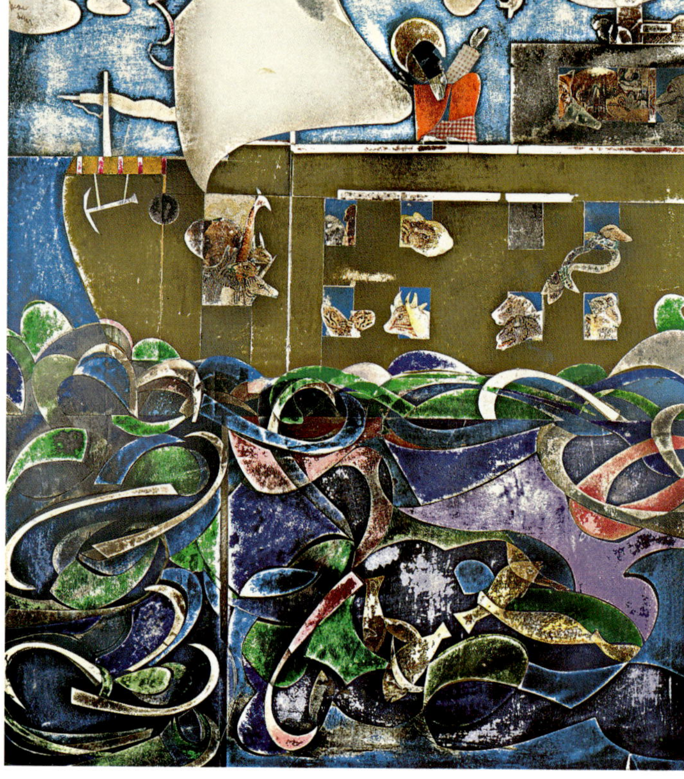

80

79
Delilah, 1973, collage of various papers with paint, ink, and graphite with surface abrasion on fiberboard, 142.2 x 116.8 (56 x 46). Collection of Jane & Raphael Bernstein

80
Noah, Third Day, 1972, collage of various papers with fabric, paint, and surface abrasion on fiberboard, 102.9 x 90.2 (40½ x 35½). High Museum of Art, Atlanta, Georgia; gift in memory of Peter Rindskopf and purchase, 73.14

81
Untitled (Prevalence of Ritual), c. 1971, collage of various papers with fabric on fiberboard, 70.5 x 53 (27¾ x 20⅞). From the Collection of Raymond J. McGuire

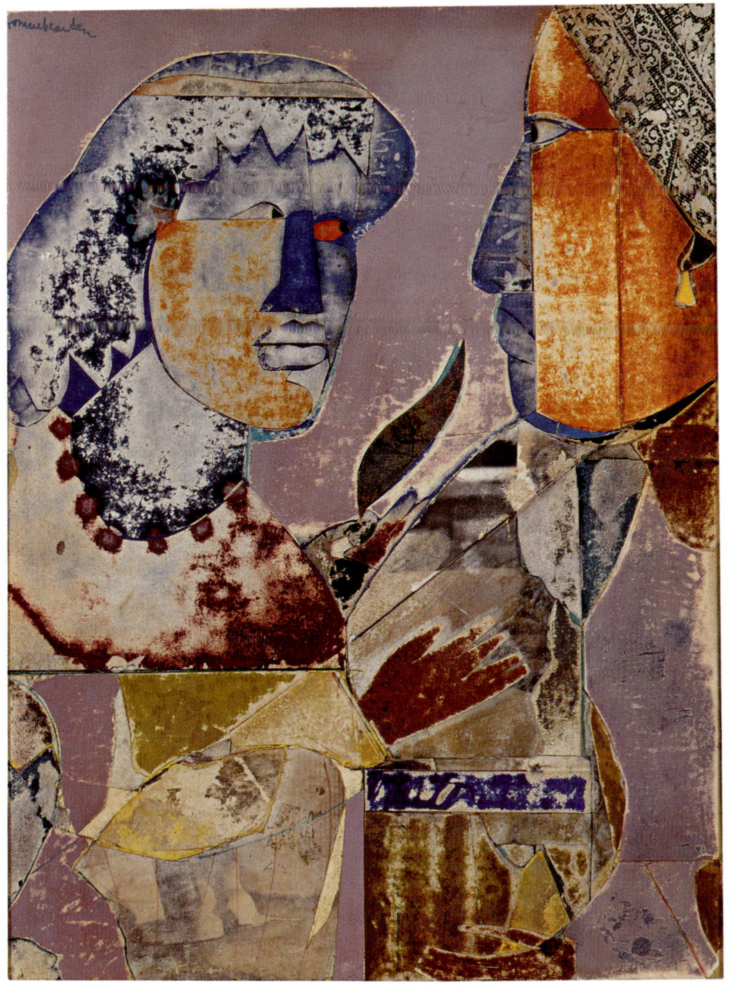

81

home. From that time on, the couple spent part of each year there, near what the artist referred to as his favorite mountain. About the same height as Paul Cézanne's Mount Sainte-Victoire:

> Paradise Peak on Saint Maartens [which shoots] straight up alone, a 2,500 foot green fountain of splashing, cascading elephant ear leaves, wild orchids, avocadoes, and bamboo canes, seemingly rising out of the sea... showing off for me how green green can be, how blue is blue until, absorbing yellow, it too is green....[in the morning] the sun is rising, brilliantly lighting the mountain, a dazzling green against the blue sky, dotted with puffs of clouds.... Yet evening brings a more spectacular show...the low-lying cumulus clouds, bumper-to-bumper on the skyway on one day or loafing lazily distant on another, may be colored by the sun's late-orangish rays or reflect the blue green of the sea or the green cast by the forest.[174]

Praising his Caribbean experience within an expansive world view as was Bearden's métier, he made the case that:

> the sparkle and pulsations of water give men and women a certain energy [and that] we have always found the great sources of art near rivers, such as along the Yellow or Yangtze River in China, or in America along the Mississippi, Missouri, and Hudson Rivers, in South America along the Amazon, and in Africa along the Congo and Nile.[175]

Perhaps life by water triggered Bearden's 1977 Odysseus series, a response to the *Odyssey*, the epic poem in twenty-four books that recounts the trials endured at sea by the Greek hero of the Trojan War, Odysseus, during ten years of wandering as he struggled home to Ithaca. In embracing ancient Greek literature, Bearden returned for inspiration to Homer whose *Iliad* had inspired watercolors and ink drawings almost thirty years earlier. In a profusion of architectural and natural form, the underlying geometry essential to Bearden's compositions is nowhere more vivid than in the twenty Odysseus collages. As with most of Bearden's series, Odysseus varies considerably in size and in its use of horizontal and vertical formats (from 14 x 11 to 44 x 56 inches with most measuring 32 x 44 in either direction). *The Fall of Troy; Poseidon, the Sea God—Enemy of Odysseus; The Sea Nymph;* and *Odysseus Leaves Circe* (nos. 82–85) demonstrate the variety in the internal scale of individual works and in his handling of collage. In many, such as *Odysseus Leaves Circe,* Bearden went to his most extreme in bold use of flat, colored papers with little surface manipulation and few if any directly drawn or painted areas. One sees these as a logical next step from the fields of fabric the artist used for the *Captivity and Resistance* textile. Others, such as *Poseidon, the Sea God,* employ painterly manipulations and multiple elements including shimmering foils. This series represents Bearden's most extended homage to Matisse (as suggested by critic John Russell when first exhibited).[176]

In addition to his large, highly finished collages, Bearden executed multiple small versions of the Odysseus imagery in series of carbon paper drawings that functioned as the equivalent of a coloring book line, which he "colored in" with watercolor, sometimes adding bits of collage. Selections from a complete set are included here—*Poseidon, the Sea God; Circe; Odysseus Rescued by a Sea Nymph; Battle with the Cicones;* and *Odysseus Enters at the Door Disguised as an*

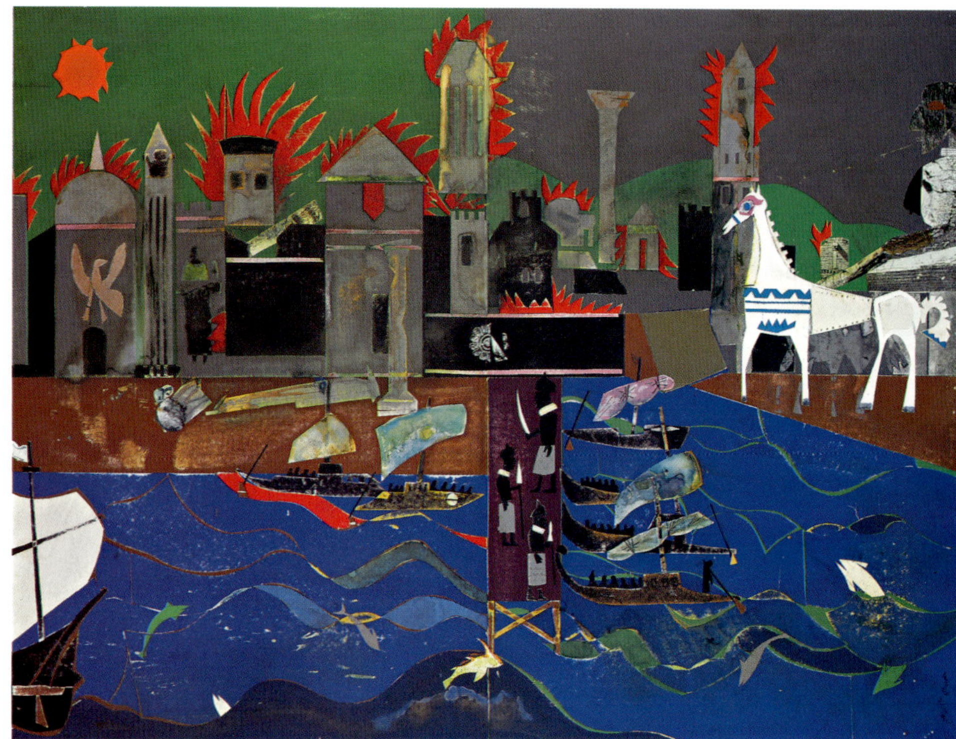

82

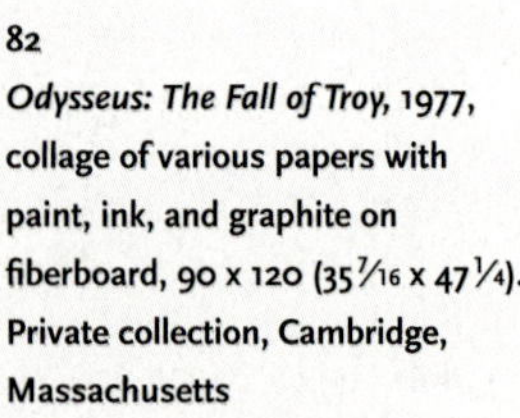

82
***Odysseus: The Fall of Troy*, 1977, collage of various papers with paint, ink, and graphite on fiberboard, 90 x 120 (35 7/16 x 47 1/4). Private collection, Cambridge, Massachusetts**

83
***Odysseus: Poseidon, The Sea God—Enemy of Odysseus*, 1977, collage of various papers with foil, paint, ink, and graphite on fiberboard, 110.2 x 79.7 (43 3/8 x 31 3/8). The Thompson Collection, Indianapolis, Indiana**

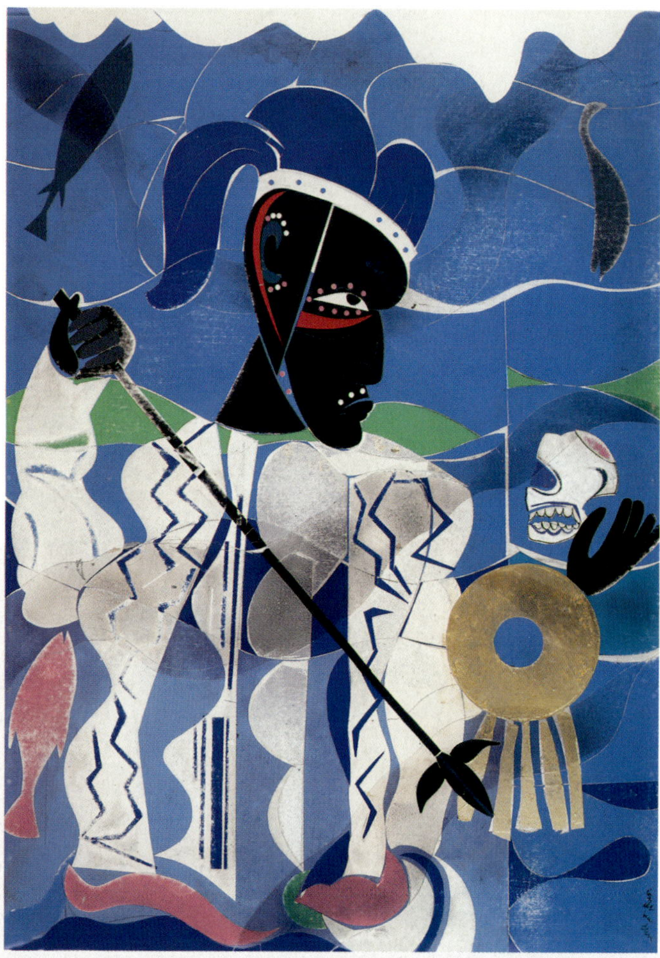

83

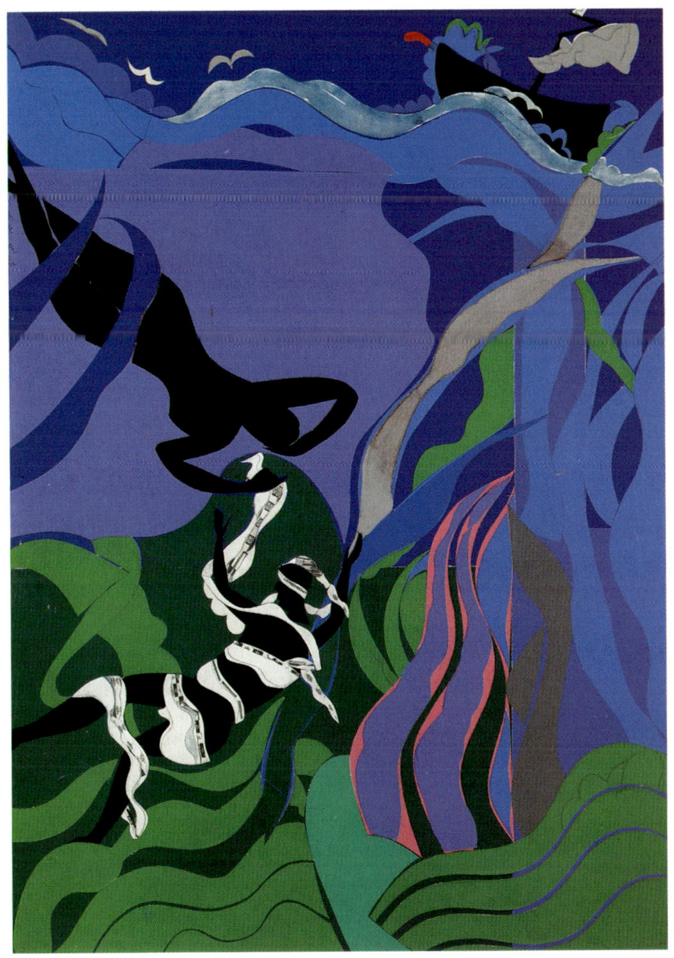

84

Old Man (nos. 86–90). They convey the variety with which Bearden also imbued such small sheets, different from but equally diverse as the larger works. Most likely they were made after the collages rather than as studies.[177] Many works using carbon paper lines exist in multiple versions in addition to these Odysseus subjects, his experimentation in them generally having to do with color and touch. But Bearden did not always use the carbon paper in this way; there are individual works for which the character of carbon line itself (rather than its usefulness for duplication) seems the attraction, its greasy properties serving to repel the watercolor and therefore to maintain discrete color areas of the sort Bearden had used in works of the late 1940s in which the calligraphic ink line served a similar purpose.

Like the population of images in his photostat-reversal museum without walls, in Bearden's Odysseus narrative, the lush environment is inhabited by dark-skinned figures rooted in both classical myth and African-American culture. When queried about this, Bearden explained that the series "involves Poseidon who always has to come up from Africa, where he wants to be with his friends there. And it is universal. So if a child in Benin or in Louisiana…sees my paintings of Odysseus, he can understand the myth better."[178]

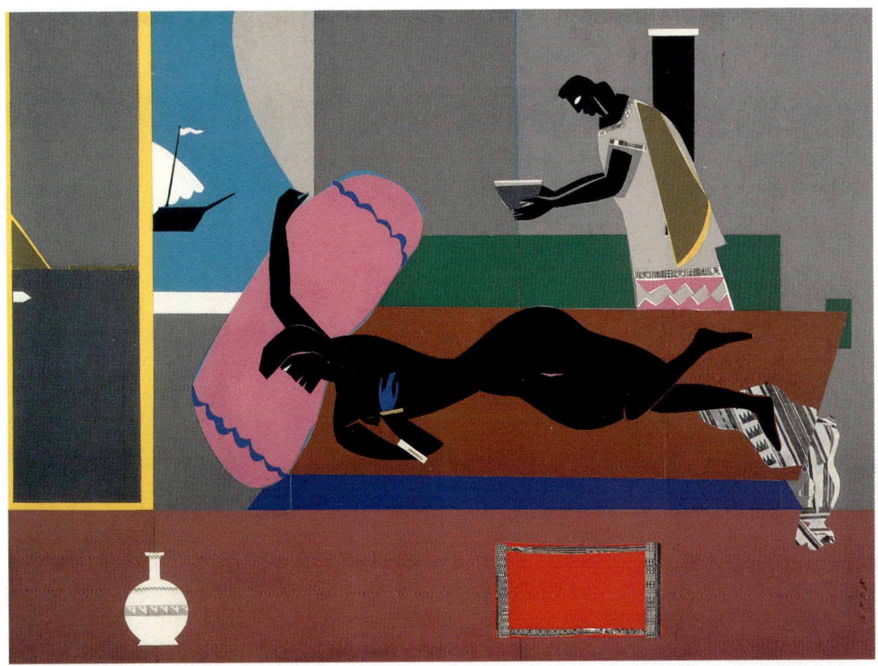

85

84
Odysseus: The Sea Nymph, **1977, collage of various papers with paint and graphite on fiberboard, 111.8 x 81.3 (44 x 32). Glen and Lynn Tobias**

85
Odysseus: Odysseus Leaves Circe, **1977, collage of various papers with foil, paint, and graphite on fiberboard, 81.3 x 111.8 (32 x 44). Collection of Jane & Raphael Bernstein**

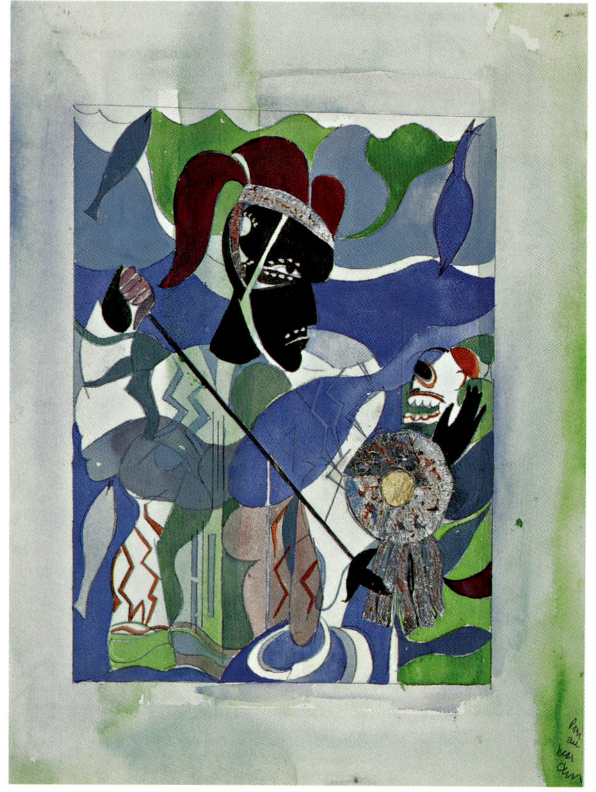

86

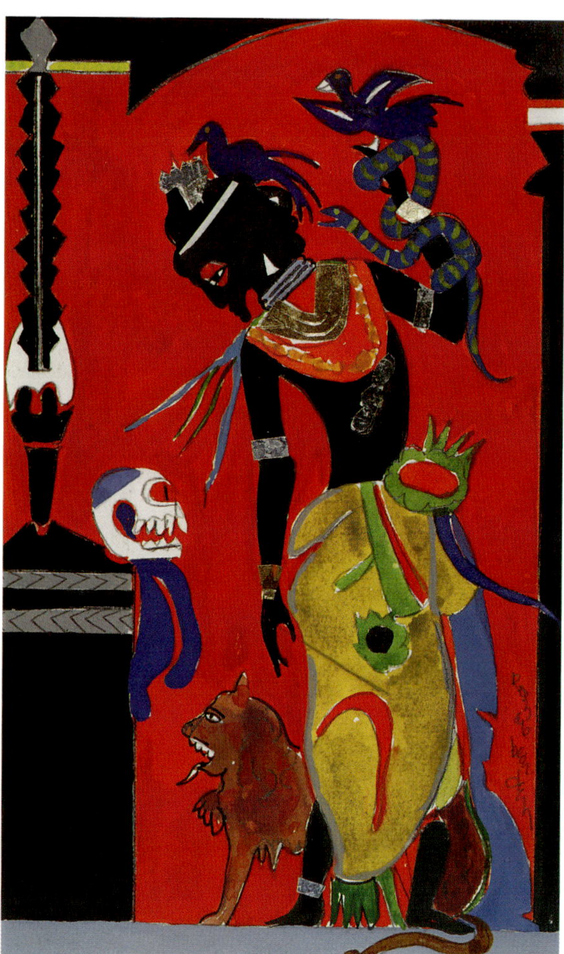

87

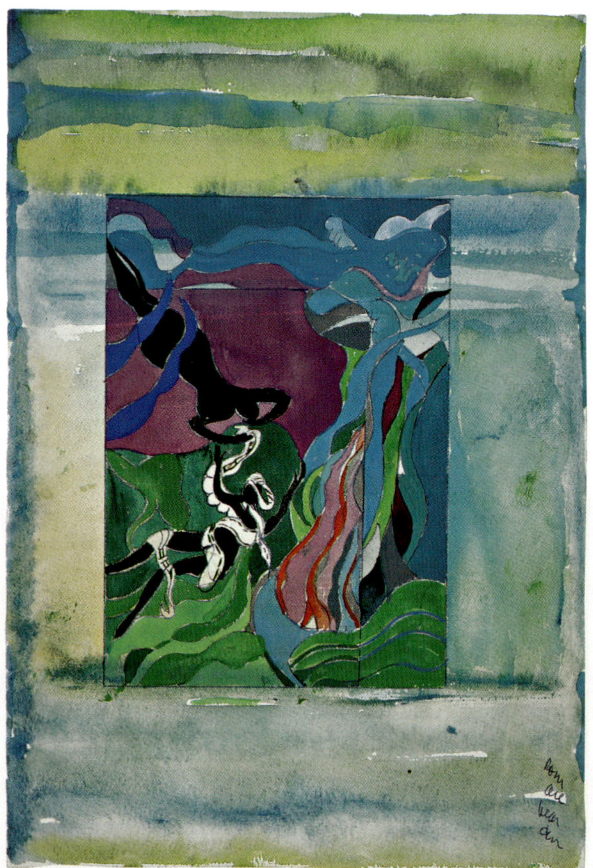

88

86
Odysseus: Poseidon, The Sea God, c. 1977, watercolor, gouache, ink, and foil collage over carbon-paper line on paper, 41 x 31 (16⅛ x 12$\frac{3}{16}$).
Evelyn N. Boulware

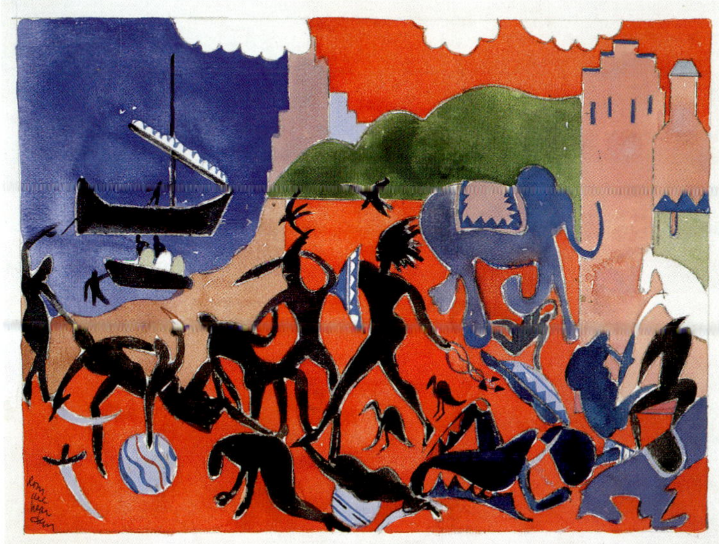

89

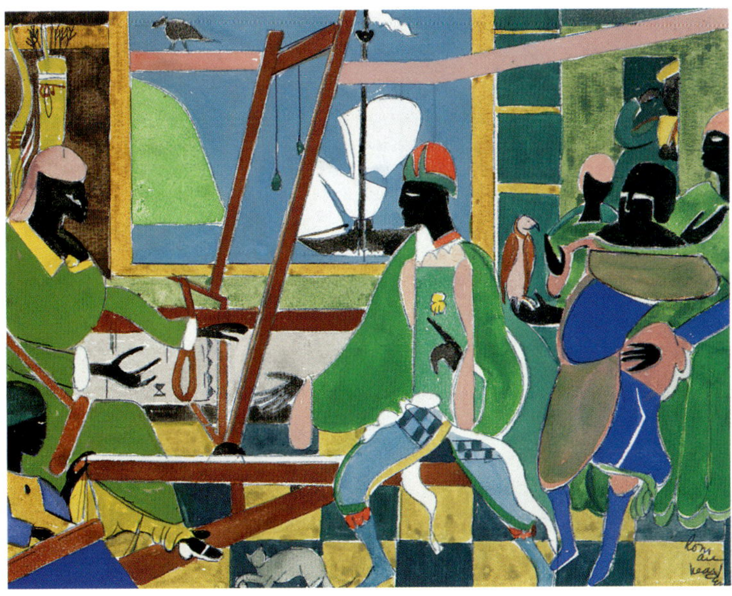

90

87
Odysseus: Circe, c. 1977, watercolor, gouache, ink, graphite and foil collage over carbon-paper line on paper, 25 x 16 ($9\frac{13}{16}$ x $6\frac{5}{16}$). Evelyn N. Boulware

88
Odysseus: Odysseus Rescued by a Sea Nymph, c. 1977, watercolor, gouache, and ink over carbon-paper line on paper, 37.5 x 26.4 ($14\frac{3}{4}$ x $10\frac{3}{8}$). Evelyn N. Boulware

89
Odysseus: Battle with the Cicones, c. 1977, watercolor and gouache over carbon-paper line on paper, 23.3 x 32.1 ($9\frac{3}{16}$ x $12\frac{5}{8}$). Evelyn N. Boulware

90
Odysseus: Odysseus Enters at the Door Disguised as an Old Man, c. 1977, watercolor, gouache, and ink over carbon-paper line on paper, 32.4 x 39.7 ($12\frac{3}{4}$ x $15\frac{5}{8}$). Evelyn N. Boulware

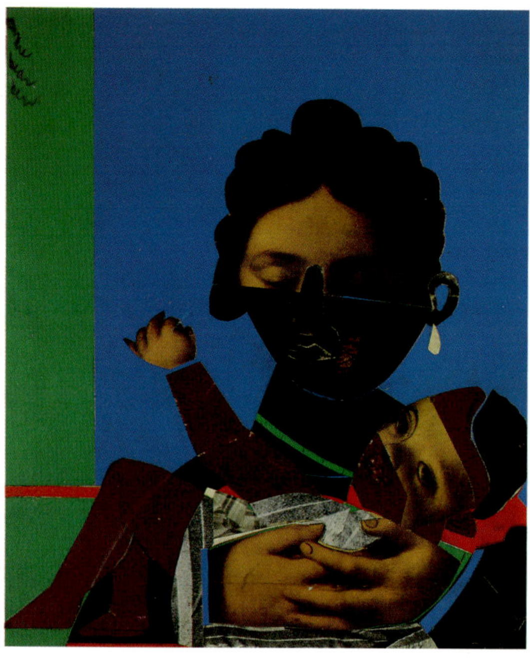

91

Bearden cited "the beauty of a black woman" as a subject of immense importance to him, and over the years it provided one of his abiding motifs.[179] Nude, muse, lover, mother, grandmother, sister, protector, friend, healer—her persona varies. She is at the center of home and family; in verdant gardens; quietly bathing in tropical pools (calling to mind Paul Gauguin's island women); awaiting clients in brothel parlors; on stage in New York's jazz clubs; dancing in Mecklenburg County; as Conjur and Obeah woman; and in numerous literary guises. The exhibition *Mysteries: Women in the Art of Romare Bearden,* organized by Mary Schmidt Campbell, addressed this crucial aspect of his work in 1975, suggesting that Bearden's perception of women places them at "the heart of the Black community and his concept of woman is particularly well suited to the sensuousness of his collage technique."[180]

In gouaches of the early 1940s such as *The Visitation* Bearden depicted strong, self-reliant African-American women like those of his youth, his great-grandmother, grandmothers, and mother. With the exception of the Lorca series that shows women engaged in ceremonial rites, in works from the later 1940s and the abstractions of the 1950s, the specific characters of the women are superseded by formal concerns; and in 1963–65, gender concerns, present in *Conjur Women* images and others such as *Mysteries,* are less emphatic than they will be in the Mecklenburg County collages that followed. These vividly portray woman as partner to a male counterpart, and as the central and essential, strong and nurturing component of family life where no welcoming father figure is seen. It is not unusual, in fact, for Bearden's family, as in *The Family* (Museum of Fine Arts, Boston), to be composed of multiple generations of women, from grandmother or great-grandmother to swaddled infant. He particularly celebrated the mother and child relationship, for example, the dramatic *Mother and Child* (no. 91) that served as a model for a c. 1984 screenprint/photo-lithograph and a unique double-sided proof *Woman and Child Reading/Untitled* (no. 92a, b) related to the lithograph *The Lamp,* 1984 (fig. 43).[181]

Remarking upon the paucity of black nudes in black artistic production prior to 1960, art historian Judith Wilson pointed out that "Romare Bearden managed to transcend the widespread stigmatization of black sexuality [visualizing] the historic conjunctions of black female beauty and eroticism with jazz, blues, African-American folklore and religion, as well as African-derived visual practices."[182] Among such collages, *Susannah at the Bath* (no. 93) is a subject of deep erotic symbolism replete with ritualistic and art-historical links. These include the purification ritual related to the baptism (the cleansing of both body and soul) and a story from the apocrypha in which truth overpowers false witness in the eyes of God (the triumph of good whatever its erotic content), tradition-based subjects Bearden would have associated with paintings and drawings by Rembrandt and others. Voyeuristic at base, we the viewers replace the elders. The image is emblematic of many of Bearden's collage interiors in which a sultry young female, usually nude or seductively draped and often alone in a room at the back of the house, suggests complex and diverse psychological interactions between herself and the foreground figures (what Wilson called the "domestication of the nude"). These may include a male/female or female/female family, but usually show an older female such as the one seen in *Susannah at the Bath.*

Susannah was cleared of charges of prostituting herself, but the subject of prostitution (another of Wilson's categories) was essential to many of Bearden's images. *Mecklenburg County, Railroad Shack Sporting House* from *Profile/Part I, The Twenties* (see no. 113) represents one type of brothel setting that appears in Bearden's work. The parlors of the legendary turn-of-the-century district of New Orleans comprise another, for example, *New Orleans: Storyville Entrance* (fig. 44). As pointed out by Patton, Storyville scenes appeared in Bearden's collages about the time MoMA exhibited images of Storyville's prostitutes by E. J. Bellocq, the glass-plate negatives for which photographer Lee Friedlander had discovered in the late 1950s and eventually purchased,

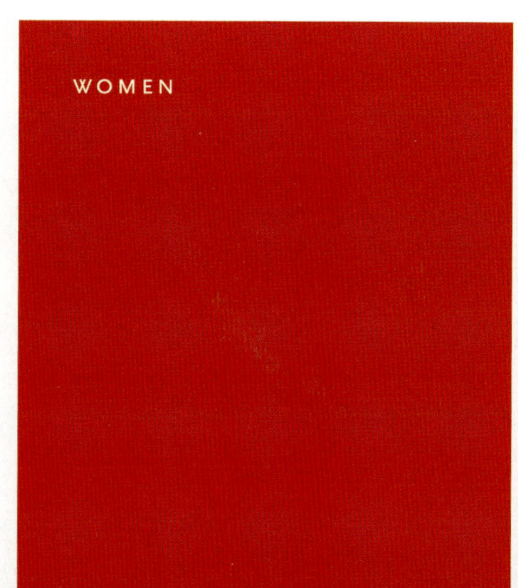

91
Mother and Child, **c. 1972, collage of various papers with ink and graphite on fiberboard, 34.9 x 30.2 (13¾ x 11⅞). Peg Alston**

92a, b
Woman and Child Reading **(recto); *Untitled* (verso); c. 1984, unique lithograph on paper, 64.8 x 47 (25½ x 18½). Collection of Professor and Mrs. David C. Driskell**

figure 43
Romare Bearden, *The Lamp,* 1984, lithograph commission commemorating the thirtieth anniversary of the United States Supreme Court's decision ending officially imposed segregation in public education. Courtesy Jerald Melberg Gallery

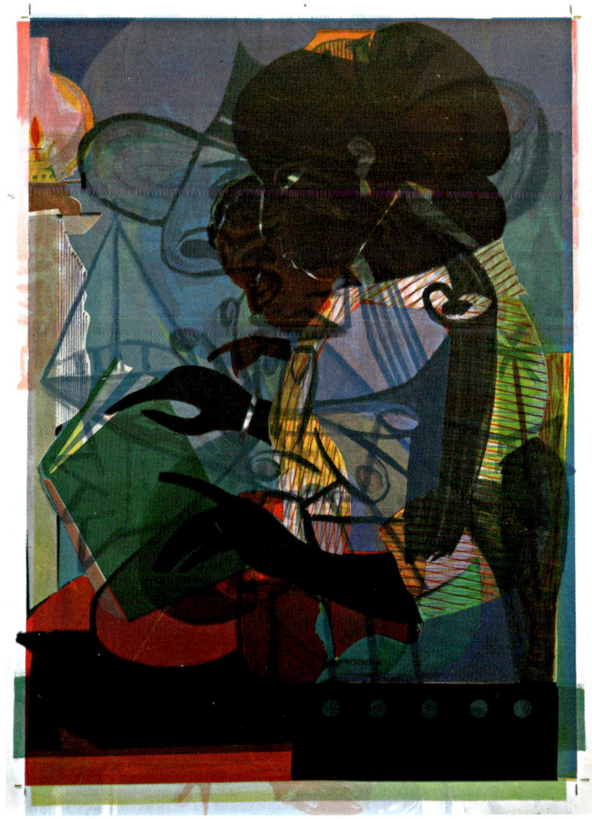

92 a

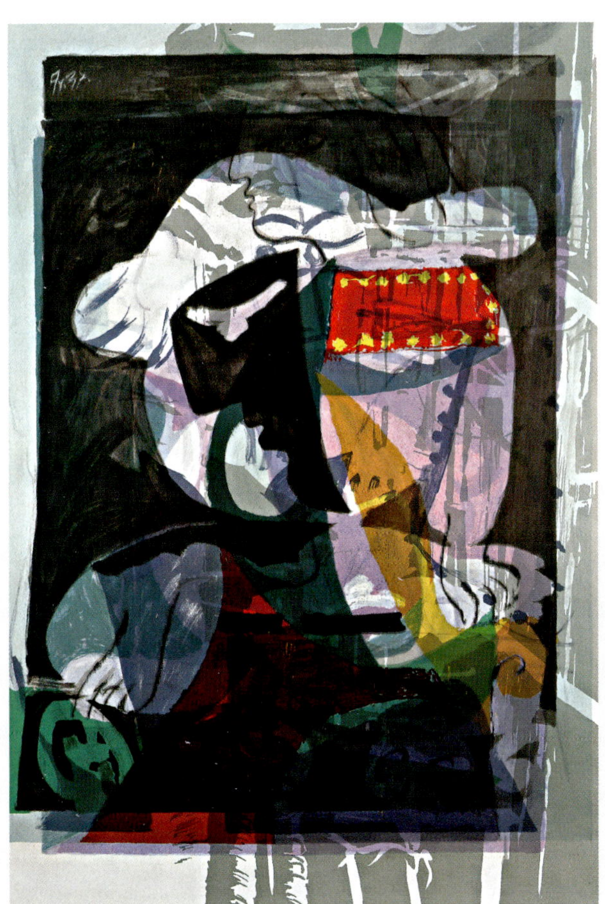

92 b

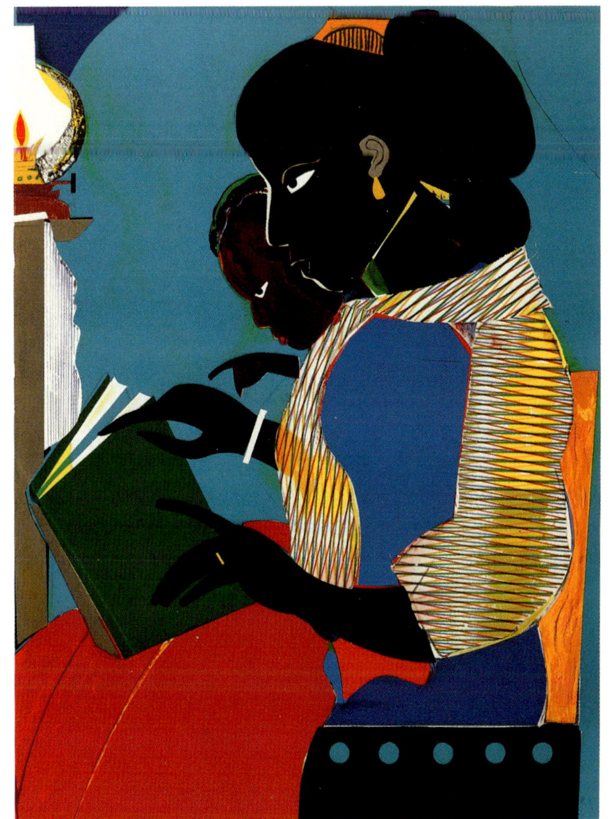

43

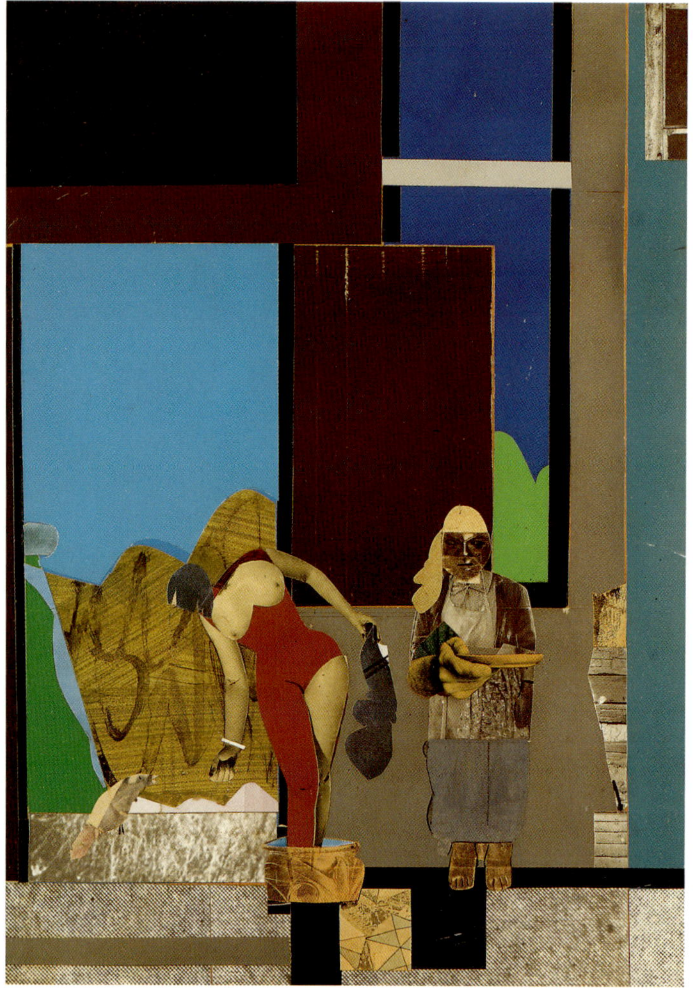

93

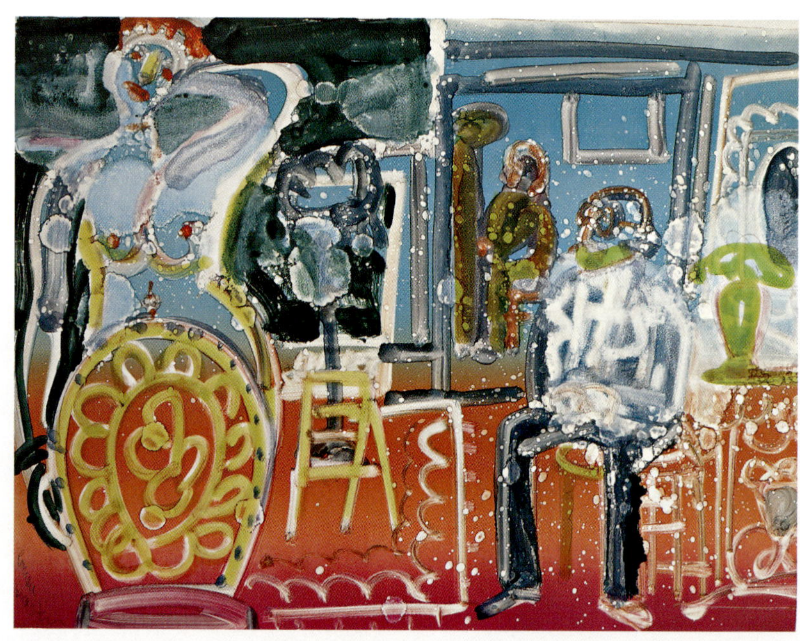

44

93
Susannah at the Bath, **1969, collage of various papers with paint, ink, and graphite on fiberboard, 60.3 x 42.6 ($23\frac{3}{4}$ x $16\frac{3}{4}$). Collection of Eileen and Peter Norton, Santa Monica**

figure 44
Romare Bearden, *New Orleans: Storyville Entrance,* c. 1976, monotype, with graphite. Estate of Romare Bearden, courtesy of Romare Bearden Foundation, New York

restored, and printed.[183] Both Bellocq and Bearden used the parlor as their setting, approaching these women of the night as did Degas and Toulouse-Lautrec in depicting their Parisian counterparts a century earlier—as observers of a slice of a life into which their artistic practice welcomed them on unique terms that enabled them to simultaneously be part of the scene and a distant "other." Deborah Willis' and Carla Williams' comments about arrests of black women who worked the streets of Storyville provoke questions about Bearden's renditions.[184] Given that the women in the parlors and thus Bellocq's photographic subjects are white and light creole, that dark-skinned prostitutes were forced to become women of the street, one wonders if Bearden's vision here was again specifically responsive to an exhibition and political, placing the black women he admired and loved in an elegant setting from which Bellocq erased them.[185] New Orleans jazz parlors beyond the Storyville years were part of Bearden's cultural memory, too, as for example, *The Apprenticeship of Jelly Roll Morton* (no. 94).

One might position Bearden's nudes between those of de Kooning and Gerhard Richter as the perfect exemplar "of a strategic preoccupation with different modes of painting and indeed different art histories concurrently inhabiting one work."[186] Bearden was fully aware of the academic tradition of the nude as a subject rich with art-historical precedent; reclining figures such as *Two Moons of Luvernia* and *Reclining Nude* (nos. 95, 96) are basic to that tradition.[187] Most certainly his admiration for Matisse played a role in both, especially *Reclining Nude*, with its spare forms

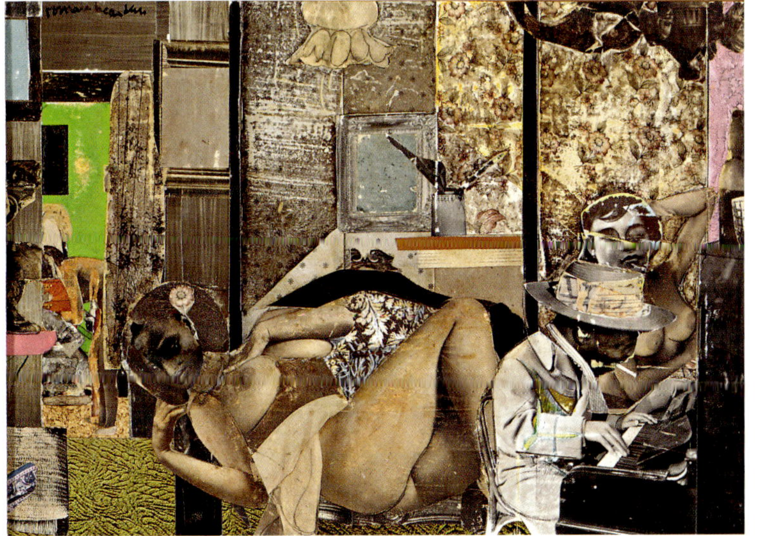

94

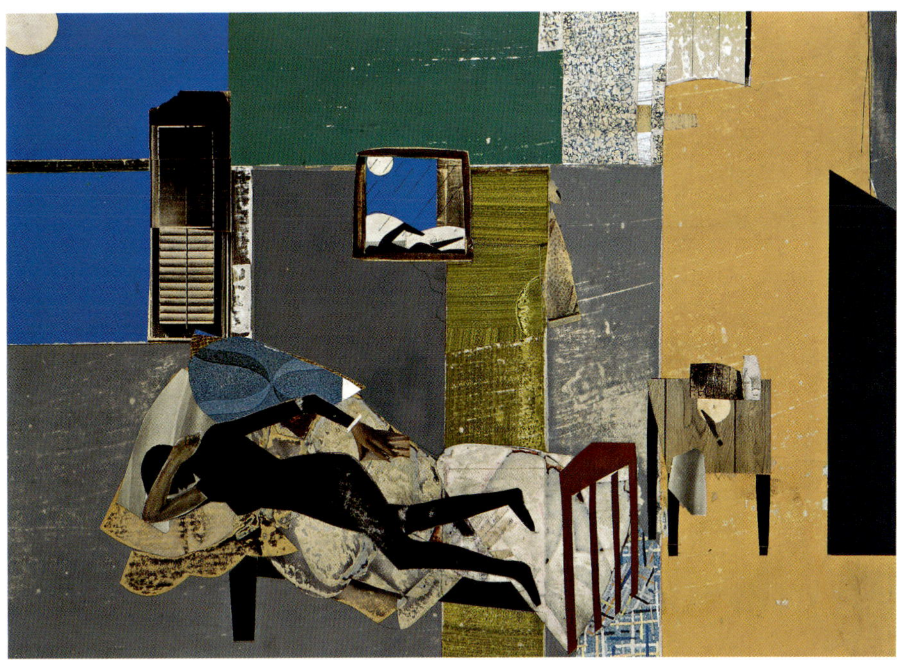

95

94
***The Apprenticeship of Jelly Roll Morton*, 1971, collage of various papers with ink and graphite on fiberboard, 24.1 x 34.9 (9½ x 13¾). James D. Fishel and Barbara L. Micale**

95
***Two Moons of Luvernia*, 1970, collage of various papers with paint and graphite (on fiberboard?), 40 x 57.2 (15¾ x 22½). Ann and Harold Sorgenti**

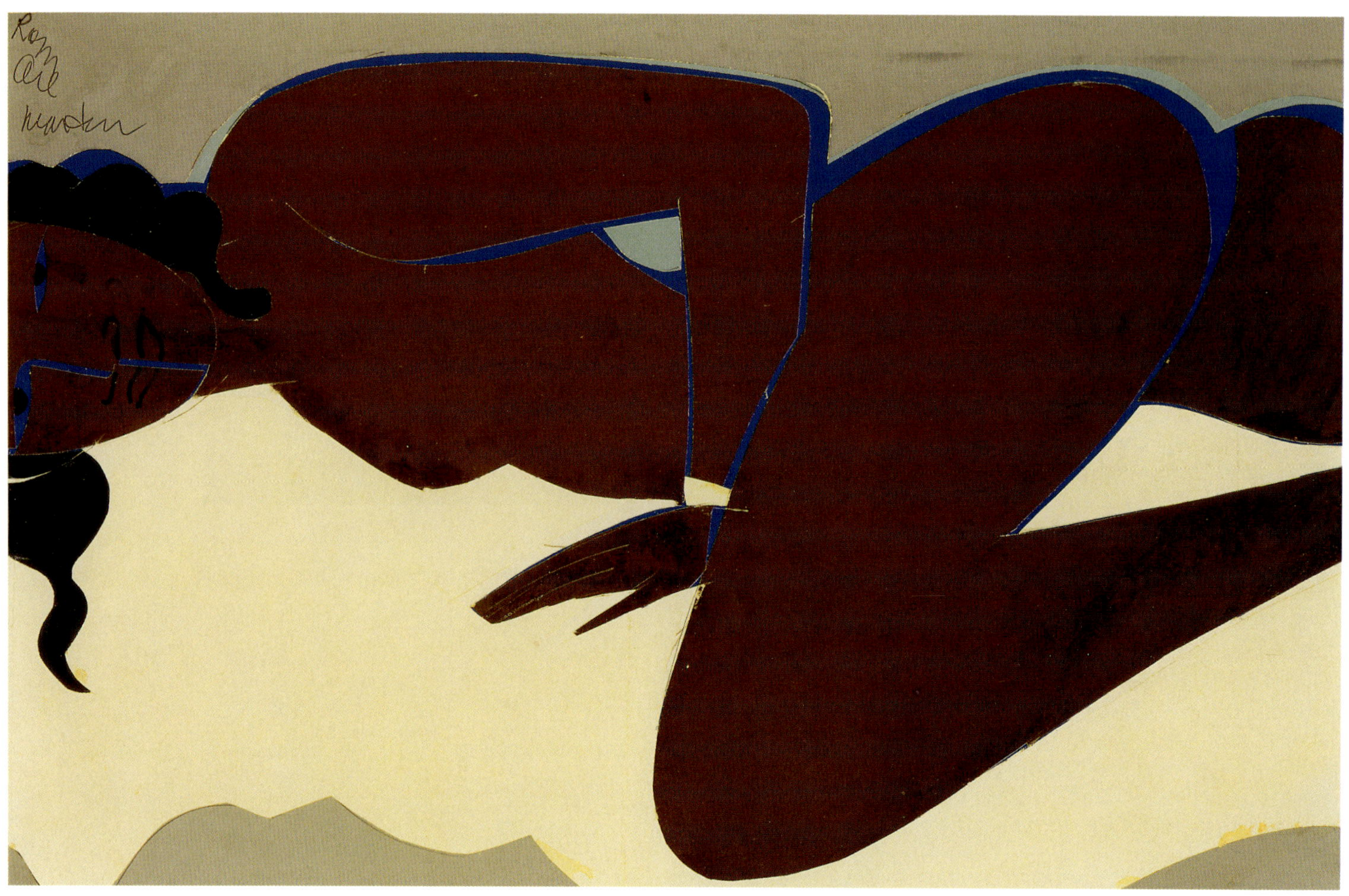

96

96
Reclining Nude, c. 1977, collage of various papers with ink and graphite on fiberboard, 27.9 x 44.5 (11 x 17½). Billie Allen

97
Conjur Woman, 1975, collage of various papers with paint and ink on wood, 116.8 x 91.4 (46 x 36). Allen Memorial Art Museum, Oberlin College, Oberlin, Ohio, R.T. Miller, Jr. Fund, 2001

close to those in the Odysseus collages. The long tradition of the nude as a subject for painters suggests that Bearden would have inevitably incorporated it into his combined world of art and popular culture (including his use of pornographic or erotic magazines—where else would he have readily obtained magazine or other photographic images of nudes?), paralleling de Kooning in the 1950s and numerous pop-oriented artists in the 1960s and 1970s. But he also depicted the nude in what may be read as relaxed and loving relationships in Mecklenburg County, as evident in the graceful *Down Home, Also* (see Kennel in this volume, no. 137).

Although the conjure woman had taken part in the Great Migration north and was a presence in Pittsburgh and Harlem as well, in Bearden's art she remains primarily associated with the south and the Caribbean (here, at times in the form of Obeah Woman). In a 1975 *Conjur Woman* (no. 97), the landscape is more densely articulated and highly colorful than in earlier versions. Depending upon viewpoint, Bearden's other Caribbean-based women are isolated in places of quiet concentration, primarily bathing pools, or in provocative settings that conceptually transform them into objects of desire (recalling Wilson's reiteration of the equation of woman with nature, the female body with the landscape). *Ritual Bayou, Untitled (Girl in a Pond),* and *Caribbean Forest* (nos. 98–100) offer variations on this theme during the 1970s and suggest the range of Bearden's collage techniques during that decade, moving from the richly colored *Ritual Bayou,* replete with detailed landscape elements; to the strength of the cliffs that dominate *Untitled (Girl in a Pond),* as reminiscent as any collage of Bearden's abstract paintings of circa 1960; to the almost monochromatic

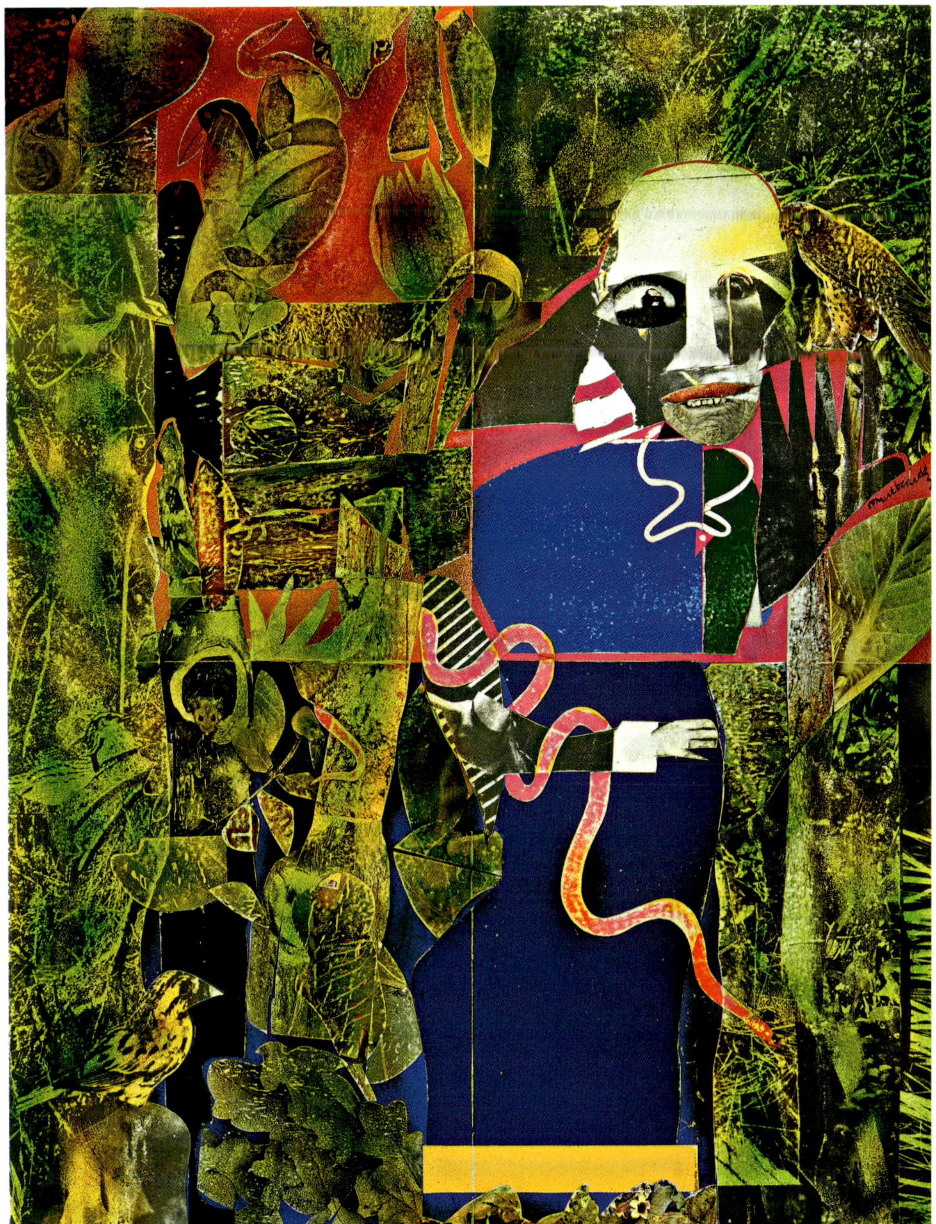

97

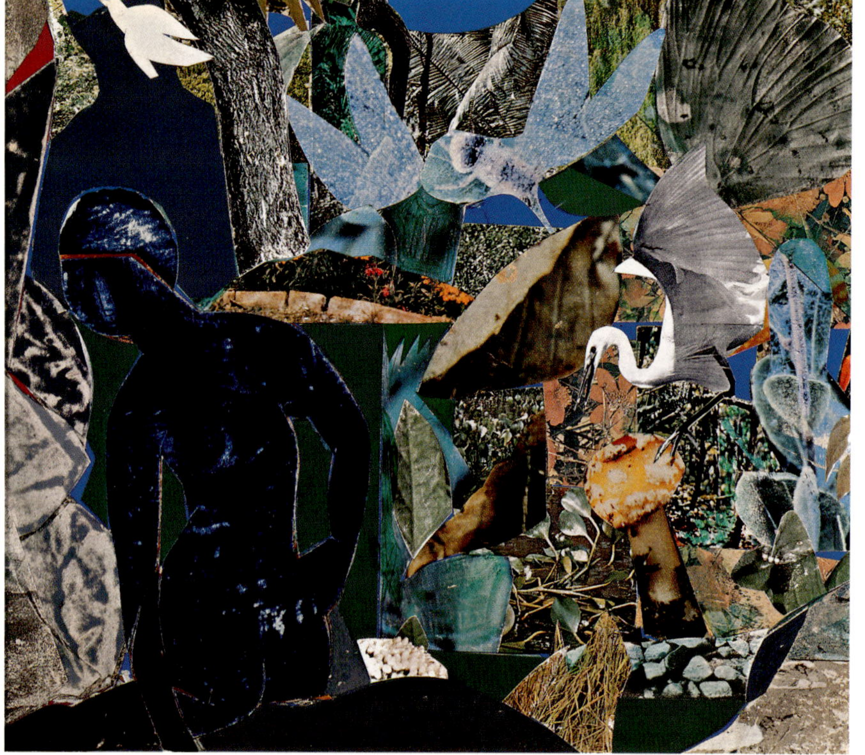

98

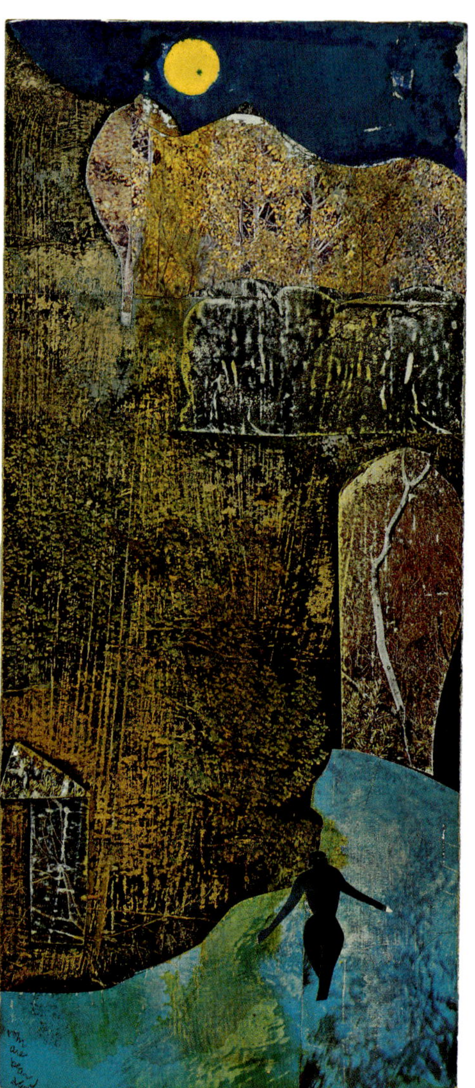

99

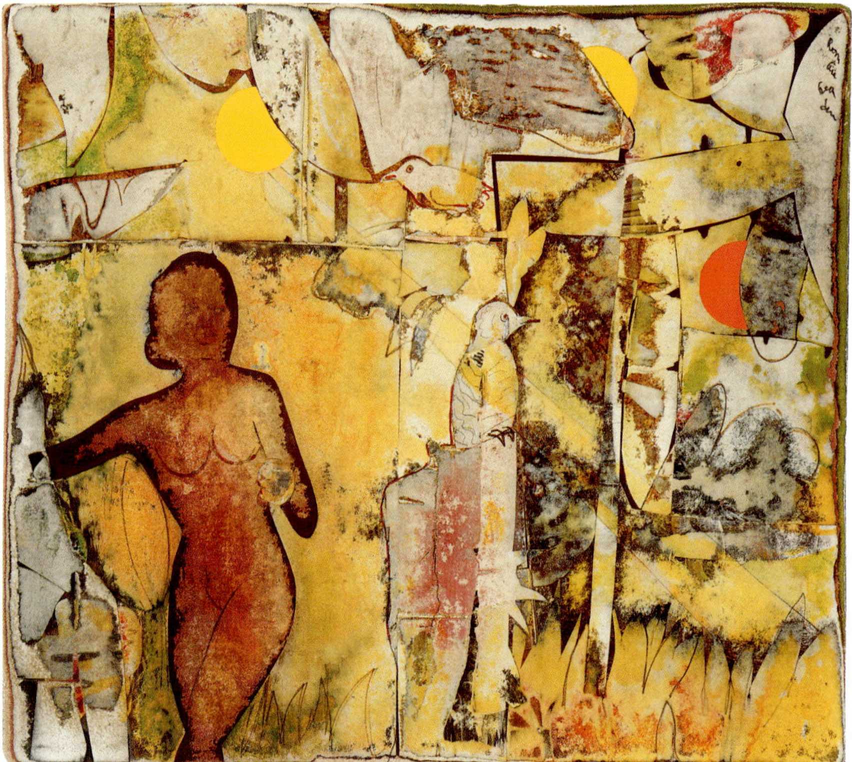

100

Caribbean Forest, with surface abrasion that softens all details to create a misty romanticized setting.[188] Bearden suggested that the relationship between men and women was different in the Caribbean than in New York:

> The women feel of themselves more as women. They can easily relate both to each other and to men on a human level. There is a direct relationship with people, which we don't have [in New York] because we have so many things in front of us, so many closed doors to try to enter to get to another person's personality.[189]

The conflation of woman and nature takes its ultimate form in Bearden's many versions of Maudell Sleet and Madeline Jones and their effusive gardens. While *Madeline Jones' Wonderful Garden* (no. 101) shows Jones surrounded by floral abundance, Bearden pushed this concept further in *Summer (Maudell Sleet's July Garden)* (see no. 125) where the figure is replaced entirely by the brilliant fullness of the garden itself.

Exemplary of Bearden's reuse of his earlier imagery are three works that feature women in intimate interiors: *Carolina Interior,* 1970 (no. 102), an image included in a series of six collage editions titled as a group Ritual Bayou, 1971, for which this is the prototype; *Mecklenburg Morning,* c. 1978; and *Mecklenburg Morning,* c. 1979 (nos. 103–104), which share a common background configuration as well as a closely related central figure. But they differ in most other details throughout. The earlier two have as their base image photostatic enlargements of an as yet unidentified source, each of them to a different size. The circa 1979 collage is considerably smaller than its predecessors and has as its base image a color photocopy from a photographic slide, probably made from the 1970 *Carolina Interior* version. All are then reworked with collage as well as painted and drawn elements. This use of a range of photographic duplication methods to develop variations of an image at different sizes over many years is a central component of Bearden's creative methodology.

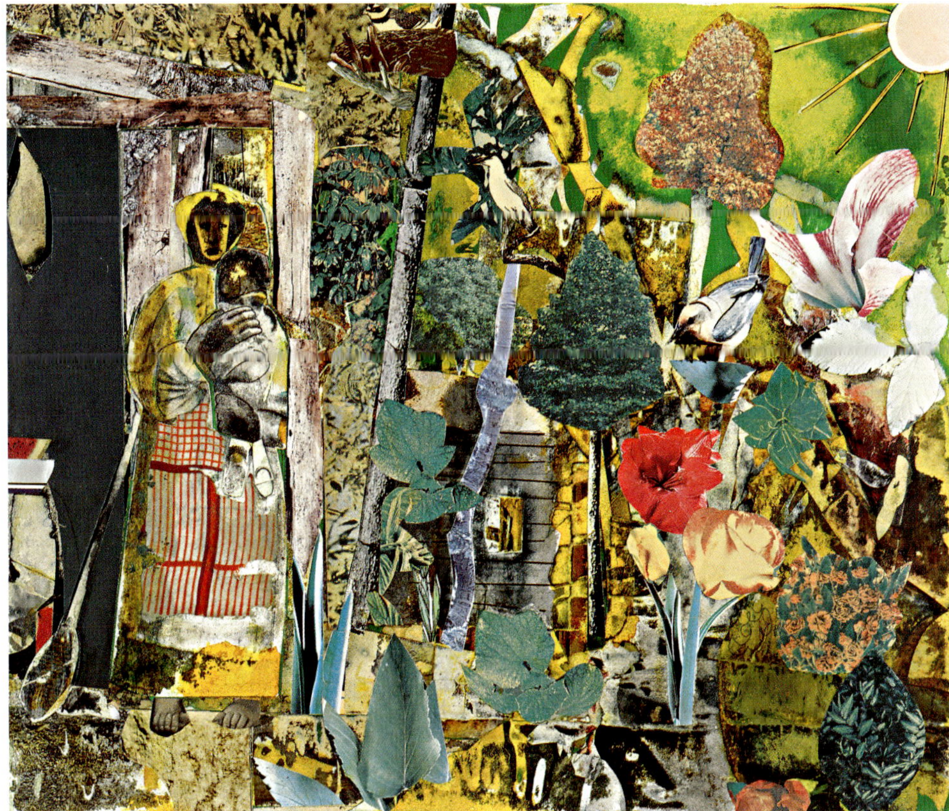

101

98
Ritual Bayou, **1970, collage of various papers with graphite and surface abrasion on wood, 32.7 x 38.1 (12 7/8 x 15). The Thompson Collection, Indianapolis, Indiana**

99
Untitled (Girl in a Pond), **1972, collage of various papers with paint and surface abrasion on fiberboard, 45.1 x 19.7 (17 3/4 x 7 3/4). Judy and Patrick Diamond**

100
Caribbean Forest, **1977, collage of various papers with paint, ink, graphite, and surface abrasion on fiberboard, 34.3 x 39.4 (13 1/2 x 15 1/2). The Walter O. Evans Collection of African American Art**

101
Madeline Jones' Wonderful Garden, **1977, collage of various papers with ink, graphite, and surface abrasion on fiberboard, 34.3 x 40.6 (13 1/2 x 16). Frederick L. Brown**

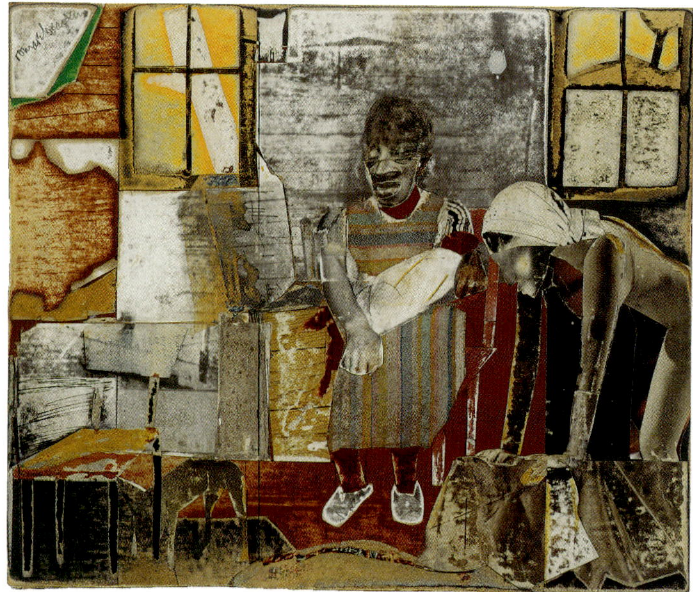

102

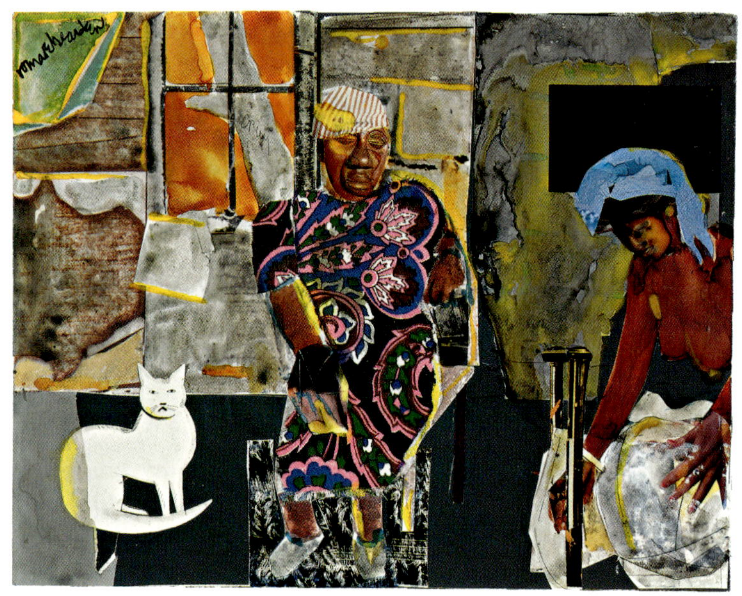

103

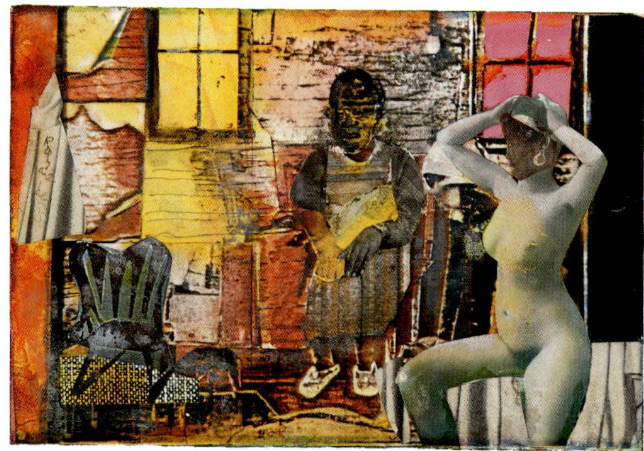

104

102
Carolina Interior, 1970, collage of various papers with fabric, paint, ink, graphite, and surface abrasion on fiberboard, 33 x 40 (13 x 15¾). Private collection: Stephen and Francine Taylor, Huntington Woods, Michigan

103
Mecklenburg Morning, c. 1978, collage of various papers with fabric, paint, ink, and graphite on fiberboard, 34 x 44.5 (13⅜ x 17½). Melvin Holmes Collection of African American Art

104
Mecklenburg Morning, c. 1979, collage of various papers with paint, ink, and graphite on fiberboard, 15.2 x 22.9 (6 x 9). The Walter O. Evans Collection of African American Art

During the years when Bearden spent extended periods in the Caribbean, he increased his use of watercolor and colored inks, and back in New York he made collages marked more extensively with painted elements and painterly additions. It is likely that his renewed interest in these materials, not employed independent of collage with regularity since the 1940s, precipitated his foray into a totally new method of working: the monotype.

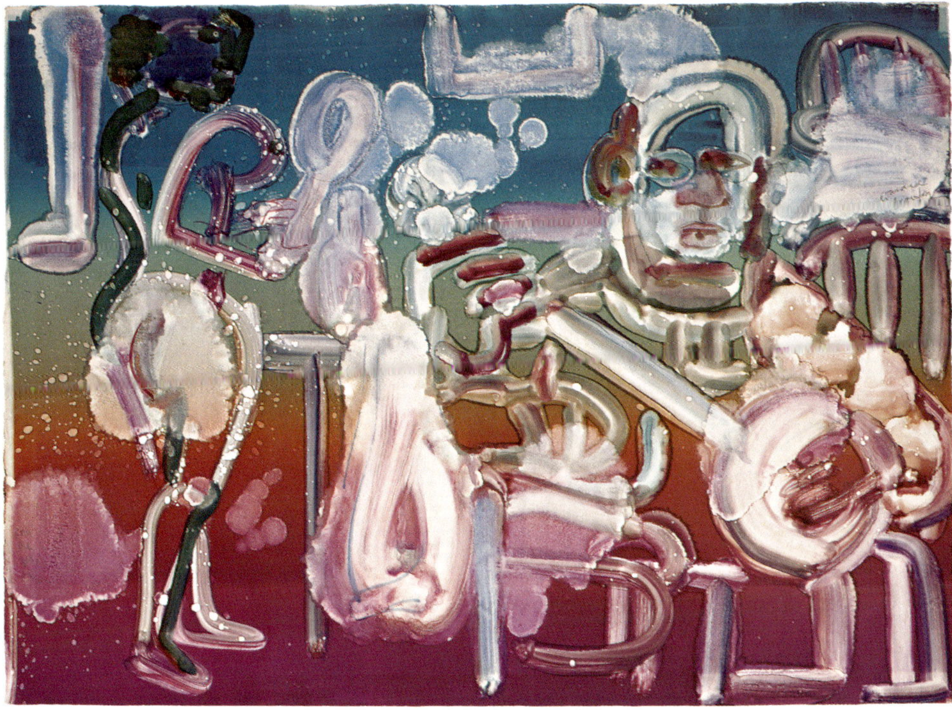

105

Produced from 1974 through 1983, Bearden's dozens of monotypes picture a variety of motifs, primary among them the blues (*Mirror and Banjo,* no. 105); jazz (*Zach Whyte's Beau Brummell Band* and *Celebrations: Trumpet Spot, Wynton,* nos. 106, 107); and portraiture (*Blues Singer,* no. 108). Fewer and less well known are the lush landscapes (*Rain Forest—Pool* and *Waterfall,* nos. 109, 110). Again building on their firm professional relationship and long-standing friendship, Robert Blackburn introduced Bearden to this hybrid process that conflates aspects of drawing and painting with printmaking and that was employed prior to Bearden by such distinguished artists as Giovanni Benedetto Castiglione, William Blake, Edgar Degas, and Milton Avery.[190]

The method requires that an image be drawn or painted onto a flat surface such as a metal plate or sheet of plastic (Bearden and Blackburn used the latter) from which it is offset to paper using hand-pressure or a printing press (again, they used the latter). Over the years Bearden's monotypes have been referred to as "oils on paper" in keeping with language used when they first were made. While not incorrect, this designation is incomplete and misleading regarding the actual process. It probably was coined to emphasize that these works are unique; calling them monotypes would have associated them with printmaking and in turn with multiple impressions generating the same kind of economic and philosophical issues discussed above in relation to the Projections. Following Degas' practice, however, Bearden sometimes created "ghost" impressions of his monotype images.[191] In other words, after offsetting (printing) an image in one impression, he made a second one without reinforcing the initial drawing or painting. Exemplary is *Fish Market,* 1975, known in a bright first impression and a beautifully delicate second one, as well as a preliminary sketch in reverse of the printed motif (figs. 45–47).[192] Apparently smitten with monotype, Bearden nonetheless engaged it only intermittently, but exploring every possible variation.[193] *Mirror and Banjo,* for example, is composed of broad color areas employing a "rainbow" or "blended" surface, a progressive chromatic rolled (rather than painted or drawn) onto the plastic sheet. Into this color field Bearden formed linear arabesques using a benzine-laden brush, removing color to establish broad white "lines" surrounded by his bright hues. By contrast, the marchers and their instruments in *Zach Whyte's Beau Brummell Band* were directly painted onto a blank field. This monotype, like *The Street* ink drawing (see no. 67), illustrated a *New York Times* article, in this instance on 17 June 1990, accompanying Jon Pareles' and Peter Watrous' "Some Riffs on a Dream Jazz Festival."

105
***Mirror and Banjo,* c. 1983, oil monotype with crayon and graphite on paper, 74.3 x 104.1 (29¼ x 41). Herbert Gentry and Mary Anne Rose**

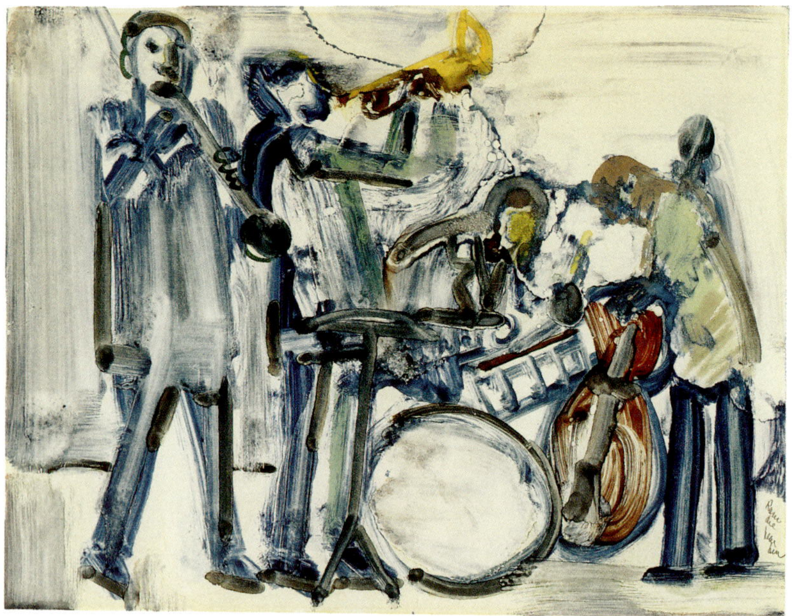

106

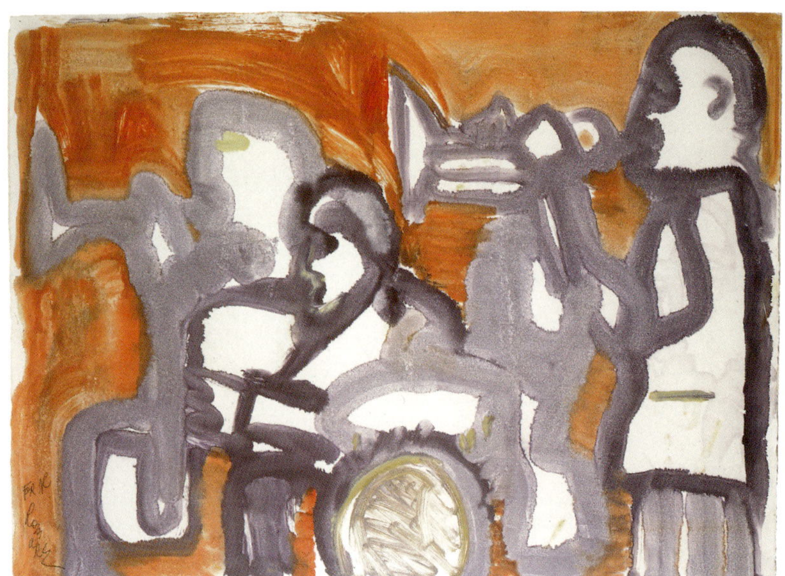

107

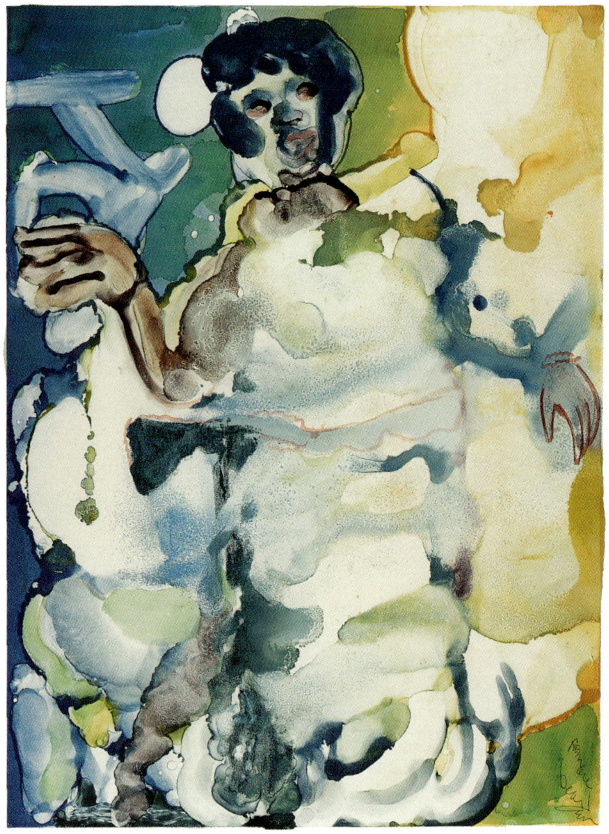

108

106
Zach Whyte's Beau Brummell Band, 1980, oil monotype with paint on paper, 43.2 x 59.7 (17 x 23½). Garth Fagan

107
Celebrations: Trumpet Spot, Wynton, c. 1983, oil monotype on paper, 74.9 x 106.7 (29½ x 42). Albert Murray

108
Blues Singer, 1975, oil monotype with paint and graphite on paper, 60.3 x 44.8 (23¾ x 17⅝). Richard A. Long

109
Rain Forest—Pool, c. 1978, oil monotype with paint on paper, 60.3 x 44.8 (23¾ x 17⅝). Private collection, Cambridge, Massachusetts

Again following Degas' lead, Bearden reworked many transferred images by drawing onto them with graphite or ink (Degas often used pastel, Bearden did not), or painting with watercolor, gouache, or acrylic, making forms more incisive, enhancing details, adding new hues, and reinforcing printed colors to enrich overall what already were very sensuous sheets. This kind of work may be seen, particularly in the performer's hands and dress in *Blues Singer* and throughout *Waterfall.* The latter, laden with added marks in great variety, presents a stark contrast to *Rain Forest—Pool* which parallels *Reclining Nude* as among Bearden's most minimalist works. Both of these landscapes, very different from each other in their use of monotype, are essentially monochromatic essays capturing the density and wetness of the island.

Bearden's monotypes were first exhibited at Cordier & Ekstrom in 1976 in another show focusing on music, *Of the Blues (Second Chorus).* Thirty-seven "oils on paper" were divided into thematic sections: "Folk Sources (Sacred, Secular)"; "New Orleans (Storeyville [*sic*], Mardi Gras, Street Band)"; "New York"; "Chicago"; "Kansas City"; "Performers"; and "Abstract Sounds." The works were made on two paper sizes, 22 x 30 inches and 29 x 40 inches. A radical departure, the show was enthusiastically received. Critic Susan Howe referenced William Blake in her appreciation, reporting that Bearden's "work is now freer in both painterly and personal ways: Songs of Experience turned back on the path of a long career to Songs of Innocence. 'Of the Blues' is a celebration both of color and of the joy of being alive."[194]

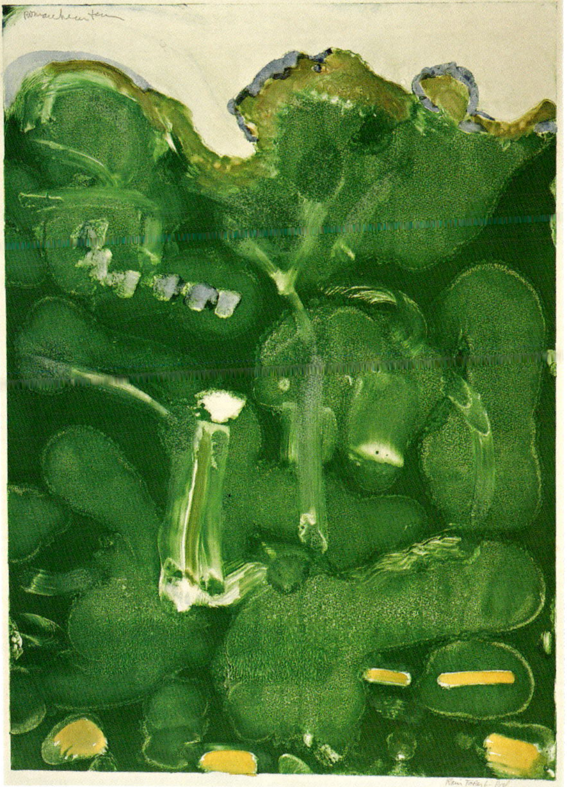

109

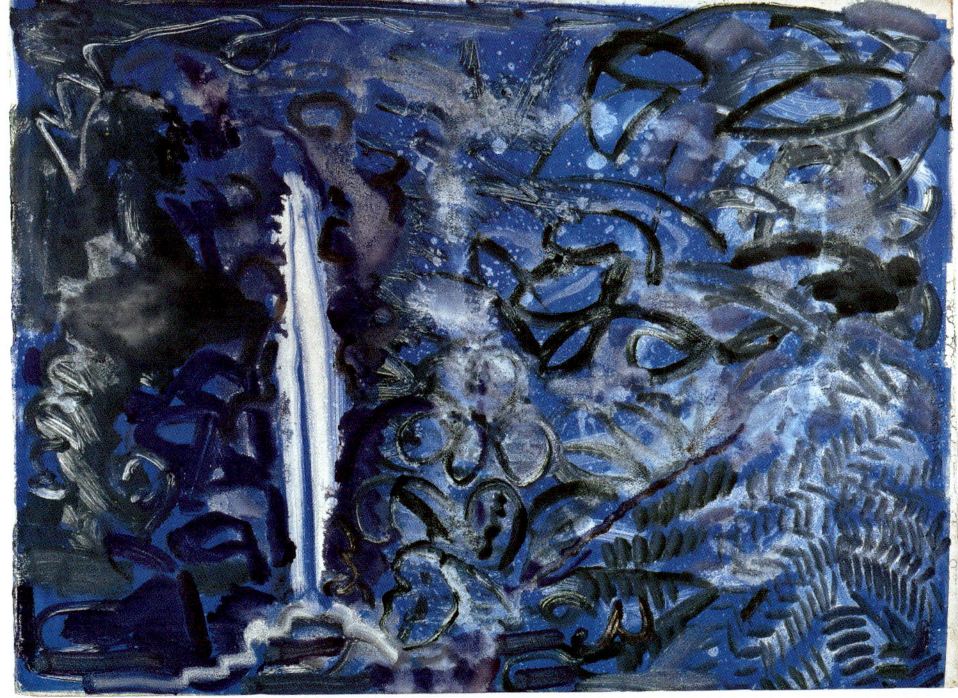

110

110
***Waterfall,* c. 1980, oil monotype with paint on paper, 74.9 x 106.7 (29½ x 42). Billie Allen**

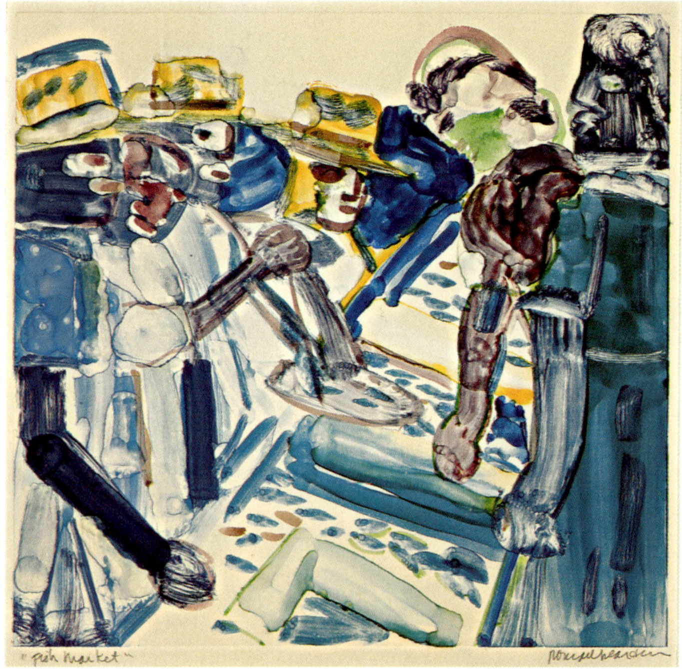

45

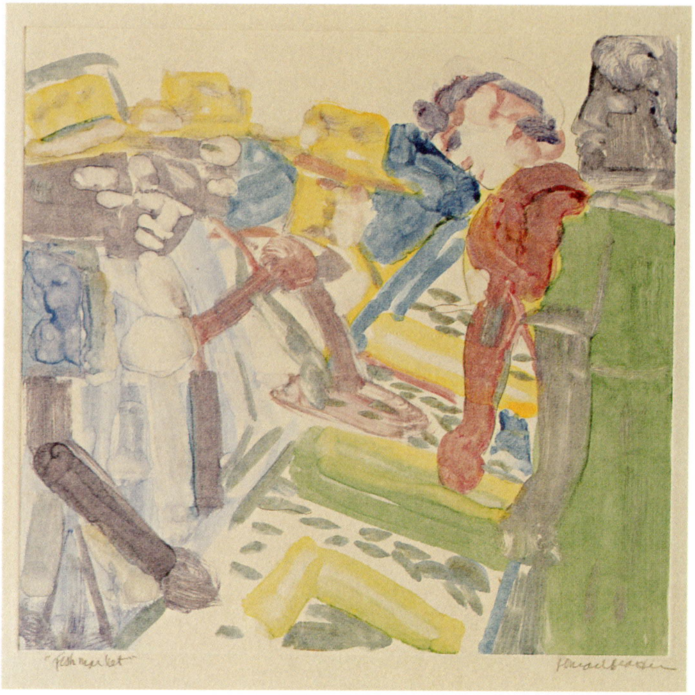

46

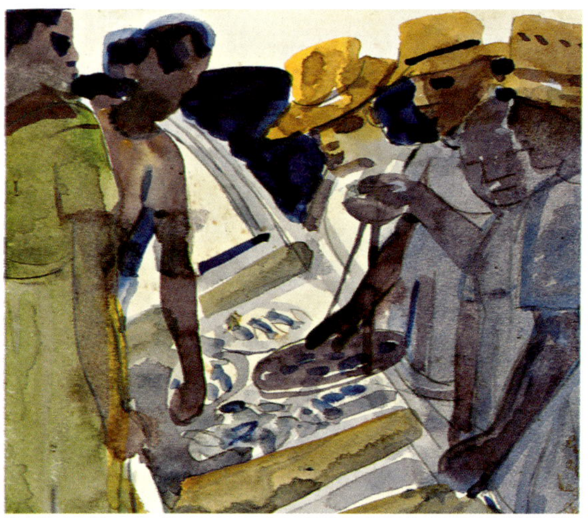

47

figure 45
Romare Bearden, *Fish Market*, 1975, monotype with paint and graphite. Harvey and Phyllis Bauman Collection

figure 46
Romare Bearden, *Fish Market*, 1975, monotype with graphite. Courtesy Bill Hodges Gallery

figure 47
Romare Bearden, *Study for Fish Market*, c. 1975, watercolor with graphite. Harvey and Phyllis Bauman Collection

Late in life Bearden commented that working quickly was "a very 20th century attitude. The development of the machine, and now of the computer, killed man's capacity for patience."[195] It seems apt, then, that working with the speed the monotype demanded and the fluidity of form it encouraged, opened new avenues of expression, adding renewed exuberance and gestural freedom to his work in other media.[196] Having gone to the opposite extreme with the stark, flat surfaces of Odysseus collages soon after the earliest monotypes, Bearden tended from that point on consistently to employ painterly additions in his collages. In great measure these replaced the abraded papers that had played so key a role. Many works of the 1980s may more accurately be called "watercolor with collage" than "collage with watercolor." Bearden's work had truly developed into "collage paintings," the term he had always used to describe it. This is not to say these changes were comprehensive. In fact, Bearden almost never completely stopped using a method just because he added a new one. For many collages made between 1974 and 1987 his means were similar to those he used in the late 1960s: various cut papers with linear additions and little if any painted enhancement at all, as in, *Falling Star, Fitting for the New Dress* (nos. 111–112), and *Profile/Part II, The Thirties: Artist with Painting and Model* (see Kennel in this volume, no. 141).

THE PROFILES

During Bearden's last decade, with Caribbean subjects added to his repertoire, he continued to probe childhood experiences and shared cultural memories in collages, watercolors, prints, and

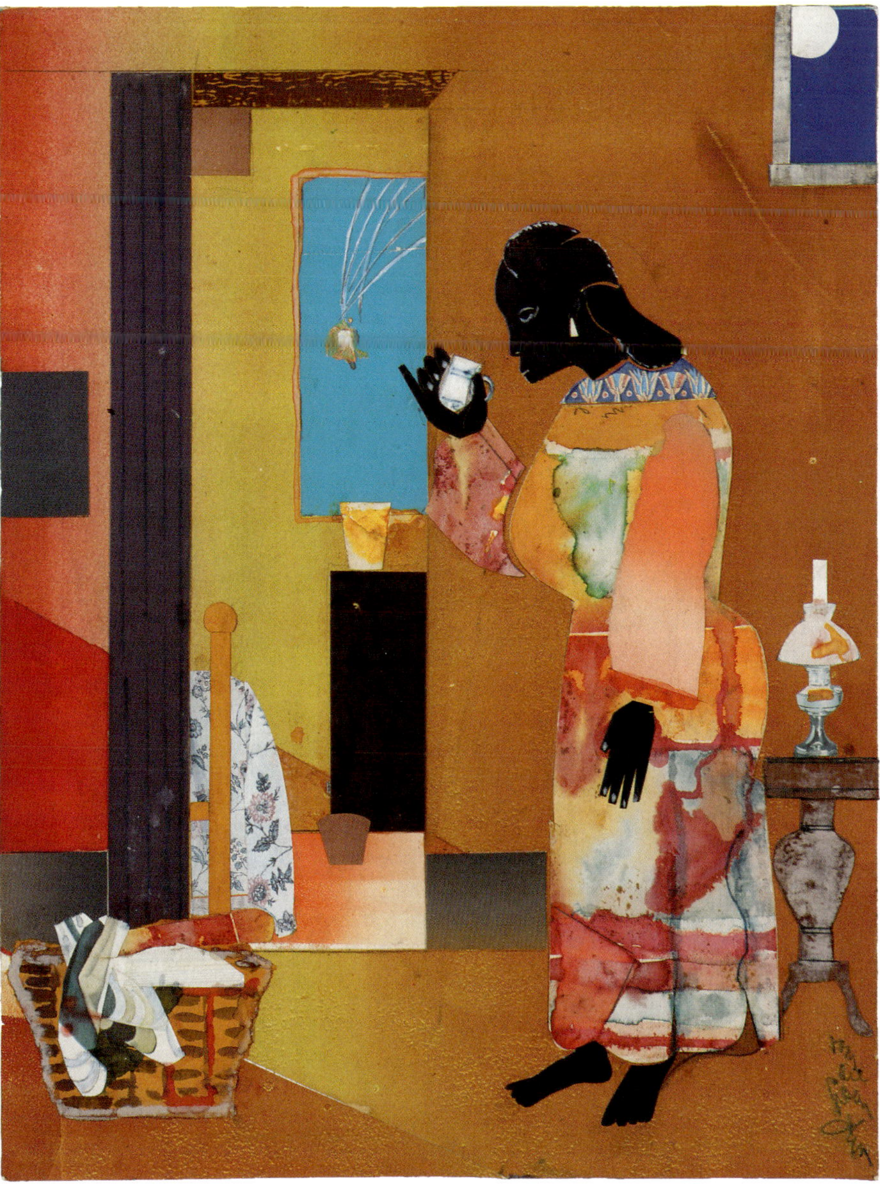

111

111
Falling Star, 1979, collage of various papers with paint, ink, and graphite on fiberboard, 35.6 x 45.7 (14 x 18). Private collection

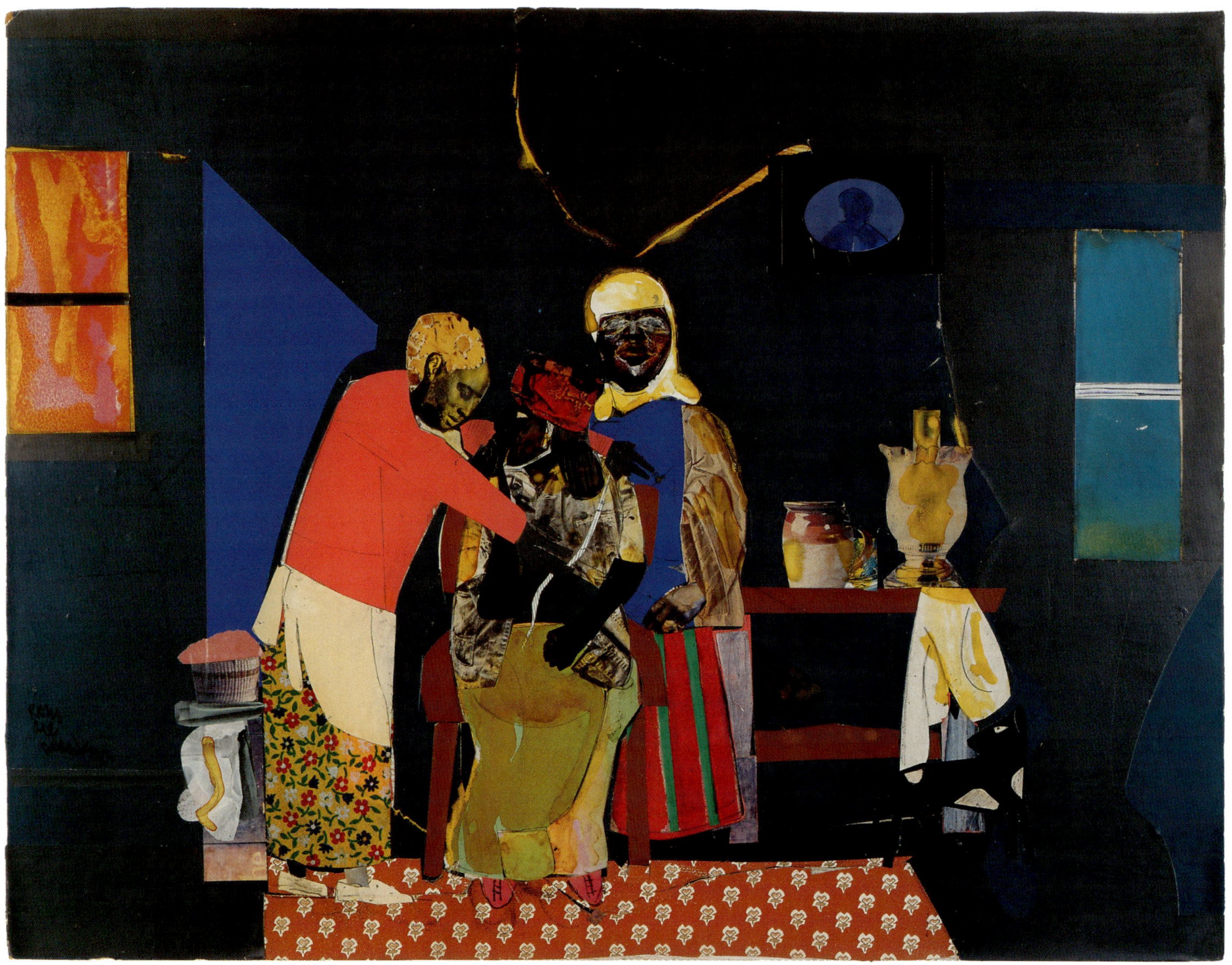

112

112
Fitting for the New Dress, 1982, collage of various papers with fabric, paint, ink, and graphite on fiberboard, 45.1 x 60.3 (17¾ x 23¾). Private collection

113
Profile/Part 1, The Twenties: Mecklenburg County, Railroad Shack Sporting House, 1978, collage of various papers with fabric, paint, ink, graphite, and bleached areas on fiberboard, 28.3 x 41.9 (11⅛ x 16½). Paul and Karen Izenberg

murals. Interviews with journalist Calvin Tomkins in 1975 in preparation for a fascinating 1977 *New Yorker* "Profile" may have deepened the artist's need to identify important people and events in his life and caused him to rethink yet again subjects that had preoccupied him for decades.[197] Inspired by the Tomkins essay, Ekstrom suggested a visual version resulting in *Profile/Part I, The Twenties,* which went on view in 1978. Various reviewers suggested it would be the first installment of a projected autobiography.[198]

Profile/Part I, The Twenties included twenty-eight collages, as usual varying greatly in size (approximately 7 x 10 through 30 x 40 inches), referencing characters and situations associated with Bearden's early life: Miss Pinkney, his school teacher; Miss Bertha and Mr. Seth who rented their home from his great-grandparents; Maudell Sleet and Madeline Jones who had wonderful gardens; Liza, his playmate, whom he depicted picking cotton; Mamie Cole in the living room of her brothel; and the Pittsburgh steel mills. Trains remained key, each named to mark the time of day it raced through the region *(Daybreak Express; The Afternoon Northbound; Sunset Limited; Moonlight Express)*. Several collages in the series recall religious rituals and biblical motifs: revival meetings; group baptisms of as many as forty or fifty people; the Sunday school picnic; Joshua at Jericho. These religious subjects were in fact quite specific to Bearden's early life: "After a certain age, I would say eighteen or nineteen, when I started college, and I didn't have to go to church any more I just never went."[199] The rituals rather than the doctrine remained of lasting importance in his memory, as did his concern with the cultural continuity these practices fostered.

Titles and texts written in chalk directly on the gallery's walls accompanied each collage in the exhibition; the language had been reviewed and edited by Murray, whose collaboration with Bearden on exhibition language dated back at least to 1964.[200] Works from *Profile/Part I, The Twenties* represented here (with related texts) are *Mecklenburg County, Railroad Shack Sporting House* (When I was old enough I found out what Liza's mother did for a living); *Mecklenburg County, Holiness Church Revival* (You could hear the tambourines from a Holiness Church as far away as you could hear the dance bands); *Pittsburgh Memories, Farewell Eugene* (The sporting people were allowed to come but they had to stand on the far right); and *Mecklenburg County, Conjur Woman and the Virgin* (Everything they said a Conjur woman could do I believed) (nos. 113–116). All represent kinds of subjects that entered Bearden's repertoire many years earlier, but, for example, in *Conjur Woman and the Virgin* Bearden's increasing attention to landscape detail plays a prominent role. In other works, the handling of the motifs is new, reflecting his late painterly style. In *Railroad Shack Sporting House* one is as aware of painted as of printed paper fields, aware of an open fluidity essential to the surfaces, but also the clear painterly delineation in the slats of the walls and other touches throughout. There is also a new visual/technical element starting in the late 1970s and continuing to the end of his life: a luminosity Bearden achieved through the use of a bleaching agent. This may be seen in the shape that bonds the breast and arm of the left figure. The method appears to be an outgrowth of the monotypes in which Bearden removed (or lightened) colors from the printing surface, using benzine. Following that practice in some of his late watercolors and collages, he lightened and eliminated color by using a liquid such as Clorox or hydrogen peroxide as he had used benzine, removing color to make color.

Bearden's (final) *Profile/Part II, The Thirties* was exhibited in 1981, accompanied by a catalogue with titles and texts again reviewed by Murray. An *Artforum* reviewer enthusiastically homed in on the complexity of Bearden's project:

> What better medium than collage to express the accumulation of memories? And isn't collage the emblematic [*sic*] medium of the century? Collagists... take bits of chaos to... investigate, organize and present evidence of the activity of a culture... Bearden's work acknowledges the vitality of the American crafts tradition

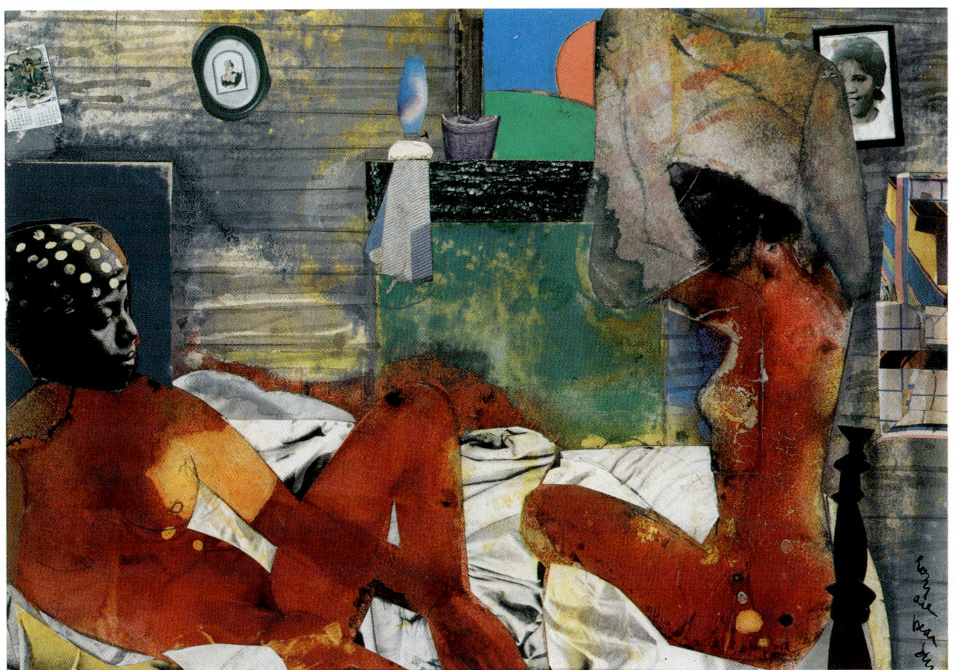

113

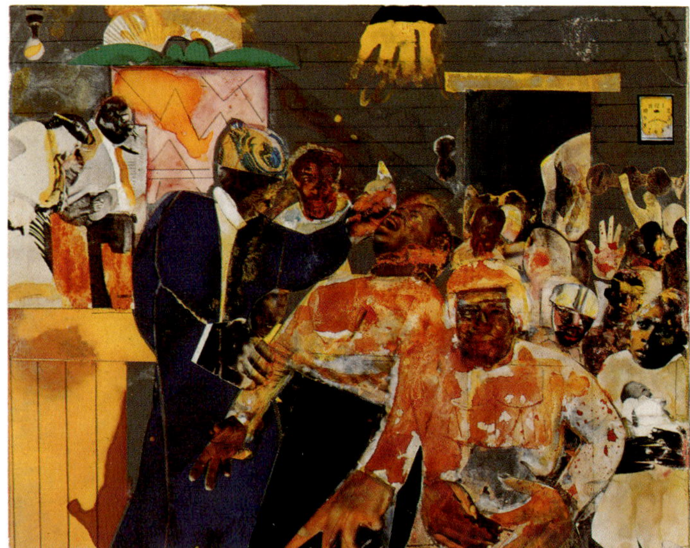

114

115

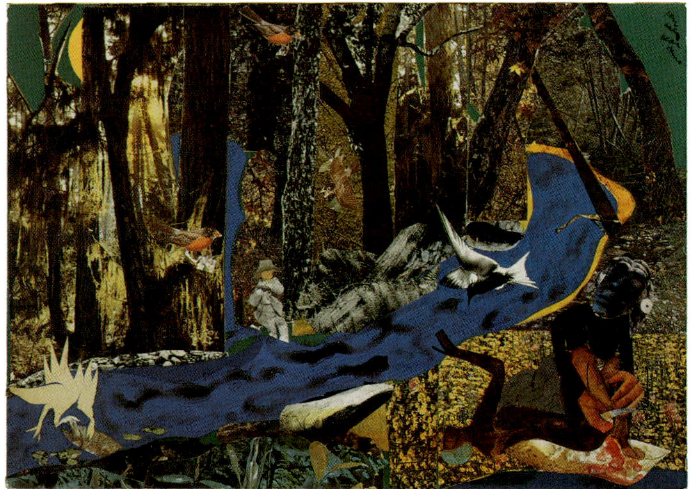

116

114
Profile/Part I, The Twenties: Mecklenburg County, Holiness Church Revival, 1978, collage of various papers with paint, ink, graphite, and bleached areas on fiberboard, 30.8 x 40 (12⅛ x 15¾). Dr. David H. Moore

115
Profile/Part I, The Twenties: Pittsburgh Memories, Farewell Eugene, 1978, collage of various papers with paint, ink, graphite, and bleached areas on fiberboard, 41.3 x 52.1 (16¼ x 20½). Laura Grosch and Herb Jackson

116
Profile/Part I, The Twenties: Mecklenburg County, Conjur Woman and the Virgin, 1978, collage of various papers with ink on fiberboard, 35.6 x 50.8 (14 x 20). Collection of The Studio Museum in Harlem, New York, Museum Purchase 1993

117
Profile/Part II, The Thirties: Uptown Sunday Night Session, 1981, collage of various papers with foil, paint, ink, and graphite on fiberboard, 111.8 x 142.2 (44 x 56). Collection of George and Joyce Wein

of quiltmaking, rug-looping, and decoration that was a lively art before the appropriation of its ideas by the Cubists.... His collages knowingly embrace every influential art movement of the century. The accomplished cut paper forms evoke Matisse, the unsubtle juxtaposition of screwball images hilariously recalls Richard Hamilton, his autobiographical underpinning echoes the structure of so much contemporary art.[201]

The second profile focuses on life in Harlem, including the Bearden family's first home there, with "Mrs. Hairston whose living room was furnished with gifts from wealthy families she had worked for over the years"; one of his many versions of Susannah bathing in a Harlem kitchen, where baths and sinks were located (toilets usually were in hallways). Bearden included Mecklenburg County images as well, such as *The Pepper Jelly Lady* (The trains in the stories she told always ran North), which served as inspiration for a lithograph. The two methodological poles in the nineteen collages are *Profile/Part II, The Thirties: Artist with Painting and Model* (no. 141) and *Uptown Sunday Night Session* (no. 117).

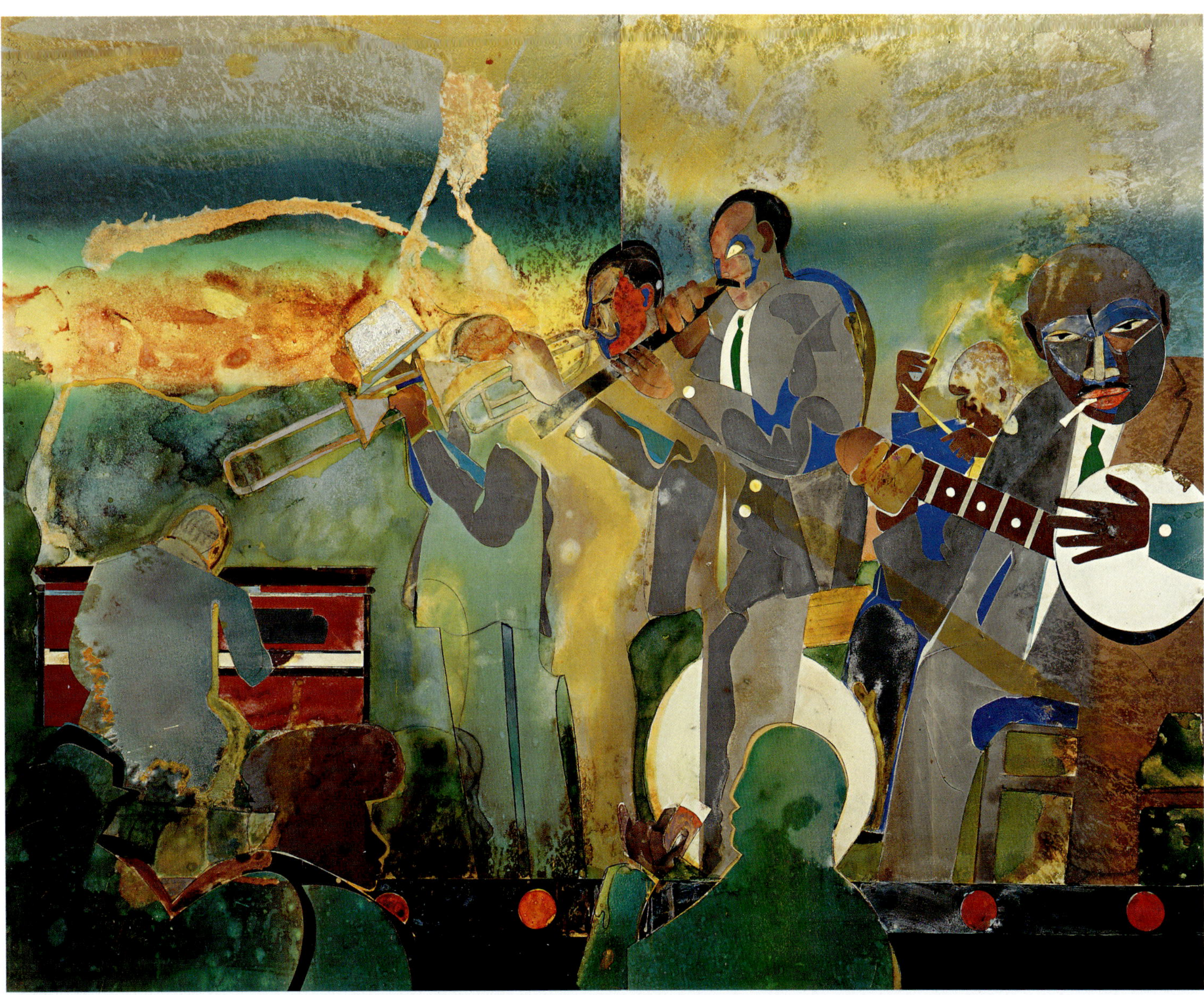

117

Structurally contained, the studio scene depicts Licia, who came every Friday to model for Bearden above the Apollo Theater: its important role in Bearden's oeuvre is discussed in this volume by Sarah Kennel. Bearden's smoky, moody *Uptown Sunday Night Session* takes us to "The Legendary Sunday nites at Leroy's on the corner of 135th Street and Lenox Avenue, [which] also included a floor show. Unlike Connie's Inn and the Cotton Club, Leroy's was mostly off limit to tourists." The Lafayette Theater and a club called Barron's were referenced in *Profile/Part II, The Thirties,* which includes one of Bearden's most sublime city views: *Midtown Sunset* (no. 118), a brilliantly balanced combination of collage and painting, described as "my last view of daylight as I entered the subway on my way home from N.Y.U."

NEW YORK AT NIGHT

Midtown (no. 119) presents the city in full night, with reference to Cinque [Gallery] on what functions as a movie marquee among the city's lights, round moon above round fixtures and period piece cars suggesting a theater or film set rather than a contemporary street scene. In contrast to the collage/paint balance of *Midtown Sunset, Midtown* exemplifies works that essentially are watercolors with collage. *City Lites* (no. 120) takes that one step further. Entirely in watercolor and inks, it highlights Bearden's bleaching technique, the most brilliant light areas appearing to have been made this way (rather than a more traditional method of removal with water).

Fluidly painted New York scenes, many at night, were used as a backdrop for titles in John Cassavetes 1980 film, *Gloria.*[202] Bearden's longtime friend Sam Shaw was the producer, and he also did the title designs that incorporated Bearden's images. The film opens with a long shot of a wall covered by Bearden's watercolors, then moves to close-up details as a foil for the starting credits. Bearden made approximately thirty watercolors, many more than were eventually used in the film. Among those not seen there is *Midtown Manhattan* (no. 121), which emphasizes the atmospheric sky that Bearden so beautifully captured in the free-flowing watercolor medium. Several others, both vertical and horizontal in format, focus on the buildings themselves, including one that sets the stage for the shift from Bearden's watercolors to a photographic view of the city.

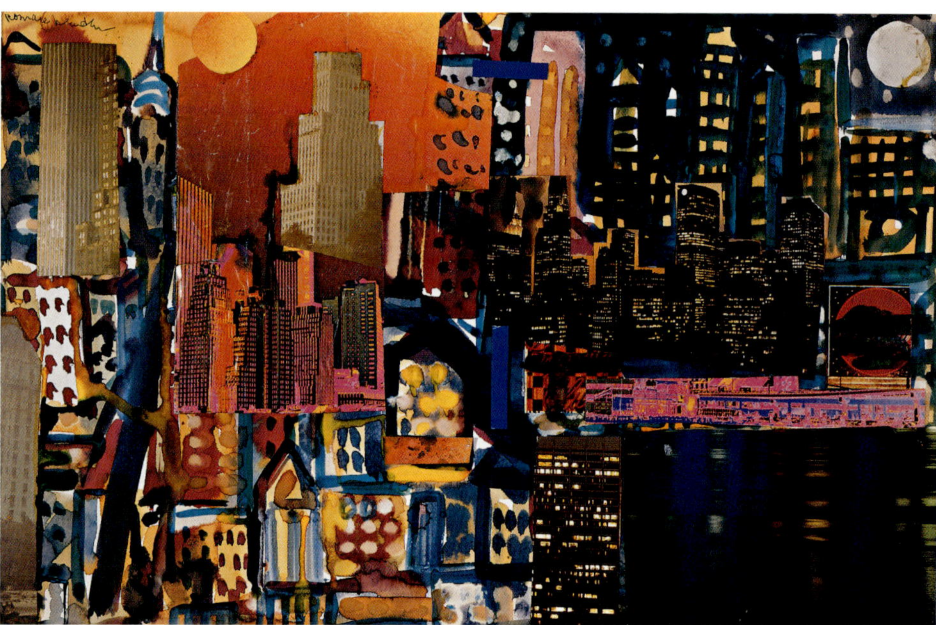

118

118
Profile/Part II, The Thirties: Midtown Sunset, **1981, collage of various papers with paint and bleached areas on fiberboard, 35.6 x 55.9 (14 x 22). Private collection**

119
Midtown, **1982, collage of various papers with paint and graphite on paper mounted on cardboard, 52.1 x 69.9 (20½ x 27½). David A. Hagelstein, Bloomfield Hills, Michigan**

120
City Lites, **1982, watercolor, ink, and bleached areas on paper, 49.5 x 35.2 (19½ x 13⅞). Anonymous lender**

121
Midtown Manhattan, **1979/1980, watercolor, gouache, graphite, and bleached areas on paper, 24.1 x 32.4 (9½ x 12¾). Harvey and Phyllis Baumann**

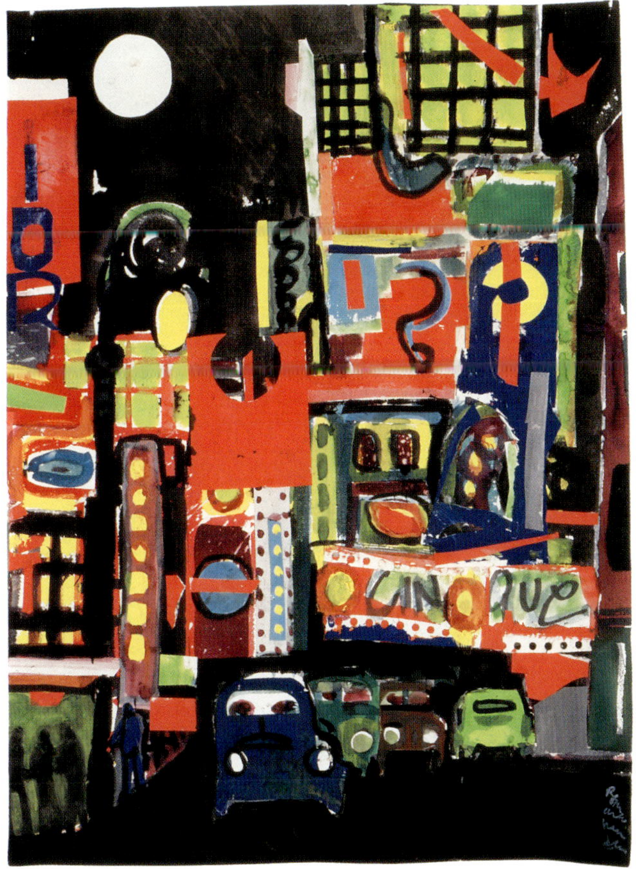

119

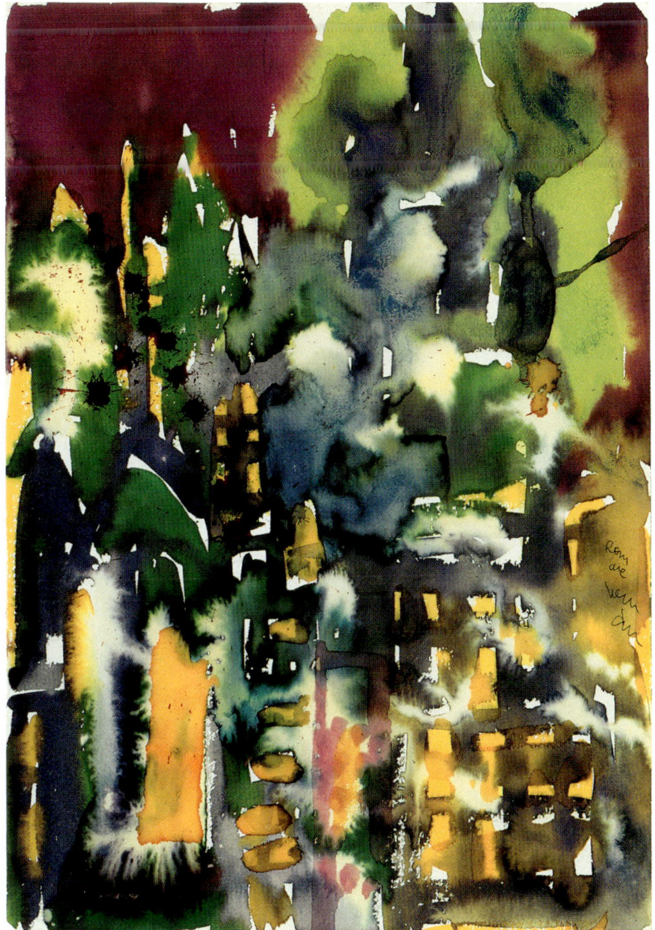

120

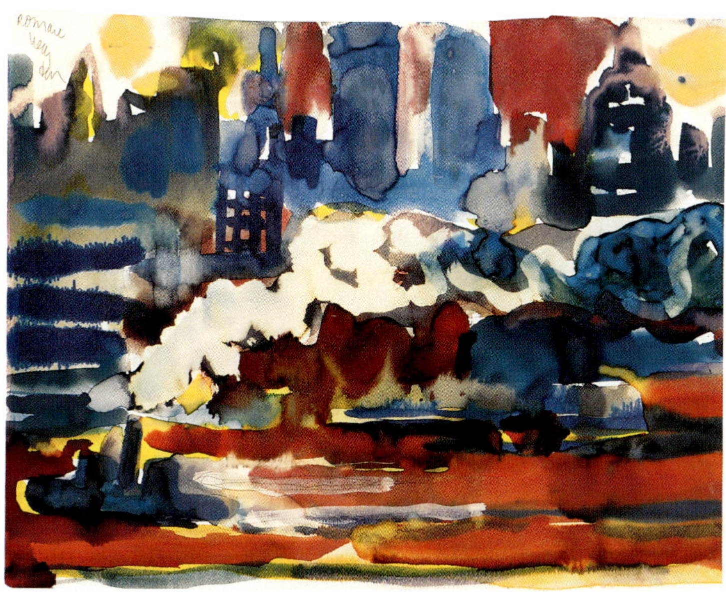

121

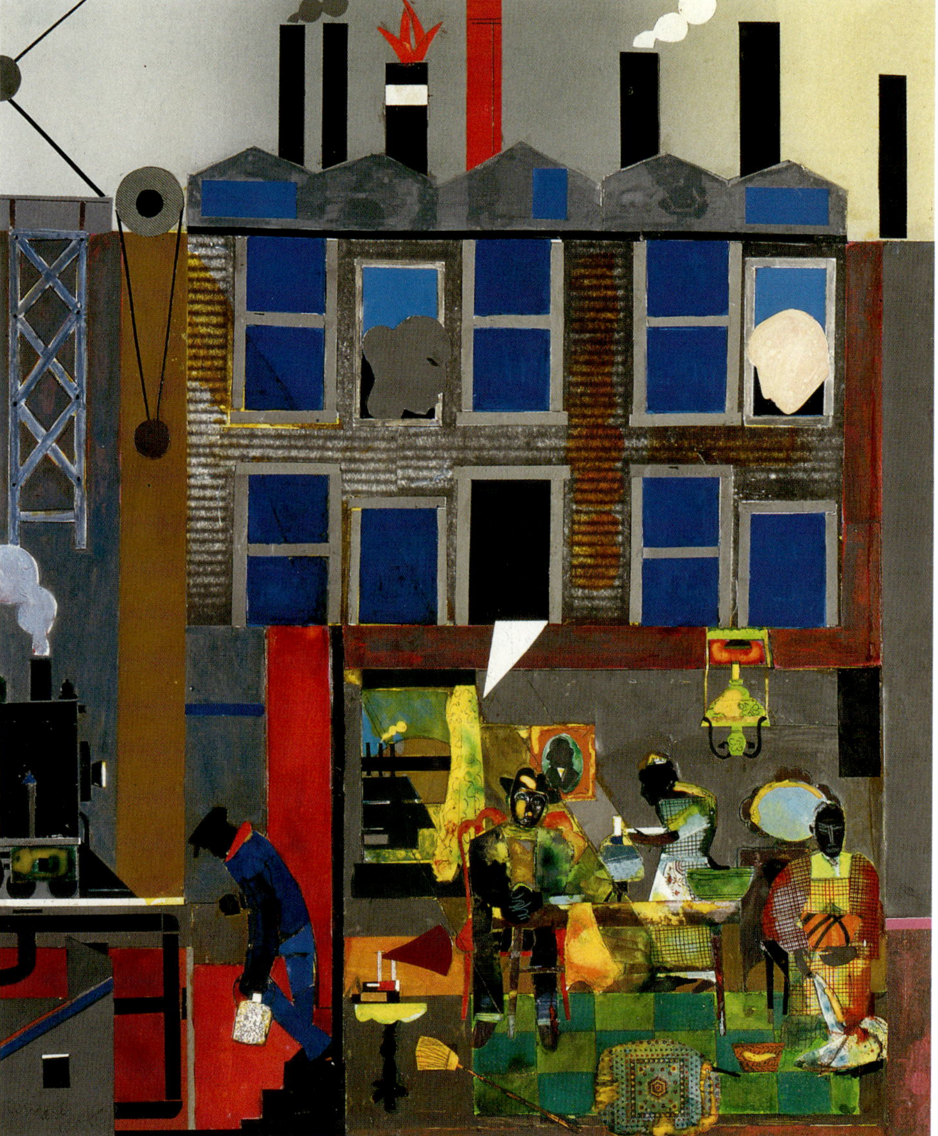

122

Bearden also revisited Pittsburgh during this last decade, most beautifully in *Pittsburgh Memories,* 1984 (no. 122), commissioned for donation to the Carnegie Museum of Art located in that city.[203] Composed of the horizontal/vertical structure Bearden always favored, it functions as a technical cornerstone of his late work and also may be viewed as a summation of much earlier imagery. According to curator John Caldwell, the interior view filling the lower right quadrant of the composition represents Banks' boardinghouse.[204] This seems an apt reading of the scene, but the room itself (in a work of a different title) could just as readily be in Bearden's great-grandparents' home in North Carolina or in one of his family's New York apartments. A cozy interior, it is marked by motifs Bearden had engaged over decades: a family photograph on the wall, a mirror, window curtains blowing in the wind, a wonderful hanging glass lamp, a broom, the oft-repeated checkered tile floor, and a new element, that extraordinary gramophone, which may be viewed as alluding to jazz music.

Smokestacks rise against the sky, with flames and smoke of different colors emanating from them. (Henderson, who also spent childhood years in this region, recalled how the blast furnaces and open hearth furnaces were "fabulous at night; it was like looking at hell itself.") A pulley system, remarkably close in form to an image in a photograph by Eugene Smith of the Pittsburgh Screw and Bolt Company, also tells us of Bearden's Pittsburgh memories.[205] So does the man walking down the steps holding a lunch-bucket of the sort Bearden depicted in other Pittsburgh collages (e.g., *Mill Hand's Lunch Bucket* from the 1978 Profile). But *Pittsburgh Memories* also encompasses an apartment block that, while it might have existed in Pittsburgh, is more reminiscent of Harlem's *The Block* and *The Block II,* with two Picassoesque heads facing each other across the expanse of windows. The space constructed by this apartment block, however, is impossible: a view out the dining room window reveals a field of the sort associated with Bearden's Mecklenburg memories, in a location in the image that logically would be filled by the rising urban buildings. Bearden, thus, has simultaneously engaged all of his boyhood cities. In addition, a train, the single most pervasive signifier in Bearden's art and an essential symbol for both Charlotte and Pittsburgh, hides part of the field through the window, and a second train enters the scene from the left, as if heading straight into the house.

In facture, *Pittsburgh Memories* is a splendid embodiment of Bearden's practices. A photostat stands for the exterior wall of the apartment block, its windows made of both printed Color Aid papers and papers with painted surfaces. Where the windows are painted the window-frames are not, and vice versa. The gray sky is spray-painted, most densely at the center, with a lighter layer as it moves out to the left. To the right a ruler-straight edge keeps the far right sky essentially clear, suggesting Bearden used a mask of the sort noted a decade earlier in *The Blues.* Both women's dresses are composed of snippets of fabric, the man's lunch pail of crinkled foil. There are linear additions as well, like the blue pencil line used both to define the clasped fingers of the seated man and the decorative pattern on the white triangular shape above his head. Bleached areas appear in several places, among them on the seated man's jacket, the outer border of the patterned rug atop the checkered floor, and the shade of the hanging lamp.

Geometric structure coordinated with a romantic handling of materials come together with a superb sense of color and space to convey a lifetime of autobiographical motifs and art-historical homages. But this already packed collage does even more than that. *Pittsburgh Memories* is the only collage we have identified that depicts two couples, two men and two women, with no children and no additional adults. It seems possible, therefore, that Bearden meant it to function as a personal homage to the two African-American couples who commissioned the collage for donation to a major museum in one of his favored cities.

A very different view of Pittsburgh, more fully specific to the city, may be seen in *Pittsburgh Recollections,* 1984, installed at Pittsburgh's downtown Gateway Center Station, a subway stop under the auspices of the Port Authority of Allegheny County (fig. 48). Composed of ceramic tile from Bennington Potters in Vermont, it measures 13 x 60 feet and using a combination of flatly colored and painterly surfaces presents a panorama of the city's history tied together by its three rivers, the Allegheny, the Monongahela, and the Ohio. Early industry embodied in the waterwheel and the spinning wheel shifts to factory gears and belts, industrial barges, and workers with lunch boxes, and then to the modern age with a microscope signifying the city's engagement with research. Included as well is what must be perceived as a self-portrait—a hand wielding a paintbrush. Like the Berkeley mural of the previous decade, *Pittsburgh Recollections* suggests the extensive historical research Bearden would have undertaken to create an appropriate image, but also the strong personal identity he embedded in every major project.

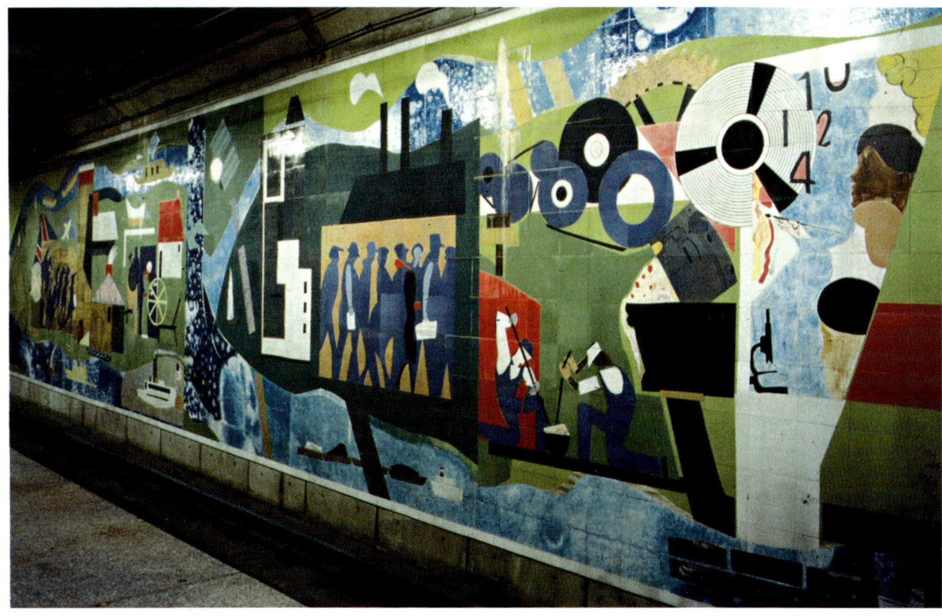

48

122
***Pittsburgh Memories,* 1984, collage of various papers with fabric, foil, paint, ink, color pencil, graphite, and bleached areas on fiberboard, 72.7 x 59.7 (28⅝ x 23½). Carnegie Museum of Art, Pittsburgh; gift of Mr. and Mrs. Ronald R. Davenport and Mr. and Mrs. Milton A. Washington, 1984**

figure 48
Romare Bearden, *Pittsburgh Recollections*, 1984, ceramic tile mural at Gateway Center Station. The Port Authority of Allegheny County Public Art Program for the Light Rail Transit System

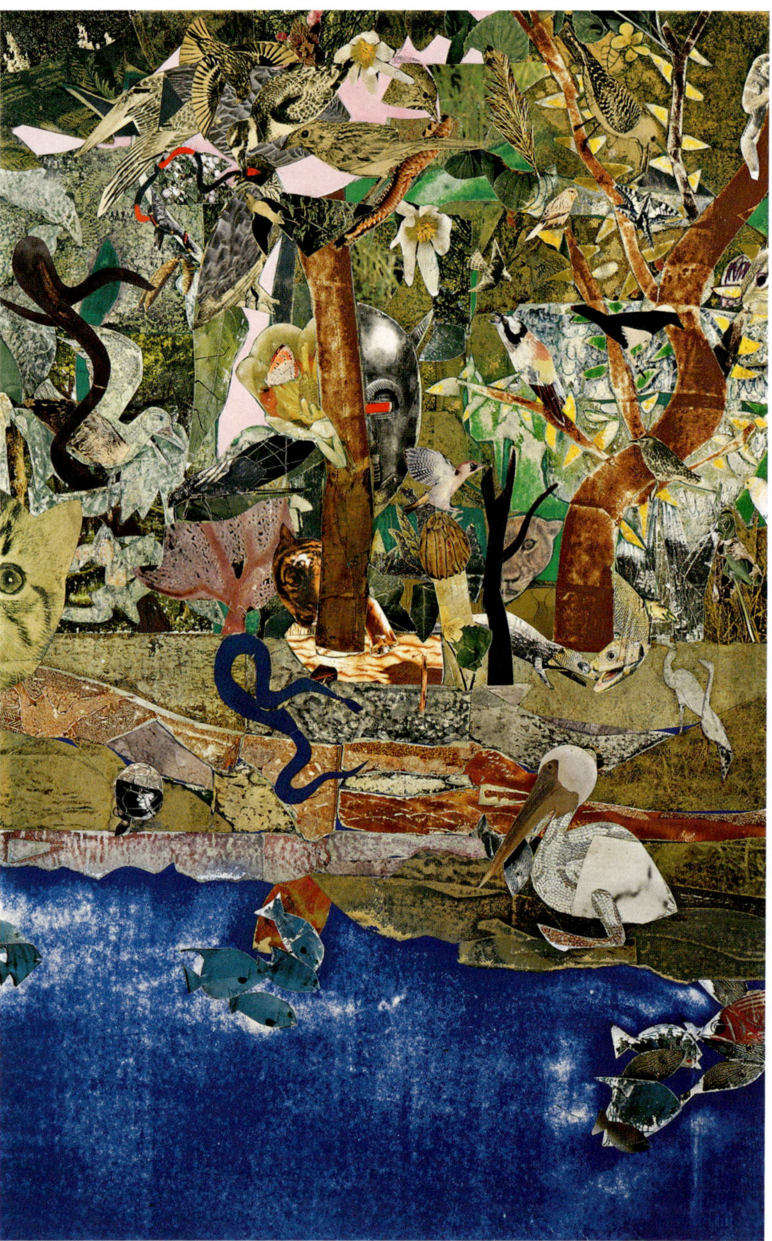

123

LANDSCAPE

Landscapes are among Bearden's most glorious late works, and to the degree they were devoid of figures, a new subject for him, one rarely associated with his name. Landscape played a role in Bearden's political cartoons for the Baltimore *Afro-American* in the mid-1930s; in many the setting was a nonspecific outdoors. In the early 1940s and through the 1960s, the Mecklenburg County landscape again served primarily as an environment, specifically for farming-oriented figure-based narratives. Lush tropical views appeared in collages of the early 1970s, but likewise primarily as a setting for figures, as in *Ritual Bayou.* Rarely at this early date do we see a pure landscape, such as *Blue Snake* (no. 123). Populated with birds, turtles, snakes, fish, cats, lizards, butterflies, a sense of *horror vacuii* is here at its most extreme. This density is suggestive of the *Unicorn Tapestries,* brilliant in their coordination of secular and religious motifs, which were among the works mentioned in *The Painter's Mind.* Reproductions of these masterpieces were among Bearden's papers; and in a letter of 3 October 1966 to a Mr. McIllhony, he referred to the Unicorn suite as a work "resolved in perfect harmony." The details are quite different in *Blue Snake,* however, where feathers, fur, fins, fronds, and flowers mesh with leaves, branches, trunks, and stems. Together they are set dramatically against the modulated (abraded) blue water and striated rocky bank to form a visual tapestry of staggering richness within which each element maintains its own individual character, very different from his landscapes of the following decade.

In the 1980s, as landscape took on a greater importance, Bearden looked anew at Mecklenburg County. The radical changes his landscapes under-

123
***Blue Snake,* 1971, collage of printed papers with paint, ink, graphite, and surface abrasion on fiberboard, 91.4 x 60.3 (36 x 23¾). Priscilla T. Grace, Promised gift to the Philadelphia Museum of Art**

124
***Mecklenburg Autumn: October—Toward Paw's Creek,* 1983, collage of various papers with paint, ink, graphite, and bleached areas on fiberboard, 76.2 x 101.6 (30 x 40). Estate of Romare Bearden, courtesy of Romare Bearden Foundation, New York**

went become clear when comparing the controlled and contained manner in which specific plant and animal forms are handled in *Blue Snake* with the loose, expressionistic coordination of paint and collage in such effusive landscapes as *Mecklenburg Autumn: October—Toward Paw's Creek* (no. 124). Bearden's late collages incorporate new elements, as in the vertical "striped" pattern of the sky, a printed paper of a sort made especially for this purpose by Blackburn. Bearden's landscapes of the 1980s call to mind that his abstract watercolors had been praised in 1955 for their "suggestiveness of season and mood." That the same was true thirty years later can be seen in *Summer (Maudell Sleet's July Garden)* and *Winter (Time of the Hawk)* (nos. 125, 126). The suggestion of intense heat by means of a profusion of bright color brilliantly conveys the summer garden, highlighting its stark contrast to the icy landscape in the winter scene. Bearden's oeuvre is an unlikely place to find a winter scene. Yet he captured that season's character with rigor equal to that of the torrid Caribbean beaches, just as his unique rendition of Berkeley equaled in his understanding of the subject that of his oft-depicted New York. While adding the Mecklenburg landscape to his imagery he continued as well to depict Southern interiors as he had been doing for three decades.

During most of the years Bearden painted in the Caribbean he worked at a table in the family house (a separate studio was not added until the mid-1980s) at a smaller scale than he would use in New York. He became increasingly engaged by the lush tropical woodlands, rocky precipices surrounding pools of water, and vistas facing the sea. Back in New York the freshness achieved in his quickly worked smaller sheets was put to expansive use in larger pieces such as *Birds in Paradise* and *In a Green Shade (Hommage* [sic] *to*

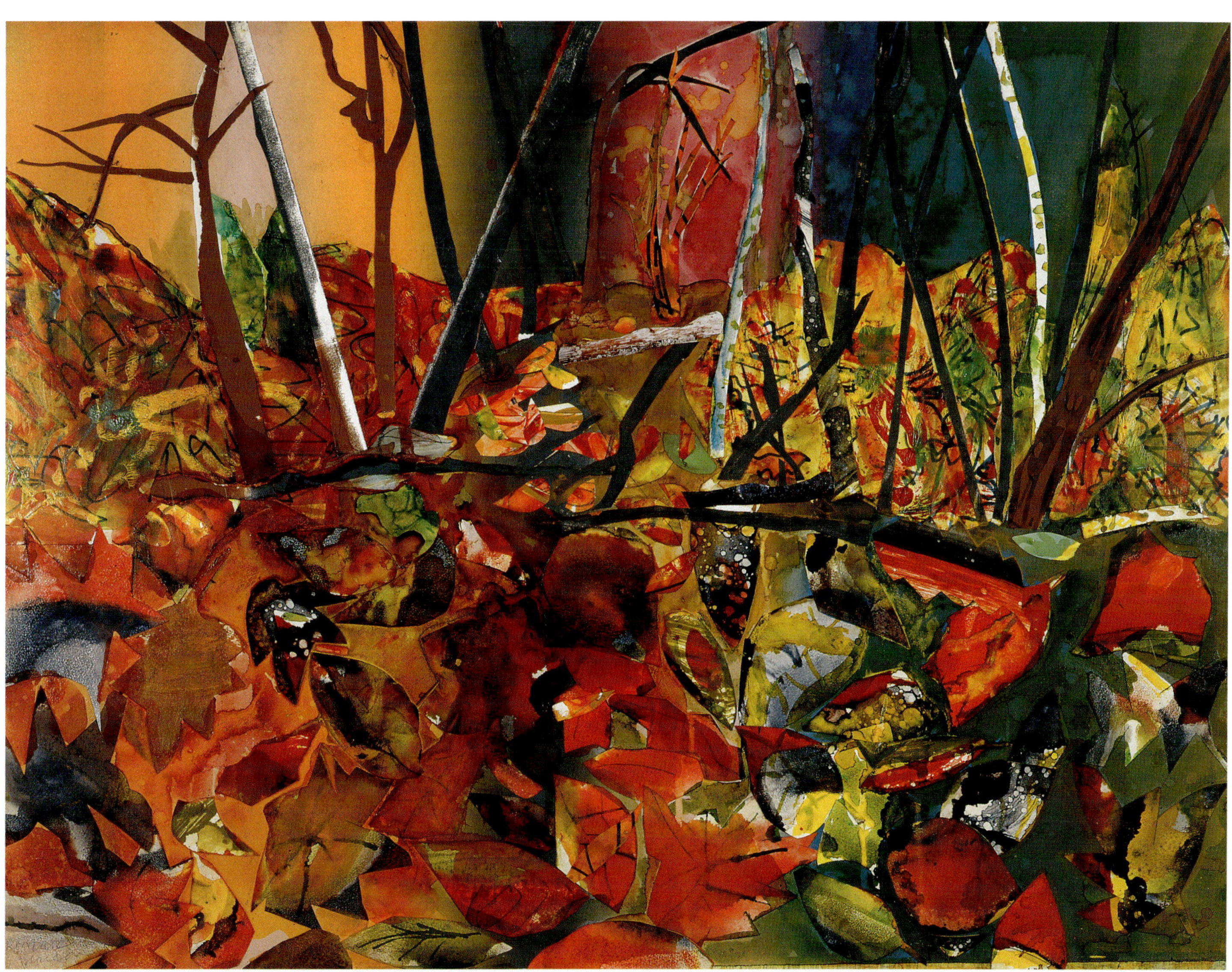

124

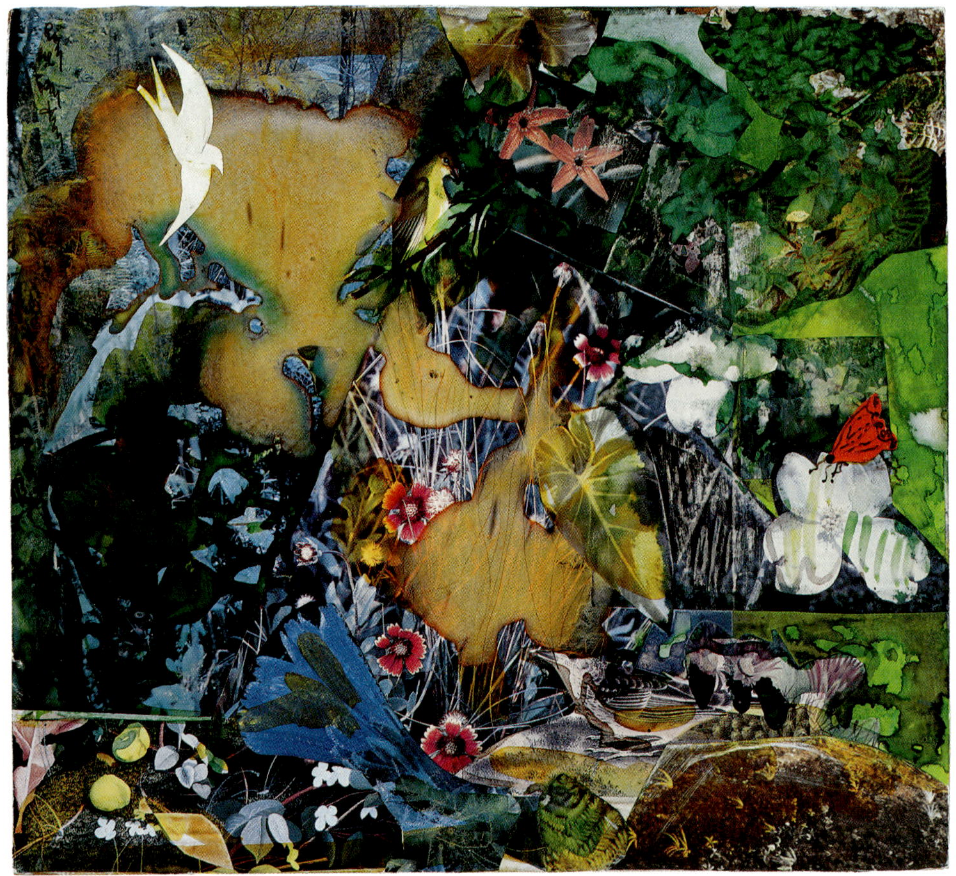

125

Marvell) (nos. 127, 128). The title of the latter taken from the last line of verse six of Andrew Marvell's poem "The Garden," reminding us of Bearden's continuing preoccupation with literature:

Meanwhile the mind, from pleasures less,
Withdraws into its happiness:
The mind, that ocean where each kind
Does straight its own resemblance find,
Yet it creates, transcending these,
Far other worlds, and other seas,
Annihilating all that's made
To a green thought in a green shade.[206]

The compositional lushness of *Birds in Paradise* is reminiscent of *Blue Snake* from more than a decade earlier, although its technique is very different, the later work being more painting than collage. Both speak to great mysteries in the natural world, suggesting a spiritual component in Bearden's landscapes, equally intense but of quite a divergent order than his figurative gouaches of the early 1940s. Similarly, *In a Green Shade (Hommage* [sic] *to Marvell)*, shows an integrated world of land, sun/moon, water, foliage, women, birds, and other creatures. It weds all of Bearden's late preoccupations in collage, a peaceable kingdom charged with romantic, perhaps erotic, overtones, reinforced by the fiery red tree backdrop for the figure.

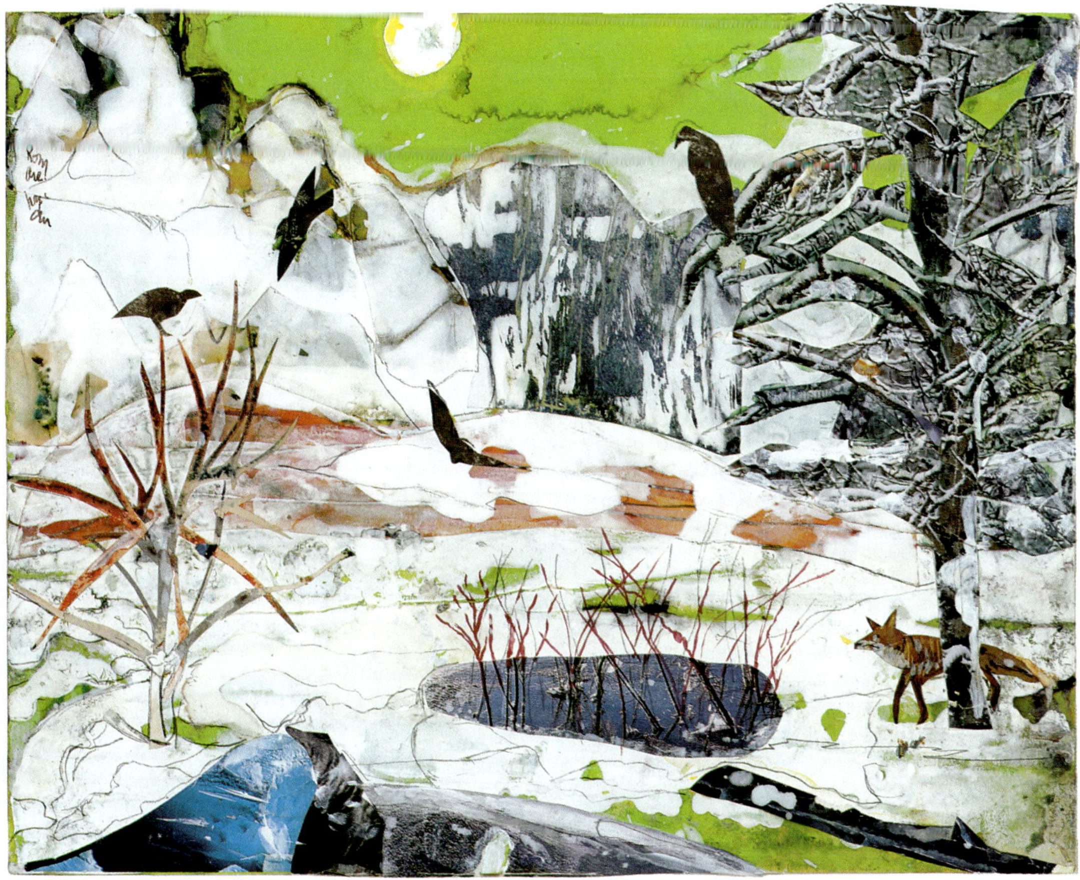

126

125
Summer (Maudell Sleet's July Garden), 1985, collage of various papers with paint, ink, graphite, surface abrasion, and bleached areas on fiberboard, 30.2 x 34.3 (11 7/8 x 13 1/2). Private collection, Charlotte, North Carolina

126
Winter (Time of the Hawk), 1985, collage of various papers with paint, ink, and graphite on fiberboard, 27.3 x 34.9 (10 3/4 x 13 3/4). Private collection, Charlotte, North Carolina

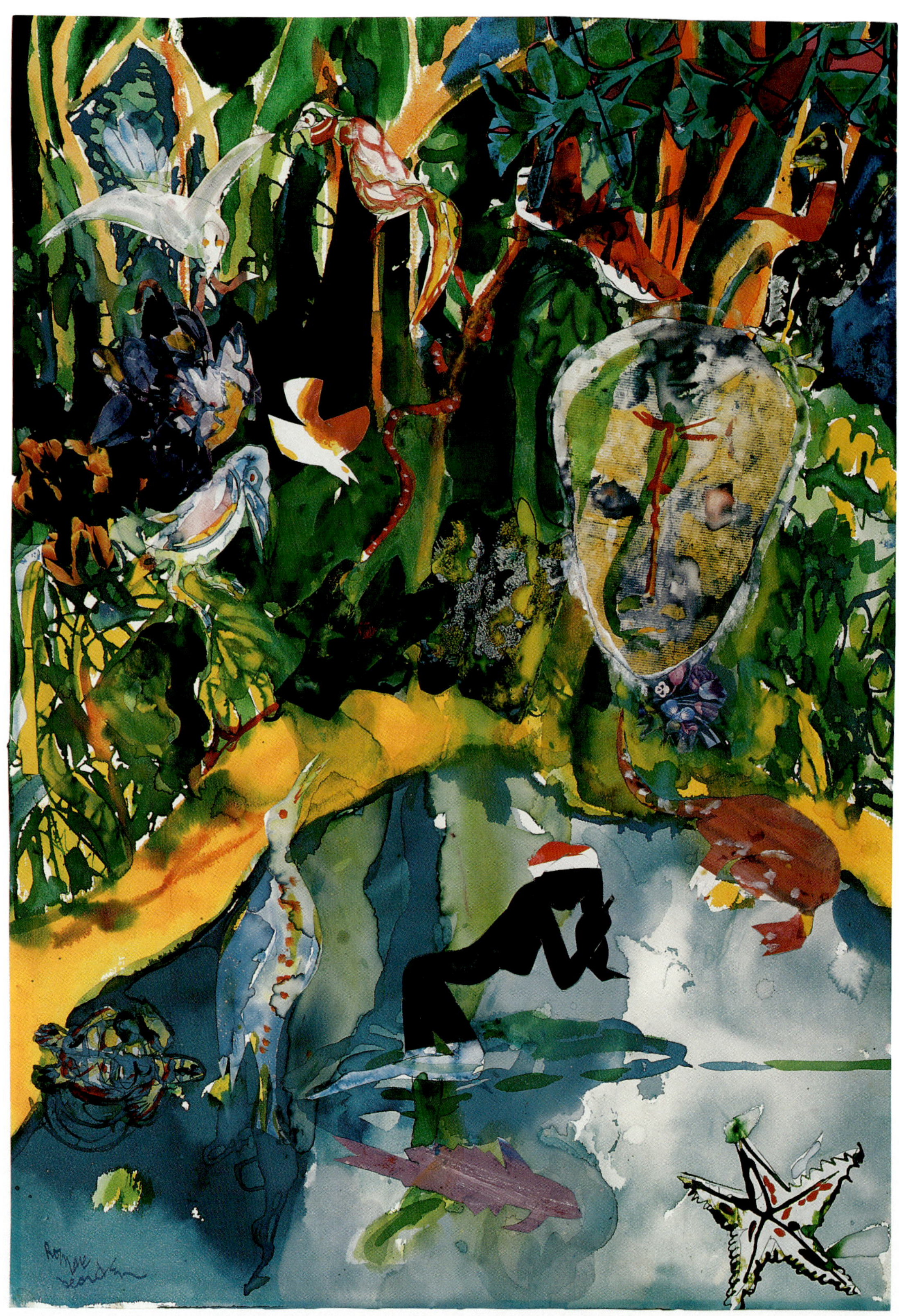

127

127
Birds in Paradise, c. 1982, collage of various papers with paint, ink, and graphite on paper, 74.3 x 52.7 (29 1/4 x 20 3/4). Collection of Dr. and Mrs. Mark Couture, Cramerton, North Carolina

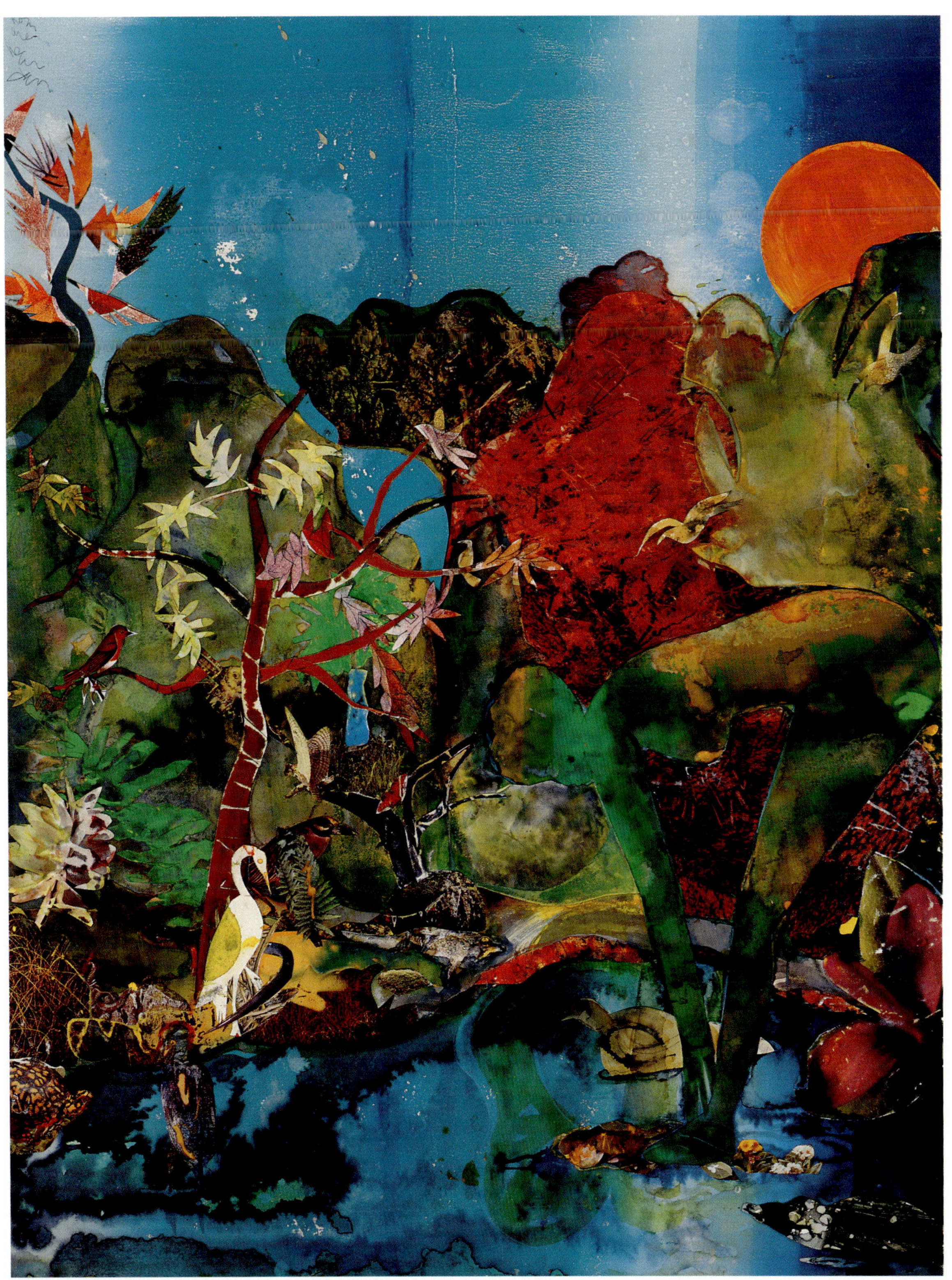

128

128
In a Green Shade (Hommage [sic] *to Marvell)*, 1984, collage of various papers with paint, ink, and graphite on fiberboard, 99.7 x 76.8 (39 ¼ x 30 ¼). Yvonne and Richard McCracken

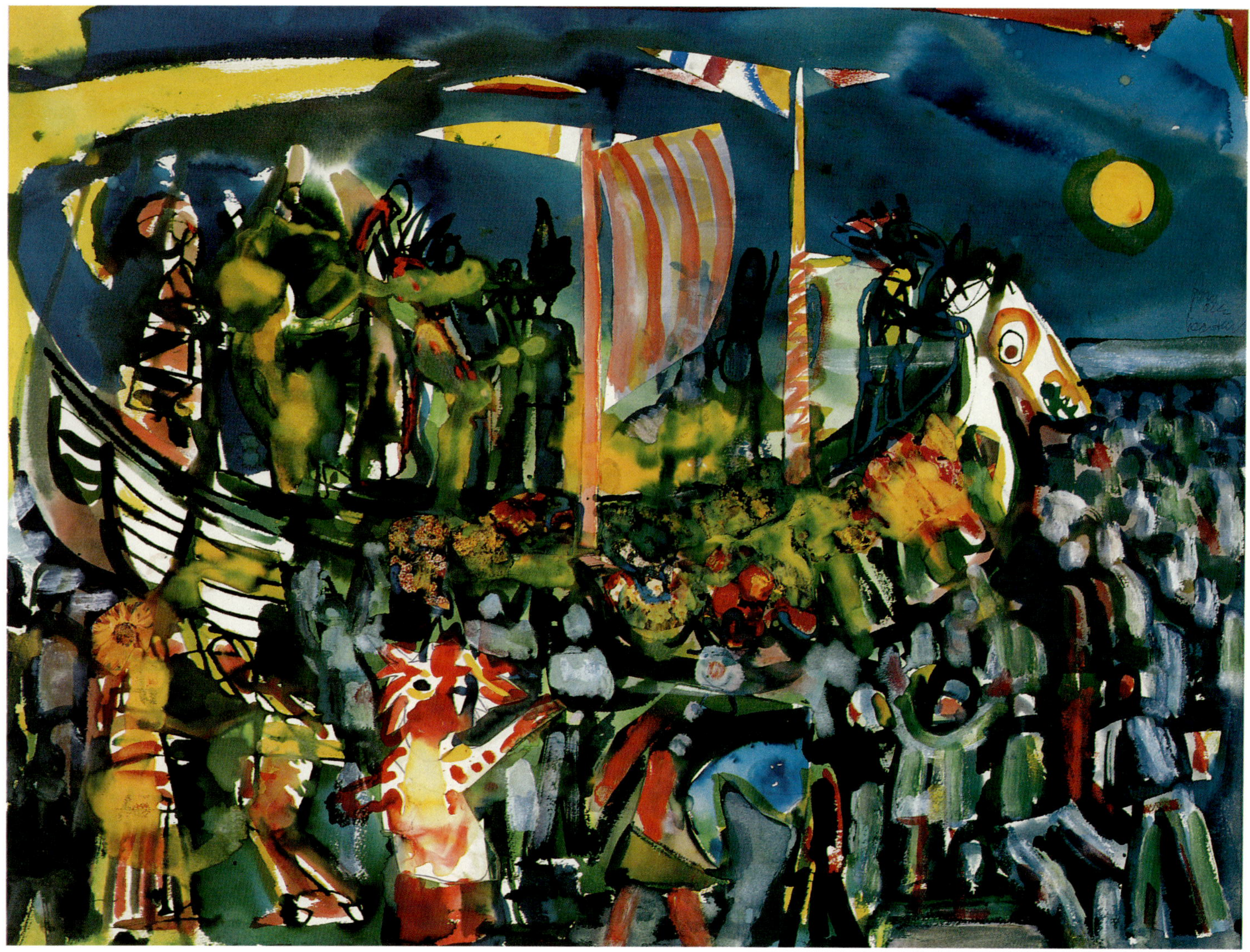

129

129
The Carnival Begins, 1984, watercolor and collage, 54.6 x 76.2 (21½ x 30). Estate of Romare Bearden, courtesy of Romare Bearden Foundation, New York

130
Obeah in a Trance, 1984, watercolor and gouache on paper, 75.3 x 49.1 (29⅝ x 19$\frac{5}{16}$). Estate of Romare Bearden, courtesy of Romare Bearden Foundation, New York

Bearden also investigated exotic spiritual rites rooted in the Caribbean as well as colorful island festivals, as in *The Carnival Begins* (no. 129). The Obeah Woman, a Caribbean parallel of the southern Conjur Woman, became a key figure. Bearden's 1984 Cordier & Ekstrom exhibition *Rituals of the Obeah* included sixteen watercolors, among them *Obeah in a Trance* (no. 130). The catalogue for the show provided titles in English, French, and Creole. Critic Michael Brenson's description of the exhibition suggests that "if the Obeah holds such an attraction for Bearden, it is clearly because its mixture of rules, improvisation, trust, and sacrifice is characteristic of art-making itself [noting specifically about *Obeah in a Trance* that the] watery murk that eats into the figure like acid [tells] us that her personality has been dissolved by her trance."[207] Several works in the *Rituals of the Obeah* exhibition engaged the Loa, a god that takes on various forms from the demonic to that of a beneficent guide within Caribbean cultures, and associated with voodoo. For Bearden the importance of the Loa figure continued over time as seen in the 1986 *An Obeah Princess, Her Loa Leaves at Dawn* (no. 131), a splendid example of his late work. In it, loosely applied fields of watercolor probably mixed with inks are juxtaposed with forceful defining lines, similar in materials and types of forms, but radically different in appearance and emotional impact from the works on paper of forty years earlier. In December 1984 Bearden discussed his belief that the Obeah people defied the rationality of the Western mind:

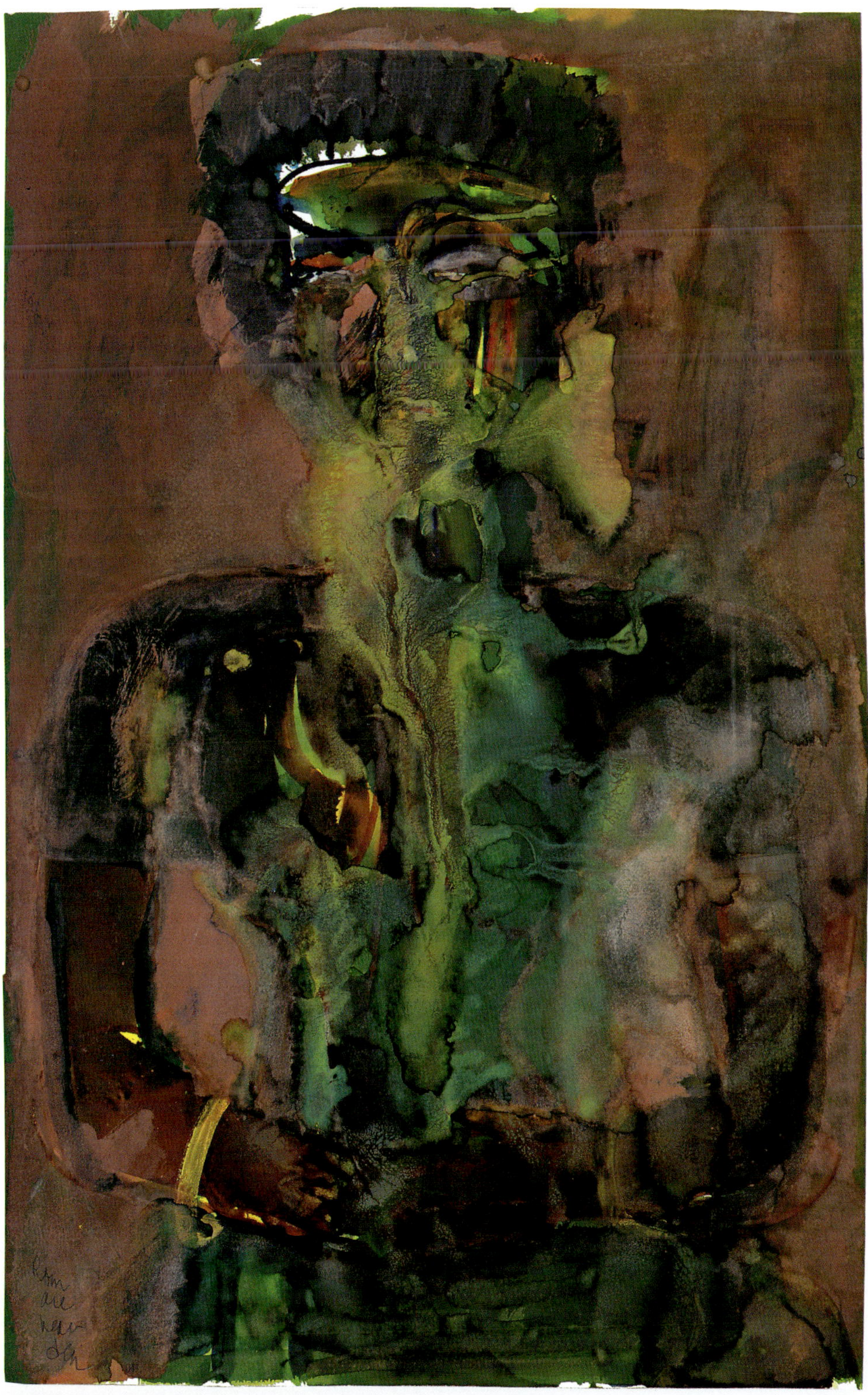

130

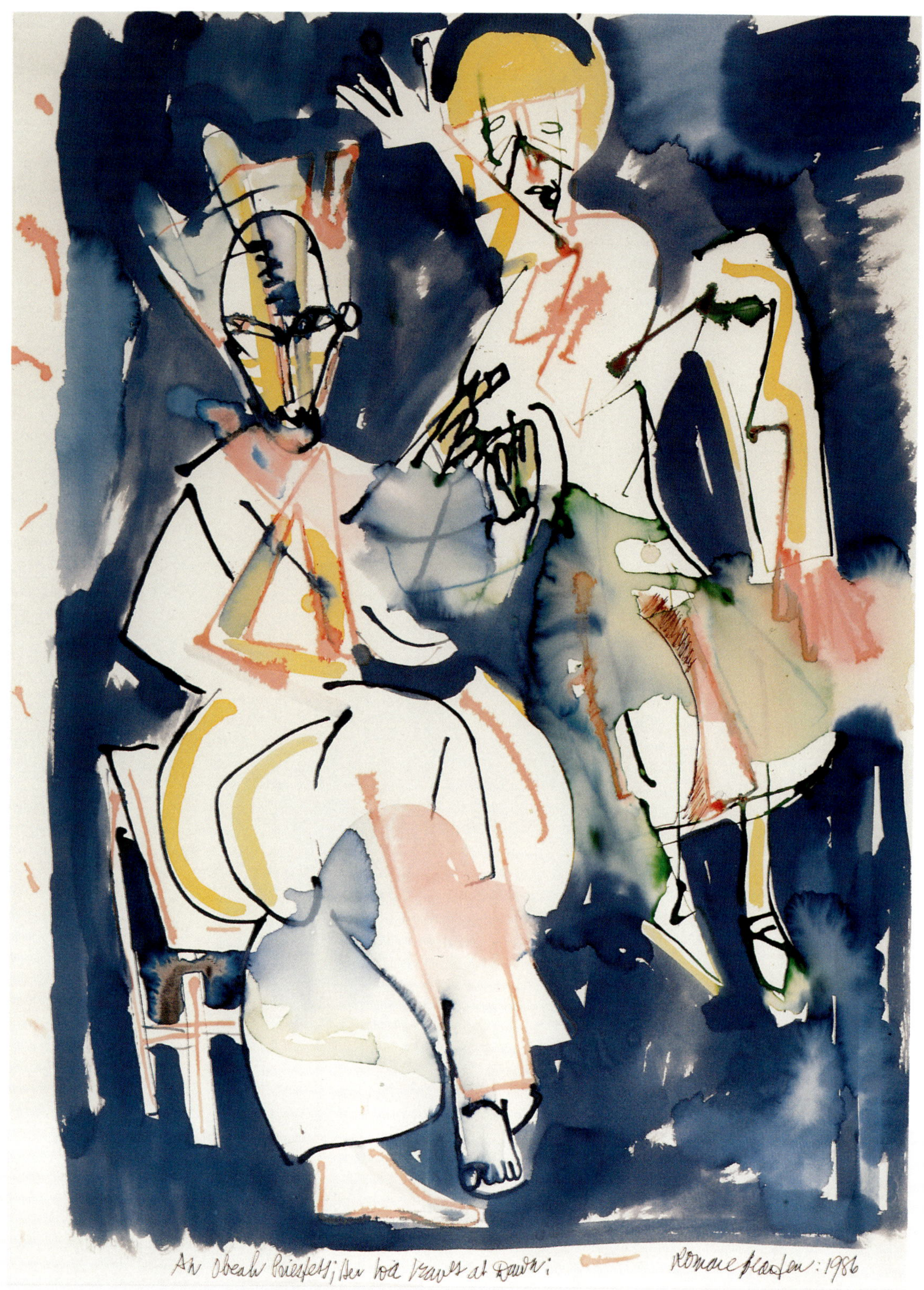

An Obeah Priestess; Her Loa Leaves at Dawn;
Romare Bearden: 1986

131

One Obeah woman thought that she made the sun rise. Each night she held back the moon and conceived a rooster which she hurled out into the sky, and it became the sun.... the darker side of things... is what the Obeah are mostly about. The Obeah go back to the Ashanti. This is magic, not religion, although it is not voodoo. Sometimes the magic and religion interweave, but as I see it, it is more about magic.... I was very interested in the fact that the Obeah and their roots could be traced back to Africa.[208]

By this time Bearden was suffering from a variety of ailments, or so he said, although it seems likely that the bone cancer from which he died in 1988 began taking its toll well before he was willing to acknowledge its presence even to close friends. He worked until the last few months of his life, at the end with frequent assistance from André Thibault/Teabo.[209] Many late works employ a heavier weight paper, or light board, that might have been easier for the artist, in pain, to manipulate. And in some collages one finds shapes with corrugated edges, as if a pattern-making punch tool, rather than scissors, was used, again, perhaps, for easier manipulation. Bearden apparently remained in high spirits, however, and he continued not only to work on watercolors and collages but also to consider mural projects, as evident from the mural for the Charlotte/Mecklenburg County Public Library under consideration at the time of his death. In addition to more than a dozen commissions for murals, throughout his career Bearden completed illustrated books, posters, journal and record album covers, performance brochures, and designs for ballet, theater, and film mentioned in this volume's chronology.

Bearden was a book man at heart, as reader and writer/illustrator/designer. Among his most beautiful book projects are the 1983 Limited Editions Club publication *The Caribbean Poetry of Derek Walcott,* selected and illustrated by Bearden with colorful island scenes (fig. 49); and *Ma Chance's French Caribbean Creole Cooking,* 1985, for which he created a dozen section markers—animated brush drawings of women bearing baskets or other vessels laden with foodstuffs appropriate to each chapter.[210]

At least two projects remained unpublished at the time of his death. One, related to photographer Sam Shaw's 1961 film *Paris Blues,* was to be a collaboration among Bearden, Murray, and Shaw documenting the film's making. Early sketches on tracing paper (fig. 50) suggest its proposed collage-like format, more vividly apparent in the highly finished maquette that recently

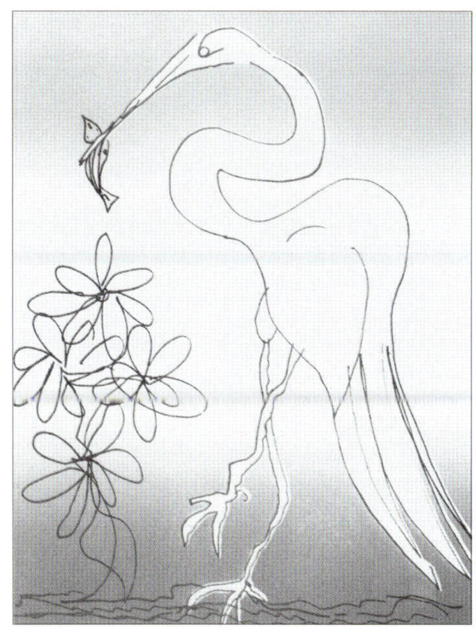

49

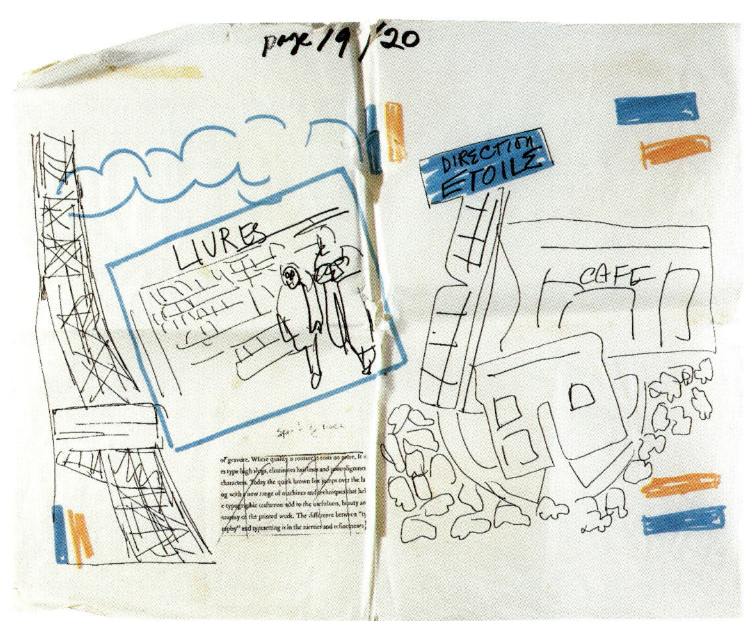

50

131
***An Obeah Princess; Her Loa Leaves at Dawn,* 1986, watercolor and ink on paper, 74.9 x 60.3 (29½ x 23¾). Collection of Stan and Marguerite Lathan**

figure 49
Romare Bearden, lithograph from *The Caribbean Poetry of Derek Walcott and the Art of Romare Bearden,* Limited Editions Club, c. 1983. National Gallery of Art, gift of Jane and Raphael Bernstein

figure 50
Romare Bearden, Layout for *Paris Blues,* c. 1960, collage of various papers with ink and graphite. Collection of Albert Murray

came to light.[211] The other, a book for children both written and illustrated by Bearden, is titled *Li'l Dan, The Drummer Boy: A Civil War Story.* Dated to the early 1980s, it is a poignant story of an African-American boy living on a cotton plantation who made a drum all by himself that played an important role in saving the lives of Union troops who befriended him. Multiple drawings, watercolors, and collages explore variations of more than twenty-five images. Three are included here (nos. 132 a, b, c) revealing the brilliant color and dynamic energy Bearden embedded in the series.[212]

Bearden's art contributed to the accomplishments of Alvin Ailey's American Dance Theater for which he designed costumes and sets. And he set aside specific works for sale on behalf of the Nanette Bearden Contemporary Dance Theater, founded by his wife, and designed covers for program brochures (fig. 51). Like the book projects, designs for at least two ballet productions got no further than the idea stage. The *Conjur Woman* (no. 133), incorporating fabric, safety pins, and string, is exemplary of Bearden's more finished costume conceptions, relating to *The Buzzard and the Snake* in the series for *Bayou Fever.*[213] Similarly *Village of Yo* (no. 134) from about the same date recalls imagery of the 1960s, but also relates to one of two backdrops accompanying watercolor designs for fourteen costumes (two with collage) for a ballet, *Conjur: A Masked Folk Ballet* (nos. 135 a–p). They were given by Bearden to Parmenia Migel Ekstrom, a ballet historian and

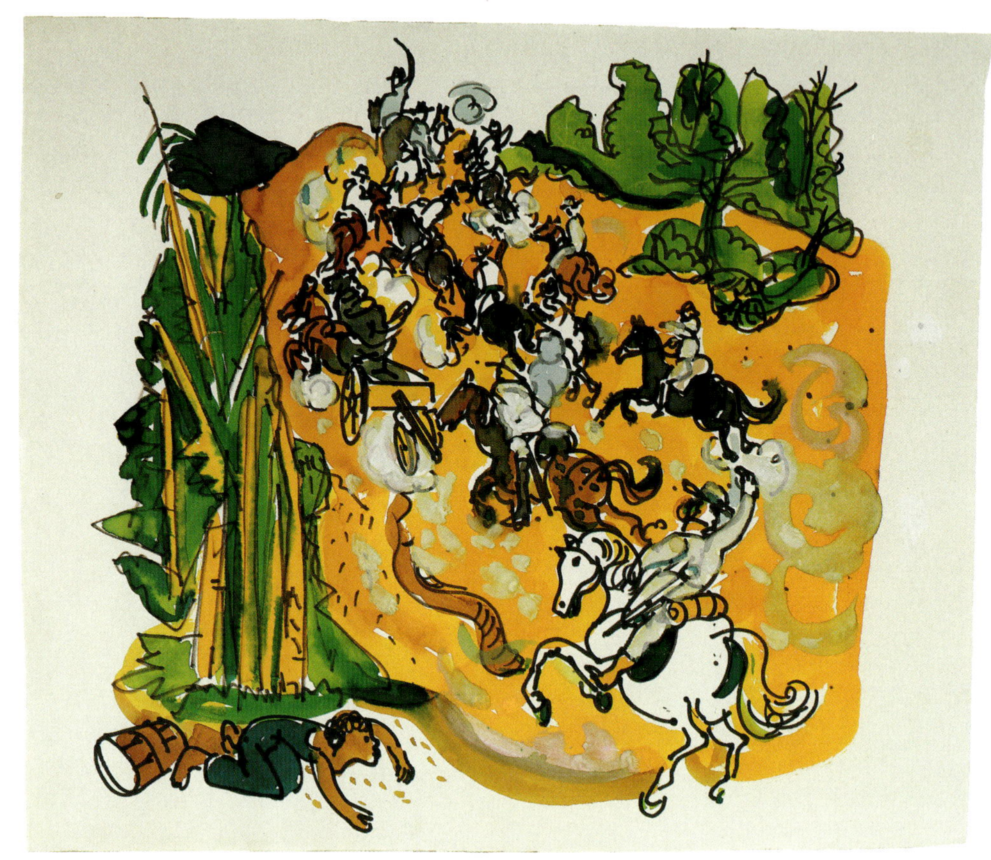

132 a

132 a
***Li'l Dan, The Drummer Boy: A Civil War Story*, c. 1983, watercolor, gouache, and ink on paper, 45.7 x 55.9 (18 x 22). Estate of Romare Bearden, courtesy of Romare Bearden Foundation, New York**

132 b
***Li'l Dan, The Drummer Boy: A Civil War Story*, c. 1983, watercolor, gouache, and ink with paper collage on paper, 33 x 44.5 (13 x 17 1/2). Estate of Romare Bearden, courtesy of Romare Bearden Foundation, New York**

132 c
***Li'l Dan, The Drummer Boy: A Civil War Story*, c. 1983, watercolor and ink on paper, 33.7 x 48.3 (13 1/4 x 19). Estate of Romare Bearden, courtesy of Romare Bearden Foundation, New York**

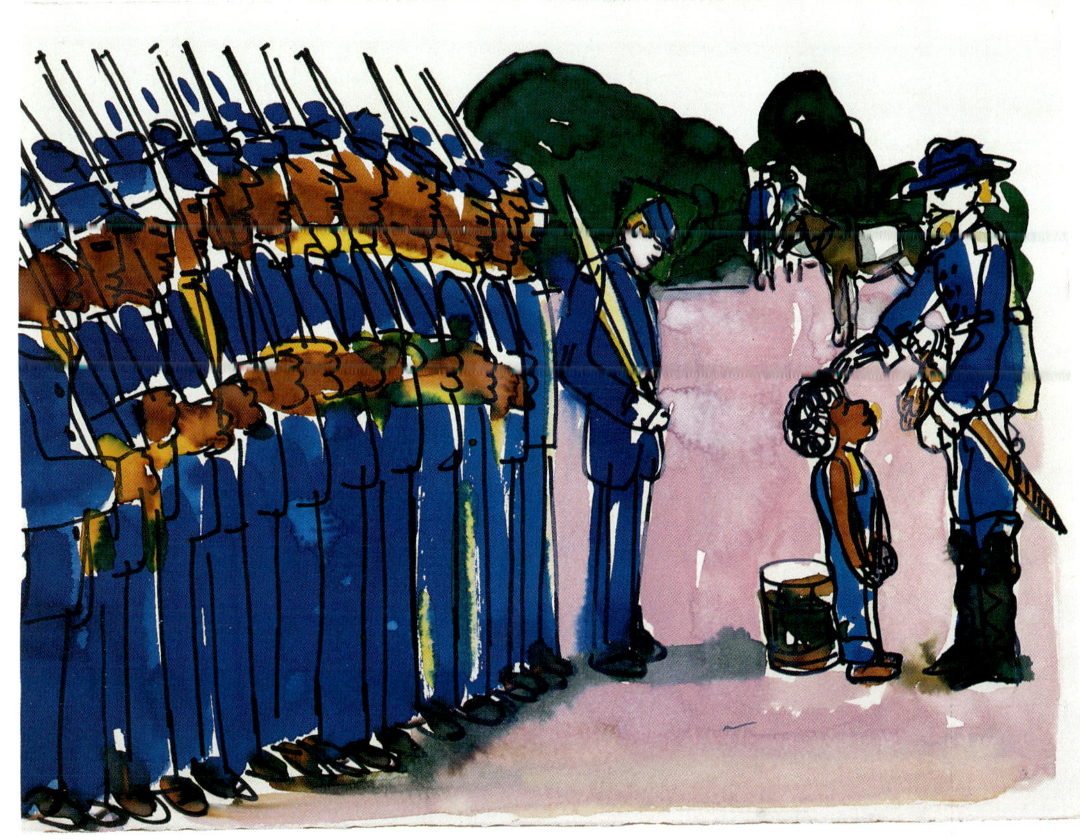

132b

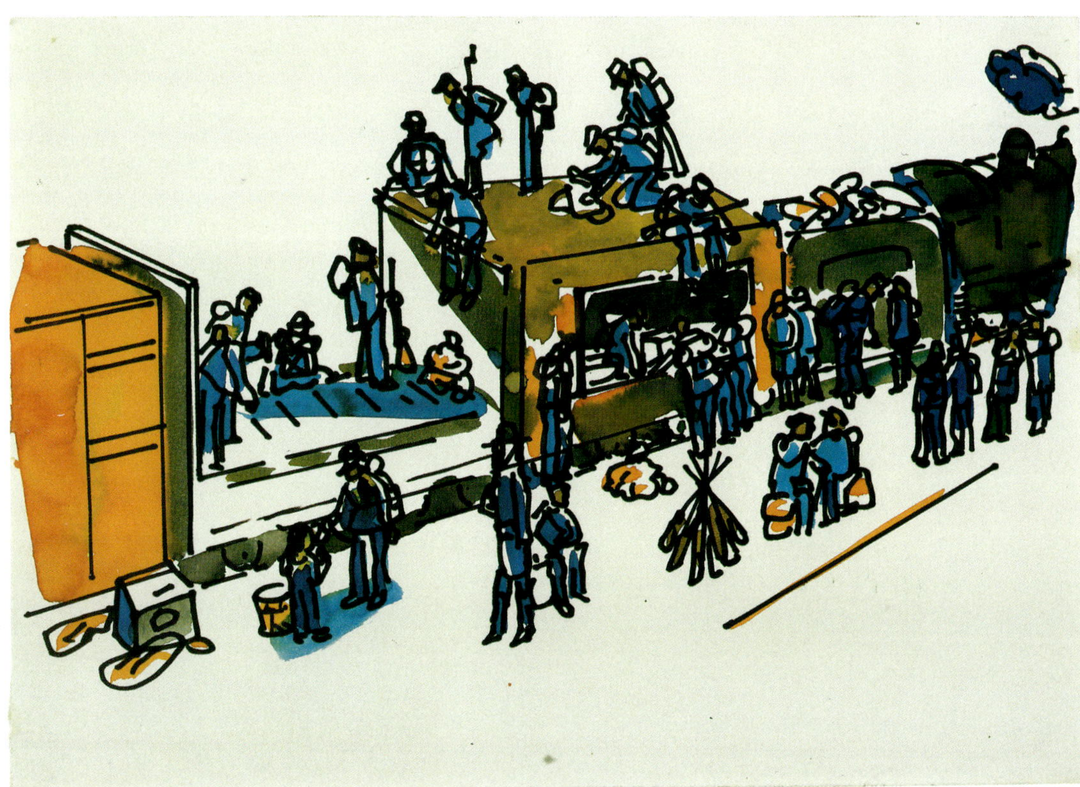

132c

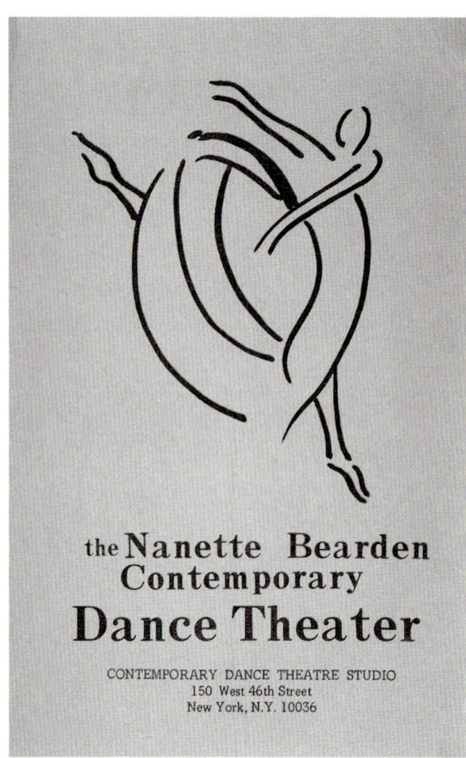

51

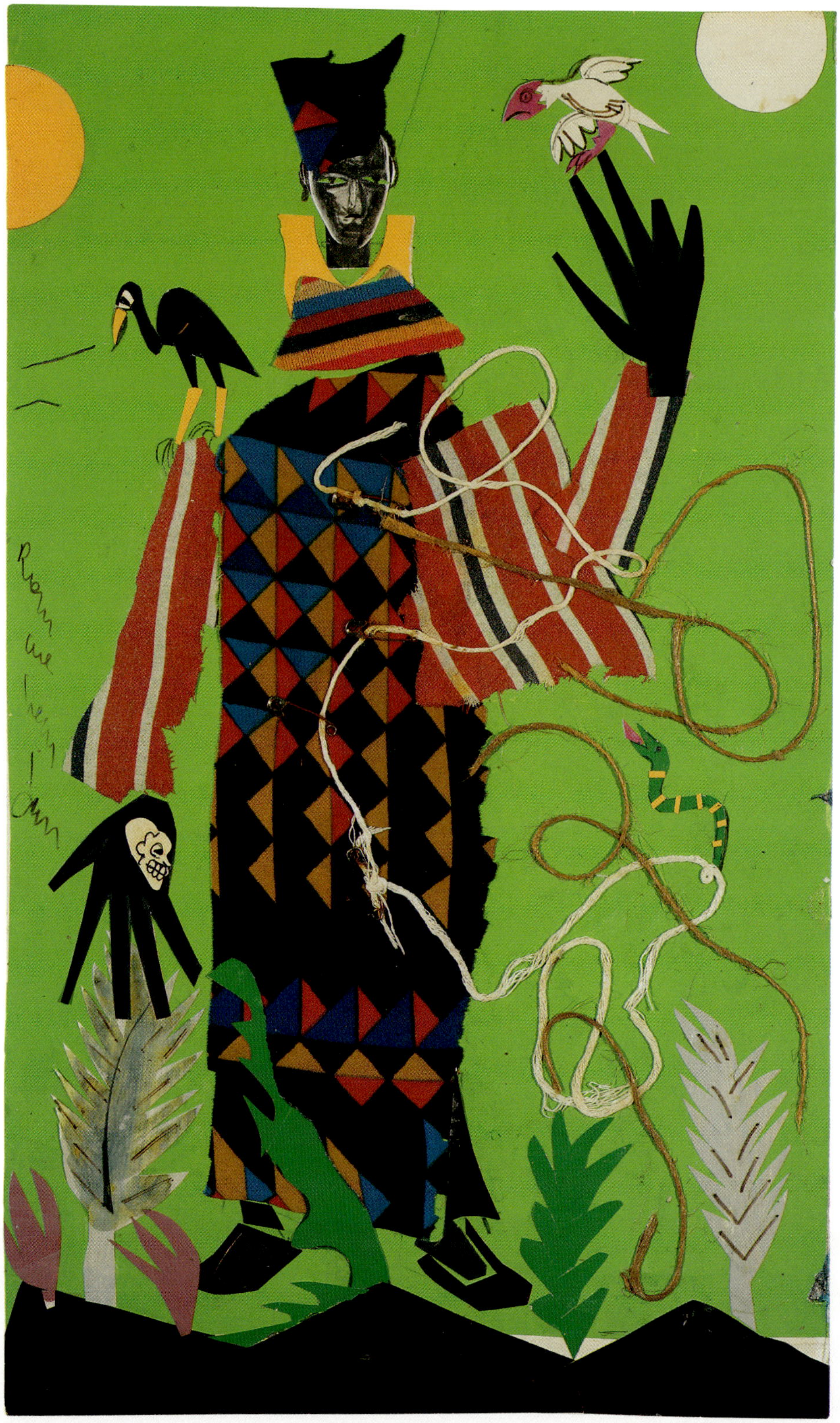

133

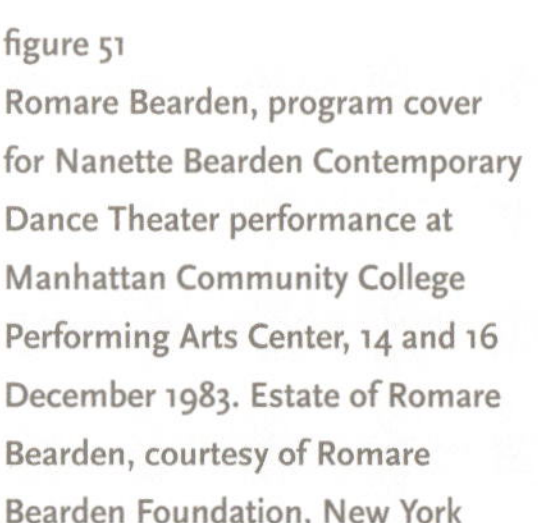

figure 51
Romare Bearden, program cover for Nanette Bearden Contemporary Dance Theater performance at Manhattan Community College Performing Arts Center, 14 and 16 December 1983. Estate of Romare Bearden, courtesy of Romare Bearden Foundation, New York

the wife of Arne Ekstrom, accompanied by a two-act libretto written by Bearden and several pages of suggested choreography (it is not clear by whom). The story is a fascinating visualization of the assembled costumed figures, set before the backdrops, a battle between good and evil with the first act set in the square of a southern village and the second in the City of Brass; the train and the Conjur Woman, two of Bearden's primary motifs throughout his life, play central roles.

While ballet was primary, Bearden also made his mark in film, as seen in the *Gloria* watercolors, and theater, designing a set for the initial presentation of Ed Bullins' play, *House Party*, at the American Place Theatre (1973). His idea for this design is recorded in a collage, *Urban Street Scene* (the David C. Driskell Collection), and a related screenprint.[214]

Bearden's immense career was a stellar one. In 1987 he was awarded the National Medal of Arts by Ronald Reagan. He had some ten successful solo museum exhibitions during his lifetime, participated extensively in group exhibitions (more than one hundred fifty are listed in the Chronology in this volume), was elected to the American Academy of Arts and Letters, the National Academy of Design, and the Black Academy of Arts and Letters. In 1960 he formed a professional relationship with the Michel Warren Gallery that evolved into Cordier & Ekstrom, Inc. This association with Arne Ekstrom

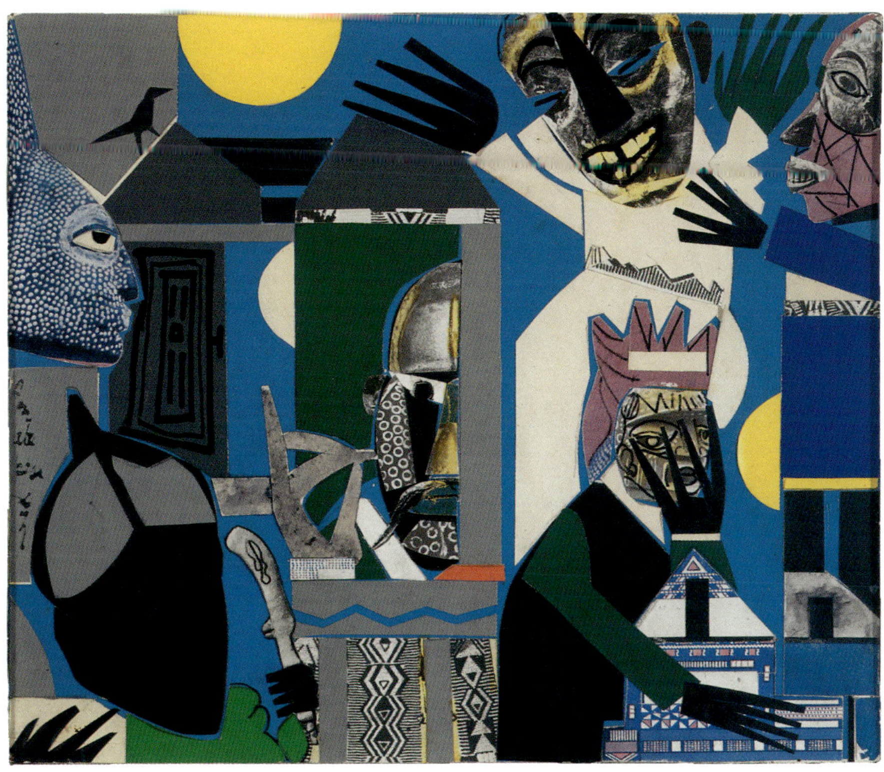

134

133
***The Conjur Woman*, c. 1977, collage of various papers with fabric, string, pins, and ink on cardboard, 58.4 x 38.1 (23 x 15). Evelyn N. Boulware**

134
***Village of Yo*, 1977, collage of various papers with ink on fiberboard, 24.8 x 29.9 (9¾ x 11¾). James R. Haynes, Washington, D.C.**

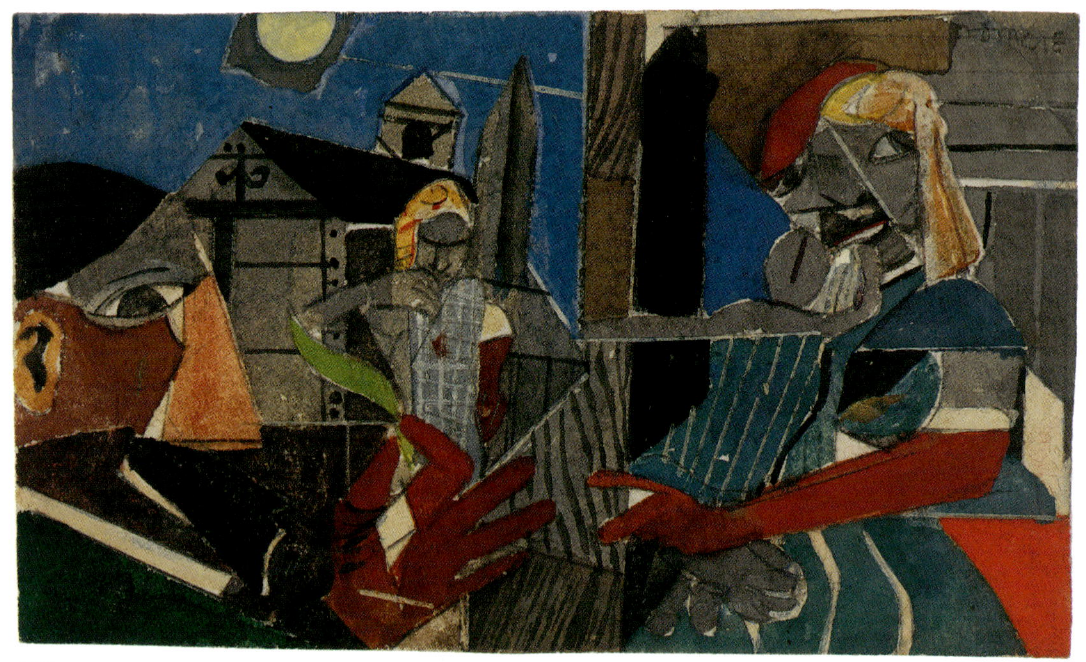

135a

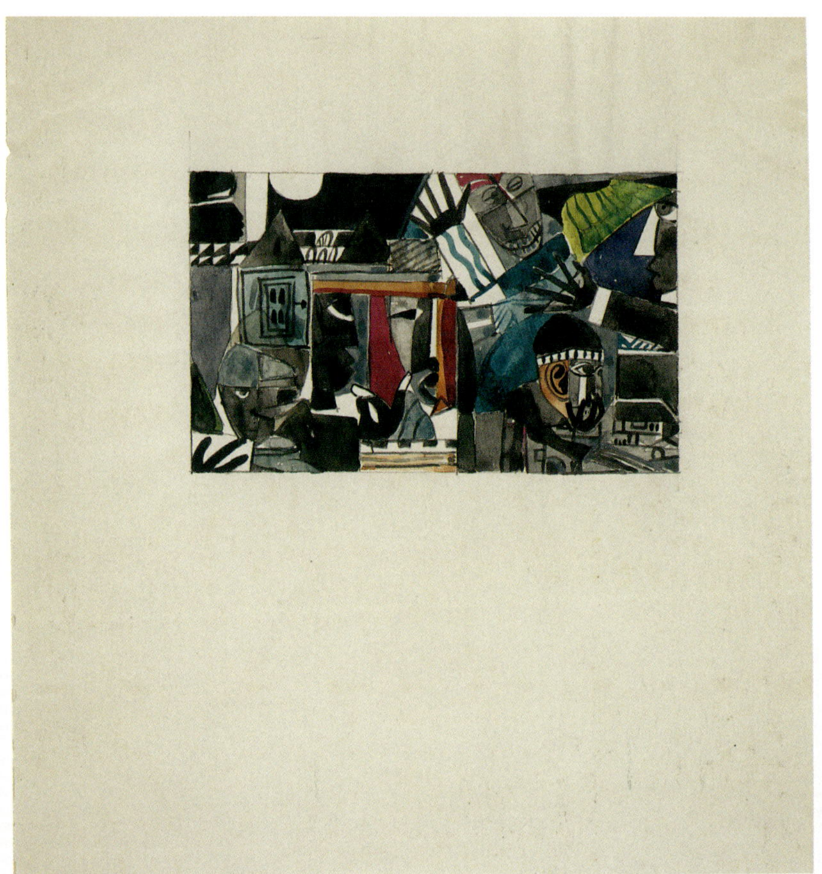

135b

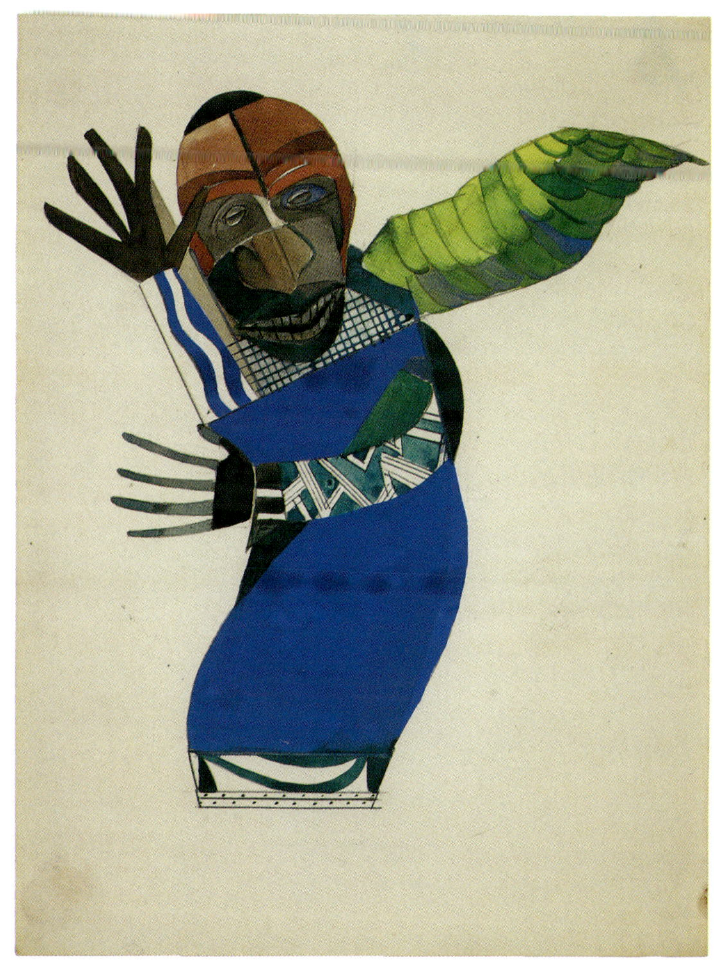

135c

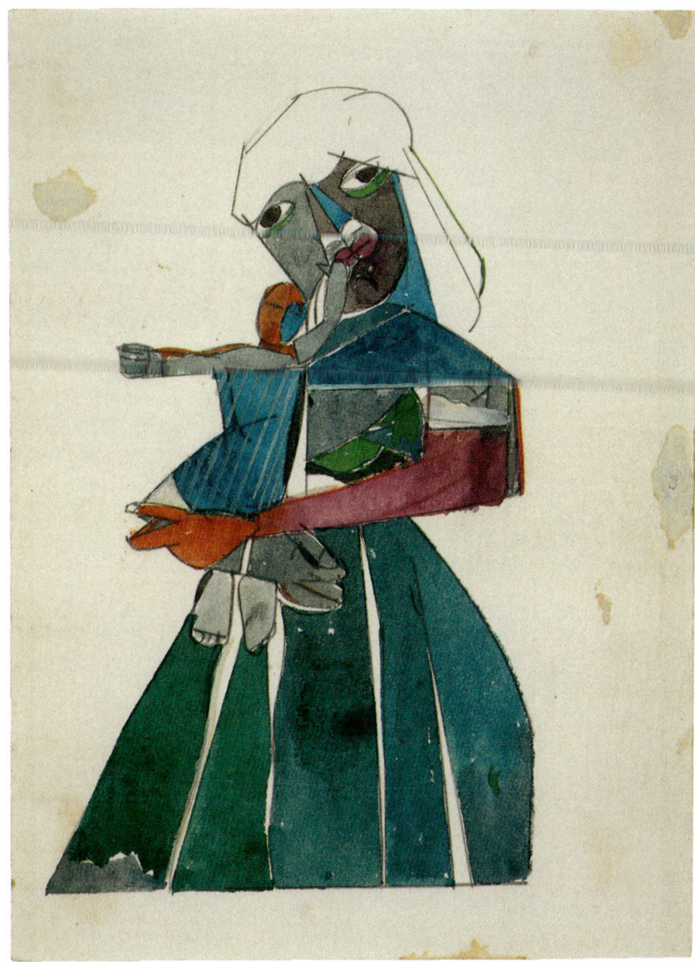

135d

135a
Conjur: A Masked Folk Ballet [La Primavera], c. 1970, watercolor and graphite on paper, 40.6 x 30.5 (16 x 12). Courtesy of Ekstrom & Ekstrom, Inc., New York

135b
Conjur: A Masked Folk Ballet [City of Brass], c. 1970, watercolor, ink, and graphite on paper, 40.6 x 30.5 (16 x 12). Courtesy of Ekstrom & Ekstrom, Inc., New York

135c
Conjur: A Masked Folk Ballet [Conjur Woman], c. 1970, watercolor, gouache, ink, and graphite on paper, 38.1 x 30.5 (15 x 12). Courtesy of Ekstrom & Ekstrom, Inc., New York

135d
Conjur: A Masked Folk Ballet [Mother and Child], c. 1970, watercolor, gouache, ink, and graphite on paper, 38.1 x 30.5 (15 x 12). Courtesy of Ekstrom & Ekstrom, Inc., New York

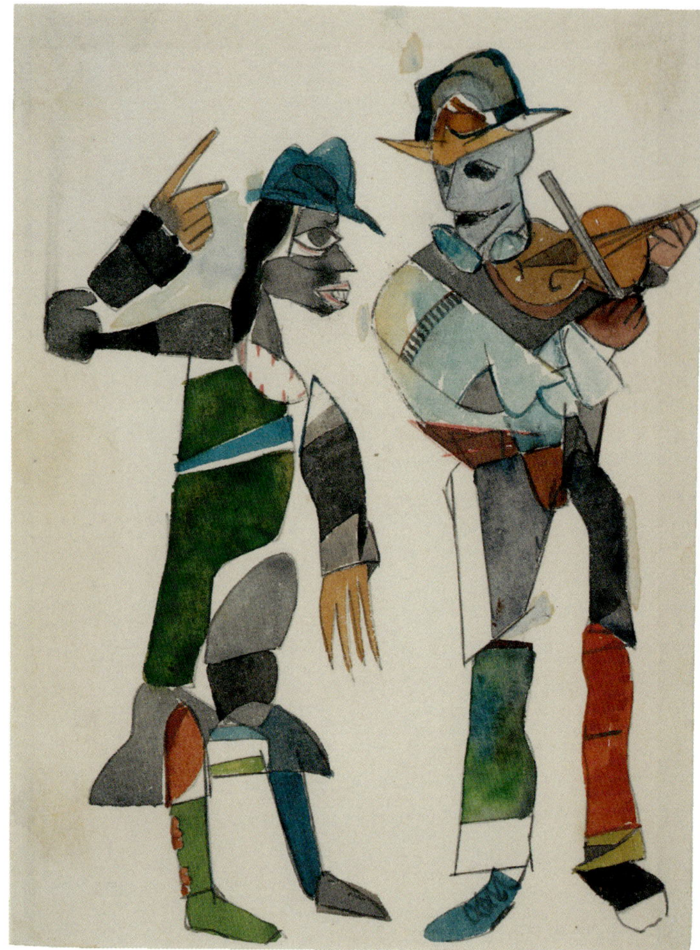

135f

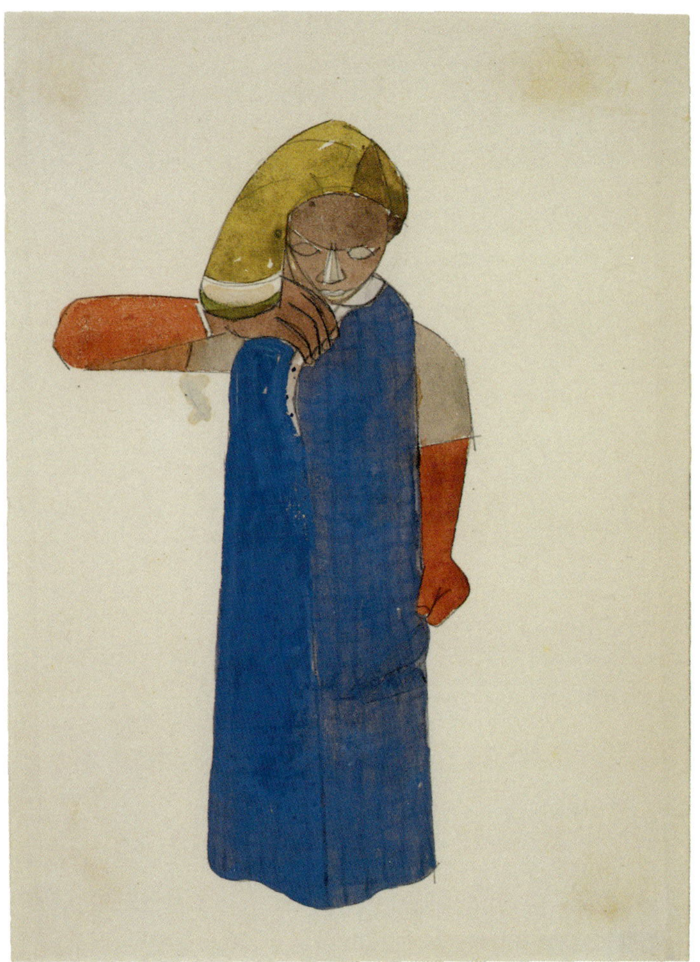

135e

135e
Conjur: A Masked Folk Ballet [Woman in Blue Dress], c. 1970, watercolor, gouache, and graphite on paper, 38.1 x 30.5 (15 x 12). Courtesy of Ekstrom & Ekstrom, Inc., New York

135f
Conjur: A Masked Folk Ballet [Two Men, One Playing Violin], c. 1970, watercolor, ink, and graphite on paper, 38.1 x 30.5 (15 x 12). Courtesy of Ekstrom & Ekstrom, Inc., New York

135g
Conjur: A Masked Folk Ballet [Two Men with Palm Leaves], c. 1970, watercolor, gouache, and graphite on paper, 38.1 x 30.5 (15 x 12). Courtesy of Ekstrom & Ekstrom, Inc., New York

135h
Conjur: A Masked Folk Ballet [Two Men Wearing Masks], c. 1970, collage of various papers with watercolor, gouache, and graphite on cardboard, 38.1 x 30.5 (15 x 12). Courtesy of Ekstrom & Ekstrom, Inc., New York

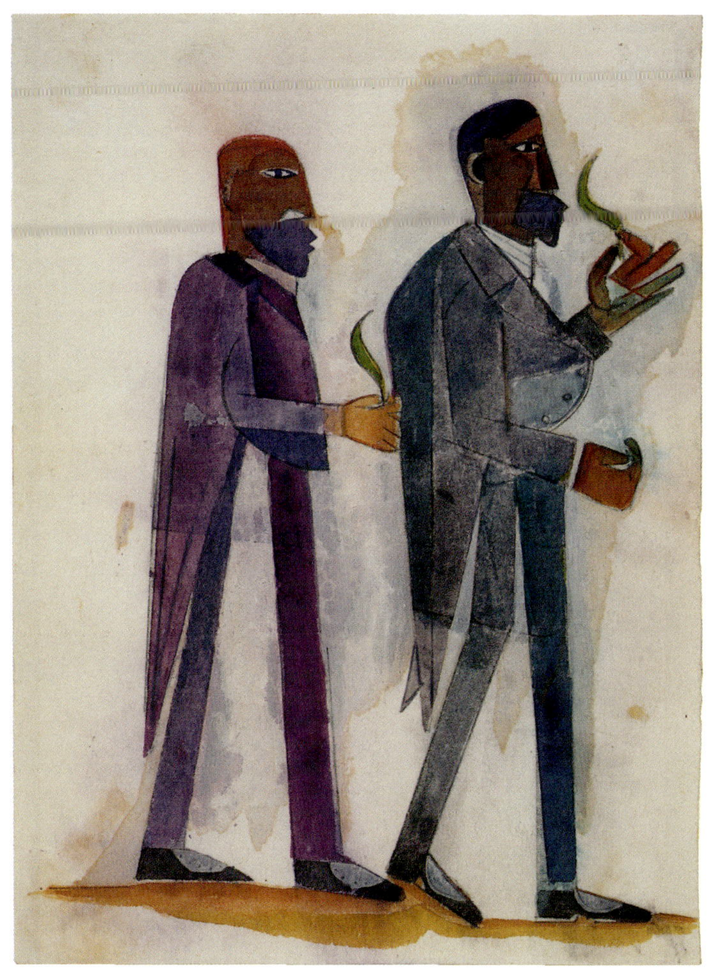

135g

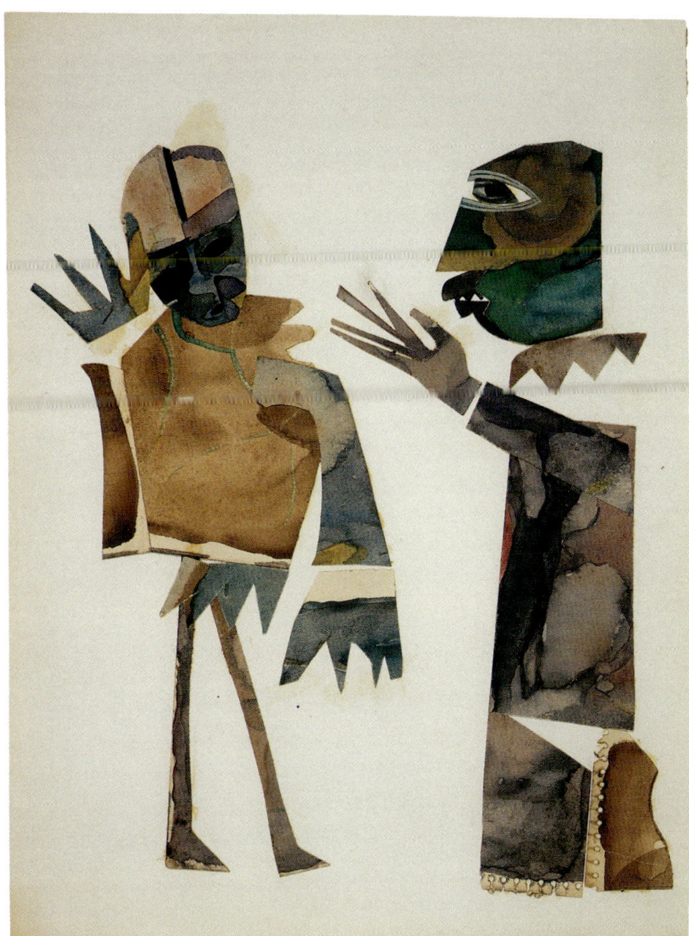

135h

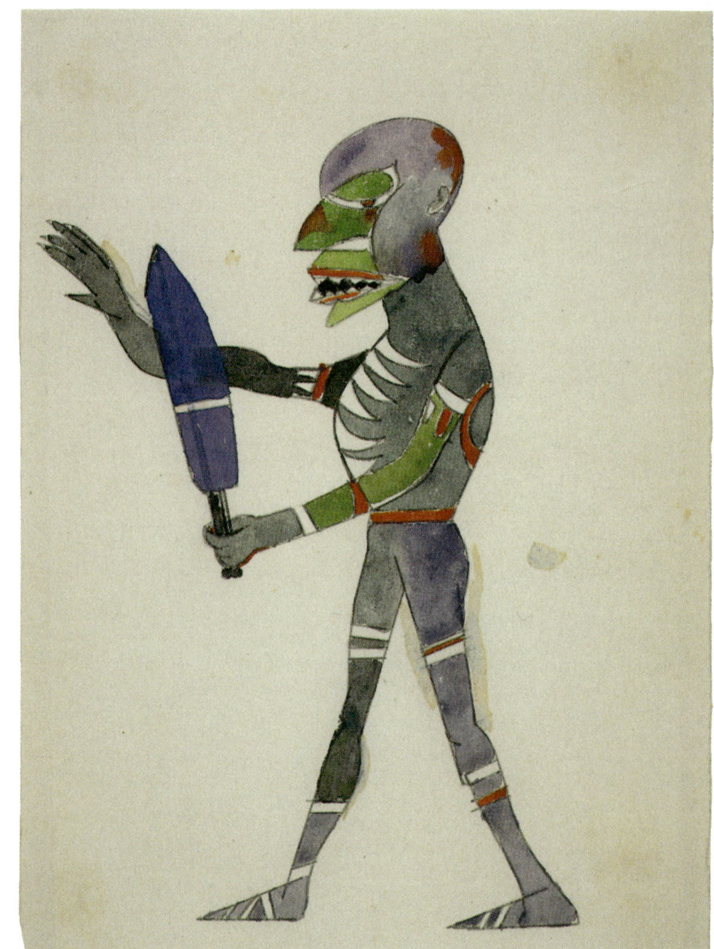

135j

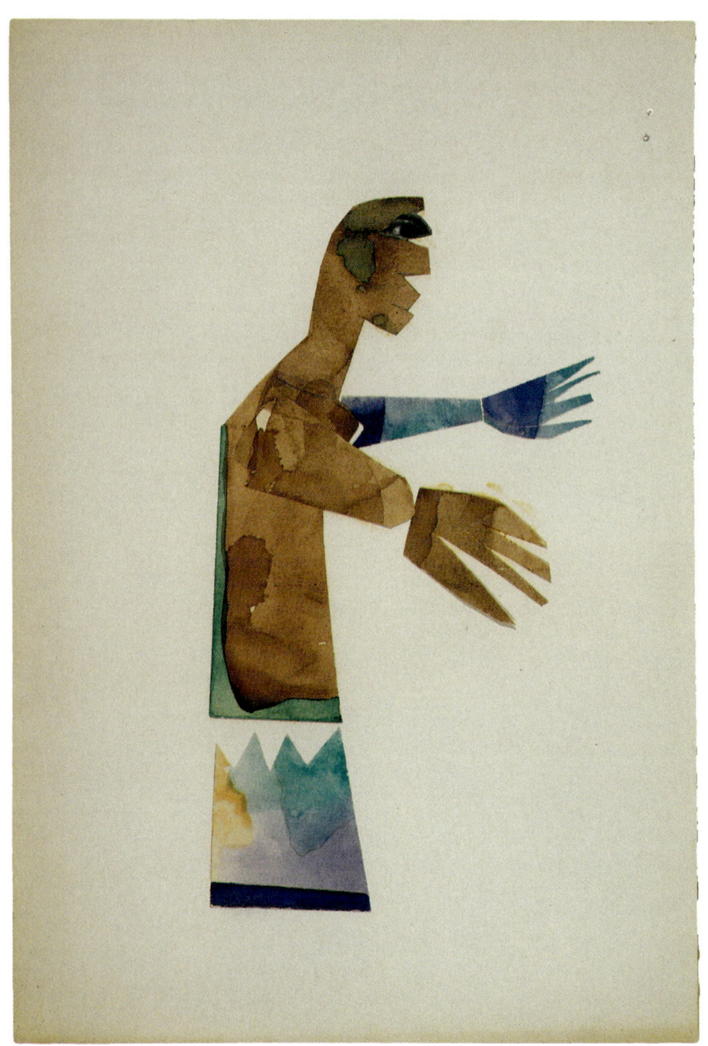

135i

135i
Conjur: A Masked Folk Ballet [Man with Arms Outstretched], c. 1970, collage of various papers with watercolor and graphite on cardboard, 38.1 x 30.5 (15 x 12). Courtesy of Ekstrom & Ekstrom, Inc., New York

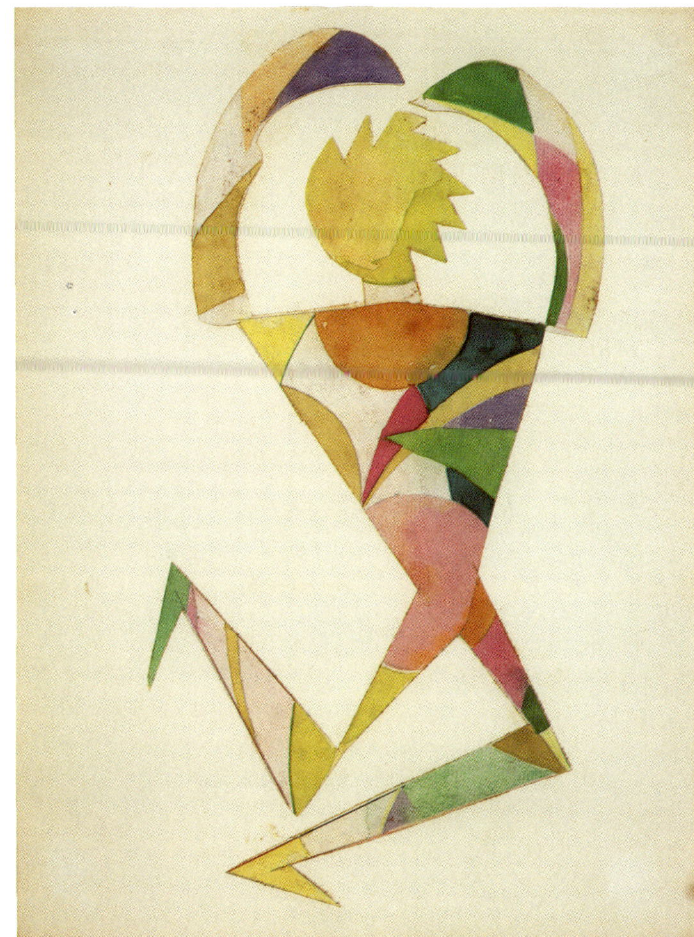

135l

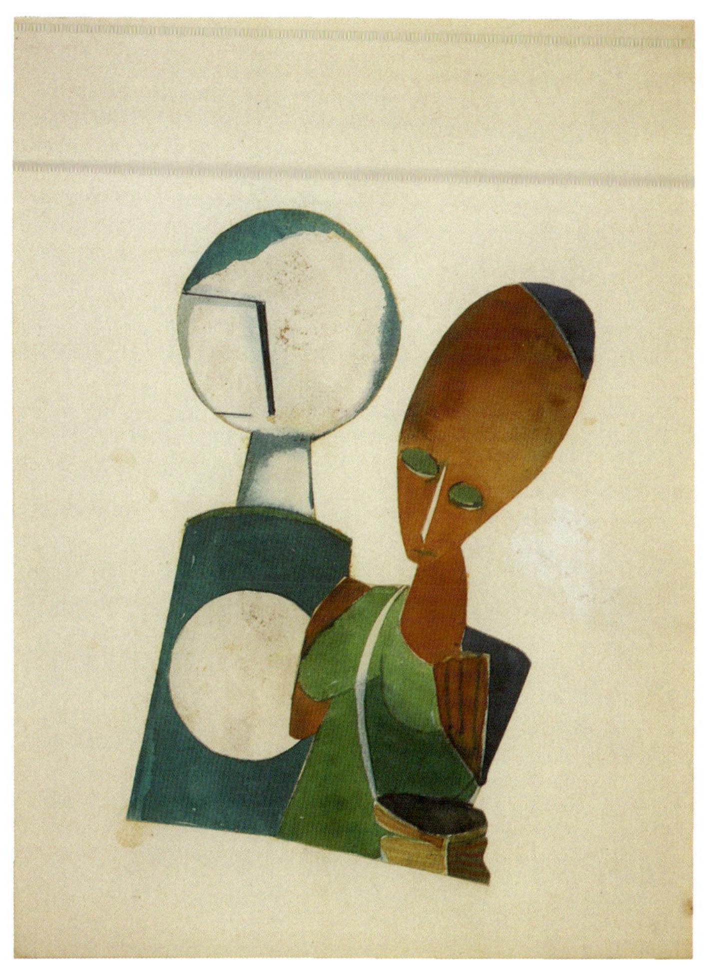

135k

135j
Conjur: A Masked Folk Ballet [Man with Dagger], c. 1970, watercolor, gouache, ink, and graphite on paper, 38.1 x 30.5 (15 x 12). Courtesy of Ekstrom & Ekstrom, Inc., New York

135k
Conjur: A Masked Folk Ballet [Two Figures], c. 1970, collage of various papers with watercolor, gouache, ink, and graphite on paper, 40.6 x 30.5 (16 x 12). Courtesy of Ekstrom & Ekstrom, Inc., New York

135l
Conjur: A Masked Folk Ballet [Harlequin], c. 1970, collage of various papers with watercolor, gouache, ink, and graphite on paper, 40.6 x 30.5 (16 x 12). Courtesy of Ekstrom & Ekstrom, Inc., New York

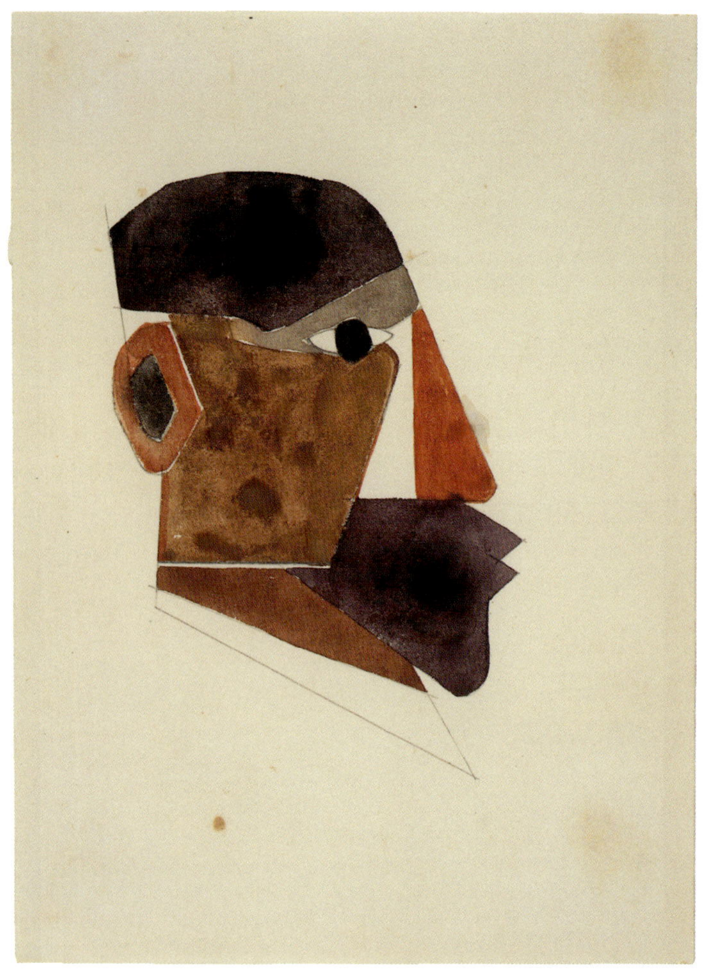

135 m

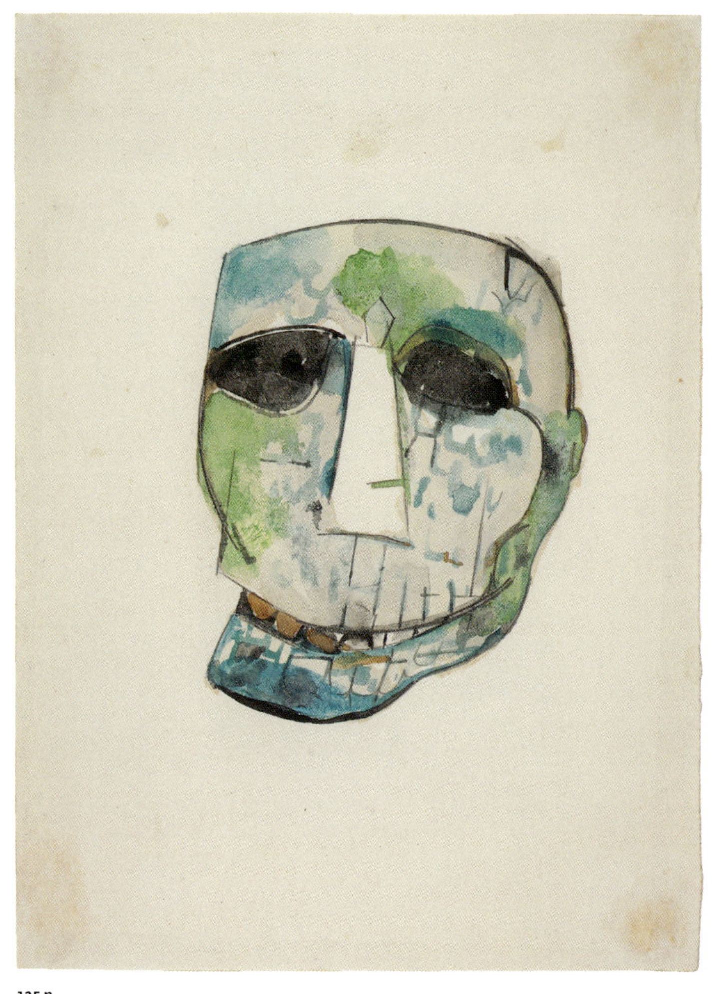

135 n

135 m
Conjur: A Masked Folk Ballet [Multi-color Profile Facing Right], c. 1970, watercolor and graphite on paper, 38.1 x 30.5 (15 x 12). Courtesy of Ekstrom & Ekstrom, Inc., New York

135 n
Conjur: A Masked Folk Ballet [Skull], c. 1970, watercolor, gouache, ink, and graphite on paper, 38.1 x 30.5 (15 x 12). Courtesy of Ekstrom & Ekstrom, Inc., New York

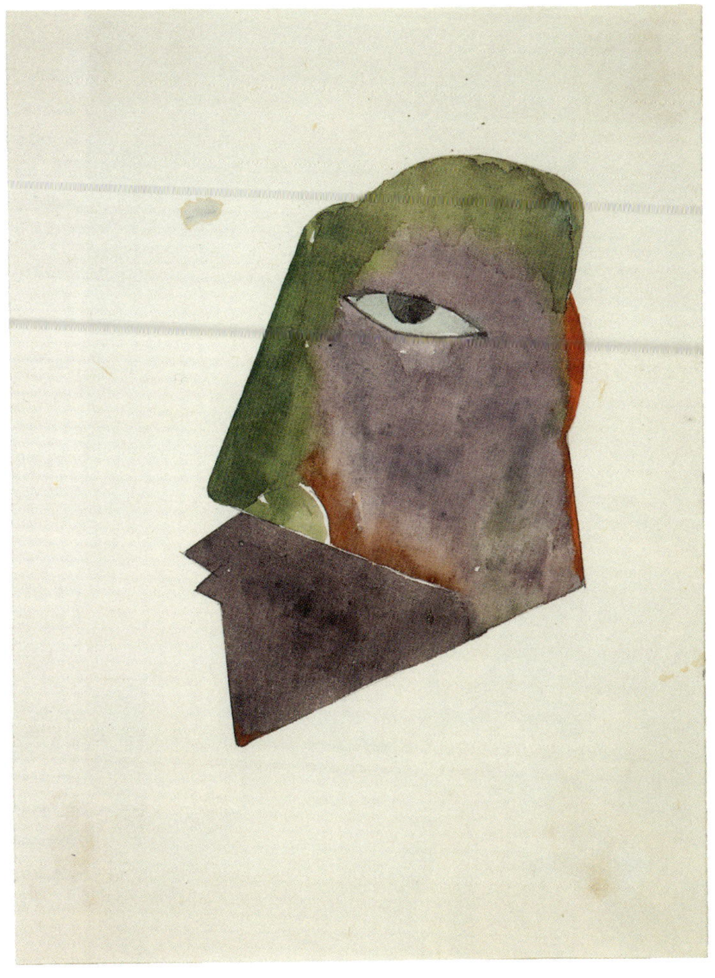

135o

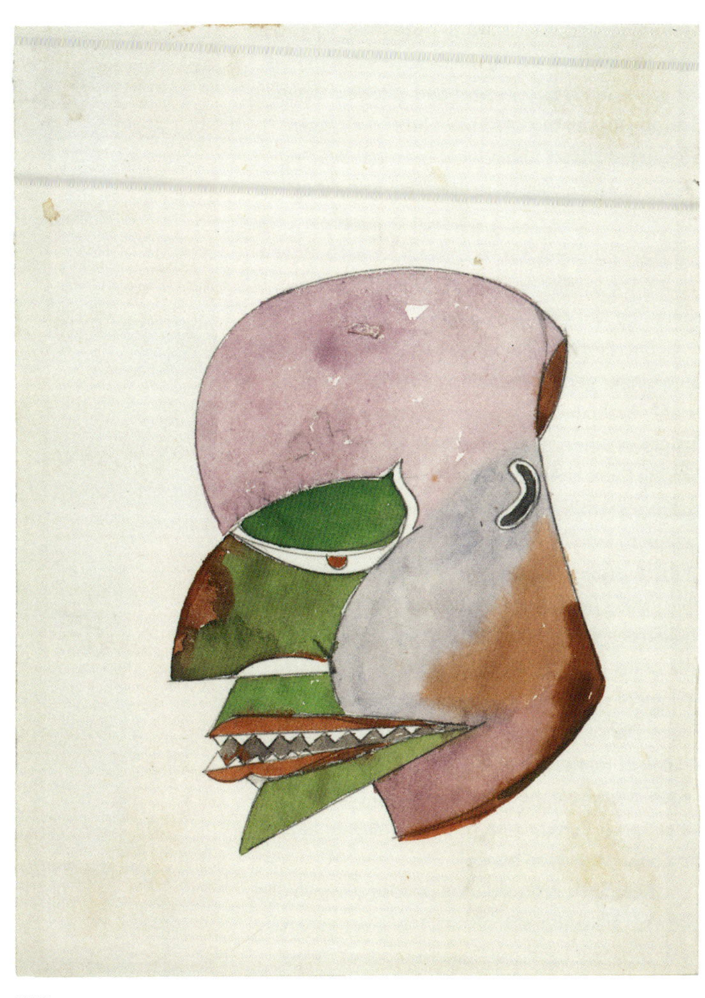

135p

135o
Conjur: A Masked Folk Ballet [Multi-color Profile Facing Left], c. 1970, watercolor, gouache, and graphite on paper, 38.1 x 30.5 (15 x 12). Courtesy of Ekstrom & Ekstrom, Inc., New York

135p
Conjur: A Masked Folk Ballet [Profile with Jagged Teeth], c. 1970, watercolor, gouache, and graphite on paper, 38.1 x 30.5 (15 x 12). Courtesy of Ekstrom & Ekstrom, Inc., New York

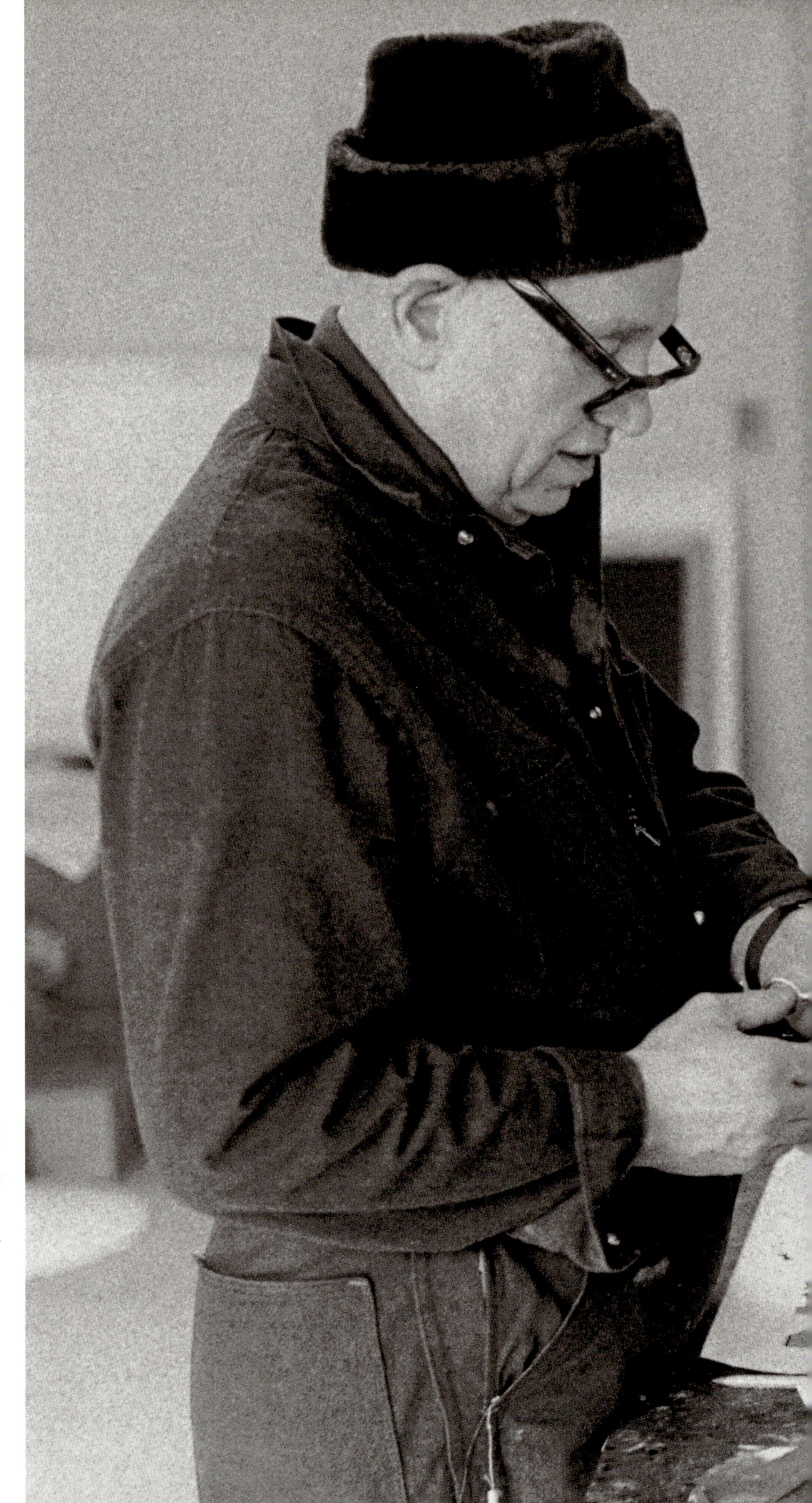

Bearden's Musée Imaginaire

SARAH KENNEL

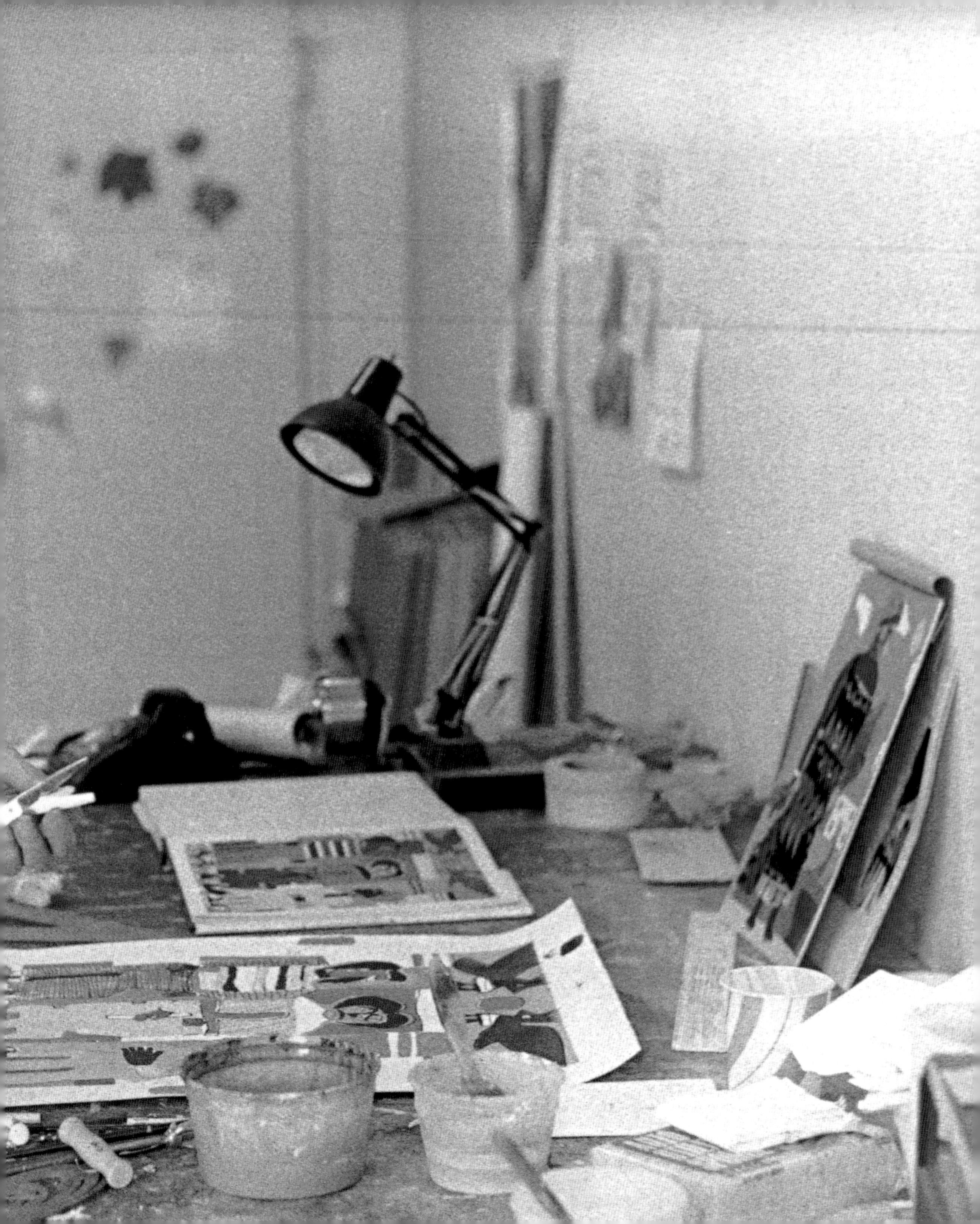

Writing to friend and fellow painter Carl Holty in the spring of 1953, Romare Bearden proposed the following experiment. "Take some of the Poussains [*sic*] and have reverse plate Photostats made, so that the figures are all black against a white background, and I bet you'd arrive at the damnest 'mau-mau' dance ever. This is a thought, maybe I'd just like to see how you would do it, before I try something like it."[1] As far as we know, Holty did not pursue Bearden's suggestion. However, Bearden's proposal to create new imagery through a reverse-plate photostat of the work of the French seventeenth-century painter Nicolas Poussin is telling because it neatly encapsulates three artistic strategies that Bearden consistently employed over the course of his rich and varied career: first, the copious use of photographic and photomechanical reproductions, whether as visual source, study aid, or as pictorial element within an original composition; second, the selective appropriation of canonical images from an inherited tradition of Western painting; third, the conscious historical revision of that tradition in order to represent the complexity of twentieth-century African-American subjectivity and identity. In using photomechanical means of reproduction to transform Poussin's classical figures into exotic dancing ones, "all black against a white background," Bearden not only imagines the inversion of painting's traditional "color" values but also locates within the very forms of Western art the possibility for a celebratory reconfiguration of its established conventions.

Taking the art of the past as a starting point for the production of new forms was second nature to Bearden. Throughout his forty-plus year career, Bearden studied, copied, and revised images culled from the painterly traditions of Western art, an endeavor greatly aided by the widespread availability of photographic reproductions of art works. Of course, Bearden was not alone in these practices. The Western tradition of image making has been built upon acts of copying, creative appropriation, and outright citation.[2] The artistic copy, whether produced for a market or as part of a pedagogical program, boasts a long history within visual culture. Similarly, the selective poaching of visual motifs has played an integral part in both the development and institutionalization of an established canon of Western art as well as in modernist and post-modernist revisions of that canon.[3] While each act of artistic appropriation is undoubtedly motivated by a specific combination of historical conditions, aesthetic and intellectual demands, and individual intentions, the impetus to borrow and transform from an inherited legacy of visual riches has been more or less a constant force in the history of Western art.

The notion that art produces art via dynamic processes of repetition, identification, and transformation forms the basic argument of André Malraux's 1951 book *Les Voix du Silence* (translated in 1953 as *The Voices of Silence*), a work to which Bearden often referred.[4] In their coauthored book *The Painter's Mind: A Study of the Relations of Structure and Space in Painting,* Bearden and Holty assert that "Malraux's principle 'art through art' remains of paramount importance."[5] This principle is first encountered in the opening section of *The Voices of Silence,* entitled the "Musée Imaginaire," or the "Museum without Walls." In what is the book's core argument, Malraux describes how the invention of photography, and consequently the enormous proliferation of visual reproductions, enabled the creation of a virtual "museum without walls" which "will carry infinitely farther that revelation of the world of art, limited perforce, which the 'real' museums offer us within their walls."[6] While the photographic reproduction of art works denuded them of specific qualities—Malraux admits that "in our museum... picture, fresco, miniature and stained glass window seem one and the same family... all have become color plates"—the aleatory and mobile nature of the photograph enables the viewer to rewrite the history of art. Thus, although it imposes a "specious unity" on a diverse world of forms, the photographic reproduction transforms the history of art into an immediately available, expanded visual field in which the viewer is free to discover formal and psychological affinities across historical and cultural boundaries. Ultimately, for Malraux, the photographic reproduction functions as a democratizing and universalizing force: "While photography is bringing a profusion of masterpieces to the artists, these latter have been revising their notion of what it is that makes the masterpiece."[7] And just as the photographic reproduction enables artists to rewrite the artistic canon, it also opens up to viewers a "new domain... [which] is for the first time the common heritage of all mankind."[8]

CREATING THE COPY

While Malraux's book contributed to Bearden's understanding of the history of art as a repository of forms and objects available to, and awaiting transformation by, the modern viewer/artist, Bearden's grasp of both the pedagogical and democratizing possibilities of a photographic history of art preceded the publication of *The Voices of Silence.* Though he had studied some art history as a student at New York University, Bearden began to systematically analyze old master paintings and drawings under the tutelage of George Grosz at the Art Students League. Bearden recalled in 1969 that it was Grosz who first "led me to study composition, through the analysis of Brueghel and the great Dutch masters, and who in the process of refining my draftsmanship, initiated me into the magic world of Ingres, Durer, Holbein, and Poussin."[9] Although none of Bearden's student studies of old masters appear to have survived, we may assume on the basis of this statement that the pedagogical formation at the Art Students League included the study of old master paintings and drawings.[10]

The extent to which Bearden's art historical investigations shaped his pictorial production during the late 1930s and early 1940s is less clear. There is no doubt Bearden was aware of the knotty issues surrounding "influence" and the quest for artistic originality. In his article "The Negro Artist and Modern Art," published in 1934 in *Opportunity: A Journal of Negro Life,* Bearden recognized that "Practically all the great artists have accepted the influence of others. But the difference lies in the fact that the artist with vision sees his material, chooses, changes, and by integrating what he has learned with his own experience, finally molds something distinctly personal."[11] Bearden later recalled that his move away from his social realist, Mexican muralist influenced idiom of the early 1940s toward a more abstract and geometric style was driven in part by a desire "to discover a personal way of expression that might be called new... I was trying to find out what was in me that was common to other men."[12] Increasingly bold and abstract, Bearden's visual language of the mid-to-late 1940s bristles with a bellicose energy that sharply distinguishes these images from stylized paintings he produced in the early years of the decade.

While this goal—to discover a personal mode of expression that was nevertheless "common to other men"—may have provided the impetus for change, Bearden's thorough study of the spatial and coloristic qualities of Byzantine and early Renaissance painting offered the means through which this change could be effected. In a 1945 letter to friend and fellow artist Walter Quirt, Bearden reported that his investigations into the design and space of Byzantine and early Italian Renaissance painting was finally bearing fruit: "I honestly believe the new stuff is better than anything before. I've studied *space* rather hard, so that the paintings are more unified now—and the fantasy is held together... I've tried to learn the design of pictures studying Byzantine painting, and the old Italian primitives, etc."[13] In another letter to Quirt dated July 10, 1945, Bearden describes his attempts to instill a sense of time through the construction of pictorial space: "I'm beginning to see what time sense means in a picture.... I'm trying to get things held together, but lead the eye from section to section—taking the time say as music does—a composition extended in time.... So, now I'm looking hard at Poussain [*sic*], Gozzolli, Byzantine mosaics, but I believe in a good sense—not to seek surface elements but essences."[14]

The search for "essences" did not stop Bearden from integrating—sometimes quite literally—into his watercolors the compositional and spatial lessons gleaned from his study of Byzantine and early Renaissance painting. For example, in his c. 1945 watercolor *You Are Dead Forever* (fig. 1), which was exhibited at the Samuel M. Kootz Gallery in 1946 as part of the series of works inspired by Lorca, Bearden adapted the composition of the panel of *The Burial of Christ* from the *Maestà* altarpiece by the Sienese artist Duccio di Buoninsegna (fig. 2).[15] Duccio's masterwork, a multipanel altarpiece that illustrates the life of the virgin, the life of Christ, and the passion of Christ, seems to have held particular sway over Bearden, for the latter modeled several of the watercolors in the Passion of Christ series after narrative panels of the Maestà altarpiece.

Duccio was not the only artist to whom Bearden looked for pictorial instruction. German Renaissance artist Dirk Bouts' painting *John the Baptist Pointing to Christ: "Behold the Lamb of God" (Ecce Agnus Dei)* (c. 1462/1464) served as the basis for the compositional structure of Bearden's 1946 watercolor *Untitled (Baptism)* (figs. 3, 4).[16] Though it lacks the exquisitely refined detail of Bouts' brushwork, Bearden's representation of three figures in a landscape retains the architectonic structure and essential compositional relationships of Bouts' composition. Additionally, Bearden's use of color, while distinct from Bouts' modulated, naturalistic palette, is nevertheless similarly disposed in fairly discrete areas across the compositional plane. Even Bearden's deployment of a large band of rosy pink in the right quadrant of the image visually mirrors the bright vermilion hue of John's cloak. In this respect, Bearden's study of Byzantine and Renaissance painting may also have encouraged him to experiment with applying brighter colors in local areas. As he wrote to Quirt, "My color is *high* now and with primaries and direct combinations of these—rather than grays and modulations—So, while the work is hard, painting has an element of fun for me now."[17]

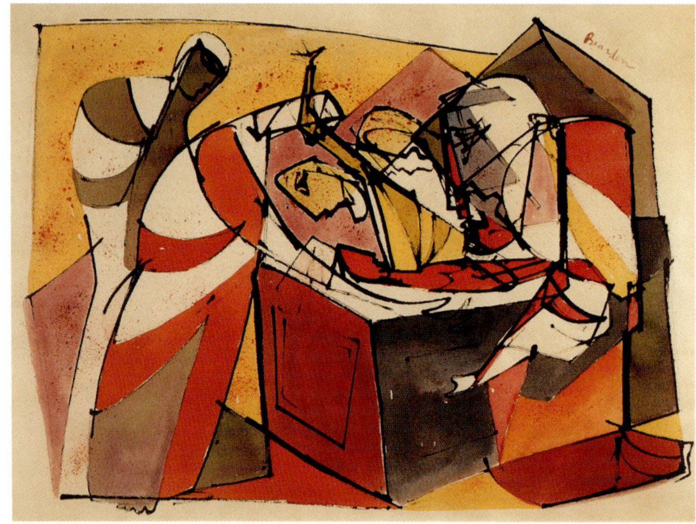

1

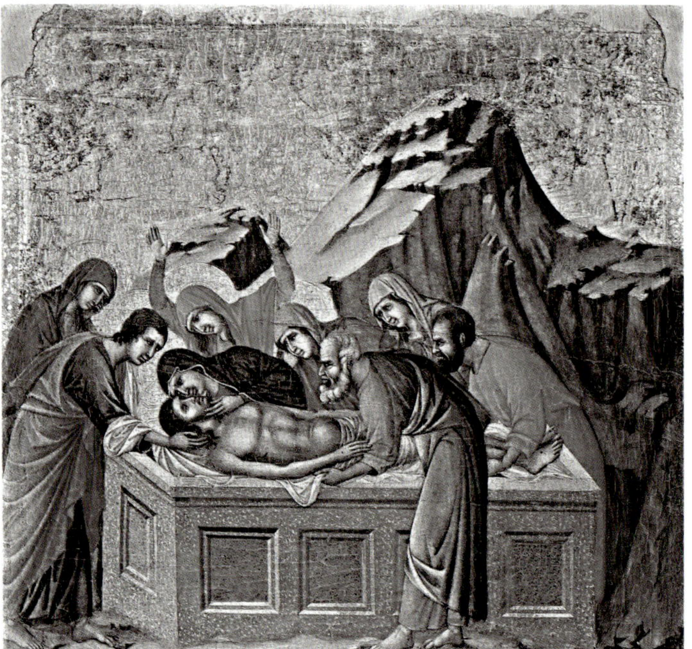

2

figure 1
Romare Bearden, *You Are Dead Forever,* c. 1945, watercolor and ink on paper. Private collection

figure 2
Duccio di Buoninsegna, *The Burial of Christ,* detail from *Maestà* altarpiece, 1308–1311, tempera and gold on panel. Museo dell'Opera Metropolitana, Siena

figure 3
Dirk Bouts, *John the Baptist Pointing to Christ: "Behold the Lamb of God" (Ecce Agnus Dei),* c. 1462/1464, tempera on panel. Bayerische Staatsgeimäl desammlungen, Alte Pinakothek, Munich

figure 4
Romare Bearden, *Untitled (Baptism),* 1946, watercolor and ink on paper. Collection Raymond L. McGuire, New York

While several of the watercolors and oils Bearden executed in the mid-1940s draw specifically upon early Renaissance paintings and frescoes (in addition to Duccio and Bouts, Giotto also seems to have been a favorite of Bearden's), these images are not copies per se, but rather free or loose transpositions of existing compositions into new visual idioms. Toward the end of the decade, however, Bearden turned his energies to the systematic copying of works of art. Once again, the photograph played a vital role. Using a photostatic process to enlarge reproductions to the size of his chosen canvases or boards, Bearden devoted about a year to copying works of art by both the old and the modern masters. As he later explained, the use of photostatic reproductions enabled him to work in the privacy of his studio: "Not wanting to work in museums, I again used Photostats, enlarging works by Giotto, Duccio, Veronese, Grunwald [*sic*], Rembrandt, De Hooch, Manet, and Matisse. I did reasonably free copies of each work substituting my own color for that of the older artists, except, of course, for the Manet and Matisse when I was guided by color reproductions."[18]

What prompted Bearden at this particular juncture to direct almost all of his energies to the production of copies? After all, in the three years following his discharge from the army, Bearden had achieved both critical and commercial success. However, toward the end of the decade, the tides of American art were swiftly changing. Kootz's decision to close down his gallery in 1948 and reopen a year later without Bearden, [George] Byron Browne, or Holty—the only three figurative artists of the original Kootz Gallery stable—was a sign that abstract expressionism was quickly emerging as the dominant avant-garde movement. No longer part of Kootz's gallery, Bearden quietly withdrew from the hectic pace of the New York gallery world, and in 1950, moved to Paris on the G.I. Bill. Though he returned to New York before the end of 1950, Bearden did not hold a solo exhibition again until 1955, when he showed a series of abstract paintings at the Barone Gallery in New York.

Bearden would later describe the period after the closing of the Kootz Gallery as "a time of getting my head together. American painting was coming to the fore (internationally). But I felt the Abstract Expressionist style was not for me as I wanted a more formal discipline, somehow. Then too, I wanted to explore the art of painting more—to see where I stood in the nature of the art."[19] Though Bearden claimed he felt little affinity for abstract expressionism, his desire to more fully understand the practice of painting at a moment when the dramatic, large-scale, and determinedly "painterly" ethos of abstract expressionism was emerging as a dominant trend is understandable. Bearden even admitted that "at a certain period [after his last Kootz Gallery exhibition] I really didn't know enough about painting, that I hadn't really gone to art school enough, my training with Grosz hadn't given me much training in oil painting."[20]

That Bearden felt he lacked facility in oil painting is suggested by his description of his working methods: "When I started to paint in oil I simply wanted to extend what I had done in watercolors. To do so, I had the initial sketch enlarged as a Photostat, traced it onto a gessoed panel and with thinned color completed the oil as if it were indeed a watercolor."[21] Thus, in the late 1940s and early 1950s, Bearden employed the photostat in a variety of ways, including effectively producing copies of his own paintings and systematically copying works culled from the history of European painting. In this endeavor Bearden was, he claimed, inspired by the journal of Eugène Delacroix. Bearden, who had read the nineteenth-century French painter's journal in 1947 and begun to keep a journal of his own at that time, described how "Delacroix almost to the end of his life was always going to the Louvre and copying paintings... I took perhaps two years and made a very systematic study of the Old Masters...."[22] Because few copies are known, Bearden's fidelity to his pictorial sources cannot be determined. But

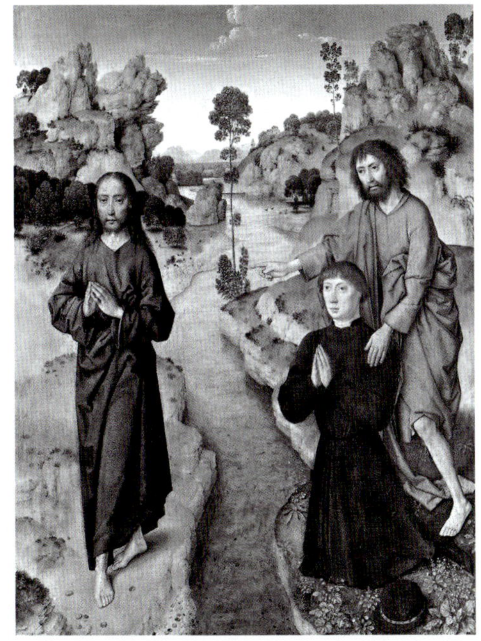

3

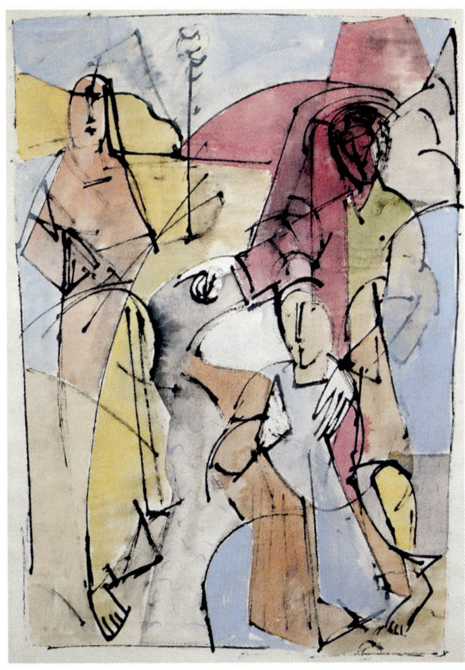

4

when asked by Karl Fortress whether his copies were "literal" or free improvisations on a given picture, the artist replied "I did it in two ways. Some I just took and did in watercolor. I was just doing a free rendering of the work. When I got down to the oils, I would...try to do a fairly literal copy, not exact, but a literal idea."[23]

Though Bearden produced little in the way of "original" work during this period, he considered copying a useful exercise: "The studies I did, I feel, gave me a lot of information as to the way a painting is put together. As I look back, this was very valuable. We put too much emphasis on being immediately creative—to damn an artist, mention is made of his influences."[24] Bearden had previously weighed in on the question of "influence" in an exchange of letters with Quirt. Puzzled at Quirt's description of his own painting as "rather automatic in concept and...not predetermined," Bearden asked Quirt:

> Does not one of the main springs of the art impulse come from an artist's admiration of the work of other artists? My point is that your unconscious impulses are in the final analysis, hampered by a thorough knowledge of painting. Or do you feel that [it] would have been better if you could have originally begun to paint with your same freedom and without your acquired knowledge. But I doubt if this had been the case, your work would be of the same quality.[25]

In asserting that art is inspired by the experience of looking at art, Bearden refuses the modernist dream of the "innocent eye" and instead chooses to embrace "influence" as at once necessary and valuable. This is not to say that Bearden considered his work derivative. Rather, we can interpret Bearden's drive to systematically paint copies following a canonical history of Western art—from Duccio to Matisse, or early Renaissance to modern—as a bid to position himself in relation to that tradition, or more specifically, as the legitimate legatee of that tradition. Thus in a 1980 interview, Bearden described the process of becoming an artist as the recognition of a "void" in art history to be filled. As he continued, "you go to see art in the museum...all the paintings. You say 'Well, this is fine; there's only one missing.'"[26]

In *The Anxiety of Influence: A Theory of Poetry,* literary critic Harold Bloom offers a psychoanalytically-inflected model of how particular poets simultaneously draw upon and deform their artistic progenitors as a way to grapple with the potentially conflicting desires to create original work and to claim authority in relation to an artistic tradition.[27] However, not all artists greet the work of their predecessors with an anxious sense of belatedness or competition. The manner in which Bearden utilized the pictorial riches of the past—particularly in his post-1964 works—was not solely directed toward the containment of influence; rather, plunging into a traditional history of painting offered Bearden the means through which he could productively shape an artistic identity and reshape the historical and cultural representations of race. While the immediate impact of Bearden's practice of copying is difficult to ascertain—few of the copies are known, and upon his return from France in 1950, Bearden turned to both songwriting and a progressively abstract, lyrical mode of painting seemingly divorced from both the literature-based works of the 1940s and his more recent foray into copying—the payoff of this practice emerged in the 1960s. Indeed, it was at precisely the moment Bearden seemed to have turned away from the art of painting altogether that he once again integrated and drew upon his vast knowledge of the history of Western painting, albeit in a dramatically new way that mediated between the humanist aspects of the Western tradition of painting that Bearden admired and the contemporary cultural politics of the multiethnic and racially divided American society in which the artist lived.

COPY TO COLLAGE

In 1964 Bearden employed the photostatic techniques he had used to copy reproductions of old masters to enlarge a series of collages constructed out of fragments of cut-up photographs culled from a diverse array of sources, including *Life* and *Ebony* magazines and possibly other forms of pictorial ephemera. Exhibited in 1964 at Cordier & Ekstrom, Inc., in New York under the title *Projections,* the photostatic enlargements combined the formal languages of cubism and abstraction and the cinematic techniques of montage and jump cuts with the material traces of mass culture to create trenchant, enchanting visual narratives. Recognized as a special achievement by its first viewers, the Projection series has remained an anchor in art historical accounts of Bearden's artistic development—the turning point, as it were, between Bearden the painter and Bearden the collagist, or between Bearden the artist primarily devoted to the exploration of "universal" themes through painting and Bearden the artist acutely aware of the issues of race, identity, and their representation through a self-consciously modern art practice.

There is no doubt that the context out of which the Projection series emerged, in particular Bearden's participation in Spiral (see Fine, "1964," in this volume) and its active engagement with the Civil Rights movement, left an indelible mark on Bearden's production from 1964 onward. While the artists in Spiral grappled with questions concerning the role of the artist in social change and whether or not race was an essential determinant of aesthetic sensibilities, the media-saturated 1960s provided the broader context for an artistic avant-garde increasingly engaged with the rhetorical and representational techniques of advertising, marketing, television, and cinema. Born of the pictorial detritus of mass culture and placed in the service of countering stereotyped images of African-American life, Bearden's photostatic enlargements were regarded as topical, socially engaged, and aesthetically avant-garde. With few exceptions, the ways in which Bearden continued to examine and exploit a canonical history of European painting in his post-1964 works has remained unexplored. While the Projection series and many of the collages that followed drew manifestly upon Bearden's experiences as an African American growing up in North Carolina, Pittsburgh, and Harlem, much of Bearden's post-1964 production alludes subtly to both his own development as an artist and his place within a wider history of art.

In this vein, it is significant to note that Bearden considered his collages as continuous with his painterly practice. In an interview with Karl Fortress, Bearden explained that "I paint on the collages. I consider them not collages but paintings...instead of putting down color...I use paper, cloth I painted myself."[28] If Bearden considered his collages as paintings, he also considered them contiguous with a historical and geographic range of artistic styles and media. Asked around 1967 about how he related to his collages, the artist replied: "Not through any one particular incident, but through Art: Zurburan, African Sculpture, Bosch, Jan Steen, Chinese Calligraphy, Mondrian. As Malraux says, 'art is made from art.'...I cannot deny that there is something transactional in these works."[29]

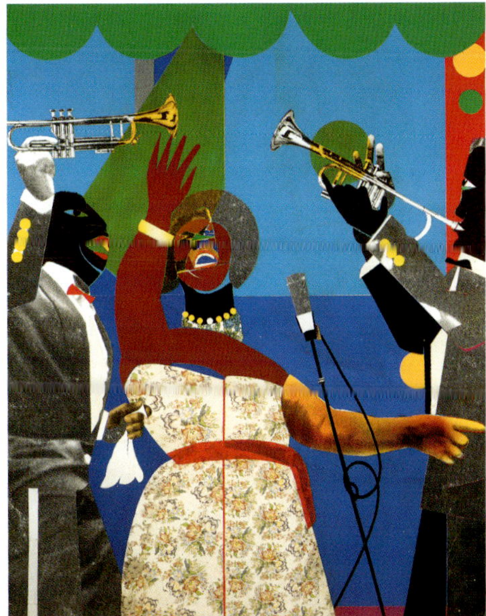

5

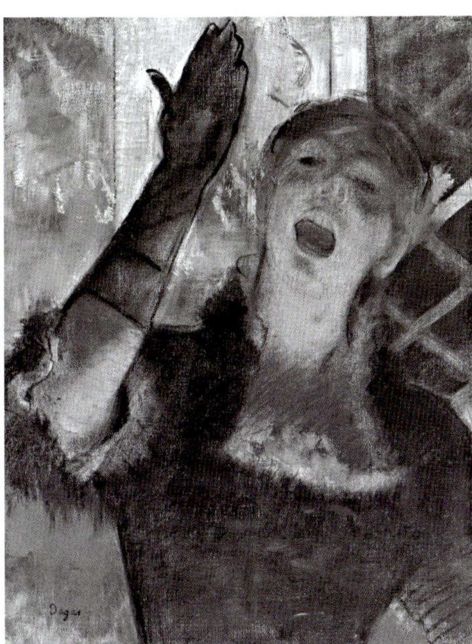

6

figure 5
Romare Bearden, *Of the Blues: Showtime*, 1974, collage with acrylic and lacquer on board. Courtesy of ACA Galleries, New York

figure 6
Edgar Degas, *Café Singer*, 1879, oil on canvas. © The Art Institute of Chicago, Bequest of Clara and Margaret Lynch in memory of John A. Lynch

In post-1964 appropriations of earlier imagery, Bearden not only drew specifically upon the compositional principles of a "source image" but also enacted a series of allusive pictorial and thematic transpositions that slyly evoke and transform that source. Take, for example, the wonderfully brazen 1974 collage *Of the Blues: Showtime* (fig. 5). Blaring trumpets intruding from both sides of the image frame the figure of a female singer whose husky, wailing voice we can almost hear. Her right arm, upraised in a dramatic gesture, her open mouth, even her flowered strapless dress revealing a deep décolleté and a neck tightly encircled by a string of pearls seem plucked straight from the smoky Harlem nightclubs Bearden frequented. Like the other collages featured in the 1975 exhibition *Of the Blues, Showtime* confirms Bearden's prominence as "a contemporary griot, or bard, of African-American musical culture, especially African-American music."[30]

What then, do we make, of the fact that Bearden's innovative collage bears an uncanny resemblance to the dance-hall singer in Edgar Degas' 1879 pastel *Café Singer*? (fig. 6). Similarly, how do we account for the ways in which Bearden's wonderful *Mother and Child* of circa 1972 (fig. 7)—itself a reworking of an eponymous 1968 composition—recalls the tight, slightly awkward embrace of Agnolo Bronzino's *A Young Woman and Her Little Boy*? (fig. 8).[31]

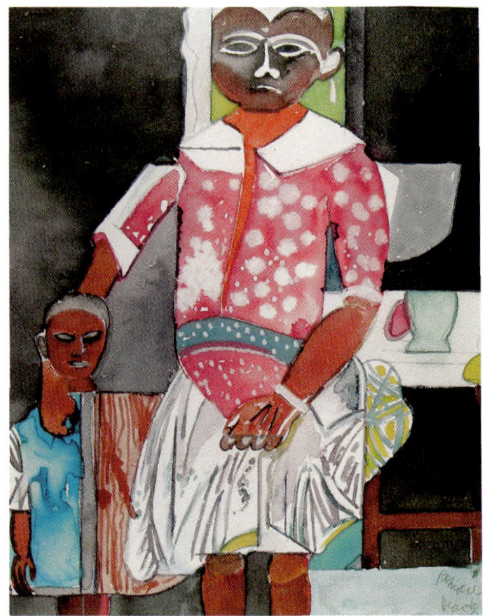

7

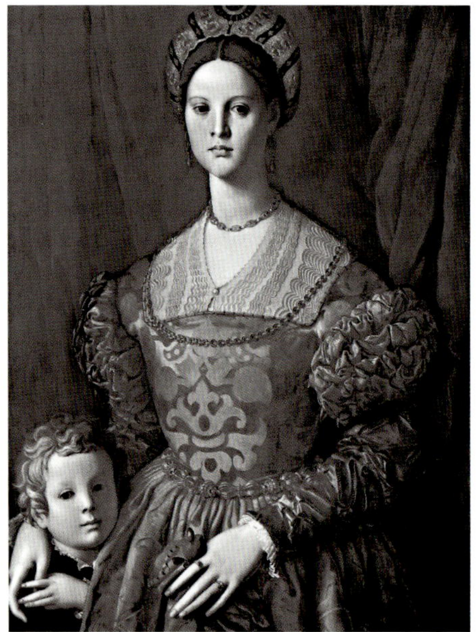

8

In all of these works, Bearden has enacted a series of brilliant pictorial transformations that establish visual and cultural affinities between distinct historical and artistic moments. In recasting Degas' chanteuse into *Showtime*'s blues crooner, Bearden not only posits an artistic kinship between himself and Degas, an artist feted for his acute ability to portray the shifting social and psychological mores of modern urban life, but also casts the blues, an early twentieth-century African-American form of music, as the cultural equivalent of the Belle Epoque's racy and wildly popular café concerts.[32] In *Mother and Child,* Bearden recasts Bronzino's aristocratic lady into a domestic African-American mother whose flat princess collar, exposed knobby knees, and hands thickened by work offer a stark image of life as toil for modest comfort. Even Bearden's technical processes—rubbed colors and collaged papers, which suggest a manipulated, worked, effortful surface—mark its distance from the seamless finish of Bronzino's oil canvas. Nevertheless, in her proud bearing and protective embrace, Bearden's figure compels the viewer to recognize both the historical affinities and distances between Bronzino's and Bearden's representations.

Thus while many of Bearden's collages take the representation of daily life in the African-American community of Mecklenburg County, Pittsburgh, or Harlem as their principal subject matter, Bearden's work reaches beyond the immediate and the familiar to suggest the complex heritage of his artistic and cultural identities. When asked in 1964 about the representation of "subject and identity" in his work, Bearden replied "I am a man concerned with truth, not flattery, who shares a dual culture that is unwilling to deny the Harlem where I grew up or the Haarlem of the Dutch masters that contributed its element to my understanding of art."[33] Bearden literalized this statement in several works of art, including *Back Home from the Up Country,* a collage based on Pieter de Hooch's *A Dutch Courtyard.* Exchanging banjo player and smoking chimney for pipe smoker and church tower, Bearden's collage posits visual and social analogies between seventeenth-century Haarlem and the memory of the southern landscapes of Bearden's childhood.[34] Whether proposing affinities between the musical scene in fin de siècle Paris and that of Harlem in the 1920s or recognizing the sociability of the courtyard across diverse cultures and temporalities, Bearden's collages draw upon the work of older artists in order to transpose these "sources" into an idiom that is at once individually and culturally resonant. That he was highly conscious of what it meant to appropriate older works of art is suggested by the fact that Bearden seemed to be drawn to those artists who themselves regularly copied or appropriated works of art by other artists.

REPLICATION AND TRANSFORMATION, OR CALL AND RECALL

In the foreground of Bearden's 1971 *Down Home, Also* (no. 137), a black couple nestled against each other relax on a patch of green grass, sinking into an afternoon snooze. The atmosphere is not one of exhaustion, however, but of languid eroticism. Bare-breasted, the woman reclines against her partner with her right leg bent at the knee, left hand draped against her belly, and her eyes closed as if in dreamy sleep. Fully clothed, the male figure is partially obscured, but the slightly askew position

figure 7
Romare Bearden, *Mother and Child,* c. 1972, watercolor, graphite, and ink on paper. Private collection, Cambridge, Massachusetts

figure 8
Agnolo Bronzino, *A Young Woman and Her Little Boy,* c. 1540, oil on panel. National Gallery of Art, Washington, D.C., Widener Collection

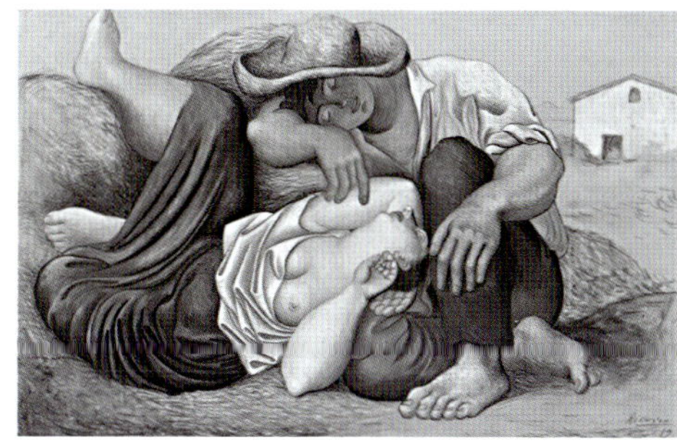

9

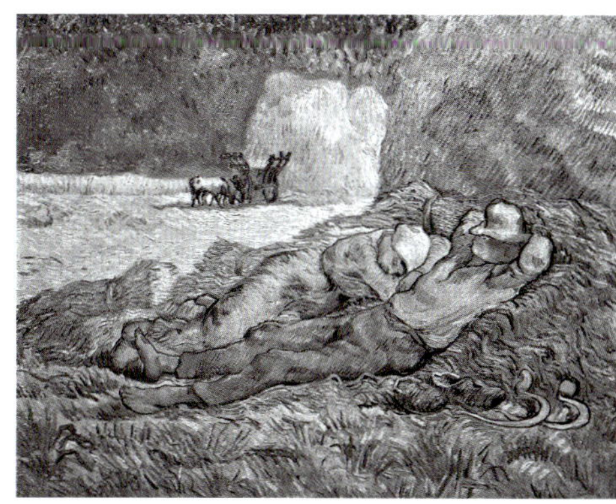

10

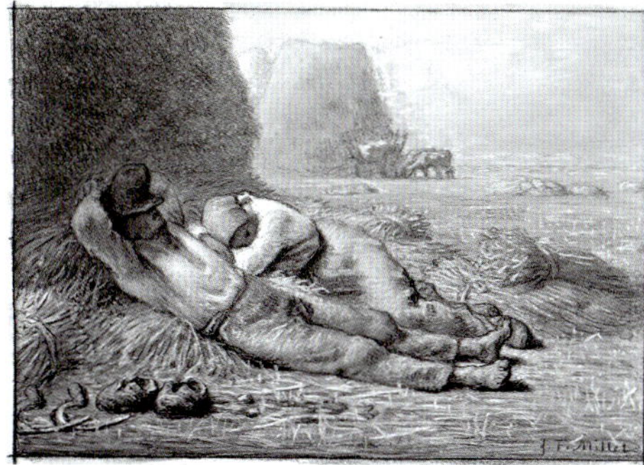

11

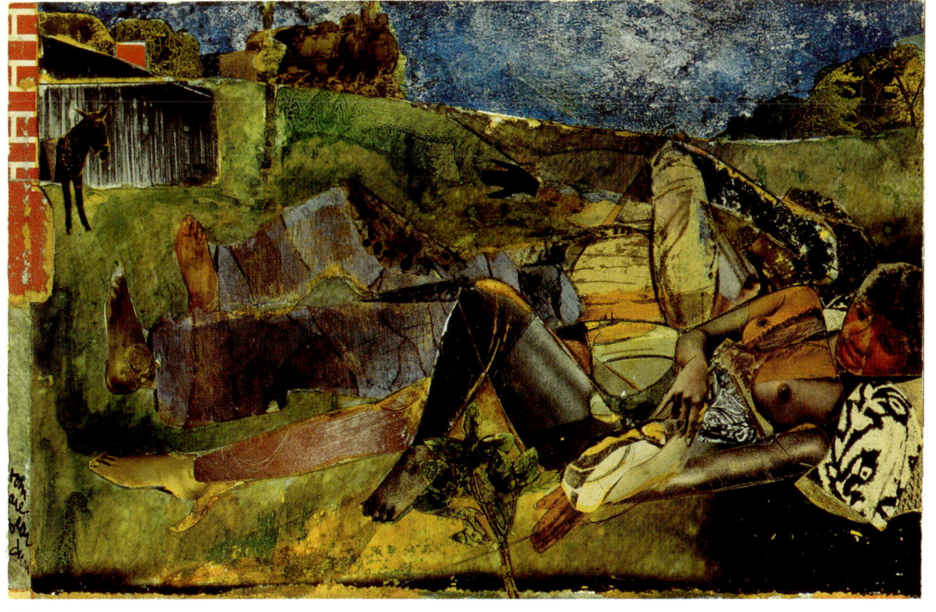

137

137
Romare Bearden, *Down Home, Also,* 1971, collage of various papers with graphite and surface abrasion on fiberboard, 24.1 x 38.1 (9½ x 15). Garth Fagan

figure 9
Pablo Picasso, *Sleeping Peasants,* 1919, tempera, watercolor, and pencil on paper. The Museum of Modern Art, New York; Abby Aldrich Rockefeller Fund

figure 10
Vincent van Gogh, *Noon: Rest from Work (After Millet),* 1889/1890, oil on canvas. Musée d'Orsay, Paris

figure 11
Jean-François Millet, *Noonday Rest,* 1866, pastel and black conté crayon on buff woven paper. Museum of Fine Arts, Boston; gift of Quincy Adams Shaw through Quincy Adams Shaw, Jr., and Mrs. Marian Shaw Haughton

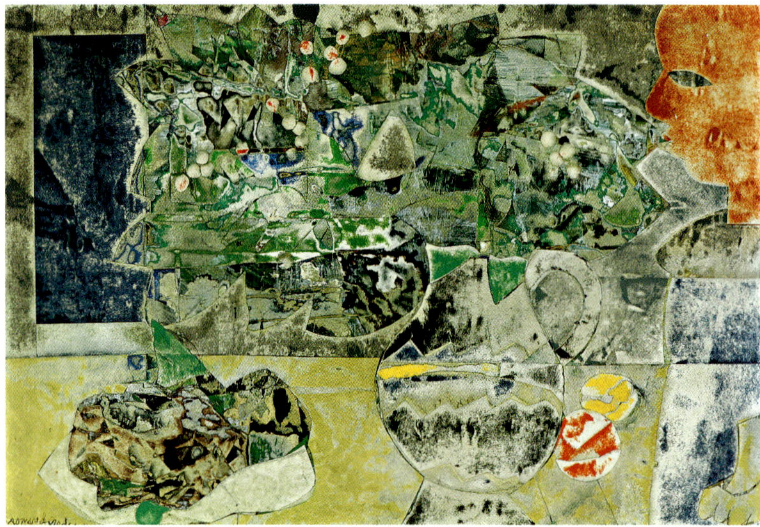

12

of his legs suggests that he has given up to deep sleep. In the background of this verdant landscape stands the edge of a simple wooden structure that might be a barn or farmhouse, and in front of that, a donkey, thus establishing the rural nature of this scene, which is certainly related to Bearden's representations of life in Mecklenburg County, North Carolina.

In contrast to the gentle, almost deliquescent color that bleeds green land into blue sky, the joins and seams of the collaged elements are vivid and stark. Body parts—composed of both photographic and painted and drawn bits—are especially subject to cuts and joins, reminding the viewer that this bucolic scene is nevertheless a thoroughly constructed one. The constructed nature of Bearden's collage accrues further significance when *Down Home, Also* is compared to Pablo Picasso's drawing, *Sleeping Peasants* (1919) (fig. 9), a work that Bearden may have known from his frequent visits to the Museum of Modern Art in New York. The two works are thematically and compositionally similar, especially in the ways each artist has rendered the rhythmic intertwining of figure with figure to impart both tenderness and sensuality.

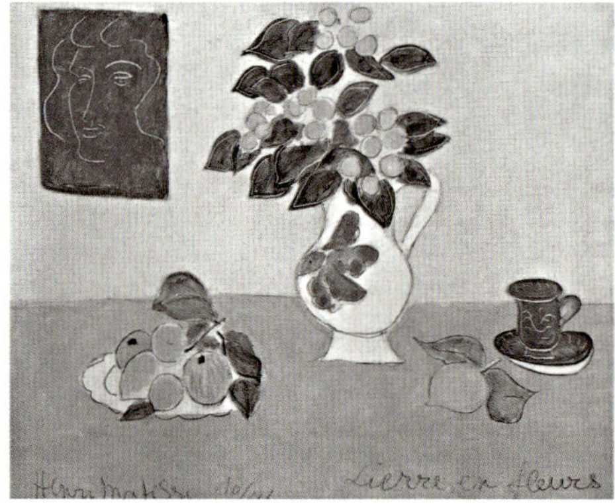

13

Before asking whether Picasso's drawing may have served as the "source" for Bearden's composition, we should note that Picasso made his drawing in response to Vincent van Gogh's painting, *Noon: Rest from Work (After Millet)*, 1889/1890 (fig. 10). Van Gogh's painting echoes the compositional structure of *Noonday Rest* (fig. 11), a pastel drawing by the French nineteenth-century artist Jean-François Millet. This pastel was itself based on an earlier drawing by Millet that was engraved (and thus reproduced in reverse) by Jacques-Adrien Lavieille under the title *Midi*. This engraving is arguably the "source" of Van Gogh's and indirectly, Picasso's and Bearden's images. In other words, while *Down Home, Also* attests to Bearden's commitment to the representation of African-American life in the rural south, the particular construction of this motif suggests that the artist was also deliberately inserting himself into an art historical chain of theme and variation and, more subtly, aligning his practice of poaching with that of Picasso's. That Bearden would suggest an affinity between his artistic practice and that of Picasso, the twentieth-century artist who more than anyone else was responsible for transforming the profligate plundering of the artistic past into an impeccably modern, highly individualistic (and marketable) enterprise, speaks as much to Bearden's ambitions as to Picasso's fame.

Running a close second to Picasso in the game of theme and variation was Henri Matisse, another figure of great and lasting importance to Bearden. While Bearden seems to have thoroughly digested into his art many lessons gleaned from Matisse, including the use of broad areas of pure color, an exquisite sense of linear design, and an interest in erotically charged representations

figure 12
Romare Bearden, *Still Life*, 1970, collage. Lauren Rogers Museum of Art, Mississippi; gift of the Edward John Noble Foundation

figure 13
Henri Matisse, *Ivy in Flowers*, 1941, oil on canvas. Private collection

of the female form (Bearden's "Storyville" prostitutes certainly beg comparison with Matisse's Odalisques), Bearden also seems to have based at least one work, the 1970 *Still Life* (fig. 12) on Matisse's 1941 canvas *Ivy in Flowers* (fig. 13). While the disposition of colored shapes (in particular the patch of blue in the left quadrant of both canvases, as well as the distinctive form of the pitcher and the pointed ivy leaves) are similar, Bearden's collage—with its mottled, bleached, and worked surface and its addition of a Vuillard-like silhouette profile—functions as a liberal interpretation of Matisse's still life, a work that Bearden may have known from the period in which he systematically copied paintings.

Indeed, Bearden's practice of copying extended beyond the old masters to include three of the most prominent modern artists of the twentieth century: Picasso, Matisse, and Cézanne. We know, for example, that a reproduction of Cézanne's *Card Players* (the version now in the Barnes Foundation) hung on the wall in Bearden's studio in the early 1940s (fig. 14). Forty years later Bearden painted two improvisations upon this Cézannien motif: *Card Players* (1982) (no. 138) and *Sunset Express* (1984). In each case, Bearden

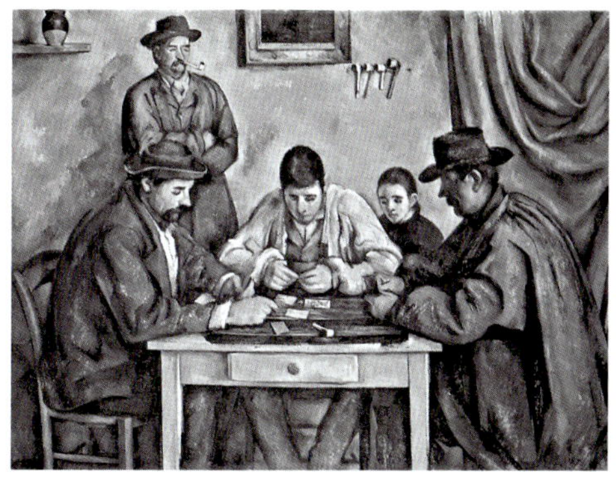

14

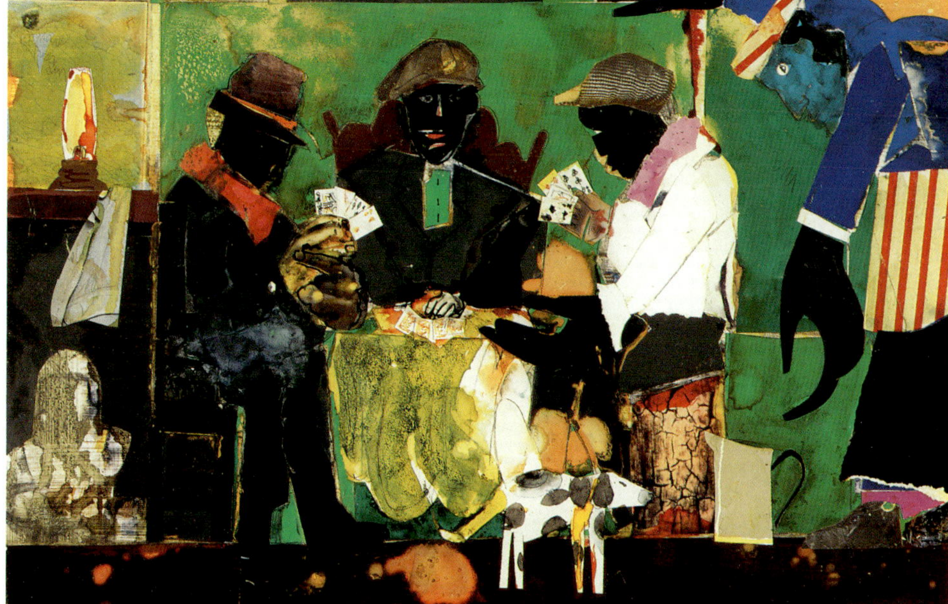

138

figure 14
Paul Cezanne, *Card Players*, 1890–1892, oil on canvas. Barnes Foundation, Merion, Pennsylvania
BF 564

138
***Card Players,* 1982, collage of various papers with paint, ink, graphite, and bleached areas on fiberboard, 45.1 x 61.3 (17¾ x 24⅛). Lent in memory of Elaine Lebenbom**

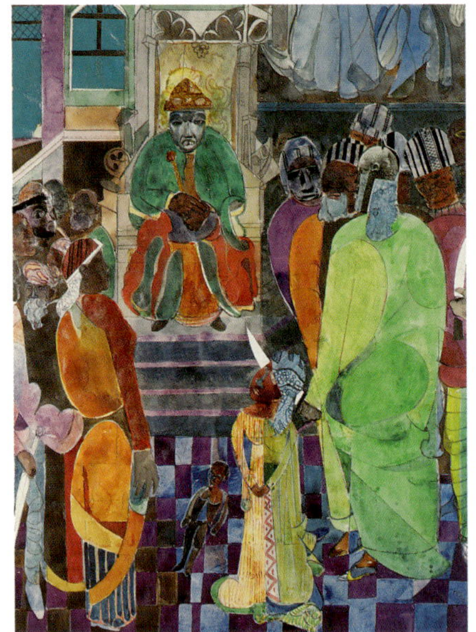

139

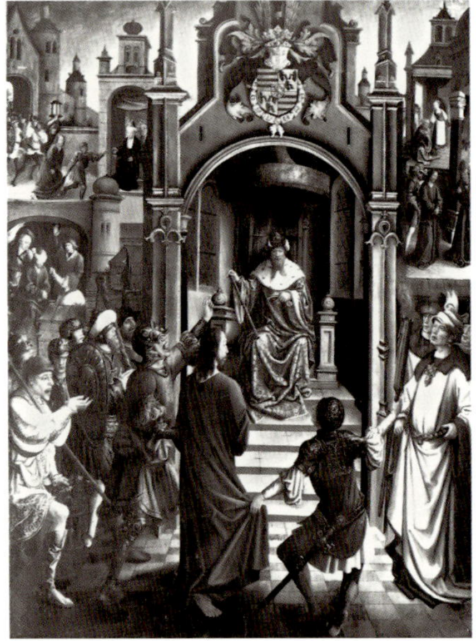

15

makes the image his own, not only through the increasingly painterly, saturated palette but also through the articulation of distinctive details, such as the glow of the gas lamp in *Card Players* and the train whistling through the landscape in *Sunset Express*—details that construct an intimate and sensitive portrait of African-American sociability. Indeed, the motif of card playing was also popular among Bearden's African-American contemporaries; both Palmer Hayden and Hale Woodruff depicted African-American men engaged in card games, a pastime that took place at both the "rent-parties" and the back rooms of many Harlem nightclubs in the 1930s and 1940s.[35]

Of course, Western art was by no means the only artistic tradition that fueled Bearden's pictorial production. African art was of particular importance to Bearden's work, and many of Bearden's most compelling images incorporate African motifs into a complex signifying structure (see Elleh in this volume). One of the most fascinating images in this vein is the undated watercolor and collage *Untitled (Shrouds)* (no. 139). This image, which seems to illustrate the biblical narrative of the Judgment of Solomon, draws upon the compositional principles of a northern Renaissance painting, *Christ Before Pilate,* by the Flemish sixteenth-century painter known as the Master of the Beighem Altarpiece (fig. 15), but liberally integrates into its narrative African visual motifs. Bearden's composition adapts the compositional structural and figural disposition of the bottom two-thirds of the painting (the bottom of the robes of the figures in the upper right corner of oil painting have been transformed by Bearden into curtains) and condenses the Flemish painter's sequential narrative, the full title of which is *Christ Before Pilate, with Christ Led to Annas, the Mocking of Christ, the Denial by Peter, and Christ Before Caiaphas),* into a single, dramatic scene. But this narrative of royal authority and biblical judgment has been transposed into an imaginative African court; faces, including that of the king, are constructed out of photographic reproductions of African masks, and clothing is a mélange of Renaissance robes cut from cloth bearing African motifs. That Bearden not only transposed one cultural setting onto another but also substituted one biblical narrative for another underscores the lability of Bearden's approach to pictorial form as a carrier of meaning. It also points to the ways in which Bearden continually strove to link the distinctiveness of African-American identity with what he understood as the universal or archetypal aspects of religion and myth. Not only is Bearden's Odysseus black, but so too is Paris and the three beauties he courts in *Prelude to Troy,* a modern reworking of Lucas Cranach's *Judgment of Paris* (no. 140, fig. 16). Similarly in another work based on Cranach's painting *Samson and Delilah,* Bearden does not merely borrow a pictorial composition but transcribes it into what Bearden described as a "Black circumstance."[36] Given these working methods, we might conclude that much of Bearden's art was directed toward the reconciliation of the categories of "blackness" and "universality" in a culture that so often saw them as mutually exclusive.

A 1967 article by Charles Childs entitled "The Artist Caught between Two Worlds" revealed the extent to which the identification and definition of a "black aesthetic" was a pressing issue among African-American artists in the 1960s.[37] Using the subtitle, "many ride the pendulum back and forth between the urge to be racial and the wish to be universal," Childs describes the "precarious

139
Romare Bearden, *Untitled (Shrouds)*, early 1980s, watercolor and collage, 24 x 18 (61 x 45.7). Hammonds House Galleries, Atlanta

figure 15
Attributed to Master of the Beighem Altarpiece, *Christ Before Pilate, with Christ Led to Annas, the Mocking of Christ, the Denial by Peter, and Christ Before Caiaphas,* c. 1520, oil and gold on panel. Philadelphia Museum of Art, John G. Johnson Collection, 1917

tightrope" many black artists walk between a desire to represent the authenticity and specificity of African-American history and subjectivity and the dangers of essentializing race.[38] According to Childs, Bearden responded to this conflict by seeking analogies between the particular and the universal. Bearden later supported this analysis when he wrote of his relation to the Afrocentric philosophy of Léopold Senghor: "I was affected by the African concepts that run through Senghor—the land, the beauty of the black woman, the protective presence of the dead, and the acceptance of intuition. But the biggest thing I learned was reaching into your consciousness of black experience and relating it to universals."[39]

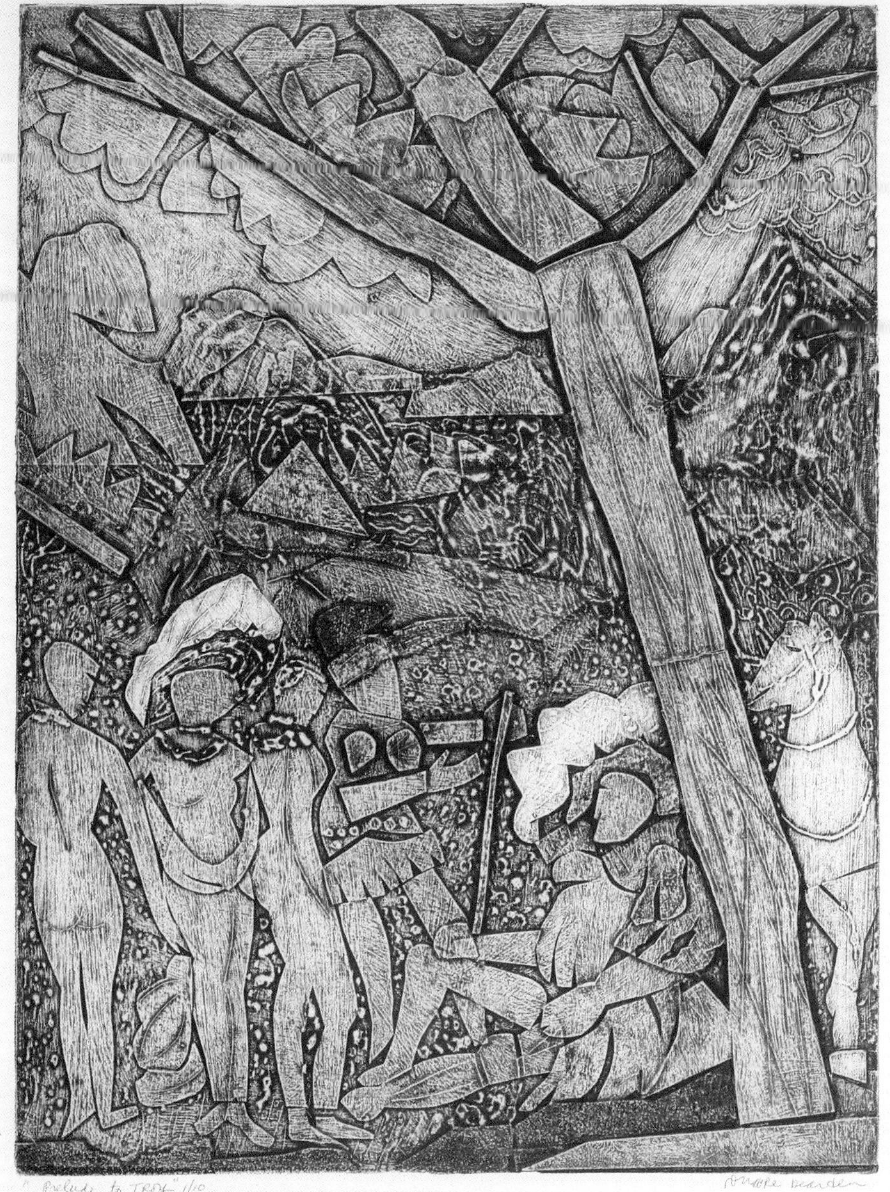

140

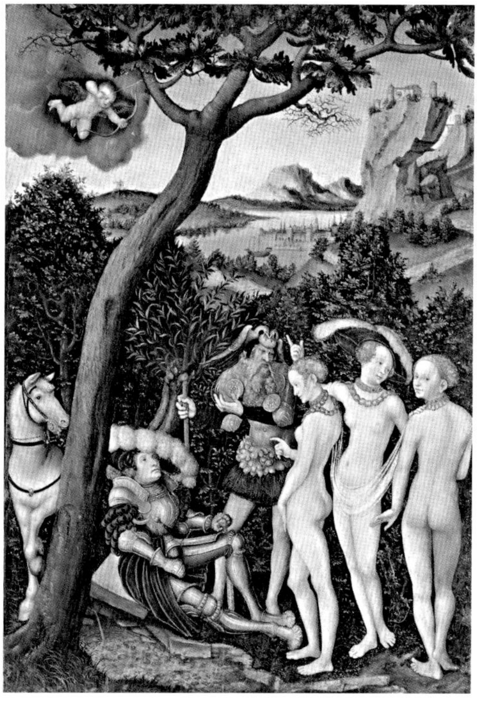

16

140
Romare Bearden, *Prelude to Troy*, c. 1969, collagraph on paper, 60.9 x 46.8 (24 x 18 7/16). National Gallery of Art, Washington, gift of Yvonne and Richard McCracken and Mary and Jerald Melberg

figure 16
Lucas Cranach the Elder, *The Judgment of Paris*, c. 1528, oil on wood. The Metropolitan Museum of Art, Rogers Fund, 1928 (28.221)

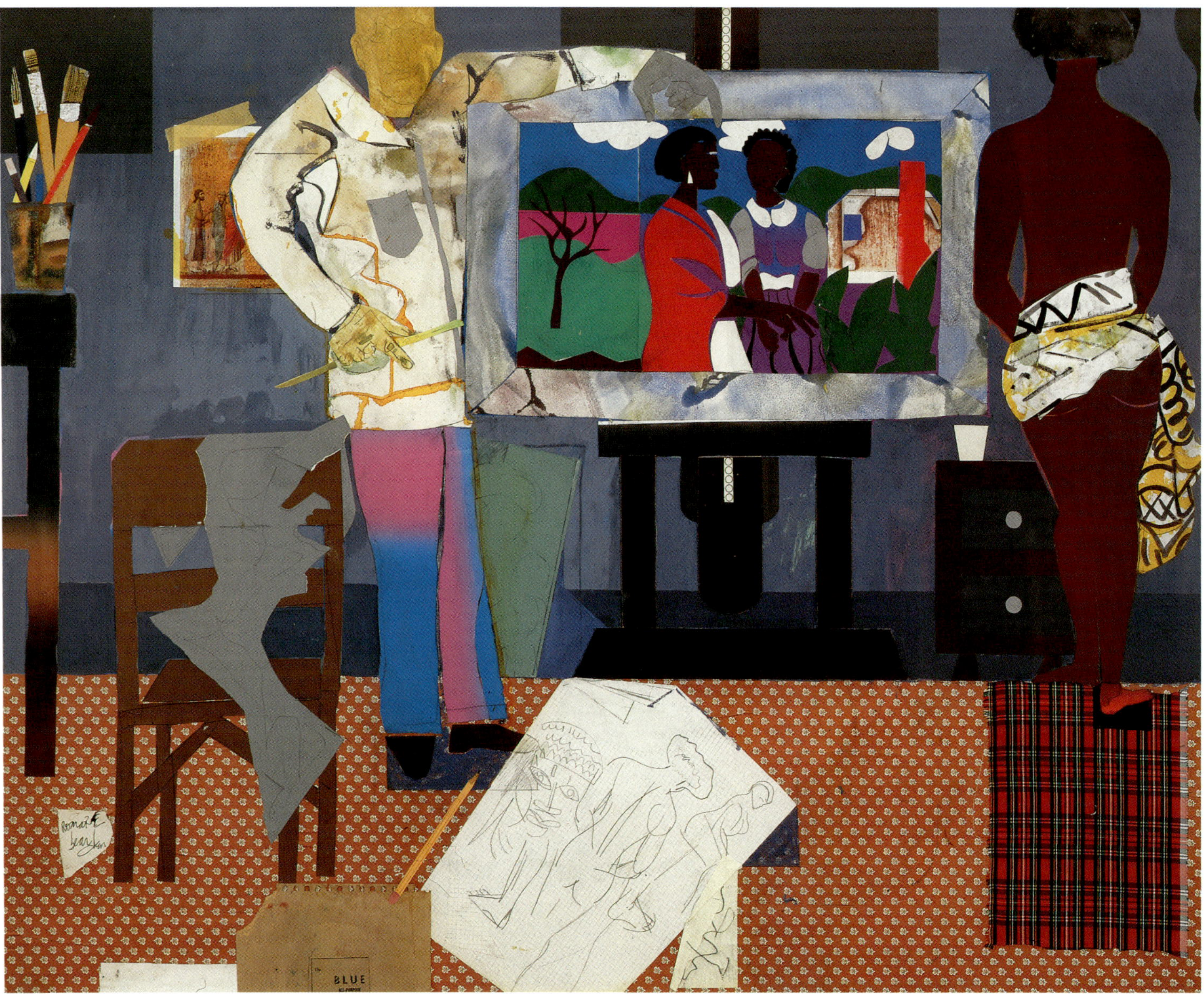

141

141
Romare Bearden, *Profile/Part II, The Thirties: Artist with Painting and Model,* 1981, collage of various papers with fabric, foil, tape, paint, and graphite on fiberboard, 111.8 x 142.2 (44 x 56). Glen and Lynn Tobias

figure 17
Sam Shaw, series of photographs (proofs) of Bearden with model, late 1940s. The Shaw Family Archives; Estate of Romare Bearden, courtesy of Romare Bearden Foundation, New York

At their best, however, Bearden's collages do more than establish analogies between the particular and the universal. They physically and psychically integrate the specificities of African-American experiences into a coherent signifying structure that seeks to simultaneously draw upon and revise stereotyped representations of race and culture. The process is not always smooth going; particularly in the late 1960s works, the fragmentary bits of photographs, the terse and elliptical narratives, the serrated and cut edges of paper and photograph, the bleeding and scratchy colors, and the disconcerting distortions of scale and perspective betray the thoroughly constructed nature of the collages. It was precisely these visual qualities that led some early commentators to characterize the works as surreal, a term that perhaps implies that the worlds imagined within Bearden's collages—worlds in which the possibilities for representing African-American subjectivity far exceeded in both richness and complexity the mere fact of skin color—remained distinct from the reality or lived experiences of many Americans in the 1960s.[40]

ARTIST WITH PAINTING AND MODEL

Profile/Part II, The Thirties: Artist with Painting and Model, 1981 (no. 141), the only known self-portrait executed by Bearden, is at once a personal history and a testament to Bearden's abiding interest in alluding to and transforming the world of art through collage. In this large (44 x 56 inches) collage, the artist, paintbrush (not scissors) in hand, stands next to an easel upon which rests a brightly colored reworking of Bearden's c. 1941 gouache, *The Visitation* (see Fine in this volume, no. 1). A nude black model, draped in a patterned scarf, stands to the right of the easel, her back toward the viewer. A fragment of a color reproduction of Duccio's *Road to Emmaus* from the *Maestà* altarpiece is tacked against the wall. A collaged sheet of graph paper covered with pencil studies of a nude woman and an African mask lies at the artist's feet.

On one interpretative level, Bearden's collage functions as a form of pictorial autobiography. The references to Duccio and to Bearden's own painting, *The Visitation,* gesture back to Bearden's development as a painter in the 1940s. But the collage makes reference to this period in Bearden's life through another pictorial allusion. This time, the "source" is not a work of art, but rather a series of photographs of Bearden in his studio taken by photographer Sam Shaw sometime in the 1940s (fig. 17). The photographs document Bearden's working space and methods. We see that Bearden not only hung several of his own watercolors on the wall, but that they were accompanied by a large-scale reproduction of Giotto's *Lamentation* (1304–6; a work that Bearden would later reproduce in his book coauthored with Carl Holty, *The Painter's Mind,* 1969), the lower portion of which is visible in one of the frames. The photographs also purport to reveal Bearden's working

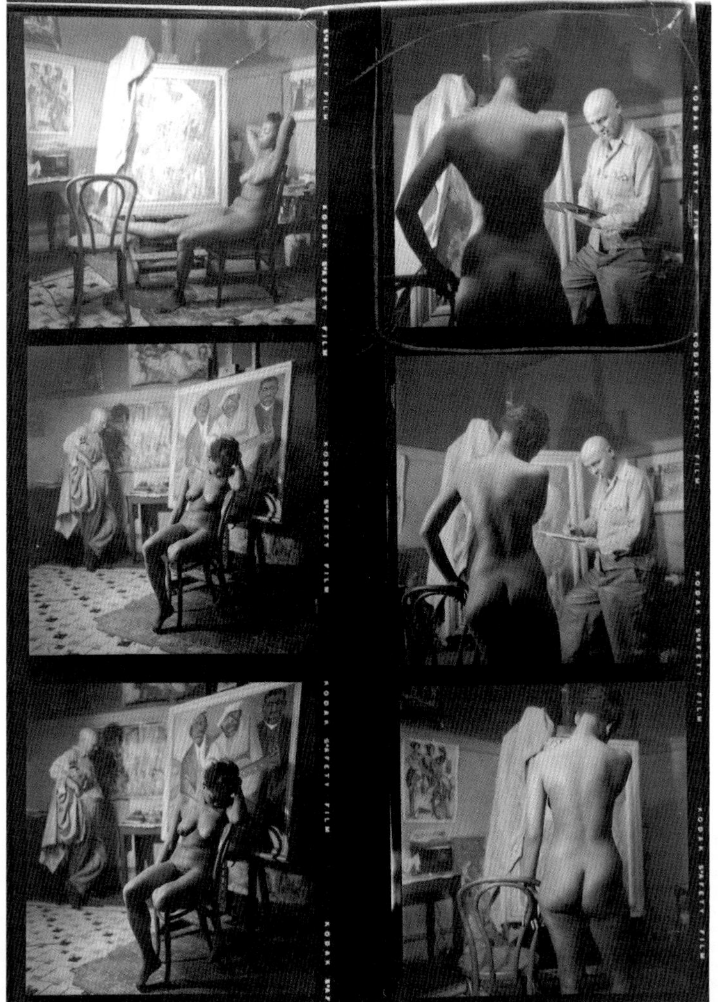

17

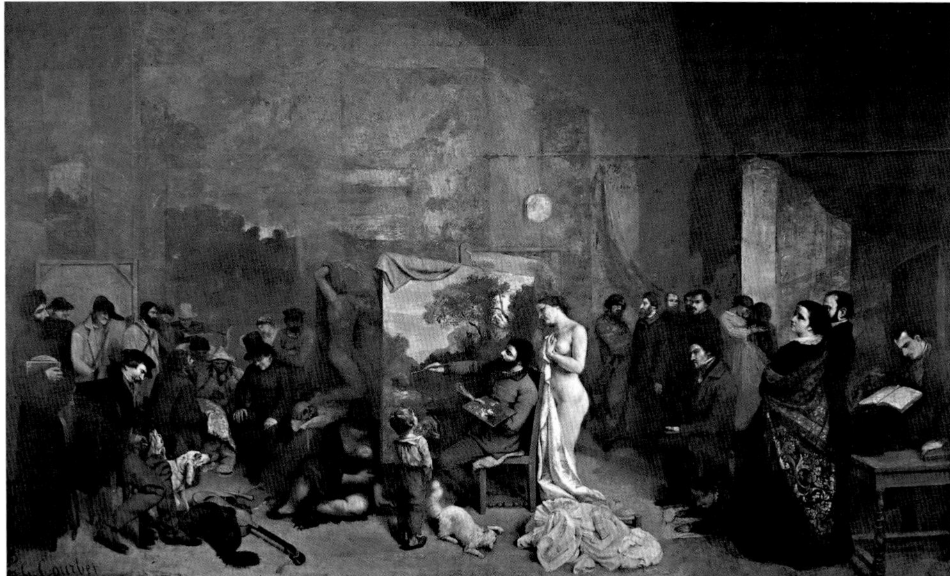

18

both a painter and a politically-engaged citizen. Courbet acknowledged these sources not only through symbolic representation, but by adapting a composition that itself possessed an art-historical pedigree, for the subject of the artist at work was a favorite of Rembrandt, an artist whom Courbet intensely admired and often copied. Similarly, Bearden, who once named Courbet one of his artistic heroes and admired the latter's "realism, his type of approach, his type of objectivity," subtly acknowledges this relationship in *Artist with Painting and Model.*[42] Like Courbet's *The Painter's Studio,* Bearden's *Artist with Painting and Model* represents artistic identity as a richly layered, highly complex interaction not only between self and world but also between (art) history and the present.

processes: thoroughly engrossed in his artistic labor, Bearden sketches the nude model, who is gracefully posed next to Bearden's gouache *Folk Musicians* (1942; see Fine in this volume, fig. 27). The photographs, like the collage *Artist with Painting and Model* (see no. 141), function as carefully staged performances of an artistic identity formed by both early Renaissance and modern art, both the female nude and abstract visual form, both the specificity of African-American life and the universal aspects of ritual and myth.

In the collage's intermingling of "real" and "represented," *Artist with Painting and Model* also serves as an homage to yet another image: Gustave Courbet's *The Painter's Studio: A Real Allegory Summing Up Seven Years of My Artistic Life* (fig. 18). Exhibited in 1855, Courbet's image depicts the painter in the center of his studio in the process of painting a landscape while a nude model holding drapery to the right of the easel looks on. Like Bearden, Courbet seems to have worked from photography in the construction of this image; Aaron Scharf has persuasively argued that a photograph of Julien Vallou de Villeneuve's (undated) *Nude Study* aided Courbet in the representation of the nude figure and has made the case for Courbet's use of photography in other figure and landscape paintings.[41]

While Courbet's enigmatic painting has generated much speculation concerning its meaning, most scholars agree with the basic premise that the image functions as a symbolic representation of the major influences—personal, political, and artistic—upon the artist's development as

BEARDEN'S MUSÉE IMAGINAIRE IN CONTEXT

While Bearden's revisions of tradition interrogate the past as vehicle for reflecting upon the present and assert the place of both invention and difference within that canon, they also reveal the complexity and self-consciousness with which Bearden approached his work as an artist. Bearden was not alone in this endeavor. In the 1960s, many of Bearden's contemporaries engaged in explicit visual dialogues with their artistic forebears. Whether as a means to articulate questions concerning the identity of the modern artist in relation to his or her artistic predecessors, an exploration of the impact of mass reproduced imagery on the construction and dispersal of an artistic canon, or a commentary on the transformation of artworks into everyday commodities, the artworks of the 1960s and 1970s that took

figure 18
Gustave Courbet, *The Painter's Studio: A Real Allegory Summing Up Seven Years of My Artistic Life,* 1855, oil on canvas. Musée d'Orsay, Paris

Art itself as their subject matter clearly reflect upon the relationship between an institutionalized history of Western art on the one hand and the status of the artist and the artwork in modern culture on the other. An important 1978 exhibit entitled *Art about Art* at New York's Whitney Museum provided a critical lens on this issue by presenting a group of contemporary artists including Robert Colescott, Jasper Johns, Roy Lichtenstein, Robert Rauschenberg, Larry Rivers, and Andy Warhol who explicitly referred to, drew upon, reproduced, or transformed in various ways canonical works of Western art. As the preface to the exhibition catalogue suggested, the works in question were often ironic in tone and satirical in intent; both the original "sources" and the processes by which these contemporary artists had transformed them were meant to be easily recognized by viewers.[43]

Although Bearden frequently exhibited in group shows with the artists who participated in *Art about Art,* and although Bearden selectively borrowed from a wide range of artistic sources throughout his career, the extent to which many of his creations deliberately revised and transformed an inherited visual lexicon has rarely been acknowledged.[44] In part, this failure to appreciate how Bearden appropriated a canonical history of Western painting stems from the nature of Bearden's artistic processes. Unlike many of the works featured in the *Art about Art* exhibition, Bearden's borrowings from tradition were not meant as a satire of art history or as a commentary on the status of the art object as such. Although drawing heavily and sometimes quite directly on a variety of rich visual traditions, including African, Byzantine, and European art, Bearden's sophisticated manipulations of pictorial form and content often served to deflect the facile identification of a work with its "source" in the history of art.

Critical assumptions about the relationship between art, race, and identity have also hindered full recognition of the complexity of Bearden's art. As one of the premiere American artists of the twentieth century who strove to "establish a world through art in which the validity of my Negro experience could live and make its own logic," Bearden has sometimes been cast as an artist whose work mainly draws upon, and speaks exclusively to, the black experience in America.[45] Such an assumption fails to take into consideration the ways in which Bearden continually struggled to make his art exceed limiting definitions of racial identity not by ascribing to a putative notion of universality but by producing sophisticated images which posit *and* elicit visual, thematic, and historical affinities among a range of artistic traditions. The result is a body of allusive and often witty representations that reveal not only the extent and sophistication of Bearden's knowledge of art history but also his enormous talent in transforming that legacy into a highly distinctive, visually compelling mode of signifying what Bearden once described as "the richness of a life I know."[46]

Bearden's Dialogue with Africa and the Avant-Garde

NNAMDI ELLEH

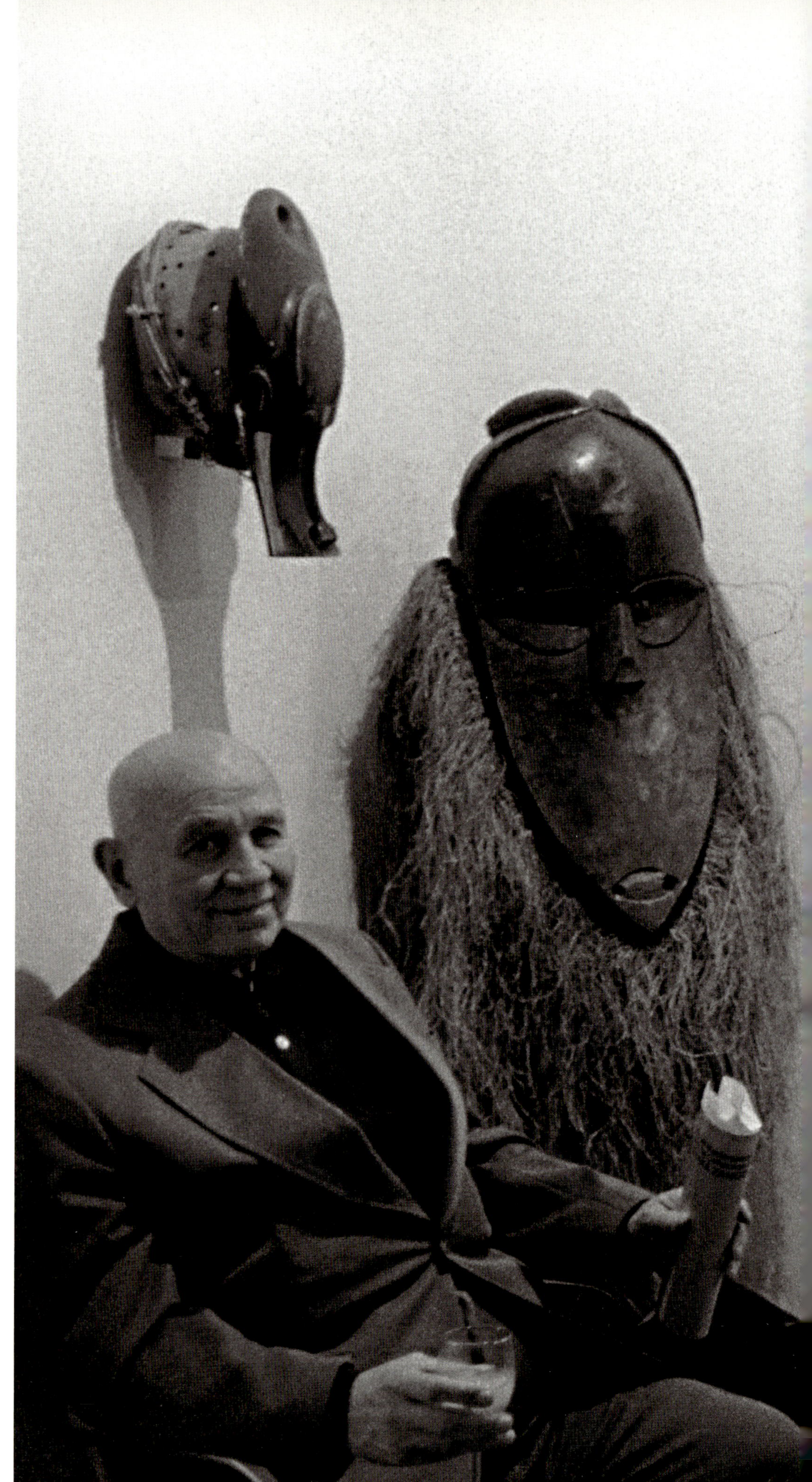

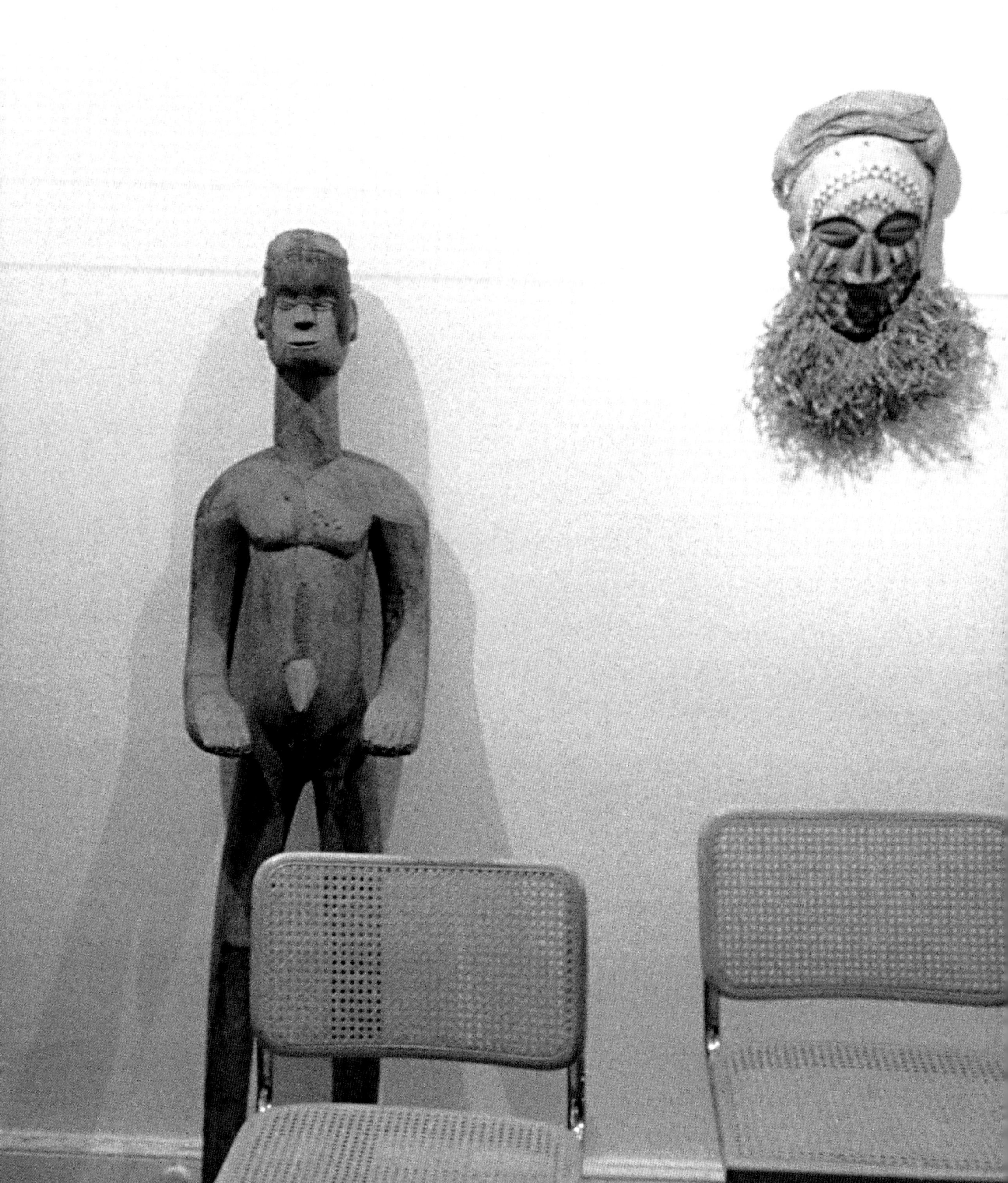

Looking at Bearden's *Sermons: The Walls of Jericho* (1964) (no. 142), from top left to right, one can observe how the earth floats in the void of space, surrounded by stars, looking like a fragile egg that is tossed into the air. From this distant view, one cannot observe any sign of life on earth and it appears to be a peaceful place. But as the viewer moves his eyes slightly to the right, the serene picture is immediately interrupted by the violence inflicted on the broken arms that are stretched upward toward the top of the image. Wedged between the two arms is a highly disfigured face that resembles a beast, yet the source of this face is recognizable. The representation of woven beads on the lower right cheek gives the broken face away as a composite object that is partly derived from twelfth-century Ife (a city in Yorubaland) antiquity. The remaining part of this beast with a badly broken face, nose, bulging eyes, and skull was derived from the woven bead-crowns of Benin bronze or brass heads (figs. 1, 2). Although the origin of the raised disfigured hand that frames this beast on the left is not easily recognizable, the raised hand that frames the broken face on the right has bracelets that suggest Bearden's familiarity with the 500 BC to 200 AD Nok terracotta objects from the Nigerian central plateau.

Sermons: The Walls of Jericho is pivotal in exploring Bearden's dialogue with the avant-garde. After a closer look at the painting, I will focus on the African ancestral elements that are represented in a select group of Bearden's work, consider how some of those traditional elements are applied to the works of modern and contemporary African artists, and finally, I will propose that the relationship between the avant-garde and minority artists is stronger than the link suggested by the scholars of cubism in the middle of the twentieth century —the belief that non-European art was merely a source of inspiration for the pioneers of modern art. It will be shown that by adopting the visual language of cultures categorized as primitive, the avant-garde—particularly the Parisian surrealists —also gave access to minority artists to engage in the larger modernist movement that dominated twentieth-century art.

Again, reading the *Sermons: The Walls of Jericho* collage from the left, under the floating earth, a collapsed Renaissance-inspired Corinthian entablature with a set of engaged columns is tilted at an approximate forty-five-degree angle to the left edge of the image with a gothic-inspired structure behind it. This fallen entablature and its engaged columns is counterbalanced on the right edge of the collage by a similarly tilted, ruined, Roman-inspired triumphal arch. Visually, the entablature and the arch are on a diagonal axis from each other but the arch is situated on a slightly lower plane. A sixteenth-century bronze head of a Benin queen mother (fig. 3) whose face is cut off can be seen under the entablature. Conversely, on the right edge of the collage and underneath the fallen arch, one can observe two broken twelfth-century brass or bronze heads of an Oni (King) of Ife. The coiffures of the Oni heads and the simulated bead screens that resemble scarifications on the faces are legible.

In order to highlight the diagonal spatial rhythm, Bearden centered a conical woven hood in the middle of the ensemble. This central object could be from China, Japan, or Vietnam, and it can be seen as a representation of the roof of the traditional African round hut, a composition that confirms Gail Gelburd's observation that "Bearden

142
Romare Bearden, *Sermons: The Walls of Jericho,* 1964, collage of various papers with paint, ink, and graphite on cardboard, 30.2 x 23.8 (11 7/8 x 9 3/8). Hirshhorn Museum and Sculpture Garden, Smithsonian Institution, gift of Joseph H. Hirshhorn, 1966

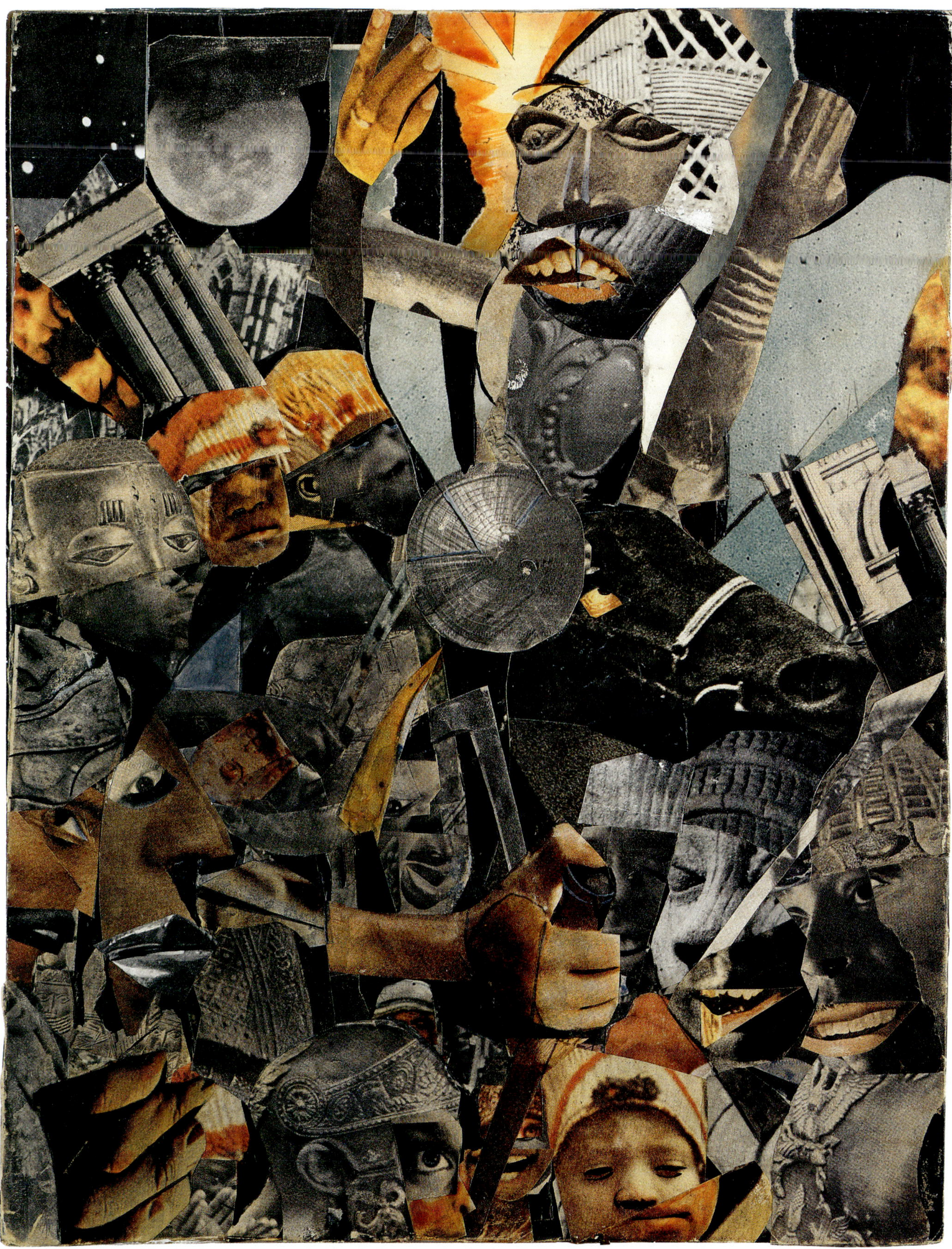

142

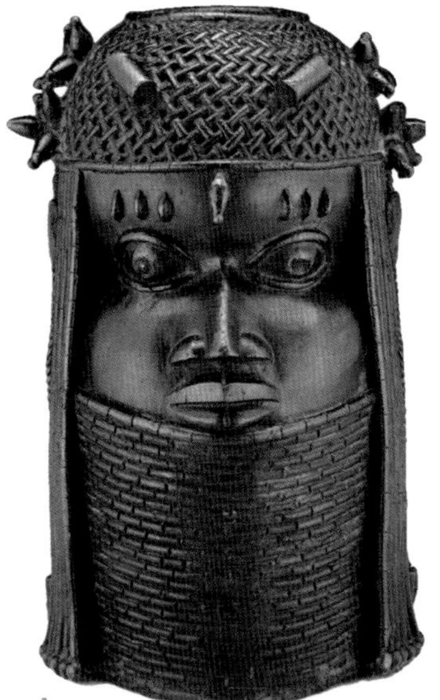

1

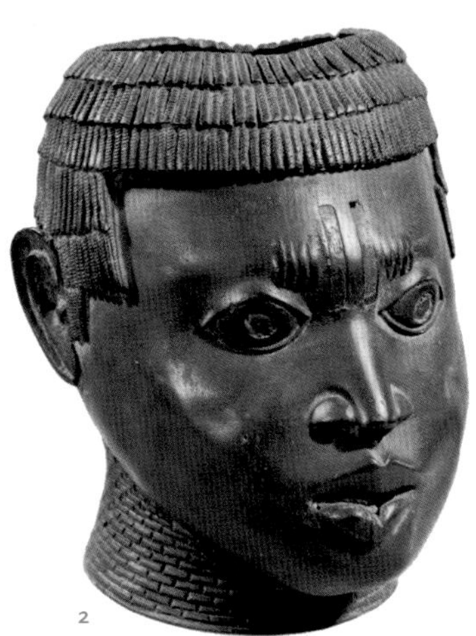

2

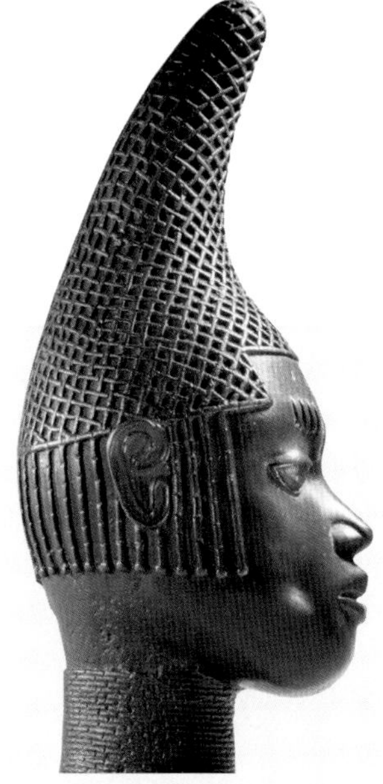

3

looked to Western and African iconography, but frequently referred to classical Chinese painting as a philosophical base for his compositional format."[1] Certainly, Bearden intended the viewer to recognize the cone as a shelter from the dangers in our environment. The hood is staged as if the earth, the battered faces, the broken heads, hands, noses, and eyes, revolve around it. The manner in which the cone is woven also serves another important purpose in this composition—the thin fiber strands that form the ribs of the fiber radiate from the tip of the cone to its rim at diagonal angles. The interlocking circular strings that hold the thin strands together form equal matrices that ripple in continuous motion from the tip of the cone to its rim. As a result the matrices and waves impose orderliness in the midst of the chaos that dominates the collage. Locating the cone in the center of the collage solved the problem of perspective for Bearden. The perspective created an illusion of depth by forming a bottomless dark pit in the center of the ensemble. From this depth, the cone generates a centrifugal force that pulls all the images from the edges to the center, the result being a unified composition. No element in the composition is too big or too small. They enhance each other's visibility.

The most prominent object in the lower end of the collage resembles the head of a Roman soldier with a helmet. Looking outward toward the viewer, this soldier's eye, like the sharp eyes of the numerous broken faces in the collage, invades the space of the viewer like the eyes of a hungry hawk that is searching for prey. On the other hand, when the viewer looks inward into these eyes, they serve the function of windows through which the viewer can see the traumas of our world and the pains we have inflicted upon one another. By slashing the faces of the objects from African antiquity and juxtaposing them with broken photographed faces of people, Bearden succeeded in deleting the lines between sculptures and people, the past and the present, and the boundaries between life and death. Based on this composition, Bearden made *Sermons: The Walls of Jericho* to rise from the ashes of ruins as if the biblical event in Joshua is taking place before the viewer. "The Lord said to Joshua, 'see, I have handed Jericho over to you, along with its king and soldiers. You shall march around the city, all the warriors circling the city once....'"[2] At last, from the title of the collage, one can see how Bearden provided the viewer with clues on how one might experience the picture—one should proceed along the wall of Jericho, observing the collage from its edges to its center.

The African objects that inhabit Bearden's wall of Jericho are altar figures that commemorate ancient queens, kings, and warriors. In Benin each Oba maintained several altars for his ancestors and guardian spirits, and the heads were the central objects in each altar. Large elephant tusks were placed inside deep cavities that were left on the top of the bronze heads. Cows, goats, sheep, and chickens were sacrificed before the objects, and the blood of the sacrificed animals was allowed to drip on the bronze head. Priests uttered incantations and poured libations to the spirits of the ancestors during the offerings. Depending on the specific occasion, masquerade dances and music were part of the offerings. It is believed that the offerings could persuade the gods and the ancestor spirits to open the liminal space in which communications can take place between the spirits and the living.

figure 1
Head of Oba, Benin, Nigeria, possibly sixteenth century, bronze. Museum für Volkerkunde zu Leipzig. Compare with the broken, top-middle object in Bearden's *Sermons: The Walls of Jericho* (no. 142).

figure 2
Royal head from altar, Benin, Nigeria, probably fifteenth century, brass and iron. University of Pennsylvania Museum, Philadelphia. Compare with the shattered middle figure at the left corner of *Sermons: The Walls of Jericho* (no. 142).

figure 3
Queen Mother head, Benin, Nigeria, c. 1500–1550, bronze. Musuem of Mankind, British Museum, London

It should not be surprising that in *Sermons: The Walls of Jericho* Bearden evoked African ritual customs and superimposed them on Euro-American and African-American cultural practices. Trans-Atlantic cultural exchanges between Africa, Europe, and the Americas influenced religion as well as the visual and the performing arts.[3] Juxtaposing ancient icons with new ones or European icons with indigenous elements has been an established practice in African art since the sixteenth century, perhaps even earlier. Such juxtapositions always delineated symbols of power and rituals. Here, we are reminded that the Portuguese and the people of Edo (Benin) have been trading since the fifteenth century. In those years, the Portuguese unsuccessfully proselytized to the Edo monarchs and their people. As a result, even when there was no conversion, certain Christian icons such as the cross were still adopted and incorporated into Edo representations of power in the ancestor altar. A good example is the altar that Oba (King) Ewaka II maintained for his father, Oba Ovonramwen, in the late nineteenth century (1888–1897). In the ensemble, Oba Ovonramwen, the central figure, is represented holding the traditional Edo sword of power on one hand and a Christian cross on the other.[4] According to Suzanne Preston Blier, "...the cross traditionally symbolizes the cosmos and temporal transition in Benin, but may also here be linked to Christianity as the Osa cult and priesthood is known to have adopted certain Christian motifs and practices."[5] In addition to the altar objects, there are several sixteenth- and seventeenth-century sculptures that are described as Afro-Portuguese ivories, brass, bronze, and terracotta because the African artists who made them juxtaposed European and African elements together.

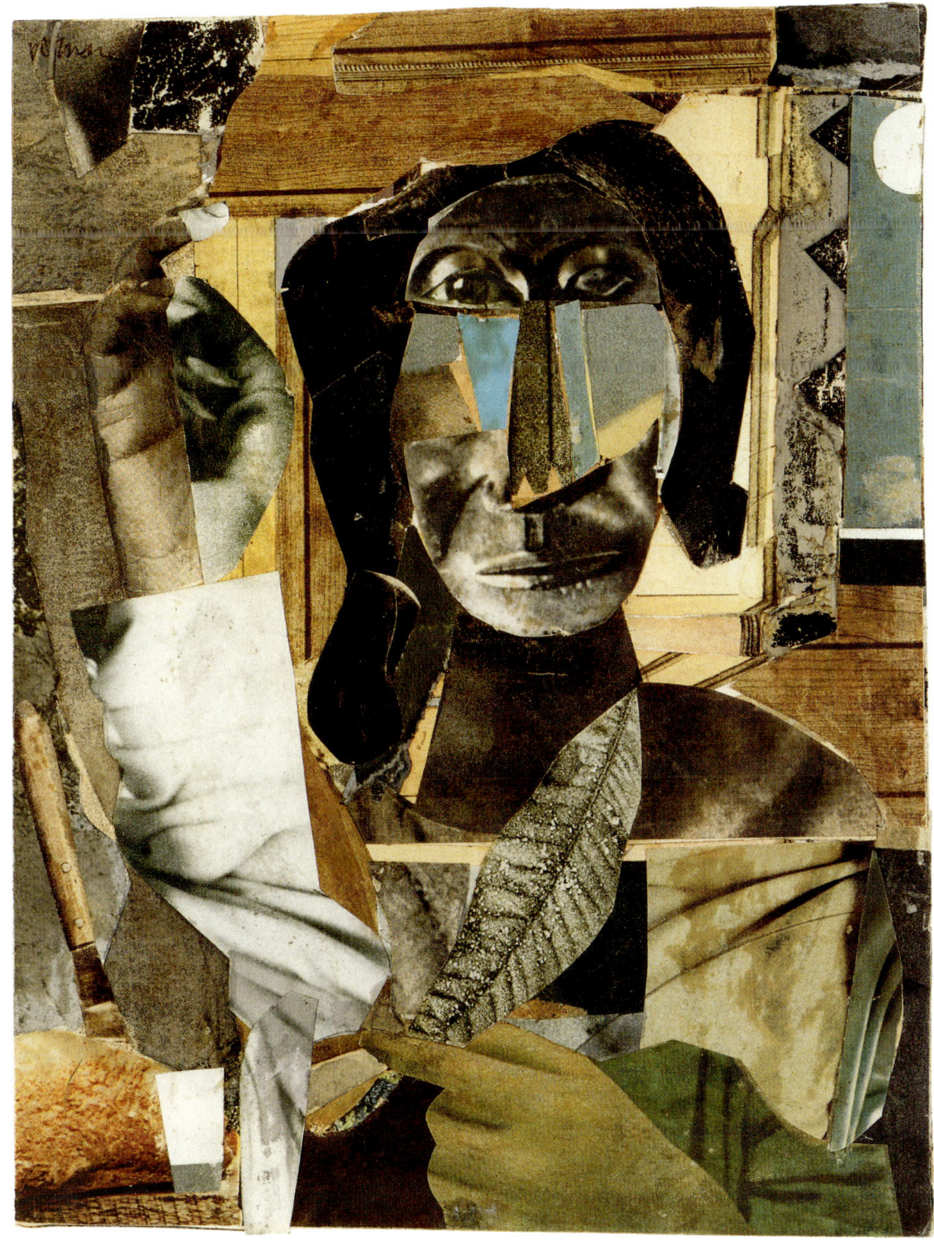

143

143
Romare Bearden, *Prevalence of Ritual: Conjur Woman*, 1964, collage of various papers with foil, ink, and graphite on cardboard, 23.8 x 18.4 (9 3/8 x 7 1/4). Anonymous lender

When exploring the cultural exchanges between Africa and the Caribbean in the *Divine Horsemen* (1953), Maya Deren elaborates on how certain traditional Yoruba religious rituals inspired Haitian religion, culture, and arts. According to Deren, such rituals are designed to serve as social discipline—they are tedious and do not really afford any self-expressive pleasure to the participants.[6] In Haiti, participation in voodoo rituals recapitulates one's relationship with ancestors and culture and also confirms the "first principles" (destiny, strength, love, life, and death). The objective of a ritual is not in the process or what transpired in it; it is focused on what the participant becomes when the ritual is over.

I do not intend to position Romare Bearden as a mediator between the avant-garde and minority groups in Africa, the Caribbean, and the United States. His work stands comfortably among the works of his contemporaries. However, by mastering the media of collage, one of the styles (mode of visual representation) of cubism, Bearden was able to create order out of chaos, produce emotions and desired focus in *Sermons: The Walls of Jericho,* and convey meanings in complex compositions that are derived from multiple cultures and time periods. The orderliness in which Bearden arranged the archetypal objects can be compared to the challenge that one will encounter if one were to speak Chinese, Edo (Benin language), Greek, Italian, Latin, Japanese, and Yoruba simultaneously and ensure that the speech makes sense to an audience.

The manner in which Bearden juxtaposed African and Euro-American elements in *Sermons: The Walls of Jericho* brings me to a second point—how some modernist and contemporary African artists apply elements we find in Bearden's works in their own oeuvre (collages, paintings, sculptures, and textiles). This is shown by connecting the possible relationships between how Bearden used African antiquities and the manner in which certain African artists applied the same objects in their works to a specific era. The decade in which Bearden prepared images such as *Sermons: The Walls of Jericho* (1964), *Prevalence of Ritual: Conjur Woman* (1964; no. 143), *Two Women* (1969; see fig. 11), and *Green Times Remembered: The Wishing Pond* (1970; fig. 4) and many of his well known collages is significant in both African-American and African history. It coincides with the Civil Rights movements in the United States, and several African countries gained their independence from European colonial powers during that decade. In the immediate post-independence era, the governments of the emancipated states were eager to build new national identities and binding memories and also to rid themselves of colonialist identities. They called upon some of their freshly trained modernist artists to represent major events that took place during their struggles for independence and to create objects that glorified the heroes who fought for the independence movements. One can cite Kwame Nkrumah's *Independence Arch* (1959) in Accra, Ghana, as an example.[7] Ghana was not the only country that evoked history in order to celebrate its independence and national aspirations. Although exclusive

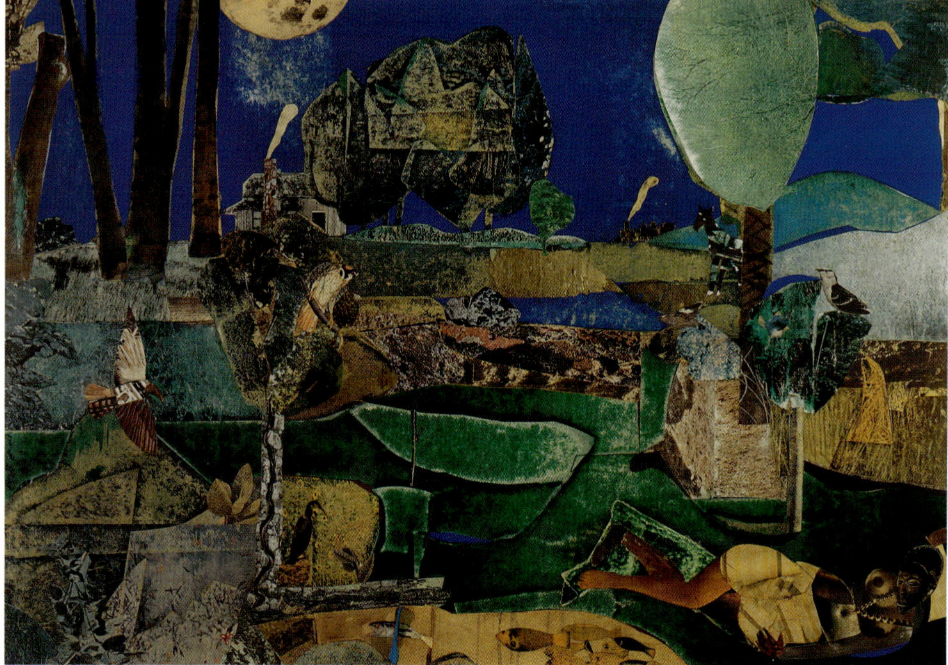

4

figure 4
Romare Bearden, *Green Times Remembered: The Wishing Pond,* 1970, collage and mixed media. Collection of Seth Taffae

figure 5
A currency of French-speaking West African states

to the Yoruba cultures of southwestern Nigeria, one of the dominant figures in the 5000-franc note (fig. 5) currently in use by several countries that were once French colonies (Senegal, Mali, Togo, Gabon, Burkina Faso, and many others) comes from Ife sculptural tradition.[8] Ife, the religious center believed to be the origin of Yoruba culture is located in southwestern Nigeria, but the emergent governments of former French colonies in Africa do not have a problem identifying with such images that can be traced to the twelfth century. This currency can be seen as a collage that exhibits Yoruba culture just as Bearden utilized such objects to tell his stories in the lower right corner of *Sermons: The Walls of Jericho.*

A brief sketch of the international scene in which Ghana's Independence Arch was created is important. This is an era in which, on the international scene, the relationships between the industrialized countries of Europe and the United States and the newly independent nations of Africa were given a new meaning under different terminologies such as first world versus third world, developed versus underdeveloped countries, industrialized versus nonindustrialized countries, and modern versus primitive countries. Along these lines of thinking, if you were an African artist and you practiced modern art, you were automatically evaluated as a non-Westerner who was aspiring to acquire Western culture and taste. If you were an African American and you practiced modern art, either you were seen as unable to make the leap beyond your cultural heritage or you were running away from your cultural heritage. If you were an American of European heritage and you shared an interest in modern art, it was seen by critics as modern art regardless of whether or not you included native American and Asian elements in your work. As a result, in Africa, to practice modern art in the immediate postcolonial era was conflated with the idea of progress, infrastructure development, and industrialization. On the other hand, in Europe and North America, to practice modern art was to engage in a particular cultural movement, and simply to be an artist.

The internal aspirations of the African nations and the politics of art in the international scene during the immediate postcolonial era convinced the newly emergent postcolonial African artists that they could be perceived as cultural traitors if they created works that did not make references to their own indigenous cultures. And, those who were interested in the practice of modern art as a discipline faced the problem of overcoming the perception that they were imitating Euro-American culture. The fact that this group of emergent African artists were educated in their homelands and abroad within the colonial educational systems that had perpetuated social injustices to their peoples did not make their problems easier. Many of the artists who studied abroad returned to their countries, assumed prominent positions, and helped in the development of modern and contemporary art. In order to articulate the artistic concerns of their era, these groups of artists drew from African myths, history, literature, and music, as well as the visual conventions that they had acquired from art academies in Europe and North America.

Here, we are reminded of the numerous African-American writers and artists who settled in Paris after World War II. Most of the artists derived their influences from the earlier Harlem Renaissance. The works of these artists transcend nineteenth-century American cultural heritage and speak more of a larger global movement that is tied to the European avant-garde as well as pan-Africanist movements in the Caribbean, Europe, and North America. Sketching the educational profile of some of the African artists might help us to see how, although residing in different continents, they shared educational experiences that one might compare to the kind of education that Bearden had received before he began to produce his collages of the 1960s. Sharon Patton writes that:

> In 1950, encouraged by Claude McKay and Barry [*sic*] Stavis, Bearden traveled to Paris to study philosophy part-time at the Sorbonne on the G.I. Bill. With letters of introduction from Samuel Kootz, Bearden met Constantine Brancusi and Georges Braque. On his own, he met other writers and artists, among them Fernand Léger, Jean Hélion, Wilfredo Lam, and Hans Reichel.[9]

In Africa, one can name Ben Enwonwu (born 1921) who studied in England in the 1940s before he returned to Nigeria.[10] He served as the art adviser to the federal government of Nigeria in the 1950s and 1960s. He carved in stone and wood, painted, and cast several bronze sculptures, including one for Queen Elizabeth II. Enwonwu created several objects that made reference to known Nigerian cultural motifs. His *Anyawnu* (literary translation from Igbo language: "the eye of the sun, a bright light, the illuminator"), has details that derive from a sixteenth-century Benin queen mother head, but the Edo (Benin) people did not cast their queen mother as Enwonwu did.

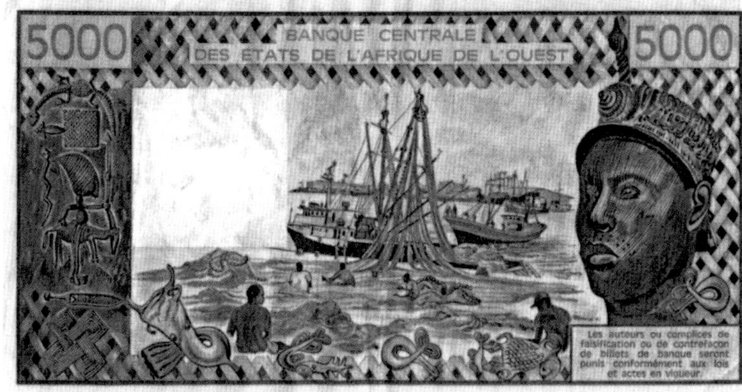

5

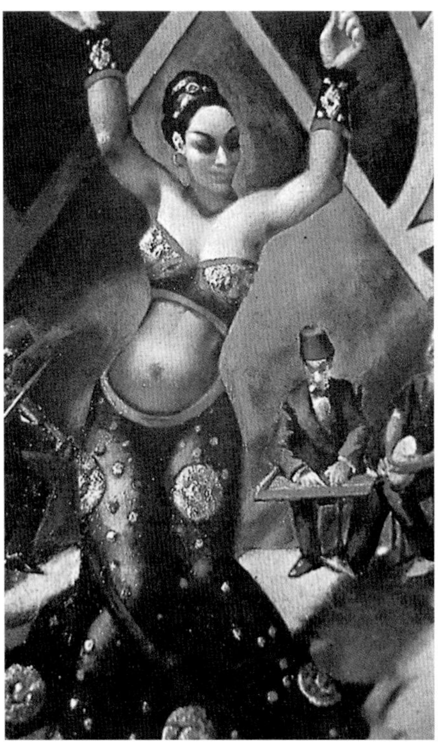

6

He elongated the figure by giving her a body and a tail that serves as her feet. The traditional woven pangolin dress that is common among Benin royalties was cast to look like the scales of a reptile and her thin limbs were streamlined to match her curved body as she stood on her feet/tail. Looking at this object creates the illusion of a sudden encounter with the ghost of a sixteenth-century Benin queen mother that is rising from a deep sea. Working with stone, the sculpture he prepared for the Nigerian National Electric Power Authority evokes the powers of Shango, the Yoruba god of thunder. Enwonwu used Shango to represent the power of electricity. Enwonwu's Shango has a great resemblance to the Greek-inspired Renaissance ideal body, however, its coiffure and the loincloth around his waist betray the fact that it is mostly derived from Ife sculptural traditions.[11]

Papa Ibra Taal (born 1935) suggests that his works emanate from the rhythms of negritude poetry and prose that celebrated the cult of the ancestors. Taal began his studies in painting at the École des Beaux-Arts in Paris and at the Centre Pédagogie Artistique de Sèvres after completing secondary school in Senegal and winning a scholarship to study abroad. Upon returning to Senegal, Taal became a professor of art and was appointed to head the Department of Black Plastic-Arts at the École des Beaux-Arts, Dakar, Senegal.

Moroccan-born Farid Belkahia (born 1934) was educated at the École des Beaux-Arts in Paris (1954–59) before he was appointed the director of the École des Beaux Arts in Casablanca. Belkahia was influenced by the works of Georges Rouault and Paul Klee when he was studying in Paris. As a result, his later work on Arabic calligraphy incorporated the influences from his foreign education.[12]

From Egypt, we have Mahmoud Said (1887–1964), a trained lawyer who later changed careers and studied painting in Alexandria under the Italian teachers Emilia Casanato and Antonio Zanin between 1914 and 1916. He traveled extensively in Europe and lived in Paris where he joined the Academie de la Grand Chaumière. His painting, *Dancer with Takht* (1949; fig. 6), articulates a new image for the modern Egyptian woman. The irony is that while countering certain orientalist stereotypes that one might observe, for example, in Jean-Léon Gérôme's *Snake Charmer* (fig. 7), Said also reinforces some of those stereotypes because he worked in the orientalist visual mode of representation. This is fuel for certain critics who marginalize modern and contemporary African art as a pastiche of Euro-American cultural productions. As indicated earlier, one cannot ignore the problems that can result when citizens of former colonies depend on the colonialist educational system and language in order to rehabilitate their culture.

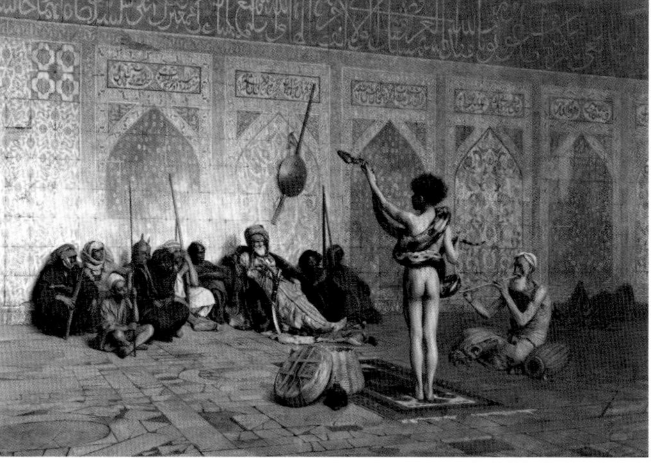

7

figure 6
Mahmoud Said (1887–1964), Egypt, *Dancer with Takht,* 1949, oil on canvas, Ministry of Culture, Cairo, Egypt. It derives from the same orientalist visual mode of representation as Gérôme's *Snake Charmer* (fig. 7)

figure 7
Jean-Léon Gérôme, *The Snake Charmer,* c. 1870, oil on canvas. Sterling and Francine Clark Art Institute, Williamstown, Massachusetts

If the Egyptian-born Said adopted a visual mode of representation that was used by the European-born Gérôme in order to express his artistic concerns, is that act any different from what happens when the Egyptian-born Mahmoud Mukhtar produces a work, *Egyptian Awakening* (1919, the gate of Cairo University; fig. 8), which echoes an exact theme of an earlier work by Meta Warrick Fuller, *Ethiopia Awakening* (1914; fig. 9)? If we were to eliminate racial differences such as African (Said) versus European (Gérôme) from the equation, then the particular contexts in which Said expressed his artistic concerns in the visual language by which Gérôme completed his orientalist projects would no longer be an issue. In this case, if race and legitimacy are raised, they function as a mechanism for enforcing distinctions and subsequently denying participation of the "other" in the modernist agenda. After all, upon examining the details of Fuller's and Mukhtar's sculptures, one might find that Mukhtar might have addressed a theme that is highly related to an earlier theme by an African-American artist but the issues of race and legitimacy are not raised here. Fuller and Mukhtar produced sphinxes, emblems of great African kings who lived three thousand years before Christ. If we consider Fuller's and Mukhtar's sphinxes as similar to Bearden's use of African images in his collages, we will observe that although the African Americans are far from the Egyptians who reside in northern Africa, African history provided them a forum for exploring a common theme in their works just as the orientalist visual language provided Said and Gérôme a way to address their artistic concerns.

We can extend the same analogy to Aaron Douglas' *Aspects of Negro Life: The Negro in an African Setting,* completed in 1934, and the

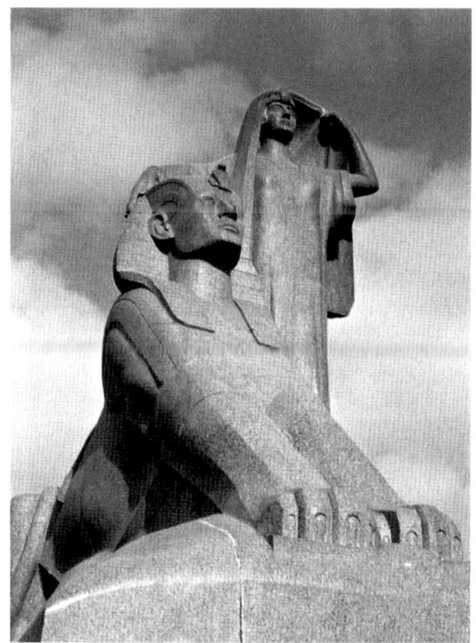

8

Jamaican-born Edna Manley's sculpture, *The Negro Aroused,* completed in 1935, two closely related works although the former is a painting and the latter is a sculpture. Following in the steps of Edna Manley, at about the same time that the sculpture was completed, the Jamaican author George Campbell composed a poem with the same title, "The Negro Aroused." The first two lines and the last three lines of the poem read as follows:

Negro Aroused! Awakened from
The ignominious sleep of dominance!...

Freedom! Let them beat down this house,
Muscle built, stifle this screaming voice,
Let them! We are aroused![13]

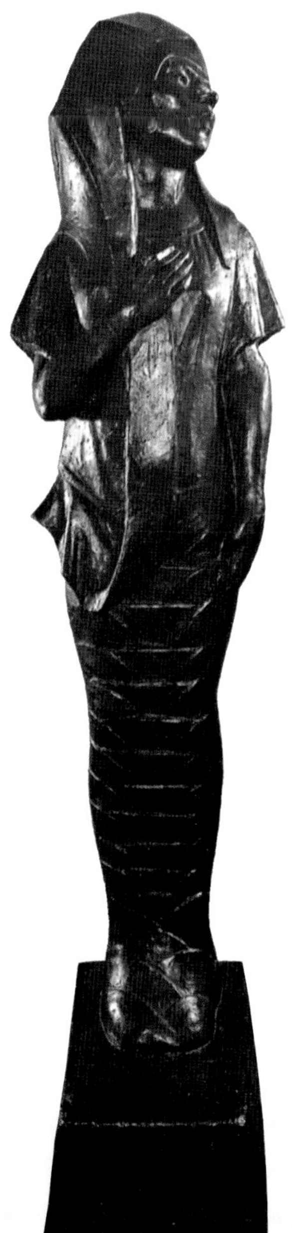

9

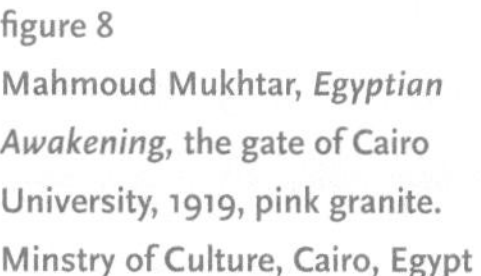

figure 8
Mahmoud Mukhtar, *Egyptian Awakening,* the gate of Cairo University, 1919, pink granite. Minstry of Culture, Cairo, Egypt

figure 9
Meta Warrick Fuller, *Ethiopia Awakening,* 1914, bronze. The Schomburg Center for Research in Black Culture, Art and Artifacts Division, The New York Public Library, Astor, Lenox, and Tilden Foundations

The sculpture by Manley and the poem by Campbell are connected by shared social and historical experience. The poet and the sculptor expressed similar ideas using the media that are available to them. By doing so the works of Manley and Campbell became the voices that spoke their concerns and emphasized their comradeship within a defined struggle for social, political, cultural, and economic freedom. Similarly, upon reading Bearden's poems, one can see that Bearden tried to put in collages things he has pondered in words.

What is it?
I'm trying really to remember
The clock has stopped
Now I can never know
Where the edge of my world can be
If I could only enter that old calendar
That opens to an old, old July
And learn what unknowing things know. . . .[14]

While this excerpt from Bearden's poem does not speak about a single collage, one can see traces of memory and social recollections, fragments of cultural aspirations, economic marginalization, and political disenfranchisement. To Bearden, such memories evoked dreams and experiences that he wanted to forget but he could not forget. Like Manley and Campbell, Bearden was left with the option of expressing his concerns —speaking out as eloquently as he could using the media he knew best, his collages. One can see how Bearden saw his world as a collage in the statement, "Now I can never know where the edge of my world can be." Bearden saw a world in which time stood still, a world that did not have boundary and cultures, history, experiences, emotions, celebrations, and defeats mixed up within one's experiences all at the same time. Perhaps, this is one of the reasons that Bearden could move to all parts of the world and draw images for a collage such as *Sermons: The Walls of Jericho*. In this collage, Bearden tried to put into images, the world he saw in his mind's eye.

George Campbell's poem leads to a third concern. Starting from the middle of the twentieth century, relationships between the avant-garde and minority groups (those who operate on the margin, not recognized by the establishment) have been closer than previously thought.

Among the many propositions that are put forward concerning modern and contemporary African art, there is a school of thought that espouses the viewpoint that modern and contemporary African art is a pastiche of modern European art because modernist African artists have deviated from their traditional art—the original, innocent, primitive art of their ancestors. This questioning of the originality of modern and contemporary art of Africa stems from the manner in which the scholars who first addressed cubism presented the relationships between minority groups and the avant-garde. One can mention Edward Fry's *Cubism* (1966), Robert Goldwater's *Primitivism in Modern Art* (1938), Robert Rosenblum's *Cubism and Twentieth Century Art* (1966), and several essays on the subject written during the middle of the twentieth century.

Goldwater popularized the viewpoint that cubism was inspired by the curiosity of artists from civilized European cultures who were drawn to the arts of "retarded peoples" (primitive cultures) for the benefit of realizing pure and original art that is unadulterated by civilization.[15] One has to give Goldwater credit for elucidating the point that the cubists did not go to non-European cultures only and that the practice of looking toward the archaic for artistic inspiration predated cubism. Nevertheless, by failing to indicate the exact nature of the relationships between the cubists and the avant-garde, he inadvertently marginalized the contributions of the non-Western groups to the role of contributing only archaic forms to the development of cubism. As such, minority artists were not participants in the development of cubism, instead, they were observers whose cultures met the exotic needs of the bored and civilized European artist who was looking for adventure.

This trajectory of thought encouraged Goldwater, Fry, and Rosenblum to focus on the rebellious intentions of cubism against the established canons of European modes of visual representations.[16] This approach postulates that cubism is a visual performance and a cultural mode of communication among a rebellious group. In this context, the ability of cubism to perform depended on its own visual language. Visual language is the process by which cubism transformed nature, culture, and political narratives, as well as materials into works of art. The most important element in the transformative process is the exploitation of alterity (the other) through the appropriation of non-European cultural modes of visual representation. When describing the creative forces and the motivations that shaped Picasso's *Dancer* (1907) Robert Rosenblum writes:

When comparing the *Dancer* with the African funerary figure from Bakota, the dual nature of this influence soon becomes clear. For one thing, primitive sculpture apparently exemplified, for Picasso, the freedom to distort anatomy for the sake of creating a rhythmic structure that can merge solids and voids and invent new shapes. For another, its terrifying power and suggestion of a supernatural presence seem to have been equally stimulating. Looked at in the context of the Western artistic tradition of the nude, the African sculpture, like Picasso's dancer, is unbearably ugly. As such it provides Picasso with an artistic stimulus of man-made grotesquerie that could, perhaps, surpass even the God-made grotesquerie of his earlier *Dwarf Dancer* of 1901.[17]

Thomas Crow expanded on the early thesis regarding the development of cubism by clarifying the reasons the cubists decided to rebel against the established canons. Unlike Goldwater's "primitivism" as a source of curiosity for the civilized avant-garde, the marketplace dictated how the avant-garde handled its artistic concerns. Crow suggests that the cult of novelty and sometimes the strange, which emphasizes rituals, individual experience, and alterity, as well as the desire to claim the public sphere in avant-garde art can be traced to the social tensions caused by the industrial bourgeois society. According to this point of view, the mistrust of the bourgeois-dominated society allowed the avant-garde to visualize itself as a "minority movement" functioning alongside the bourgeois-dominated modern art movement. Crow recognized the tension that existed between modernism and the avant-garde in his thesis and in order to diffuse the tension, he proposed that modernism designates "the characteristic practice that goes on within the social and ideological formation we call avant-garde."[18]

On the other hand, the term avant-garde is more inclusive and often it does not place social or international boundaries on its sources; it includes low-culture, group survival mechanisms, as well as provocative styles.[19] In Crow's dichotomy between modernism and the avant-garde, the latter went to the low-culture as a tactical approach during its battle against the bourgeois-dominated market. The traditional motifs that the avant-garde retrieved from the cultures of the lower classes provided it with the weapons for its war. Having appropriated such weapons, it retreated and restored to "itself the high-cultural autonomy it had momentarily abandoned."[20] Crow does not stand alone in proposing this market-driven avant-garde. Clement Greenberg also articulated the thesis as "kitsch."

Kitsch, using for raw material the debased and academicized simulacra of genuine culture, welcomes and cultivates this insensibility [the appropriation of lower culture]. It is the source of its profits. Kitsch is mechanical and operates by formulas. Kitsch is vicarious experience and faked sensations. Kitsch changes according to style, but remains always the same. Kitsch is the epitome of all that is spurious in the life of our times. Kitsch pretends to demand nothing of their customers except their money—not even their time.[21]

I am in agreement with Crow's and Greenberg's proposals regarding the self-entrapment of the avant-garde in the marketplace. There is no doubt that the "enormous profit" of kitsch was a "source of temptation to the avant-garde itself, and its members have not always resisted this temptation."[22] However both Crow and Greenberg failed to take advantage of the strong theoretical foundations they contributed because they narrowed their investigations to European viewpoints.[23]

One might ask, what is missing from the versions of the dialogue between the avant-garde cubists and their minority (African and African-American) counterparts that Crow and Greenberg provided? It is the fact that the minority groups were full members of the surrealist movement, i.e., the avant-garde, starting from the 1930s.

I emphasize that Crow and Greenberg are indispensable here as we attempt to bridge the missing aspect of the dialogue between the surrealists and the minority groups. Both scholars clearly elucidated the point that the obsession of the avant-garde with the exploitation of language as a tool for group survival enabled the avant-garde, especially the Parisian surrealists, to see themselves as minorities. Here, I will extend Crow's and Greenberg's foundations by suggesting that the avant-garde did not just take from the "other" and return to their bourgeois culture, leaving nothing behind. In this extension, I argue that in relation to what the avant-garde obtained from minority groups, the search for kitsch was obtained with a strong alliance that enabled the minority groups to become full members of the surrealist movement.

Seeing themselves as minorities as Crow and Greenberg have stated, the surrealists developed certain radical values that enabled them to form a strong alliance with other minority groups who were suffering in what they saw as bourgeois-dominated society. The minority groups with whom the surrealists joined hands came from the colonies of France. They included Africans; they came from the Caribbean islands, Asia, and the United States. Although the government of the United States did not officially declare the black communities in the country as colonies,

African Americans were living under oppressive conditions that were comparable and sometimes worse than the ways of life in some of the French colonies. The latter point is yet to be fleshed out by scholars of the avant-garde. As such, there is a lacuna in the literature of surrealism regarding the full participation of minority artists who helped to invigorate the movement in the middle of the twentieth century.

It is not an overstatement to suggest that the surrealist movement holds a privileged position in the internationalization of avant-garde culture that gave more minority access to the modern movement than any other avant-garde group. One thing that set the surrealists apart from all the other avant-garde movements was their stance on colonial issues. For example, between 1925 and 1926, during the province of Rif rebellion in Morocco, the surrealists sided with Abdul Karim of Morocco. They joined forces with the French communist party in the condemnation of the French government and openly called upon French soldiers to rise up and fraternize with the colonized people of Morocco and all over the French colonies. It was during these early years that the surrealists gave an unreserved commitment to what they called the "color question,"[24] meaning the "other." The surrealist's emphasis of cultural rejuvenation as a means to political freedom obviously came out of their own self-reflections as a marginalized group in the bourgeois-dominated European society—their fear of bourgeois appropriation of language, the tools of education, and "mass culture" for social domination.

The surrealists seized the opportunity during the 1931 Paris Colonial Exhibition, which was specifically staged to display the splendors of the French empire and the relationships between the metropole, France, and the peripheries, the colonies, to act out their disdain for bourgeois domination of European society and to condemn cultural domination of colonized people. They published and distributed a tract called "Murderous Humanitarianism," which later appeared in Nancy Cunard's 1934 *Negro Anthology.* The objective of the tract was to present the government and the sponsors of the exhibition as hypocrites who had the sinister intention of subjugating the cultures of colonized peoples while taking away their identity under the guise of enhancing them with the cultures of "Greater France."

Signed by André Breton, Roger Caillois, René Char, René Crevel, Paul Éluard, Jules-Marcel Monnerot, Benjamin Péret, Yves Tanguy, André Thirion, Pierre Unik, and Pierre Yoyotte,[25] in "Murderous Humanitarianism," the surrealists asserted that they were in favor of taking up the problems of the suppressed colored people in Africa, Europe, Asia, the Caribbean, North America, and South America and bringing them into France as civil war. With the support of the communist party, the surrealists staged a counter exhibition. Their major feature was a starving African child holding a bowl and begging for food. They called it the "European Fetish, and the Real Truth about the colonies" which the hypocritical bourgeois who were staging the 1931 Paris Colonial Exhibition did not tell the world.

By focusing on the psychology of colonialism against colonized people and by positioning the cultures of colonized people as a means of combating colonial domination, the 1931 tract set a revolutionary precedent that was adopted by several future anticolonialist groups and pan-Africanist cultural movements. The radical and explosive 1931 publication by the surrealists left no doubt in the minds of minority artists that they could trust and work with the surrealists.

On 1 June 1932, a group of students from the French colony of Martinique who were studying in Paris took a decisive political cue from André Breton's 1926 *Surrealist Manifesto* and published a document called *Légitime Défense.* The authors of the document include Etienne Léro, Thélus Léro, René Ménil, Monnerot, Michel Pilotin, Maurice-Sabas Quintman, Auguste Thésée, and Pierre Yoyotte. The text focused on the liberation of colonized people from European imperialism and from its own highly assimilated [Martinique] bourgeoisie community, through a Marxist framework of social transformation.[26] The uncompromising tone of the journal and its extreme left-wing affiliation caused the French government to cut off the students' scholarships. In addition, the French government put pressure on the students and succeeded in closing down the journal in 1934.[27]

One serious criticism of *Légitime Défense* is that it did not concentrate on the problems of African peoples around the world. It was too concerned with universal problems that could be resolved by Marxism and the French avant-garde movement. As Michael Richardson points out, "Certainly, considered in its unity and structure, the discourse of *Légitime Défense* is not a discourse of negritude,"[28] a movement that dedicated itself to the promotion of African culture and identity. This accusation stuck despite the fact that the students who published the document, while declaring their full fidelity to the surrealist movement, wanted to retain a certain autonomy in order to concentrate on their socio-ethnic problems. This also explains why we did not have to wait long before *Pigments* (1937) by Damas and *Notebook of a Return to My Native Land* (1939) by Aimé Césaire came out in order to respond to the kind of literature that was missing in *Légitime Défense.* According to Gendzier, "When Senghor's [Léopold Sédar Senghor] anthology appeared, and when *Présence Africaine* (1947) was first published, the movement known as negritude was no longer a novelty. It had its roots in the political and literary experiments that had involved men of different continents and political orientations."[29]

In December 1945 André Breton visited Haiti and gave several lectures. Breton's first lecture on 20 December at the Rex Theater, Port-au-Prince, concentrated on the themes of culture, as well as political and economic freedom. According to Breton, in Haiti, "Surrealism verifies one of its fundamental propositions, that the first condition of a people's persistence, as of a culture's viability, is that both can endlessly re-immerse themselves in the great affective currents that bore them at birth, without which they rapidly collapse."[30] Breton was also of the opinion that several Haitian painters like Hector Hypolite derived their creative inspiration from the Haitian voodoo religion, without which their works would not be authentic.[31] Seen as a subversive rebel who had come to cause an uprising in Martinique, Breton was expelled from the country in 1946 after a military coup that took over the government of President Elie Lescot, who could not contain the insurgency that was inspired by Breton's lectures. A surrealist journal *La Rouch* (1945), published by Lézignan-Corbiès, Réne Depestre, Théodore Baker, J. S. Alexis, and G. Bloncourt, was closed down by the military government and the insurrection was repressed, paving the way for François Duvalier to assume power in Haiti.

In Paris and in Martinique the allegiance of Africans from the Caribbean continued to inspire the publication of journals such as *L' Etudiant Noire* (1934) and *Tropiques* (1941–1945). Frantz Fanon, a Martinique-born French psychiatrist, whose intellectual associates were members of the surrealist movement in France, went to Algeria to help the French community, but he switched sides and fought alongside the native Algerian soldiers against the French army whom he was sent to Algeria to help.[32] Based on his experiences in the Algerian war, Fanon published his landmark books, *Black Skin White Masks* (1952) and *The Wretched of the Earth* (1961).[33]

I have maintained that drawing from the socioeconomic concerns of the artists, the avant-garde, especially surrealism, an offshoot of cubism, can be seen as a visual language that incorporates action in order to achieve its artistic objectives. This language-based thesis is best elucidated in the essay "Black Orpheus" (1948), by Jean-Paul Sartre, who proposed that Francophone minorities have mastered the French language to the extent that they could use it as a tool for subverting and displacing the dominant French culture. Like the surrealists, Sartre believed that language is a tool for cultural, economic, and political domination. Any society that does not have its own language will not be able to sustain its own culture, identity, and independence. Written as a preface for the first anthology that was compiled by Senghor and his fellow black poets in France (1948), Sartre's "Black Orpheus" encapsulates the major idealistic and universal goals of the visual language of the avant-garde. According to Sartre:

> The Negro as we have said creates an anti-racist racism. He does not at all wish to dominate the world; he wishes the abolition of racial privileges wherever they are found; he affirms his solidarity with the oppressed of all colors. At a blow the subjective, existential, ethnic notion of Negritude "passes" as Hegel would say, into the objective, positive, exact notion of the proletariat.[34]

In order to justify the polemically charged anti-European sentiments that are expressed in the anthology, Sartre condensed the most important aspects of his essay as follows:

> In fact, Negritude appears as the weak stage of a dialectical progression: the theoretical practical affirmation of white supremacy is the thesis; the position of Negritude as antithetical value is the moment of the negativity. But this negative moment is not sufficient in itself and the blacks who employ it well know it; they know that it serves to prepare the way for the synthesis or the realization of the human society without racism. Thus Negritude is dedicated to its own destruction, it is a passage and not objective, means and not the goal.[35]

Sartre's "Black Orpheus" is both numinous and prophetic in that it demonstrates how minority groups engaged their political and economic concerns through the media of architecture, dance, film, literature, music, paintings, the performance arts, sculptures, and textiles, just as their European allies were doing. I would like to add that Sartre's views can be extended to Crow's and Greenberg's thesis about the activism of the avant-garde for the purposes of combating bourgeois domination.

If we extend Crow's, Greenberg's, and Sartre's visual language thesis to Bearden's *Sermons: The Walls of Jericho,* then this collage can be seen as

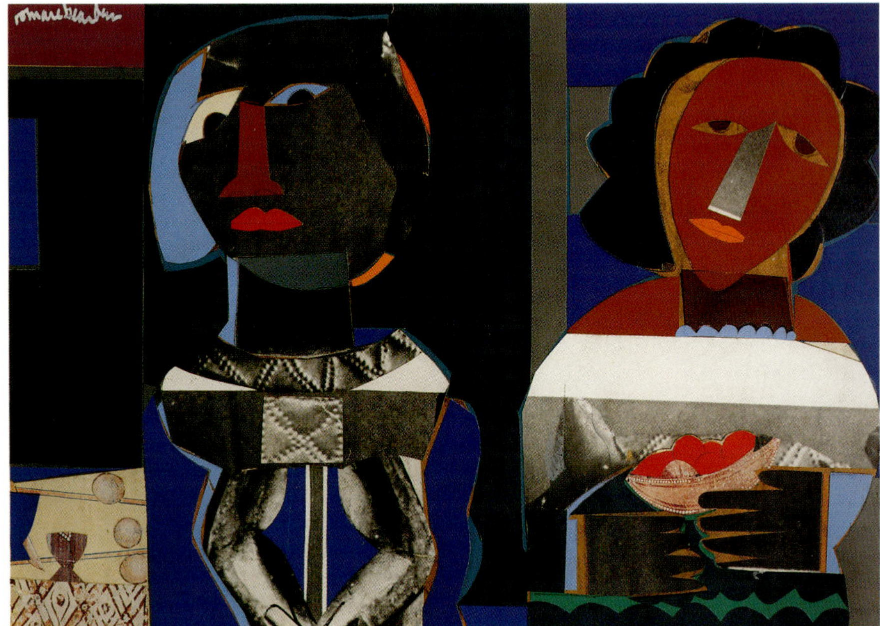

11

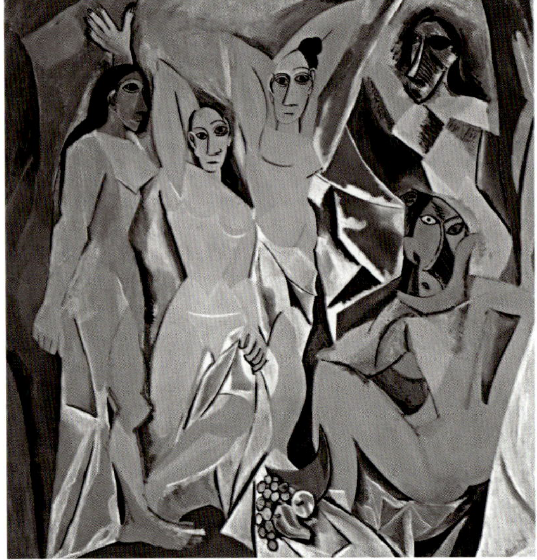

10

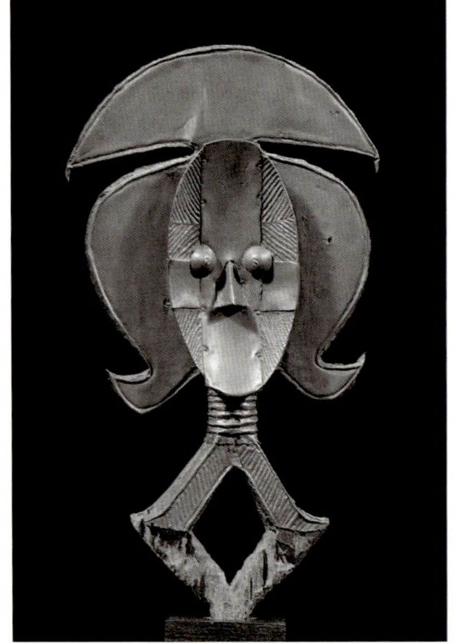

12

figure 10
Pablo Picasso, *Les Demoiselles d'Avignon,* 1907, oil on canvas. The Museum of Modern Art, New York. Acquired through Lillie P. Bliss Bequest

figure 11
Romare Bearden, *Two Women,* 1969, collage. Collection of Fanny Ellison, New York

figure 12
Reliquary ancestor guardian figures, nineteenth century, Kota, Gabon. The Chaim Gross Studio Museum, New York

a visual language of cubism, a technique that was pioneered by Georges Braque and Pablo Picasso. Like any user of language, the artist Bearden had the responsibility of communicating to his audience. Even in its most abstract and esoteric form where meaning might be difficult to decipher and comprehend, the absence of meaning becomes the meaning of the language because the artist was reflecting on cues from human experiences. In addition, the fact that Braque and Picasso developed the technique of collage does not add or remove from the meaning that Bearden wanted to communicate to his audience, just as Gérôme's orientalist inspiration should not take away from whatever meaning that Said wanted to convey to his audience, and Fuller's *Ethiopia Awakening* does not take away from Mukhtar's *Egyptian Awakening.* In a similar vein we can look at Picasso's *Les Demoiselles d'Avignon* (1907) (fig. 10) and Bearden's *Two Women* (1969) (fig. 11), both of which drew heavily from the nineteenth-century Kota, Gabon, reliquary ancestor guardian figures (fig. 12) and from several Euro-American sources. The former focuses on the subject matter of a Spanish brothel, while the latter deals with African-American life and spirituality.[36] Each of these pictures met the needs for which the artist produced it without taking away from the other, regardless of the fact that Picasso's picture is sixty-two years earlier than Bearden's picture.

To that effect, all these projects say more about the flexibility of cubism than the authenticity or inauthenticity of the works that different artists produced within the modernist tradition. Seen from this perspective, *Sermons: The Walls of Jericho* speaks more to the fact that Bearden's collages contain elements from many cultural, geographical, historical, political, and stylistic conventions, regardless of my Africanist focus on its visual contents and meanings. *Sermons: The Walls of Jericho* is a ruptured space in which one can observe how Bearden thematically utilized portraiture, landscape, folklore, literature, history, music, mythology, and religion to present his concerns in the form of a social narrative. Sharon Patton writes that "the visual eloquence of Bearden's art recalled the prose of African-American life as he reconstructed his own life's history and the culture of African Americans."[37] John A. Williams shares Patton's view by suggesting that "looking at Bearden's work, I seem to be looking at subjects distorted by the soft movement of water in a shallow creek. In those 'distortions' I see the black psyche pulsating mysteriously with contradictions of joy, defeat, victory, endurance, and this in relationship to the whole of humankind."[38]

Yes, along the line of thought expressed by Williams, I conclude that minority artists contributed their share to the development of surrealism in relationship to the rest of humankind. If there is an absence in the literature that speaks to the contributions of minority groups in the development of surrealism, the absence speaks more to the historical fact that many people from around the world (Africa, Europe, Asia, the Americas), who have worked very hard and continue to invest most of their lives toward the production of the goods of capitalism and its high culture, have often been excluded from participating in the enjoyment of its benefits. Bearden's *Sermons: The Walls of Jericho* eloquently conveys this message.

Reading Bearden

JACQUELINE FRANCIS

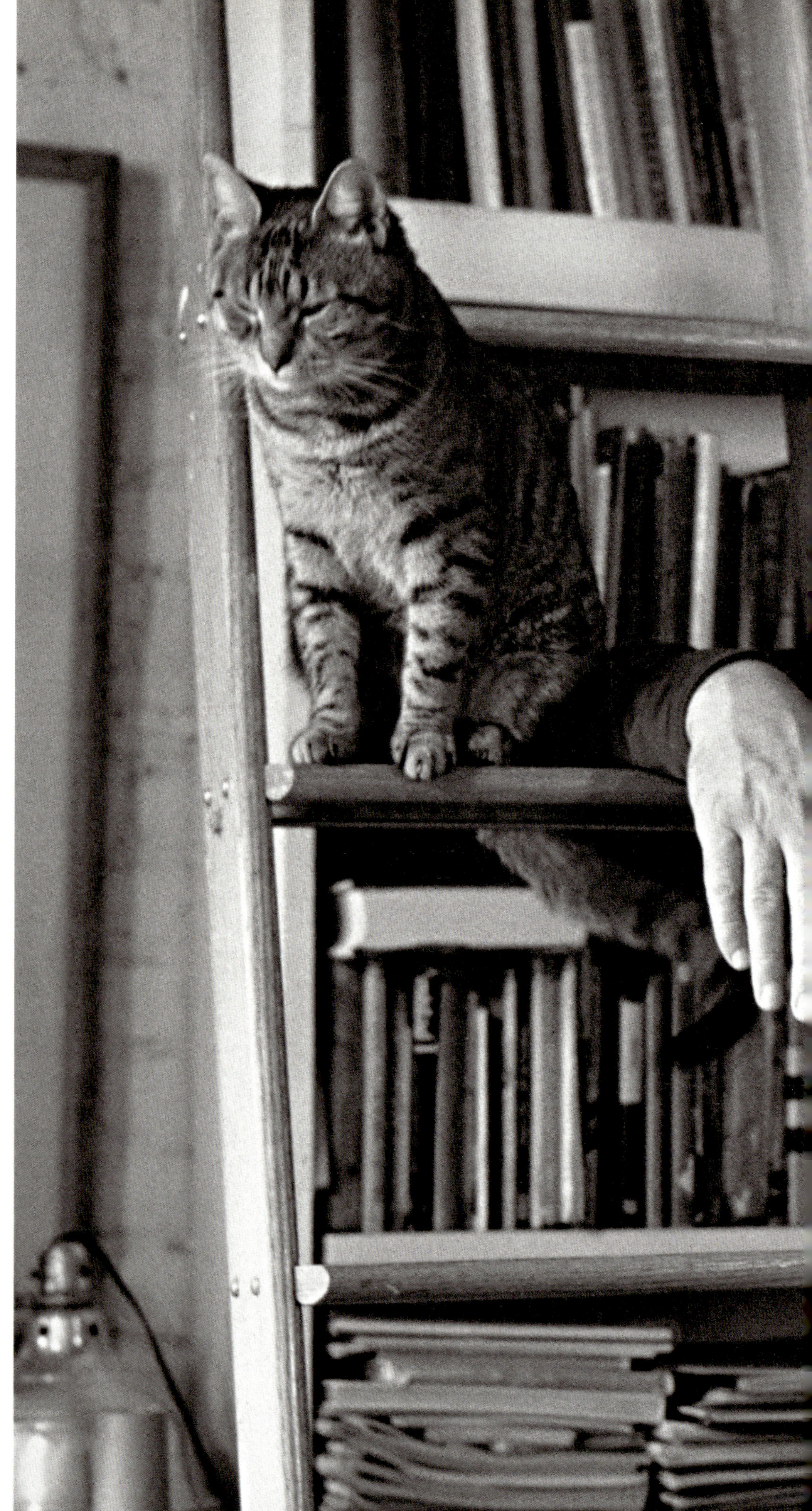

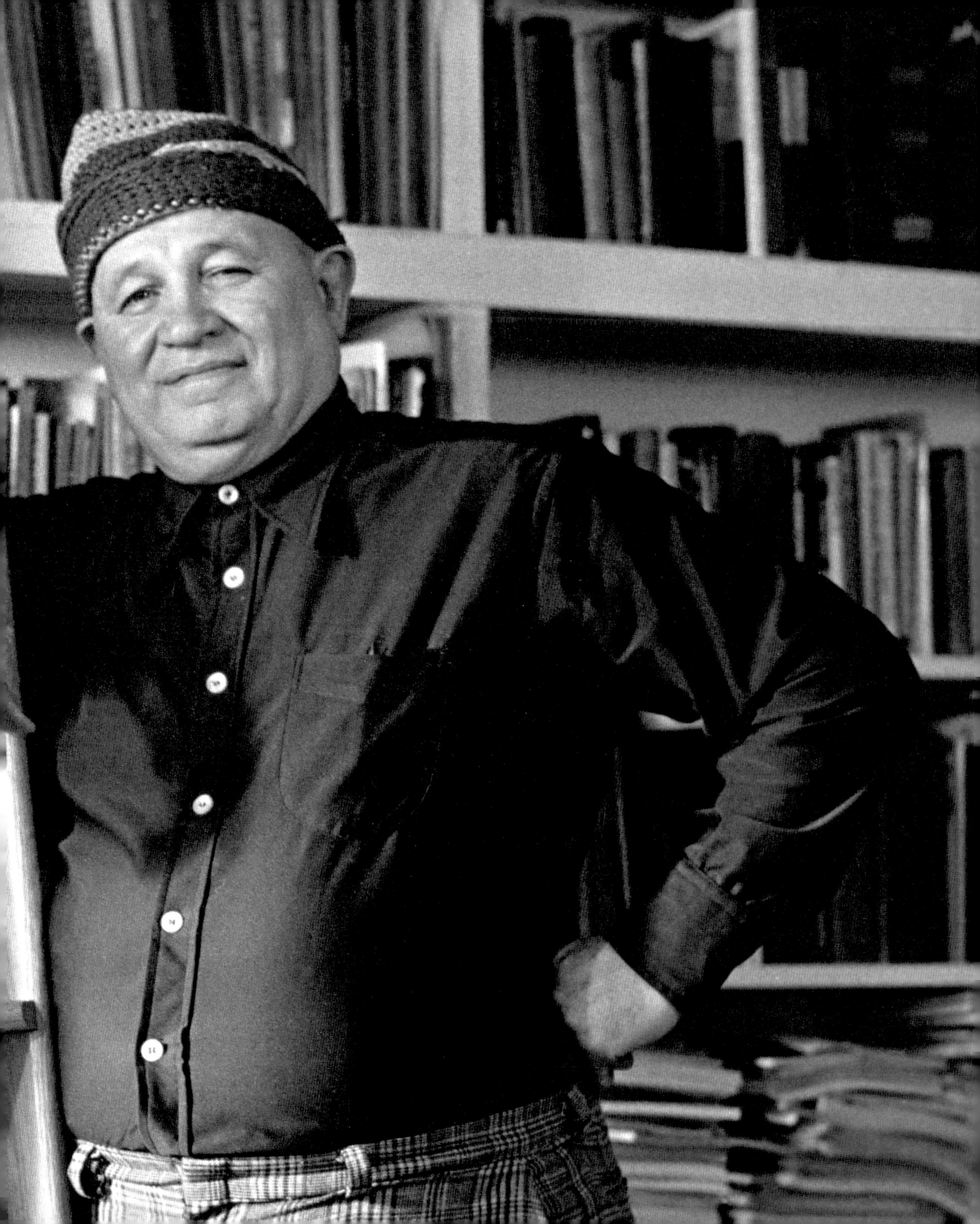

Romare Bearden's tastes as a reader and paths as a writer were myriad. He read and studied history, art history, politics, literature, music, religion, psychology, and philosophy throughout his life. He was a bibliophile who amassed hundreds of books and magazines on these subjects, mining dictionaries and encyclopedias for definitions and aphorisms, jotting these down along with charts of poetic meter and diagrams of compositional theories such as the "Golden Section" (figs. 1, 2). He read criticism and treatises from Aristotle to Henri Bergson, sources that he deemed authoritative, and hence, helpful to his reflections on art and experience. Luxuriating in language in his notebooks, diaries, song lyrics, correspondence, and published histories and articles about African-American artists' production (including his own), Bearden wrote to think through ideas—his and those of the artists and writers he admired. His writings reveal fascination with a variety of creative approaches and lay bare his efforts to conceive the artist's vocation on a heroic scale.

Why look to the writing of an artist, especially one whose corpus still demands much formal analysis and art historical contextualization? And, don't Bearden's publications—among them cultural histories, art surveys, biographies, exhibition reviews, reminiscences—speak eloquently for themselves? Neither the published nor unpublished writings can fully explain this artist or his oeuvre; moreover, much of the material in the latter category is fragmentary and generates more questions than definitive answers. His personal books only occasionally bear annotations that would direct scholars to the indisputable origins and clear outcomes of his particular artistic projects. Nonetheless, the written record left behind by Bearden affords a rare opportunity to consider

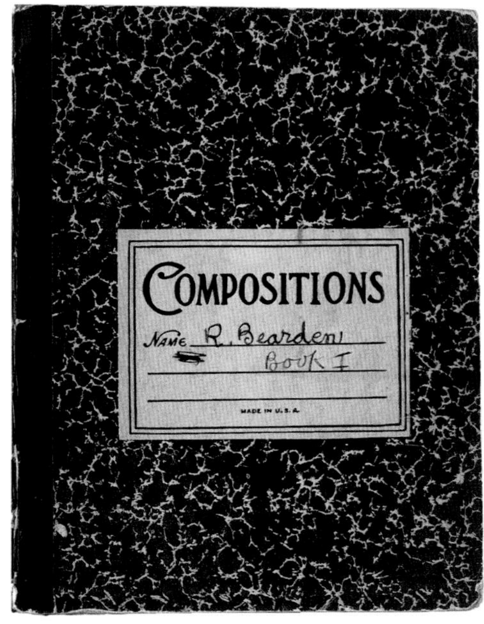

1

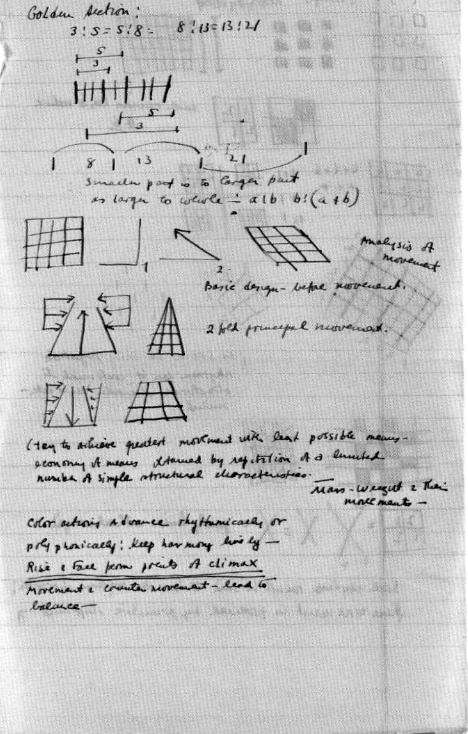

2

art as a result of thinking and reasoning, for even in the twenty-first century, the prevailing view is a romantic one, namely, that the purest art springs from the sensitive soul's churning depths. In the art histories of our time, the power accorded to artists is framed as magic and mystery, only loosely connected to conceptualizing plans and preparatory sketches. And what is written about African-American (and other) artists of color as an undifferentiated whole generally aligns them to such metaphors' exotic alchemy: that is, the black artist-subject is a translator, able to restate the ever-present rhythms of black culture into a legible visual analogue.[1] For all of the sincere appreciation for African-American art, it has been effectively relegated to the categories of autobiography and documentary—something illustrative of that buzz-phrase, "the black experience." At the least, attention to Bearden's writing is perhaps a breakthrough toward retiring such an oversimplified characterization of how art comes to be.

Albert Murray played a crucial collaborative role in the organization of Bearden's writing in the 1960s and afterward. The two met in Paris in 1950, and when reunited in New York in the following decade, Murray, an African-American novelist and critic, became the artist's close friend and sounding board. He often came up with titles for Bearden's work, and he gave shape to talks and essays such as the 1969 article "Rectangular Structure in My Montage Paintings" and Bearden's 1975 Carnegie-Mellon University address, subsequently published in the *New York Times* as "Humility"[2] (figs. 3, 4). Bearden downplayed his writing efforts on occasion,[3] and it would be easy to accept his self-dismissals as admissions of a ghostwriting conspiracy. Murray did do just that for others, such as jazz musician Count Basie.[4] Yet, about Bearden, with whom he haunted bookstores and museums and with whom he discussed aesthetic theories and Pablo Picasso, Paul Cézanne, and André Malraux, Murray has said: "Romie was an intellectual. . . . We'd work out the outlines because Romie really knew the stuff. Another thing, he liked writers and I was his writer."[5] Murray's explanation may be extended to Bearden's relationship with artist Carl Holty and journalist Harry Henderson for they, too, were the lead architects in their coauthored publications, which are considered in this essay. Nonetheless, Bearden's singular voice, known to us through his letters, private notebook entries, and public interviews, is recognizable in the solo and joint projects.

Leonardo, Vol. 2, pp. 11–19. Pergamon Press 1969. Printed in Great Britain

RECTANGULAR STRUCTURE IN MY MONTAGE PAINTINGS

Romare Bearden*

Abstract—*The author describes his change from being a student of mathematics to that of being a painter, after studying with George Grosz. Through Grosz, the author was led to study Brueghel, and the Dutch masters and their art, together with Byzantine mosaics and African sculpture, have remained a major influence in his work.*

A study of the paintings of De Hooch and Vermeer was also helpful from the point of view of the way those artists were able to control their large shapes, even when disparate elements were included within these shapes. Also, the author describes the influence upon him of examples of Chinese paintings and his method of working with mounted layers of torn papers.

Both the similarities as well as the differences to Cubism in his style are described in detail, with the hope that the structural content of his work will be understood and even more valued than its social message.

I

When I first started to make pictures I was particularly interested in using art as an instrument of social change. As far as I was concerned at the time, which was in the mid-1930's, art techniques were simply the means that enabled an artist to communicate a message—which, as I saw it then, was essentially a social, if not a political one. My original objective as an artist was to become a political cartoonist. I was an undergraduate majoring in mathematics at New York University when I started producing a steady stream of caricatures and satirical sketches for *The Magpie*, the campus magazine of humor; by the time I received my degree I had already become something of a semi-professional cartoonist with a weekly feature in the Baltimore *Afro-American*, a Negro newspaper of nationwide reputation and circulation.

It was my search for better ways of getting a social message into my cartoons which led me to the works of Daumier, Forain and Kathe Kollwitz, to the Art Students League and to George Grosz. The artists in the 1930's were deeply conscious of social problems, and Diego Rivera, José Orozco and David Siqueiros in Mexico, and Thomas Hart Benton, John Steuart Curry and Grant Wood in the United States were then at the height of their popularity. But what impressed, engaged and challenged me most were the corrosive line drawings and the watercolors of Grosz.

It was during my period with Grosz, under whom I began studying several months after graduating from New York University, that I began to regard myself as a painter rather than a cartoonist. The drawings of Grosz on the theme of the human situation in post World War I Germany made me realize the artistic possibilities of American Negro subject matter. It was also Grosz who led me to study composition, through the analysis of Brueghel and the great Dutch masters, and who in the process of refining my draftsmanship initiated me into the magic world of Ingres, Dürer, Holbein and Poussin.

I had decided that I wanted to make painting, not mathematics, my life's work, but it was not until several years after leaving the League that I managed to do a group of paintings with any stylistic continuity. The subject matter of almost all of these paintings was drawn from Negro life. This is also true of my painting now, but at that time my emphasis was more on the rural south of the United States, than the urban north. Everything that I have done since then, has been, in effect, an extension of my experiments with flat painting, shallow space, Byzantine stylization and African design.

All of my first paintings were done in tempera. I completed about 20 before going into military service in 1942. When I returned to civilian life in 1945, I began a series of watercolors based on such themes as the Passion of Christ, the Bullring and the Iliad. My temperas had been composed in closed forms and the coloring was subdued, mostly earthy browns, blues and green. When I started working with watercolor, however, I found myself using bright color patterns and bold, black lines to delineate semi-abstract shapes. I never worked long on a

*Artist living at 357 Canal Street, New York, N.Y. 10013, U.S.A. (Received 27 April 1968.)

11

3

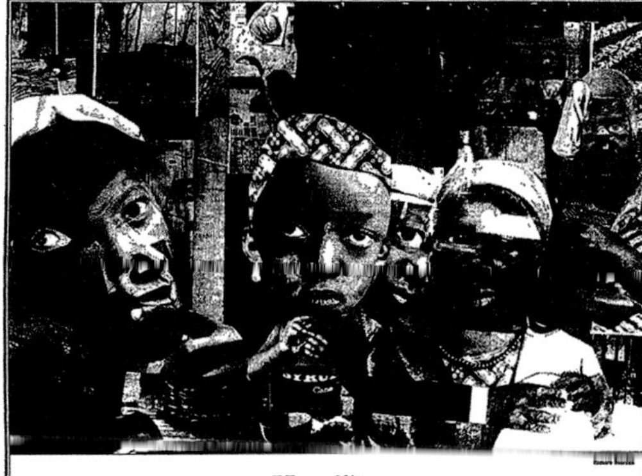

Humility

By Romare Bearden

PITTSBURGH—Alfred North Whitehead was convinced of the indispensable relationship of science, technology, art and religion. I can believe that the administration and faculty of Carnegie-Mellon University have based your training on assumptions entirely compatible with Whitehead's imperatives. They have invited me, an artist, to speak to you [graduating students], who are for the most part in various scientific and technological disciplines.

After all, when we talk about the human ends of science and technology we are concerned with aesthetics—indeed the world of art. Science is greatly absorbed with mankind's perceptions of the objective world. Art, whether it be literature, dance, music, or painting, sculpture and the graphic arts, is concerned with the conceptions men and women have of themselves, and of their relation to the world around them. However, neither the scientist, the technologist, nor the artist works in a vacuum; all are involved with human ends. That is to say, human impulses, drives, urges, desires, motives and ideals.

Thomas Mann has described man as the means through which nature becomes aware of itself. Mankind, then, is nature with consciousness, and men and women are aware of themselves, and those things around them, to a greater extent than any other form of life on this planet. In acquiring consciousness we also acquired a conscience, which is a concern about the consequence of action, and, naturally, a desire for that which is most serviceable to mankind.

I like to believe for all the specialized demands of your chosen fields, you do not lose sight of human ends, which are of primary importance to the artist. Before our age of specialization, the artist, scientist, technician and religious servant often existed in one person as a matter of course. In the Western world, this was the time of the Renaissance, and with Leonardo Da Vinci, we certainly have the embodiment of all these faculties.

Among his many other accomplishments, Leonardo devised something similar to our modern submarine. When Leonardo was once asked to build this device and use it to set fire to an enemy fleet blockading an Italian city, Leonardo refused because he felt that water was a divine element and should not be violated by subterfuge. Since Leonardo, in all he did, never lost sight of human ends, in this instance, I'm sure, his conscience told him not to use his submarine in the way suggested.

While it may be easy for the scientist and technologist, busy in their own efforts, to ignore the artist, the artist cannot ignore them, because they are constantly altering the world the artist must relate to.

As students you are part of a generation that has been much involved with social and political change. The desire to participate in improving our world is most commendable; but, from the recent mishaps around the world, it should be apparent, change is most effective when we have an understanding of what we intend to change. No one is going to alter our world for the better anymore with technology alone, or with military might, which is a force of technology, often placed in the wrong hands. The demands of the world require much more than good intentions—they require insight and wisdom. For wisdom in the face of complexity is likely to produce the necessary humility that keeps mankind human.

And all this is to say that great productive changes never occur through the influence of one dominant force, whether it be art, science, or religion, but through a confluence of many forces, which in unison have the power to transcend the contributions of all individual elements. For the highest order of the human experience is in building a fit world where we can all live in peace.

4

NOTEBOOKS AND DIARIES

Of the unpublished writings, letters are numerous; poems, fragments of plays, diaries, and sketchbooks substantial. To wit, throughout 1947 Bearden kept a journal in an ordinary ledger book that offers insight into his artistic anxieties and ambitions (fig. 5). However, the entries shorten in length toward the end of that year, and he abandoned diary keeping during 1948.[6] Thereafter, only a small fraction of his many notebooks are dated; a greater number are undated, though their topics and references suggest that they were composed after 1970. By then, Bearden had retired from a full-time caseworker position in New York City's Department of Social Services, allowing him to

figure 1
Romare Bearden, cover, notebook, undated. Estate of Romare Bearden, courtesy of Romare Bearden Foundation, New York

figure 2
Romare Bearden, page, notebook, undated. Estate of Romare Bearden, courtesy of Romare Bearden Foundation, New York

figure 3
Romare Bearden, page, "Rectangular Structure in My Montage Paintings" (1969). *Leonardo* 2 (January 1969): 11. Estate of Romare Bearden, courtesy of Romare Bearden Foundation, New York

figure 4
Romare Bearden, page, "Humility," (1975). *New York Times*, 31 January 1975, 27. Estate of Romare Bearden, courtesy of Romare Bearden Foundation, New York; *New York Times*

65

Dec 1st

Great artists live on in a peculiar way like vampires roaming in time.

Somewhere in ~~[struck out]~~ the adventure of art one may find immortality—the immortality that has been the touchstone of man's desires throughout the ages. For most of us, either we serve by having our blood sucked by these mighty vampires, or else the stave is nailed through our hearts; thus fast us forever to the sepulcher of our own times and condition.

Dec 5th

More and more painters will begin to find it fruitful to compose out of the big ornaments of the object; rather than to seek form impressions. The days of the strict cubist disciplines are over, yet many painters who would not even acknowledge cubism as a source, use arbitrary shapes

5

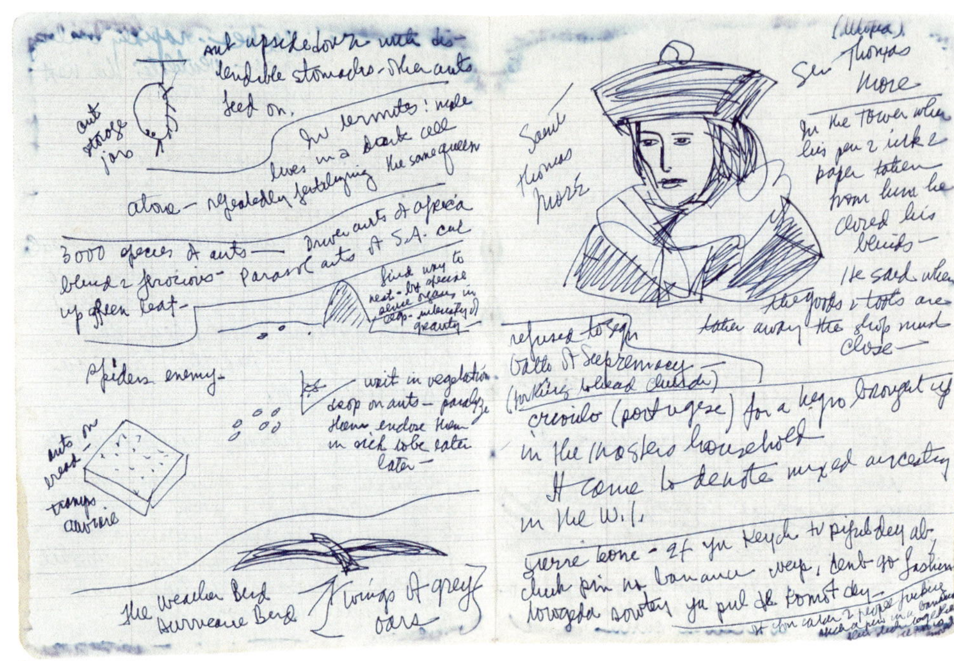

6

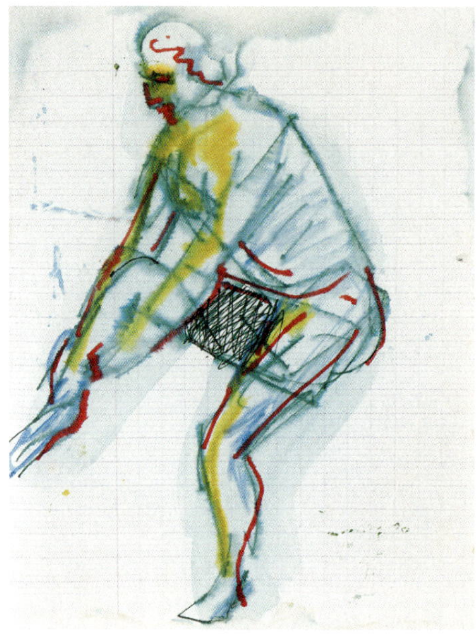

7

devote all his energies to art. The pages of these late notebooks are filled with paragraph-length quotes, doodles and academic sketches, tables, and diagrams—all shorthand forms, much like the fragments he reworked and transformed into collages (figs. 6, 7). In one undated notebook, Bearden wrote out the principles of fiction writing. As early as September 1955, he was researching this interest in the New York Public Library, borrowing E.M. Forster's *Aspects of the Novel* (1927; fig. 8) and reading magazine articles on story revision. Working from these and other sources, he defined key terms for himself, e.g., plot, crisis, denouement, picaresque, and even diagrammed the literary structure of texts such as *Don Quixote*, Coleridge's epic "Rime of the Ancient Mariner," *Othello*, and *Faust*.[7] Such notations abound in

figure 5
Romare Bearden, diary, 1 December 1947, page 65. Estate of Romare Bearden, courtesy of Romare Bearden Foundation, New York

figure 6
Romare Bearden, page, undated diary (after 1960). Estate of Romare Bearden, courtesy of Romare Bearden Foundation, New York

figure 7
Romare Bearden, page, undated diary (after 1960). Estate of Romare Bearden, courtesy of Romare Bearden Foundation, New York

Bearden's notebooks and provide convincing evidence of his desire to devise and undertake intellectual challenges. His notes, moreover, suggest that he saw such investigations as useful to narrative painting. Rules, while recorded in inconsistent outline form, are readily applicable both to fiction writing and picture making:

Don't fill page with tertiary material—no art of omniscience—

—Keep in mind these factors for [?]

(1) "Picturize" your material—so appeal can be made to readers imagination—Then author knows if he strays from *fire* [?] of *action*—or from *intention*.

(b) Make essential situation the nucleus of story, from which action springs—

By picturing we mean the transformation of abstract thought into statement of home in negative but so important as it is statement of intention in positive form.[8]

Bearden studied the formulas for creating setting, heroic characterization, and epic stories throughout his life, and his papers include beginnings and extended efforts in poetry, short stories, and playwriting. "Until I Find" is an undated radio drama that he scripted with "Corporal Jack Kaufman," who likely was a friend made in the army (fig. 9). Set on the Italian front and in the heartlands of the United States and Germany during World War II, the play strikes a balance between patriotic and pacifist sentiments. Combat scenes and somber speeches about death convey the message that "war is hell" for all sides—for Americans at home and in the trenches and for their Axis enemies. Bearden also tapped the themes of war in "A Matter of Brimstone," a short story distinguished for its descriptions of places and events undeniably drawn from his own experiences. Notably, the nameless protagonist is an army sergeant on leave to care for his ailing parents. The locale is New York City, and we learn that this serviceman enjoys visiting the Metropolitan Museum of Art. Information conveyed in a barroom conversation demonstrates that "A Matter of Brimstone" has its inventions, too, for while Bearden was stationed in the United States during World War II, his main character is a world traveler. A slightly inebriated woman who has listened to this soldier's description of a Metropolitan Museum painting of Christ descending into hell asks:

"A picture upset you so much? You aren't worrying about going to Hell are you?"

"No, I don't believe in that stuff, but my mother is sick and I've been uneasy about her. This picture kinda set my mind in a whirl."

"Well, we might all be better off if we had definite things to believe in like Heaven and Hell. What can you believe in today?"

"You talk like a lot of fellows do in the Army."

"I can't get my grips on a damn thing these days. I'm like a scarecrow flapping in the wind."

"You should believe in something. When I was in Iceland we used to orient our guns on the star Polaris. I always got a kick out of finding the Big Dipper and tracing a path from the two pointers out across to the North Star. Then I'd look around and watch the pattern of the big guns all training on the same star. Just locating that star each night gave me confidence and a belief in something."

She looked at me, her eyes were a bit hazy. "I'd like to know you better…"[9]

Such matter-of-fact realism has its parallels in many mid-twentieth-century cultural forms, from gunfighter movies and Edward Hopper tableaus, to the novels of Richard Wright and Ernest Hemingway. And like those, "A Matter of Brimstone" explores themes of alienation and the tense gender divide. Recognizably specific to Bearden, it presents the artist's preoccupations of the 1940s and 1950s: mortality and loss at home and in war, life's meanings, and Christian iconography as a response to existential crises.

USE A SEPARATE SLIP FOR EACH TITLE

CLASS MARK (In upper right hand corner of card)

Author: Forster, Em

Title:

BOOKS MUST NOT BE TAKEN FROM THE ROOM

Use of false name or address may mean exclusion from use of the Library

SEAT NUMBER

Name R Bearden

Address 50

8

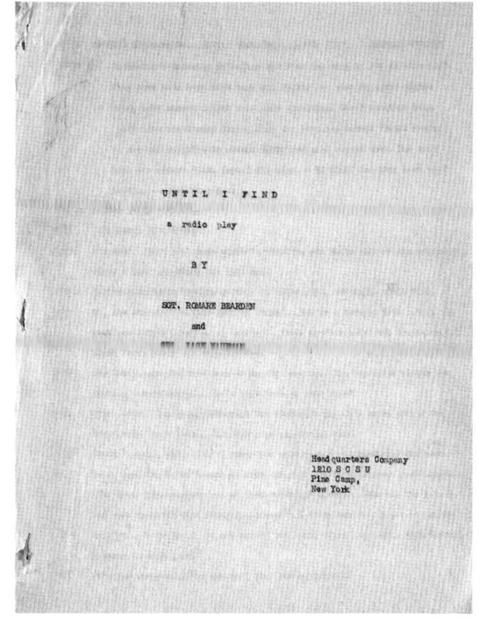

UNTIL I FIND

a radio play

BY

SGT. ROMARE BEARDEN

and

[illegible]

Headquarters Company
1210 S C S U
Pine Camp,
New York

9

figure 8
Romare Bearden, call slip, New York Public Library, undated. Estate of Romare Bearden, courtesy of Romare Bearden Foundation, New York

figure 9
Romare Bearden, cover page, "Until I Find," manuscript, undated (after 1941). Estate of Romare Bearden, courtesy of Romare Bearden Foundation, New York

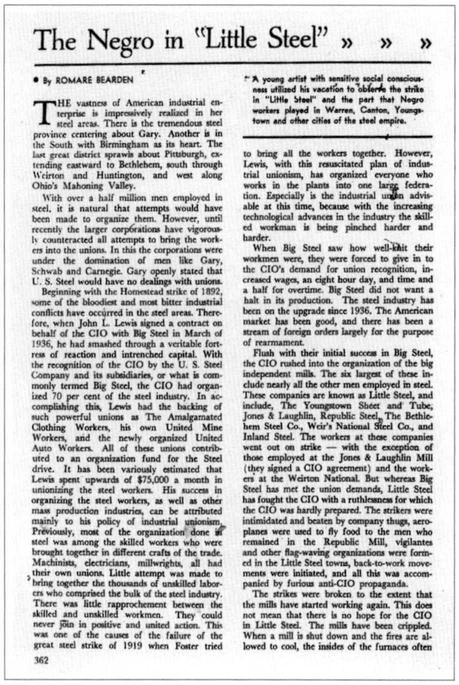

Bearden wrote in fits and starts, much in the manner that he painted during the decades from 1930 to 1960. One of his earliest known publications is "The Negro in 'Little Steel,'" a substantial essay that appeared in the National Urban League's monthly magazine *Opportunity* in 1937 (fig. 10).[10] Traveling through Ohio and Pennsylvania during the summer of 1936, Bearden photographed and described the steel-working industry and its laborers' hardships in unblinkingly realistic terms. His journeys to rural America, like those of many of the decade's artists (including his cousin Charles Alston, and fellow New Yorker Ben Shahn), informed Bearden's monumental interpretations of what he saw—in both his art and his writing. The article opens with an overview of the ultimately successful unionizing efforts by the Congress of Industrial Organizations (CIO) at Bearden's one-time place of employment, "Big Steel," that is the U.S. Steel Company of Pittsburgh. Bearden then turns to "Little Steel," which consisted of the major independent mills spread across Ohio and Pennsylvania, and notes its brutal campaigns against the CIO during the first decades of the twentieth century. Interviewing black and white workers at both "Little Steel" and "Big Steel" plants, Bearden reveals both warm alliances and deep-seated antagonisms in various settings. While some black workers had joined the CIO, many remained stuck in menial jobs with little opportunity of advancement, and he reported the instances in which their white brethren moved slowly to eliminate discriminatory practices. But as Bearden discovered, most protected the privileges afforded them as white men, and their racism was stoked by the episodes of black strikebreaking, antiunionism, and desperate aspirations to earn a living wage at the height of the Great Depression. In one anecdote, Bearden's progressive, prounion stance is audible and his sympathy for the black steelworkers' predicament clear:

> Here in these small towns the colored worker is in a position analagous [sic] to Mohammed's coffin—"suspended between heaven and earth." On one hand he is faced with the disrespect of organized labor if he refuses to join its ranks. And if he sides wholly with labor he must face the wrath of his employers and the fascist-minded vigilante groups. The whole pattern and background of his life tend to make him faithful to the employer. He is isolated in his social life. He is under the influence of inept and backward leaders. He thinks in terms of his stomach and pocket book and does not understand the broader issues of the labor struggle. His feelings are typified in an experience the writer had with a colored steelworker in Warren. After a talk with the man on the street, the writer was invited home for dinner. The man said he had gone back to the mills after the back-to-work movement had started. "You know," he said, "a man can't stand to see his kids go hungry." He was definitely interested in the CIO and listened closely during the meal to an explanation of the workings of the CIO and of industrial unionism. Finally he stopped chewing his food, and [sic] "Son," he said, "what you say sounds pretty good. But what I go by is this. Here on my plate I got one chop. If I join the CIO can I get two chops?"[11]

Bearden placed his hopes in integration as a shared responsibility among blacks and whites in the running of the mills and the organization of its labor and offered a "Little Steel" operation as a case study of progress. Pennsylvania Iron and Steel Company in Tarentum, Pennsylvania, was

The Negro in "Little Steel" » » »

• By ROMARE BEARDEN

A young artist with sensitive social consciousness utilized his vacation to observe the strike in "Little Steel" and the part that Negro workers played in Warren, Canton, Youngstown and other cities of the steel empire.

THE vastness of American industrial enterprise is impressively realized in her steel areas. There is the tremendous steel province centering about Gary. Another is in the South with Birmingham as its heart. The last great district sprawls about Pittsburgh, extending eastward to Bethlehem, south through Weirton and Huntington, and west along Ohio's Mahoning Valley.

With over a half million men employed in steel, it is natural that attempts would have been made to organize them. However, until recently the larger corporations have vigorously counteracted all attempts to bring the workers into the unions. In this the corporations were under the domination of men like Gary, Schwab and Carnegie. Gary openly stated that U. S. Steel would have no dealings with unions.

Beginning with the Homestead strike of 1892, some of the bloodiest and most bitter industrial conflicts have occurred in the steel areas. Therefore, when John L. Lewis signed a contract on behalf of the CIO with Big Steel in March of 1936, he had smashed through a veritable fortress of reaction and intrenched capital. With the recognition of the CIO by the U. S. Steel Company and its subsidiaries, or what is commonly termed Big Steel, the CIO had organized 70 per cent of the steel industry. In accomplishing this, Lewis had the backing of such powerful unions as The Amalgamated Clothing Workers, his own United Mine Workers, and the newly organized United Auto Workers. All of these unions contributed to an organization fund for the Steel drive. It has been variously estimated that Lewis spent upwards of $75,000 a month in unionizing the steel workers. His success in organizing the steel workers, as well as other mass production industries, can be attributed mainly to his policy of industrial unionism. Previously, most of the organization done in steel was among the skilled workers who were brought together in different crafts of the trade. Machinists, electricians, millwrights, all had their own unions. Little attempt was made to bring together the thousands of unskilled laborers who comprised the bulk of the steel industry. There was little rapprochement between the skilled and unskilled workmen. They could never join in positive and united action. This was one of the causes of the failure of the great steel strike of 1919 when Foster tried to bring all the workers together. However, Lewis, with this resuscitated plan of industrial unionism, has organized everyone who works in the plants into one large federation. Especially is the industrial union advisable at this time, because with the increasing technological advances in the industry the skilled workman is being pinched harder and harder.

When Big Steel saw how well-knit their workmen were, they were forced to give in to the CIO's demand for union recognition, increased wages, an eight hour day, and time and a half for overtime. Big Steel did not want a halt in its production. The steel industry has been on the upgrade since 1936. The American market has been good, and there has been a stream of foreign orders largely for the purpose of rearmament.

Flush with their initial success in Big Steel, the CIO rushed into the organization of the big independent mills. The six largest of these include nearly all the other men employed in steel. These companies are known as Little Steel, and include, The Youngstown Sheet and Tube, Jones & Laughlin, Republic Steel, The Bethlehem Steel Co., Weir's National Steel Co., and Inland Steel. The workers at these companies went out on strike — with the exception of those employed at the Jones & Laughlin Mill (they signed a CIO agreement) and the workers at the Weirton National. But whereas Big Steel has met the union demands, Little Steel has fought the CIO with a ruthlessness for which the CIO was hardly prepared. The strikers were intimidated and beaten by company thugs, aeroplanes were used to fly food to the men who remained in the Republic Mill, vigilantes and other flag-waving organizations were formed in the Little Steel towns, back-to-work movements were initiated, and all this was accompanied by furious anti-CIO propaganda.

The strikes were broken to the extent that the mills have started working again. This does not mean that there is no hope for the CIO in Little Steel. The mills have been crippled. When a mill is shut down and the fires are allowed to cool, the insides of the furnaces often

362

10

figure 10
Romare Bearden, first page, "The Negro in 'Little Steel'" *Opportunity: Journal of Negro Life* 15 (Dec. 1937): 362. Estate of Romare Bearden, courtesy of Romare Bearden Foundation, New York. Reprinted by permission of The National Urban League

entirely unionized, its CIO leader a black man who had the support of the minority white workforce. Its owners told Bearden that their hiring practices were fair and nondiscriminatory, and the young artist documented his own optimism in a photo of happy coworkers:

In the plant, as well as on the outside, there is a fine relationship between the workers. They live near each other. Their children play together in a large ballfield back of the mill. The writer took some pictures of Howell, the president of the local, in the mill yard. After snapping several pictures, one of the white workmen came over and asked the writer to take his picture with Howell. When the picture was completed, the white worker said, "I wanted you to take my picture with Howell because he's my best friend in the mill. And if I'm not his friend he hasn't a friend in this mill."[12]

Bearden's critical commentaries, "The Negro Artist and Modern Art" (1934) and "The Negro Artist's Dilemma" (1946), broadly invoked the standards of Western art history and his individual efforts to develop a meaningful, cautiously abstract visual language. In the former essay, Bearden defined the artist in romantic terms:

...with the Negro artist—he must not be content with merely recording a scene as a machine. He must enter wholeheartedly into the situation he wishes to convey. The artist must be the medium through which humanity expresses itself. In this sense the greatest artists have faced the realities of life, and have been profoundly social.[13]

To explain the "social," Bearden summoned the examples of Rembrandt's genre scenes, William Hogarth's drawings of prostitutes, Jean Baptiste Siméon Chardin's still lifes, and Diego Rivera's, and José Clemente Orozco's depictions of Mexican peasants: these artists, he asserted, successfully represented everyday life. Decrying the absence of a "definite ideology or social philosophy" among African-American artists, Bearden chided his peers for their interest in European locales; he wrote:

...the Negro artist will proudly exhibit his "Scandinavian Landscape," a locale that is entirely alien to him. This will of course impress the uninitiated, who through some feeling of inferiority toward their own subject matter, only require that a work of art have some sort of foreign stamp to make it acceptable.[14]

With this remark Bearden singled out the work of William H. Johnson, the South Carolina-born artist who had lived in Denmark and traveled in Europe and north Africa during the 1930s. His rebuke may have extended to Palmer Hayden, Albert Alexander Smith, Hale Woodruff, and several other African-American artists who studied art in Europe and produced picturesque scenes of its cities and villages. Bearden's charge is one among many leveled at all American artists during the early twentieth century; as a body, they were regularly criticized as slavish imitators of European art who had failed to develop a representative, national art. African Americans faced similar charges, albeit ones especially freighted by essentialist stereotypes constructed around race. Hence, while Bearden conceded that it was "almost impossible for the Negro artist not to be influenced by other men,"[15] he nonetheless anticipated "racial art," a particularist aesthetic that has been discussed in the cultural commentary and exhibition reviews, and among black artists themselves since the 1920s. Bearden's critique was consistent with the clamor for racial art. Chastising African-American artists for "not taking advantage of the Negro scene," he surmised: "When he [the African-American artist] learns to harness his great gifts of rhythm and pours it into his art—his chance of creating something individual will be heightened."[16] In sum, black artists' production had to index Harlem and urban locales as New Negro archetypes and the stereotypical signs of blackness as well: Harlem, the rural South, the African jungle, rhythmic patterns, and bright color.

Bearden variably positioned himself in both universal and culturally specific frameworks throughout his life. "As a Negro," he wrote in a 1967 artist's statement, "I do not need to go looking for 'happenings,' the absurd or the surreal, because I have seen things that neither Dali, Beckett, Ionesco, nor any of the others, could have thought possible."[17] The pronouncement not only placed his work above fads and "isms" of Western modernism; it also effectively suggests that black experiences were defined by racism's absurd aspects, and a fortiori, heroic survival and a distinctly racial cultural achievement. Two decades before, blackness for Bearden and many of his progressive contemporaries was still conceptualized within liberal, Western humanism. In "The Negro Artist's Dilemma" Bearden renounced the "racial art" credo of "The Negro Artist and Modern Art"; in the former essay, he asserted: "The work of the Negro artists reflects all the artistic trends of the time, ranging from the academic to the modern. There is no single characteristic that would stamp their individual works as having been done by a Negro."[18] Furthermore, like many post–World War II enunciations, "The Negro Artist's Dilemma" contemplates the reasons for art after the mass destruction and genocide of the global conflict. The artist, Bearden wrote:

> searches for values that are permanent and relevant to all men and not those related to the fluctuating needs of any group, or the transitory social situation. A good painting has its own world. What ideas it arouses are integral and in relation to itself.
>
> . . . We cannot calculate what new forms will emerge, but the artist, of whatever race, must explore with integrity and sensitiveness the processes of life that he sees and feels. The Negro artist must come to see himself not primarily as a Negro artist, but as an artist. Only in this way will he acquire the stature which is the component of every good artist.[19]

Both "The Negro Artist and Modern Art" and "The Negro Artist's Dilemma" make evident Bearden's lifelong ambition to situate his and other African-Americans' art in the discourse of art history. In both essays, his voice is easy and confident when relating African sculpture's influence on modernism, Ashcan School realism and its portrayal of black subjects, and the diversity of black artistic production in the work of Richmond Barthé, Norman Lewis, Horace Pippin, and Charles W. White. Furthermore, these essays are stands against all-black exhibitions. In "The Negro Artist's Dilemma," he railed against the Harmon Foundation, a philanthropy that organized such events in the 1920s and 1930s:

> ...the attitude of the Foundation toward the Negro artists was patronizing: it firmly established the pattern of segregated exhibits; it fostered artificial and arbitrary artistic standards, stemming from a sociological rather than aesthetic interest in the exhibitors' work. This concept of the Negro as an odd personality, rather than a mature individual, has been both insulting and harmful.[20]

Within two years Bearden had lodged a similar complaint with the organizers of the Atlanta University annual exhibition of black artists' work. In a 1948 letter to them, Bearden justified his opposition to the all-black shows, saying that "An artist profits by association and competition with other artists, which the racial shows drastically limits [sic]."[21] By all measures Bearden's career advancement in the 1940s supported such an assertion, for he had exhibited in open forums in New York, Chicago, Washington, D.C., and Paris. Yet, sometime afterward, Bearden, who had shown in only a few galleries during the 1950s, shifted his perspective and embraced the "black show."[22] Indeed, black racial identity as a coherent and cohesive sign in culture and rhetoric informed his art, alliances, and publications: the founding of the New York black artists' group Spiral in 1963; the organization of the City University of New York exhibition *The Evolution of Afro-American Artists, 1800–1950* in 1967; and the survey texts he co-authored with Harry Henderson, *Six Black Masters of American Art* (1972) and *A History of African-American Artists: From 1792 to the Present* (1993).

Bearden's 1969 essay, "Rectangular Structure in My Montage Paintings," outlines the artist's influences and goals, presenting the names and movements that consistently show up in his journals and sketchbooks.[23] At a time when abstract expressionism was no longer an avant-garde mode, but rather, the accepted institutional one, *and* when cultural nationalists issued the call for "a black aesthetic," Bearden reasserts his guiding principle, a "social modernism" forged decades earlier. Like a School of Paris painter versed in the formalism of Clive Bell, Roger Fry, and Alain Locke, he offers: "I do not burden myself with the need for complete abstraction or absolute formal purity but I do want my language to be strict and classical, in the manner of the great Benin heads, for example."[24] In addition to this Yoruba court style that dates to the fifteenth century, the art of antiquity elsewhere inspired him, namely, the simplified color arrangements of Pompeii's Villa of the Mysteries murals and the spatial organization strategies of large-scale, canonical Chinese painting. As the essay's title suggests, in the 1960s Bearden focused his energies on establishing a compositional space governed by planes and energized by the assemblage of disparate materials. His debts, he asserts, were not only to cubism, but also to the "masters of flat painting": Japanese portraitists, the Sienese School of Duccio and the Lorenzettis, the Dutch Pieter de Hooch and Jan Vermeer, and, in particular, the "flatly modeled drapery" of Francisco de Zurburán's baroque portraiture.[25] An underutilized map in Bearden scholarship to date, the essay situates his efforts as the outcome of imagination as opposed to mere pastiche or autobiography.[26] The passage below refutes one-note readings of Bearden's art as literal record of his past; found in the last section of the essay, these lines respond to critical assessments of his best-known work that cited its fragmentariness, randomness, shocking juxtapositions, and perceived racial personality.

> First, I feel that some photographic detail, such as a hand or an eye, is taken out of its original context and is fractured and integrated into a different space and form configuration, it acquires a plastic quality it did not have in the original photograph....

Secondly, I think a quality of artificiality must be retained in a work of art, since, after all, the reality of art is not to be confused with that of the outer world. Art, it must be remembered, is artifice, or a creative undertaking, the primary function of which is to add to an existing conception of reality.... I am afraid, despite my intentions, that in some instances, commentators have tended to overemphasize what they believe to be the social elements in my work. But while my response to certain human elements is as obvious as it is inevitable, I am also pleased to note that upon reflection many persons have found that they were as much concerned with the aesthetic implications of my paintings as with, what may possibly be, my human compassion.[27]

Bearden's career coincided with the arrival of African-American artistic production in increasingly larger and more prominent exhibition spaces. In the first half of the twentieth century, he had witnessed and decried the impact of the Harmon Foundation's simultaneously liberal and paternalistic patronage, and the cultural autonomy and circumscription characteristic of "Negro," and later, "black" shows. As an organizer of exhibitions, Bearden, too, thought (as curators have since the twentieth century) "racially," mounting the comprehensive survey, such as the previously mentioned *The Evolution of Afro-American Artists* in 1967, as well as the modestly-scaled presentation of Staten Island artists in the *Black Experiences Through Art* show of 1968. Yet he always returned to his universalist ideals about art, its service to society, and his early formed humanist ideas of art transcending everyday realities. In "Humility," featured on the op-ed page of the *New York Times* in 1975, Bearden situated Leonardo da Vinci as his paragon: "artist, scientist, technician, and religious servant." Implicitly, he referenced his own life trajectories as social worker, artist, and writer, and aligned himself with the Italian Renaissance man. Bearden's expressions were lofty and apropos to the nation's post–Vietnam War recovery: art, he asserted, was "one dominant force" that, when conjoined with moral applications of religion and scientific knowledge, brought about "great productive changes" and the "building of a fit world where we can all live in peace."[28]

In the essays, "Eating at Ma Chance's" (1978) and "An Artist's Renewal in the Sun" (1983), Bearden describes his second home and neighbors in St. Martin with the passion of an explorer.[29] There is a rich visuality to each of these travel articles and an undisguised sense of wonder. What is also striking is that amidst the specific references to the splendor of Caribbean flora and fauna are comparisons with the touchstones in European and European-American cultural production. For instance, Bearden writes that dawn on the island nation reminds him of "Turner's watercolors." And his interest in the stars led him to buy a constellation chart that he ultimately discarded because "Down here, at least, I feel very much as Walt Whitman did when, after listening to the lecture of a learned astronomer, he left the hall and looked up at the distant stars in 'perfect silence.'"[30] Complementing what Bearden had, symbolically, brought to St. Martin was his encounter with Obeah, a system of spiritual practices informed by African sources and transformed by the experiences of Africa-descended people in the diaspora. Through an American anthropology student, Bearden gained entrée to an Obeah circle, and his account to his friend and collector, Walter O. Evans, brims with boyish excitement:

These are the for *very* real sorcerers. I got into their language, which is a kind of broken French, creole that's spoken so fast, you can't understand even if you can speak it. Then, there is a language the High Priest speaks, that's only given to him/or her orally—and from what I have been told, is a very ancient African language —only spoken by the priests. As a scientist, and a rational person, you might find them quite irrational—but, on the other hand, they live, *in the mind anyway,* way apart from our Western orientation. The High Priest knew I was an artist (how I don't know) and I saw *some (parts)* of ceremonies, one, unbelievable, was a marriage of a young girl to a viper—startling. I did a large watercolor of it.[31]

THE CORRESPONDENCE

Unsurprisingly, many of Bearden's occasional correspondents were kindred spirits, among them figures who anchor the histories of twentieth-century Western culture: Alexander Calder, Stuart Davis, Marcel Duchamp, Ralph Ellison, George Grosz, Yasuo Kuniyoshi, Jacob Lawrence, Archibald MacLeish, Albert Murray, Man Ray, and Faith Ringgold. Bearden's affable nature and restless intellect illuminate his letters (fig. 11). While far from stiff, these carefully composed missives are characterized by the politesse of his generation's approach to the art of letter writing. That is to say, letters open with cheery greetings and close with sincere expressions of goodwill to the correspondent, and when appropriate, to mutual friends and family. In his newsy style, Bearden wrote to amuse and engage his readers; to his most trusted friends, he described his creative process and anxieties, experiences while traveling, and even, conversations with strangers. He hungrily

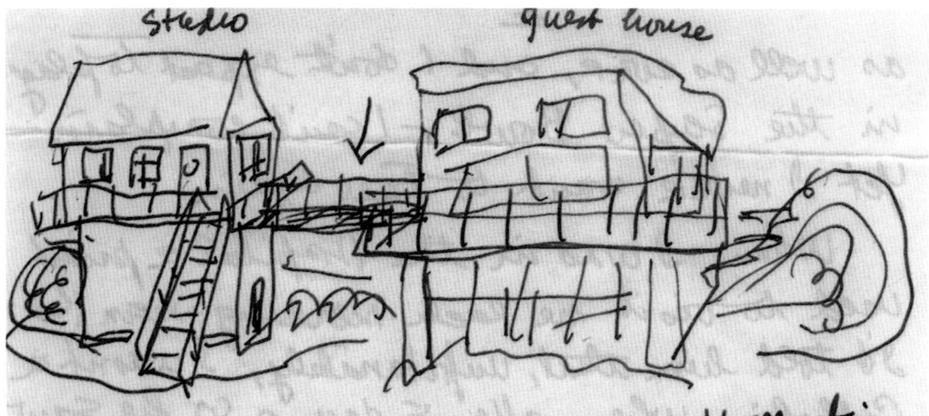

Hi Walter. We've been down in St. Martin since 12/15 - And when I got down I was glad to see the new studio, built over the garage. It also connects with the bridge like passage way I've marked by the arrow above. We modern artists have forgotten perspective; but I think you get the idea, at least.

They tell me (the doctors at N.Y. Hospital) that I'm making a nice recovery. I'm able to walk up the 109 steps to the studio & have just about put aside the cane. That aint to say that "ole rockin' chair" isn't often very welcome. But since I am painting

11

figure 11
Romare Bearden, first page (sketch of Beardens' St. Martin's studio and guest house), letter to Walter O. Evans, undated (envelope postmarked 19 January 1987). Collection Dr. Walter O. Evans, Savannah, Georgia

sought similar information from his closest colleagues, clearly determined to keep up with their doings as well. Even the most self-conscious passages convey an urgency to connect with a fellow artist, one aware of the struggles and triumphs of the creative endeavor.

Bearden's letters, like his essays, were sites of political and cultural activism. As discussed above, in the 1940s he wrote to the Atlanta University annual exhibition's organizers urging them to open it to artists of all races. Although that appeal failed to change the show's format, Bearden found an ally in the annual's founder, painter Hale Woodruff; together, they lobbied the International Business Machines (IBM) Corporation to adopt a race-blind approach to patronage: namely, "to remove all racial references in the catalogue of their art collection, and to abolish all racial preferences in their art acquisition policies."[32] Furthermore, Woodruff and Bearden, who were jurors for IBM's *Contemporary Art of the American Negro* exhibitions, ended that event in 1947.[33] Bearden's moves reflect his idealistic and universalist outlook and are made all the more significant when considered alongside later interventions. In 1968 he argued with officials at the Metropolitan Museum of Art about *Harlem on My Mind: Cultural Capital of Black America, 1900–1968,* an exhibition they planned to open the following year. In a letter to organizer Allon Schoener, Bearden suggested the overhaul, if not abandonment of this project, which featured few examples of painting and sculpture:

> I know the artists are not going to tolerate color transparencies of their work in an Art Museum.... the sort of show you are putting together should be in the Museum of the City of New York, The New York Historical Society, or some similar place.[34]

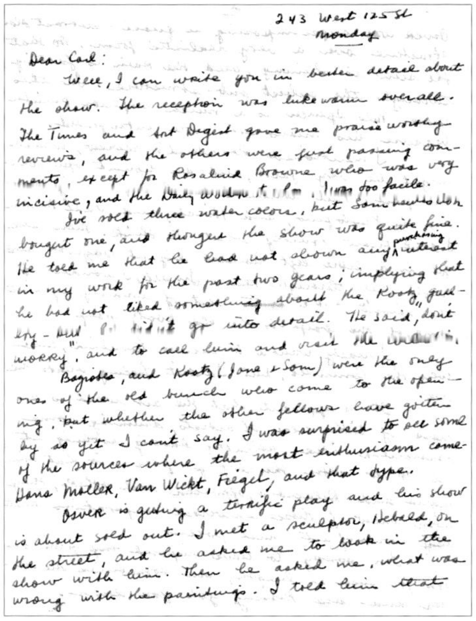

12

13

14

He generously offered his help and that of his New York artist-peers, Alston, Lawrence, Norman Lewis, Richard Bruce Nugent among them—and also appealed to Met director Thomas P. F. Hoving. Again, he failed to bring about the results he sought, and yet, it is notable that Bearden was committed to facilitating exposure of African-American artists to the public.

The correspondence between Bearden and his fellow artists Carl (Robert) Holty (1900–1973)—figs. 12, 13—and Walter Quirt (1902–1968)—fig. 14—is the most extensive to be found in his existing papers. Holty and Quirt were among Bearden's friends made on the New York art scene in the late 1930s and early 1940s. When Holty and Quirt left the city to take teaching posts elsewhere in the mid-1940s, Bearden felt their absences acutely. They were his trusted confidantes, and in the younger artist's eye, senior statesmen of American painting. Rarely mentioned in contemporary accounts of modernism, Holty, in fact, was an influential player in its development in New York: he was a key spokesman for the American Abstract Artists (AAA) group founded in 1936 and a teacher at the Art Students League where he mentored Ad Reinhardt, a principal of abstract expressionism. Bearden himself worked to ensure Holty's place in that movement in "A Painter in the Fifties," a 1974 *Arts Magazine* feature that posthumously honored the older artist's vision. While both Holty and Quirt were articulate, outspoken personalities, Holty was exceptionally opinionated and readily aired his likes and dislikes. To historians, he retrospectively recounted fierce arguments with Arshile Gorky during the first AAA meeting in 1936; he spoke proudly of having met Edvard Munch and Robert Delaunay while traveling in Europe in the 1920s, and irreverently of well-known artist-gurus, from Fernand Léger to his own teacher Hans Hofmann.[35] Of his own place in inter- and postwar painting produced in New York, Holty set his colorful and geometric abstraction far apart from contemporaneous naturalistic and realistic modes as well as figural abstraction. His work was not about communication as his contemporary Ben Shahn's was, he explained to interviewer Paul Cummings in 1968; in fact, Holty asserted that he had "told Bearden one time that I didn't think I was a painter anyway."[36] Painting meant figuration to Holty, whose artistic concerns were informed by Piet Mondrian's

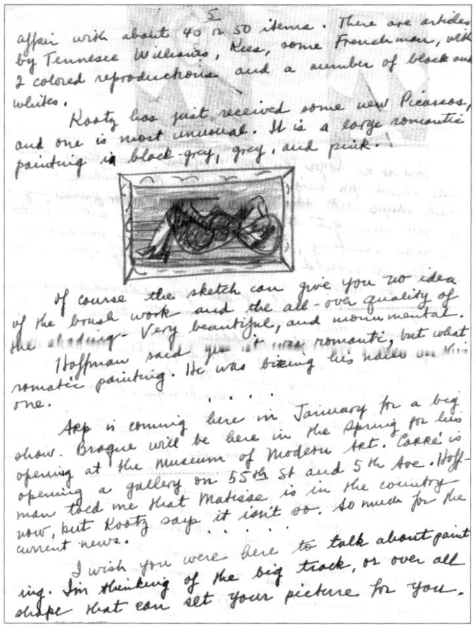

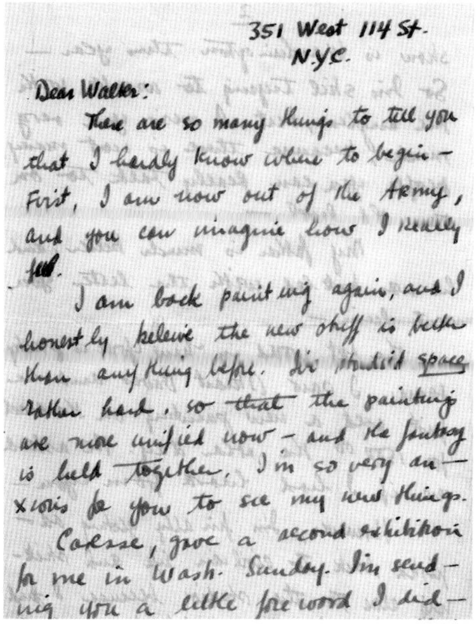

figure 12
Romare Bearden, first page, letter to Carl Holty, undated (probably 1946 or 1947). Carl Robert Holty Papers 1916–1972, Archives of American Art, Smithsonian Institution, Washington, D.C.

figure 13
Romare Bearden, fifth page, letter to Carl Holty, undated (probably 1946 or 1947). Carl Robert Holty Papers 1916–1972, Archives of American Art, Smithsonian Institution, Washington, D.C.

figure 14
Romare Bearden, first page, letter to Walter Quirt, undated (probably c. June 1945). Collection Dr. Walter O. Evans, Savannah, Georgia

neoplasticism, and hence, expectedly privileged the pictorial unity and structure that could be realized in nonobjective painting.[37] Although Bearden kept the figure in his works of the 1940s, Holty's fidelity to abstraction as pure expression clearly influenced him. In a letter to Holty written during the late 1940s, Bearden observed wryly:

Isn't it strange in this painting business that you work harder and harder to put less and less on the picture plane [?]... What concerns me, is when I move about the entire surface adjusting the planes, trying to get certain shifts going across each other, I run into choppiness (like Gris). I believe that I have a tendency now to overwork. The picture comes like a great puzzle that I hate to leave. So now I can do only one watercolor a day. I make a lot of little pencil sketches while (and before) I work, but when I get going I constantly see new chances—but the work gets overloaded.

When I do the whole thing over, using what I think are the best directions the whole picture looks good—but this is such a tedious procedure. Actually, I'm pretty exhausted when I finish an evening's work.[38]

Indeed, Bearden frankly discussed the challenges of painting and his efforts to meet them with both Holty and Quirt. "I've studied space real hard," he wrote to Quirt in a letter written sometime in the 1940s. "I've tried to learn the design of pictures studying Byzantine painting, and the old Italian primitives, etc. till I finally think I'm beginning to understand what makes a picture move—what *time sense* in a picture means—leading *plane by plane*—step by step in a series of counterpoints."[39] In the same period, he revealed to Quirt: "I'm dying to get things held together, but hold the eye from section to section—taking the time say as music does—a composition extended in time."[40]

If Holty's geometric abstractions seem to inform Bearden's known 1940s production, Quirt's surrealist automatism is less evident. In his art Quirt pursued pictorial dynamism with flat colored and doodle-like forms that are evocations of nature and romanticized symbols of Native American rituals, and his own dreams.[41] As was the case with many white European and American modernists, Quirt viewed non-Western cultures as utopian and admired nonwhite peoples for their perceived proximity to a natural state of grace. Quirt wrote confidently to Bearden in 1947:

The greatest creative asset of the Negro is his natural affinity with nature, for that produces in him greater amounts of energy of a constructive kind than the historically conditioned white, whose energies are, by and large, neurotically destructive... because... the white primarily responds to society.[42]

Quirt's cultural primitivism apparently did not get in the way of his friendship with Bearden, who probably encountered "noble savage" formulations from New York School artists in the 1940s.[43] Mortality preoccupied many post–World War II American artists, Quirt and Bearden among them, after the casualties of combat and atomic bomb explosions. In a manner, Bearden's response—a search for unbounded themes in art that led him to comb through Judeo-Christian narratives, Homeric literature, and Rabelais' and Federico Garcia Lorca's heroic epics—perhaps parallels Quirt's primitivist reasoning. Yet where Quirt framed whiteness as a bankrupt subject-position, Bearden's oft-quoted description of his efforts—"I was trying to find out what was in me that was common to other men"—indicates a less-divided sense of identity and perception of the world at large. Irrespective of these disjunctive opinions among friends, Bearden's letters exude his admiration for Quirt's and Holty's achievements and appreciation for their advice about art practices and the art market. Bearden, furthermore, expressed his shared empathy with creative struggle and artistic desire for recognition. A January 1942 letter to Quirt is rich with confession, opinion, and supportive words for his friend, who had just begun to publish art criticism:

What you are doing is very important. First, because we need some decent art critics in this country. Most of the art criticism only concerns itself with a painter's relationship to the art movements of the past. We painters are catalogued and fitted into neat little piles.... Then, most of the critics have arrived at some personal equation of what art should be—and if a painter does not fit into a narrow niche—he is damned. Good analitical [*sic*] criticism is as important to the developement [*sic*] of a culture as are those persons involved in the creative process.[44]

Underscoring his point about the necessity of criticism, Bearden added that he too intended to make public his ideas:

I am starting an article myself on the Negro artist... Alain Locke gave a talk last Thursday on his book, "The Negro in Art," and James Sweeney indicated in so many words that the Negro painter should direct his efforts largely from the standpoint of the heritage left him from his African ancestors. Naturally to try and carry on in America where African sculptors left off would be to start on a false basis—the gap of the years, the environment, and ideology is too great. So I would like to treat these points in an article, and discuss this question with you beforehand.[45]

The article referred to was probably "The Negro Artist's Dilemma," not published until 1946. This essay directly confronts Quirt's theories of racial atavism, for Bearden both reiterated and advanced his objections to "all-black" exhibitions, from those organized by African-American social clubs, to those of the white philanthropy, the Harmon Foundation, and the historically black institution, Atlanta University. Bearden's perspective, of course, was informed by his experiences as a moderately successful New York exhibitor in the 1940s, when he regularly showed at the Kootz Gallery and had his watercolor, *He Is Arisen,* purchased by the Museum of Modern Art. In the above-cited January 20, 1942, letter to Quirt, Bearden's ambivalence is undisguised:

> The press was often enthusiastic about the work—but I realize that doesn't really mean much—for I am interested in much more than being a popular success. But I have had so many divergent opinions passed about my work. One painter wrote from the South that my stuff was forced and deliberately painted to cater to what the critics think a Negro should paint like. To many of my own people, I learn, my work was very disgusting and morbid—and portrayed a type of Negro that they were trying to get away from. One man bought a painting and brought it back in three days because his wife couldn't stand to have it in the house.
>
> So I ask myself, is what I'm doing good or bad [?] Are my paintings an honest and valid statement [?] Have you ever felt like this? Recently, I've gotten so I want to paint and then put the paintings away except to show them to a few people.

Without overdetermining Bearden's story, we might view his resignation and frustration as omens of his near abandonment of painting in the early 1950s, when he strove for Tin Pan Alley fame and fortune.[46]

BEARDEN'S SONGS

Bearden was an afficionado not only of jazz and blues, as many have observed, but also the popular American musical forms they influenced and were influenced by, namely, vaudeville, the Big Band sound, and Broadway show tunes. He filled notebooks and scrapbooks with the printed lyrics—cut out from publications and pasted in—for hit tunes such as "All of Me," "I Got Rhythm," "It Had to Be You," "Jeepers Creepers," and "You'll Never Walk Alone." These assemblages served as reference textbooks on the craft of songwriting, and Bearden's favorite "teachers" included Duke Ellington, Oscar Hammerstein II and Richard Rodgers, Jerome Kern, George and Ira Gershwin, Johnny Mercer and Harold Arlen, Cole Porter, Thomas "Fats" Waller, and Andy Razaf. On a few occasions, Bearden hand copied lyrics and annotated them with accent marks in order to closely analyze rhythmic structures: Hollywood composer Jimmy McHughes' "I'm in the Mood for Love" (1934) and Frank Loesser's "On a Slow Boat to China" made popular by the Kay Kyser Band (1948) were among the standards under his examination. His self-directed study was more than a hobby, for in 1951 Bearden founded the Bluebird Music Company with David (Dave) Ellis. Bearden wrote lyrics for Ellis' music, "Hello and Good-bye," "Little Girl," "Night Wind," "Promise of Spring," "Upside Down," and also collaborated with Ellis on the lyrics for Ruth Frank's score "Street Without a Name." "Promise of Spring" typified Bearden's compositions; spare and melancholy, it spins a reassuring metaphor about love's cycles:

> In winter remember there's always
> the promise of spring.
> Tho' fortune frowns,
> The world turns 'round,
> Night turns to day.
> The love you lost,
> The one you miss may come back one day.
> So dry your eyes and smile—There's always
> the promise of spring.

Bearden also formed a productive partnership with newspaper columnist and composer Laerteas "Larry" Douglas, who ran his own sheet music publishing firm. Together, they wrote about twenty songs including "Missus Santa Claus" and "My Candy Apple," both recorded by the emerging child performer Leslie Uggams (Crayne) during the 1950s (fig. 15). In these and other published songs, Bearden delivered catchy, playful lines; in the 1951 "You Say That You're Joe," written to J. Lee's music, Bearden's ear is attuned to street slang and accents, and probably, Cab Calloway's romping vocal riffs as well:

> You say that you're Joe.
> (I am Joe.)
> You're too tall to be little Joe.
> (Can't you see a'-tall?)
> Too short to be big Joe.
> (I'm tall.)
> You mustn't be Joe a'-tall.
> (Whaddye mean I ain't Joe?)
> Now if you ain't Joe.
> (I told you I'm Joe.)
> I guess then you must be Moe.
> (I don't know no Moe.)

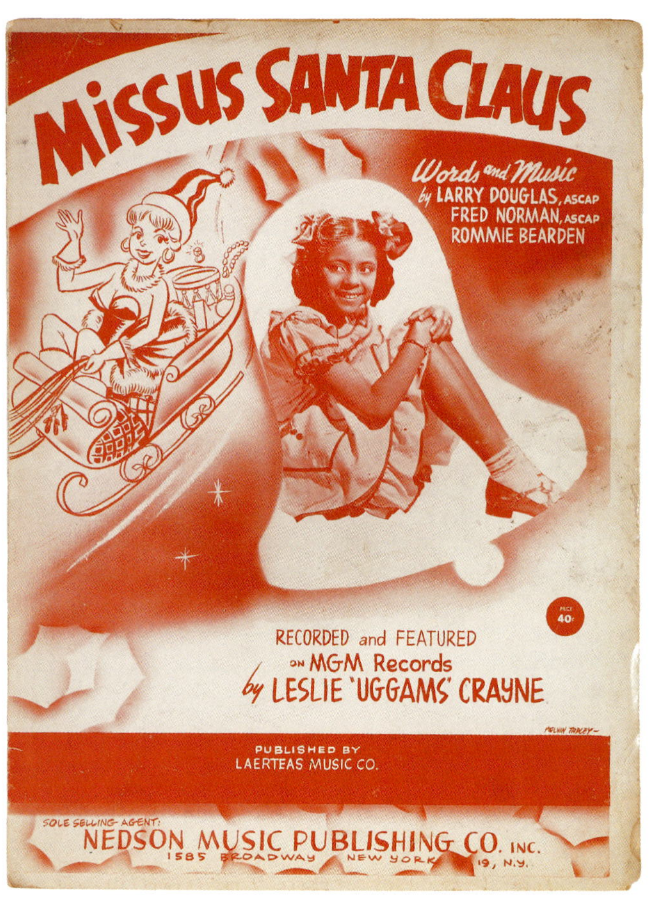

15

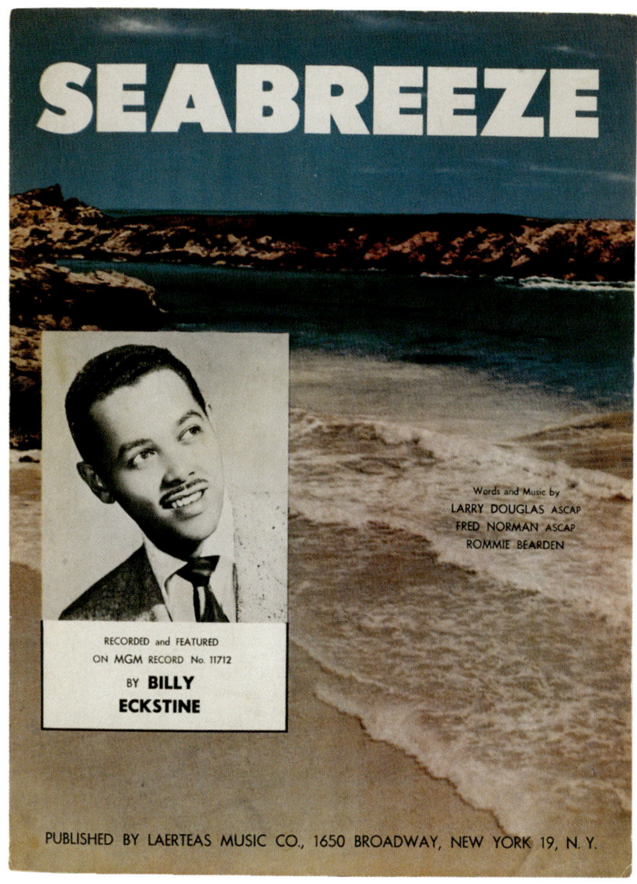

16

figure 15
"Missus Santa Claus" sheet music cover with Bearden's name among writer credits. Estate of Romare Bearden, courtesy of Romare Bearden Foundation, New York

figure 16
"Seabreeze" sheet music cover with Bearden's name among writer credits. Estate of Romare Bearden, courtesy of Romare Bearden Foundation, New York

Aside from farces, airy romance seemed Bearden's favorite subject, the wistful ballad his preferred genre. Titles such as "Dry Is My Cup" (cowritten with Douglas, for music by Nelson Glover), and "It's Twilight in My Heart" and "Just You Are" (both with music by Martin Lagunoff) bear out his propensity toward reverie. "Seabreeze," another escapist ballad, brought Bearden his greatest acclaim (fig. 16). Cowritten with Douglas and Fred Norman in 1954, the song was performed and recorded by several musicians including the silken-voiced Billy Eckstine; his version hewed to the sheet music directive of "medium slow, with a tropical beat."

It seems only yesterday,
In that Cafe, a tropic isle
Those golden drinks
Icy foamed like the ocean spray hear it say,
Seabreeze....

"Seabreeze" was so effectively suggestive of paradise that Seagram's liquor company used the song in its advertisement for a cocktail of the same name. As an elected member of the American Society of Composers, Authors and Publishers (ASCAP) from 1955, Bearden earned royalties each time his songs were performed, but the yields were modest and too few in number. Friends, such as philosophers Hannah Arendt and her husband Heinrich Blücher, encouraged him to focus on his art.[47] By 1956 he had rededicated himself to painting: "Now, I'm going to do nothing but paint—no more wildcat schemes to get rich with a hit song, etc.," he wrote to Holty.[48]

A HISTORY OF COLLABORATION

Like Bearden's songwriting efforts of the 1950s, his book-writing projects were collaborative ventures. With journalist Harry Henderson, he produced the posthumously released *A History of African-American Artists* and *Six Black Masters of American Art.* With fellow artist Carl Holty, he wrote *The Painter's Mind* (1969), an appreciative study of Western artistic techniques and creative psychology from the Middle Ages to the book's present. With St. Lucia–born writer (and later, Nobel Laureate) Derek Walcott, he published *The Caribbean Poetry of Derek Walcott* (1983), a selection of Walcott's verse, illustrated by Bearden watercolors. A children's book, *A Visit to the Country* (1989), was similarly born of Bearden's alliance with another artist, writer Herschel Johnson.[49] Was Bearden's desire to work with respected peers yet another manifestation of his famously sociable nature? The inclination of an artist who enjoyed the synergy of collectives, from his youthful days in Alston's 306 circle to his founding role in Spiral in 1963? Both explanations seem feasible. Moreover, the pace at which he formed collaborations quickened after he retired from social work, as he finally had time to develop long-simmering ideas.

If *A History of African-American Artists* and *Six Black Masters of American Art* can be assigned to the category of "race as culture"–driven art histories, then, *The Painter's Mind* was a markedly different endeavor for Bearden. In *The Painter's Mind,* he and coauthor Holty advise their readers theirs is not "a book of art history," even as they point out "certain continuities in the long history of picturemaking."[50] *The Painter's Mind* self-consciously belongs to the genre of art appreciation, and it embraces a recognizable Western canon whose titans are Cézanne, Mondrian, Rembrandt, Picasso, and Tiepolo. While European objects dominate it, the authors' list of exemplars is widened to include several twentieth-century American artists, their contemporaries Norman Lewis, Richard Lindner, and Robert Rauschenberg among them. Each man (for no women artists are considered) discussed in *The Painter's Mind* is put in the artistic lineage of Bearden's and Holty's construction. For instance, comments on the three African-American artists mentioned in the text—Lewis, Lawrence, and Raymond Saunders—focus on style or stylistic school: Lewis is described as a lyrical abstractionist; Lawrence a social realist in the vein of Jack Levine and William Gropper; and Saunders a mixed-media artist with a pop art sensibility. Moreover, *The Painter's Mind* goes against the tack of viewing African-American artists' production exclusively through the prism of race, and specifically, race as nonwhite particularity. Instead, Bearden and Holty posit artistic identity determined by the era in which the painter lived, the influence of national schools, and key innovations, from Italian Renaissance space and the impressionist palette, to cubist form and neoplasticism. And since these authors frequently address their comments to the "young artist" or the "modern student," it seems clear that they hope to persuade this audience of an artistic legacy and aesthetic debts to precursors.[51]

All collaborations run the risks of unevenness and discordance, pitfalls that Bearden deftly skirted. The unified voice—didactic and seasoned—of *The Painter's Mind* sounds like both authors' published articulations, a function, no doubt, of their close relationship and influence on each other. Although Bearden and Holty modestly absent their own works from *The Painter's Mind,* this text is suffused with the dialogic tone of their correspondence, and probably, their ongoing conversations about the masterworks and innovations they revered. Subtitled "A Study of the Relations of Structure and Space in Painting," *The Painter's Mind* seeks to explain visual strategies, which Bearden and Holty believed were rarely analyzed:

> Curiously, there are any number of books such as ours in the fields of poetry, prose fiction, and music, where it is not at all unusual to analyze structure and the principles of composition. There are precious few for painting —and the resistance to such books has been as long as it is unfortunate and misguided.[52]

The book's main planks—the import of pictorial unity, powerful variably modeled forms, and rhythmic balances marshaled to generate interest —are the same preoccupations articulated in the authors' letters to each other and in their individual interviews and publications. *The Painter's Mind,* a reservoir of their experiences that they want to share with a younger generation of artists, also forecasts the future they desire for themselves. In the book's concluding chapter, "The Artist's Maturation," they write:

> Young artists, carried on the wings of spontaneity and enthusiasm, are often the innovators and heralds of new styles.... But in the old age of the truly gifted artist, unique and wonderful things often occur. The striving for originality, the pursuit of skills for their own sake, and all other irrevelancies disappear. The master artist tends to forego surface refinements and to abjure all that is not of the deep wisdom of poetry. Secure in his space and structure, he is at one with the world he was born into and that world of difficulties he has overcome, and can now be seen for what he truly represents.[53]

The desire to teach similarly fueled Bearden's history-writing projects. The first, *Six Black Masters of American Art,* focused on the careers of Joshua Johnston, Robert S. Duncanson, Henry O. Tanner, Horace Pippin, Augusta Savage, and Jacob Lawrence.[54] Bearden and his coauthor, journalist Harry Henderson, summoned anecdotes from the artist's biographies and scripted dramatic dialogues that enlivened the tones of the individual narratives.[55] Equally dramatic is the unprecedented designation by Bearden and Henderson of their subjects as "masters," a denomination still infrequently applied to consummate artists who are black, female, or both. Although mastery has rightfully been scrutinized by scholars of cultural production since the 1970s for its presumption of universal evaluative criteria and its top-to-bottom hierarchies, this paradigm survives in art historical discourse, and especially in the popular arenas of museums, galleries, and their publications. In these forums, as in *Six Black Masters of American Art,* mastery (and its attendant, the masterpiece) galvanize public attention, conferring worth, significance, and legitimacy on the topic at hand. An early entry in the niche market of black history for general audiences, *Six Black Masters in American Art* especially slaked the thirst of black readers in search of documentation of black creativity and accomplishment.

Like the survey texts that preceded it—Alain L. Locke's *The Negro in Art* (1940), James A. Porter's *Modern Negro Art* (1943), Cedric Dover's *American Negro Art* (1960), and Samella Lewis' *Art: African-American* (1978)—Bearden's and Henderson's *A History of African-American Artists* is an invaluable reference for its breadth. In this second collaborative undertaking, they retained the biographical approach of *Six Black Masters of American Art* and increased the number of subjects by sixfold.[56] More women artists are included in *A History of African-American Artists*, and while a greater percentage of it is devoted to their male counterparts, the careers of Edmonia Lewis, Augusta Savage, Lois Mailou Jones, Elizabeth Catlett, and Alma W. Thomas are well-researched and contextualized for their centrality to the authors' overall objective: to compile "a record of the triumph of the artistic drive of African-American artists over social conditions and despair, closely linked to and profoundly influenced by their concern for their people and their identification with them."[57] Their utmost concern was that these artists be remembered.[58] Germane to such archaeological, historical, and sociological aims, Bearden and Henderson also chronicle the significant impact of nonartists Locke, the Harlem bibliophile Charles Christopher Seifert,[59] and the Harmon Foundation director Mary Beattie Brady, and of the art departments at historically black colleges and universities for, as instructors, patrons, and advocates, these individuals and institutions nurtured black artists' professional development in the twentieth century and introduced their work to wider audiences. The most underrecognized contribution of *A History of African-American Artists,* perhaps, is its reproduction of rarely seen objects and documents, which, in turn, provided material for further research, exhibitions, and other projects that study, assess, and advance the valuation of black artistic production. Certainly, earlier publications were successfully scripted toward similar ends; nonetheless, the voluminous *History of African-American Artists* was the most ambitious of the twentieth-century books to conjoin history, heritage, and an argument for a black canon.

A History of African-American Artists is written as a lively narrative, for Bearden had long sought to make the public "more art conscious, or more aware of the Negro artist."[60] As a result, the text is conversational and varied with biographical facts, anecdotes gathered from interviews, and pithy evaluations of artistic talent and historical import. For the reader who may find abstraction and expressionism strange and maladroit, Bearden and Henderson have gentle explanations of modernist strategies; they point out conspicuous manipulations of color, line, and form, and pictorial captions often say something about artistic inspiration or intention. Undermining prevalent notions of artistic eccentricity and bohemianism, subjects are presented as everyday people, albeit exceptional ones whose talents and efforts improve society as a whole. It is in this manner that Bearden modestly includes himself in *A History of African-American Artists*; his work is not discussed (as it had been in survey texts dating back to Porter's *Modern Negro Art* of 1943), but instead, his membership in artists' circles and his interventions in the public discourse about black aesthetics and identity earn mention.[61] Such attention to activism—broader than the most conventional approaches to writing art history—is applied throughout *A History of African-American Artists*: measuring both the work and lives of the artist-citizen, Bearden and Henderson posited their terms for artistic success.

A Refracted Image: Selected Exhibitions and Reviews of Bearden's Work

ABDUL GOLER

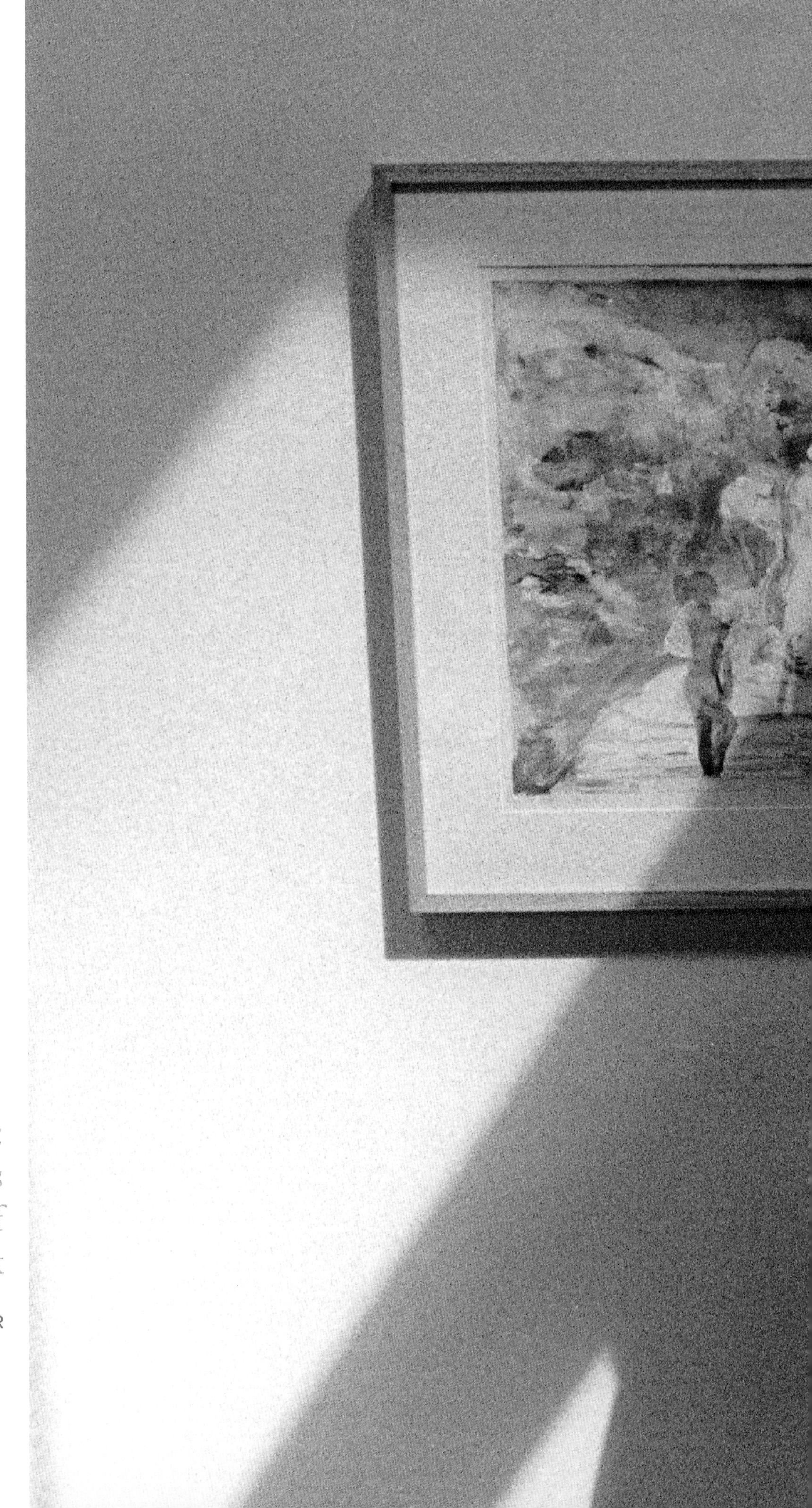

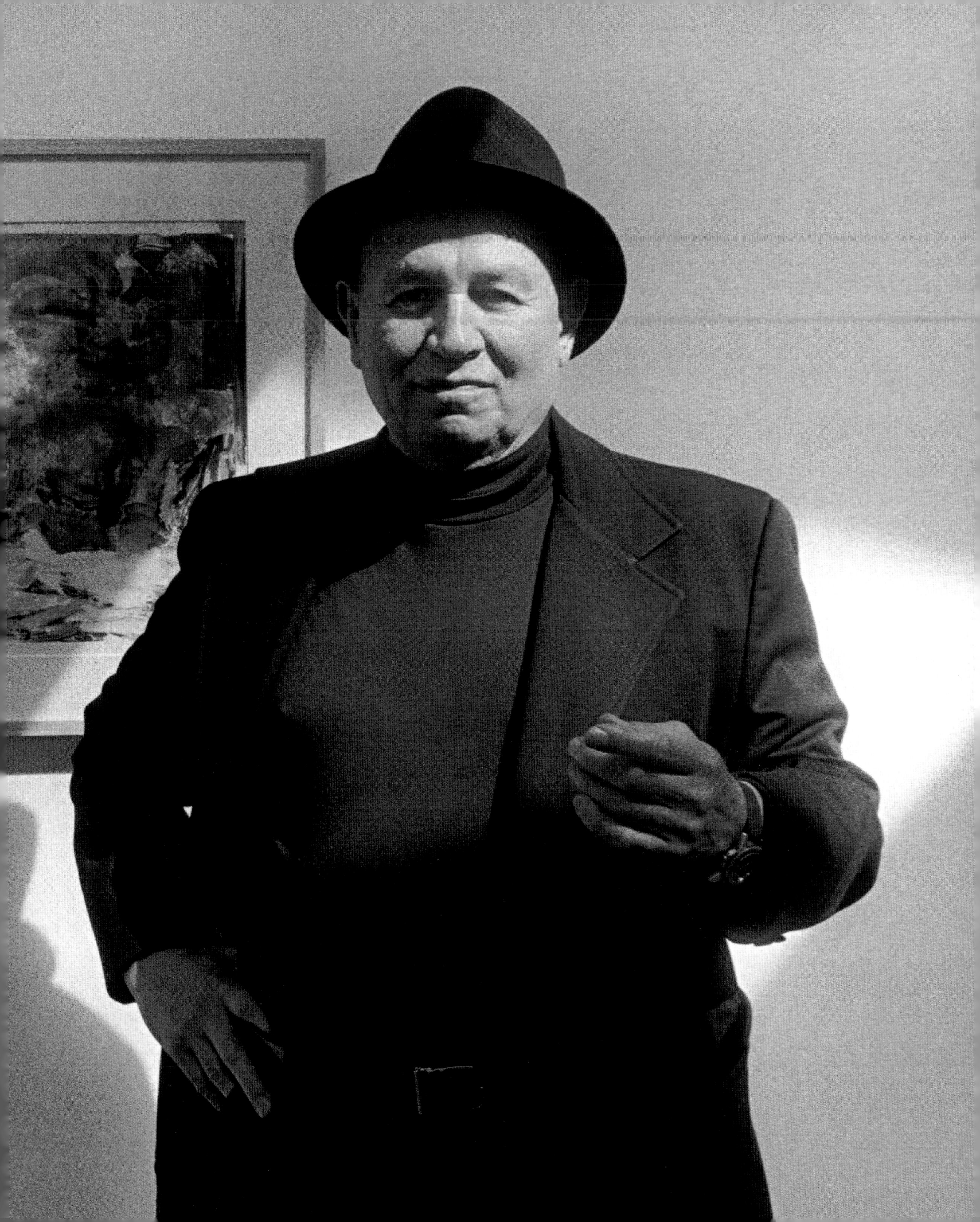

Selected from both the mainstream and the African-American press, as well as European publications,[1] these are excerpts from newspaper articles, journals, and essays that accompanied or responded to exhibitions of Romare Bearden's art during his lifetime. Included are reviews of exhibitions in which Bearden's work appeared with that of other artists. As Richard Powell has pointed out, Bearden not only knew and discussed art with major figures in European modernism such as Joan Miró and his teacher George Grosz, he also kept close ties to African-American artists and intellectuals.[2] The group shows are a reflection of his cosmopolitan associations.

The historical differences between the African-American press, the mainstream press in the United States, and the diversity of press to be found in major European cities served as an impetus for the selection of the reviews. During part of the era conveyed by this selection—just prior to American involvement in World War II through the 1980s—the African-American press was not only focused on the life and culture of people of African descent, it was also a means of propaganda: a bulwark against the negative impact of racism. The mainstream press usually minimized race as a significant factor while simultaneously referring to race as an element of exotic fascination. In the 1960s and 1970s race became a divisive issue for some mainstream critics and for others—bewildering, given the obvious impact ethnicity was having in "dividing" the art world. There are some early important exceptions to this trend that emerge in the writing of certain individuals not associated with the African-American press or institutions. In reviews of Bearden's work, beginning with Barrie Stavis' comments on the 1947 exhibition *New Paintings by Bearden* at the Samuel M. Kootz Gallery, we see the emergence of nuanced and balanced criticism of Bearden's work. The one Parisian review of Bearden's work included here does not mention or even allude to the artist's ethnicity nor make any claims to there being racial overtones in his work; rather his work is reviewed in art historical terms, solely on artistic merit. Bearden had only two exhibitions in Paris that we know of, although he did show in a group exhibition that was organized by Henri Ghent and exhibited in Geneva, Switzerland; the one article previewing the development of the group show by an American journalist is included here and for the most part reflects the sentiments of the curator of the exhibition.

This compilation is organized into seven chronological sections. The artist's first solo exhibition was in 1940, but this selection starts with his first show at the Kootz Gallery in 1945 and ends with his last exhibitions at Cordier & Ekstrom Inc. in 1987. The title "Refracted Image" was appropriated from Ralph Willis' essay that appeared in the catalogue for *Fragments of American Life: An Exhibition of Paintings* held at Princeton University in 1976.[3]

REFLECTIONS OF DEPRESSION-ERA HARLEM AND THE NEW NEGRO MOVEMENT

The series of paintings shown at the Kootz Gallery in the fall of 1945 was entitled ***Romare Bearden: The Passion of Christ,*** and the brochure for the show announced it as Bearden's "first New York exhibition" (fig. 1). The exhibition originated at G Place Gallery in Washington, D.C., in the summer of 1945. The downtown art scene's discovery of Bearden was repeatedly reinforced in both the

figure 1
Brochure for Bearden's "first New York exhibition" at Samuel M. Kootz Gallery, New York, 1945. Brooklyn Museum of Art Library Collections

mainstream and African-American press.[4] Writing in *Art Digest*, critic Ben Wolf cited Bearden as being "one of the most exciting creative artists" to emerge in "a very long time." Wolf went on to praise Bearden for the developed structure of his painting and the projection of "an uncanny sense of space" as well as his use of color all combined to create "an experience not soon to be forgotten."[5]

In the *New York Amsterdam News* Nora Holt praised Bearden's achievement as a family member back home would praise a native son who had found success in the big city: "Romare Bearden, young American painter, son of Howard and the late Bessye Bearden, prominent Harlem civic and social leader, opened his first New York exhibition at the Samuel Kootz Galleries ... and has already created a spirited interest among critics and artists bordering on sensational."[6]

Reviews from both of these streams of the U.S. press suggest that this exhibition in New York showcased Bearden as a new and promising talent to the world at large. Chronologically, however, the artist's first exhibition ***Romare Bearden: Oils, Gouaches, Water Colors, Drawings (1937–1940)*** was held in May of 1940 in the studio of the dancer and Harlem community activist Addison Bates at 306 West 141 Street. "306," as the space was called, was a place where during the Great Depression young artists of the Harlem community often began their careers, and where Jacob Lawrence's work was first exhibited.

In an article in the *New York Amsterdam News* announcing the upcoming exhibition at 306, Bearden's work was described as "distinctive." "He is among the few of the young Negro artists who have been interested in showing the transition of the colored worker from the agricultural to the urban industrialized community. Not only that, but he completely has absorbed the environment of such a change in the life of these people."[7]

As indicated by the paintings in the show—*Behind the "El," Men Eating, Women at a Pump*—at this stage in his career Bearden was creating readily identifiable images stylized yet realistic depictions of people and communicable social events, i.e., common folk in common places.

The use of folk and so-called primitive themes—often intertwined—in the organization of group exhibitions of African-American artists, in which Bearden participated in the early 1940s, was of great interest to the press. In "Art by Negroes," a review of the McMillen interior decorating firm's 1941 exhibition ***Negro Art: Contemporary***, the unidentified critic asserted a simplistic connection:

> In addition to canvases by contemporary Negroes, the ... show presents the pure African background of Negro art—primitive sculpture—through examples from the famous Frank Crowninshield Collection. From this section is the *Seated King*, a Pahouin piece from the Gabon country reproduced on the Digest's cover [see fig. 2]. Like the best of the primitive exhibits, it is marked by an austere nobility, by a flawless, native sense of design and by an anatomic distortion that helped the work express the religious purposes of its creator.... Typical of the innate sensitivity of these canvases are Ernest Crichlow's *Young Mother*, a Madonna-like conception ... Romare Bearden's strong, rhythmically designed *Woman Picking Cotton* and *The Visitation*....[8]

The critic has made a direct connection between the principles of design and motif found in sub-Saharan African art and those found in the art of the contemporary African-American artists shown in the exhibition. Such a suggestion overly simplifies the influences and borrowings that may have been present in the work on display, as being inherent, one might even say inherited, rather than an aesthetic choice based on social and political concerns as proposed by Alain Locke and the New Negro Movement.

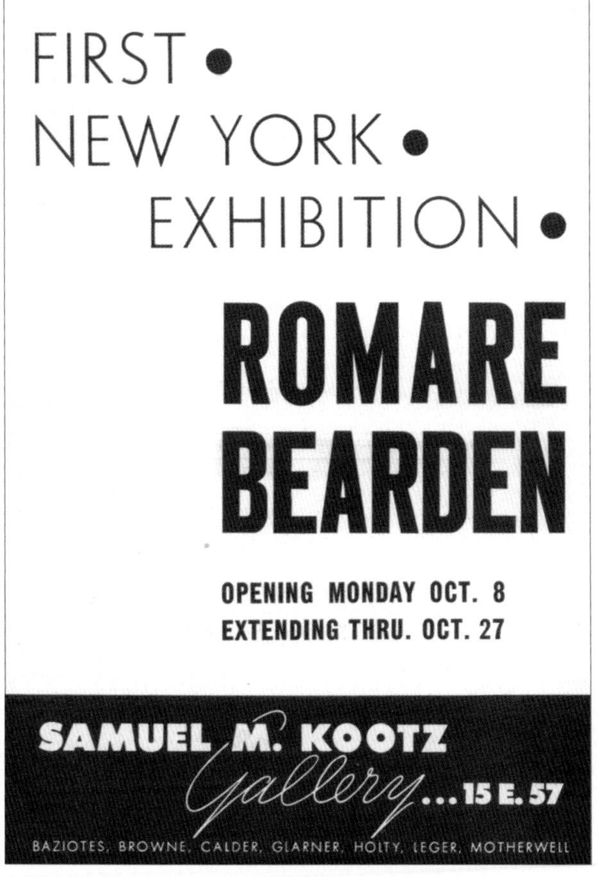

1

Not all of Bearden's forays into semiabstraction were judged as successful. In response to his second solo exhibition at the Kootz Gallery in 1946 (see fig. 4), Marion Summers offered decidedly cautionary advice to the young artist:

Romare Bearden, a young Negro painter, is exhibiting at the Kootz Gallery a series of oils and water colors based on the Spanish poet Garcia Lorca's 'Lament for a Bullfighter.' Bearden is clean, fresh and brilliant, and he composes with breadth and ease. Throughout his work there is a sense of spontaneity and control.

[Yet] Bearden has taken at second-hand the tragedy of Lorca and the horror of Picasso and transformed them into exercises in design. Bearden should be reminded that although it is a common and valid practice to borrow from one's artistic heritage, it is the element of personal experience which transforms that borrowing into something original and important. Until he gives us more of himself he will be creating pleasant but second-rate merchandise for the current art market.[21]

Whether this statement should be viewed as a critique of Bearden's use of Picasso-inspired imagery or of Bearden's borrowing from traditions thought to be outside the cultural heritage of "a young, Negro painter" is debatable.

Seeming to ignore the criticism of his borrowing from the non-biblical Western literary tradition, Bearden would continue to explore political and satirical aspects of the canon. His deployment of Rabelaisian themes in his third show at the Kootz Gallery, ***New Paintings by Bearden*** (see fig. 5), in 1947 was discussed in the press as a kind of humanist triumph.[22] In his untitled essay for the exhibition catalogue, Barrie Stavis offered his opinion as to the impulse underlying Bearden's work:

Though this may not appear on the surface, there is a continuity in Bearden's work; the Christ, the Lorca and the Rabelais are all related...[Bearden] felt that Christ, his humanness, his fathomless capacity for suffering, his infinite dignity, could best express Man. In Garcia Lorca's "Lament for the Death of a Bullfighter," Man,

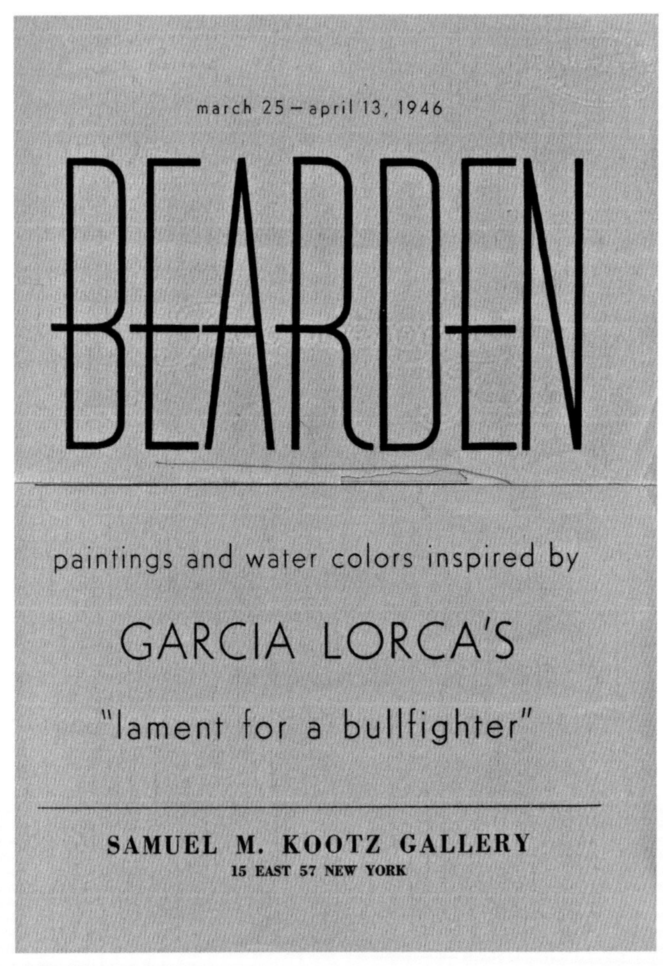

4

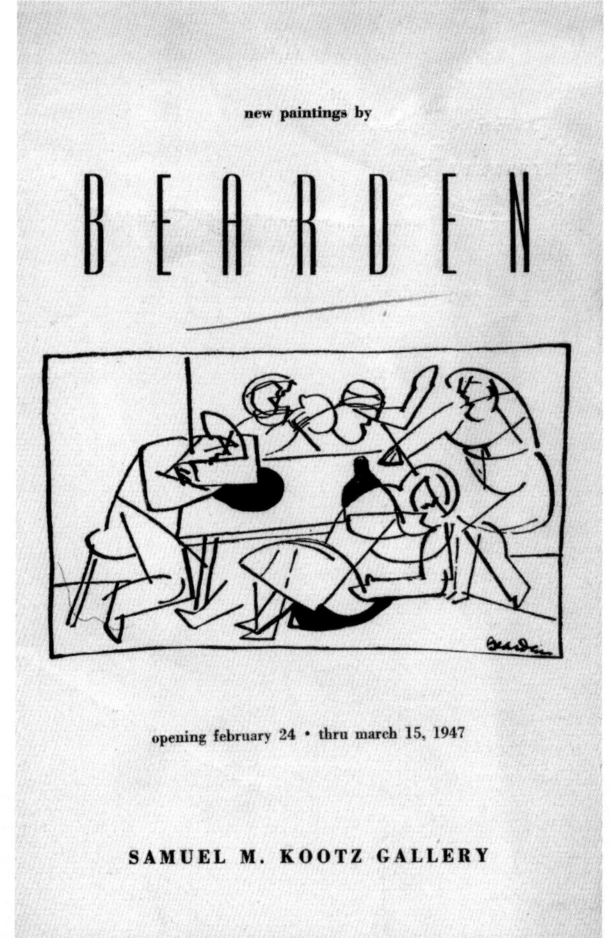

5

this time invested in ritualistic garb (the traditional costume of the bullfighter), is portrayed in another aspect of man's struggle against darkness, prejudice and ignorance symbolized by the brute force of the bull charging.[23]

In "Bearden Sings of the Cup That Cheers" appearing in *Art Digest*, Ben Wolf also aligned this series with social interests: "Bearden provides an antidote for those who feel that the human denominator must necessarily be sacrificed in the realm of the abstract."[24]

Bearden's participation in a group exhibition at the Kootz Gallery entitled *Women: A Collaboration of Artists and Writers* in the fall of 1947 was reviewed in *Art News* as a continuation of previous semiabstract archetypal explorations: "Picasso's monumental Woman in a Green Costume, 1943, dominates the show.... More realistic are the ladies conceived by [Carl] Holty and Bearden. Flat streamlined planes respectively describe the actions of pouring water and consulting an oracle."[25]

The essay by poet William Carlos Williams written to accompany Bearden's "woman" highlighted the social context in which the painting was exhibited:

With woman there's something under the surface which we've been blind to, something profound, basic. We need, perhaps more than anything else today, to discover woman; ... Such a show as this, almost flippant, certainly 'wrong' as it may seem, at least avoids the more malicious flippancy which masquerades as 'woman' today. Such a picture as Bearden's (taken with the others, good and bad) if it can link the basic conception of woman I have sketched with an art that is in the condition painting is in today becomes important....

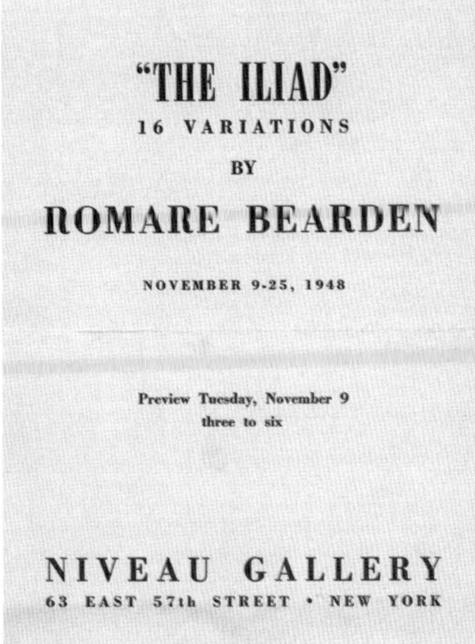
"THE ILIAD"
16 VARIATIONS
BY
ROMARE BEARDEN
NOVEMBER 9-25, 1948
Preview Tuesday, November 9
three to six
NIVEAU GALLERY
63 EAST 57th STREET • NEW YORK

6

It is altogether fitting at such a time that her traits (no face) be celebrated—by the artist who alone among men resembles her.[26]

The social status that women and African Americans shared in the United States as second-class citizens is alluded to as Bearden's resemblance to "her."

The Kootz Gallery would close its doors in July of 1948 and reopen in September 1949 without Bearden and Holty. Shortly thereafter, however, in November of 1948, Bearden would have his only solo exhibition at the Niveau Gallery, New York; it highlighted another venture into the Western literary tradition, *The Iliad,* a series of sixteen watercolors (see fig. 6). The exhibition pamphlet stated:

The great gods of Homer—Zeus, Apollo, Athena—have remained for 3000 years as ideal types for all subsequent poetry and sculpture. His personages—Helen, Achilles, Hector, etc.—live for the imagination today as no others save those of Shakespeare's greatest tragedies.... The brilliant watercolors by Romare Bearden are not *illustrations*, as they do not necessarily refer to any particular episodes or personages in the Iliad, which has rather served only as an inspiration for these works.[27]

Bearden would create a second series of works inspired by Homer—the Odysseus series of 1977. In the exhibition catalogue for the second series Calvin Tomkins' essay discussed the psychological impact of the work (see note 63).

STUDIES OF TEXTURE AND COLOR—POST PARIS

Between the fall of 1948 and 1955, reviews of solo and group exhibitions that provide critical analysis or specifically cite Bearden's achievements are scarce. In 1950 Bearden departed New York to study at the Sorbonne in Paris for several months. He explored philosophy, including Buddhism, and did very little if any painting. Bearden was in Paris from February through August and then traveled through France, Italy, and Spain and back to New York. One might look at the period between the fall of 1948 and that of 1955 as a period of contemplation—a coming to terms with seemingly opposing forces Bearden encountered in society, in the art world, and in his personal life.

figure 4
Brochure for *Bearden: Paintings and Water Colors Inspired by Garcia Lorca's "Lament for a Bullfighter,"* 1946, Samuel M. Kootz Gallery, New York. Brooklyn Museum of Art Library Collections

figure 5
Brochure for *New Paintings by Bearden,* 1947, Samuel M. Kootz Gallery, New York. Brooklyn Museum of Art Library Collections

figure 6
Brochure for *The Iliad: 16 Variations by Romare Bearden* exhibition, 1948, Niveau Gallery, New York. Brooklyn Museum of Art Library Collections

An article reviewing Bearden's first solo exhibition since his return at the Barone Gallery in New York (see fig. 7) in the fall of 1955 was positive, but mistaken in its assertion that he had "...profited by a long stay abroad, notably in color and in a new freedom in his space-filling figure paintings." Bearden was in Europe for less than a year. However, the review did stress the psychological and emotive quality of Bearden's new work. The oil paintings, for example, were described as "heavily charged" and the watercolors "quite abstract in their fluent interpenetrating washes and yet he has contrived to suggest remoteness in space and seasonal moods. Mountain contours and loneliness are implicit in these statements, which are intrinsically and appealingly decorative."[28]

Bearden's contributions to several exhibitions from 1955 to 1961 together demonstrate his further progression toward a synthesis of subject matter, form, and color. ***Eight New York Painters,*** an exhibition organized by Hale Woodruff as part of the University of Michigan's summer session—"Patterns of American Culture: Contributions of the Negro at the University of Michigan Museum of Art," July 1–31, 1956, directly addressed the issues of race, representation, and African-American artistic production—issues that Bearden actively discussed.[29] The exhibition included in addition to Bearden's the work of Eldzier Cortor, Jacob Lawrence, Norman Lewis, Merton Simpson, Charles W. White, Ellis Wilson, and Woodruff, whose catalogue foreword "The American Negro Artist," asserted that:

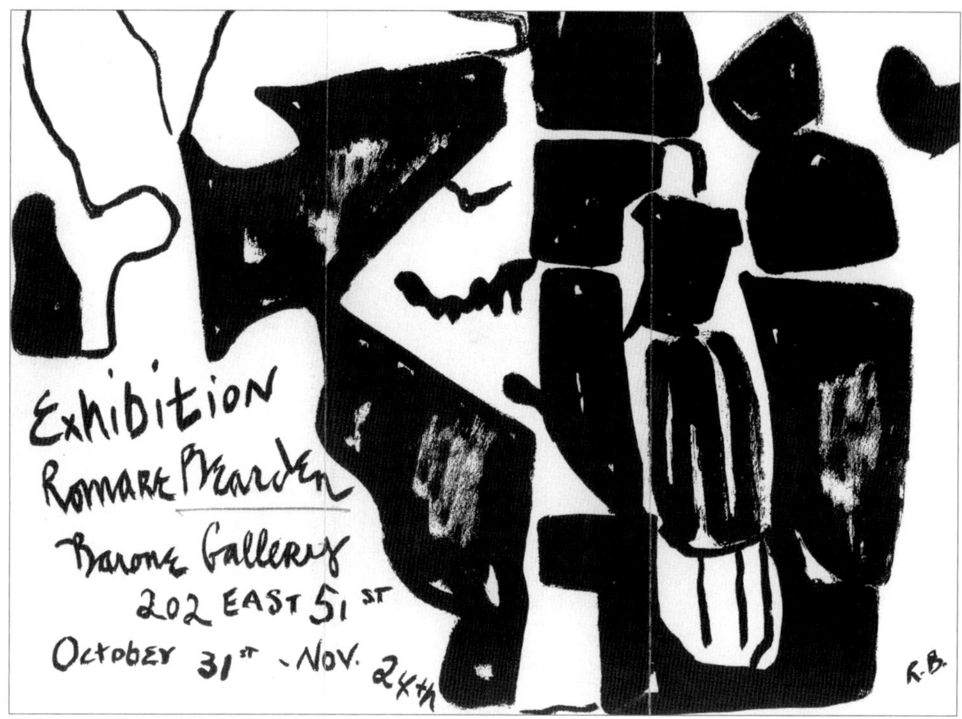

7

> The 'Decade of the Depression' may be marked as the coming of age of the Negro artist.... Any racial elements that might have identified his works were submerged in the mainstream of the general and specific qualities of all art produced in this period.... His aspirations toward full integration in American life found expression in his art.[30]

Again we see discussion of the sublimation of content that first appeared with Porter's writing for the exhibition ***Ten Hierographic Paintings by Sgt. Romare Bearden*** in 1944. Similar discussions as to the psychology and social relevance of Bearden's work, as well as the work of other African-American artists, resurface in reviews of exhibitions in the 1960s.

Bearden's show of new work at the Michel Warren Gallery in New York in 1960 was seen as a successful return to the New York art scene by the *New York Herald Tribune*:

> Major interest in the show of non-objective paintings at the new Michel Warren Gallery (857 Madison Ave.) is that an artist once as well regarded here as Romare Bearden is exhibiting again.... That which materializes on the walls of the gallery is not specific but remote and poetic. Thus paintings like those entitled *Wine Star* and *Wings of the Dragon* are a sublimation of private experiences, more than realizations of communicable

subject matter. Forms and colors seem filtered into the canvases, gaining remarkable hues and textures as though they were strained through a sieve. Grays and quiet brick-reds and blues are used, with the luminosity of the color of an insect's wing, or the flaring form of a mysteriously lovely flower.[31]

The following year in a review of Bearden's exhibition at the new Cordier-Warren Gallery, the successor to the Michel Warren name, Brian O'Doherty stated that:

> The remote soundings of natural fact continue...in the exhibition by Romare Bearden....These large paintings suggest that Mr. Bearden, like Empedocles, divides nature into the primary elements—air, water, earth and (in one warm painting full of glowing embers) fire. For they are full of suggestions of stratified earth, subaqueous suspensions and clear auroras or atmosphere. ...It is a most inventive and a fully controlled style, capable—and this is most unusual in this genre—of wide ranges of expression and mood.[32]

In May of 1961 Bearden and his wife, Nanette, left for a month-long tour of Europe, visiting Geneva, Paris, and historically important Italian centers of art production. Upon his return to New York a month later, figurative elements began to reappear in his work.

In the early 1960s the Cordier-Warren Gallery, where Bearden appeared in two solo exhibitions between 1961 and 1963, was renamed Cordier & Ekstrom Inc. Semirepresentational collages appeared in 1962, but Bearden's use of figuration did not come to the media's attention until his *Projections* show two years later. The exhibition included black-and-white photostatic enlargements of small detailed color collages. The enlargements, because of what was perceived as their graphic nature within the politically charged times of the mid-1960s, became the focus of the media.

COLLAGE

The opening of *Projections* at Cordier & Ekstrom in October of 1964 was referred to by one press source as "propagandist in the best sense."[33] Many of the reviews included here spoke specifically of the photostatic enlargements as a type of semiabstract social documentary film.

One review began by describing Bearden's process of creating collage, in general, from diverse sources such as newspapers, magazines, and photographs in order to tell "the saga of the American Negro as it has filtered through his memories and experience." The reviewer continued with an explanation of how the collages were created around a theme such as cotton workers and then ended by stating that they were enlarged to make "photo-murals...It is these photomurals that are being exhibited."[34]

The social dimension of the iconography is emphasized again and again in reviews:

> But as his people's fight for integration gained intensity, his early childhood memories returned to haunt his thoughts—and his art. He began to make tiny collages—tormented faces of Southern Negro women hanging upside down on the cracked stoops of Harlem tenements, New York bridges soaring out of Carolina cotton fields, African sorcerers, leaning against Egyptian pyramids....Bearden then had these collages, which were in color, blown up into huge black-and-white photographs, which he called 'projections.'[35]

A review in *Time* magazine described the work as a "compelling vision of beauty and horror": "From cut-outs—crooked nose, laughing eyes, tear-stained cheek—he has collaged and carefully distorted images of Negro life, then photographed and enlarged them, to make the most moving show on the avenue."[36]

An insightful review appearing in the *New York Herald Tribune* by an anonymous author praised *Projections* and Bearden's successful synthesis of content and form.

> Transcending the pitfalls of race-problem painting, Bearden, long known as a skilled abstractionist, has, in this new show, produced a startling—if not spectacular—series of collages on Negro themes. Hundreds of faces, houses, streets and objects seem to collide and mesh into fugue-like networks that in each instance tell strong and often poignant tales. 'The Burial,' 'The Street,' or 'Woman in a Harlem Courtyard' have the shock and impact of a swift cinematic passage. Easily one of the best shows in town.[37]

The sentiments expressed echo those of Porter and Woodruff's and are uncannily similar to Ralph Ellison's statements four years later that accompanied the State University of New York, Purchase, exhibition *Romare Bearden: Paintings and Projections.* Furthermore, unlike the other reviews included here of this seminal showing of the enlargements, this review generally referred to all of the work on display as collage and did not differentiate between the black-and-white enlargements and the small color compositions; the filmlike quality was seen to be embodied in the totality of works in both media.

figure 7
Announcement for *Romare Bearden,* Barone Gallery, 1955, New York. Brooklyn Museum of Art Library Collections

Following the critical success of the 1964 *Projections* show, the number of opportunities for Bearden in ever more diverse venues proliferated. Collage was now his primary medium.

Between 1964 and the mid-1970s the press presented Bearden as working on two fronts: he was part of the mainstream and was represented in collective showings of contemporary art; he also displayed his own work in exhibitions with fellow African-American artists. These shows often had as their focus historical issues such as tracing the lineage of African-American artistic development (***The Evolution of Afro-American Artists, 1800–1950*** [1967]). Some others were simply shows of unity during particularly turbulent times.

The critical acclaim awarded ***Romare Bearden, New Collages*** (see fig. 8) in the fall of 1967 at Cordier & Ekstrom, marked a high point in the artist's career. Although Ralph Pomeroy's review of the exhibition, "Black Persephone," referred specifically to one painting, *The Rites of Spring,* the title of the article suggests Bearden's use throughout the exhibition of classically stylized images of black women issuing from his synthesis of color, composition, and archetype:

She stands like a tribal saint, formal, mysterious and significant: Black Persephone with attributes of earth and leaf.... She wears a costume of blues, greens and whites—Mediterranean hues—and a hat like that of any field worker. Her face is like an African mask.

The total effect is airy, legendary, formal, hieratic, tender, archetypal. These garden deities, these spring impersonators, are subjects in a large collage by the American painter Romare Bearden. He titled it (no surprise now), "The Rites of Spring."

The somewhat stiff gestures and the frontal-profile switches have a rather Egyptian air about them.... It could almost be a painting of the Two Marys. The color-scheme is lovely—blues, roses, lavenders, greys, indigoes and blacks harmonized with tans. And again we have the African mask-like faces.

Romare Bearden is a Negro (which is like writing, 'Picasso is Spanish; Chagall, Russian-born').[38]

The type of recognition of Bearden's artistic prowess and ethnicity seen in the review above is very different from references in reviews from the 1940s to supposed racial affinities said to be exhibited in his work and the work of other African-American artists. Here we have a sense of the thoughtful process of synthesis that informed Bearden's cultural borrowing.

Cathy Aldridge's review of the same show, "Bearden's Collages Sold Though Exhibit Goes On," in the *New York Amsterdam News* pointed out that "The artist... adroitly built up his figural works of Afro-American subjects, using variously colored pieces of paper in a mosaic-like technique." The article continued: "His collages, an interesting and exciting technique using bits of magazine photos, poster art, subway signs, and other photographic flotsam-jetsam so usual in the commercialism of our times, come to life in ways which are at once emotional, perceptive, and sensual." Aldridge concluded that "While some squeamish individuals may scream 'stereotype in a new medium' the art world recognizes at once the majestic dignity of Bearden's subjects."[39]

The concluding statement by Aldridge may be seen as an allusion to the use of imagery by many African-American artists of this period that sought to valorize black urban existence. Such artists may have been associated with black nationalism and more overt forms of protest in comparison to Bearden's artistic statements, that would have shunned the depiction of cotton pickers, watermelon eaters, and other "negative" images associated with African-American rural culture.

In contrast to the sentiment Aldridge said might have been held by some, John Canaday offered his summation of the artist's achievements in the exhibition:

Romare Bearden achieves, several times over, what has been impossible for other painters of Negro subjects during our recent years of troubled conscience and violent protest. He has managed to invest his Negroes with dignity instead of trying to wrap them in it as if it were a cloak out of a stage wardrobe.

He has employed motifs of setting and costume peculiar to Negro life—from the Southern cabin to Harlem—without falling into the traps of picturesqueness, pathos and righteous indignation. He frequently speaks poignantly, never sentimentally... he shows us what has happened to the Negro but he shows it as a fact, not an accusation. The accusation is built-in, and thus is more effective than the mawkish tirade that so many painters end up with no matter how good the cause or how sincere their convictions in this difficult area. He evokes a past alive in the present, and evokes it not in historical terms but as part of an infinitely complex inheritance—and he does so in a twentieth-century medium that he employs with masterly structural skill.[40]

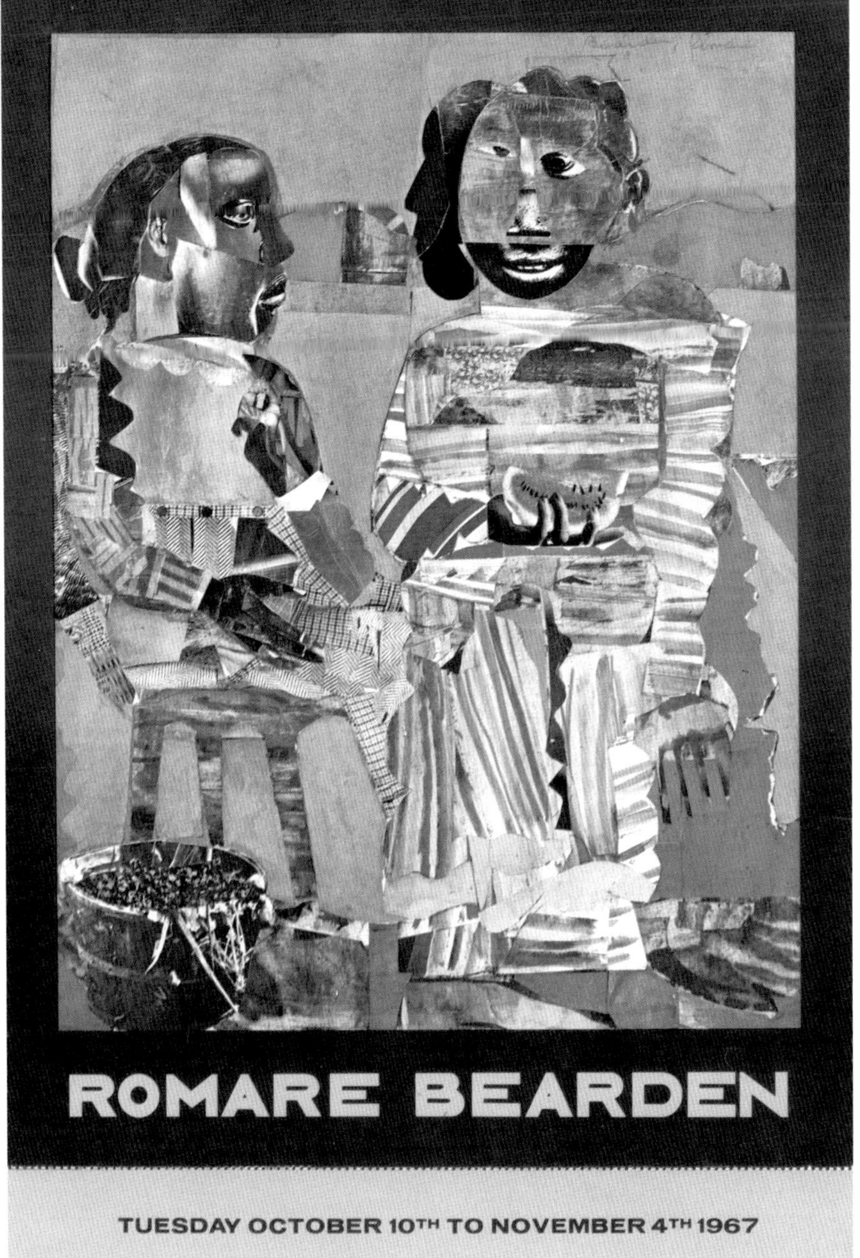

8

The poignant nature of Bearden's work, and this 1967 exhibition in particular, was also discussed in *Time* magazine:

In material as well as topic, they are timely…the pictures illustrate the difference between journalism and art, for Bearden brings to his panoramas a poet's fantasy, a professional's technique, and a philosopher's understanding of reality.

What makes the final product so fresh and captivating is the skill with which Bearden employs his polyglot artistic heritage…All this intermingling has the effect of broadening his pictures from the specific into the universal…Finally, what is true for his Negro subjects becomes true for every man.[41]

Novelist and social critic Ralph Ellison may have offered the best summation of Bearden's perceived role in the art world and within the social fabric of the 1960s and 1970s as it was being shaped by the Civil Rights movement:

Romare Bearden…is an artist whose social consciousness is no less intense than his dedication to art; his example is of utmost importance for all who are concerned with grasping something of the complex interrelations between race, culture and the individual artist as they exist in the United States.

One suspects…that as an artist possessing a marked gift for pedagogy, he has sought…to reveal a world long hidden by the clichés of sociology and rendered cloudy by the distortions of newsprint and the false continuity imposed upon our conception of Negro life by television and much documentary photography.

Thus in the poetic sense these works give plastic expression to a vision in which the socially grotesque conceals a tragic beauty, and they embody Bearden's interrogation of the empirical values of a society which

figure 8
Promotional poster for *Romare Bearden, New Collages*, 1967, Cordier & Ekstrom Inc., New York, featuring *Melon Time*, an early stage of *Melon Season*, in the Neuberger Museum of Art, Purchase College, State University of New York. Brooklyn Museum of Art Library Collections

mocks its own ideals through a blindness induced by its myth of race. All of this ironically, by a man who visually at least (he is light-skinned and perhaps more Russian than "black" in appearance) need never have been restricted to the social limitations imposed upon easily identified Negroes. Bearden's art is thus not only an affirmation of his own freedom and responsibility as an individual and artist, it is an affirmation of the irrelevance of the notion of race as a limiting force in the arts. These are works of a man possessing a rare lucidity of vision.[42]

In his review of *Romare Bearden: Recent Collages* at Cordier & Ekstrom (1970), Hilton Kramer raised an extremely important issue regarding the nature of Bearden's achievements in relation to cubism's historic borrowings from African art and possible relation to African-American culture:

The collage paintings of Romare Bearden, with their fragmented images of Negro life locked into an elegant cubist design, are fairly well known on the New York art scene...the works...raise some interesting questions about the relation of black experience to modernist forms of painting and sculpture. Mr. Bearden uses a great many photographic fragments in his collages. He also occasionally uses pictorial fragments of African masks in a sort of montage synthesis with contemporary black figures. There is an interesting idea at work in the use of these African mask motifs—a suggestion of the morphology of certain forms that derive originally from African art, then passed into modern art by way of cubism, and are now being employed to evoke a mode of Afro-American experience.[43]

A concurrent review of the same show in *Arts Magazine* provided examples of more tangible influences in Bearden's work:

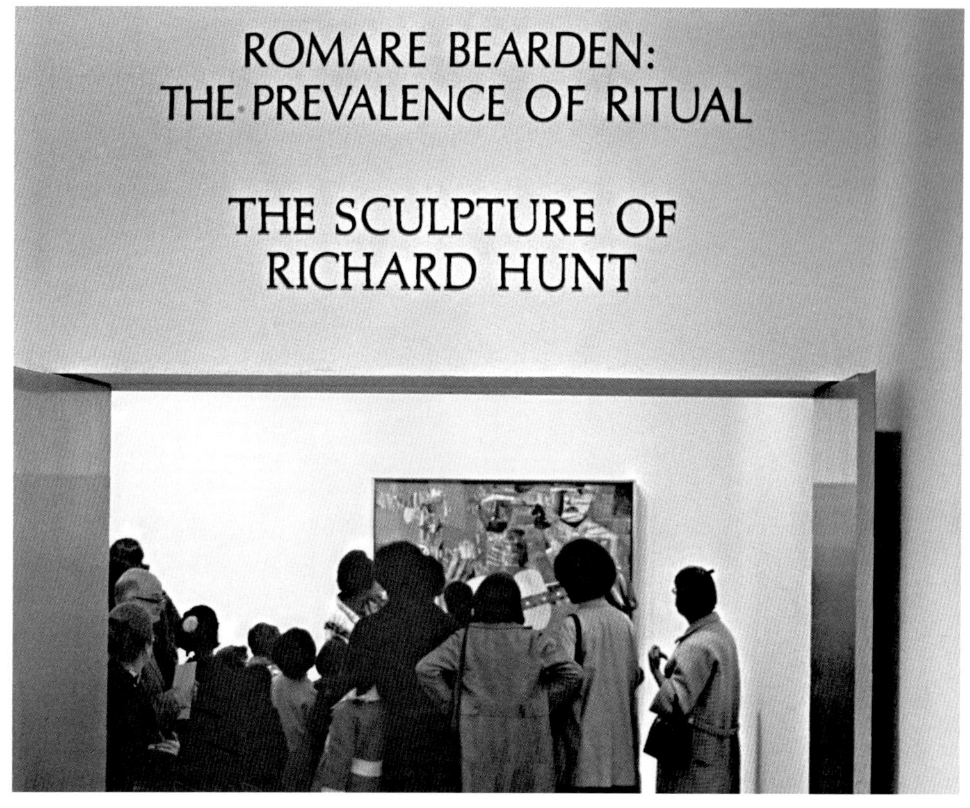

9

The recent collages by Romare Bearden create a formal aesthetic meriting highest praise, while maintaining his familiar interest in social themes—particularly the life and times of the American Negro. It is difficult in this medium to maintain a harmonious order between artistic aims and literal subject matter; yet, as always Bearden maintains complete control. His images form a pulsating rhythm, color and movement, vividly akin to modern jazz while simulating a pictorial "folk song of American life."...In all his collages, a unification both sensitive and intelligent exists between the figures and backgrounds....The city scenes show a dominance of architectural façade over the subjects themselves as if stifling the air and the freedom they were born to. Windows and doorways are exaggerated as symbols of escape, as well as implying imprisonment....[44]

Romare Bearden: The Prevalence of Ritual, Bearden's one-person show at the Museum of Modern Art (MoMA) in 1971 was a high point in his career (see fig. 9).[45] Emily Genauer's article "Black Artists, But Black Art?" discussed the exhibition and the issues surrounding its organization:

figure 9
Visitors to *Romare Bearden: The Prevalence of Ritual,* 1971, at the Museum of Modern Art, New York

figure 10
Romare Bearden, left, at the *Art of the American Negro* exhibition, 1966

Two major and exceptionally fine one-man exhibitions by black artists, Richard Hunt, sculptor, and Romare Bearden, painter and collagist, have simultaneously opened in adjoining galleries at the Museum of Modern Art. Their joint presentation, says the museum, is entirely coincidence.

A critic would be justified, then, in considering each exhibition as a separate, unrelated event. He would also be singularly obtuse. There is no issue in the American cultural world more painful and divisive right now than that involving art created by blacks. Notice that I don't use the increasingly popular term, black art.

That, in fact, is the core of the question. Is there a black art, as many black artists maintain, meaning an expression growing out of the creator's unique experience as blacks in America? Or is there only art, of widely disparate intention and form, created by artists who happen to be black?[46]

Charles Allen's review of the MoMA show suggested formal antecedents for Bearden's work in addition to a critique of the status quo in his article "...the Walls Come Tumbling Down?":

Interestingly, and to his credit, Bearden manages a successful fusion of two rather disparate elements—the mosaic and the Byzantine, and the monumental and the African. The entire series has a starkness more akin to cinema vérité than to painting. And this is achieved by the artist's freely borrowing from that 20th-century medium, film. He uses its multiple imagery technique to obtain a simultaneity and immediacy of vision. This makes the collages not only more filmic than painterly; it also enables them to violate Renaissance concepts of space.

But Bearden's art is truly less modern than it is the culmination of a traditional art. For despite the intervention of found objects, polymer paint, photo-mechanical process and techniques of the cinema, Bearden looks backward to the hard-edge classicism of the 19th-century, triumphing in a style best described as Afro-American Baroque. Bearden's art...[is] an art nurtured by, inseparable from and, indeed, impossible without the Black Experience.

Some critics will be made apprehensive by my referring to [Bearden] as Black. They will doubtless allege that color is irrelevant. But it will not cease to be relevant until such time as Black artists are fully integrated into the Museum of Modern Art's mainstream. For the exhibition of the works of two Black artists does not make a non-racist policy, although it could well mark the beginning.[47]

CONTEXT AND COMMUNITY: AN ONGOING DIALOGUE

Two of Bearden's collages, *The Dove* and *Jazz: (N.Y.) Savoy—1930's*, both from 1964, appeared in the exhibition *Art of the American Negro* (see fig. 10), which Bearden was involved in organizing for the Harlem Cultural Council in the summer of 1966. The catalogue essay stated:

This exhibition will give an opportunity for the Harlem community to view the work of Negro artists in greater scope than has been possible in a number of years. The Harlem Cultural Committee is, therefore, privileged in presenting these outstanding artists. The committee is hopeful, that as a consequence of this show, artists will find a more receptive audience within the community.

Today, there is an increasing interest in the effort of the Negro painters and sculptors. Exhibitions similar to this one are already being planned throughout the country. This is important, because the most momentous factor in American life, is the Negro's drive for self-identification and art has a power to enlarge the vision and understanding people have of themselves and of other people.

In spite of the inequities of his life, the Negro artist has maintained a freedom and independence in exploring the various facets of his art. This is clearly reflected in this exhibition, in an engaging variety of styles, as all artists must explore the nature of reality in their own way. But in whatever manner the Negro artist may approach his art—whether lyrical, abstract or realistic—nothing is so important as his identifying with the self-reliance, the hope, and the courage of those who, in this crucial hour, are marching in the interest of man's freedom and dignity.[48]

The following year in the fall of 1967 another group exhibition of work by African-American artists—*Evolution of Afro-American Artists, 1800–1950*—organized by Bearden and Carroll Greene, Jr., was held at the City University of New York. In her *Newsday* review, "Does Race Color a Painter's Work?," Emily Genauer spoke of the complex issue of race and its impact on the art world:

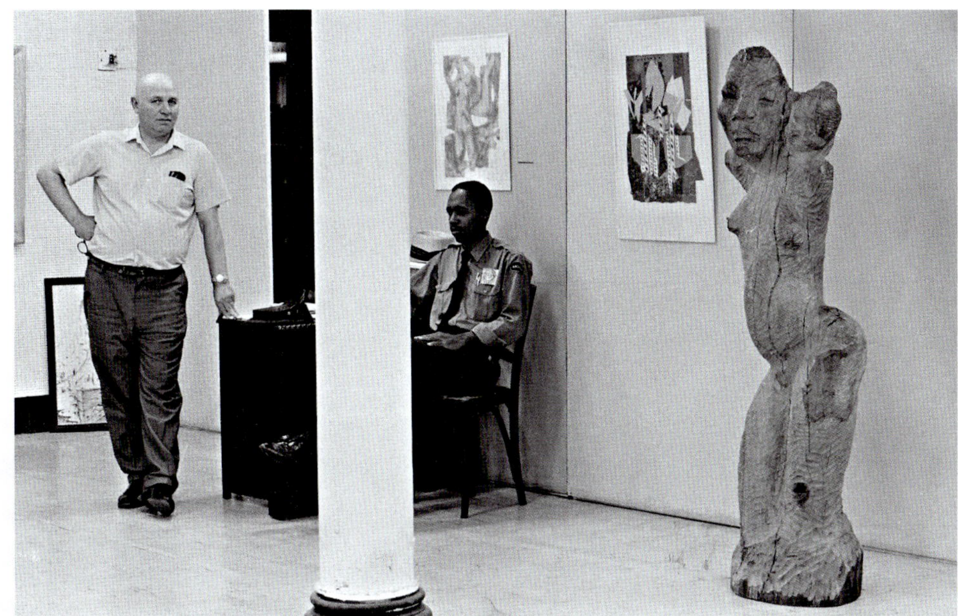

10

The creator's color is not apparent to his audience. It may have determined the character of his art, since art is the reflection of total experience, and surely the experience of being an American Negro is of greatest importance to the artist.

[But] the gallery audience can't tell from the pattern of geometry on a canvas, any more than it can from the sound of music, the color of the man who made it. And yet the fact remains—and the new exhibit is evidence—that Negroes have made a good but not greatly distinguished contribution to painting and sculpture in this country....

The critic went on to make the qualitative comparison that "Among the gifted artists represented in the new display are Jacob Lawrence, Romare Bearden, Charles Alston, Norman Lewis, Richard Mayhew. They are not of the caliber of de Kooning, Hans Hofmann, Stuart Davis, Rivers, Rauschenberg, Shahn...." She concluded that what bothered her was "a premise and a label implying not a challenge so much as a self-constructed barrier [and that it was] startling to find deliberate emphasis on a separateness based on race."[49]

In a more factual review of the exhibition by Grace Glueck that appeared in the *New York Times,* we learn that Bearden got the idea for the show after visiting Howard University in Washington, D.C., and seeing the exhibition organized by James A. Porter, entitled ***Ten Afro-American Artists of the Nineteenth Century***. The critic cites the impetus the organizers had for the New York show:

To "give history the opportunity of appraising the contributions that Negro artists have made," Mr. Bearden and associates have organized a historical survey of American Negro art.

The 150 works—oils, water-colors, sculptures, drawings and prints [by 55 artists]—are divided into four periods: "The Nineteenth Century," "The Negro Renaissance" (1920's); "The Depression Years to World War II," and "World War II to 1950." The show also includes the retrospective work of living artists who were established by 1950.

A small collection of African sculpture, dating from the 16th century, forms a prelude to the chronological presentation. The sculpture, Mr. Bearden notes, is interesting not only as "heritage" but also as an influence on the works of such men as Picasso, Matisse and Modigliani, who in turn influenced modern American painters.[50]

Bearden's involvement in exhibitions devoted to showcasing African-American artists continued through the 1970s. Opinions as to the quality of these exhibitions varied from positive to nonchalant to dismissive, but Bearden's work was usually well received. An exception to this trend was a review by Joseph Mashek in *Artforum*:

In a group show called "Black Artists 1970," at the Visual Arts Gallery,[51] only three figures out of sixteen evidence any talent. Bill Howell... Warren L. Harris [and]... Romare Bearden's Morning collage [that] includes one very fine Legeresque female figure, but the piece suffers from an unbalanced and overcomplicated, pseudo–De Stijl background.

The exhibition is billed as "the first professional Black Art exhibit," and, aside from the fact that it is hardly of a professional mean standard, it does focus attention on what must be a real problem for blacks in relation to culture at large: romantic identification with peasant life and values as against civilization... there is no reason why art like this should not be made and enjoyed in some informal communal milieu, but exhibiting it as "professional" work is another story.... Blacks, like everybody else, are going to have to move out from the realm of the merely sincere and decide for themselves whether they want the kibbutz or Paris.[52]

Henri Ghent, curator of the Community Gallery (affiliated with the Brooklyn Museum of Art), provided his "qualitative" analysis of the Boston exhibition ***Jubilee: Afro-American Artists on Afro-America***[53] and of African-American group shows in general in his review "Black Critic Takes a Look at 'Jubilee,'" which appeared in the *Boston Globe*:

In the late 1960s black artists lost their invisible status almost literally overnight. Major museums, colleges and universities began to stage "black" art shows with staggering rapidity. The heretofore unvocal black artistic community was saying—quite lucidly—that it wanted to enter the mainstream of American art, and the white art establishment flung open its doors with abandon.

Ethnic-oriented exhibits were not only expedient but indeed desirable in the late 60s and early 70s when the "Black Consciousness" movement was at its zenith, a highly significant period in contemporary Afro-American history. The movement served among other things, to give countless numbers of black artists a renewed sense of pride in both African and Afro-American cultural achievement.

This seeming advancement by Afro-American artists would be cause for rejoicing—that is, if gestures of recognition had indeed been motivated out of sincere concern for excellence in art created by blacks, rather than being—as time has certainly proved—merely token efforts to appease social critics, as well as to assuage deep-seated guilt feelings about black people.

While the white art establishment must assume responsibility for the gross lack of artistic standards exercised in the vast majority of the "black" shows that have inundated us in the past seven years, our black "cultural leaders" must also stand accountable for their share of the damage as well. All of which is pertinent to the large and colorful exhibition, "Jubilee: Afro-American Artists on Afro-America."…The exhibition is comprised of more than 159 paintings, sculpture, graphics and crafts by some 32 artists who are based, for the most part, in Boston, New York, Philadelphia and Washington.

Judging by the paucity of overall concern for quality and innovation…[it] would seem that involvement in the black artistic community—like…much present-day activity therein…is more politically than artistically motivated.

The most satisfying of the figurative artists in the older age group are William H. Johnson, Allen Crite, Archibald Motley, Jacob Lawrence, Eldzier Cortor and Romare Bearden.[54]

In contrast to Ghent's critique of *Jubilee* and the African-American art exhibition phenomenon, Glueck's review of the Brooklyn Museum of Art's showing of ***Two Centuries of Black American Art,*** organized by David Driskell, Jr., offered an analysis similar to James Porter's of Bearden's work in *Ten Hierographic Paintings* and Hale Woodruff's tracing of black artistic development in his foreword to *Eight New York Painters*:

Ignored for the most part by those committed to "mainstream" art, blacks have seen "ethnic" shows as a way of compelling attention. The tactic has been useful (for women as well): Though such shows are deplored by critics who rightly wish to consider art as an esthetic, not an ethnic matter, their very existence has forced the examination of work that might otherwise be bypassed, and given it a context that may shed light on its conception. Top-notch artists are represented here (if not always by their best works): the primitive painter Horace Pippin, Jacob Lawrence, Romare Bearden, Alma W. Thomas.

Though Professor Driskell feels obliged to flirt, in his catalogue essay, with the idea of a "black esthetic," he never defines it, nor does he come to grips with it in terms of the work shown. Perhaps the truth is that there is no "black esthetic," and there is no such thing as "black art." There are simply black artists, working in one mode or another, who sometimes deal with black themes. And that is the way they should be judged, as they are increasingly accepted in the "mainstream" art world.[55]

While black group shows became an ever more persistent presence in the United States, such exhibitions were rare in Europe. The review by *New York Times* critic Glueck entitled "No Bones in Their Noses" cites an exception:

Staid old Geneva (Switzerland)…will nevertheless be first in Europe to stage a show of art by black Americans. Titled "Eight Afro-American Artists," directed by Henri Ghent…director of the Brooklyn Museum's Community Gallery, the exhibition will inhabit Geneva's Rath Museum from June 11 through Sept. 5.

In the black art world, its exclusivity has already earned it the title of "Henri's Show."…Limited by a shipping budget (the tab will be shared by Swissair and Ernst Teves, a German industrialist), he has deliberately confined the show to eight artists, ranging in repute from old master Romare Bearden…to painter-printmaker Ruth Turnstall.…Ghent…think[s] the show will provide a needed introduction for Europeans to the work of contemporary black artists ("At a reception, some of the Swiss came up to me and said how exciting it would be to see a 'primitive' show," reports Ghent).

"We hope to change a few stereotypes," says Ghent, "show them that we've removed the bone from our noses. I think what we're sending them is more black—black in depth—than the rebels who scream and criticize."[56]

LYRICAL INTERPRETATIONS

After the recognition of his MoMA show, Bearden's art was widely exhibited in commercial galleries and museums. The presentation of his work in both mainstream and university museums contributed significantly to the depth and character of critical analysis of his achievements.

Unlike the 1971 showing with a related title at MoMA, which provoked discussion regarding the black artist in society, his 1973 show at Cordier & Ekstrom, ***Romare Bearden: Prevalence of Ritual, Martinique/The Rain Forest,*** was reviewed by Hilton Kramer as "Art: Drawings with Graphic Subtlety":

In this new series of collage-paintings, based on Mr. Bearden's personal mythological variations on episodes in black history, there is a more evident sensuousness in the handling of surfaces and a less evident reliance on the cubist matrix that used to dominate the artist's forms. A great deal of iconographic detail is crowded into a single plane, where the poetic "content" engages the mind with no loss of visual power. Part of the increased power in these new pictures seems to derive, too, from a more effective synthesis of painting and collage, for it is the painterly impulse that now dominates the discrete collage components and confers on them a greater unity of impulse.[57]

Mary Schmidt Campbell revisits issues of iconography in the catalogue for the 1975 retrospective exhibition at the Everson Museum of Art of Syracuse and Onondaga County, ***Mysteries: Women in the Art of Romare Bearden*** (see fig. 11):

> [Bearden's] women . . . are a part of [his] search for an appropriate vehicle for his ideas on myth and ritual. A number of avant-garde artists of the period shared his interest in the mythic. Robert Motherwell, Adolph Gottlieb, Carl Holty, and Mark Rothko—all painters with whom Bearden exhibited after World War II—were exploring various pictorial means of conveying timeless archetypal themes. Bearden found his solution in his choice of subjects from western literature and his stress on ceremony and ritual.[58]

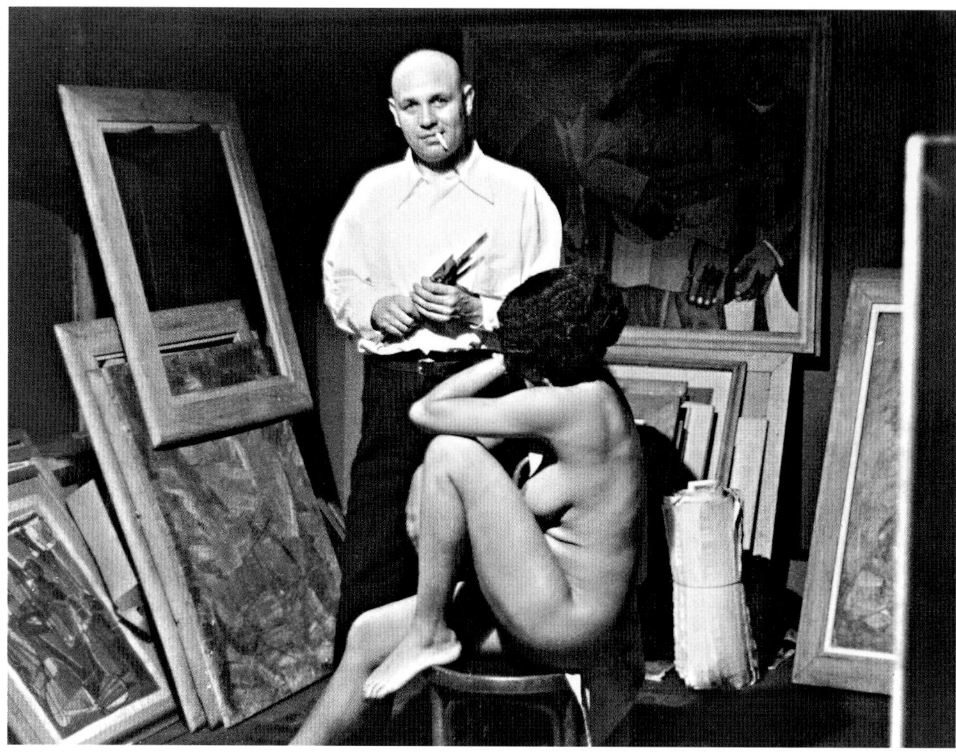

11

Reviews of the artist's work in the mid-1970s continue to allude to the symbolic aspects of his compositions, but tend to discuss the complex nature of his constructions and their success.

David Bourdon reviewed ***Of the Blues: Romare Bearden,*** 1975, in "Music to the Eyes" *(Village Voice)* as "his best show to date . . . All of the nearly two dozen new collages celebrate black musicians, and they do so in a style that is more evocative than it is descriptive of specific people and places. They are, in effect, Bearden's imaginative impressions of archetypal performers and performances, as indicated by such titles as 'Ancestral Rythyms,' 'One Night Stand,' and 'Empress of the Blues.'"[59]

A review of the same show in *Art News* stated that:

> Romare Bearden literally shared a studio for 16 years with the Apollo Theater; Fats Waller and Duke Ellington were first patrons. It's not surprising, then, that Bearden's new show—a pictorial history of jazz—contains his best work. They are collages overlaid with acrylic and lacquer. . . . This is historical painting, and photography, interestingly, has supplied it with specific information. . . . Bearden cuts these photos into formal elements, then blows them up to create, as in a Lichtenstein, giant Pop dots.[60]

Susan Howe's review of Bearden's 1976 show ***Romare Bearden: Of the Blues (Second Chorus)*** in *Art in America* continued the comparison of Bearden's technique and deployment of stylistic devices to other modern masters:

> His long-time love for jazz . . . was combined here with his love of French painting. The musicians, musical instruments and rooms of people sitting or standing that have appeared in many of his earlier collages were all here. But now the faces are nearly featureless. When there are features, they are reminiscent of those on African masks—but African masks as we know them through Picasso and the Fauves. One of the best paintings in the show, *Young Louis Listening to King Oliver,* illustrates this ambience. An asymmetrical head, with elliptical contours, heavy bold cross-hatching and rich dark crimsons, ochers, cerulean and violet, is a portrait of Louis Armstrong, but it is strongly reminiscent of *Les Demoiselles d'Avignon,* too.[61]

figure 11
Sam Shaw, Bearden and model in his Harlem studio, late 1940s.
The Shaw Family Archives; Estate of Romare Bearden, courtesy of Romare Bearden Foundation, New York

Hale Woodruff revisited the sentiment offered by James Porter some thirty years earlier in his catalogue essay for Bearden's showing at the Firehouse Gallery, in Garden City, New York (1976). "Who are these folk who populate the collage panels of Romare Bearden?" he asked and then answered: "Their true reality... lies in the roles and in the appearances they assume as they are transformed, through Bearden's art, into 'art-life' imagery of 'art-life' expression." Woodruff goes on to paraphrase Ellison: "And as these places and faces confront us thus in these works, we realize that they have been released from the restrictions of the anecdotal and the journalistic by the artist. Although they are still characterized by a quality of the contemporary, they now reveal themselves as timeless, transcendental."[62]

Bearden returned to the Western classics he had explored in the 1940s with his 1977 Odysseus series, which was seen by critics as a unique refining of the boundaries of the ancient world.

In his catalogue introduction, Calvin Tomkins, who that year also wrote a *New Yorker* magazine profile of Bearden, focused on the psychological ramifications of his new work:

> In *The Odyssey* it is men and women who control events, acting sometimes in contravention of divine will. The poem's great theme, the wandering of the hero who longs for home, has been described by Julian Jaynes in his recent study as "an odyssey toward subjective identity and its triumphant acknowledgement out of the hallucinatory enslavements of the past (*The Origin of Consciousness in the Breakdown of Bicameral Mind*)."
>
> Romare Bearden's Odyssey series is not literature but painting, of course, and his technique is that talismanic twentieth century one, collage.... An act of necromancy, requiring cunning, grace, nerve, intelligence and luck (defined as the ability to take good advantage of chance—or the gods).[63]

John Russell's review of the same show commented on Bearden's relationship with Matisse:

> It is a rash nature that invokes "The Odyssey" in one department of its activity and Henri Matisse in another. But this is what Romare Bearden does in the series of collages on the subject of Odysseus that makes up his new show at Cordier & Ekstrom... it says much for the quality of his imagination that we see two giant progenitors... as friendly allies of Mr. Bearden [rather than enemies].
>
> It would be useless to pretend that Mr. Bearden's collages do not draw on the example of Matisse in their treatment of the human figure, in their treatment of exotic foliage, and in their treatment... of submarine life. But this does not at all put them out of account... much of what Homer has to tell us can quite logically be given an African context.[64]

IMPROVISING A WORLD OF HIS OWN

The autobiographical nature of Bearden's work was more frequently discussed in the press with his 1978 show *Profile/Part 1, The Twenties,* the first of two shows inspired by Tomkins' 1977 *New Yorker* article. Recalling the expressive and narrative uses of collage dating back to twelfth-century Japan and seventeenth-and nineteenth-century Europe, Hilton Kramer suggested:

> It is in this respect that the work of Romare Bearden sets itself apart from the more familiar conventions of collage. What is remarkable about his vein is that it permits Mr. Bearden to do many of the things that modernist art is not supposed to do. He attaches his art to a story—in this case, the story of his own life. He is anecdotal. He is affectionate—in fact, tender—in the attitude he takes toward his subject, and there is never any doubt that he does, indeed, *have* a subject, and that the subject is not art itself.
>
> The style that serves this personal iconography might best be described as patchwork Cubism. The folk art conventions of the patchwork quilt have often been used by Mr. Bearden in the past, and they are again used here. Actual quilts, too, are depicted in appropriate settings. I think there is a key here to the special quality Mr. Bearden achieves in his collages. The patchwork quilt is, after all, a kind of primitive Cubism in itself, and its use allows the artist both a free play on personal memory and the discipline necessary for art.[65]

Another review of the same show that appeared in *Art News* referred to the collage painting *Miss Mamie Singleton's Quilt* and suggested that, "For an artist of Bearden's stature to undertake such a work there is value not only in artistic terms but in social history as well. Highly subjective, as all history becomes in the final analysis, this group of collages pinpoints past moments in a real life like a collection of rare and luminous butterflies."[66]

"Bearden's Sentimental Journey," Gylbert Coker's review of the show in the *New York Amsterdam News,* also highlighted the autobiographical nature of the exhibition:

This is a lovely exhibition. The finest Mr. Bearden has done to date. As a whole unit the exhibition is made complete by Bearden's use of the handwritten statements, giving us the feeling of traveling through a personal diary.[67] It's a very sensitive touch, reminding me of Roy De Carrava's [sic] book, *The Sweet Flypaper of Life*. Here, as in the book there exists the honest quality of presenting life as it was and is.

Holding on to the old southern tradition of storytelling, Bearden reveals not only his own story but one that belongs to many Americans—Black and white.... The individual pieces are very exciting. Bearden's collages have taken on a more painterly feel to them. His touch has softened and in some of the works like Lula Hayes & Son Remembered, Maudell Sleet's Magic Garden and Morning he has captured the gentle touch of Pierre Auguste Renoir, lending a misty element to the works visually capturing the mental process of remembering.[68]

In 1980 Romare Bearden had a second major museum exhibition ***Romare Bearden: 1970–1980***, which included work that had been completed since his 1971 MoMA retrospective. Paul Richard's *Washington Post* review of the exhibition's Baltimore venue was critical of the "black" content critics often cited in the artist's work:

The art of Romare Bearden... tends to wear a label.

Harlem, it is true, is Romare Bearden's home, and frequently his subject. The odalisques, the witches, the farmhands and musicians he so masterfully portrays are almost always black, and the blues may be heard singing in his sweet-yet-rough collages. But to screen his work for blackness does it a disservice. For Romare Bearden's art is an art of integration. So layered are its messages, so numerous its sources, that his 10-year retrospective—which goes on view today at the Baltimore Museum of Art—in the end affirms the irrelevance of race.[69]

This idea, that Bearden's borrowings from diverse sources affirmed "the irrelevance of race," is a very different notion from Ellison's analysis of such borrowing as affirming the "irrelevance of race as a limiting force" in art. Bearden's concept of race may be found in the life and work of the Harlem Renaissance existentialist writer Jean Toomer. In the 1920s Toomer spent time in Europe studying and teaching the transcendental philosophy of George I. Gurdjieff.[70] Similarly, Bearden studied Buddhism while in Paris in 1950. While Bearden was in Paris, he associated with leading thinkers of the negritude movement, such as Léopold Sédar Senghor, the future first president of the independent West African state of Senegal, and Martinique writer Aimé Césaire. They were attempting to translate the existential character of being a black person in a colonized world in their literary journal *Présence Africaine*. Taking these influences into account, Bearden may have considered race as grounded in a false sense of reality, yet he clearly acknowledged its social and psychological ramifications.

Comparisons to Roy Lichtenstein are made in Amei Wallach's review of Bearden's 1970–1980 retrospective at the Brooklyn Museum of Art:

Item: "Roy Lichtenstein 1970–1980" recaps the pop king's years since his Guggenheim Museum Retrospective. Item: "Romare Bearden: 1970–1980" tunes into the collage master's development since his Museum of Modern Art retrospective.

The two approaches appear to be similar: Take an artist long admired and catch up on what has happened since we last heard from him. But in execution, the difference is vast.... Lichtenstein's slickly mounted exhibit inhabits the entire fourth floor of the Whitney Museum in Manhattan and has been accorded all the attention due to the work of a media darling.

The Bearden show is tucked away in a series of small galleries on the fifth floor of the Brooklyn Museum, and there is no money available to reprint enough catalogs to make them available to all prospective buyers...

After viewing the Bearden exhibit... the difference in treatment between the two artists becomes all the more incomprehensible.

Lichtenstein is a clever, often amusing commentator on contemporary values. He adds up to somewhat more than a stand-up comedian of art history.... But Bearden is simply an extraordinary painter. Like most of the artists who have made more than a passing impact on human events, he has found a way to transform his own highly personal experience into a metaphor for his times. The fact that his experience is a black one—and his means of [capturing it] calls as much on folk art traditions and rhythms of jazz as it does on the cubism of Picasso and the odd placements of the Renaissance master Duccio—has done much to obscure his universality.

The characters in Bearden's pictures [are] often presented with the misleading simplicity of a patchwork quilt. But the sophisticated complexity with which his paintings capture a corner of humanity and make it stand for the whole is rivaled by only a few artists painting today.[71]

Larcelia Kebe's review of ***Profile/Part II, The Thirties*** spoke of the evocative nature of Bearden's work: "The artist has captured the people, sight, sounds and smells of his world in Harlem during the thirties. You can almost see yourself in those smoke-filled rooms listening to Bearden's favorite musicians. He has reached another dimension, artistically, by combining painting skills, sense of balance, mathematical abilities and construction acumen into a unified and successful whole."[72]

The artist's continued explorations of other dimensions were seen in *Romare Bearden: Jazz* at the Birmingham Museum of Art in 1982. "In these works inspired by jazz can be seen fascinating visual parallels or equivalents to certain musical considerations, such as variations on a theme and improvisation. As in creating jazz, the particular expression at a specific moment, whether premeditated, spontaneous, or altered according to plan, is central to Bearden's creative process in realizing these images."[73]

Maryanne Conheim emphasized the artist's creative process in conjunction with the exhibition, *The Worlds of Romare Bearden,* at the Jenkintown Fine Art Gallery in Jenkintown, Pennsylvania (a suburb of Philadelphia) also in 1982. Her review was entitled "A Magical Master Who Is Thriving on 'Painting the Blues'" and appeared in the *Philadelphia Inquirer.* The reporter described her experience of watching Bearden work:

> A great artist is one who creates a magical world that people can enter and, like a magician, usually is loath to reveal his secrets. Romare Bearden is different.... Seizing an envelope on the cluttered work table in his New York studio, he draws a rectangle. Rapidly, he sketches in several smaller rectangles until a Mondrian-like grid emerges, perfectly balanced...."I have no idea what it's going to be," he says, his pencil poised. Suddenly he fills in a large area with a frieze-like female figure. "First, I do the abstract thing," he says. "Then I let the content come out of it."[74]

Calvin Tomkins described Bearden's use of underlying structure and increasingly "free" use of color and collage elements in his catalogue essay "The Intelligent Hand," which accompanied the exhibition *Romare Bearden: Mecklenburg Autumn: Oil Paintings with Collage* in November of 1983:

> "I keep going back, for some reason, to Mecklenburg. To the county. I can't explain it." In his mind's eye, Bearden means.
>
> Now Bearden has brought back from that lost country of his imagination paintings unlike any we have seen before. His color has a new license, an almost violent intensity. Forms disintegrate in these molten reds and greens. The center holds, though, as it always does in Bearden's work. What has not changed is the structural basis....His formal language, which is as strict as Vermeer's, allows him to do things that many a neo-expressionist thinks he ought to be able to do, too, which may be why so much neo-expressionist work fails to convince us.[75]

Discussion about the structure of Bearden's art continues in reviews of the exhibition *Rituals of the Obeah* in 1984. In this show of new work, Bearden uses themes inspired by African-derived religious ceremony. The preface to the catalogue placed the context for inspiration in the forefront, citing *Webster's* definition of Obeah:

> A religion, probably of Ashanti origin, practiced esp. formerly among the blacks, chiefly of the British West Indies, The Guianas, and the Southeastern U.S., and characterized by the use of sorcery and magic ritual.[76]

In his review of the show Michael Brenson noted that "Bearden's...compositional devices are...filled with intention. As with his teacher at the Art Students League, George Grosz, Bearden pushes the figures right up to the picture plane. There is no air, no space. The figures are stuck where they are, and we cannot get away."[77]

Bearden's showing of new work at the Jerald Melberg Gallery in Charlotte, North Carolina, the following year, according to Richard Maschal, emphasized the use of color:

> Approaching his 71st birthday, Bearden is leaving things out. As the 16 collages at Melberg's demonstrates [sic], his work has gotten leaner, and paradox of art, richer. He seems less interested in the architecture of his collages and more interested in communicating his feelings....The vegetation in "Lady & A Blue Bird" is tropical, almost suffocatingly lush. For such a work, Bearden's earlier method, dividing the picture plane into flat geometric forms of color, would not serve....These works breathe a sense of time, a celestial time removed from everyday clamor. They have an elegiac quality, a sense of quietness that is highly appealing.[78]

The theme of improvisation and its association with music continued with the Real Art Ways Gallery exhibition *Sound Collages and Visual Improvisations* in Hartford, Connecticut, in 1986.

Bernard Hanson's review of the exhibition, "In Innovative Exhibit, Bearden Executes Jazz on Canvas," pointed out that:

> Bearden is highly respected for his use of collage, and collage elements are visible in a number of the works here. There are also areas which look like collage but are not; they might well be done with stencils, although it is hard, if not impossible, to tell.
>
> There is the suggestion of an air brush here which seems implausible for an artist such as Bearden (a little easy and obvious). Several areas look as though the paint had been applied with a sponge and others suggest finger painting....There is a softness of surface, an almost watercolor look, and a looseness of organization in most of the works here.[79]

In her review of ***Romare Bearden: Recent Collages*** at the McIntosh Gallery in Atlanta in 1986, Barbara McKenzie described the artist's apt use of collage: "Collage suits Bearden thematically ... Its kaleidoscopic surfaces are similar to the shifting patterns and experiences of life itself, and the layering of fragments parallels the working of memory.[80]

The Cordier & Ekstrom exhibition ***Mecklenburg: Morning and Evening,*** 1987, was reviewed in *Art in America* expressly as a nonpolitical return to the artist's southern roots:

A man of wide-ranging interests and active political involvement, Bearden was hardly unsympathetic to the social issues that his work was seen to address. Still, he resisted such a limited reading.

In the collages recently shown at Cordier and Ekstrom, Bearden has returned to Mecklenburg but seemingly left his political concerns behind. Mecklenburg is now pictured as a place of unremitting sunshine, benign poverty and languid conviviality.

Photographs have retained only a vestigial place in Bearden's work—they occasionally appear as tiny, painted-over scraps lurking beneath the surface of a nude of the contours of a face—but their use is particularly deft and subtle. They speak for the secondary role of tangible reality in the collages.[81]

The artist's last retrospective during his lifetime, but the first to include many aspects of his early work, ***Romare Bearden: Origins and Progressions*** organized by the Detroit Institute of Art in 1986, was heavily criticized by Joy Colby of the *Detroit News*:

So they loaded the running of the show with 29 works from 1945–1949, when Bearden was strongly influenced by Picasso and other artists from Giotto to Stuart Davis. They've left it light at the end, with only 18 smallish collages from the crucial period 1966–1985, counting on the mosaic mural and its maquette to provide most of the weight of the late work. What resulted is an art historian's exhibit with a pedantic cast rather than an absorbing cross-section of Bearden's art. Ms. Taragin [the curator] justifies the emphasis on the Picassoesque works by pointing out that Bearden, the colorist, was visible even then.

It's true that these pieces are done with finesse, that the color is delectable, that the exploration of Cubist space was to serve Bearden throughout his career. But few of these pictures would tell the story quite well, rather than devoting more than half the show to a period when the artist was experimenting to find the personal vision that would come nearly 20 years later.

Despite its debatable emphasis, the exhibit does make the point that Bearden always worked in the mainstream of American art.[82]

The *New York Times'* Vivien Raynor focused her review of the exhibition's showing at the Bronx Museum of the Arts on Bearden's nonobjective, nonfigurative, experimentations of the 1950s:

The best of these collage-paintings are the few that are entirely nonobjective. Each consists of irregular but similarly sized slab-like shapes that are cut from brownish rice paper and, shingled at all angles, are again marked with streaks and blots of diluted colors—mostly dark blue, gray and rusty brown. All-over images, they are the first in the show to reveal the musician in the artist. They look as if he did them while listening to jazz, just as Jackson Pollock tossed his paint to the accompaniment of Jimmy Yancey records, and they are beautiful.

Nevertheless, the artist as represented here continues the struggle to reconcile the abstract with the figural until 1963. Nor is it hard to understand why it was the old art—of Byzantium, Florence, Siena—that impressed him and, in this view, delayed his development.[83]

A touching review of the 1987 Wendell Street Gallery exhibition, ***Bearden—Watercolors and Collages,*** in Cambridge, Massachusetts, spoke of the restorative quality of his work:

A nighttime helicopter ride around Manhattan led to a series of cityscapes Bearden did in the early 1980s. In "Night Dream," bright colored buildings jostle for space, ragged little bursts of paint seem like urban energy made tangible, and dashes of white light up the teal blue sky. Bearden does for the city what he also does for North Carolina and the island of St. Martin, making each seem a place of color and vibrant life.[84]

This was Bearden's last solo exhibition before his death in March 1988.

By the time of his death Romare Bearden had become America's foremost "black artist"—a title that previously had been given to Jacob Lawrence and a type of categorization Bearden deplored in the characterization of his own work and achievements. Despite his dislike of the title, Bearden was very much an activist in his efforts to portray African-American life in a complex way that was directly opposed to many of the pat assumptions held on both sides of the social-political debates held during his lifetime.

What remains of paramount importance regarding Bearden's activism is that he attempted to materialize it primarily through his artistic output. The efficacy of such activism has yet to be properly gauged, but if anything it will be most felt psychologically, rather than manifest itself in ways that could be succinctly measured. This is in many ways the paradox of Bearden the artist, the African American, and the socially aware philosopher and teacher: his life and art resisted and still resist easy categorization. As a result Bearden's art is a useful educational tool that positions aesthetics not only as an appreciation of beauty but also as an area of social and political critique—a practice that connects him with such artists as his teacher George Grosz, and European masters such as Daumier, Goya, and Brueghel. Since Bearden's death there have been efforts made to elucidate examples of such critiques embodied in his oeuvre, particularly his 1963 and 1964 photomontages. These investigations are commendable, but the record of Bearden's artistic output supports a longer and more dynamic history of the artist's layering of social and artistic concerns.

Romare Bearden: A Chronology

ROCÍO ARANDA-ALVARADO
AND SARAH KENNEL WITH
CARMENITA HIGGINBOTHAM

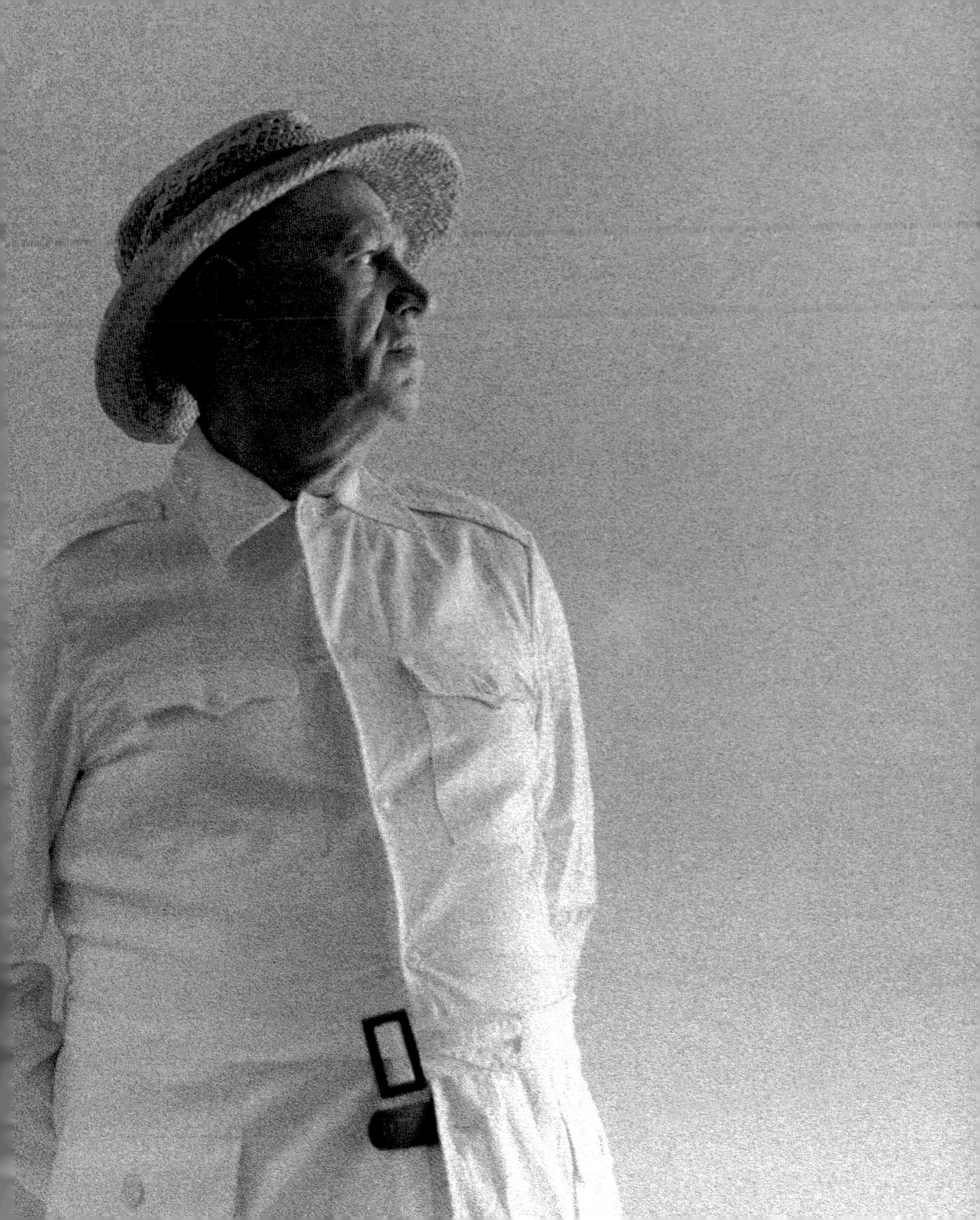

NOTE TO THE READER

Within each year, events in Romare Bearden's life are followed by solo, then group exhibitions. Inconsistencies of information given for exhibitions reflect the data we have been able to locate and confirm. Titles and dates are given for exhibited works in group exhibitions if known and for solo shows prior to 1963 if known. Medium is given for works dating prior to 1963 if known. References to 1964 titles produced as collages and photostats are followed by medium to clarify which was on view, if known. Titles for works of later date are assumed to refer to collages; if they are known to refer to works in other media, it is noted. Wherever possible, wording for titles is based on earliest known listing. References to catalogues include brochures, checklists, and other printed material as listed in the bibliography, followed by a question mark (?) if unconfirmed.

1911

2 September: Fred Romare Harry Bearden, named for family friend, Fred Romare, born in Charlotte, North Carolina, to Bessye Johnson Bearden and (Richard) Howard Bearden. Artistic talent ran in Howard Bearden's family; his grandfather had painted and his mother sketched in charcoal.

19 November: RB is baptized at St. Michael's and All Angels Episcopal Church.

c. 1914

Family moves to New York City.

1917

Fall: Enrolls at Public School (P.S.) 5, 141st Street and Edgecombe Avenue.

1918

Howard Bearden finds work with Canadian railroad between Edmonton, Alberta, and Moose Jaw, Saskatchewan. Bessye and RB join him in Saskatchewan.

1920

Bearden family settles permanently in Harlem; Bearden home becomes hub for writers, intellectuals, and artists, including Charles Alston (RB's cousin by marriage), Aaron Douglas, W. E. B. Du Bois, Duke Ellington, Langston Hughes, Paul Robeson, and Fats Waller.

Spends periods of time with relatives in Pittsburgh, Pennsylvania; Mecklenburg County, North Carolina; and Lutherville, Maryland.

1921

Attends fourth grade in Pittsburgh; lives with maternal grandparents. Grandmother Carrie and step-grandfather George Banks owned Banks' Boardinghouse on Pennsylvania Avenue near steel mills.

1922

Bessye Bearden is elected to New York City School Board No. 15. The first black woman elected to a local school board, she serves until 1939.

1924

Transfers to P.S. 139, Seventh Avenue.

1925

Completes P.S. 139 and enters De Witt Clinton High School, 116th Street annex.

Frequents Augusta Savage's Savage Studio of Arts and Crafts on West 143d Street.

1926

Summer: Eugene Bailey, a young Pittsburgh neighbor, gives RB drawing lessons.

1927–28

Grandparents move to East Liberty, Pittsburgh; RB lives with them and attends Peabody High School.

Summer 1927: Works various jobs on night shift at United States Steel, Pittsburgh.

Wins $25 and one-year movie pass for poster design based on research about World War I movies; wins second poster contest for city campaign to clean up Pittsburgh.

Bessye Bearden becomes New York editor for the *Chicago Defender,* African-American weekly newspaper with largest circulation in nation. RB writes occasional short pieces on such topics as baseball for the newspaper.

1911 1920 1930

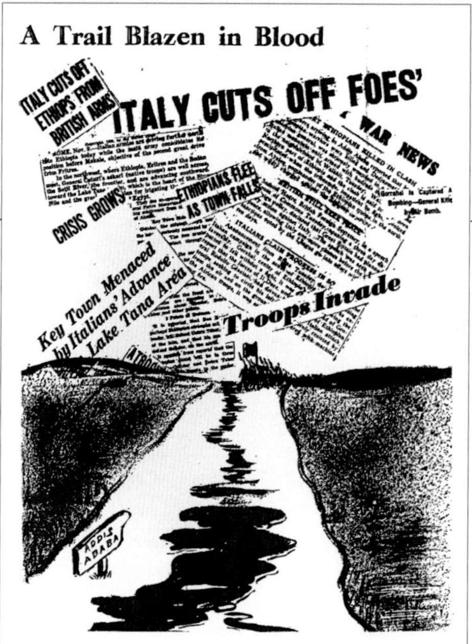

1

figures 1–4
Romare Bearden, *The Afro American* (Baltimore): (1) 16 November 1935; (2) 21 December 1935; (3) 6 June 1936; (4) 13 June 1936. Used with permission of the Afro-American Newspapers Archives and Research Center

Summer 1928: Works at Pittsburgh speakeasy. Earns college funds and a large reward for saving owner's money during a robbery.

1929

Graduates from Peabody High School. Enters Lincoln University, Oxford, Pennsylvania.

1930

Transfers from Lincoln University to Boston University for two years; takes many art courses and becomes star pitcher on varsity baseball team. Pitches for Boston Tigers, all-black minor-league baseball team; refuses offer from owner of Philadelphia Athletics a place in professional baseball if he agrees to pass for white. Creates covers and illustrations for university publication, *The Beanpot.*

1931

Meets Elmer Simms Campbell, first black cartoonist for such publications as *Saturday Evening Post, Esquire,* and *New Yorker.*

1932

Transfers from Boston University to New York University (NYU) under name Howard Bearden; continues to take numerous art courses. Does cartoon illustrations for NYU publication, *The Medley.*

March: Publishes cover of National Urban League-sponsored *Opportunity: A Journal of Negro Life.*

1933

Produces political cartoons for *The Crisis,* activist journal sponsored by the National Association for the Advancement of Colored People.

August: Takes night class at Art Students League.

1934

24 February: Cartoon published in *Collier's,* signed Howard Bearden, Jr. There may have been others in 1934 and 1935.

April 1934–January 1936: Cartoons published in several monthly issues of *The Crisis.*

December: Publishes "The Negro Artist and Modern Art" in *Opportunity,* criticizing African-American artists for lack of commitment to the representation of contemporary life.

1935

June: Graduates from NYU with Bachelor of Science in Education.

September: Takes night class at Art Students League.

Fall: Becomes case worker for Harlem office of New York City Department of Social Services. Frequents Harlem nightclubs, including Savoy Ballroom, Lafayette Theater, Small's Paradise, Barron's, and Connie's Inn, places that later appear in images. Attends meeting of about fifty black artists at 135th Street YMCA. Group becomes Harlem Artists Guild, led by Augusta Savage. Visits Museum of Modern Art exhibit *African Negro Art* with artists led by "Professor" Charles Seifert, Harlem intellectual and collector of African art and books on African and African-American history.

Alston becomes director of Works Progress Administration/Federal Art Project-sponsored Harlem Art Workshop at the 135th Street branch of the New York Public Library. At another artists' meeting place, 306 West 141st Street, in a studio shared by sculptor Henry (Mike) Bannarn and Alston, the community included artists Robert Blackburn, Ernest Crichlow, Jacob Lawrence, Norman Lewis, and Savage; writers Countee Cullen, Hughes, Claude McKay, and Richard Wright; philosopher and art historian Alain Locke; choreographer Katherine Dunham; and furniture maker, dancer, and artists' model Addison (Ad) Bates; from downtown, writer William Saroyan, artist William Steig and his brother Arthur, and photographer Carl Van Vechten.

1935–1937

September 1935–May 1937: Publishes weekly cartoons in *The Afro-American* (Baltimore) (figs. 1–4).

Befriends photographer Sam Shaw, with whom he later collaborates on several projects, and lawyer Maxwell T. Cohen, who came to represent RB and his estate.

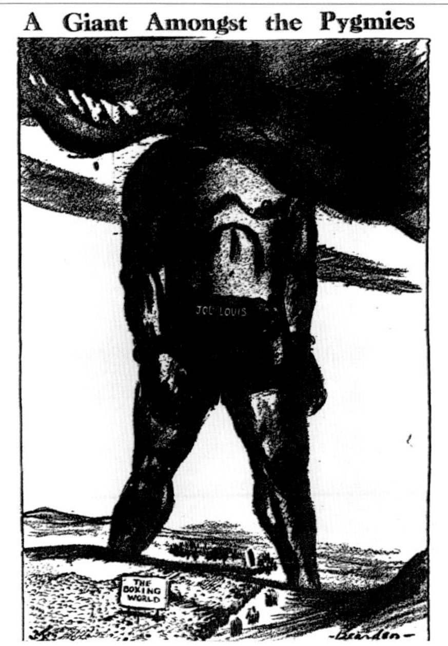

2

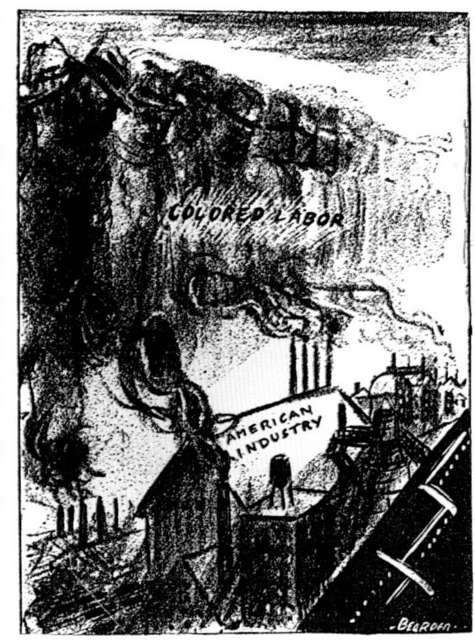

3

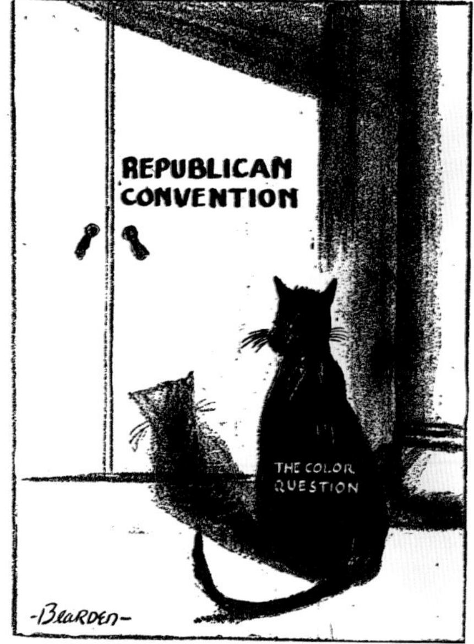

4

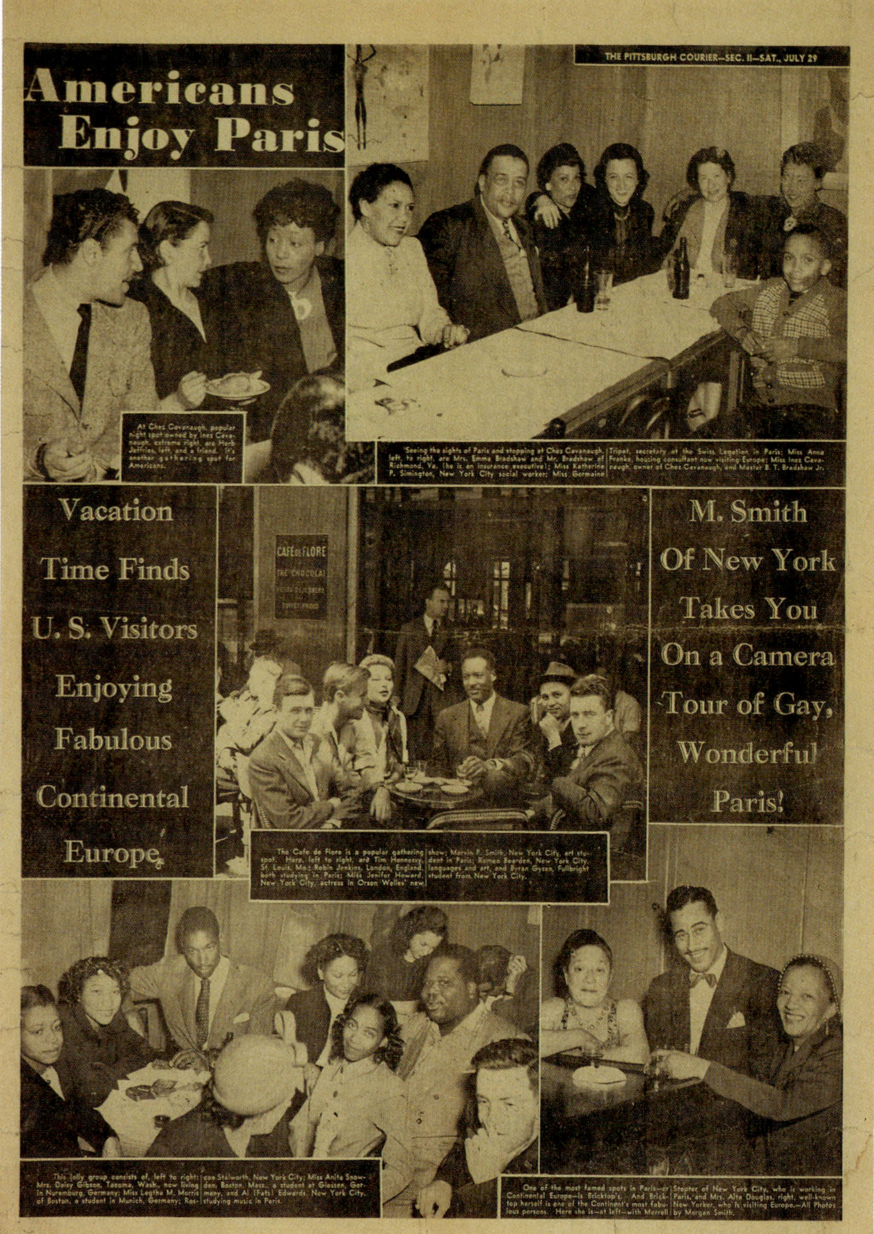

THE PITTSBURGH COURIER—SEC. II—SAT., JULY 29

Americans Enjoy Paris

At Chez Cavanaugh, popular night spot owned by Ines Cavanaugh, extreme right, are Herb Jeffries, left, and a friend. It's another gathering spot for Americans.

Seeing the sights of Paris and stopping at Chez Cavanaugh, left, to right, are Mrs. Emma Bradshaw and Mr. Bradshaw of Richmond, Va. (he is an insurance executive); Miss Katherine P. Simington, New York City social worker; Miss Germaine Tripet, secretary at the Swiss Legation in Paris; Miss Anna Franke, housing consultant now visiting Europe; Miss Ines Cavanaugh, owner of Chez Cavanaugh, and Master B. T. Bradshaw Jr.

Vacation Time Finds U. S. Visitors Enjoying Fabulous Continental Europe

M. Smith Of New York Takes You On a Camera Tour of Gay, Wonderful Paris!

The Cafe de Flore is a popular gathering spot. Here, left to right, are Tim Hennessy, St. Louis, Mo.; Robin Jenkins, London, England, both studying in Paris; Miss Jenifer Howard, New York City, actress in Orson Welles' new show; Marvin P. Smith, New York City, art student in Paris; Romeo Bearden, New York City, languages and art, and Byran Gysen, Fullbright student from New York City.

This jolly group consists of, left to right: Mrs. Daisy Gibson, Tacoma, Wash., now living in Nuremburg, Germany; Miss Leatha M. Morris of Boston, a student in Munich, Germany; Roscoe Stalworth, New York City; Miss Anita Snowden, Boston, Mass., a student at Giessen, Germany, and Al (Fats) Edwards, New York City, studying music in Paris.

One of the most famed spots in Paris—or Continental Europe—is Bricktop's. And Bricktop herself is one of the Continent's most fabulous persons. Here she is—at left—with Merrell Stepter of New York City, who is working in Paris, and Mrs. Alta Douglas, right, well-known New Yorker, who is visiting Europe.—All Photos by Morgan Smith.

7

1950

February–August: Takes leave from Department of Social Services, travels to Paris under GI Bill of Rights, studies philosophy with Gaston Bachelard at Sorbonne and French at Institut Britannique; also studies Buddhism. Has letters of introduction from Kootz to Picasso, Braque, Constantin Brancusi, Henri Matisse, and Mary Myerson (who ran Cinématique Français); letters from Holty to painters Jean Hélion and Hans Reichel; meets Wifredo Lam. Associates with other Americans in Paris, including poets Myron O'Higgins and Samuel Allen; writers James Baldwin and Albert Murray; painters William Rivers and Herbert Gentry; and engineer Jim Moseley. Frequents Café Dome, Gentry's and Honey Johnson's Club Galerie, a salon by day and jazz club by night. Also meets with Harlem friends in Paris, who include jazz musicians Sidney Bechet and Roy Eldridge, photographers Morgan and Marvin Smith; writers Wright and Howard Swanson (fig. 7).

Travels in Italy, France, and Spain; stays with Nellie Barnes, an acquaintance from New York, in Saint-Tropez. Visits Picasso in Juan les Pins and spends time in Málaga.

GROUP EXHIBITION

8 December–25 February 1951: Metropolitan Museum of Art, *American Painting Today—1950: Woman with a Bird* (1949). Other artists include Alston, Hopper, Sheeler, Wyeth. Catalogue.

figure 7
"Americans Enjoy Paris," *Pittsburgh Courier*, 29 July 1950. Center photograph shows Bearden at Café de Flore with (left to right) Tim Hennessy and Robin Jenkins; Jennifer Howard, cited as an actress in Orson Welles' new show; photographer Marvin P. Smith; Bearden, cited as studying languages and art; and Byran Gysen. Newspaper Courtesy June Kelly. The Pittsburgh Courier/GRM Associates, Inc.

figure 8
Romare Bearden offering cake to Nanette Rohan Bearden at their wedding party, 4 September 1954. Estate of Romare Bearden, courtesy of Romare Bearden Foundation, New York

figure 9
Certificate of Romare Howard Bearden's membership in the American Society of Composers, Authors, and Publishers, 22 March 1955. Estate of Romare Bearden, courtesy of Romare Bearden Foundation, New York

1950

1951–1954
RB and Dave Ellis found Bluebird Music Company. RB writes lyrics for Ellis' songs "Hello and Goodbye," "Little Girl," "Promise of Spring," and "Street Without a Name" (music by Ruth Frank); none of these songs appear to have been published. Over the next several years, RB writes about twenty songs with Fred Norman and Laerteas "Larry" Douglas, which are published by Laerteas Music Company. "Seabreeze" is most successful; used by Seagrams to promote mixed drink of same name. Other successes include "Missus Santa Claus," "My Stocking Is Empty," and "My Candy Apple," sung by child star Leslie Uggams. With Douglas and Norman, RB also publishes "Who Can Say," "So Much More" (recorded by Mitzi Mason), and "My Love for Dorothy" (dedicated to actress Dorothy Dandridge). Also writes lyrics to "Dry Is My Cup," with Nelson Glover and Douglas, published by Citation Music, and "It's Twilight in My Heart" and "Just as You Are" with music by Martin Lagunoff.

1951
GROUP EXHIBITIONS
17 March–16 May: Whitney Museum of American Art, New York, *Sculpture, Watercolors, Drawings,* second half of *Annual Exhibition of Contemporary American Sculpture, Watercolors and Drawings: Walls of Troy* (1946–47, watercolor). Other artists include Calder, Naum Gabo, Lawrence, Ad Reinhardt. Catalogue.

2 November–2 December: Metropolitan Museum of Art, New York, *The Lewisohn Collection: Untitled—Golgotha* (1945, watercolor). Other artists include Paul Cézanne, Paul Gauguin, Matisse, and Picasso. Catalogue.

1952
Returns to New York City Department of Social Services.

1953
Philosopher Hannah Arendt and husband, Heinrich Blücher, urge RB to focus more on painting and less on music.

1954
4 September: Marries Nanette Rohan whom RB met at New York benefit for hurricane victims in West Indies (fig. 8). They live with RB's father in apartment at 351 West 114th Street.

GROUP EXHIBITION
17 November–19 December: Whitney Museum of American Art, New York, *Roy and Marie Neuberger Collection: Mary Supporting Christ* (1945). Other artists include Dove, Lawrence, O'Keeffe, Pollock. Exhibition travels to Arts Club of Chicago (4–30 January 1955); Art Gallery, University of California, Los Angeles (21 February–3 April); San Francisco Museum of Art (26 April–5 June); City Art Museum of St. Louis (27 June–7 August); and Cincinnati Art Museum (29 August–25 September). Catalogue.

1955
22 March. Becomes member of American Society of Composers, Authors and Publishers (ASCAP) (fig. 9).

SOLO EXHIBITION
31 October–24 November: Barone Gallery, New York, *Romare Bearden: Blue Lady* (1955), *John at Patmos, Mountains of the Moon, The Oracle, River Merchant's Wife.* Oils and watercolors. Catalogue.

GROUP EXHIBITIONS
12 May–15 June: Arts Club of Chicago, Illinois, *World at Work 1930–1955: Twenty-five Years of Art for Fortune.* Sponsored and circulated by the American Federation of Arts. *Factory Workers.* Exhibition travels to California Palace of the Legion of Honor, San Francisco (15 July–5 September); Albright Art Gallery, Buffalo, New York (15 September–15 October); Houston Museum of Fine Arts (26 October–26 November); Seattle Art Museum, Washington (11 December–8 January 1956); Los Angeles County Museum of Art (18 January–15 February 1956); Detroit Institute of Arts, Michigan (1–31 March 1956); City Art Museum of St. Louis, Missouri (15 May–15 June 1956). Catalogue.

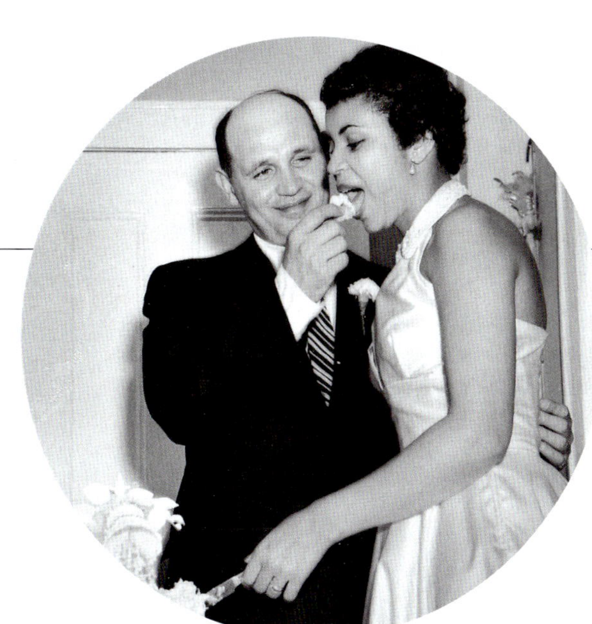
8

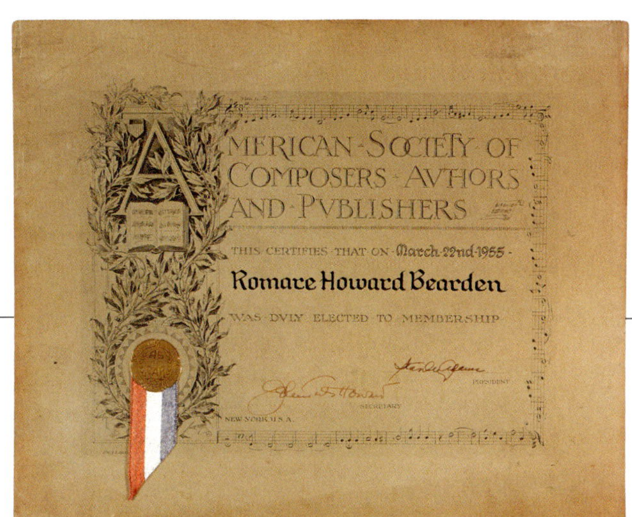
AMERICAN SOCIETY OF COMPOSERS AVTHORS AND PVBLISHERS
THIS CERTIFIES THAT ON March 22nd 1955
Romare Howard Bearden
WAS DVLY ELECTED TO MEMBERSHIP
NEW YORK U.S.A.

9

9 November–8 January 1956: Whitney Museum of American Art, New York. *Annual Exhibition of Contemporary American Painting: John at Patmos.* Other artists include Baziotes, Richard Diebenkorn, Joan Mitchell, O'Keeffe. Catalogue.

1956

RB seeks a cure for "stomach cancer" and a "heart attack"—false alarms. Improper diet, overwork, and tension contribute to period in Bellevue Hospital.

Moves with Nanette to loft at 357 Canal Street, Manhattan, where he lives for the rest of his life.

Studies calligraphy with a bookseller, Mr. Wu, on Bayard Street.

GROUP EXHIBITIONS

1–31 July: University of Michigan Museum of Art, Ann Arbor, *Eight New York Painters: Golden River, Repose* (oils). Exhibition organized by Woodruff for university summer session program, "Patterns of American Culture: Contributions of the Negro." Other artists include Cortor, Lawrence, Lewis, Woodruff. Catalogue.

26 October–26 November: Pyramid Club, Philadelphia, *Second Annual Fall Review of Painting and Sculpture: The Oracle* (oil). RB honored by club for achievement in writing and painting. Contributes essay "The Artistic Imagination" to event program. Other artists include Larry Day, Humbert L. Howard, Woodruff. Catalogue.

1959

November: Gallery owners Arne Ekstrom and Michel Warren visit RB's studio, express interest in showing new work.

1960

Cedric Dover's *American Negro Art,* published by New York Graphic Society, includes RB's *He Is Arisen.*

SOLO EXHIBITION

20 January–19 February: Michel Warren Gallery (later renamed Daniel Cordier & Michel Warren, Inc.), New York. Large abstract canvases from late 1950s, including *Friends of the Night, Night Watches in Silence, Wine Star, Silent Valley of the Sunrise, South of the Great Sea, Wings of the Dragon.* Catalogue.

GROUP EXHIBITION

12 December–12 February 1961: Museum of Modern Art, New York, *Recent Acquisitions: Silent Valley of the Sunrise* (1959, oil).

1961

Daniel Cordier & Michel Warren, Inc., later renamed Cordier & Ekstrom Inc., represents RB until his death.

January: Golden Dawn (1960?, oil) installed in pre-inaugural suite of President John F. Kennedy, Hotel Carlyle, New York.

May–June: Tours Europe with Nanette; visits Paris, Florence, Venice, Genoa, and Geneva. Begins to reintroduce figurative elements in work.

SOLO EXHIBITION

6–25 April: Daniel Cordier & Michel Warren, Inc., New York, *Romare Bearden: New Paintings.* Includes *Gold Sound, Ariadne's Answer* (both oils).

GROUP EXHIBITIONS

22 September–8 October: Institute of Contemporary Art, Boston, *New Painting: Among Constellations, Winds of Spring* (1960), *A Poem for Far Away* (oil). Other artists include Julius Bissier, Freidel Dzubas, Al Held, Robert Nakian.

27 October–7 January 1962: Carnegie Institute of Technology, Department of Fine Arts, Pittsburgh, *1961 Pittsburgh International Exhibition of Contemporary Painting and Sculpture: Golden Day* (1960). Other artists include Jean Arp, Picasso, David Smith, Mark Tobey. Catalogue.

1962

GROUP EXHIBITIONS

9 March–15 April: Virginia Museum of Fine Arts, Richmond, *Americans, 1962: Winds of Spring* (1960, oil).

7 May–18 June: Massachusetts Institute of Technology, Cambridge, untitled exhibition. *Winds of Spring* (1960, oil).

1963

July: RB invites artists to meet at his Canal Street studio to discuss political events related to civil rights and plight of blacks in America. Named "Spiral," the group seeks to answer question "What is black art?" Group rents space on Christopher Street and begins to meet weekly, plan exhibitions, and make arrangements for attending march on Washington led by Martin Luther King, Jr., in August.

1964

RB appointed first art director of newly established Harlem Cultural Council, a prominent African-American advocacy group with several hundred members.

1960

SOLO EXHIBITION

6–24 October: Cordier & Ekstrom, Inc., New York, *Projections* (fig. 10). Twenty-one photostatic enlargements (photostats) of collages. Catalogue.

GROUP EXHIBITIONS

6 May–16 May: Gallery of American Federation of Arts, New York, *Artists for CORE* [Congress of Racial Equality]. *Third Annual Art Exhibition and Sale: Evening Meal of Prophet Peterson* (1964). Other artists include Calder, Jim Dine, Joe Overstreet, Ray Saunders. Catalogue.

20 October–20 November: Fairleigh Dickinson University Art Gallery, Madison, New Jersey, *Some Negro Artists,* sponsored by Morris County Tercentenary Committee. Other artists include Beauford Delaney, Lorenzo Gilcrist, Ellis Wilson. Catalogue.

1965

SOLO EXHIBITION

1–31 October: Corcoran Gallery of Art, Washington, D.C., *Projections.* Five collages, twenty-two photostats. Catalogue.

GROUP EXHIBITIONS

3–12 March: Rockford College, Illinois, *Contemporary Negro Art* in *Festival of the Arts: Creativity and the Negro.* Other artists include John Biggers, Richard Hunt, Lam, White. Catalogue.

19 March–4 April: National Institute of Arts and Letters, Academy Art Gallery, New York, *An Exhibition of Contemporary Painting, Sculpture and Graphic Art.* Exhibits two 1964 collages and five 1964 photostats: *The Burial; Jazz: (Chicago) Grand Terrace—1930s; Mysteries; Prevalence of Ritual: Baptism; Prevalence of Ritual: Conjur Woman as an Angel.* Other artists include Nell Blaine, Bruno Lucchess, Joyce Reopel. Catalogue.

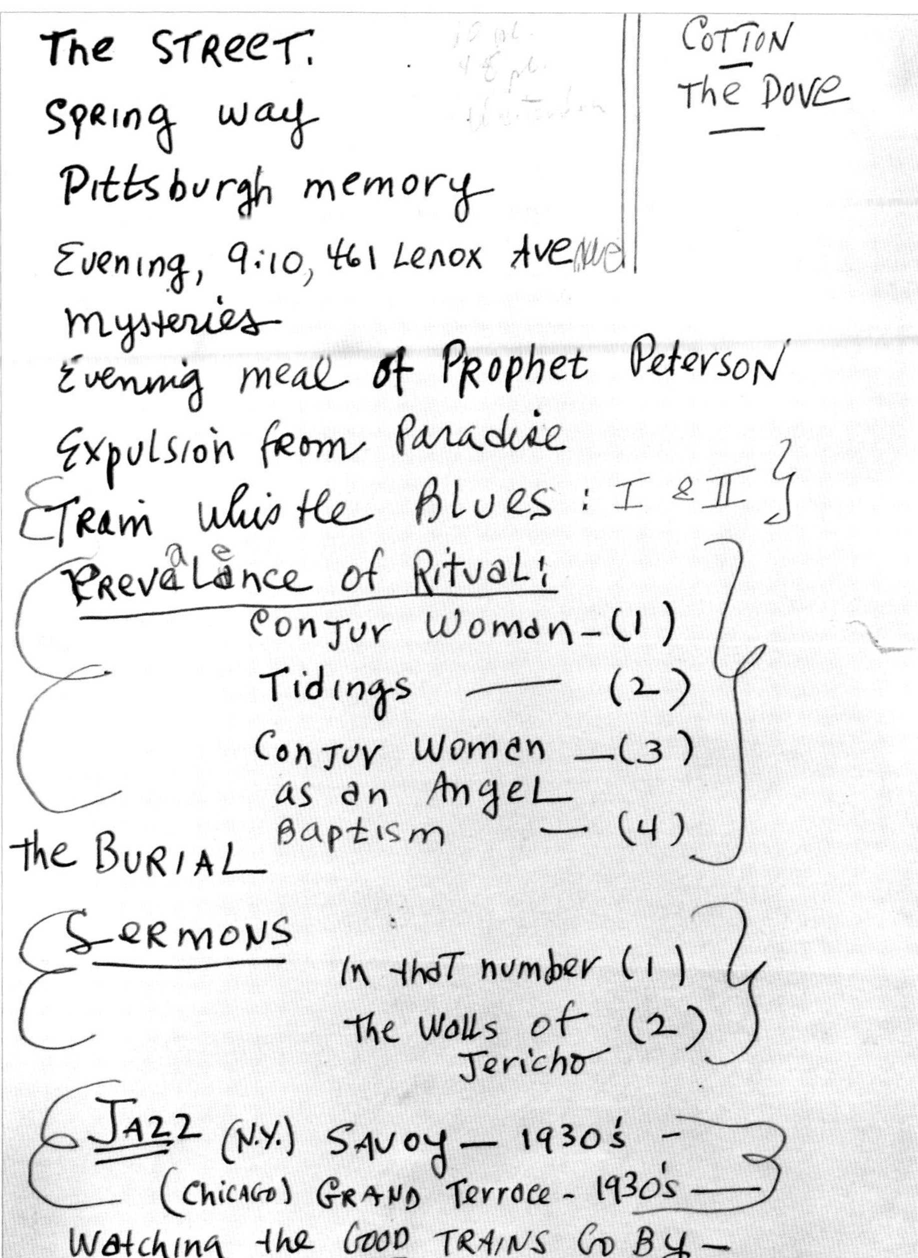

The STREET.
Spring way
Pittsburgh memory
Evening, 9:10, 461 Lenox Avenue
mysteries
Evening meal of Prophet Peterson
Expulsion from Paradise
Train whistle Blues: I & II
Prevalence of Ritual:
Conjur Woman – (1)
Tidings — (2)
Conjur Women as an Angel — (3)
Baptism — (4)
the BURIAL
Sermons
In that number (1)
The Walls of Jericho (2)
JAZZ (N.Y.) Savoy – 1930's –
(Chicago) Grand Terrace – 1930's —
Watching the GOOD TRAINS GO BY –
COTTON
The DOVE

10

figure 10
Romare Bearden's handwritten, annotated, list of works in his 1964 *Projections* exhibition at Cordier & Ekstrom, Inc. Courtesy of Ekstrom & Ekstrom, Inc.

(3–31 January 1969); De Pauw University, Greencastle, Indiana (21 February–16 March 1969); Sloan Galleries of American Painting, Valparaiso University, Indiana (8–28 April 1969); Mankato State College, Minnesota (19 May–19 June 1969). Catalogue.

8 May–30 June: Rhode Island School of Design and Brown University, Providence, *An American Collection: The Neuberger Collection.* Other artists include Stuart Davis, Lawrence, Quirt, Tamayo, Tobey. Travels to the National Collection of Fine Arts, Washington (15 August–25 September). Catalogue.

10–30 May: Wilcox Gallery, Swarthmore College, Pennsylvania, *Black Artists in America, 19th and 20th Centuries: Monday Morning, 1967.* Other artists include Edward M. Bannister, Lawrence, Saunders, Tanner. Catalogue.

June: Salon Zacheta, Warsaw, Poland, *Biennale Internationale de l'Affiche.* Catalogue (?).

17 October–24 November: Minneapolis Institute of Arts, Minnesota, *30 Contemporary Black Artists: Tomorrow I May Be Far Away* (1966/1967), *Family, Palm Sunday Procession* (1967 collages). Exhibition travels to High Museum, Atlanta, Georgia (15 December–12 January 1969); Flint Institute of Art, Flint Michigan (31 January–1 March 1969); Everson Museum of Art, Syracuse, New York (16 March–13 April 1969); IBM Gallery of Arts and Sciences, New York (28 April–29 May 1969); Roberson Center for the Arts and Sciences, Binghamton, New York (12 July–9 August 1969); Memorial Art Gallery, Rochester, New York (22 August–5 October 1969); San Francisco Museum of Art, California (16 November–31 December 1969); Contemporary Arts Museum, Houston (20 January–16 February 1970); New Jersey State Museum, Trenton (13 March–26 April 1970); Museum of Art, Rhode Island School of Design, Providence (1–31 July 1970); Art Galleries, University of California, Santa Barbara (12 October–15 November 1970). Other artists include Amos, Sam Gilliam, Alvin Hollingsworth, Hunt, Saar. Catalogue. All works may not have been shown at all venues.

31 October–3 November: Museum of Modern Art, New York, *In Honor of Dr. Martin Luther King, Jr.: Soul Three* (1968). Other artists include Donald Judd, Tom Wesselman. Sale of works benefits Southern Christian Leadership Foundation Conference. Catalogue.

November–December: Johnson C. Smith University, James B. Duke Library, Charlotte, North Carolina, *Encounters.* Catalogue (?).

19 November–5 January 1969: Studio Museum in Harlem, New York, *Invisible Americans: Black Artists of the 30s.* Other artists include Barthé, Catlett, Cortor, Motley, Savage, Woodruff. Catalogue (?).

1969

Retires from Department of Social Services to work full-time in studio (fig. 13).

March: "Rectangular Structure in My Montage Paintings" published in *Leonardo,* journal published by International Society for Arts, Sciences, and Technology.

20 April: Soul History appears on cover of *New York Times Magazine* (fig. 14).

June: The Painter's Mind: A Study of the Relations of Structure and Space in Painting, written with Carl Holty, released by Crown Publishers.

December: With seed money from Ford Foundation, RB, Lewis, and Crichlow open Cinque Gallery in a studio next to Joseph Papp Public Theater, New York. First exhibition devoted to works by Malcolm Bailey.

SOLO EXHIBITION

27 November–11 January 1970: Memorial Union Gallery, Iowa State University of Science and Technology, Ames, untitled exhibition. Twenty-three photostats (all 1964), two collages.

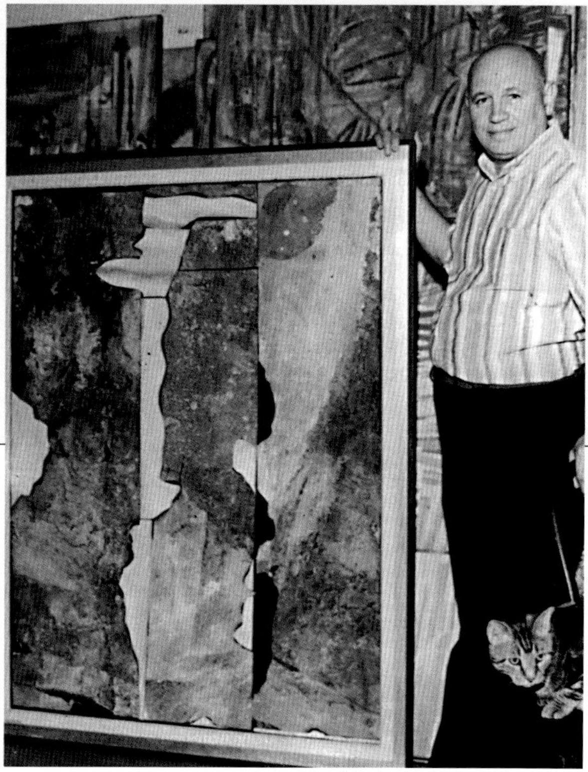

13

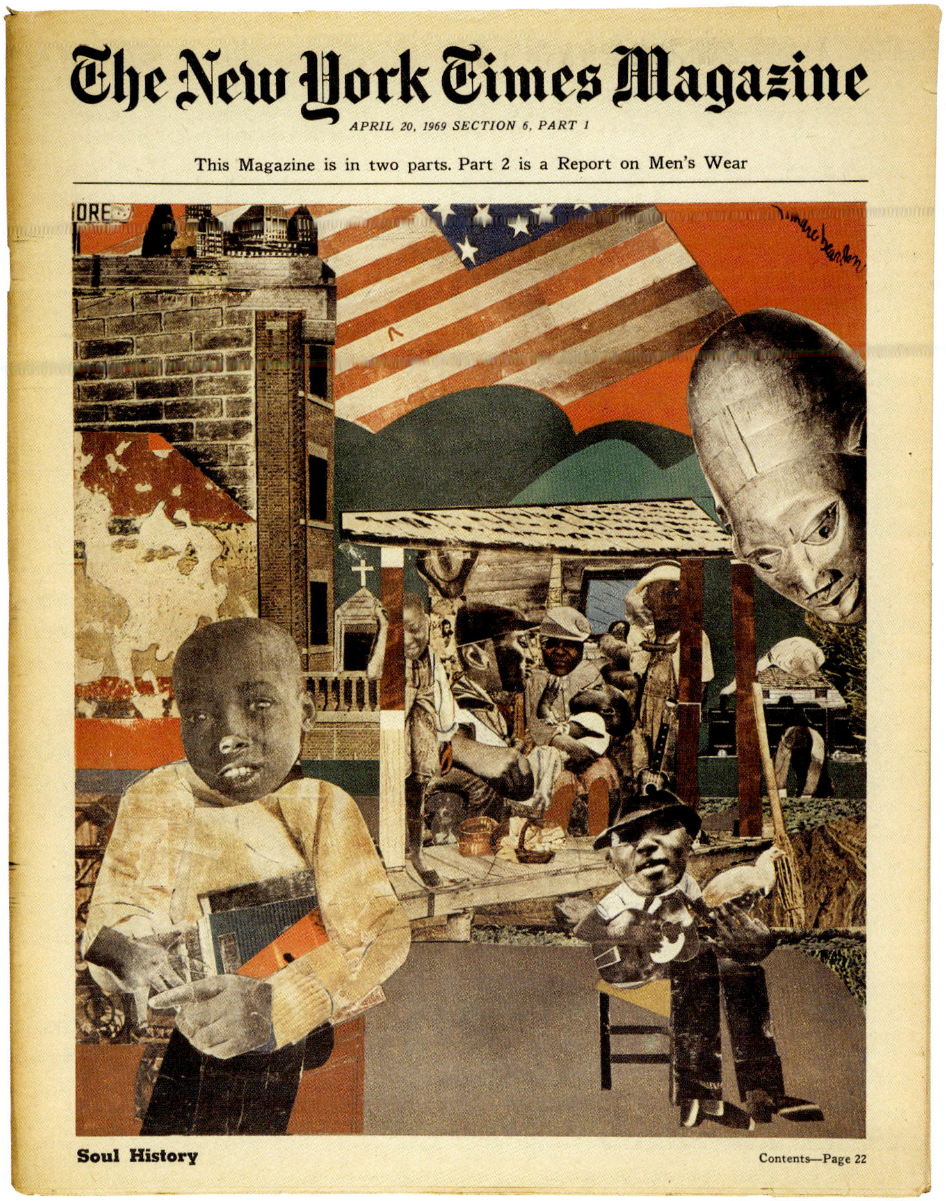

The New York Times Magazine

APRIL 20, 1969 SECTION 6, PART 1

This Magazine is in two parts. Part 2 is a Report on Men's Wear

Soul History

Contents—Page 22

14

GROUP EXHIBITIONS

Spring: University of Oklahoma Museum of Art, *Paintings by Contemporary Afro-American Artists.*

1 March – 28 February 1970: Crosscurrents USA, organized by Detroit Institute of Arts and Project Outreach, travels to additional museums in Michigan. Catalogue.

1 – 27 April: Cranbrook Academy of Art, Bloomfield Hills, Michigan, *Sixth National Biennial: Religious Art Exhibition: Madonna and Child* (1968). Other artists include Kenneth Callahan, Jack Levine, Robert Andrew Parker. Catalogue.

1 April – 2 May: Purdue University, Lafayette, Indiana, *Collage: Beardon* [sic], *Bultman, Motherwell, Nickle, and Roeber.* Catalogue.

25 April – 8 June: New School for Social Research, New York, *Inaugural Exhibition, Graduate Faculty Center: Carolina Morning* (1969), *Circe Preparing a Banquet for Odysseus* (1968). Other artists include Diebenkorn, Seymour Lipton, Louise Nevelson, Rivers. Catalogue.

15 May – 22 June: Whitney Museum of American Art, New York, *Recent Acquisitions: Eastern Barn* (1968).

2 – 30 June: J. L. Hudson Gallery, Detroit, Michigan, *Twentieth-Century American Painting and Watercolors.* Catalogue (?).

18 June – 5 October: Museum of Modern Art, New York, *The New American Painting and Sculpture: The First Generation from the Collection of the Museum of Modern Art including Promised Gifts: Silent Valley of the Sunrise* (1959, oil). Catalogue.

figure 13
Romare Bearden in his Manhattan studio with his cat "Gypo," 1969. Copyright 1969 SchoolArts Magazine

figure 14
Romare Bearden, *Soul History, New York Times Magazine* cover, 20 April 1969. Estate of Romare Bearden, courtesy of Romare Bearden Foundation, New York/ The New York Times

October: Lincoln University, Oxford, Pennsylvania, Black Arts Festival, *The Black Experience.* Other artists include Moe A. Brooker, Gilliam, Ellen Powell, John Wade. Catalogue.

16 October–30 November: Finch College Museum of Art, New York, *Posters by Artists.* Other artists include Mel Bochner, Nancy Grossman, Robert Mangold, David Smith. Catalogue (?).

6–26 November: Dwight Art Memorial, Mount Holyoke College, South Hadley, Massachusetts, *Ten Afro-American Artists,* sponsored by Mount Holyoke Friends of Art and organized by Henri Ghent, director of the Community Gallery of the Brooklyn Museum. *Circe Preparing a Banquet for Ulysses* (1968), *Carolina Morning* (1969). Other artists include Floyd Coleman, Lewis, Saunders, Bob Thompson. Catalogue.

3–31 December: Cordier & Ekstrom, *Blocked Metaphors.* RB exhibits *Mauritius* (1969), his sole sculpture. Other artists include Jasper Johns, Man Ray, Andy Warhol. Catalogue (?).

5–29 December: Municipal Arts Gallery, Museum of the Philadelphia Civic Center, *Afro-American Artists 1800–1969,* sponsored by the Division of Arts Education of the School District of Philadelphia in cooperation with the Museum of the Philadelphia Civic Center. *Morning.* More than two hundred paintings, sculptures, and works on paper. Other artists include Barthé, Gammon, Hollingsworth, Dox Thrash. Catalogue.

16 December–1 February 1970: Whitney Museum of American Art, New York, *Contemporary American Painting Exhibition: Interior with Profiles* (1969). Other artists include John Baldessari, Brice Marden, Barnett Newman, Rauschenberg. Catalogue.

1970

One of fifty founding members of the Black Academy of Arts and Letters, designed to "define, preserve, promote and develop the arts and letters of black people."

January: Teaches five-week course in history of culture at Williams College, Williamstown, Massachusetts. Last four weeks of class taught at RB's own studio, due to his difficulties coping with Massachusetts winter.

February: RB appears with Ossorio on "You're Part of Art," on WNBC-TV.

March: Designs cover for *The Crisis,* which features essay by Ellison on RB (fig. 15).

Early May: Spends one week at University of Delaware, Newark, participating in seminars, critiques, and informal discussions with faculty and students as part of semester-long residency program, *Twelve Black American Artists, 1970.*

June: Receives John Solomon Guggenheim Foundation grant to write history of African-American art.

1–31 July: Gallery Museum, Hall of Springs at Saratoga Performing Art Center, New York, *Fifteen under Forty: Paintings by Young New York State Black Artists.* Crichlow served as director of exhibition with RB as consultant. Artists include Amos, Bailey, Hollingsworth. Catalogue by RB.

SOLO EXHIBITIONS

11 February–7 March: Cordier & Ekstrom, *Romare Bearden: Recent Collages.* Twenty-four works including 1969 sculpture *Mauritius* and screenprint with collage based on and titled *Carolina Blue* (1969), published in edition of 100. Catalogue.

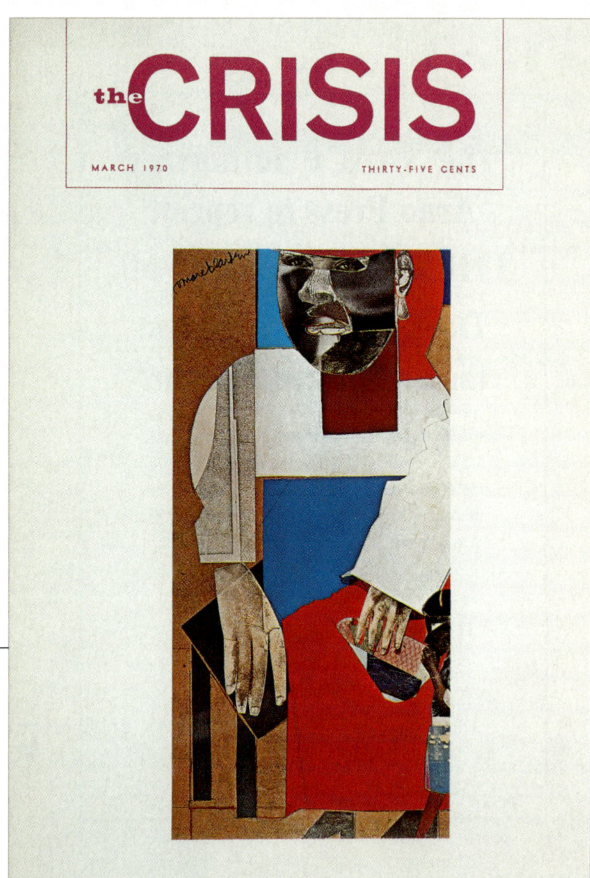

15

figure 15
Romare Bearden, *The Crisis* cover, March 1970. Estate of Romare Bearden, courtesy of Romare Bearden Foundation, New York

1970

14–20 August: Tirca Karlis Gallery, Provincetown, Massachusetts, *Romare Bearden: Collages.* Twelve collages and *Carolina Blue,* screenprint with collage.

GROUP EXHIBITIONS

9 January–20 February: Gallery 303 of the Composing Room, New York, *Black Artists in Graphic Communication.* Other artists include George Olden, Gordon Parks, Mozelle Thompson. Catalogue (?).

26–31 January: Martha Jackson Gallery, New York. Benefit exhibition for Studio Museum in Harlem: *Black Madonna and Child* (1969). Sixty works by sixty artists.

9 February–10 March: Museum of the National Center of Afro-American Artists, Boston, *Five Famous Black Artists: Jazz: (Chicago) Grand Terrace—1930s, Watching the Good Trains Go By, Evening Meal of Prophet Peterson,* all 1964 collages. Other artists are Lawrence, Pippin, White, Woodruff. Catalogue.

14 February–29 March: La Jolla Museum of Art, San Diego, California, *Dimensions of Black: Pittsburgh Memory, Evening, 9:10, 461 Lenox Avenue* (both 1964 collages). Other artists include Biggers, Joshua Johnston, Lawrence, Simpson. Also includes large selection of African sculpture. Catalogue.

8 March–19 April: Staten Island Museum, New York, *Coalition 70: Family Dinner, House in Cotton Field* (both 1968). Other artists include Hollingsworth, Lewis, Mayhew. Catalogue.

April: George Washington Carver Museum, Tuskegee Institute, Alabama, *Festival of Arts Exhibition.*

6–30 April: California State College, Los Angeles, *Two Generations of Black Artists: Continuities.* Catalogue (?).

7–30 April: Association of the Bar of the City of New York, *Contemporary Graphic Art on Contemporary Law and Justice, 1870–1970: Saturday Night.* Exhibition celebrates one hundredth anniversary of Bar Association of New York. Other artists include Lawrence, Rauschenberg, James Rosenquist, White. Catalogue.

30 April–20 May: Bayonne Public Library, New Jersey, *GEIGY Art Collection.* Other artists include Nevelson, Mitchell, Rauschenberg.

19 May–23 June: Museum of the National Center of Afro-American Artists, School of Museum of Fine Arts, Boston, and Museum of Fine Arts, Boston, organize *Afro-American Artists, New York and Boston: Circe Preparing a Banquet for Ulysses, Serenade* (both 1968 collages). Other artists include Amos, Blackburn, Barbara Chase-Riboud, Jones. Catalogue.

19 May–21 June: Philadelphia Museum of Art, Pennsylvania, *Peace Exhibition,* organized by students from Philadelphia College of Art, Tyler School of Art, Pennsylvania Academy of Fine Arts, and Moore College of Art. *Family Dinner* (1968). Other artists include Ellsworth Kelly, Motherwell, Nevelson, Newman.

September: Visual Arts Gallery, New York, *Black Artists 1970: Morning.* Other artists include Elton C. Fax, Bill Howell, Warren L. Harris. Catalogue (?).

September: American Federation of Arts, New York. *Still Life Today: Still Life* (1970). Exhibition travels throughout United States through 1972. Supported by the Edward John Noble Foundation to encourage contemporary artists via the purchase of their work for public collections. As works were donated to museums, new ones were purchased to replace them in the circulating exhibition.

3–16 December: Cordier & Ekstrom, *She. Patchwork Quilt* (1970) (fig. 16); later acquired by Museum of Modern Art, New York. Catalogue (?).

1971

***Five,* film produced by Seagrams Distillers Company that focuses on the life and work of five artists, RB, Chase-Riboud, Betty Blayton Taylor, Hunt, and White, released for noncommercial viewing.**

***10 June–1 September:* RB and Nanette travel to London, Geneva, and Basel.**

SOLO EXHIBITIONS

4–25 March: Middle Earth Gallery, Detroit, Michigan. Collages including *Ritual Bayou* (1970), a series of six collage editions.

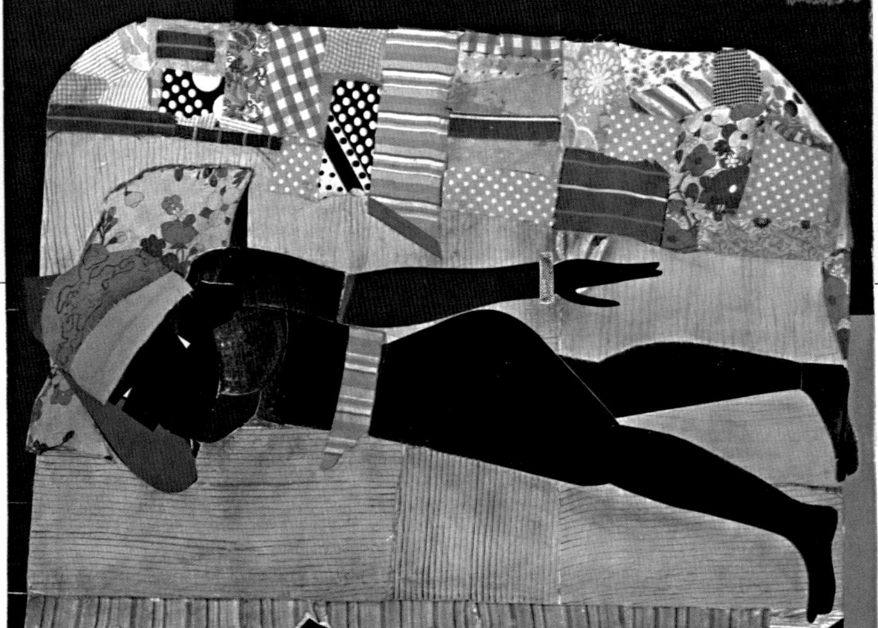

16

figure 16
Romare Bearden, *Patchwork Quilt,* 1970, collage of various papers with fabric and paint on fiberboard. The Museum of Modern Art, New York, Blanchette Rockefeller Fund

25 March–7 June: Museum of Modern Art, New York, *Romare Bearden: The Prevalence of Ritual.* Retrospective of fifty-six works, travels to National Collection of Fine Arts, Washington, D.C. (16 July–12 September); University Art Museum, Berkeley (25 October–5 December); Pasadena Art Museum, California (20 December–30 January 1972); High Museum, Atlanta, Georgia (27 February–9 April 1972); North Carolina Central University, Raleigh (2 May–11 June); Studio Museum in Harlem, New York (16 July–30 September 1972). Catalogue.

GROUP EXHIBITIONS

13 January–5 February: Lobby Gallery, Illinois Bell Telephone, Chicago, *Black American Artists/71: Spring Planting* (1969). Other artists include Andrews, David C. Driskell, Gilliam, David Hammons. Exhibition travels to Illinois State Museum, Springfield (22 February–19 March 1971); University of Wisconsin, Milwaukee (27 March–23 April); Sloan Galleries, Valparaiso, Indiana (1 May–29 May); Peoria Art Guild, Peoria, Illinois (6 June–3 July); Burpee Gallery, Rockford, Illinois (11 July–7 August); Davenport Municipal Gallery, Davenport, Iowa (16 August–10 September). Closing at the Museum of Art, University of Iowa, 2 January 1972. Catalogue.

13 May–6 September: Newark Museum, New Jersey, *Black Artists: Two Generations: Adoration of the Wise Men, Dream* (1970). Exhibition combines reconstruction of *American Negro Art—Contemporary Painting and Sculpture* held in 1944 at Newark Museum with work of younger contemporary artists. Other artists include Chase-Riboud, Lewis, Mayhew, Overstreet. Catalogue.

12 June–5 September: Rath Museum, Geneva, Switzerland, *Eight Afro-American Artists.* Five 1964 photostatic enlargements: *Jazz—1930s* [no city specified in title], *Prevalence of Ritual: Conjur Woman, Prevalence of Ritual: Conjur Woman as Angel, The Street, Pittsburgh Memory;* and seven collages: *The Farmer* (1968), *Mother and Child* (1968), *Morning* (1970), *Urban Blues* (1971), *Express to Memphis* (1971), *Carolina Family* (1971), *The Basket Woman* (1971). Other artists include Frederick John Eversley, Marvin Harden, Wilbur Haynie, Sue Irons, Alvin Smith, Thompson, Ruth Tunstall. Organized by Henri Ghent, director of Brooklyn Museum of Art's Community Gallery; travels to Brooklyn, June 1972. Catalogue.

9 December–9 January 1972: Peale Galleries, Pennsylvania Academy of the Fine Arts, Philadelphia, *Return to the Figure: Expulsion from Paradise* (1964), *Memory of a Dream, The Green Room, Green, Enchanted Region* (all 1971). Other artists include Sydney Goodman, Alex Katz, Mitzi Melnicoff, Armando Morales, Philip Pearlstein. Catalogue.

1972

Elected sixth president, board of directors, Harlem Cultural Council.

Six Black Masters of American Art by RB and Harry Henderson, published by Zenith Books, examines the work of Duncanson, Johnston, Lawrence, Pippin, Savage, and Tanner.

17 May: Elected to National Institute of Arts and Letters. Other new members are Adolph Gottlieb, Philip Guston, Constantino Nivola, and Stuyvesant Van Veen.

July: Justice appears on cover of *Contact,* a journal for black artists. RB also serves on board of directors for the journal.

30 August: Dedication in Times Square of temporary mural designed for New York City's Department of Cultural Affairs (fig. 17).

GROUP EXHIBITIONS

January: Solomon F. Guggenheim Museum, New York, *10 Independents: An Artist-Initiated Exhibition: Monday Morning* (1967), *Two of Them* (1969), *Junction, Conjunction, Sunday After Sermon* (all 1971). Other artists include Red Grooms, Irving Kriesberg (who helped organize the show), Peter Schumann, H.C. Westermann. Works were selected by the artists. Catalogue.

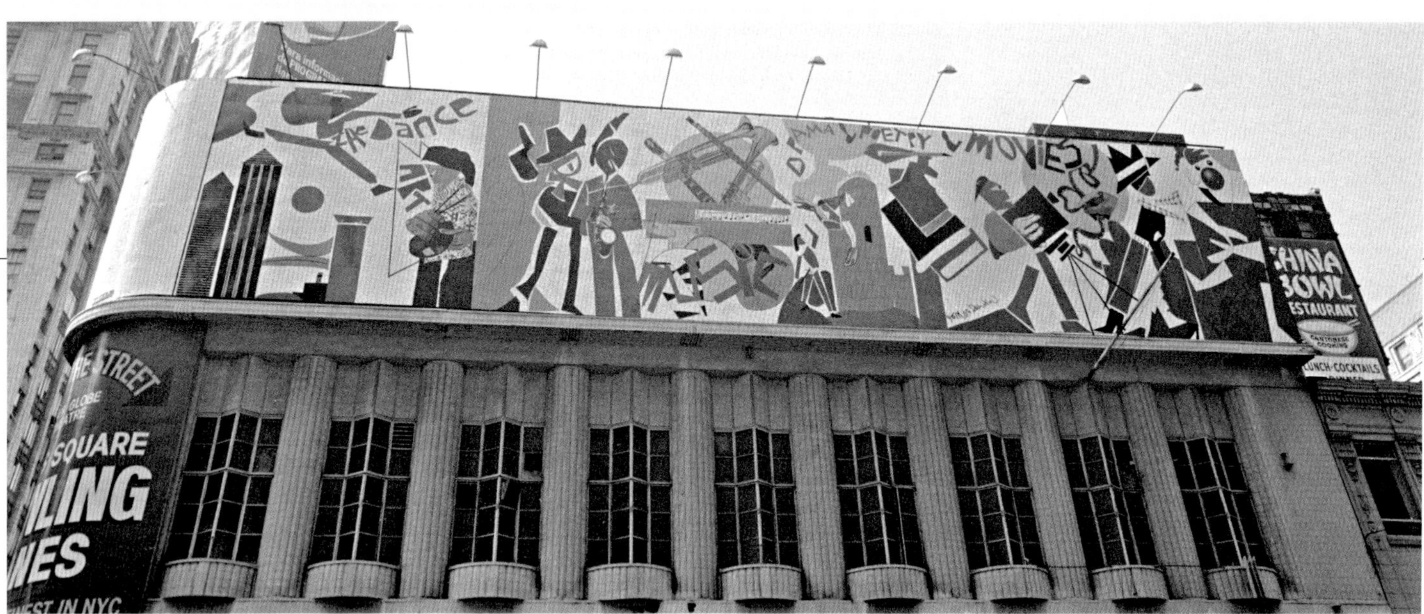

17

25 January–19 March: Whitney Museum of American Art, New York, *Annual Exhibition of Contemporary American Painting: Byzantine Dimension* (1972). Other artists include Chuck Close, Helen Frankenthaler, Lichtenstein, Frank Stella. Catalogue.

9 March–9 April: Reynolda House, Museum of American Art, Winston-Salem, North Carolina, *Black American Artist Seminar: The Trojan War* (c. 1950). Conference and exhibition. Cochaired by Hayward Oubre and Carroll Greene, Jr. Other artists include Lawrence, Bannister, Johnston, Hughie Lee Smith, Tanner, Hayward Oubre, Roland Watts. Catalogue.

18 May–18 June: American Academy of Arts and Letters and National Institute of Arts and Letters, New York, *Exhibition of Work by Newly Elected Members and Recipients of Honors and Awards: Mama's Knee, Woman in a Blue Dress, The Block II* (1972), *Blue Maternity, Girl in a Garden, Tidings II, Sketch for Block II, Ancestral Legend.* Other artists include Gottlieb, Guston, Clyfford Still. Catalogue.

14 August–1 October: Colorado Springs Fine Arts Center, *New Accessions USA, 14th Biennial Exhibition of Contemporary Paintings Acquired by Leading Art Museums of United States for Their Permanent Collections: Before the Dark* (1971). Other artists include Albers, Lichtenstein, O'Keeffe. Catalogue.

8–15 October: Benton Convention Center, Winston-Salem, North Carolina, *Reflections: The Afro-American Artist,* sponsored by Winston-Salem Alumnae Chapter of Delta Sigma Theta. *The Block II, Memories No. 2* (both 1972). Other artists include Alston, Lawrence, Charles Sebree, Tanner. Catalogue.

10 November–17 December: American Academy of Arts and Letters and National Institute of Arts and Letters, New York, *Paintings by Members: Conjunction* (1971). Other artists include Bishop, Lawrence, Motherwell, Tobey. Catalogue.

12 November–19 December: Weatherspoon Art Gallery, University of North Carolina, Greensboro, *1972 Art on Paper: Soul Three* (1969).

1973

Poems from Africa, anthology edited by Samuel Allen with illustrations by Bearden, published by Thomas Y. Crowell Editions.

Appointed to New York State Council on Arts.

Commissioned to create ceramic tile mural for P.S. 84 in the Bronx.

Builds house on St. Martin, Antilles, ancestral home of Nanette Bearden's family.

January: Appointed to three-year term on American Academy of Arts and Letters/National Institute of Arts and Letters Awards for Art committee. Awarded honorary doctorate in fine arts, Pratt Institute, Brooklyn, New York.

24 April–8 May: Teaches week-long workshop/seminar for students at California State University, Hayward, followed by multiday tour of Berkeley, California, to gather visual material for City Council Chambers, City Hall, Berkeley, mural commission.

June: Awarded Ford Foundation grant to compile comprehensive biographical information on African-American artists born before 1925.

Fall: Designs scenery for Ed Bullins' play, *House Party,* American Place Theater, New York City.

Fall: Named Rockefeller Fellow at Metropolitan Museum of Art, New York.

November: The Art of Romare Bearden: The Prevalence of Ritual by M. Bunch Washington, published by Harry N. Abrams.

SOLO EXHIBITION

28 March–28 April: Cordier & Ekstrom, *Romare Bearden: Prevalence of Ritual, Martinique, The Rain Forest* series. Twenty-four collages. Catalogue.

GROUP EXHIBITIONS

Dates unknown: Brooklyn College of Educational Services Union, *The First Tribute to Caribbean Heritage.*

9 March–6 May: La Jolla Museum of Contemporary Art, *Kurt Schwitters and Related Developments: Back Home from the Up Country* (1967). Catalogue (?).

11 May–15 June: Shorewood Atelier Gallery, New York, *Romare Bearden / Richard Lindner.*

10 June–12 August: University Art Museum, University of Texas at Austin, *Visual R & D: A Corporation Collects, The CIBA-GEIGY Collection of Paintings: The Witnesses* (1970). Other artists include Elaine De Kooning, Guston, Katz, Betty Parsons. Catalogue.

Fall: New School Art Center, New York. Group exhibition.

October: High Museum of Art, Atlanta, Georgia, *Highlights from the Atlanta University Collection of Afro-American Art: Snow Morning* (1959, oil). Travels to the Baltimore Museum of Art (January 15–February 24); the Jacksonville Art Museum,

figure 17
Romare Bearden, *Times Square Mural,* 1972. Photograph copyright Chester Higgins Jr. All Rights Reserved

9–31 August: Jamaica Arts Center, Jamaica, New York, *Tribute Exhibition to Master Printer and Printmaker Robert Blackburn.* Other artists include Andrews, Will Barnet, Kathy Caraccio, Sue Fuller.

9 September–5 October: Cordier & Ekstrom, untitled group show. *The Blues* (1975). Other artists include Peter Bardazzi, Grossman, Margaret Israel.

21 September–31 October: Hunter Museum of Art, Chattanooga, Tennessee, *A Southern Sampler: American Paintings in Southern Museums: Still Life* (1970). Other artists include Stuart Davis, Franz Kline, Grosz. Catalogue.

Winter: Pace Editions, New York. Group exhibition.

3 November–4 January 1976: Museum of the City of New York, *New York by Artists of the Art League of New York. In Celebration of the Centennial Year of the Art Students League of New York: Show Time* (1974). Other artists include Milton Avery, Barnet, Bishop, Grosz, Marsh. Catalogue.

14 November–4 January 1976: Museum of Fine Arts, Boston, *Jubilee: Afro-American Artists on Afro-America: Of the Blues: Wrapping It Up at the Lafayette* (1974). Other artists include William H. Johnson, Motley, Faith Ringgold, Savage. Catalogue.

1976

Awarded Gold Medal for achievement in the arts by the governor of North Carolina.

Contributes "The Black Man in the Arts" to the *New York Amsterdam News* special bicentennial issue on black contributions to United States history and culture.

Serves on executive board of the Rainbow Art Foundation, New York City, which offers scholarships, training, and exhibitions to young minority printmakers.

Completes collage mural *Cityscape* for Health and Hospitals Corporation; community controversy prevents its installation in Lincoln Medical Center, Bronx. Eventually installed at Bellevue Hospital Center, New York.

Nanette Rohan Bearden founds the Nanette Bearden Contemporary Chamber Dance Group, later renamed Nanette Bearden Contemporary Dance Theater. Over the years RB designed costumes, sets, and programs.

May: Invited by Mint Museum in Charlotte, North Carolina, to give talk on occasion of permanent installation of *Of the Blues: Carolina Shout (1974)*.

11 August: Alvin Ailey American Dance Theater performance of *Night Creature* introduced by projections of collages from RB's Of the Blues series.

30 September: Presents slide lecture on work of Tanner at Philadelphia Museum of Art, sponsored by Brandywine Graphic Workshop; receives workshop's first annual James VanDerZee award for excellence and contributions to history of Afro-American art, named for and presented by photographer VanDerZee.

November: Declared honorary citizen of Atlanta at a ceremony dedicating his design for mural in Kutz Building. (Mural lost when building was demolished.)

SOLO EXHIBITIONS

23 January–2 February: Graphis Gallery, Toronto. First show in Canada.

11 February–13 March: Cordier & Ekstrom, *Romare Bearden: Of the Blues (Second Chorus).* Thirty-seven monotypes.

22 February–14 March: Firehouse Gallery, Nassau Community College, Garden City, New York, *Romare Bearden.* Three collages, eleven prints. Exhibition cosponsored by Art Department and Afro-American Studies Department to celebrate United States bicentennial. Held simultaneously with an exhibition of prints by John Romano and Claire Ross. Catalogue.

21 November–18 December: Sheldon Ross Gallery, Birmingham, Michigan, *Romare Bearden: Recent Collages.* Fifteen collages, one print. Inaugural exhibition of Sheldon Ross Gallery.

GROUP EXHIBITIONS

25 January–28 March: Art Museum, Princeton University, Princeton, New Jersey, *Fragments of American Life: Folk Musicians* (1941–42), *Prevalence of Ritual: Baptism* (1964), *Conjur Woman* (1971), *Byzantine Dimension* (1971), *Mother and Child* (1968), *Intimacy of Water* (1973), *Prologue to Troy No. 1* (1972), *Intermission Still Life* (1974), *Ancestral Rhythms* (1974–75). Other artists include Delaney, Jones, Hughie Lee Smith, Woodruff. Catalogue.

Spring: Pratt Graphics Center Gallery, New York, *Printed Quilts—Quilted Prints: An Exhibition Marking Completion of a Special Project.* Circulates.

4 March: Exhibition marking opening of Clark, Phipps, Clark and Harris, Inc., New York: *Spring Procession* (1973). Other artists include Alston, Camille Billops, Hollingsworth, Lawrence, Lewis, Ringgold, Saunders. Catalogue.

30 March–6 September: Hirshhorn Museum and Sculpture Garden, Washington, D.C., *Bicentennial Banners* (published by Chuck Levitan): *Prince Cinque* (1976). Other artists include Richard Anuszkiewicz, Edward Clark, William King, Marisol Escobar. Exhibition circulated by Smithsonian Institution Traveling Exhibition Service. Catalogue.

14 April–14 June: Metropolitan Museum of Art, New York, *Selected Works by Black Artists from the Collection of the Metropolitan Museum of Art.*

29 July–8 August: Philadelphia Civic Center, *Exhibition of Liturgical Arts.* Other artists include Robert Arneson, Day, William Daley, and Alice Neel. Catalogue.

31 August–2 October: Berliner Festwochen Kunstamt Wedding, Wather-Rathenau-Saal, Rathauswedding (Altban), Berlin, *Art Students League of New York, 1875–1976: Drückgraphic: Prevalence of Ritual* (1974, screenprints). Other artists include Barnet, Blackburn, Stuart Davis. Catalogue.

12 September–24 October: North Carolina Museum of Art, Raleigh, *Two Hundred Years of the Visual Arts in North Carolina.* Catalogue.

30 September–21 November: Los Angeles County Museum of Art, *Two Centuries of Black American Art,* organized by David C. Driskell. *Death in the Afternoon* (1946), *Thirst Goes Away with Drinking* (1946, watercolor), *Trojan War Series: At the Oracle* (1949), *Gardens of Babylon* (1955), *Sermons: The Walls of Jericho* (1964), *The Woodshed* (1969). Exhibition travels to High Museum, Atlanta, Georgia (8 January–20 February 1977); Dallas Museum of Fine Arts, Texas (30 March–15 May 1977); and Brooklyn Museum, New York (25 June–21 August 1977). Other artists include Biggers, Lawrence, Lewis. Catalogue.

1–21 December: Pratt Institute Gallery, Brooklyn, *14 Afro-American Artists.* Other artists include Blackburn, Crichlow, Hunt, Lewis. Catalogue.

1977

January: Designs set and costumes for Alvin Ailey American Dance Theater's performance of Diane McIntyre's *Four Elements.*

22–28 January: Homage to Roots appears on *TV Guide* to mark airing of miniseries *Roots* based on novel by Alex Hailey (fig. 20).

18 April: The Street (Composition for Richard Wright) published in *New York Times.*

May: Gives commencement speech and receives honorary doctorate in fine arts from Maryland Institute College of Art, Baltimore. Receives honorary doctorate from North Carolina Central University, Durham.

May: Designs scrim for Alvin Ailey American Dance Theater's premiere of "Ancestral Voices" choreographed by McIntyre.

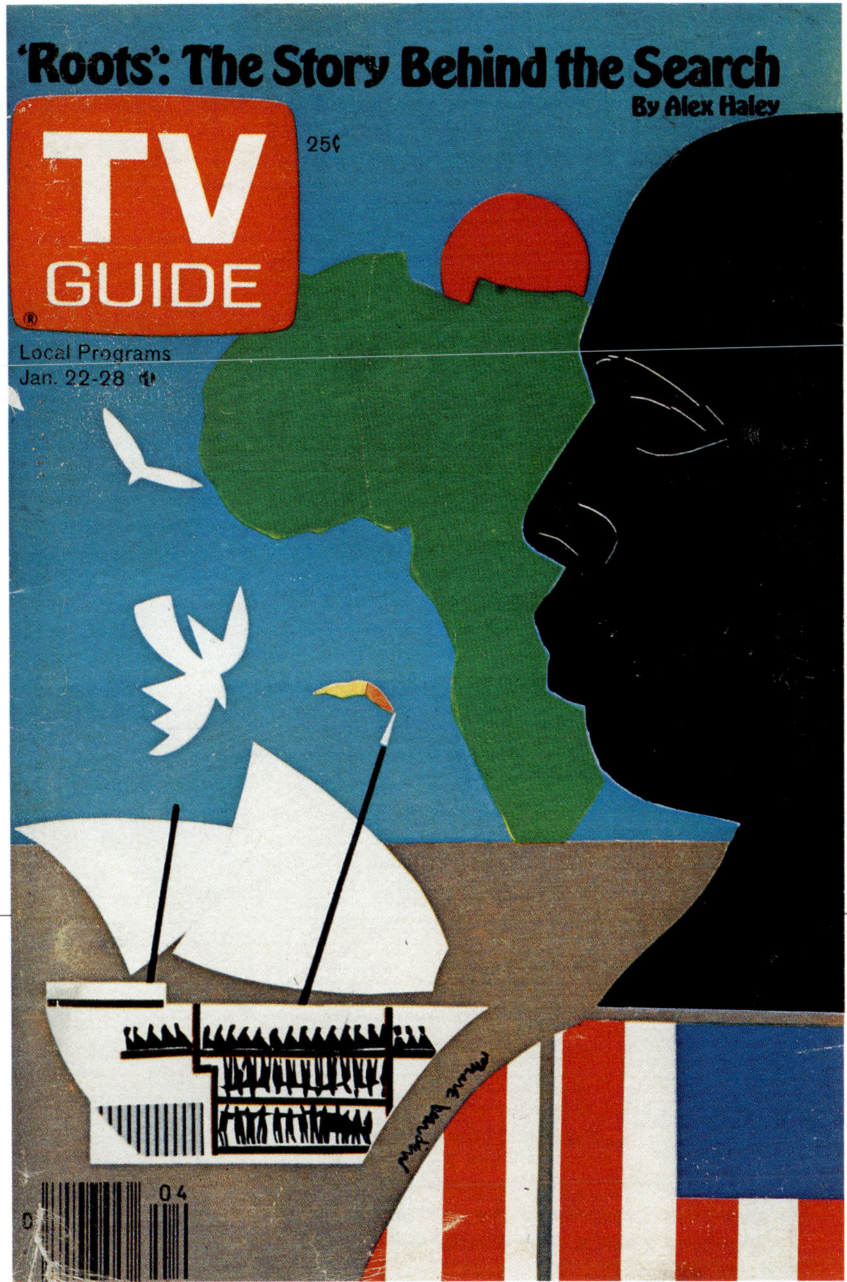

figure 20
Romare Bearden, *Homage to Roots,* design for *TV Guide* cover story, "'Roots': The Story Behind the Search," by Alex Haley, 22–28 January 1977. Estate of Romare Bearden, courtesy of Romare Bearden Foundation, New York/TV Guide Magazine Group, Inc.

20

June: Participates in International School Biennial Art Exhibition and Sale organized in honor of Alexander Calder at General Assembly of United Nations, Manhattan.

18 June: "Homage to Charles 'Spinky' Alston," obituary published in the *New York Amsterdam News.*

September: Resigns as director of Cinque Gallery to spend more time in St. Martin.

28 November: New Yorker publishes Calvin Tomkins' "Profiles: Romare Bearden" (fig. 21).

December: Interviewed for educational filmstrip, *Contemporary Artists at Work,* produced by Harcourt-Brace Jovanovich. Other artists in film include Close, Katz, Anuszkiewicz.

SOLO EXHIBITIONS

3 April–7 May: Graphis Gallery, Toronto, *"And all that jazz."*

27 April–28 May: Cordier & Ekstrom, Odysseus series. Travels to the Hudson River Museum, New York. Twenty collages. Catalogue.

21 November–21 December: Gallery One, Montclair State College, New Jersey, *Romare Bearden.*

GROUP EXHIBITIONS

1–26 February: Roko Gallery, New York, *The American Collagists.* Other artists include Beverly Chessler, Grossman, Saar.

10–31 March: Bard College, Annandale-on-Hudson, New York, *Aspects of the Collage.* Other artists include Grace Hartigan, Motherwell, Howardena Pindell, Adja Yunkers. Catalogue (?).

6 May–5 June: Oklahoma Art Center, Oklahoma City, *Manscape: 77: Show Time* (1974). Other artists include Grooms, Grossman, Lawrence, White. Catalogue.

1 June–1 July: Grey Art Gallery and Study Center, New York University, New York, *Drawing and Collage: Selections from the New York University Art Collection: Adoration of the Magi* (1945, oil). Other artists include Avery, Otto Dix, Diego Rivera, Rothschild. Catalogue.

15–21 July: Tirca Karlis Gallery, Provincetown, Massachusetts, *Graphic Show.*

Fall: Cordier & Ekstrom. Group exhibition.

20 September–20 November: Indianapolis Museum of Art, *Perceptions of the Spirit in Twentieth Century Art.* Travels to University Art Museum, University of California at Berkeley (20 December 1977–12 February 1978); Marion Koogler McNay Art Institute, San Antonio, Texas (5 March–16 April 1978); Columbus Gallery of Fine Arts, Ohio (10 May–19 June 1978). Other artists include Willem de Kooning, Gottlieb. Catalogue.

23 September–2 October: Florida International University, North Miami Campus. *Contemporary Black Art: A Selected Sampling: Show Time* (1974). Other artists include Andrews, Melvin Edwards, Gilliam, Ringgold, Saunders. Also shown at Tamiami Campus 4–22 October. Catalogue.

4–30 November: North Carolina Central University, Museum of Art, Durham, *Heralds of Life: Artis, Bearden, Burke.* Catalogue.

17 November–30 December: Andrew Crispo Gallery, New York, *Twelve Americans: Masters of Collage: Early Morning; Train Whistle Blues I* (as *Untitled*); *Evening 9:10, 461 Lenox Ave.; Pittsburgh Memory; Conjur Woman* (all 1964); *Four Figures* and *Two Figures* (both 1968); *Flights and Fantasy* and *Ritual Bayou* (both 1970); *Memory of a Dream* and *Late Afternoon* (both 1971); *Prevalence of Ritual: Prologue to Troy No. 1* (1972); *Spring Procession* (1973); *Of the Blues: Mecklenburg County, Saturday Night* (1974); *Odysseus: Cattle after Sun;* and *Odysseus: Odysseus and Penelope Reunited* (both 1977). Other artists include Joseph Cornell, Robert Courtright, William Dole, Dove, Lee Krasner, Motherwell, Rauschenberg, Reinhardt, Ann Ryan, Joseph Stella, Wesselman. Catalogue.

1978

Receives Freedom Fighter Award from Atlanta Chapter of National Association for the Advancement of Colored People.

4 May: Receives thirteenth annual Frederick Douglass medal from New York Chapter of National Urban League. Event hosts over fifteen hundred guests and half a million television viewers.

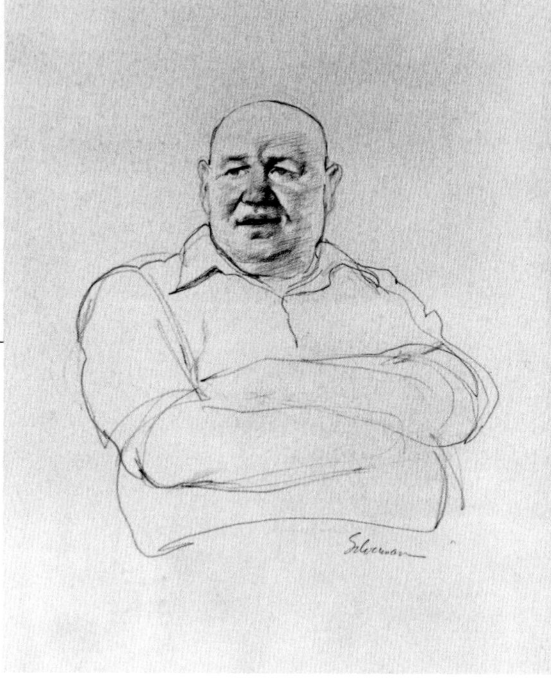

21

figure 21
Burton Philip Silverman, *Romare Bearden*, 1977, graphite. Made at the time of the *New Yorker* "Profiles: Romare Bearden." National Portrait Gallery, Smithsonian Institution/Art Resource, NY

April: Receives honorary doctorate in fine arts from Davidson College, North Carolina.

June: President and Mrs. Carter invite Nanette and RB to attend concert and buffet dinner at White House.

June: RB's cover appears on *Black Enterprise* magazine.

17 September: RB's cover appears on *TV Guide.*

SOLO EXHIBITIONS

23 March–22 April: Neighborhood Arts Center, Inc., Atlanta, Georgia, *Romare Bearden.* Thirteen collages and photostats. Catalogue.

11 April–5 May: Davidson College Art Gallery, North Carolina, *Romare Bearden.* Eighteen collages, six screenprints.

8 November–16 December: Cordier & Ekstrom, *Profile/Part I, The Twenties.* Twenty-eight collages. Catalogue.

16 December–13 January 1979: Sheldon Ross Gallery, Birmingham, Michigan, *Romare Bearden.* Twenty-two watercolors and collages inspired by St. Martin.

GROUP EXHIBITIONS

23 February–16 April: Ringling Museum of Art, Sarasota, Florida, *Contemporary Tapestries Created by Gloria Ross: Recollection Pond* (1975), *Mille Fleurs* (1977). Other artists include Frankenthaler, Richard Lindner, Nevelson, Lucas Samaras. Catalogue.

15 August–8 September: Whitney Museum of American Art, New York, *Collage: Selections from the Permanent Collection: Eastern Barn* (1968). Other artists include Sam Middleton, Motherwell, Rauschenberg, Joseph Stella.

18 September–30 November: Gallery 62, National Urban League, New York, *Golden Opportunity: Christ's Entry into Jerusalem* (1945). Other artists include Barthé, Selma Burke, Hayden, Savage, Tanner, White. RB is member of advisory board for Gallery 62. Catalogue.

7 October–10 November: Schenectady Museum, New York, *Black Artists in Historical Perspective, Part II.* Catalogue (?).

26 October–14 November: Temple University, Tyler School of Art Galleries, Elkins Park, Pennsylvania. Untitled exhibition related to painting department's visiting speakers program in which RB participated. Two works.

1979

13 October: Presentation of Carol Jenkins' interview, "Profile of Romare Bearden," on "Positively Black," WNBC-TV, channel 4.

GROUP EXHIBITIONS

March: Newhouse Gallery-North, Snug Harbor Cultural Center at Staten Island, New York, untitled exhibition. *Memories* (oil monotype). Sponsored by Black Educators United of Staten Island.

7 March–6 May: Montgomery Museum of Fine Arts, Alabama, *Art Inc.: A Selection of American Paintings from Corporate Collections: Blue Interior, Morning* (1968). Exhibition travels to Corcoran Gallery of Art, Washington, D.C. (12 June–14 July); Indianapolis Art Museum (8 August–23 September); San Diego Art Museum (17 November–30 December). Other artists include Calder, Dove, Frankenthaler, Krasner. Catalogue.

1 April–29 July: Huntsville Museum of Art, Alabama, *Black Artists/South: Carolina Blue* (1969), *Sun and Candle* (1971), *Untitled.* Other artists include Amos, Biggers, Gilliam, Samella Lewis. Catalogue.

8 April–20 May: Rockland Center for the Arts, West Nyack, New York, *Works on Paper USA.* Other artists include Carl Andre, Frankenthaler, Johns, Agnes Martin.

2 July–15 September: North Park National Bank, Dallas, Texas, *Gloria F. Ross Tapestries: Recollection Pond* (1975). Other artists include Avery, Frankenthaler, Frank Stella.

October: Creativity—The Human Resource, sponsored by Chevron. Exhibition travels to numerous venues, including Pacific Science Center, Seattle, Washington; Union-Carbide Building, New York; John F. Kennedy Center for the Performing Arts, Washington, D.C.; Franklin Institute Science Museum, Philadelphia (12 November 1980–12 January 1981); Museum of Science, Boston, through 29 March 1981. Other artists include John Cage, Buckminster Fuller, Margaret Mead. Catalogue.

1980

Approximately thirty New York cityscapes in watercolor executed for opening credits of John Cassavetes' film *Gloria.*

Selects images for new edition of W. E. B. Du Bois' *Dusk of Dawn: An Essay Toward an Autobiography of a Race Concept* (first edition, 1940), published by Franklin Library, Pennsylvania.

1980

May: Exhibition at Massachusetts College of Art, organized by Wendell Street Gallery, Cambridge. Watercolors of St. Martin.

17–21 May: Rochelle and Irwin Lowenfeld Hall, Hofstra University, Hempstead, New York, *An Exhibition of Prints by Romare Bearden.* Twelve works in conjunction with commencement speech. Catalogue.

? May–2 June: Jenkintown Fine Art Gallery, Pennsylvania, *The Worlds of Romare Bearden.*

14 November–30 December: Malcolm Brown Gallery, Shaker Heights, Ohio, *Romare Bearden.* Sixteen collages. Catalogue.

GROUP EXHIBITIONS

6 February–?: Newark Museum, New Jersey, *Black Artists: Dream Storybook Scene, Landscape.* Other artists include Bannister, Clark, Robert Reid, Raymond Steth.

4 April–6 June 1982: Mississippi Museum of Art, Jackson, *The Modern Figurative Tradition: Conjunction* (1971).

27 April–14 May: Equitable Gallery, New York, *Black Achievement in the Arts: Circe Turning a Companion of Odysseus into a Swine* (1977). Other artists include Loving, Mayhew, Parks, Saar, VanDerZee. Catalogue.

7 May–20 June: Oklahoma Arts Center, Oklahoma City, *American Masters of the Twentieth Century: Mamie Cole, Odyssey.* Other artists include John Marin, O'Keeffe, Nevelson, David Smith. Travels to Terra Museum of American Art, Evanston, Illinois (11 July–15 September). Catalogue.

20 June–1 November: Studio Museum in Harlem, New York, *Ritual and Myth: A Survey of African American Art.* Catalogue.

11 July–3 October: Contemporary Art Museum, Houston, *The Americans: The Collage: Patchwork Quilt* (1970), *The Street* (1975). Catalogue.

3 October–3 November: Hickory Museum of Art, Hickory, North Carolina, *The Afro-American Presence in the Arts, Past and Present from North Carolina Collections: In the Garden* (1976), *Morning of the Rooster: Mecklenburg County* (1980); both lithographs. Catalogue (?)

2 December–January 1983: Schomburg Center for Research in Black Culture, New York Public Library, *The Art of Jazz: Solo Flight* (1978), *Jamming at the Savoy* (1981). Other artists include Middleton, Walter Davis, Roy DeCarava.

1983

Limited Editions Club publishes *The Caribbean Poems of Derek Walcott,* Derek Walcott's poems illustrated with RB's watercolors (see fig. 24).

Completes designs for Alvin Ailey American Dance Theater presentation of "Blueshift," choreography by Talley Beatty.

20–21 April: Lectures at Columbia Museum of Sciences and Arts, South Carolina, as part of the first South Carolina Visual Artist Forum, sponsored by the South Carolina Arts Commission and the National Endowment for the Arts. Other artists in the series include Alice Aycock, Jack Beal, Duane Michals, Susan Peterson, Jerome Witkin.

May: Unveiling of *Baltimore Uproar* mosaic for Laurens Street subway station, Baltimore.

September: Unveiling of mural based on *Spring Way* (1964) at new Chambers Street campus, Borough of Manhattan Community College, City University of New York.

2 October: "An Artist's Renewal in the Sun" about life on St. Martin appears in the *New York Times Magazine.*

26 October: Awarded Studio Museum in Harlem's "Artist Award" with Catlett and Lawrence.

December: Alvin Ailey American Dance Theater adapts RB's *Under the Bridge* as scrim for world premiere of "The Stack-Up" by Talley Beatty, choreographer who later works with Nanette Bearden's Contemporary Dance Theater.

SOLO EXHIBITIONS

11–26 March: Sheldon Ross Gallery, Birmingham, Michigan, *New York at Night: Recent Watercolors.* Twenty watercolors.

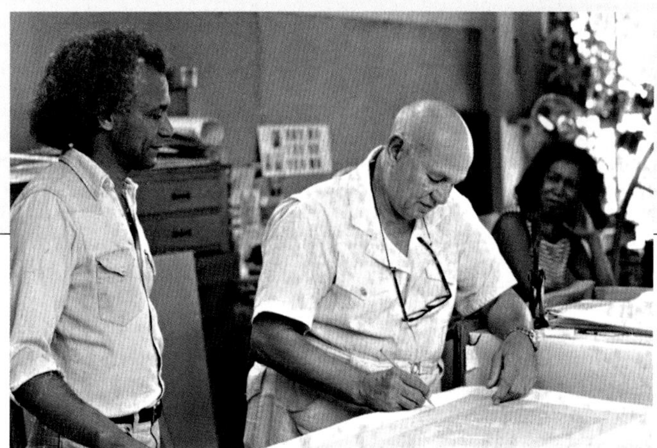

23

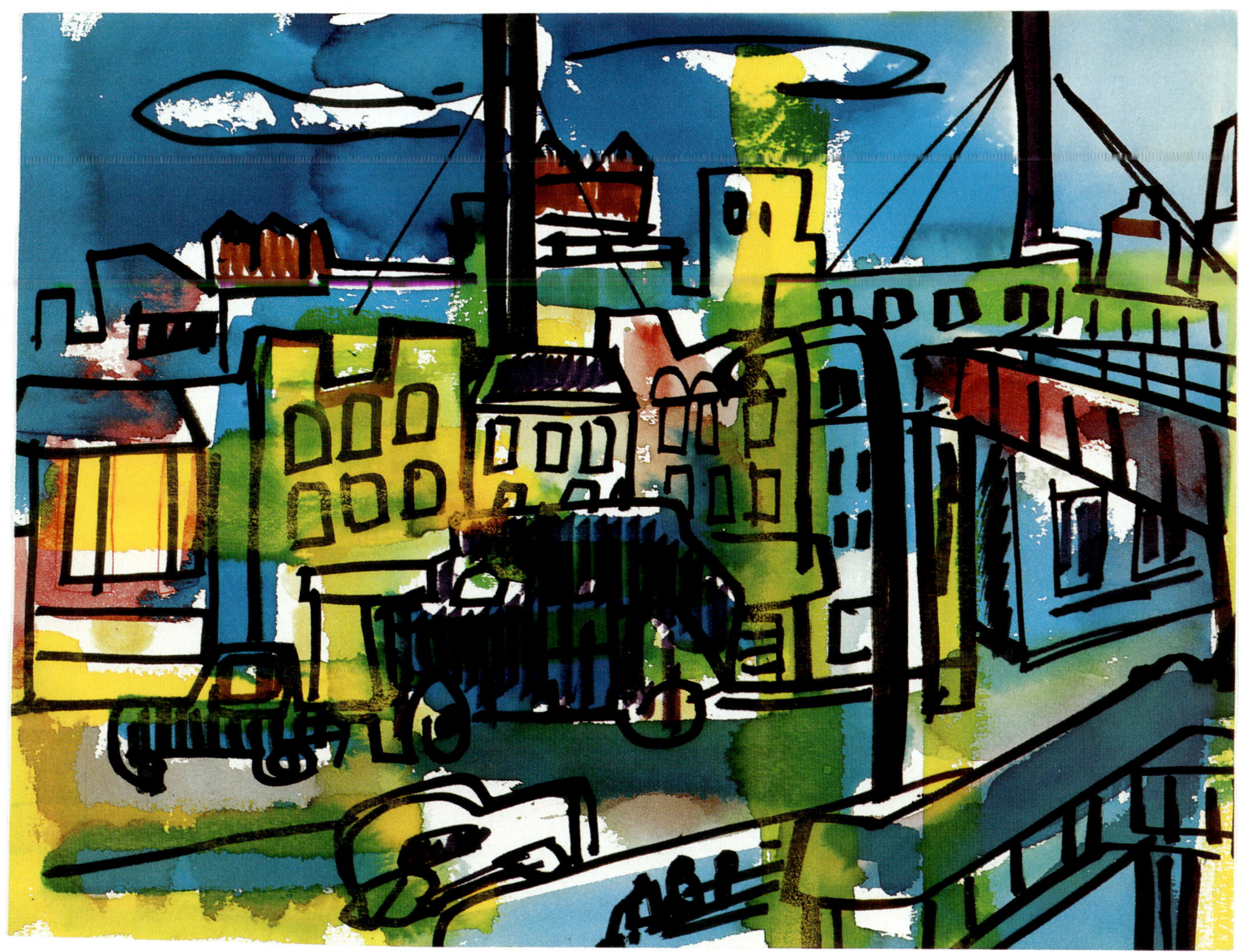

24

figure 23
Romare Bearden, center, signing the etching edition *Jamming at the Savoy;* Mohammad Khalil and June Kelly looking on. Courtesy June Kelly

figure 24
Romare Bearden, *Untitled (Long Island City)*, 1980s, watercolor and ink. Collection James Craig

24 September–16 October: New Jersey State Museum, Trenton, untitled exhibition from the permanent collection and recent works. Concurrent with 25 September benefit performance of Nanette Bearden's Contemporary Dance Theater on behalf of the museum's collection of works by African-American artists.

12 November–17 December: Cordier & Ekstrom, *Romare Bearden: Mecklenburg Autumn: Oil Paintings with Collage.* Fourteen works. Catalogue.

GROUP EXHIBITIONS

10 April–22 May: Mississippi Museum of Art, Jackson, *New York, the Influence: The Street* (1975).

14 September–27 November: Virginia Museum of Fine Arts, Richmond, *Painting in the South, 1564–1980: Prevalence of Ritual: Tidings* (1964). Exhibition travels to Museum of Art, Birmingham, Alabama (8 January–4 March 1984); National Academy of Design, New York (12 April–27 May 1984); Mississippi Museum of Art, Jackson (24 June–26 August 1984); J. B. Speed Art Museum, Louisville, Kentucky (16 September–11 November 1984); Museum of Art, New Orleans, Louisiana (9 December–3 February 1985). Other artists include Gorky, Johns, William H. Johnson. Catalogue.

26 September–10 November: Godwin-Ternbach Museum, Queens College, City University of New York, *20th Century Prints from the Godwin-Ternbach Museum: Tidings* (1977). Other artists include Grosz, Rouault, Jose Clemente Orozco, Rauschenberg. Catalogue.

October: McCoy Gallery, Philadelphia, *Sometimes I Feel Like…* Fourteen artists.

28 October–4 December: Kenkeleba Gallery, New York, *Jus' Jass: Correlations of Painting and Afro-American Classical Music: Saxophone Solo* (1980). Other artists include Billops, David Hammons, Ringgold. Catalogue.

1984

Pittsburgh Recollections, mural for Gateway Center "T" Station, Pittsburgh Allegheny Rapid Transit.

17 May: RB and Nanette attend NAACP Legal Defense Fund (LDF) Annual Civil Rights Institute. LDF commissions lithograph *The Lamp* to celebrate thirtieth anniversary of *Brown v. Board of Education.* Printed at J. K. Fine Arts Editions, New York, to benefit fund; edition of 100.

24 May: National Academy of Design, screening of film, *Bearden Plays Bearden* by Billie Allen and Nelson Breen, followed by RB lecture about influence of jazz on his work.

27 November: Receives Mayor's Award of Honor for Art & Culture, New York City, from Edward Koch at Gracie Mansion. RB introduced by Calvin Tomkins. Other recipients include musician Mario Bauza, choreographers Martha Hill and Twyla Tharp, architecture critic Ada Louise Huxtable, and set designer Ming Cho Lee.

SOLO EXHIBITIONS

4–25 April: Capen Gallery, Amherst Campus, University of Massachusetts, *Romare Bearden: Prints.*

6 May–1 July: Grand Rapids Art Museum, Michigan, *The Art of Romare Bearden.* Twenty watercolors and collages. Catalogue.

30 August–22 September: Sheldon Ross Gallery, Birmingham, Michigan, *Romare Bearden: Watercolors from St. Maarten.* Twenty-four watercolors, three collages.

14 November–22 December: Cordier & Ekstrom, *Rituals of the Obeah.* Sixteen watercolors. Catalogue.

GROUP EXHIBITIONS

10 January–4 March: Montgomery Museum of Art, Alabama, *Advancing American Art: Politics and Aesthetics in the State Department Exhibition, 1946–48: Five in the Afternoon* (1946, oil); *Mad Carousel* (1946, watercolor). Reconstruction of State Department Exhibitions of 1946–48. Travels to the William Benton Museum of Art, Storrs, Connecticut (17 March–6 May 1984); National Museum of American Art, Smithsonian Institution, Washington, D.C. (1 June–8 October); Terra Museum of American Art, Evanston, Illinois (21 October–9 December). Catalogue.

3 February–10 March: Alexandria Museum of Art, Louisiana, *The Rhythm of Life: Bearden, Gwathmey, and Lawrence.* Travels to Greater Lafayette Museum of Art, Indiana (4 May–17 June). Catalogue.

5 February–18 March 1984: Emily Lowe Gallery, Hofstra University Library, Hempstead, New York, *A Blossoming of New Promises: Art in the Spirit of the Harlem Renaissance.*

13 April–6 June: Center Gallery, Bucknell University, Lewisburg, Pennsylvania, *Since the Harlem Renaissance: 50 Years of Afro-American Art: The Rites of Spring* (1967). Travels to Amelie A. Wallace Art Gallery, State University of New York, College at Westbury (1 November–9 December); Museum of Art, Munson-Williams Proctor Institute, Utica, New York (11 January–3 March 1985); the Art Gallery, University of Maryland, College Park (27 March–3 May 1985); the Chrysler Museum, Norfolk, Virginia (19 July–1 September 1985); Museum of Art, Pennsylvania State University,

University Park (22 September–1 November); the Freedman Gallery, Albright College, Reading, Pennsylvania; the Tyler Art Gallery, State University of New York, Oswego. Other artists include Middleton, Gilliam, Pindell, Jack Whitten. Catalogue.

29 June–30 September: Museum of African American Art, Los Angeles, *Artists of the Thirties and Forties: Study for Trojan Series* (1947–48). Other artists include Catlett, Cortor, Crichlow, Parks.

22 July–15 January 1985: California Afro-American Museum, Los Angeles, *East-West: Contemporary American Art: Bayou and Heron* (1982). Other artists include Gilliam, Hunt, Martin Puryear, Saar, William T. Williams. Catalogue.

30 November–18 January 1985: Schomburg Center for Research in Black Culture, New York Public Library, New York, *Art in Print: A Tribute to Robert Blackburn: Tidings* (1977), *Conjunction: Three Women* (1981, both lithographs). Other artists include Adger Cowans, Edwards, Herbert Gentry, Krishna Reddy. Catalogue (RB wrote introduction).

2 December 1984–26 January 1985: Association of Community-Based Artists of Westchester, Mt. Vernon, New York, *Tribute to Robert Blackburn: Mecklenburg Spring, Folk Singer.* Other artists include Amos, Billops, Catlett. Catalogue.

1985

20 April: Honored by New York Artists Equity Association for lifetime of artistic achievement and devotion to fellow artists' interests.

20 May: Receives honorary doctorate in literature from Atlanta University.

6 October: Contributes article on St. Martin, "Clouds in the Living Room," to *The Sophisticated Traveler,* special section of *New York Times.*

3 November: Book signing at the Studio Museum in Harlem for *Ma Chance's French Caribbean Creole Cookery* (Jeanne Louise Duzant Chance) illustrated by RB.

6 December: Drawing reproduced with *New York Times* article, "A South African Fights from Exile."

14 December: With Mayor Edward Koch, E.L. Doctorow, Sylvia Fine Kaye, Brendan Gill, Robert Klein, Joseph Papp, and Steven Sondheim, RB took part in award presentation to eight New York City teachers, principals, and cultural organizations for helping introduce children to the arts. Program sponsored by Alliance for the Arts and funded by the Schubert Foundation.

SOLO EXHIBITIONS

29 January–3 March: Lehman College Art Gallery, Bronx, New York, *Romare Bearden: Selected Prints.*

February: Nanette Bearden Gallery of Fine Art, St. Martin, *Rituals of the Obeah.*

1–28 February: Bacardi Art Gallery, Miami, Florida, *Romare Bearden: Drawing, Collage, Printing, and Watercolor.* Thirty-nine works. Catalogue.

17 May–29 June: Jerald Melberg Gallery, Charlotte, North Carolina. Sixteen collages accompanied by short narratives on gallery walls.

GROUP EXHIBITIONS

27 January–30 June: Studio Museum in Harlem, New York, *Tradition and Conflict: Images of a Turbulent Decade, 1963–1973.* Among the fifty-five artists included are Malcolm Bailey, Catlett, Dana Chandler, Chase-Riboud, Gilliam, Lawrence, Parks, Pindell, Ringgold, Saunders. Catalogue.

February: Schomburg Center, New York Public Library. Group exhibition.

Spring: Lehman College Art Gallery, Bronx, New York, *The Subway Show.*

2 April–11 May: Washington Project for the Arts, D.C., *Art in Washington and Its Afro-American Presence.*

8 July–14 October: Newark Museum, New Jersey, *20th-Century Afro-American Artists.*

Fall: Evans-Tibbs Collection, Washington, D.C., *The Art of Collage: Romare Bearden, David Driskell, Kenneth Falana, Sam Gilliam, Ulysses Marshall, Barbara Mosley, Betye Saar, Sharon Sutton: Catfish Morning* (1983), *Fitting for the New Dress* (1984), *Conversation II* (1983), *Middle Region* (1984), *Up at Minton's* (1982), *Two Nudes* (1973). Catalogue.

Fall: Studio Museum in Harlem, New York. Group exhibition.

5 September–27 October: Bergen Museum of Art and Science, Paramus, New Jersey, *Collage: The State of the Art.* Other artists include Grossman, Ann Ryan, Miriam Shapiro. Catalogue.

14 September–10 November: Bellevue Art Museum, Washington, *Hidden Heritage: Afro-American Art, 1800–1950: Bullfighter, Warriors* (both 1947/48, watercolors). Other artists include Grafton T. Brown, Mary Edmonia Lewis, Savage, White. Organized by David C. Driskell for the Bellevue Art Museum and the Art Museum Associates of America, exhibition travels to Bronx Museum of the Arts, New York (14 January–10 March 1986); California Afro-American Museum, Los Angeles (7 April–2 June); Wadsworth Atheneum, Hartford,

Connecticut (14 July–31 August); Mint Museum of Art, Charlotte, North Carolina (22 September–17 November); San Antonio Museum of Art, Texas (15 December–9 February 1987); Toledo Museum of Art, Ohio (8 March–3 May 1987); Baltimore Museum of Art, Maryland (1 June–27 July 1987); Pennsylvania Academy of the Fine Arts, Philadelphia (23 August–18 October 1987); Oklahoma Museum of Art, Oklahoma City (15 November–10 January 1988). Catalogue.

15 November–20 December: Baruch College Gallery, Baruch College, City University of New York, *Figural Art of the New York School: Selections from the CIBA-GEIGY Collection.* Other artists include Stanley Boxer, Lester Johnson, Parsons, Nora Speyer. Travels to school of Art Gallery, Foster Hall, Louisiana State University, Baton Rouge, 2–21 February 1986. Catalogue.

1986

Mural, *Quilting Time,* installed in conjunction with retrospective exhibition at Detroit Institute of Arts.

August: Health continues to deteriorate. Corresponds with long-time student, André Thibault/Teabo, who becomes his assistant.

Autumn: Studio built adjacent to house in St. Martin.

October: Awarded Fourth Annual North Carolina Prize; $10,000 prize given by four newspapers, subsidiaries of the *New York Times,* to a North Carolinian for outstanding work in visual or performing arts.

5 November: Lectures at New York Public Library.

SOLO EXHIBITIONS

6 February–22 March: Flushing Gallery, Queens, New York, *Romare Bearden.* Monotypes, watercolors, edition prints.

7–28 February: Center Gallery, Carrboro, North Carolina, sponsored by North Carolina Arts Council, *Bearden: An American Master.*

?–21 June: McIntosh Gallery, Atlanta, *Recent Collages by Romare Bearden.*

30 April–28 June: Artworks Gallery and Real Art Ways Gallery, Hartford Arts Center, Connecticut, *Sound Collages and Visual Improvisations.* Works with jazz themes. In conjunction with exhibition, RB and musician Jackie McLean perform "Sound Collages and Visual Improvisations" at the Wadsworth Atheneum on 4 May. While McLean played piano, RB discussed his art and executed a portrait of McLean. Catalogue.

1–25 September: McKissick Museum, University of South Carolina, Columbia, *Romare Bearden: Jazz Collages.* Travels to Jerald Melberg Gallery, Charlotte, North Carolina (3–31 October).

12 September–25 October: Sheldon Ross Gallery, Birmingham, Michigan, *Romare Bearden: Recent Collages.* Twenty-one works from 1985–86 include Mecklenburg and St. Martin themes.

16 September–16 November: Detroit Institute of Arts, Michigan, *Romare Bearden: Origins and Progressions,* retrospective exhibition of fifty-seven works travels to Bronx Museum of the Arts, New York. Catalogue. Nanette Bearden's Contemporary Dance Theater, with sets and costumes designed by RB, performs at New York's Music Hall in conjunction with Bronx showing.

23 September–1 November: Cordier & Ekstrom, *Romare Bearden: Mecklenburg: Morning and Evening.* Fourteen collages. Catalogue.

3 October–16 November: Afro-American Cultural Center, Charlotte, North Carolina, *Romare Bearden: Prints.*

GROUP EXHIBITIONS

Fall: Tougaloo College, Mississippi, *Graphic Art by Afro-American Artists from the Collections of Tougaloo College: Sun and Candle* (1971), *The Street* (1975), *Tidings* (1977). Other artists include Lawrence, Catlett, Woodruff, White. Exhibition travels over two years to Alabama State University, Montgomery; Stillman College, Tuscaloosa, Alabama; Arts Experiment Station, Tifton, Georgia; Okefenokee Heritage Center, Waycross, Georgia; Neighborhood Arts Center, Atlanta, Georgia; Shelton State University, Tuscaloosa; African-American Museum, Bishops College, Dallas, Texas; University of Kentucky, Knoxville; Transylvania University, Lexington, Kentucky; Jackson State University, Mississippi. Catalogue.

3 December–?: Forum Gallery, New York, *Collages.* Other artists include Hannelore Baron, Varujan Boghosian, Gregory Gillespie, Saar.

16 December–28 February 1987: Jamaica Arts Center, New York, *Masters and Pupils: The Education of the Black Artist in New York, 1900–1980: Three Figures* (1946). Other artists include Alston, Benton, Delaney, Gwathmey, Holty, Lawrence, Lewis, Ringgold, Saunders, Vytlacil, Whitten, Woodruff. Exhibition travels to Metropolitan Life Gallery, New York (10 March–24 April 1987).

figure 25
Bearden in St. Martin, 1980s

1987

Illustrates *A Visit to the Country,* children's book by Herschel Johnson, published by Harper and Row in 1989.

January: After *Romare Bearden: Origins and Progressions* opens at Bronx Museum, RB travels to St. Martin (fig. 25).

March: Returns to New York, resumes work with André Thibault/Teabo.

23 May–16 August: San Diego Museum of Art exhibits *Perspectives: Angles on African Art,* juried by RB and nine others including artists Nancy Graves, Lela Konakou, Iba N'Diaye, writer James Baldwin, art historians Robert Thompson and Susan Vogel, and collector David Rockefeller. Show travels to the Center for African Art, New York, and Birmingham Museum of Art, Alabama.

June: Receives National Medal of Arts from President Reagan at White House. Attends dinner hosted by chair of National Endowment for the Arts, Frank Hodsell, and congressional reception hosted by Senator Edward Kennedy. Other recipients include singer Ella Fitzgerald, writer and scholar Howard Nemerov, choreographer Alwin Nikolais, sculptor Isamu Noguchi, composer William Schumann, and writer and poet Robert Penn Warren.

July: Makes final trip to St. Martin where he helps organize annual carnival celebration.

18 October: Bearden Day declared in Philadelphia, Pennsylvania, to celebrate achievements of RB and Nanette. In conjunction with celebration, Port of History Museum hosts exhibition of RB's works and performance by Nanette Bearden Contemporary Dance Theater.

SOLO EXHIBITIONS

Date unknown: Sheldon Ross Gallery, Birmingham, Michigan, *Recent Collages/Watercolors.* Thirteen works.

January: Nanette Bearden Fine Arts Gallery, St. Maarten. Twenty-seven works.

1–31 January: Delta Art Center, Charlotte, North Carolina. Eleven edition prints.

6 February–28 March: St. John's Museum of Art, Wilmington, Delaware, *Romare Bearden: Collages and Prints.* Seventeen collages and ten prints.

21 November–24 December: Thomas Segal Gallery, Boston, *Romare Bearden: Jazz.*

8 November–2 December: Wendell Street Gallery, Cambridge, Massachusetts, *Romare Bearden—Watercolors and Collages.*

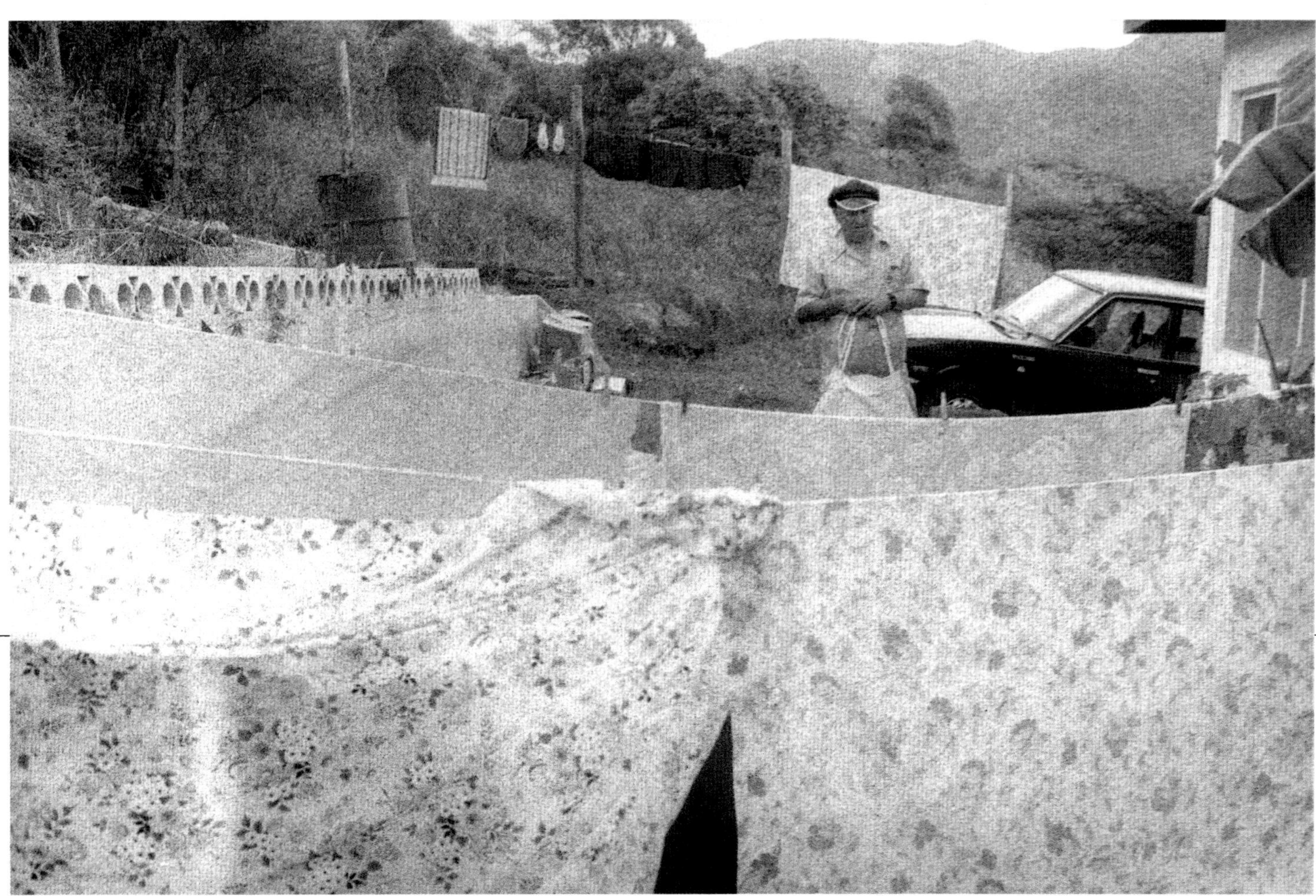

25

GROUP EXHIBITIONS

14 February–22 March: Mint Museum, Charlotte, North Carolina, *Charlotte Collects: Train Whistle Blues: 1* (1964), *Lady and a Bluebird* (1985).

Spring: Studio K, Long Island City, Queens, New York, *Second Annual Invitational Show.*

Spring: Hofstra University Library, Hempstead, New York, *An American Portrait.*

7 March–14 August: California Afro-American Museum, Los Angeles, *The Portrayal of the Black Musician in American Art: New Orleans Farewell* (1975), *Encore (Jazz)* (1980). Other artists include Lewis, Pippin, Saar. Catalogue.

November–27 December: Museum of African American Art, Los Angeles, *Los Angeles Collects.* Other artists include Barthé, Hammons, Saunders.

1988

26 January: Enters New York Hospital, goes into coma.

12 March: Romare Bearden dies.

6 April: Memorial service at Cathedral of St. John the Divine. Derek Walcott, Ralph Ellison, and Mary Schmidt Campbell, Commissioner of Cultural Affairs for New York City, speak at service. An exhibition of works by RB is installed at the cathedral.

May: Nanette accepts for her husband posthumous Lifetime Achievement Award from Studio Museum in Harlem.

SOLO EXHIBITIONS

23 January–3 April: North Carolina Museum of Art, Raleigh, *Riffs and Takes: Music in the Art of Romare Bearden.* Catalogue.

February: Nanette Bearden Fine Arts Gallery, St. Maarten. Exhibition of carnival-themed works.

1989

11 May–10 June: ACA Galleries, New York, *Romare Bearden (1911–1988): A Memorial Exhibition.* Catalogue.

1991

14 April–11 August: Studio Museum in Harlem, New York, *Memory and Metaphor: The Art of Romare Bearden.* Retrospective exhibition of 141 works. Published itinerary: Museum of Contemporary Art, Chicago (28 September–10 November 1991); Wight Gallery, University of California, Los Angeles (8 December 1991–2 February 1992); High Museum of Art, Atlanta (10 March–3 May 1992); the Carnegie Museum of Art, Pittsburgh (30 May–25 July 1992); National Museum of American Art, Smithsonian Institution, Washington, D.C. (2 October 1992–4 January 1993). Catalogue.

1993

Pantheon Books, New York, publishes *A History of African-American Artists: From 1792 to the Present,* cowritten by RB and Harry Henderson who together dedicated many years to researching and writing this comprehensive survey of African-American art.

Mural, *City of Glass,* based on 1982 maquette, installed at East Tremont Avenue and Williamsburg Road (elevated) Station, Bronx, Metropolitan Transit Authority, New York (figs. 26, 27).

2003

14 September–4 January 2004: National Gallery of Art, Washington, D.C., *The Art of Romare Bearden.* One hundred and forty works. Exhibition travels to San Francisco Museum of Modern Art; Dallas Museum of Art; Whitney Museum of American Art, New York; High Museum of Art, Atlanta. Catalogue.

1990

2000

figure 26
Romare Bearden, *Proposal for "Untitled (City of Glass),"* 1982, collage with paint and graphite on paper. Commissioned and owned by Metropolitan Transportation Authority Arts for Transit

figure 27
Romare Bearden, *City of Glass,* 1993, faceted glass triptych, 9½ feet x 20 feet, installed at Westchester Square (elevated) Subway Station, Bronx, New York. Commissioned and owned by Metropolitan Transportation Authority Arts for Transit

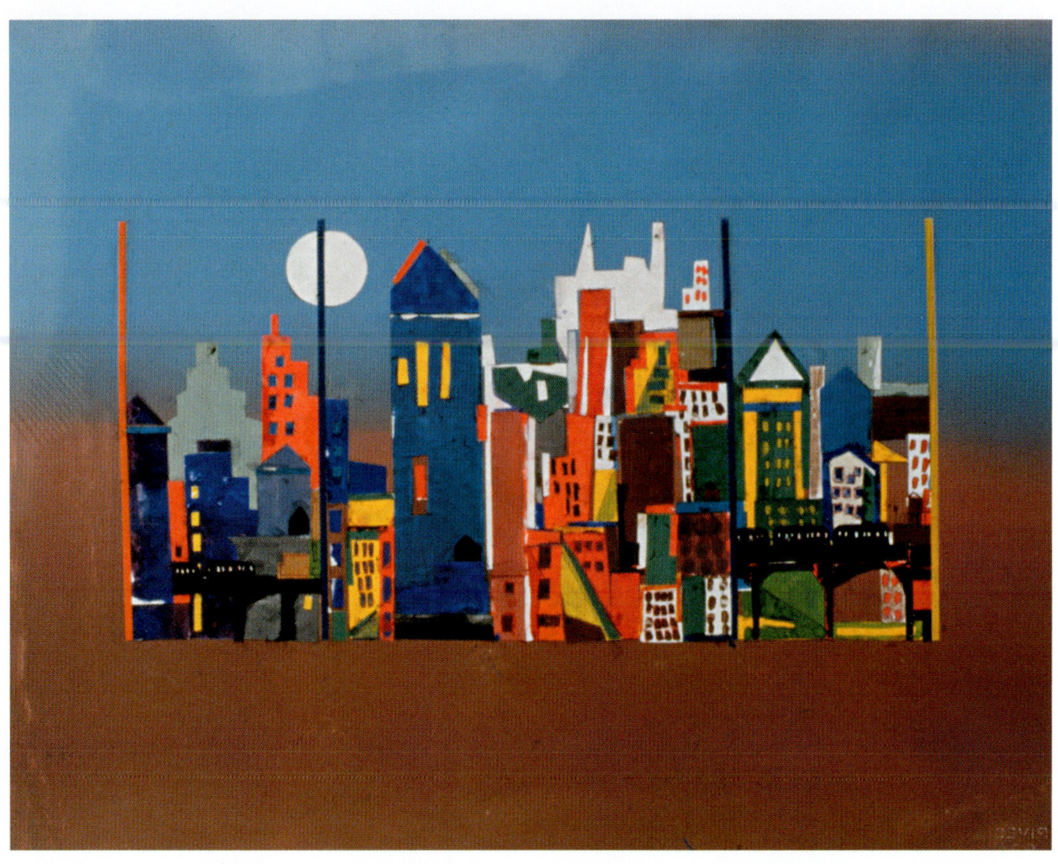

26

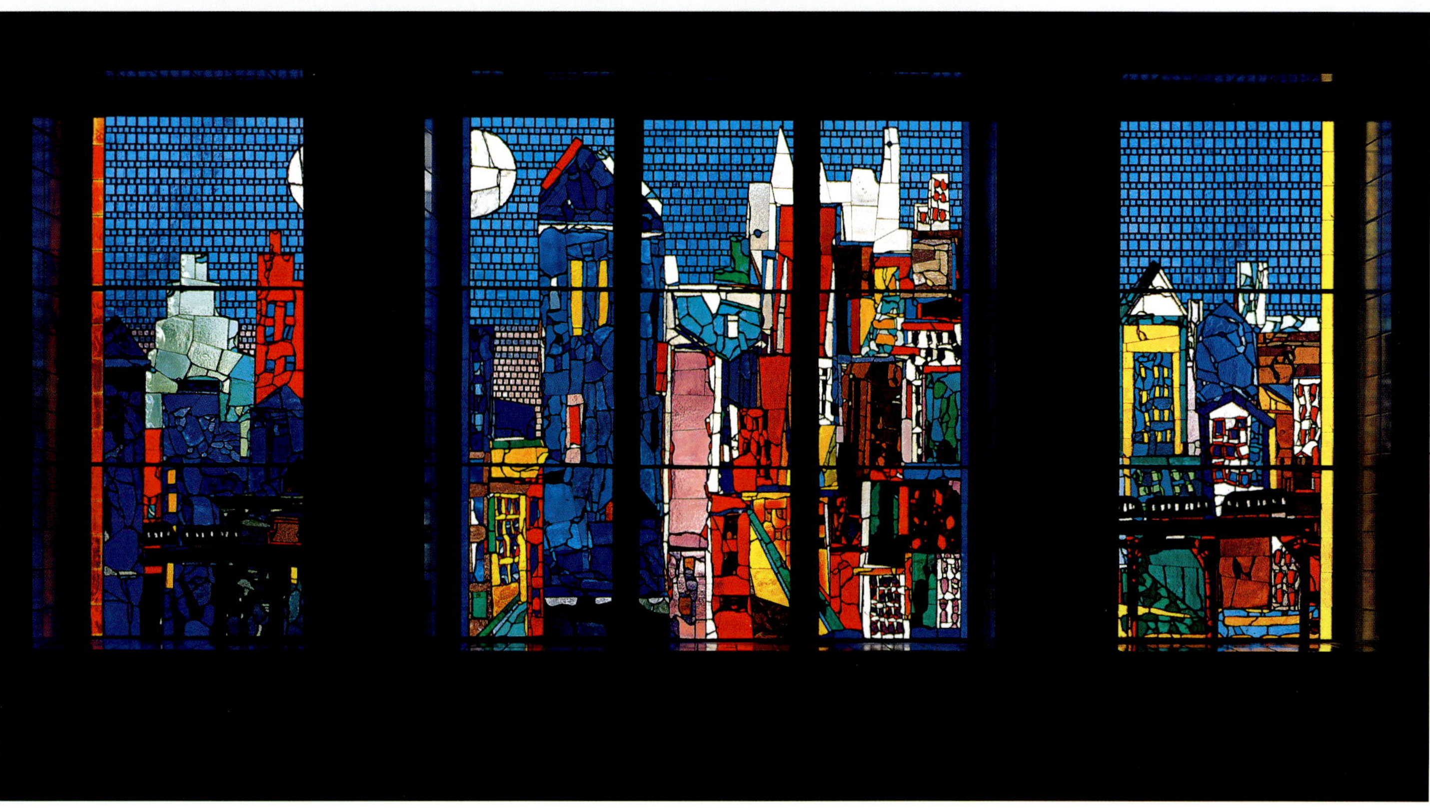

27

CHRONOLOGICAL LIST OF WORKS IN THE EXHIBITION

NOTES

BIBLIOGRAPHY

PHOTOGRAPHY CREDITS

INDEX

CHRONOLOGICAL LIST OF WORKS IN THE EXHIBITION

Within each year, firmly dated works are listed alphabetically. Works of uncertain date are placed before and after firmly dated works, depending on where they are judged to belong.

Works will be exhibited in all of the following venues, unless locations are specifically indicated.

W: National Gallery of Art, Washington

S: San Francisco Museum of Modern Art

D: Dallas Museum of Art

N: Whitney Museum of American Art, New York

A: High Museum of Art, Atlanta

The Visitation, 1941 (no. 1)

The Family, c. 1941 (no. 2)

They That Are Delivered from the Noise of the Archers, 1942 (no. 3) WSDN

Presage, c. 1942 (no. 4)

Madonna and Child, 1945 (no. 13)

Untitled (Crucifixion), 1945 (no. 6)

Untitled (En Route to Calvary), 1945 (no. 5)

Untitled (He Is Arisen), 1945 (no. 7)

Untitled (The Resurrection), 1945 (no. 8)

The Ascension of Christ in Glory, c. 1945/1946 (no. 11)

Untitled (Lorca Series), c. 1946 (no. 10)

Now the Dove and the Leopard Wrestle, 1946 (no. 9)

Two Figures, c. 1946 (no. 12)

A Walk in Paradise Gardens, 1955 (no. 14)

Harlequin, c. 1956 (no. 16)

North of the River, 1962 (no. 15)

Baptism, 1964 (no. 23)

The Burial, 1964 (no. 21)

Cotton, 1964 (no. 25) D

Evening Meal of Prophet Peterson, 1964 (no. 17)

Evening, 9:10, 461 Lenox Avenue, 1964 (no. 18)

Expulsion from Paradise, 1964 (no. 19) WN

Expulsion from Paradise, 1964 (no. 20)

Mysteries, 1964 (no. 30) SD

Pittsburgh Memory, 1964 (no. 29)

Prevalence of Ritual: Baptism, 1964 (no. 24) S

Prevalence of Ritual: Conjur Woman, 1964 (no. 143)

Prevalence of Ritual: Conjur Woman as an Angel, 1964 (no. 41)

Prevalence of Ritual: Tidings, 1964 (no. 37)

Prevalence of Ritual: Tidings, 1964 (no. 38)

Sermons: The Walls of Jericho, 1964 (no. 142) W

Spring Way, 1964 (no. 31)

The Street, 1964 (no. 32) W

The Street, 1964 (no. 33)

Train Whistle Blues: I, 1964 (no.27)

Train Whistle Blues: II, 1964 (no. 28) WN

Untitled, 1964 (nos. 40a,b)

Watching the Good Trains Go By, 1964 (no. 26)

Village of Yo, c. 1964 (no. 43) WS

Early Morning, c. 1964 (no. 35)

City of Brass, c. 1965 (no. 42)

Farm Couple, c. 1965 (no. 46) WN

Ritual, c. 1965 (no. 22) N

Pittsburgh, 1965 (no. 45) DNA

Southern Recall, 1965 (no. 47)

Childhood Memories, 1965/1966 (no. 34)

Three Men, 1966–1967 (no. 48)

Tomorrow I May Be Far Away, 1966/1967 (no. 50)

Backyard, 1967 (no. 54)

Illusionist at 4 P.M., 1967 (no. 56)

Monday Morning, 1967 (no. 55) WN

Old Couple, 1967 (no. 51) WSDN

La Primavera, 1967 (no. 52)

Sunday Morning Breakfast, 1967 (no. 53)

Three Folk Musicians, 1967 (no. 49)

Palm Sunday Procession, 1967–1968 (no. 57)

Strange Morning, Interior, 1968 (no. 58)

Mauritius, 1969 (no. 77)

Susannah at the Bath, 1969 (no. 93)

Prelude to Troy, c. 1969 (no. 140)

City Lights, c. 1970 (no. 68)

Conjur: A Masked Folk Ballet, c. 1970 (nos. 135a–p)

Carolina Interior, 1970 (no. 102)

Family, 1970 (no. 44)

Ritual Bayou, 1970 (no. 98)

Two Moons of Luvernia, 1970 (no. 95)

The Visitor, 1970/1974 (no. 39)

Untitled, c. 1971 (no. 69)

Untitled (Prevalence of Ritual), c. 1971 (no. 81)

The Apprenticeship of Jelly Roll Morton, 1971 (no. 94)

Blue Snake, 1971 (no. 123)

Conjunction, 1971 (no. 59)

Down Home, Also, 1971 (no. 137)

Sun and Candle, 1971 (no. 36)

Mother and Child, c. 1972 (no. 91)

The Block II, 1972 (no. 63)

Noah, Third Day, 1972 (no. 80)

Untitled (Girl in a Pond), 1972 (no. 99)

Berkeley—The City and Its People, 1973 (no. 62)

Delilah, 1973 (no. 79) WSDN

Of the Blues: At the Savoy, 1974 (no. 70)

Of the Blues: Carolina Shout, 1974 (no. 73)

Of the Blues: Kansas City 4/4, 1974 (no. 74) A

Of the Blues: Mecklenburg County, Saturday Night, 1974 (no. 72)

Of the Blues: Wrapping It Up at the Lafayette, 1974 (no. 71) WS

The Blues, 1975 (no. 64) WSDN

Blues Singer, 1975 (no. 108)

Conjur Woman, 1975 (no. 97) WDN

Departure from Planet Earth, 1975 (no. 65)

The Family, 1975 (no. 61)

The Street, 1975 (no. 66)

Captivity and Resistance, 1976 (no. 78)

The Street (Composition for Richard Wright), c. 1977 (no. 67)

Caribbean Forest, 1977 (no. 100)

Madeline Jones' Wonderful Garden, 1977 (no. 101)

Odysseus: The Fall of Troy, 1977 (no. 82)

Odysseus: Odysseus Leaves Circe, 1977 (no. 85) SDNA

Odysseus: Poseidon, The Sea God—Enemy of Odysseus, 1977 (no. 83)

Odysseus: The Sea Nymph, 1977 (no. 84)

Village of Yo, 1977 (no. 134)

The Conjur Woman, c. 1977 (no. 133) WSDN

Odysseus: Battle with the Cicones, c. 1977 (no. 89) WSDN

Odysseus: Circe, c. 1977 (no. 87) WSDN

Odysseus: Odysseus Enters at the Door Disguised as an Old Man, c. 1977 (no. 90) WSDN

Odysseus: Odysseus Rescued by a Sea Nymph, c. 1977 (no. 88) WSDN

Odysseus: Poseidon, The Sea God, c. 1977 (no. 86) WSDN

Reclining Nude, c. 1977 (no. 96)

Profile/Part I, The Twenties: Mecklenburg County, Conjur Woman and the Virgin, 1978 (no. 116) SDNA

Profile/Part I, The Twenties: Mecklenburg County, Holiness Church Revival, 1978 (no. 114)

Profile/Part I, The Twenties: Mecklenburg County, Railroad Shack Sporting House, 1978 (no. 113)

Profile/Part I, The Twenties: Pittsburgh Memories, Farewell Eugene, 1978 (no. 115)

Thank You... For F.U.M.L. (Funking Up My Life), 1978 (no. 75)

Mecklenburg Morning, c. 1978 (no. 103)

Rain Forest—Pool, c. 1978 (no. 109)

Mecklenburg Morning, c. 1979 (no. 104)

Falling Star, 1979 (no. 111) DNA

Midtown Manhattan, 1979/1980 (no. 121)

Waterfall, c. 1980 (no. 110)

Zach Whyte's Beau Brummell Band, 1980 (no. 106)

Conversation II, 1981 (no. 60)

Profile/Part II, The Thirties: Artist with Painting and Model, 1981 (no. 141)

Profile/Part II, The Thirties: Midtown Sunset, 1981 (no. 118)

Profile/Part II, The Thirties: Uptown Sunday Night Session, 1981 (no. 117)

Untitled (Shrouds), early 1980s (no. 139) DNA

Card Players, 1982 (no. 138)

City Lites, 1982 (no. 120)

Fitting for the New Dress, 1982 (no. 112) WS

Midtown, 1982 (no. 119)

Birds in Paradise, c. 1982 (no. 127)

Celebrations: Trumpet Spot, Wynton, c. 1983 (no. 107)

Li'l Dan, The Drummer Boy: A Civil War Story, c. 1983 (nos. 132a–c)

Mirror and Banjo, c. 1983 (no. 105)

Mecklenburg Autumn: October—Toward Paw's Creek, 1983 (no. 124)

Piano Lesson, 1983 (no. 136)

Woman and Child Reading, Untitled, c. 1984 (nos. 92a,b)

The Carnival Begins, 1984 (no. 129) DNA

In a Green Shade (Hommage [sic] to Marvell), 1984 (no. 128)

Obeah in a Trance, 1984 (no. 130)

Pittsburgh Memories, 1984 (no. 122) WS

J Mood, c. 1985 (no. 76)

Summer (Maudell Sleet's July Garden), 1985 (no. 125)

Winter (Time of the Hawk), 1985 (no. 126)

An Obeah Princess; Her Loa Leaves at Dawn, 1986 (no. 131)

NOTES

Romare Bearden: The Spaces Between

RUTH FINE

1 Marshall McLuhan's *Understanding Media: The Extensions of Man,* published in 1964, includes a chapter titled "The Medium Is the Message." This language and its implications were topics of wide-ranging discussion among artists of the period, especially those like Bearden who were concerned with experimental artistic practices.

2 This 1914 date appears in many solo and group exhibition catalogues during his lifetime as well as in most biographical data on file at Cordier & Ekstrom, Inc., his long-term dealer. It also appears in Mary Schmidt Campbell, "Romare Bearden: A Creative Mythology," Ph.D. diss., Syracuse University, 1982, 3. Campbell worked closely with Bearden and his wife, Nanette, on this and other projects for which he supplied important data. This body of evidence suggests that Bearden had adopted 1914 as his birthdate for public use. Campbell's study was an invaluable resource during work on this book.

3 The Baptismal Registry was first reported by Myron Schwartzman in *Romare Bearden: His Life and Art* (New York, 1990), 15. Dr. Schwartzman's text remains a primary resource for biographical information about Bearden and his family. In addition, we are extremely grateful for his generosity in sharing the recorded interviews he conducted with Bearden on June 4 and 19, 1984; May 7 and 14, 1985; October 15, 1985; and April 8, 1986 (accompanied by painter Gwendolyn Wells); and with Leonard Bates on January 12, 1988. These provided data and opinions he did not publish that are included here. All quotations from Bearden and references to Bearden's remarks to Schwartzman not otherwise cited are from these conversations.

4 Given these 1927 and 1942 documents, one wonders if Bearden assumed the 1914 birthdate in the early 1950s, perhaps when he met Nanette Rohan, who is recorded as having been born in 1927 and thus was considerably younger than a man born in 1911 or 1912. A New York University transcript documenting his studies beginning in the 1932–1933 school year records his date of birth as "9-2-11," his place of birth as "Pittsburgh," and his name as "Howard Bearden, Jr."

5 Howard has been among the names used by Bearden. However, it does not appear in the Baptismal Registry where Fred Romare Bearden is recorded, with Harry written in below Fred Romare. Jean M. Frye's search of the Baptismal Registry in October and November 2002 revealed no record for a child similarly named and baptized in 1912. We are indebted to Ms. Frye for her research into both the church and civic records, aiding our effort to determine Bearden's birthdate.

6 See Janette Thomas Greenwood, *Bittersweet Legacy: The Black and White "Better Classes" in Charlotte, 1850–1910* (Chapel Hill, North Carolina, 1994); and John R. Rogers and Amy T. Rogers, *Charlotte, Its Historic Neighborhoods* (Dover, New Hampshire, 1996).

7 Bearden's memories of Lutherville included Mrs. Johnson who made "watermelon cake," which Bearden delivered to her customers. He was often accompanied by her husband, E.C. Johnson, a blind guitarist (Schwartzman 1990, 24–26).

8 *Colored Charlotte,* printed by A.M.E. Zion Job Print (Charlotte, North Carolina, 1915), 7, on file in the Carolina Room at the Charlotte/Mecklenburg County Library. *Colored Charlotte* was published by the Hon. C.H. Watson in connection with the fiftieth anniversary of the freedom of the negro in the county of Mecklenburg and the city of Charlotte, North Carolina, with an introduction by Bishop G.W. Clinton. Among business statistics were included three real estate companies, 31 restaurants, 30 nurses, 12 doctors, 87 ministers, 20 professors and 103 city and county teachers, 40 bricklayers, and 222 insurance agents.

9 Documentation of the year the family moved north has not been located. Bearden reports that he thought his parents were living in New York and that he was born during a visit to Charlotte; he also cites this as taking place in 1914. Tape-recorded interview of Bearden by Henri Ghent, June 1968, transcription in Archives of American Art (AAA), Smithsonian Institution, Washington, D.C., 4 (here referred to as Ghent transcription).

10 See *Langston Hughes and the Chicago Defender: Essays on Race, Politics, and Culture, 1942–1962,* ed. Christopher C. De Santis (Urbana, Illinois, 1995).

Bessye Bearden was a dynamic figure. She was the first woman appointed to the New York City school board, a member of the executive board of the New York Urban League, an organizer of the National Council of Negro Women, and the founder and first president of the Negro Women's Democratic Association. She also played a small role in Oscar Micheaux's 1921 film *The Gunsaulus Mystery* and functioned as the first "chaperone" of the Girl Friends, a sorority or social club for young, college-educated African-American women. See the invaluable resource, Calvin Tomkins, "Profiles: Romare Bearden, Putting Something over Something Else," *New Yorker* 53 (November 28, 1977): 55; Charles Musser, Corey K. Creekmur, Pearl Bowser, J. Ronald Green, Charlene Regester, and Louise Spence, "An Oscar Micheaux Filmography: From the Silents through His Transition to Sound, 1919–1931," appendix B in *Oscar Micheaux & His Circle: African-American Filmmaking and Race Cinema of the Silent Era,* Pearl Bowser, Jane Gaines, and Charles Musser, eds. (Bloomington, Indiana, 2001), 241; and Lawrence Otis Graham, *Our Kind of People: Inside America's Black Upper Class* (New York, 2000 edition), 116.

11 Ellison's remark was in a memorial address for Bearden, delivered April 6, 1988, and printed, in part, in "Bearden," *Callaloo* 11 (Summer 1988): 417. Harry Henderson, in conversation with the author, December 21, 2001, told of the elder Bearden's pride in his son's far-reaching success, the artist's mother having died prior to his first show outside of Harlem. All information and quotations attributed to Henderson, unless otherwise noted, are from this conversation.

12 Henderson has recounted that about 1940 he was managing editor for the magazine *Friday* for which photographer Sam Shaw was art director. A *Friday* article about Horace Pippin introduced them to the work of African-American artists. When *Friday* closed in 1941, Henderson and Shaw became a freelance writer/photographer team, creating stories for a variety of magazines and remaining extremely interested in art by African Americans.

They met Bearden after the war and he "often visited the Henderson-Shaw office, telling stories of a mythical character, 'Slow-down Brown.' Another visitor was playwright Barrie Stavis [who] became so excited by a Bearden on their mantel that he interviewed Bearden and wrote the essay for [an upcoming show] at the Samuel Kootz Gallery. . . . [Henderson] and Shaw frequently visited Bearden's 125th Street studio and Shaw made many pictures of him that are among the important visual documents of Bearden at that time." Henderson "later became a medical writer-editor. Bearden often visited [him] and they would take sandwiches to the East River and discuss developments in art, especially the development of abstract art which initially excited Bearden. However, it was remote from the life of African Americans which bothered him." After a summer of discussion in 1966 the two men began work on what became *Six Black Masters of American Art* (1972) and *A History of African-American Artists: From 1792 to the Present* (1993). "Bearden selected the artists to be covered and [Henderson] interviewed many of the artists. . . . To complete the book they met every Wednesday evening for more than 15 years and then met sporadically. Unfortunately, Bearden died before the book was published, but he was proud of what had been achieved." Letter from Henderson to the author, February 4, 2003. I am extremely grateful to Mr. Henderson for sharing his voluminous memories of Romare Bearden and for other assistance.

13 In Campbell 1982, 40, note 3, Bearden's academic major is given as education, citing the archives of New York University. The degree itself, as well as Bearden's NYU transcript, are at the Romare Bearden Foundation, New York. We are particularly grateful to Pam Henly for information about Bearden's year at Lincoln University.

14 According to Katherine Kominis, March 14, 2003, e-mail to Carmenita Higginbotham, "Howard Bearden" created three covers and seven illustrations for the student publication at Boston University, *The Beanpot*. Bearden's cartoons appeared in the following issues of *The Medley:* December 1933; January, March, April, and December 1934; and March and May 1935. One of his cartoons is featured on the cover of the October 1934 issue. The issues for December 1935 and March and May 1936 list Howard Bearden as a member of the Art Board for the publication. Also, in "Rectangular Structure in My Montage Paintings," *Leonardo* 2 (January 1969): 11, Bearden mistakenly gives the name of the New York University journal as the *Magpie*, which was, rather, the name of the journal at DeWitt Clinton High School.

As to Bearden's essay on the history of cartooning, an untitled manuscript by Howard Bearden (the name Bearden was using at that time) is on file at the Schomburg Center for Research in Black Culture, New York Public Library. At the end of it Bearden noted, "I am a cartoonist myself, so a lot of the material I already knew, from my work and contacts in the field." The sources he cited in his article (corrected here for spelling and details of titles) are Clifford K. Berryman, *The Development of the Cartoon;* Clare Briggs, *How to Draw Cartoons;* John Campbell Cory, *The Cartoonist's Art;* George Paston, *Social Caricature in the 18th Century;* and Laurance Shaffer, *Children's Interpretations of Cartoons.*

15 See also Gary A. Reynolds, "American Critics and the Harmon Foundation," in Gary A. Reynolds and Beryl J. Wright, *Against the Odds: African-American Artists and the Harmon Foundation* (Newark, N.J., 1989), 107–119.

16 Romare Bearden, "Sharing Yesterdays with Norman Lewis (1909–1979)," *New York Amsterdam News,* December 15, 1979, 27. See also *Augusta Savage and the Art Schools of Harlem* [exh. cat., Schomburg Center for Research in Black Culture, New York Public Library] (New York, 1988).

17 Published in *Romare Bearden: A Memorial Exhibition* [exh. cat., ACA Galleries] (New York, 1989), unnumbered leaf between 30 and 31.

18 The descriptive categories are from James Hall, *Mercy Mercy Me: African American Culture and the American Sixties* (New York, 2001), in his chapter "The Prevalence of Ritual in an Age of Change: Romare Bearden," 159.

19 See Carl Senna, *The Black Press and the Struggle for Civil Rights* (New York, 1993) for a discussion of the African-American press during the period Bearden worked for it.

20 In the introduction to *Romare Bearden: Paintings and Projections* [exh. cat., The Art Gallery, State University of New York at Albany] (Albany, 1968), not paginated, Ralph Ellison recalled becoming aware of Bearden's work in the late 1930s when he was "painting scenes of the Depression strongly influenced by the Mexican muralists." Although the paintings we have seen from that period show little of the muralists' impact, based on these political cartoons from the mid-1930s, one can imagine that impact playing a role in paintings as well. Ellison's essay remains one of the most useful introductions to Bearden's work.

21 "Romare Bearden: Visual Artist," interview with Camille Billops and James V. Hatch, December 6, 1972, in *Artist and Influence* 17 (New York, 1998), 32 (cited hereafter as Billops and Hatch 1998).

22 Stephanie Cassidy, archivist at the Art Students League of New York, to Carmenita Higginbotham, letter, November 11, 2002, with copies of Bearden's registration records. We are grateful to Ms. Cassidy for her assistance. Bearden's address in 1933 is listed as 1902 Seventh Avenue, in 1935 as 50 Morningside Avenue. Ms. Cassidy also reported that Bearden was elected to membership in the League on January 15, 1936, and dropped from membership in September 1938. He later was made an honorary member, an acknowledgment of service to the school and to the art world.

23 Author's telephone conversation with James Rosenquist, May 15, 2002.

24 Widespread respect for Grosz's draftsmanship is reflected in the fact that his graphite portrait of his mother-in-law, *Anna Peter,* 1926–27, purchased for the Museum of Modern Art by Paul J. Sachs, was the first drawing to enter the permanent collection, in 1929. See William S. Lieberman's introduction to *The Museum of Modern Art, Drawings: Recent Acquisitions. An Announcement of the Paul J. Sachs Committee* (New York: 1962).

For the rest of his life Bearden's practice included the close study of works by these and other masters. See Kennel, in this volume, which provides an extended discussion of this topic.

25 The connection with Dada is discussed in Hall 2001 in his chapter on Bearden, 151–86.

26 Ghent transcription, 4.

27 For the quotation about Baziotes, see Ghent transcription, 9. Graham's text was first printed in 1937 by l'Imprimerie Crozatier in Paris in an edition of one thousand copies and was published in the United States later that year by Delphic Studios. It was reissued by Johns Hopkins University Press in 1971, annotated from unpublished writings by Graham and with an introduction by Marcia Epstein Allentuck and a foreword by artist Dorothy Dehner.

In conversation with Schwartzman, Bearden spoke at length about Graham; in addition to praising his text, Bearden said he had studied drawing with him.

28 Campbell 1982, 117.

29 In January 1936, just months after the Museum of Modern Art (MoMA) mounted the exhibition *African Negro Art,* Graham organized a loan exhibition for New York's Jacques Seligmann Galleries that included work from his own collection as well as that of MoMA curator James Johnson Sweeney. See "African Sculpture Show Illustrates One of Oldest Art Traditions," *Art Digest* 10 (January 1, 1936): 5–6.

30 "The studio" was the designation used throughout the taped conversation between Schwartzman and Leonard Bates (January 12, 1988). Leonard was the younger brother of Addison Bates, and he reported living at the studio in 1936 and 1937, and again, with Myrtle, in 1939 through 1942. His reminiscences of 306, how it looked, how it functioned, and who passed through while they were there are essential to our description. See also Bearden and Henderson 1993, 234–35, and Jeff Richardson Donaldson; "Generation '306'—Harlem, New York," Ph.D. diss., Northwestern University, June 1974.

31 This list of participants is based on several sources, including Billops and Hatch 1998, 31, and the conversation between Schwartzman and the Bateses.

32 I am grateful to Nikki Alma Rose Greene for sharing with me her master's thesis for the University of Delaware, fall 2002, "Romare Bearden and All That Jazz: Improvising within 'The Veil' of Double Consciousness." Greene's study was helpful to the clarification of my own thinking about this subject and brought to my attention Richard Cullen Rath, "Echo and Narcissus: The Afrocentric Pragmatism of W. E. B. Du Bois," *Journal of American History* 84 (September 1997): 461–95.

33 Bates told Schwartzman (taped interview, January 12, 1988) he assisted Bearden in writing this statement. If so, it sets a pattern for collaboration in many of his writing efforts, with Albert Murray and Harry Henderson playing particularly important roles.

34 Bearden in Ghent transcription, 2. Avis Berman, "Romare Bearden: 'I Paint out of the Tradition of the Blues,'" *Art News* 79 (December 1980): 64, gives 1938 as the date Bearden moved into the studio at 33 West 125th Street.

35 See Billops and Hatch 1998, 37. The quotation is from Don Bishop, "Bearden Is Rising as Modern Artist," *Charlotte Observer,* August 3, 1952, 2D.

36 See Laura Katzman "Mechanical Vision: Photography and Mass Media in Ben Shahn's Sacco and Venzetti Series," in *Ben Shahn and the Passion of Sacco and Venzetti* [exh. cat., Jersey City Museum] (Jersey City, 2001), 52–80, 126–135, for useful parallels to Bearden's use of photographic sources.

37 See Desmond Rochfort, *Mexican Muralists: Orozco, Rivera, Siqueiros* (London, 1993), 99–111 (Orozco); 130–33 (Rivera's mural was destroyed in 1934 because he refused to remove a portrait of Lenin in his composition).

38 Peyton Boswell, "Painters without Pigment," *Art Digest* 16 (October 1, 1941), 3.

39 The importance of the photographic record to African American families, repeatedly affirmed within Bearden's interiors, is documented in *Picturing Us: African American Identity in Photography* (New York, 1994), ed. Deborah Willis; and Deborah Willis, *Reflections in Black: A History of Black Photographers, 1840 to the Present* (New York, 2000). See also Jackie Napolean Wilson, *Hidden Witness: African-American Images from the Birth of Photography to the Civil War* (New York, 1999).

40 Most cultures invest the sun and moon with symbolic meaning too complex to discuss in detail here. Briefly stated, both are seen as sources of fertility and light and as symbols of death and regeneration/resurrection. Gender-specific associations vary widely. One of many sources for this data is James Hall, *Illustrated Dictionary of Symbols in Eastern and Western Art* (New York, 1994).

41 See Sharon F. Patton's essay of the same title in *Memory and Metaphor: The Art of Romare Bearden 1940–1987* [exh. cat., Studio Museum in Harlem] (New York, 1991), 24.

42 Bearden, "The Negro Artist and Modern Art," *Opportunity,* December 1934, 371–72.

43 For this reason we have re-dated to c. 1942 *Presage,* previously dated to 1944 but with no support for the later date on the painting or in the literature.

44 Crosby and Porter formed their partnership in autumn 1943, opening G Place Gallery in a "completely modernized antebellum gingerbread house" with an exhibition of work by surrealists Max Ernst, Roberto Sebastian Antonio Matta Echaurren, Yves Tanguy, and Wilfredo Lam. A[lfred].D[avidson]. in "G Place Gallery," *Art Digest* 18 [November 15, 1943]: 15. With Crosby's sights on Europe and the avant-garde and Porter's on the American midwest, it was a curious mix, but the *Art Digest* note suggested that there was "little doubt such a gallery will be welcome in the Capital City which has been inexplicably barren in centers of modern art." In October 1944, approximately eight months after Bearden's first show, *Art Digest* announced that G Place Gallery henceforth would be called David Porter Gallery, so one assumes that Crosby moved on in other directions. Despite the announcement of the name change, so far as we know, Bearden's 1945 exhibition has always been listed as taking place at G Place Gallery.

Caresse Crosby's gossipy autobiography *The Passionate Years,* Ecco Press edition (New York, 1979), mentions Bearden only once (page 234), in reference to an exhibition that followed the two shows of his work that she had organized in Washington: "It was the fall of 1945 in Paris, just after the war. I was one of the first Americans to return. I did not bring coffee and rice to my friends but I had brought them drawings by the American artists [Washington-based] Pietro Lazzari and Romare Bearden, and I arranged to show these at John Devoluy's minute gallery in the rue Furstenberg. I had invited friends and artists by telephone; Paris was starving for contact with the American world of art and everyone flocked. Gertrude Stein came stalking in with her white poodle at her heels. She sat in the center of the tiny room and almost stole the show, my show." There is no mention of the G Place Gallery as such, although on page 351 Crosby mentions a Washington gallery: "My contribution to the 'war effort' was to open the Crosby Gallery of Modern Art." I thank Bearden's long-time friend Sidney Wallach for sending me Crosby's book.

45 "The Negro Artist Comes of Age," *Art News* 43 (February 1–14, 1945): 16. The anonymous reviewer ends his or her comments (page 30) with the optimistic suggestion that the exhibition "establishes [the Negro artists'] integration with trends, styles, and standards of all American art."

46 Campbell 1982, 125. According to Henderson, Bearden was one of two specialists in the department on the gypsy community. He recalled that Bearden wrote and illustrated a pamphlet about the group to provide welfare departments throughout the country a better understanding of the gypsy culture. Henderson mentioned, in particular, Bearden's interest in fortune tellers, and one wonders if they provided him a link to the conjure women of his childhood.

47 Romare Bearden to Walter Quirt, July 10, 1945, AAA. The letter also informed Quirt that four works had been sold from the Washington show, one of them to "Saarinen, the big Finnish architect." Henderson recalled taking Bearden's cartoons to editors at *Collier's* who felt the drawings were fine but the "gags" were too politically controversial for their use.

48 Sharon F. Patton points out in "A Divine Presence in the Art of Romare Bearden," *Prism* 15 (1992): 29, that, despite the title of the exhibition, the series of twenty-four watercolors and oils embraced subjects from other parts of the Bible. Campbell 1982, 129–37, provides a lengthy discussion of the series.

49 Two related finished images are reproduced in *Memory and Metaphor* 1991: *Resurrection* (acquired by Duke Ellington), 28, figure 6; and *He Is Arisen* (acquired by MoMA, New York), 83, plate 1.

50 The admiration for Rouault by both American and European painters at midcentury is a subject yet to be explored in depth, with the exception of a 1994 Ph.D. dissertation, "The Iconography of Georges Rouault (France, Painting, Engraving)," by Soo-Yun Kang, University of California, Santa Barbara. In respect to Bearden's Passion series, Patton (1992, 30) suggests that "schematic figures defined by sweeping and angular black lines...give the appearance of French medieval stained glass windows or paintings by the French expressionist Georges Rouault."

51 Patton, *Memory and Metaphor* 1991, 27.

52 Lowery S. Sims, "Romare Bearden: An Artist's Odyssey," in *Romare Bearden: Origins and Progressions* [exh. cat., Detroit Institute of Arts] (Detroit, 1986), 13.

53 A fascinating oil, *Untitled*, late 1940s, reproduced by Ann Eden Gibson in *Abstract Expressionism: Other Politics* (New Haven, 1997), 67, demonstrates how far into abstraction Bearden moved during this period.

54 The titles of the oils and watercolors listed in the exhibition brochure do not mirror each other; we have been unable to determine the title of the watercolor included here. Campbell (1982, 137–50) includes a lengthy discussion of the Lorca series.

55 *Cordozo Studies in Law and Literature* 2 (Fall–Winter 1990) reprints Stavis' play about Galileo, *Lamp at Midnight*, and includes more than a dozen essays commenting on it and other aspects of Stavis' life and work. Although Bearden is not mentioned, Ezra Goldstein's "The Passionate, Personal Plays of Barrie Stavis," 279–88, in this volume is useful in suggesting parallels between Bearden's and Stavis' morality and ambition for their work.

56 Leslie Stainton, *Lorca: A Dream of a Life* (New York, 1999), 220–21. The chapter "New World: 1929–30," 214–42, offers an account of Lorca's stay in the United States.

57 For a discussion of Bearden's encounter with Miró, see Schwartzman 1990, 106, 146–49; photograph, 103.

58 Fred Orton, *Figuring Jasper Johns* (Cambridge, Mass., 1994), 24.

59 Marie and Roy R. Neuberger, *Modern American Paintings from the Collection of Mr. and Mrs. Roy R. Neuberger* [exh. cat., Samuel M. Kootz Gallery] (New York, 1946), not paginated.

60 Judith Kaye Reed, "Art at Christmas along Fifty-Seventh Street," *Art Digest* 20 (December 1, 1945): 15.

61 Niveau had opened its doors in May 1943 with an exhibition of works by twentieth-century French artists. In 1948, in addition to Bearden's show, exhibitions by Anna von Schusert, Raoul Dufy, and Jacques Letord were on view. One can only wonder how Bearden was meant to fit into this group. In a fortuitous confluence of data, the exhibition review that precedes the announcement of Niveau's opening in *Art Digest* 17 (May 15, 1943): 7, covers an exhibition of work by Jacob Lawrence under the headline "Effective Protest by Lawrence of Harlem." Lawrence is described by M[aude] R[iley] as a natural designer with little formal training who makes "a contribution to the arts from and for his race."

62 Edward Ellis, "Welfare Worker Arrives in Art," *New York World-Telegram*, October 21, 1949, 31.

63 In November 1951, through Gimbels department store, in a hideous act of disrespect to Browne and Holty, Kootz sold at greatly reduced prices more than three hundred of their works. Henderson reported that Sam Shaw and he had advised Bearden against accepting Kootz's offer of $2,000 per year in exchange for all of his work. Bearden's acceptance of this advice presumably saved him from similar insult. For background on Kootz, see Serge Guilbaut, trans. Arthur Goldhammer, *How New York Stole the Idea of Modern Art: Abstract Expressionism, Freedom, and the Cold War* (Chicago, 1983), 64ff.

64 This is supported by Gibson (1997, xi), who sets out the establishment hierarchy of New York galleries in the late 1940s, noting the "triumvirate composed of the now legendary galleries of Betty Parsons, Samuel Kootz, and Charles Egan, a triangle of early eminence sometimes squared by the addition of Marian Willard."

65 Hall 2001, 24.

66 The 1934 essay was in the December issue of *Opportunity: A Journal of Negro Life*, 371–72; the 1946 essay in the November issue of *Critique: A Review of Contemporary Art*, 16–22. The quotation is on page 22.

67 Keith Morrison, "Global Village of African American Art," in *African American Visual Aesthetics: A Postmodernist View*, ed. David C. Driskell (Washington, D.C., 1995), 30. The point begs the questions as to the degree formalism must be a conscious concern and whether narrative concerns necessarily diminish attention to formalist ones.

68 Romare Bearden, "Rectangular Structure in My Montage Paintings," *Leonardo* 2 (January 1969): 11; Bearden spoke of Murray's contributions to this article in his conversations with Schwartzman. Romare Bearden and Carl Holty, *The Painter's Mind: A Study of the Relations of Structure and Space in Painting*, Introduction by Ralph Ellison (New York, 1969; reprinted New York and London, 1981). These formalist concerns were widespread during the 1960s. Bearden and Holty did not include a bibliography in *The Painter's Mind*, but one assumes that they would have been familiar with Charles Bouleau's 1963 publication *The Painter's Secret Geometry: A Study of Composition in Art*, trans. Jonathan Griffin, with a preface by artist Jacques Villon, which tends to similar ideas.

69 Several of Bearden's friends and associates have confirmed that he did not do photography himself, except possibly snapshots, and was not knowledgeable about the techniques of enlarging, printing, etc. Rather he depended upon others to do this work for him, generally friends who were professionals in the field.

70 André Malraux, trans. Stuart Gilbert, *The Psychology of Art*, 3 vols.: *Museum without Walls*, *The Creative Art*, and *The Twilight of the Absolute*, Bollingen series 24 (New York, 1949–50). *The Voices of Silence* was published in English in 1953 and *The Metamorphosis of the Gods* in 1960; both were also translated by Gilbert.

Georgia, recalled that Bearden was very successful tracking down and staying in touch with the gypsy families for whom he was responsible (conversation with the author, November 26, 2001).

149 In 1970 Bearden received a John Solomon Guggenheim Foundation grant in support of his research. Henderson reports that Bearden, who selected the artists, was adamant at first that neither illustrators nor teachers be included, believing that both professions were harmful to serious artistic practice. He relented with regard to teachers, however, accepting the seriousness of the art of such teacher/practitioners as Charles Alston and Hale Woodruff. He also was adamant that he not be included, and Henderson respected this decision after Bearden's death. According to Henderson, the collaboration worked this way: Bearden made notes about the artists, Henderson drafted text, and Bearden reviewed it. They met on Canal Street weekly, usually on Wednesday nights, the discussions ending when Henderson had to race for the last train to his home along the Hudson. The book was finished in the 1970s, and publishers' delays were responsible for its not being issued during Bearden's lifetime.

Bearden published numerous catalogue introductions and exhibition reviews on behalf of other artists, including Jacob Lawrence, Alex Kosta, and Sam Middleton.

150 See Benny Andrews, "The B.E.C.C.: Black Emergency Cultural Coalition," *Arts* [magazine] 44 (summer 1970), 18–20.

151 Billops and Hatch 1998, 33. David C. Driskell et al., *Amistad II: Afro-American Art* [exh. cat., Fisk University Department of Art] (Nashville, Tenn., 1975), is an important catalogue, useful in many ways, and includes Clifton H. Johnson's "The Amistad Incident," 15–34, a cogent overview of the events and their aftermath.

152 See *The Sculpture of Richard Hunt* [exh. cat., Museum of Modern Art] (New York, 1971), with introduction by William S. Lieberman and statements by the artist.

153 Paul Allman, "Art Who," *Berkeley Gazette,* November 1971.

154 *The Block* is published in full and in several details in *The Block,* with poems by Langston Hughes selected by Lowery S. Sims and Daisy Murray Voigt and an introduction by Bill Cosby (New York, 1995). Critics' responses to the work were measured. The comment of Charles Allen in what was an essentially enthusiastic review, "Walls Coming Down?" *New York Times,* April 11, 1971, D28, is typical: "Yet *[The Block],* unlike The Projections, seems to me not monumental but lilliputian. Accompanied by a soundtrack of gospel singing and street sounds, it seems like a clever idea that doesn't quite come off. The treatment is too decorative, the color too cheerful. The lesson to be learned here is that a Harlem block is much more than the sum of its parts." He went on to say that "Bearden's art in all other respects is an art that triumphs; an art nurtured by, inseparable from, and, indeed, impossible without the *Black experience.*"

155 See Bridget R. Cooks, *Seen and Not Seen: A History of Black Representation and Self-Representation in Art Exhibitions in the United States, 1893–1998,* Ph.D. diss., University of Rochester, 2001, 54–97. The presentation of James VanDerZee's oeuvre to a large audience was one accomplishment of the *Harlem on My Mind* exhibition, on behalf of an artist based in Harlem.

156 In *Origins and Progressions* 1986, checklist 48 is listed as *Study for Block II,* 1972, a work that corresponds in size to *The Block II.* The catalogue for the May 1972 group exhibition at the American Academy of Arts and Letters and the National Institutes of Arts and Letters lists a *Sketch for Block II* (no. 26, colored ink drawing) which may be the five-part sketch for *The Block* in figs. 34–38.

157 *Atlanta City Scenes* was another; it focused on aspects of African-American history, however, so its theme was not so new to Bearden as the Berkeley environment.

158 Gordon and Saunders were members of the museum's Committee for the Acquisition of Works by Afro-American Artists; they also were advisers for the Civic Art Commission. I am grateful to Peter Selz and Carl Worth who shared with me their accounts of the mural project's evolution and documents recording aspects of Bearden's interaction with the committee (meeting on November 5, 2001). See also Thomas Albright, "Berkeley's Life Style: Impressive New Mural," *San Francisco Chronicle,* January 3, 1974, 40, and Mary Ellen Perry, "On the Art Scene," *San Francisco Post,* May 4, 1972, 4.

159 The opinion is that of City Councilman Ramon Valez, a powerful force in the Bronx, in "Hospital Art Wasting Away in Warehouses," *New York Daily News,* October 22, 1976, 4, an article that supplied other data cited here. The mural had been commissioned by New York's Health and Hospital Corporation, the State Facilities Development Corporation, and a committee of prominent art experts including representatives of the Harlem Council on the Arts. This information and dates of commission and completion are based on the note in the program for the May 26, 1999, Bellevue Hospital Center rededication ceremony for the mural, sponsored by the hospital and by the Art Commission of the City of New York, celebrating the conservation of the mural by Luca Bonetti. I am grateful to Mr. Bonetti for sharing with me both his conservation records, and, in conversation, on September 7, 2001, his insights into Bearden's technique.

160 See Marsha Miro, "Master of Mosaic," *Detroit Free Press,* September 16, 1986, C1, C2.

161 The importance of murals in the history of African-American art is documented in *The People's Art: Black Murals, 1967–1978* [exh. cat., African American Historical and Cultural Museum] (Philadelphia, [1968]); and James Prigoff and Robin J. Dunitz, *Walls of Heritage/Walls of Pride: African American Murals* (San Francisco, 2000). Bearden's murals are as follows, with available data provided: (1) *The Grill, 42nd Street,* 1972–74, and *Untitled,* 60-feet tall, two-part temporary billboard mural in Times Square; maquettes are in the Studio Museum in Harlem; (2) *Berkeley — The City and Its People,* 1973 (see no. 62); (3) *Untitled* (?), 1973, PS 84, tessera mosaic (?), Bronx, N.Y.; (4) *Untitled,* 1974, PS 346, 16 x 28 feet, tessera mosaic by Crovatto Mosaics Inc., Brooklyn, N.Y., Starrett City; (5) *Cityscape,* 1974, 7⅓ x 26⅓ feet, collage of various papers with paint, ink, and surface abrasion on fiberboard, Bellevue Hospital Center, New York; (6) *Atlanta City Scenes,* 1976, 30 x 90 feet, paint on brick wall of Kutz Building, destroyed with building; (7) *Untitled (Music), 1980,* 14 x 15, and *Olympics,* 14 x 18 feet, acrylic on two separately mounted canvases, Hartford (Connecticut) Civic Center; (8) *Baltimore Uproar,* 1983, 15 x 40 feet, tessera mosaic by Crovatto Mosaics Inc., Upton Subway Station, Baltimore; (9) *The City,* 1983, 16 x 24 feet, tessera mosaic, Borough of Manhattan Community College, City University of New York; (10) *Communications,* 1982, 10 x 5 feet, collage and oil on canvas, Howard University, Washington, D.C.; (11) *Pittsburgh Recollections,* 1984, 13 x 60 feet, painted and glazed ceramic tiles, Bennington Potters, Inc.; (12) *Quilting Time,* 1986, 9½ x 14 feet, tessera mosaic by Crovatto Mosaics Inc., Detroit Institute of Arts; (13) *Family,* 1989, Addabbo Federal Building, Jamaica, N.Y.; (14) *Before Dawn,* 1989, 9 x 13½, based on a 1985 collage, tessera mosaic by Crovatto Mosaics Inc., Public Library of Charlotte and Mecklenburg County (North Carolina);

(15) *City of Glass,* 1993, fabricated by Benoit Gilsoul and Helmut Schardt (based on a 1982 maquette), East Tremont Avenue and Williamsbridge Road (elevated) Station, Metropolitan Transit Authority, Bronx, New York.

162 Bonetti's conservation report offers a detailed description of the framing and hanging strategy used for the installation.

163 For this suggestion I am indebted to National Gallery painting conservator Jay Krueger.

164 Ellison 1988, 418.

165 Albert Murray, "The Visual Equivalent of the Blues," in *Romare Bearden: 1970–1980: An Exhibition* [exh. cat., Mint Museum] (Charlotte, N.C., 1980), 17–28.

166 Murray in *Romare Bearden: 1970–1980,* 26.

167 The quotations are from the author's conversation with Donald and Yourna Byrd, November 23, 2001.

168 Romare Bearden, artist's statement, in *Since the Harlem Renaissance: 50 Years of Afro-American Art* [exh. cat., Center Gallery, Bucknell University] (Lewisburg, Pa., 1985), 14.

169 Donald Byrd, conversation with the author, November 23, 2001.

170 Commission at this time was confirmed in e-mail correspondence between Mary Lee Corlett and Beverly Kendall, former registrar for collections and exhibitions at the museum, to whom we are grateful for her assistance. A photograph showing Bearden laying out the collage is included in Gelburd, *Romare Bearden in Black and White* 1997, 80–81. The date of c. 1978–79 must be in error given that the finished piece was accessioned by the museum in 1976. Bearden made designs for a number of professionally woven tapestries during the 1970s and 1980s, as listed in the Chronology in this volume.

171 I am grateful for the insights of Julia Burke, Head of Textile Conservation, National Gallery of Art, and to Judith Mueller, registrar at the African American Museum in Philadelphia, and her colleague, Richard Watson, preparator, for their gracious and generous assistance when we examined the work unframed at what was for them a very inopportune time.

172 It is useful as well to know that in his talk at the memorial service for Hale Woodruff, Bearden focused on Woodruff's murals on this subject for the library at Talladega College in Alabama, which he had seen with Woodruff during his 1940 visit to the south. Bearden noted that when Woodruff painted his murals there was little documentation for "this episode in our history," applauding the historical research his friend had undertaken in order to accomplish his task, and associating it with an experience en route back to Atlanta with Woodruff during which he turned off the lights of the car on a dark road. "There was something about the pitch darkness that took me back to another time and another aspect of Afro-American history—I imagined Frederick Douglass or Harriet Tubman as fugitives making their way north to freedom amid the shouts of the pursuers and the baying of the blood hounds." The association was one he carried into his own *Amistad* mural. Undated typescript on file at the Romare Bearden Foundation, New York.

173 Bearden to Gudron Vigtel, letter, June 15, 1973.

174 Undated typescript, "My Mountain in the Caribbean," in the archives of the Romare Bearden Foundation, New York.

175 Bearden, *Since the Harlem Renaissance* 1985, 13.

176 John Russell, "Art: Bearden from Homer to Henri," *New York Times,* April 29, 1977, C22.

177 These works were dated to 1972 in the 1991 *Memory and Metaphor* exhibition. It seems unlikely that Bearden would have made them so many years prior to his major collages on this theme. More in keeping with his practice would be for him to have made the small versions after completing the large ones, as he did some thirty years earlier, basing the small Passion of Christ sketches on more finished works.

178 Bearden in Charles H. Rowell, "Inscription at the City of Brass: An Interview with Romare Bearden," *Callaloo* 11 (Summer 1988), 433.

179 Quoted in Berman 1980, 67.

180 Mary Schmidt Campbell, "Introduction," in *Mysteries: Women in the Art of Romare Bearden* 1975, not paginated.

181 Other works included here that are related to edition prints reproduced in Gelburd, *Graphic Odyssey* 1992 are *Blue Snake* (no. 123) for a 1971 lithograph, *Dreams of Exile (Green Snake); Odysseus Enters at the Door Disguised as an Old Man* (no. 90) for a 1976 screenprint *Return of Ulysses; Falling Star* (no. 111) for a 1979 lithograph of the same title; *Village of Yo/City of Brass* (nos. 42, 43, 134) for a 1972 screenprint *Sorcerer (African Fantasy); Noah, Third Day* and *Delilah* (nos. 80, 79), which served as the origins for two screenprints in the five-part 1974 series The Prevalence of Ritual—the *Prelude to Troy* (no. 140) image but not based on this collagraph, was in the series; *Carolina Shout* (no. 73) for the 1975 screenprint *Baptism; Palm Sunday Procession* (no. 57) for a 1983 screenprint, *Processional;* and *Piano Lesson* (no. 136) for a 1984 lithograph, *Homage to Mary Lou* [Williams].

182 Judith Wilson, "Getting Down to Get Over: Romare Bearden's Use of Pornography and the Problem of the Black Female Body in Afro-U.S. Art," in Michael Wallace, *Black Popular Culture,* ed. Gina Dent (New York, 1970), 113.

183 Sharon F. Patton, "Romare Bearden: Narrations," in *Romare Bearden: Narrations* [exh. cat., Neuberger Museum of Art] (Purchase, New York, 2002), 11. *E.J. Bellocq: Storyville, Portraits; Photographs from the New Orleans Red-Light District* [exh. cat., Museum of Modern Art] (New York, 1970). This catalogue is in Bearden's library.

184 Deborah Willis and Carla Williams, *The Black Female Body: A Photographic History* (Philadelphia, 2002), 56–57, 202, note 95, referencing Marc Miller in *Louis Armstrong: A Cultural Legacy* [exh. cat., Queens Museum of Art] (New York, 1994). Circulated. Published in association with University of Washington Press. Text: Donald Bogle, Richard A. Long, Marc H. Miller, and Dan Morgenstern.

185 Throughout his life Bearden expressed warmth toward an aging and not very handsome prostitute whom he credited with helping break a creative block he suffered in the early 1940s by suggesting he search for the beauty within rather than on the surface.

186 The quotation is from Cornelia H. Butler's provocative essay, "The Woman Problem: On the Contemporaneity of de Kooning's Women," in *Willem de Kooning: Tracing the Figure* [exh. cat., Museum of Contemporary Art] (Los Angeles, 2002), 188, in which she states that between de Kooning and Richter there is no such example. Butler addresses issues of attitude in de Kooning's women that parallel those in Bearden's. One also might rewrite Thomas B. Hess' "Pinup and Icon," in Thomas B. Hess and Linda Nochlin, *Women as Sex Object: Studies in Erotic Art, 1730–1970, Art News Annual* 38 (1972), 223–27, fitting Bearden's nudes into the de Kooning, Rauschenberg, Lichtenstein mix.

187 Kenneth Clark's *The Nude: A Study in Ideal Form* was first published in 1956 by Pantheon Books for the Bollingen Foundation, Inc., N.Y., documenting his A.W. Mellon Lectures in the Fine Arts at the National Gallery of Art.

188 *Ritual Bayou* and *Carolina Interior* were two of six prototype images for Bearden's only collage edition series entitled *Ritual Bayou,* published by Shorewood Editions and intended as an edition of seventy-five, although fewer than that were completed (Patton, *Memory and Metaphor* 1991, 110, note 41, reports twenty-five). Other titles in the group are *Reunion, Mississippi Monday, Byzantine Frieze,* and *Memories.*

189 Bearden, *Since the Harlem Renaissance* 1985, 130.

190 See Cullen 2000. For a history of the monotype, see *The Painterly Print: Monotypes from the Seventeenth to the Twentieth Century* [exh. cat., Metropolitan Museum of Art] (New York, 1980).

191 See Eugenia Parry Janis, *Degas Monotypes: Essay, Catalogue, and Checklist* [exh. cat., Fogg Art Museum] (Cambridge, Mass., 1968). Monotypes are reproduced throughout Richard Kendall, *Degas Landscapes* [exh. cat., Metropolitan Museum of Art] (New Haven and London, 1993). Two appendices, 273–76, document the landscape monotypes.

192 We have seen no other examples of ghost impressions by Bearden, but others probably exist; nor have we seen other examples of Bearden preceding a monotype with so highly developed a watercolor as *Study for Fish Market.*

193 Cullen 2000 records Blackburn reporting that Bearden came to the Printmaking Workshop on Saturdays and an occasional Sunday from 1974 through 1983. The implication is that he made monotypes on many of these Saturdays. Yet Bearden told Schwartzman that he did not work frequently in this process because the fumes from the benzine solvent employed were unhealthy.

In the Cullen interview, Blackburn describes how Bearden "would come in with his little bag of photographs and he would work, using them as a stimulus." Contrary information comes from Kathy Caraccio, who assisted Bearden with his Storyville monotypes at Blackburn's shop and remembers him working without any visual aids. It is perfectly reasonable to assume that both accounts are accurate, that he worked in different ways at different times.

194 Susan Howe, "Romare Bearden at Cordier & Ekstrom," *Art in America* 64 (November–December 1976): 122.

195 Bearden, *Since the Harlem Renaissance* 1985, 13.

196 Bearden told Schwartzman that he worked from five to seven minutes on each of his initial monotype drawings. Caraccio confirmed the speed with which he worked, suggesting that the time for each impression was ten or fifteen minutes. If he took longer, the benzine would dry and the image would not transfer. This does not account for the time spent reworking the transferred images.

197 Tomkins 1977 (see above, note 10).

198 See for example, Carrie Rickey, "Reviews: New York," *Artforum* 17 (February 1979), 62.

199 Ghent transcription, 5.

200 The use of legends on the walls of exhibition galleries to explicate scenes in narrative sequences is something Jacob Lawrence had done previously.

201 Rickey 1979, 61.

202 See *Romare Bearden: Narrations* 2002, 13, 22–26. The catalogue includes an essay of the same title by Sharon F. Patton. The exhibition focused on three series: the watercolors for *Gloria;* an unpublished book, *Paris Blues;* and costume and set designs for an unrealized ballet, *Bayou Fever.*

203 See Steven Pajewski, "All Painting Is a Kind of Talking about Life: The Pittsburgh Memories of Romare Bearden," *Carnegie Magazine* 61, no. 3 (May–June 1992), 14–18, 20–21.

204 See John Caldwell, "Romare Bearden," *American Drawings and Watercolors in the Museum of Art, Carnegie Institute* (Pittsburgh: University of Pittsburgh Press, 1985), 238–239.

205 See *Dream Street: W. Eugene Smith's Pittsburgh Project,* ed. Sam Stephenson [exh. cat., Carnegie Museum of Art] (Pittsburgh and New York, 2001), 111. My thanks to Charles Ritchie for directing me to this catalogue.

206 Andrew Marvell, *The Complete English Poems,* ed. Elizabeth Story Donno (New York, 1974), 101.

207 Michael Brenson, "Art: Romare Bearden, 'Rituals of the Obeah,'" *New York Times,* November 30, 1984, C23.

208 Bearden, *Since the Harlem Renaissance* 1985, 13.

209 See Schwartzman, 200–203 for an interview with Thibault/Teabo regarding his assistance to Bearden.

210 In addition to eight photographically reproduced island scenes, each of the Walcott volumes includes an original lithograph. Bearden completed eight different images to be divided among the edition. "Ma Chance" is Jeanne Louise Duzant Chance. Her recipes were edited and compiled by June Kelly, and published by G.P. Putnam's Sons, New York. In the volume she acknowledges "Romare Bearden, who encouraged me so that my dream could come true."

211 This was one of the series in *Romare Bearden: Narrations* 2002 discussed and reproduced in the accompanying catalogue, 17–21.

212 Publication of Bearden's *Li'l Dan, the Drummer Boy: A Civil War Story,* with a selection of his illustrations is anticipated from Simon & Schuster Books for Young Readers in September 2003.

213 *Romare Bearden: Narrations* 2002, 13–14; illustrations, 27–34. *The Buzzard and the Snake* is no. 52. Patton reports Bearden's unfulfilled hope that Ailey would choreograph the story.

214 *Urban Street Scene* is reproduced as cat. no. 50 in *Narratives of African American Art and Identity: The David C. Driskell Collection* [exh. cat., University of Maryland Art Gallery] (College Park, Md., and San Francisco, 1998), 117, although the relationship to the *House Party* set is not mentioned. The connection between this image (in its print form) to the play was conveyed to me separately by Billie Allen and Earle Hyman. I am grateful to both for the information.

215 Jeannette Watson, Introduction [Dear Friends], in *Letters to a Bookstore: Books & Co., 1978–1988* (New York, 1988), not paginated.

216 The Romare Bearden Foundation in New York is coordinating this effort.

217 James A. Porter, *Notes on Romare Bearden,* on the verso of the checklist of *Ten Hierographic Paintings by Sgt. Romare Bearden* [exh. cat., G Place Gallery] (Washington, D.C., 1944).

Bearden's Musée Imaginaire

SARAH KENNEL

1 The passage that precedes this statement reads: "There is a show of French drawings at the Metropolitan, with a few wonderful Claudes and Poussains [*sic*],... How close Poussain is to Cezzane [*sic*], or I should have written it the other way around; but you know what I mean with the bather series—and Poussain's 'wash' studies. I'd be very interested to see what you would do with some of the Poussain drawings or paintings; while they have elements in them you don't like, I think you might do some fantastic 'take off' that would be as far removed, and as near, in the big sense, as the Cezzane watercolors of the 'bathers series.'

Poussain would be good for you now, because he is good, and also neutral, and you can let your own fantasy play." Romare Bearden to Carl Holty, undated letter, Archives of American Art (AAA), Smithsonian Institution, Washington, D.C. Although the letter is undated, Bearden mentions visiting several recent exhibitions, including a 1953 Rouault exhibition at the Museum of Modern Art and the exhibition of French drawings at the Metropolitan Museum of Art that took place from March 19 to April 20, 1953.

2 The literature concerning artistic copying, variation, and appropriation in Western art has expanded in the last two decades. See K. E. Maison, *Themes and Variations: Five Centuries of Master Copies and Interpretations* (London and New York, 1960); Richard Schiff, "Representation, Copying, and the Technique of Originality," *New Literary History* 15, no. 2 (1984): 333–63. For a discussion of how painters attempt to create original work in response to older art, see Norman Bryson, *Tradition and Desire from David to Delacroix* (Cambridge and New York, 1984); and Leo Steinberg, "The Glorious Company," in Jean Lipman and Richard Marshall, *Art about Art* [exh. cat., Whitney Museum of American Art] (New York, 1978), 8–31. On imitation in the Renaissance, see Jeffrey M. Muller, "Rubens's Theory and Practice of the Imitation of Art," *Art Bulletin* 64 (June 1982): 229–47. On the academic copy in the nineteenth century, see Albert Boime, *The Academy and French Painting* (London, 1971).

3 For discussion of modernism's relationship to old master painting, see Roger Benjamin, "Recovering Authors: The Modern Copy, Copy Exhibitions and Matisse," *Art History* 12, no. 2 (1989): 176–201; Susan Galassi, *Picasso's Variations on the Masters: Confrontations with the Past* (New York, 1996); and chapters one and two of Michael Fried's *Manet's Modernism, or the Face of Painting in the 1860s* (Chicago, 1996).

4 At the end of *The Painter's Mind: A Study of the Relations of Structure and Space in Painting* (New York and London, 1981), Bearden and coauthor Carl Holty write: "At no time in history has the art of all the world been so available to artists—at least through such information as reproductions can furnish, in what Malraux refers to as 'the museum without walls.'" Bearden also discussed Malraux's conception of "art from art" in a 1968 interview with Henri Ghent. When Ghent asked Bearden what provided him with inspiration, the artist answered, "But I think that the things that make an artist paint, early recollections of things, or a sunset—Malraux said, that few artists are impelled to painting because of these early sensations. It's seeing finally the work of other artists that makes you want to paint rather than things from nature." Interview with Henri Ghent, June 29, 1968, Romare Bearden papers, AAA. Unpublished transcript, 6, here referred to as Ghent transcription.

5 Bearden and Holty 1981, 21. For a discussion of Malraux's impact on Bearden, see Lee Stephens Glazer, "Signifying Identity: Art and Race in Romare Bearden's Projections," *Art Bulletin* 76 (September 1994): 411–26. Glazer's article provides an excellent analysis of Bearden's relationship to both Malraux's *Voices of Silence* and to an institutionalized canon of Western art. The author links Bearden's *Prevalence of Ritual: Baptism* (1964) to Francisco Zurburan's *The Virgin as Protectress of the Carthusians* (c. 1625) and *Women in a Harlem Courtyard* (1964) to Pieter de Hooch's *A Courtyard in Delft at Evening: A Woman Spinning* (c. 1658), an identification first suggested in 1964 by Charles Childs, "Bearden: Identification and Identity," *Art News* 63 (October 1964): 25. Glazer also suggests that Diego Velázquez's *The Luncheon* (c. 1617–18) inspired Bearden's *Evening, 9:10, 461 Lenox Avenue* (1964); I think that *Evening* is much closer to Velázquez's *Three Musicians*.

6 André Malraux, *Voices of Silence* (Garden City, N.Y., 1967), 16.

7 Malraux 1967, 17.

8 Malraux 1967, 46.

9 Romare Bearden, "Rectangular Structure in My Montage Paintings," *Leonardo* 2, no. 1 (January 1969): 11.

10 Janet Moore, a student at the Art Students League in 1934–35, recorded many of the comments Grosz made in class, among them the advice, "Look not too much at the modern masters, look at the old masters from whom they derive." Quoted in M. Kay Flavell, *George Grosz: A Biography* (New Haven and London, 1988), 317.

11 Romare Bearden, "The Negro Artist and Modern Art," *Opportunity: A Journal of Negro Life* 12 (December 1934): 371.

12 Quoted in Childs 1964, 61. See note 5.

13 Bearden to Walter Quirt, undated letter, c. 1945, Walter Quirt Papers, AAA.

14 Bearden to Walter Quirt, July 10, 1945, Walter Quirt Papers, AAA.

15 Although many of the Passion of Christ works were based on similar narrative scenes in the *Maestà* altarpiece, the fact that Bearden took Duccio's work as the starting point for an image in the Lorca series suggests that Bearden understood visual form as an inherently labile structure, distinct from narrative significance, which can be deployed and given new meaning by the artist.

16 My thanks to Renée Maurer who discovered the source for this image.

17 Bearden to Walter Quirt, undated letter, Walter Quirt Papers, AAA.

18 Bearden 1969, 12. Few of these works seem to have survived; Ruth Fine surmises that Bearden may have reused the surfaces for later collages.

19 Bearden to Mary Schmidt Campbell, letter, September 22, 1973, cited in Mary Schmidt Campbell, "Romare Bearden: A Creative Mythology," Ph.D. diss., Syracuse University, 1982, 560.

20 Ghent transcription, 3.

21 Undated typescript, "Lectures, Writings," Romare Bearden Papers, AAA.

22 Ghent transcription, 3.

23 Romare Bearden, interview by Karl Fortress, June 28, 1970, tape recording, AAA.

24 Bearden to Mary Schmidt Campbell, letter, September 22, 1973. See Campbell 1982, appendix D, 550.

25 Undated letter to Walter Quirt, Walter Quirt Papers, AAA.

26 Romare Bearden, interview by Avis Berman, July 31, 1980, AAA. My thanks to Avis Berman for granting access to this restricted interview.

27 Harold Bloom's now-classic analysis of artistic influence and the "anxiety" an artist feels in the face of inherited tradition can be found in Bloom's *The Anxiety of Influence. A Theory of Poetry* (Oxford, 1975), and *A Map of Misreading* (Oxford, 1975).

28 Romare Bearden, interview by Karl Fortress, June 28, 1970, tape recording, AAA.

29 Undated (but probably 1967), unpublished typescript, library of the Museum of Modern Art, New York.

30 Sharon F. Patton, "Memory and Metaphor: The Art of Romare Bearden, 1940–1987," in *Memory and Metaphor* [exh. cat., Studio Museum in Harlem] (New York, 1991), 63.

31 Bearden's image also recalls another similar painting by Bronzino, *Eleanora of Toledo and Her Son Don Garcia* (Uffizzi Gallery, Florence), which was reproduced on page 52 of *The Painter's Mind.*

32 In the catalogue introduction to Bearden's 1975 exhibition *Of the Blues,* Albert Murray notes that Bearden grew up in the

Harlem of "blues idiom musicians and entertainers... many of whom by the way had rich personal memories of Paris in the Belle Epoque. In point of fact, not a few of the figures from the world of Toulouse-Lautrec were very much on hand to greet and help make the blues idiom music and entertainment the rage of Paris after World War I." Albert Murray, introduction, *Of the Blues: Romare Bearden* [exh. cat., Cordier & Ekstrom] (New York, 1975).

33 Childs 1964, 54.

34 In this vein, Bearden wrote of his 1967 collage *Two Women in a Courtyard* (which is based on Pieter de Hooch's painting of the same title), "I try to show that the courtyard was as important to American southern life as indeed it was in the Holland of De Hooch, Terborch, and Vermeer." Bearden 1969, 17.

35 My thanks to Claude Elliott for alerting me to Hale Woodruff's oil painting *The Card Players* (c. 1978) in the collection of John H. and Vivian D. Hewitt. Palmer Hayden's watercolor is entitled *Nous Quatre à Paris*. In 1987 Bearden recalled that at the house-rent parties "the host would lay out a whole lot to eat and drink, and there would be a blackjack or poker game, and always a room for dancing, with only one dim red light." Quoted in *Riffs and Takes: Music in the Art of Romare Bearden* [exh. cat., North Carolina Museum of Art] (Raleigh, 1988).

36 Bearden to Mary Schmidt Campbell, September 22, 1973, in Campbell 1982, appendix D, 561.

37 Charles Childs, "The Artist Caught between Two Worlds," *Tuesday Magazine* (April 1967), 8–10, 23.

38 More recently, Paul Gilroy has analyzed the historical roots of this conflict, arguing that "the intellectual and cultural achievements of the black Atlantic populations exist partly inside and not always against the grand narrative of Enlightenment and its operational principles. Their stems have grown strong, supported by a lattice of western politics and letters. Though African linguistic tropes and political and philosophical themes are still visible for those who wish to see them, they have often been transformed and adapted by their New World locations to a point where the dangerous issues of purified essences and simple origins lose all meaning. These modern black political formations stand simultaneously both inside and outside the western culture which has been their peculiar step-parent." Paul Gilroy, *The Black Atlantic: Modernity and Double Consciousness* (Cambridge, Mass., 1993), 48–49.

39 Quoted by Lyneise Williams in her essay in *Such Sweet Thunder: African Elements in the Art of Romare Bearden* [exh. cat., Kent State University School of Art Gallery] (Kent, Ohio, 1997), 8. The debate continues. Recently Samir Amin has argued that while Afrocentrism functions as a counterdiscourse to Eurocentrism, it too is limited by the same culturalist assumptions which posit "the existence of irreducibly distinct cultural variants that shape historical paths of different people." In contradistinction to an Afrocentrist model, Carolyn Boyce Davies suggests that Bearden adopted a "diasporic" model of interaction by drawing inspiration from the crosscultural and transnational experiences that arose out of the interactions and collisions between African and Western cultures. See Samir Amin, *Delinking: Towards a Polycentric World* (London, 1985), vii; Carolyn Boyce Davies, "Beyond Unicentricity: Transcultural Black Presences," *Research in African Literatures* 30 (July 15, 1999): 9.

40 Ralph Ellison's description of Bearden's technique assumes a somewhat different position in which the "surreal" characterizes African-American experience itself: "Bearden's meaning is identical with his method. His combination of technique is in itself eloquent of the sharp breaks, leaps in consciousness, distortions, paradoxes, reversals, telescoping of time and surreal blending of styles, values, hopes, and dreams which characterize much of Negro American history." Ralph Ellison, "The Art of Romare Bearden," introduction in *Romare Bearden: Paintings and Projections* [exh. cat., The Art Gallery, State University of New York at Albany] (Albany, 1968), n.p.

41 Aaron Scharf, *Art and Photography* (London, 1968; reprinted 1974), 131.

42 Ghent transcription, 10.

43 Lipman and Marshall 1978, 7.

44 The notable exception is Glazer 1994.

45 Childs 1964, 62.

46 Bearden 1969, 18.

Bearden's Dialogue with Africa and the Avant-Garde

NNAMDI ELLEH

1 See Gail Gelburd, "Romare Bearden in Black-and-White," in *Romare Bearden in Black-and-White: The Photomontage Projections of 1964* [exh. cat., Whitney Museum of American Art] (New York, 1997), 29.

2 Holy Bible, Joshua 6:2, 3.

3 Such cultural exchange has been fully documented since the turn of the twentieth century by several scholars. See the following sources for further reading: M.J. Herskovits, *Dahomey, an Ancient West African Kingdom* (New York, 1938); Henry Drewal and David Driskell, *Introspectives: Contemporary Art by Americans and Brazilians of African Descent*, with contributions by Luiza Bairros and Sheila Walker (Los Angeles, 1989); Elizabeth McAlister, *Rara: Vodou, Power, and Performance in Haiti and Its Diaspora* (Berkeley, 2002); *Caribbean Cultural Identities*, ed. Glyne Griffith, *Bucknell Review* 44, no. 2 (Lewisburg, Pa., 2001).

4 For more information about the altar of Ovonramwen, see Suzanne Preston Blier, *Royal Arts of Africa* (London, 1998), 68–78. See also Paula Girshick Ben-Amos, *The Art of Benin* (Washington, D.C., 1995), 80–96.

5 Blier 1998, 69.

6 Maya Deren, "Dance as the Mediation of the Body," in *Divine Horsemen: The Living Gods of Haiti* (New York, 1953), 198.

7 Some of the works that were realized in this era are vignettes showing the national aspirations of the immediate postcolonial era, the glories of African cultures, and the challenges ahead based on unique experiences from daily life in the respective countries.

8 See Susan Vogel, Ema Ebong, et al., *Africa Explores: 20th Century African Art. Germany* (Munich, 1994), 233.

9 See Sharon F. Patton, "Memory and Metaphor," in *Memory and Metaphor: The Art of Romare Bearden, 1940–1987* [exh. cat., Studio Museum in Harlem] (New York, 1991), 18–104.

10 One can also mention Bruce Onobrakpeya, who uses the techniques of drawing, painting, etching, and engraving to represent different cultural scenes of Nigeria. He was obsessed with rituals of all kinds, ranging from the royal Edo (Benin kingship) ceremonies to Christian ceremonies. Weddings, musicians, musical instruments, kingship coronations, magical scenes, and different aspects of the everyday experiences of the ordinary Nigerian people are often legible in his works. Like Bearden, his figures always derive from known Nigerian artifacts, such as the Benin bronze objects, and people that one encounters in everyday experience. There are several self-published catalogues and portfolios of Bruce Onobrakpeya, including *Bruce Onobrakpeya* (Lagos, Nigeria, 1982). One can also name Yusuf Grillo, who was educated both in Nigeria and abroad before he became the head of the School of Art, Design and Technology, at Yaba College of Science and Technology, Lagos, Nigeria. Grillo painted different scenes of Nigerian life including religious scenes, often drawn from Nigerian antiquity and native attires, which are abundant in Bearden's collages and paintings. There is also Demas Nwoko, who worked in different media. His terra-cotta *Mother and Child* derives its visual vocabulary from the long-extinct Nok culture that Bearden incorporated in some of his collages.

11 Although there are several scholars of African art who have discussed Ben Enwonwu, the most detailed study is by Sylvester Ogbechie, *Ben Enwonwu and the Constitution of Modernity in 20th Century Nigerian Art* (Ph.D. diss., Northwestern University, 2000).

12 Among the African artists who studied abroad in the 1930s, one can also name Ahmed Cherkaoui (1934–1967), who began to experiment with abstract-style Arabic calligraphy after graduating from the École des Métiers d'Art and the École des Beaux Arts in Paris. There is also Mohammed Issiakhem (1928–1986) from Algeria, who was educated at both the Société de Beaux Arts in Algiers and at the École Nationale Supérieure des Beaux Arts in Paris.

13 David Boxer, *Jamaican Art,* 1922–1982 (Washington, D.C., 1983), 16.

14 See "The Poetry of Romare Bearden" in Romare Bearden in *Black and White Photomontage Projections, 1964* (New York, 1997), 63–73.

15 Robert Goldwater, *Primitivism in Modern Art* (Cambridge, Mass., 1966 and 1986), 51–52.

16 See Edward F. Fry, "History of Cubism," in *Cubism* (London, 1966), 11–35. See also Fry, "Cubism as a Stylistic and Historical Phenomenon," in *Cubism,* 36–41.

17 Robert Rosenblum, *Cubism and Twentieth Century Art* (New York, 1966), 25.

18 Thomas Crow, "Modernism and Mass Culture in the Visual Arts," in *Pollock and After: The Critical Debate,* ed. Franscina Francis (London and San Francisco, 1985), 233–59.

19 Crow 1985, 234.

20 Crow 1985, 234.

21 Clement Greenberg, "Avant-Garde and Kitsch," in *Pollock and After: The Critical Debate,* ed. Franscina Francis, 2d ed. (London and New York: Routledge, 2000), see page 52.

22 Greenberg 2000, 53.

23 One can make the case that Clement Greenberg's avant-garde and kitsch do reflect certain aspects of Frederic Jameson's postmodern culture where "'culture' has become a product in its own right; the market has become a substitute for itself and fully as much a commodity as any of the items it includes within itself: modernism was still minimally and tendentially the critique of the commodity and the effort to make it transcend itself. Postmodernism is the consumption of sheer commodification as a process." See Frederic Jameson, *Postmodernism or, the Cultural Logic of Late Capitalism* (Durham, N.C., 1991).

24 The Surrealist Group in Paris, "Murderous Humanitarianism," in *Negro Anthology Made by Nancy Cunard (1931–1933). Paris,* ed. Nancy Cunard, translated from the French by Samuel Beckett (London, 1934), 574.

25 Cunard 1934, 575.

26 *Refusal of the Shadows: Surrealism and the Caribbean,* ed. Michael Richardson, trans. Michael Richardson and Krzysztof Fijatowski (London and New York: Verso, 1996), 11.

27 Irene Gendzier writes that "the degree of activity among West Indians, Africans, and black Americans in Paris in the years between 1929 and 1940 was intense." Irene L. Gendzier, *Frantz Fanon. A Critical Study* (New York, 1973), 39.

28 Michael Richardson, "1978 Introduction to *Légitime Défense,*" in Richardson 1996, and pages 37–40.

29 Gendzier 1973, 39.

30 René Despestre, "André Breton in Port-au-Prince," in Richardson 1996, 232.

31 André Breton, *Haïti: Art Naïf Art Vaudou* (Paris, 1988), 120.

32 See Frantz Fanon, *Black Skin White Masks,* trans. Charles Lam Markmann (New York, 1967), and Fanon, *The Wretched of the Earth,* trans. Constance Farrington, and with a Preface by Jean-Paul Sartre (New York, 1961).

33 Frantz Fanon, *The Wretched of the Earth* (New York, 1961; reprint 1983), 39. Fanon criticized Breton for praising Aimé Césaire's eloquence in the French language following the publication of *Note of a Return to My Native Land.* In Fanon's view, "to speak a language is to take on a world, a culture," regardless of the fact that Césaire's book aimed to subvert the assimilative intentions of the French colonial policy. According to Fanon, "there is no reason why André Breton should say of Césaire, here is a black man who handles the French Language as no white man today can." African intellectuals (Anthony Appiah and V.Y. Mudimbe) from various disciplines remain preoccupied by this issue, and its implication is no less obvious in the visual arts. Nevertheless, if we consider the avant-garde as a universal movement in which minority groups and their majority counterparts drew from the same educational systems and communicated with each other the burden of cleansing the minority, then the language of the colonizer is no longer as important, especially when the minority groups are using that language to achieve their objectives. In order to achieve their objectives, they subvert the language of the colonizer.

34 Jean-Paul Sartre, "Black Orpheus," trans. S.W. Allen, in Léopold Sédar Senghor, *Anthologie de la nouvelle poésie nègre et malagache de langue Française* (Paris, 1963), 55.

35 Sartre 1963, 55.

36 I am making the connection between Picasso's *Les Demoiselles d'Avignon* (1907) and Bearden's *Two Women* (1969). See M. Bunch Washington, *The Art of Romare Bearden: The Prevalence of Ritual* (New York, 1973; reprinted 1999); Vogel et al. 1994; Robert Goldwater, *Primitivism in Modern Art* (Cambridge, Mass.: 1966, 1986); Robert Rosenblum, *Cubism & Twentieth Century Art* (New York, 1966).

37 Patton, "Memory and Metaphor," 1991, 18–104.

38 John A. Williams, "Introduction," in *The Art of Romare Bearden* 1973, 9.

Reading Bearden

JACQUELINE FRANCIS

1 Writing specifically of the "essentially fictive and entirely refashioned sensibility" in Bearden's collages and prints, Richard J. Powell draws attention to what I believe is a consistent underestimation of imagination in the history and criticism of black artists' production. See Powell, "What Becomes a Legend Most? Reflections on Romare Bearden," *Transition* 55 (1992): 66.

2 Romare Bearden, "Rectangular Structure in My Montage Paintings," *Leonardo* 2 (January 1969): 11–19; "Humility," *New York Times,* June 21, 1975, 27.

3 In 1980 Bearden told an interviewer: "I can write a letter, but I don't consider myself, as you say a writer. But writing is a very difficult type of craft." Romare Bearden, interview by Avis Berman, July 31, 1980, Archives of American Art (AAA), Smithsonian Institution, Washington, D.C., transcript, 18.

4 Henry Louis Gates, Jr., "King of Cats," *New Yorker* 72.7 (April 8, 1996): 70.

5 Author's telephone interview with Albert Murray, August 8, 2002.

6 Davira S. Taragin, "Editor's Note to the Journal of Romare Bearden," in *Romare Bearden: Origins and Progressions* [exh. cat., Detroit Institute of Arts] (Detroit, 1986), 23.

7 A bibliography in an undated Bearden notebook lists the following entries: Beach, *Outlook of American Prose;* Forster, E. M., *Aspects of the Novel;* James, *Art of Fiction;* Hamilton, C., *Materials and Methods of Fiction; Technique of Thomas Hardy;* Leggett, *Idea in Fiction;* Lubbock, *Craft of Fiction*; Uzzell, Thomas, *Narrative Technique; Technique of the Novel; Manual of the Art of Fiction;* Weston, H., *Forms in Literature.* Undated notebook, Romare Bearden Foundation, New York.

8 Undated notebook, Romare Bearden Foundation, New York, n.p.

9 Romare Bearden, "A Matter of Brimstone," undated short story, Romare Bearden Foundation, New York.

10 Romare Bearden, "The Negro in 'Little Steel,'" *Opportunity: Journal of Negro Life* 15 (December 1937): 362–65, 380. From its inception in 1910, the National Urban League targeted workplace equality and job training as key strategies for improving the lives of black Americans; its magazine, founded by the sociologist Charles S. Johnson in 1923, advanced the organization's broad aims following the motto "Not Alms, But Opportunity." Johnson and his successors published literature, scholarly studies, and art in reproduction not only to inform but also to encourage and patronize the black intelligentsia. Articles in 1934 included poems and stories by emerging talents such as the novelists Paule Murray and Dorothy West, as well as reports on black workers in the New York garment unions, Texas agriculture, and the nursing profession. Bearden's "The Negro in 'Little Steel'" placed him in the ranks of the ambitious black youth, whose voices and vision were given honored space in *Opportunity*'s pages: a few months before his article appeared, another entitled "The Negro in the Kentucky Coal Fields" presented its author to readers as "a miner and the son of a miner" who was working "to earn enough money to enter college." In similarly poignant terms, Bearden was introduced as "a young artist with sensitive social consciousness."

11 Bearden 1937, 364.

12 Bearden 1937, 380.

13 Romare Bearden, "The Negro Artist and Modern Art," *Opportunity: Journal of Negro Life* 12 (December 1934): 372.

14 Bearden 1934, 371.

15 Bearden 1934, 372.

16 Bearden 1934, 372.

17 Quoted in *Romare Bearden: Collages* [exh. cat., J. L. Hudson Gallery] (Detroit, 1967), n.p.

18 Romare Bearden, "The Negro Artist's Dilemma," *Critique: A Review of Contemporary Art* 1, no. 2 (November 1946): 21.

19 Bearden 1946, 22.

20 Bearden 1946, 19.

21 Bearden to [Atlanta University Annual exhibition organizers], October 9, 1948, letter, Romare Bearden Foundation, New York.

22 Bearden did exhibit, infrequently, in the 1950s. He had a 1955 solo exhibition at New York's Barone Gallery, owned by a friend of his wife's, and he participated in a group show exhibited at the California Palace of the Legion of Honor in San Francisco and other venues, in group shows at New York's Whitney Museum of American Art (1955), and at the University of Michigan and the Pyramid Club of Philadelphia (1956).

23 Myron Schwartzman offhandedly disclosed that Bearden cowrote "Rectangular Structure in My Montage Paintings" with Albert Murray. See Schwartzman, *Romare Bearden: His Life and Art* (New York, 1990), 194.

24 Bearden 1969, 14.

25 Bearden 1969, 14–15.

26 A few years later, Bearden made his artistic autonomy even clearer: "It's a new ball game. We don't need the academic way of painting anymore. We don't need perspective to make a good painting, or perfect anatomy, or exact color of things. The only thing you would need is that you should finish it with something of the same logic in which you began.... But otherwise, today everyone is on his own." Romare Bearden, in "Romare Bearden: Visual Artist. Interviewers: Camille Billops and James V. Hatch, December 6, 1972," *Artist and Influence* 17 (1998): 36.

27 Bearden 1969, 17–18.

28 Bearden 1975, 27.

29 "Eating at Ma Chance's," *Essence* (April 1978): 112–14; "An Artist's Renewal in the Sun," *New York Times Magazine, http://hn.umi.com/pqdweb* (August 10, 2002).

30 "An Artist's Renewal in the Sun," *New York Times, http://web.lexis-nexis.com* (August 9, 2002).

31 Bearden to Walter O. Evans, "Friday-9/6," letter, Dr. Walter O. Evans Collection, Savannah, Ga. Based on references to Bearden's visit to Evans' Detroit home, the letter likely dates to 1980 or after.

32 Richard J. Powell, *Black Art and Culture in the Twentieth Century* (London and New York, 1997), 105.

33 Ann Eden Gibson, *Abstract Expressionism: Other Politics* (New Haven, 1997), 71.

34 Bearden to Schoener, June 6, 1968, letter, Romare Bearden Papers, AAA, microfilm, N68–87.

35 Carl Holty, interview by Ruth Gurin, April 2, 1964, AAA, transcript, 6, 8, 10.

36 Carl Holty, interview by Paul Cummings, September 25, 1968, AAA, transcript, 90.

37 In a 1964 interview, Holty asserted that if a picture "doesn't hold it's not abstract. That used to be Mondrian's measure.... Whether the picture holds together, whether it has unity. Its unity was abstraction." Carl Holty, interview by Ruth Gurin, April 2, 1964, AAA, transcript, 22.

38 A reproduction of this letter, in the Archives of American Art, is undated. Nonetheless, Bearden's reference to American reviews of José Ortega y Gasset's *The Dehumanization of Art* suggests that the letter dates to 1948, the year of the book's U.S. debut. Bearden to Carl [Holty], letter, Romare Bearden Papers, AAA, microfilm, N68–87.

39 Bearden, undated letter to Quirt, Romare Bearden Papers, AAA, microfilm, N68–87. Based on Bearden's reference to his second exhibition at Caresse Crosby's G Place Gallery in Washington, D.C., the letter probably dates to June 1945.

40 Bearden to Quirt, July 10, 1945, Romare Bearden Papers, AAA, microfilm, N68–87.

41 It is also worth noting that early in his career, Quirt, like Bearden, preferred watercolor to oils for the former medium's liveliness. It might be said that both artists abandoned watercolor not because of their aesthetic dissatisfaction with it: Bearden turned seriously to oil painting because gallery owner Samuel Kootz expected him to; Quirt felt the solemnity of the Great Depression precluded expression in watercolor. Undated, unattributed manuscript about Quirt, 3, Romare Bearden Foundation, New York.

42 Undated, unattributed manuscript about Quirt, 45, Romare Bearden Foundation, New York.

43 "Cultural primitivism" was offered and clearly defined by Arthur Lovejoy and George Boas in 1935 as "the discontent of the civilized with civilization, or with some conspicuous and characteristic feature of it. It is the belief of men living in a highly evolved and complex cultural

condition that a life far simpler and less sophisticated in some or all respects is a more desirable life." See Lovejoy and Boas, *Primitivism and Related Ideas in Antiquity* (Baltimore, 1935; reprinted Baltimore, 1965), 7.

44 Bearden to Quirt, January 20, 1942, letter, Dr. Walter O. Evans Collection.

45 Bearden to Quirt, January 20, 1942, letter, Dr. Walter O. Evans Collection.

46 As has been noted by several historians, Bearden did little painting during his stay in Paris in 1950. Months after arriving, he optimistically reported to Carl Holty: "So the other night I came home late and drew with charcoal, something I've never heretofore been able to do—and I drew very well, with rich tones and nice passages felt all over the paper. I'll be able to work in Paris from now on." Bearden to Holty, April 1, 1950, letter, Romare Bearden Papers, AAA, microfilm, N68–87.

47 Sharon F. Patton, "Memory and Metaphor: The Art of Romare Bearden, 1940–1987," in *Memory and Metaphor: The Art of Romare Bearden, 1940–1987* [exh. cat., Studio Museum in Harlem] (New York, 1991), 34.

48 Bearden, undated letter to Holty, AAA, microfilm, reel 670, counter 0423. Myron Schwartzman has dated the letter to c. 1954. Schwartzman 1990, 310, note 27.

49 Similarly, many of his curatorial projects were team undertakings: *The Evolution of Afro-American Artists, 1800–1950* in 1967 (with Carroll Greene, Jr.); numerous Cinque Gallery's shows of the 1960s and 1970s (with Norman Lewis and Ernest Crichlow); *Fifteen under Forty: Paintings by Young New York State Black Artists* in 1970 (with Crichlow); *Profile/Part I, The Twenties,* a 1978 Cordier & Ekstrom show of Bearden collages with narrative titles scripted by the artist and his great friend, writer Albert Murray.

50 Romare Bearden and Carl Holty, *The Painter's Mind: A Study of the Relations of Structure and Space in Painting* (New York, 1969), 8.

51 "For a modern student to realize that the slouching nude model in the depressing art school studio is related to those from whom some of the greatest masters worked, and undoubtedly resented as much by the students of today, is to find a positive empathy with the past." Bearden and Holty 1969, 14.

52 Bearden and Holty 1969, 8.

53 Bearden and Holty 1969, 218.

54 Bearden's research on sculptor Edmonia Lewis, begun in *Six Black Masters of American Art*, greatly inspired him. With Henderson, he planned a monograph on the nineteenth-century mixed race artist. Henderson has since finished the work they began together and plans to publish the manuscript. Author's telephone interview with Harry Henderson, July 10, 2002.

55 Henderson, a white magazine journalist and medical writer, met Bearden in New York City in the 1940s. They bonded over their shared interest in black history and culture, and their connections to Pittsburgh: Henderson had been raised near the western Pennsylvania city, Bearden spent long periods there with his maternal grandparents. Author's telephone interview with Harry Henderson, July 10, 2002.

56 In the introduction to *A History of African American Artists,* Henderson wrote that the book was "basically complete" by the time of Bearden's death in March 1988. Romare Bearden and Harry Henderson, *A History of African American Artists: From 1792 to the Present* (New York, 1993), xvii.

57 Bearden and Henderson 1993, xiii.

58 Bearden's stake in documentary history extended to reminiscences written for magazines, books, and exhibition texts, and published eulogies for artist-friends. In the first category, see foreword to *Fifteen under Forty: Paintings by Young New York State Black Artists* [exh. cat., Gallery Museum] (Saratoga Springs, N.Y., 1970), n.p.; "The 1930s: An Art Reminiscence," *New York Amsterdam News,* September 18, 1971, D24; foreword to *Black Artists of a New Generation,* by Elton C. Fax (New York, c. 1977), ix–xii; "Horace Pippin," *Art/World* (April 1977): 10; "Herbert Gentry," *An Ocean Apart: American Artists Abroad* [exh. cat., Studio Museum in Harlem] (New York, 1982), 9–10; *Jacob Lawrence: Fifty Years of His Work and the "Toussaint L'Ouverture" Series* [exh. cat., Jamaica Arts Center] (New York, 1984), n.p. In the second category, see "A Painter in the Fifties," *Arts Magazine* 48, no. 7 (April 1974): 36–37; "Hale Woodruff: Tribute from Friends," *New York Amsterdam News,* November 22, 1980, 35.

59 The spelling of this Barbados-born bibliophile's name has been variable in publications. In Bearden and Henderson 1993, it is "Seifert"; as is the case in Schwartzman's monograph, the spelling in Ellen Harkins Wheat's *Jacob Lawrence: American Painter* (Seattle, 1986) is "Seyfert."

60 Interview by Henri Ghent, June 29, 1968, Romare Bearden Papers, AAA. Unpublished transcript, 21.

61 Biographical information about the authors, printed at the end of *A History of African-American Artists* and on its dust jacket, offers the most information about Bearden's art and the acclaim it garnered. In addition, his work is identified, in passing, as an influence upon sculptor Ed Wilson. Bearden and Henderson 1993, 460.

A Refracted Image: Selected Exhibitions and Reviews of Bearden's Work

ABDUL GOLER

1 The documents excerpted were originally compiled by Mary Lee Corlett and Rocío Aranda-Alvarado and were taken from many sources including the Romare Bearden Foundation, New York and the Romare Bearden Papers, Archives of American Art, Smithsonian Institution, Washington, D.C. (AAA). One of the most salient aspects revealed in the European press was a lack of preoccupation with Bearden's ethnicity.

2 Richard J. Powell, "What Becomes a Legend Most? Reflections on Romare Bearden" *Transition* 55 (1992): 63–72.

3 "Paper and cloth mingle motifs of written light; fragmented forms shimmer like colored glass—like images refracted in a shattered mirror. Natural form is sacrificed to a specific vision.... The collage frees him from the fetters of oil painting." Ralph Willis, *Fragments of American Life: An Exhibition of Paintings* [exh. cat., Art Museum, Princeton University] (Princeton, N.J., 1976), 17.

4 "Downtown" as used here refers to all of Manhattan south of 110th Street—below Harlem.

5 Ben Wolf, "Bearden—He Wrestles with Angels," *Art Digest* 20, no. 1 (October 1, 1945): 16.

6 Nora Holt, "Romare Bearden Wins High Praise for Exhibition, 'The Passions of Christ,'" *New York Amsterdam News,* October 27, 1945, 6.

7 "Romare Bearden to Have One-Man Show of Paintings," *New York Amsterdam News,* frame 0499, reel N/68-87, AAA file.

8 "Art by Negroes," *Art Digest* 16, no. 2 (October 15, 1941): 11, 23.

9 The exhibition was organized by Alain Locke and was first shown at Edith Halpert's Downtown Gallery, New York.

10 Frederic R. Sisson, "Exhibition of Negro Art Provides an Opportunity: Outstanding Works Brought to Gallery in Faunce House following Show in New York—Two Schools Discerned," *Providence Journal*, 1942 (no date or page number cited on archival material).

11 Robert M. Coates, "The Art Galleries," *New Yorker*, December 27, 1941, 52–53.

12 For an explanation of connections between hieroglyphs and the use of "hieratic" stylization by African-American artists, see Keith Morrison, "The Global Village of African American Art," in *African American Visual Aesthetics: A Post Modernist View*, ed. David C. Driskell (Washington, 1995), 17–43.

13 James A. Porter, "Notes on Romare Bearden," in *Ten Hierographic Paintings by Sgt. Romare Bearden* [exh. cat., G Place Gallery] (Washington, n.d [1944]) (archival source: Romare Bearden Papers, AAA, box 2/3).

14 Crosby introduced Bearden to Samuel M. Kootz in the summer of 1945 prior to *The Passion of Christ* exhibition opening at G Place.

15 Unidentified source, October 28, 1945, frame 0513 [?], reel N/68-87, AAA.

16 "The Passing Shows," *Art News* 44, no. 13 (October 15, 1945): 6–7, 27–29.

17 E.A.J., "Among the Local Shows," *New York Times*, October 14, 1945, Art, x7. See Ann Eden Gibson's discussion of African-American, non-Euro-American, and nonheterosexual male artists' use of abstraction in *Abstract Expressionism: Other Politics* (New Haven, Conn., 1997). Although primarily focusing on post–World War II New York and the dominance of the emerging abstract expressionist artists, Gibson provides a useful comparative analysis of the use of abstraction that may have been intended to work against prevailing notions of the primitive.

18 Unidentified source, October 28, 1945, frame 0513 [?], reel N/68-87, AAA.

19 No author cited. "Fantastic and Abstract Expressions Dominate Whitney Annual," *Art News*, December 1 (1945): 5 (frame 0513[?], reel N/68-87, NMAA file).

20 No author cited. "Sgt. Romare Bearden et Pietro Lazzari," *Arts*, October 24 (1945). Bearden Papers, AAA, Frame 0513 [?], reel N/68-87: "La galerie Crosby de Washington présente dans l'élégante petite galerie parisienne de John Devoluy des gouaches at des dessins de Romare Bearden sur La Passion et de Pietro Lazzari sur Les Chevaux. Romare Bearden, en joignant l'esthétique cubiste et l'art violemment colore des vitraux roman, a crée un art populaire aimple et impressionnant qui touche par des moyens directs renouvelés."

21 Marion Summers, "Art Today: A Talented Artist in the Picasso Idiom." Periodical source not cited in archival materials: frame 0515, reel N/68-87, AAA files.

22 The work was based on the satirical novel *Gargantua and Pantagruel*.

23 Barrie Stavis, foreword to *New Paintings by Bearden* [exh. cat., Samuel M. Kootz Gallery] (New York, 1947).

24 Ben Wolf, "Bearden Sings of the Cup That Cheers," *Art Digest* 21, no. 11 (March 1, 1947): 19.

25 Alfred M. Frankfurter, ed., "Women," *Art News* 46, no. 7 (1947): 39. Holty was part of the Kootz stable of artists. He and Bearden became friends and together wrote *The Painter's Mind: A Study of the Relations of Structure and Space in Painting* (New York and London, 1981), described as a treatise on flat painting; see Stephens Lee Glazer, "Signifying Identity: Art and Race in Romare Bearden's Projections," *Art Bulletin* 76, no. 3 (1994): 414.

26 William Carlos Williams, "Woman as Operator," in *Women: A Collaboration of Artists and Writers* [exh. cat., Samuel M. Kootz Gallery] (New York, 1948). Archival source: Romare Bearden Papers, AAA, N75.

27 Original emphasis. Romare Bearden Papers, AAA, box 2/3, "exhibition catalogues 1948–78."

28 "About Art and Artists: Exhibitions at Two Galleries Here Show Painters Profited by Their Absence," *New York Times*, November 5, 1955, 28L.

29 See, for example, Romare Bearden, "The Negro Artist's Dilemma," *Critique: A Review of Contemporary Art* 1, no. 2 (November 1946): 16–22.

30 Hale Woodruff, "The American Negro Artist," in *Eight New York Painters* (Ann Arbor: University of Michigan Museum of Art, 1956).

31 Carlyle Burrows, "Bearden's Return," *New York Herald Tribune*, January 24, 1960, 6.

32 Brian O'Doherty, "Art: O'-Keeffe Exhibition: Her Pictures Displayed at the Downtown—Bearden and Resnick Works on View," *New York Times* (Archival source: Romare Bearden Papers, AAA, frame 0519, reel N/68-87, NMAA file.

33 Stuart Preston, "Art: Summary of the Week's Events," *New York Times*, October 10, 1964, 26L.

34 C.Z.O., "Pictures on Exhibit," October 1964 review of *Projections*. Archival source: Romare Bearden Papers, AAA, frame 0383, reel N/68-57.

35 "Tormented Faces," *Newsweek* 44, no. 16 (October 19, 1964): 105.

36 "Art in New York," *Time* 84, no. 17 (October 16, 1964): NY5.

37 "Art Tour, the Galleries—A Critical Guide," review of *Projections, New York Herald Tribune* (October 10, 1964), 11.

38 Ralph Pomeroy, "Black Persephone," *Art News* 66, no. 6 (October 1967): 45, 73–75.

39 Cathy Aldridge, "Bearden's Collages Sold Though Exhibit Goes On," *New York Amsterdam News*, November 11, 1967, 23. The second half of the quotation may indicate a perceived shift in how Bearden's then current artistic production was held, in comparison to his earlier work, within the Harlem African-American community (see Holt 1945, 6).

40 John Canaday, "Romare Bearden Focuses on the Negro," *New York Times*, October 14, 1967.

41 "Painting: Touching at the Core," *Time* 90, no. 17 (October 27, 1967): 64.

42 Ralph Ellison, *Paintings and Projections* (Albany: Art Gallery, State University of New York, 1968).

43 Hilton Kramer, "Black Experience and Modernist Art," *New York Times*, February 14, 1970, 23.

44 By 'A (Artinomis),' "In the Galleries: Bearden at Cordier & Ekstrom," *Arts Magazine* 44, no. 5 (March 1970): 57.

45 *The Prevalence of Ritual* was a retrospective shown at MoMA March 25–June 7. See Chronology in this volume for dates and locations of other venues.

46 Emily Genauer, "Art and the Artist." *New York Post*, April 3, 1971, 34 (magazine p. 14).

47 Charles Allen, "...the Walls Come Tumbling Down?" *New York Times*, April 11, 1971, 27, 28.

48 Harlem Cultural Council, Inc., *Art of the American Negro: Exhibition of Painting and Sculpture* [exh. cat., Harlem Cultural Council, Inc.] (New York, 1966). Because Bearden acted as the curator of the show, he may have been the author of the passage.

49 Emily Genauer, "Does Race Color a Painter's Work?" *Newsday*, October 17, 1967, 1A.

50 Grace Glueck, "Negro Art from 1800 to 1950 Is on Display at City College," *New York Times,* October 16, 1967, L47 and L48.

51 Exhibition was held September 1970 in New York.

52 Joseph Mashek, "New York. Morris Louis, Rubin Gallery; Michael Steiner, Marlborough Gallery; Black Artists, Visual Arts Gallery," review of *Black Artists 1970, Artforum* 9, no. 1 (September 1970): 75–80.

53 Exhibition was held December 7, 1975–January 4, 1976, Museum of Fine Arts, Boston.

54 Henri Ghent, "Black Critic Takes a Look at 'Jubilee,'" *Boston Globe,* December 7, 1975, A13.

55 Glueck, "Two Centuries of Black Art at Brooklyn," *New York Times,* June 24, 1977, 14.

56 Glueck, "No Bones in Their Noses," *New York Times,* April 18, 1971, D21.

57 Hilton Kramer, "Art: Drawings with Graphic Subtlety. Romare Bearden," *New York Times,* March 31, 1973, 31.

58 Mary Schmidt Campbell, *Mysteries: Women in the Art of Romare Bearden* [exh. cat., Everson Museum of Art of Syracuse and Onondaga County] (Syracuse, N.Y., 1975), i–iii.

59 David Bourdon, "Music to the Eyes," review of *Of the Blues, Village Voice,* March 10, 1975, 84.

60 Michael Andre, "Romare Bearden," review of *Romare Bearden: Of the Blues, Art News* 74, no. 5 (May 1975): 95.

61 Susan Howe, "Romare Bearden at Cordier & Ekstrom," review of *Romare Bearden: Of the Blues (Second Chorus), Art in America* 64 (November–December 1976): 122.

62 Hale Woodruff, "The Art of Romare Bearden: A Closer Look," in *Bearden, Romano, Ross: Prints, Collages,* publishing information not provided in archival material.

63 Calvin Tomkins, Foreword to *Romare Bearden: Odysseus. Collages* [exh. cat., Cordier & Ekstrom] (New York, 1977).

64 John Russell, "Art: Bearden from Homer to Henri," *New York Times,* April 29, 1977, C22.

65 Hilton Kramer, "Bearden's 'Patchwork Cubism,'" *New York Times,* December 3, 1978, 2: 35.

66 "Romare Bearden (Cordier & Ekstrom)," *Art News* 78, no. 2 (February 1979): 172–73.

67 Bearden wrote anecdotal captions on the walls of the gallery.

68 Gylbert Coker, "Bearden's Sentimental Journey," *New York Amsterdam News,* January 6, 1979, D6.

69 Paul Richard, "The Integrated Art of Romare Bearden," *Washington Post,* April 25, 1981, H1, H5.

70 Writer Charles Johnson quotes Jean Toomer's self description in "A Sangha by Another Name," as a "psychological adventurer: one who, having had the stock experience of mankind, sets out at right angles to all previous experience to discover new states of being (p. 45)." Johnson goes on to describe Toomer's classic novel *Cane,* said to have "inaugurated the Renaissance," as "a hypnotic, language-rich montage of poetry and fiction that delivers a portrait of Southern black life as so mythic and shot through with elemental mysteries that it clearly belongs in the tradition of American transcendentalism stretching back to Emerson and Thoreau (p. 46)." In *Tricycle: The Buddhist Review* 9, no. 2 (Winter 1999): 43–47.

71 Amei Wallach, "Catching Daily Life in Visual Jazz," *New York Newsday,* October 4, 1981, pt. 2: 17, 18.

72 Larcelia Kebe, "Romare Bearden: The Artist and the Man" (no source cited in archival material, AAA), 1981.

73 Edward F. Weeks, Introduction to *Romare Bearden: Jazz* [exh. cat., Birmingham Museum of Art] (Birmingham, Ala., 1982).

74 Maryanne Conheim, "A Magical Master Who Is Thriving on 'Painting the Blues,'" *Philadelphia Inquirer,* May 6, 1982, 1D–7D.

75 Calvin Tomkins, "The Intelligent Hand," in *Romare Bearden: Mecklenburg Autumn: Oil Paintings with Collage* [exh. cat., Cordier & Ekstrom] (New York, 1983).

76 *Webster's New International Dictionary,* 2nd ed., as cited in the preface to exh. cat.

77 Michael Brenson, "Art: Romare Bearden, 'Rituals of the Obeah,'" *New York Times,* November 30, 1984, 23.

78 Richard Maschal, "New Bearden Works Leaner, Richer," *Charlotte Observer,* June 2, 1985.

79 Bernard Hanson, "In Innovative Exhibit, Bearden Executes Jazz on Canvas," *Hartford Courant,* June 15, 1986, G7.

80 Barbara McKenzie, "Collage Paintings Are Magical, Mysterious," *Atlanta Constitution,* June 6, 1986, 2B.

81 Nancy Princenthal, "Romare Bearden at Cordier & Ekstrom," *Art in America* 75, no. 2 (February 1987): 149.

82 Joy Colby, "Memories, Missions, Mosaics: A DIA Exhibit Showcases Romare Bearden's Varied Career," *Detroit News,* September 14, 1986, 7B.

83 Vivien Raynor, "A Glance at Romare Bearden at the Bronx Museum of the Arts," *New York Times,* January 4, 1987, 24.

84 Christine Temin, "Art Notes," review of *Bearden—Watercolors and Collages from the Mid 1960s On, Boston Globe,* November 28, 1987, 8.

BIBLIOGRAPHY / *Mary Lee Corlett*

Section 1
Archival Materials

Section 2
Film, Video, and Other Visual Materials

Section 3
Published Works by Bearden

Section 4
About Bearden

Section 5
General Reference

NOTES TO THE READER

This bibliography builds on the essential groundwork laid by a number of previously published bibliographies, including, but not limited to, those prepared by Judith Goldman (MoMA 1971), Theresa Cederholm (1973), Oakley N. Holmes (1978), Mint Museum (1980), and Lynn Moody Igoe (1981) and (1993). It also depends on the Herculean research efforts of everyone involved in this project, including, but not limited to, Rocío Aranda-Alvarado, Abdul Goler, Carmenita Higginbotham, and Sarah Kennel.

All the works listed (including those in Section 5: General Reference) contain some reference to Romare Bearden. Citations were confirmed by reviewing original sources whenever possible. In addition, brief annotations in brackets [ ] give further information about the source or its contents. For example, juvenile literature is identified as [children]. Exhibition reviews may be annotated with the title of the exhibition or the name of the institution (a short form is often used for both). Titles of works of art reproduced, as well as photographic images of the artist, are noted on a selective basis. Lists, including but not limited to artists' names, authors, etc. are not necessarily inclusive. If an exhibition is accompanied by a catalogue and a brochure, the brochure is noted in the catalogue citation. Many references document sources found in clipping files and other archival materials that are annotated with varying degrees of accuracy. Given time constraints, the difficulty imposed by inaccurate citations, and the unavailability of some primary sources, it has not been possible to examine firsthand every source cited. Citations not verified firsthand are followed with an asterisk and a reference to the citation source in brackets. For example [*Igoe (1981)] would indicate that I have not seen the actual material, but it was cited in Lynn Moody Igoe's 1981 bibliography. Clipping file material for which the citation has not been verified is also identified with an asterisk, followed by the name of the archive in which the clipping was found. Private archives are identified as such. —MLC

ABBREVIATIONS FOR BIBLIOGRAPHIC REFERENCES

Cederholm (1973): Theresa Dickason Cederholm. *Afro-American Artists: A Bio-bibliographical Directory.* Trustees of the Boston Public Library, 1973.

Holmes (1978): Oakley N. Holmes Jr. *The Complete Annotated Resource Guide to Black American Art.* Spring Valley, N.Y.: Black Artists in America, 1978.

Igoe (1981): Lynn Moody Igoe, with James Igoe. *250 Years of Afro-American Art: An Annotated Bibliography.* New York: Bowker, 1981. Updated version: Lynn Igoe. *African-American Artists* on Disc. New York: G.K. Hall & Co., c. 1999. [*laser optical disk, plus guide, University of Virginia Libraries (VIRGO) online catalogue; call no.XX(3527037.1); ISBN: 0783885393].

Igoe (1993): *Joy of Living: Romare Bearden's Late Work.* Exh. cat., North Carolina Central University, Durham, October 17–December 3, 1993. Text: Lynn Moody Igoe; Norman E. Pendergraft.

Mint Museum (1980): *Romare Bearden: 1970–1980.* Exh. cat., Mint Museum [of Art] (Department of Art), Charlotte, N.C., 1980. Text: Dore Ashton; Albert Murray; Jerald L. Melberg and Milton J. Bloch, eds.

MoMA (1971): *Romare Bearden: The Prevalence of Ritual.* Exh. cat., Museum of Modern Art, New York, 1971. Text: Judith Goldman; Carroll Greene; April Kingsley.

MoMA Scrapbooks: Museum of Modern Art, New York, Artists' Scrapbooks, Romare Bearden. Articles, reviews, catalogues, invitations, announcements; available on microfiche, Chadwyck-Healey, Alexandria, Va., 1986.

RB and Henderson, *Six Black Masters* (1972): Bearden, Romare, and Harry Henderson. *Six Black Masters of American Art.* New York: Doubleday & Co., Inc., 1972.

RB and Henderson, *A History of African-American Artists* (1993): Bearden, Romare, and Harry Henderson. *A History of African-American Artists: From 1792 to the Present.* New York: Pantheon Books, 1993.

RB and Holty, *The Painter's Mind* (1969): Bearden, Romare, and Carl Holty. *The Painter's Mind: A Study of the Relations of Structure and Space in Painting.* New York and London: Garland Publishing, Inc., 1981. Reprint of edition published by Crown Publishers, New York, 1969, with added introduction by Ralph Ellison.

Washington (1973): Washington, M. Bunch. *The Art of Romare Bearden: The Prevalence of Ritual.* New York: Harry N. Abrams, Inc., 1973. Introduction: John A. Williams.

OTHER ABBREVIATIONS

AAA: Archives of American Art, Smithsonian Institution, Washington, D.C.

AAA/RB: Romare Howard Bearden Papers, 1945–1981, Archives of American Art, Smithsonian Institution, Washington, D.C.

CATNYP: New York Public Library, online catalogue

C&E: Cordier & Ekstrom, Inc., New York

Kootz: Samuel M. Kootz Gallery, New York

LC: Library of Congress, Washington, D.C.

Met.: Metropolitan Museum of Art, New York

Mint Museum: Mint Museum of Art, Charlotte, North Carolina

MoMA: Museum of Modern Art, New York

NYPL: New York Public Library

NYPL/SC: Schomburg Center for Research in Black Culture, New York Public Library

NYT: *New York Times*

OCLC: OCLC Online Computer Library Center Inc., Dublin, Ohio

RB: Romare Bearden

RBF: Romare Bearden Foundation, New York

SMIH: Studio Museum in Harlem, New York

SITES: Smithsonian Institution Traveling Exhibition Service, Washington, D.C.

Whitney: Whitney Museum of American Art, New York

Whitney/Philip Morris: Whitney Museum of American Art at Philip Morris, New York, branch

Whitney/Stamford: Whitney Museum of American Art at Stamford, Connecticut, branch

Section I Archival Materials

ARCHIVAL COLLECTIONS

(Arranged alphabetically by archive.)

Archives of American Art, Smithsonian Institution, Washington, D.C.

Afro-American Historical and Cultural Museum [Philadelphia], Artists' Files, 1968–85. (microfilm).

Cinque Gallery Press Release [for opening], 1969. microfilm reel N70-48.

First World Festival of Negro Arts Photographs/Geoffrey Clements. Photograph by Clements of RB with artwork, for festival in Dakar, Senegal, 1966.

Lenore Seroka Photographs, 1977–84.

Printed Material on Romare Bearden, Alice Neel and Howard Newman, 1975–90. Donated by Estate of Dennis Florio. Exhibition announcements, catalogues, 1975–86.

Romare Howard Bearden Papers, 1945–81. [AAA/RB in subsequent citations] Correspondence, photographs, sketches, writings, clippings, catalogues, other unpublished materials.

Beinecke Rare Book and Manuscript Library, Yale University, New Haven, Conn.

Yale Collection of American Literature: Bearden, Romare. Untitled article on *The Passion;* handwritten, no date; *JWJ MSS Small Collections (James Weldon Johnson Collection).

Hatch-Billops Collection, Inc., New York

Hatch-Billops Archives of Black American Cultural History. Press clippings, slides, tapes, catalogues.

Museum of Modern Art Library, New York

Archives Pamphlet File, *Romare Bearden: The Prevalence of Ritual.* Uncatalogued material related to 1971 exhibition; call no.: MoMA 958x.

Artists' Scrapbooks, Romare Bearden. Articles, reviews, catalogues, invitations, announcements; available on microfiche, Chadwyck-Healey, Alexandria, Va., 1986.

Political Art Documentation and Distribution Archive Pamphlet File. Rainbow Art Foundation. One folder; uncatalogued material. *MoMA call. no.: PAD/D Archive; Rainbow Art Foundation.

Political Art Documentation and Distribution Archive Pamphlet File. Romare Bearden. One folder; uncatalogued material. *MoMA call. no.: PAD/D Archive; Rainbow Art Foundation.

Public Library of Charlotte and Mecklenburg County, Charlotte, North Carolina

Bearden, Romare. Biography files (7).

Romare Bearden Foundation, New York

Correspondence, video and audio recordings, manuscripts, sheet music, photographs, Bearden's library.

Schomburg Center for Research in Black Culture, New York Public Library

Art and Artifacts Division: Education Poster Collection, 1942–90. Includes one poster by RB. *CATNYP call no.: Sc Art Education posters; OCLC: 25459559.

Art and Artifacts Division: Romare Bearden Poster Collection, 1969–88. 21 posters for RB exhibitions, or that reproduce his art to advertise events; some autographed by RB. *CATNYP call no.: Sc Art Posters.

Art and Artifacts Division: Schomburg Library Events Poster Collection, 1940–91. Includes commissioned poster by RB. *CATNYP call no.: Sc Art Posters; OCLC: 26455752.

Manuscripts, Archives and Rare Books Division: (Romare) Bearden Papers, 1933–79. Correspondence, writings, notes. CATNYP call no.: Sc MG 74.

Photographs and Prints Division: Portrait Collection, Morgan and Marvin Smith [c. 1930–59]. Photographs by Morgan and Marvin Smith, Peggy Plummer. Includes group portraits with RB. *CATNYP call no.: Sc Photo Smith, Morgan & Marvin.

Photographs and Prints Division: Portrait Collection, Bessye and Romare Bearden [c. 1920–50]. Photographs by Addison Scurlock, Morgan and Marvin Smith. Includes views of RB as young boy; with Bessye. *CATNYP call no.: Sc Photo Bearden, Bessye and Romare.

University of North Carolina at Chapel Hill

Miscellaneous items on RB, 9 folios; gifts of Norman E. Pendergraft and Lynn Igoe. OCLC: 38584994; *UNC-CH call no. FFVCB B368.

MISCELLANEOUS PAPERS WITH BEARDEN CORRESPONDENCE

Archives of American Art, Smithsonian Institution, Washington, D.C.

Charles Henry Alston Papers, 1928–80

Carl Holty Papers, 1916–72

Stewart Klonis Papers, 1886–1982

Jacob Lawrence and Gwendolyn Knight Papers, 1937–79

Julian E. Levi Papers, 1846–1981

Earl Loran Papers, 1913–91

Marcia M. Mathews Papers Relating to Henry Ossawa Tanner, 1937–69

Roy R. Neuberger Papers, 1940–79; includes drawings by Bearden

Walter Quirt Papers, 1928–76

Robert Dennis Reid Papers, 1961–77

Raphael Soyer Papers, 1936–89

Saul Zalesch Collection of Artists' Letters, 1834–1973

SOUND RECORDINGS: INTERVIEWS

(Arranged alphabetically by archive.)

Interviews with Bearden

Archives of American Art, Smithsonian Institution, Washington, D.C.

Artists' Inner Vision. November 21, 1970. Discussion moderated by Alvin C. Hollingsworth, with RB, Reginald Gammon, Max Ginsburg, Alfonso Ossorio. No transcript.

Colette Roberts: Interviews with Artists. 1961–71. No transcript.

Crosscurrents U.S.A. [exhibition] Artists' Statements. Detroit Institute of Arts, March 1969. No transcript.

Esther G. Rolick Papers. 1941–85. For Rolick's course "Black Music and Art," Mercy College, c. 1970–71. No transcript.

Interview by Avis Berman. July 31, 1980. Transcript (45 pp.).

Interview by Henri Ghent. New York, June 29, 1968. Transcript (29 pp., microfilm). Oral History Program.

Irma Jaffe Interviews. 1965–77. Discussion with Spiral artists, featuring RB and Alvin C. Hollingsworth; commentary by Jeanne Siegel. No transcript.

Karl E. Fortess: Interviews with Artists. 1963–85. No transcript.

The Hatch-Billops Oral History Collection of Black Culture, New York

A Conversation with Mr. Romare Bearden. New York, December 6, 1972. Interview by James Hatch and Camille Billops. (1 cassette), no. 16; approx. 55 minutes; with abstract.

Museum of Modern Art, New York

Interview by Carroll Greene. [197?]. 2 analogue cassettes. *MoMA call no.: audio C0088.

"The Block." 1971. 1 sound tape reel, continuous loop: music, voices, street sounds for RB's *The Block,* for 1971 solo exh. *MoMA call no.: sound recording #71.28a.

Interviews with Bearden Discussed

Archives of American Art, Smithsonian Institution, Washington, D.C., Oral History Program

Charles Henry Alston. October 19, 1968. 1 sound tape reel; transcript (25 pp., on microfilm reel 4223; also available online); interviewer: Albert Murray.

Dana Chandler. March 11–May 5, 1993. 4 analogue cassettes (6 hrs.); interviewer: Robert F. Brown. [April 14: some discussion of RB.]

Herbert Gentry. May 23, 1991. 2 cassettes; transcript (22 pp.; also available online); interviewer: Liza Kirwin.

New York Public Library

Dianne McIntyre. April 1 and 8, 2000. 6 cassettes (approx. 6½ hrs.). Transcript (191 leaves). Interviewer: Jennifer Dunning in *NYT* office. Cassette 6, April 8 (10 mins.): discusses *Ancestral Voices,* Bearden designed costumes. *CATNYP call no.: *MGZMT 3-2252 (transcript); *MGXTC 3-3353 (sound cassette). [Asterisk is part of call no.]

BROADCASTS

(Arranged chronologically.)

Jeanne Siegel. "The Unknown American Negro Artists." 1967. Sound recording, 42 mins.; 1 tape reel. MoMA and WBAI-FM Radio, New York. Radio interview on October 12, 1967; published as "Romare Bearden: The Unknown American Negro Artists," in Jeanne Siegel, *Artwords: Discourse on the 60s and 70s* (Ann Arbor, Mich.: UMI Research Press, 1985), 72–83. *MoMA call no.: sound recording #67.6. Museum of Modern Art, New York.

Mike Wallace. "Romare Bearden: The Prevalence of Ritual." 1971. Sound recording. 1 tape reel. Interview. *MoMA call no.: sound recording #71.50. Museum of Modern Art, New York.

"Rhythm on Canvas." 1987. Interview with RB by Charlene Hunter Gault. *MacNeil/Lehrer Report,* on *Rhythm on Canvas,* 40-year retrospective exh. [*Origins and Progressions?*] at Bronx Museum of the Arts, New York. Public Broadcasting System, WNET, New York, June 26, 1987. *www.BeardenFoundation.org.

"Collage: The Life & Times of Romare Bearden." 1988. Vertamae Smart-Grosvenor. Sound recording; 1 cassette. National Public Radio, Washington, D.C., *Horizons,* October 4, 1988. OCLC: 30497019; *University of North Carolina, Charlotte, J. Murrey Atkins Library, online catalogue.

"Romare Bearden—Charlotte Collaborations." 2003. Steve Crump Production, Charlotte, N.C. WTVI, Charlotte, February 19, 2003.

MUSIC MANUSCRIPTS

(Arranged chronologically.)

Hello and Good-bye. 1951. Music by David Ellis; lyrics by Romare Bearden. 1 leaf; melody with chord symbols. LC call no.: M1630.2.E.

Little Girl. 1951. Music by Dave Ellis; lyrics by Romy Bearden. 1 leaf; melody with chord symbols. OCLC: 30517910. LC call no.: M1630.2.E.

The Promise of Spring. 1951. Music by Dave Ellis; lyrics by Romie Bearden. 1 leaf; melody with chord symbols. OCLC: 30508306. LC call no.: M1630.2.E.

It's Twilight in My Heart. 1954. Music by Marvin Lagunoff; words by Rommie Bearden. 1 leaf; melody only. OCLC: 30517931. LC call no.: M1630.2.L.

Just as You Are. 1954. Music by Marvin Lagunoff; words by Rommie Bearden. 1 leaf; melody only. OCLC: 30517919. LC call no.: M1630.2.L.

The Street without a Name. 1954. Music by Ruth Frank; lyrics by Romare Bearden and David Ellis. 1 leaf; melody only. OCLC: 30517924. LC call no.: M1630.2.F.

Section 2 Film, Video, and Other Visual Materials

FILM AND VIDEO

(Arranged chronologically.)

Bearden

Positively Black. [Romare Bearden] [video] New York: WNBC-TV, 1979. Producer: Bonnie B. Boswell; director: Harry J. McNeill; interviewer: Carol Jenkins. [U-matic, 28 mins., color] [Topics discussed by RB include use of recurring themes, method of working, Paris, people who have influenced his work.] *CATNYP call no.: Sc Visual VRA-48 (service copy); Sc Visual VRB-171 (original). OCLC: 20344272. Communications Excellence to Black Audiences Award Collection.

Romare Bearden: Mirrors of Life. [video] Charlotte, N.C.: Group W Productions, [WPCQ-TV], 1980. [U-matic, 25 mins., color] Producer/author: Pat Bates. [presentation of WRET-TV; RB discusses blues tradition and his work] *CATNYP call no: Sc Visual VRA-49 (service copy); Sc Visual VRB-213 (original). OCLC: 20656365. Communications Excellence to Black Audiences Award Collection.

Bearden Plays Bearden. [video] St. Petersburg, Fla.: Third World Cinema Productions, 1980. 59 mins., color, 16 mm; (short version, 28 mins.). Narrator: James Earl Jones; producer: Richard Bell; director: Nelson E. Breen; authors: Billie Allen, Nelson E. Breen. [released as motion picture 1981] [Emmy award/directing; Emmy nominee/music, 1985; CINE Golden Eagle, 1981; Houston International Film Festival Bronze Award, 1981]. *Program for Art on Film, Brooklyn, New York, online database: *www.artfilm.org.*

Black News. [Romare Bearden] [video] WNEW-TV, New York, 1981. [U-matic, 4 mins., color] Interviewer: Lynne White; producer: Robert E. Martin. [Bearden exhibition at Brooklyn Museum of Art. RB explains symbolism in his work.] *CATNYP call no.: Sc Visual VRA-97 (service copy); ScVisual VRB-313 (original). OCLC: 20657965. Communications Excellence to Black Audiences Award Collection.

Romare Bearden. [video] Interviewer: Kate Horsfield. Chicago: Video Data Bank, 1984. 28 mins., color, VHS. (coproducers: Lyn Blumenthal and Kate Horsfield) [series title: *On Art and Artists*]. *Carnegie Mellon University Libraries; Video Data Bank website: *www.vdb.org.*

Inside New York's Art World: Romare Bearden. [video] Interviewer: Barbaralee Diamonstein. 1 videocassette, 1986/87. color, VHS [originally issued as U-matic videocassette]. *Duke University Libraries, Durham, N.C. OCLC: 15273644.

Memories of Bearden. [video] 9 mins., color. CBS News, 1991. *Program for Art on Film, Brooklyn, N.Y., online database: *www.artfilm.org.*

Romare Bearden: Visual Jazz. [video]. African American Artists series. Chappaqua, N.Y.: L & S Video, 1995. 28 mins., color, VHS. Narrator: Wynton Marsalis. Producer: Linda Freeman; author/director: David Irving [footage of RB working, trumpet solos by Marsalis, comments by Robert Blackburn, Barrie Stavis]. *Program for Art on Film, Brooklyn, N.Y., online database: *www.artfilm.org.* [*Romare Bearden: The Direct Experience,* listed in Crystal Productions, Glenview, Ill., 1996 sales catalogue, was a preliminary title for *Visual Jazz.*]

Bearden and Others

Black Artists in America: Part One. [video] Alexandria, Va.: Dr. Oakley N. Holmes, Jr. [1990], © 1970. 20 mins., color, VHS. Videocassette release of motion picture. Producer: Oakley N. Holmes, Jr. [nine artists]. *Program for Art on Film, Brooklyn, N.Y., online database: *www.artfilm.org.* OCLC: 25426457.

Black Artists in America: Part Two. [video] Alexandria, Va.: Dr. Oakley N. Holmes, Jr. [1991], © 1971. 41 mins., color, VHS. Videocassette release of motion picture. Producer: Oakley N. Holmes, Jr. [sole documentation of 1971 panel: African-American sculptors, painters, curators, historians, museum directors discuss complexity of their status in United States. Historical introduction by RB with rare footage of Black Art Shows of 1930s]. *Program for Art On Film, Brooklyn, N.Y., online database: *www.artfilm.org.* OCLC: 25598703.

Black Artists in America: Part Three. [video] Alexandria, Va.: Dr. Oakley N. Holmes, Jr. [1990], © 1973. 34 mins., color, VHS. Videocassette release of motion picture. Producer: Oakley N. Holmes, Jr. [seven artists] *Program for Art On Film, Brooklyn, N.Y., online database: *www.artfilm.org.* OCLC: 26464316.

Five. [film] 29 mins., color, 16 mm. Silvermine Films, Inc., [1971 or 1975?]. Director: Alvin Yudkoff. [five artists] *Program for Art on Film, Brooklyn, N.Y., online database: *www.artfilm.org;* CATNYP call no. Sc Visual VRA-219 (service copy); Sc Visual MPB-171 (original). [NYPL date: 1975; Program for Art on Film date: 1971]

Two Centuries of Black American Art. [film] Los Angeles County Museum of Art. Santa Monica, Calif.: Pyramid Films, 1976. 26 mins., color, 1 reel. Producer/director: Carlton Moss; narrator: Stanley Waxman. [survey of black art history in America; segments by artists, including RB] *CATNYP call no.: Sc Visual MPB-109 (original); Sc Visual VRA-208 (service copy).

Contemporary Artists at Work. Volume II. [filmstrip] New York: Harcourt Brace Jovanovich Films, 1978. 2 rolls, plus 2 sound recordings (33⅓ rpm 12 in.) and 1 teacher's guide. [also issued with sound cassettes] Author: Dan Tooker; producer/director/photographer: Dan De Wilde; consultants: Henry T. Hopkins, Peter Plagens. [ten artists] *LC call no. ND212 filmstrip 3806; LCCN: 78730978.

Core of the Apple. [video] Producers: Danish Television, 1985. 5 mins., color, VHS. [RB and Herbert Gentry make collaborative painting while listening to jazz.] Available at AAA.

African-American Artists Speak: Civil Rights. [video] Producers: ARC Videodance as part of television series *Eye on Dance.* Recorded January 30, 1989, at studios of WNYC-TV, New York. Telecast February 23, 1989. 29 mins., color with b/w sequences. Producers: Celia Ipiotis and Jeff Bush; video director: Richard Sheridan; host: Celia Ipiotis. [Nanette Bearden among the guests; performance excerpts include *Homage to Mary Lou,* choreography by Walter Rutledge, Dianne McIntyre, and Alvin Ailey; sets by RB] *CATNYP call no. MGZIC 9-3099 (performing arts–dance).

Griots of Imagery: A Comment on the Art of Romare Bearden & Charles White. [video] 28 mins., color. New York: Praisesong on a Shoestring, Inc., 1993. Producer: James Macove; executive producers: Russell Goings, Evelyn Boulware; author/narrator: Primus Mason Davy. [1993 exh. at Manhattan East Gallery, New York]. Available: AAA; NYPL.

Art History and Art Criticism. [video] © J. Paul Getty Trust, 1995. Color. Director: Donald R. Ham. [includes segment on Los Angeles 2nd-grade classroom in which U.S. history and art are interwoven] *LC call no.: VAE 3160; LCCN: 96507491.

American Visions: The Empire of Signs. [video] Planet 24 production in association with BBC Television; a Time, Inc.-BBC coproduction in association with Thirteen/WNET, 1997. [PBS Home Video, Alexandria, Va.; distributed by Warner Home Video] 60 mins., color, VHS. [American Visions series, no. 7 of 8] Producer/director: James Kent [Programs for Art on Film database *www.artfilm.org* lists Julia Cave as producer/director, but most other sources cite Kent.] Author/narrator: Robert Hughes. [examines America's development toward consumer culture and art produced from 1950s to 1970s]. *Smithsonian Institution Research Information System: *www.siris.si.edu;* Program for Art on Film, Brooklyn, N.Y., online database: *www.artfilm.org.*

I'll Make Me a World: Not a Rhyme Time. [video] Boston: Blackside, Inc., in association with Thirteen/WNET, 1999. Color and b/w, VHS. [*I'll Make Me a World* series; no. 5 of 6] [producer/director: Denise Green] [African-American achievement in the arts; eleven artists and writers featured] *LC call no.: VAH 2031 (viewing copy); LCCN: 2001635497; *www.blackside.com.*

SLIDE SETS

(Arranged chronologically. All titles in brackets are works of art by Bearden.)

Afro-American Artists: 1800–1968. Baldwin, N.Y.: Prothmann Associates, 1968 [1969?]. 40 slides. Commentator: Carroll Greene, Jr. [8 pp.]. [34 artists]. *OCLC FirstSearch, WorldCat database: *http://FirstSearch.oclc.org.* OCLC: 16678184 and 5545444.

Contemporary Black Artists. New York: Sandak, [1969?]. 47 slides. [works in the revised touring exh. of *30 Contemporary Black Artists* at Minneapolis Institute of Arts, October 1968] [*Family, Palm Sunday Procession*]. *Southeastern Louisiana University, Sims Memorial Library online catalogue, slide set 22. OCLC: 4393649.

Romare Bearden: Ritual Bayou. New York: Visual Resources, Inc., n.d. [1970s?] *Saint Cloud State University (Minnesota) Library call no. N6537.B4 R65x. OCLC: 9300996.

The Painting of Romare Bearden. Educational Dimensions Corp., 1971. 20 slides, teacher's guide. *University of North Carolina, Chapel Hill, online library catalogue.

The Black Experience. Stamford, Conn.: Sandak, [1973?]. 60 slides, teacher's guide by Bearden and Philip S. Foner. [*Jazz—1930's Chicago, Prince Cinque,* in exh. *The Black Experience In Prints,* Pratt Graphic Art Center, February 1972]. *Southeastern Louisiana University, Sims Memorial Library, slide set 18. OCLC: 4284978.

Contemporary American Black Artists. Stamford, Conn.: Sandak, [1970–79?]. 25 slides. [21 artists] *OCLC FirstSearch, WorldCat database: *http://FirstSearch.oclc.org.* OCLC: 5962723.

Masters of Collage. Kenilworth, N.J.: Art Now, Inc., [1978?]. 158 slides. [12 artists] *Minnesota State University, Mankato, audiovisual collection N6494.C6 M3x. OCLC: 10426075.

American Black Artists. Sarasota, Fla.: Universal Color Slide Co., [1980? 1993?]. 50 slides. [19th- and 20th-century art; *She-ba, Return of the Prodigal Son, Interior*]. *OCLC FirstSearch, WorldCat database: *http://FirstSearch.oclc.org.* OCLC: 29306061.

Afro-American Artists. Seattle, Wash.: Shoreline Community College, 1981. 44 slides. Compiler: Bob Kelly. [17 Bearden slides]. *OCLC FirstSearch: OCLC: 43042013.

Modern Art by Black Americans. New York: American Library Color Slide Co., Inc., 1986 [?]. 24 slides [21 artists; *Blue Interior Morning, Patchwork Quilt, Ritual Bayou*] *OCLC FirstSearch, WorldCat database: *http://FirstSearch.oclc.org.* OCLC: 15128966.

Adventures in Art. Level 5. Worcester, Mass.: Rosenthal Art Slides, [1990s]. 30 slides. [accompanies textbook *Adventures in Art,* Worcester, Mass.: Davis Publications, Inc., (1994?/1998?); *Sermons: The Walls of Jericho*]. *OCLC FirstSearch, WorldCat database: *http://FirstSearch.oclc.org* OCLC: 37349713.

Western. United States. Painting. 20th Century. A–G. n.d. [1990s?]. *South Puget Sound Community College, Library-Media Center, Olympia, Wash., call no.: slide room 78-40-20. OCLC: 42486118.

Rosenthal Art Slides from the 90's Catalog. Part 5. 20th Century American Painting. Chicago: Rosenthal Art Slides, 1992. 45 slides. [*Woodshed*]. *OCLC FirstSearch, WorldCat database: *http://FirstSearch.oclc.org.* OCLC: 40893983.

African American Art. 1993. 15 slides. [*Prince Cinque, Palm Sunday Procession*] *Normandale Community College Library, Bloomington, Minn., N 6538 A7.5x. OCLC: 29332587.

African-American Experience as Depicted in XVIIIc–XXc Art. New York: American Library Color Slide Co., 1999. 48 slides. *OCLC FirstSearch, WorldCat database: *http://FirstSearch.oclc.org.* OCLC: 43720616.

ART REPRODUCTION SETS

(Arranged chronologically. All titles in brackets are works of art by Bearden.)

American Black Artists. Sandy Hook, Conn.: Shorewood Reproductions, and Flemington, N.J.: Modern Learning Press, 1985 © 1970. 9 plates, teacher's guide, artists' biographies, painting critiques. [*Summertime*]. *OCLC FirstSearch, WorldCat database: *http://FirstSearch.oclc.org.* OCLC: 21480762. [see also OCLC: 30639186 for record of similar set of 8 plates]

Contemporary Black American Artists. Chicago: Johnson Publishing Company, 1974. 16 plates. [JPC art collection; Ebony Photopak #5]. [*Two of Them*]. *OCLC FirstSearch, WorldCat database: *http://FirstSearch.oclc.org.* OCLC: 3495728.

Black Artists in America. Sandy Hook, Conn.: Shorewood Fine Art Reproductions, 1974. 12 plates, teacher's guide. [Shorewood art programs for education, no. 5014; *Summertime*]. *OCLC FirstSearch, WorldCat database: *http://FirstSearch.oclc.org.* [WorldCat cites program 5014 (12 plates)/OCLC: 12764250, and program 5024 (15 plates)/OCLC: 12764446]

How Do I Feel? New York: Shorewood Reproductions, 1974. 12 plates, teacher's guide. [*Summertime*]. *OCLC FirstSearch, WorldCat database: *http://FirstSearch.oclc.org.* OCLC: 3684334.

We All Ask "Who Am I?" Sandy Hook, Conn.: Shorewood Fine Art Reproductions, 1974. 12 plates, teacher's guide. [program 5019; *Summertime*]. *OCLC FirstSearch, WorldCat database: *http://FirstSearch.oclc.org.* OCLC: 12661126.

American Black Artists. New York: Shorewood Reproductions, 1980. 10 plates. [*Summertime*]. *OCLC FirstSearch, WorldCat database: *http://FirstSearch.oclc.org.* OCLC: 9564581.

American Artists: 1700 to the Present. Sandy Hook, Conn.: Shorewood Fine Art Reproductions, 1983. 25 plates, teacher's guide. [*She-ba*]. *OCLC FirstSearch, WorldCat database: *http://FirstSearch.oclc.org.* OCLC: 18160812.

Cityscapes. Aspen, Colo.: Crystal Productions, 1989. 5 plates, guide. Consultant: Kay Alexander. [*Pittsburgh Memories*]. *OCLC FirstSearch, WorldCat database: *http://FirstSearch.oclc.org.* OCLC: 23171835.

Davis Visuals. Color. Worcester, Mass.: Davis Publications, 1990. 24 plates, teacher's guide. Commentator: John Lidstone. [*Carolina Blue*]. *OCLC FirstSearch, WorldCat database: *http://FirstSearch.oclc.org* OCLC: 23857802.

Free within Ourselves. Washington, D.C., and Petaluma, Calif.: Pomegranate Publications, 1991. 8 plates. [*Family*]. *OCLC FirstSearch, WorldCat database: *http://FirstSearch.oclc.org.* OCLC: 31640719.

Exploring Art. Lake Forest, Ill.: Glencoe/Macmillan/McGraw-Hill, 1992. Student text, teacher's edition, teacher's resource binder, 30 transparencies with guide, 20 plates with guide. Compilers: Jane Rhoades, Rosalind Ragans. [*The Prevalence of Ritual: Tidings*]. *OCLC FirstSearch, WorldCat database: *http://FirstSearch.oclc.org.* OCLC: 38292500.

Adventures in Art. Level 1.2.3 Large Reproductions. Worcester, Mass.: Davis Publications, 1993, 1998. 25 plates, teacher's guide. [for use with *Adventures in Arts* textbooks by Laura H. Chapman, grades 1–3; editor: Cynthia Colbert] [*Serenade*]. *OCLC FirstSearch, WorldCat database: *http://FirstSearch.oclc.org* OCLC: 29347189 and 39164642.

Portfolios: African American Artists. Palo Alto, Calif.: Dale Seymore Publications, 1994. 12 plates in portfolio. Biographical and discussion material on versos by Teresa S. Unseld. [*Three Folk Musicians*]. *OCLC FirstSearch, WorldCat database: *http://FirstSearch.oclc.org.* OCLC: 37729680.

Know the Artist. Set 1. Glenview, Ill.: Crystal Productions, 1998 [1999]. 8 color posters, teacher's guide. Artchart poster series. [8 artists; posters © 1998; Teacher's Guide 1999]. *OCLC FirstSearch, WorldCat database: *http://FirstSearch.oclc.org.* OCLC: 41527716.

Interdisciplinary Connections: Art and Music. Aspen, Colo.: Crystal Productions, 1999. 5 plates, guide. Consultants: Nancy Walkup; Pam Stephens. [*Out Chorus*]. *OCLC FirstSearch, WorldCat database: *http://FirstSearch.oclc.org.* OCLC: 42857101.

African-American Artists. Orem, Utah: Art Visuals, 2000. 18 plates, brief biographies. [*The Black Man in the Building of America*]. *OCLC FirstSearch, WorldCat database: *http://FirstSearch.oclc.org.* OCLC: 47737090.

Section 3 Published Works by Bearden

INTERVIEWS AND PANEL DISCUSSIONS

(Arranged chronologically by date of interview or discussion. See also "Sound Recordings: Interviews" in Section 1 and "Film and Video" in Section 2.)

Siegel, Jeanne. "Why Spiral?" *Art News* 65 (September 1966): 48–51, 67–68.

"How Effective Is Social Protest Art? (Civil Rights)." In Jeanne Siegel, *Artwords: Discourse on the 60s and 70s.* Ann Arbor, Mich.: UMI Research Press, 1985, 84–98. Panel discussion with RB, Alvin Hollingsworth, and William Majors; moderator: Jeanne Siegel. Recorded and broadcast, December 14, 1967, WBAI.

Siegel, Jeanne. "Romare Bearden: The Unknown American Negro Artists." In Jeanne Siegel, *Artwords: Discourse on the 60s and 70s.* Ann Arbor, Mich.: UMI Research Press, 1985, 72–83. Artist interview broadcast on WBAI on October 12, 1967. [see also MoMA Archives; call no.: sound recording 67.6; one tape reel; 42 mins.]

Jacobs, Jay. "Two Afro-American Artists in an Interview." *The ART Gallery* 11, no. 7 (April 1968): 26–31. Report on separate interviews with RB and Hughie Lee-Smith, in prose format with quotations.

"Romare Bearden: Visual Artist. Interviewers: Camille Billops and James V. Hatch, December 6, 1972." *Artist and Influence* 17 (1998): 30–41. [Hatch-Billops Collection, Inc., New York: *hatchbillops@worldnet.att.net*]

D'Amico, Margarita [interviewer]. "Romare Bearden: El Ritual Negro Americano." *7° Día* (Revista dominical de *El Nacional,* Caracas), December 2, 1973, 10–11.

Kendall, Michael. "Romare Bearden Interview." *Art Worker's News* 6 (April 1977): 6–7, 12.

Staats, Margaret, and Lucas Matthiessen. "Genetics of Art—Part 2." *Quest/77* 1, no. 3 (July–August 1977): 38–43. [RB, p. 41]

Glueck, Grace. "The 20th-Century Artists Most Admired by Other Artists." *Art News* 76 (November 1977): 78–103. [RB comments, photo, p. 80]

Diamonstein, Barbaralee. "How to Redesign New York." *Art News* 77 (November 1978): 76–82. [RB comments, pp. 76, 78]

Breen, Nelson E., ed. "To Hear Another Language: Alvin Ailey, James Baldwin, Romare Bearden, and Albert Murray in Conversation." *Callaloo* 40 (Summer 1989): 431–52. [edited by Breen from transcript of conversation on December 15, 1978, recorded for the film *Bearden Plays Bearden*]

Diamonstein, Barbaralee. *Inside New York's Art World.* New York: Rizzoli, 1979. [RB, pp. 28–39]

Miro, Marsha. "Q. Romare Bearden: Beggars Can Be Kings?" *Detroit Free Press,* December 8, 1979, 1A.

Toppman, Lawrence. "Romare Bearden: Painter of Memories." *Charlotte News,* Sunday Magazine, October 4, 1980, C1–2. [exh. *Romare Bearden 1970–1980,* Mint Museum]

Magnan, George A. "Romare Bearden: Master Collage Maker." *Today's Art and Graphics* 29, no. 3 (1981): 4–8.

Peters, Joy. "Romare Bearden: Jazz Intervals." *Art Papers* 7 (January–February 1983): 11.

Schwartzman, Myron. "Romare Bearden Sees in a Memory." *Artforum International* 22 (May 1984): 64–70.

"Interview with Romare Bearden." In *Since the Harlem Renaissance: 50 Years of Afro-American Art.* Exh. cat., Center Gallery of Bucknell University, Lewisburg, Pa., April 13–June 6, 1984. Cat. published 1985. [December 9, 1984, New York; conducted by exh. curator (Joseph Jacobs?)]

Mennekes, Friedhelm. "Romare Bearden." *Kunst und Kirche* (April 1987): 267–69.

Schwartzman, Myron. "A Bearden-Murray Interplay: One Last Time." In "In Memoriam: Romare H. Bearden, 1912–1988." *Callaloo* 36 (Summer 1988): 410–15. [May 27, 1987, conversation with RB and Albert Murray]

Rowell, Charles H. "'Inscription at the City of Brass': An Interview with Romare Bearden." In "In Memoriam: Romare H. Bearden, 1912–1988." *Callaloo* 36 (Summer 1988): 428–46. [August 11, 1987]

Schwartzman, Myron. *Romare Bearden: His Life and Art.* New York: Harry N. Abrams, Inc., 1990. [extensive interviews]

WRITINGS

(Arranged chronologically by publication date.)

"The Negro Artist and Modern Art." *Opportunity: Journal of Negro Life* 12 (December 1934): 371–72. Reprinted in *The Portable Harlem Renaissance Reader,* ed. David L. Lewis, New York: Penguin Books, 1994, 138–41. [also reprinted in Lindsay Patterson, *The Negro in Music and Art,* New York: Publishers Company, 1967, 221–23 (per Mary Schmidt Campbell, "Romare Bearden: A Creative Mythology," Ph.D. dissertation, Syracuse University, N.Y., 1982); and in *Speech and Power: The African-American Essay and Its Cultural Content, from Polemics to Pulpit,* ed. Gerald Early, Hopewell, N.J.: Ecco Press, 1993, 2:10–13]

"The Negro in Little Steel." *Opportunity: A Journal of Negro Life* 15 (December 1937): 362–65, 380.

Artist's Statement. In *Romare Bearden: Oils, Gouaches, Water Colors, Drawings 1937–1940.* Exh. cat., 306 West 141st Street, New York, May 4–May 11 [1940].

Artist's Statement: "The Passion of Christ." Exh. cat., G Place Gallery, Washington, D.C. (?), June 1945. [*AAA/RB; frame 0171, reel N/68-87]

Artist's Statement. In *First New York Exhibition: Romare Bearden.* Exh. cat., Kootz, New York, 1945. [excerpt from "The Passion of Christ" (June 1945), probably published for G Place Gallery exh.]

"The Negro Artist's Dilemma." *Critique: A Review of Contemporary Art* 1, no. 2 (November 1946): 16–22.

"The Artistic Imagination." In *Second Annual Fall Review of Paintings and Sculpture: 1956.* Exh. cat., Pyramid Club, Philadelphia, October 26–November 26, 1956.

[statement] "Romare Bearden—Biography." In *Romare Bearden Projections,* exh. cat., C&E, October 6–24, 1964. [*Mary Schmidt Campbell, "Romare Bearden: A Creative Mythology," Ph.D. dissertation, Syracuse University, N.Y., 1982]

Artist's Statement. In... *Some Negro Artists.* Exh. cat., Fairleigh Dickinson University, Madison, N.J., Art Gallery, October 20–November 20, 1964.

Artist's Statement. In *Romare Bearden.* Exh. cat., Corcoran Gallery of Art, Washington, D.C., October 1–31, 1965.

Artist's Statement. In *Contemporary Urban Visions.* Exh. cat., New School Art Center, Wollman Hall, New York, January 25–February 24, 1966, 5.

"Art of American Negro on Exhibit in Harlem." *New York Amsterdam News,* July 16, 1966, 46.

Untitled poem. In *Ten Negro Artists from the United States. (Dix artistes nègres des Etats-Unis.)* Exh. cat., United States, Commission for the First World Festival of Negro Arts, and National Collection of Fine Arts, Smithsonian Institution. First World Festival of Negro Arts, Dakar, Senegal, 1966.

Bearden, Romare, and Carroll Greene, Jr. *Evolution of the Afro-American Artist, 1800–1950.* Exh. cat., City University of New York, Harlem Cultural Council and National Urban League, 1967. [includes excerpt from an essay by Carroll Greene, Jr.; brief artist biographies; checklist]

Artist's Statement. In *Romare Bearden: Six Panels on a Southern Theme.* Exh. cat., Bundy Art Gallery, Waitsfield, Vt., April 12–May 29, 1967.

Artist's Statement. In *Romare Bearden Collages.* Exh. cat., J. L. Hudson Gallery, Detroit, November 9–30, 1967. [reprints text by John Canaday, "Treatment Is Poignant but Not Mawkish," *NYT,* October 14, 1967]

Untitled poem. In *Encounters: An Exhibition in Celebration of the Charlotte-Mecklenburg Bi-Centennial.* Exh. cat., Johnson C. Smith University, James B. Duke Library, Charlotte, N.C., November–December 1968. Introduction by Eugene Grigsby. [begins: "One summer long ago I stayed With my grandfather, In Charlotte, North Carolina."]

"The Artist Responds." *Harvard Art Review* 3, no. 2 (1969): 31. [biographical note, p. 32] [RB response, among others, to letter sent to artists by associate editor David Stang soliciting commentary on art education]

Bearden, Romare, and Carl Holty. *The Painter's Mind: A Study of the Relations of Structure and Space in Painting.* New York and London: Garland Publishing, Inc., 1981. Reprint of edition published by Crown Publishers, New York, 1969, with added introduction by Ralph Ellison.

"Rectangular Structure in My Montage Paintings." *Leonardo* 2 (January 1969): 11–19.

[RB: moderator] "The Black Artist in America: A Symposium." *Metropolitan Museum of Art Bulletin* 27.5 (January 1969): 245–61. [participants: Sam Gilliam, Jr., Richard Hunt, Jacob Lawrence, Tom Lloyd, William Williams, Hale Woodruff]

"Bearden Reviews Thompson Exhibits." *New York Amsterdam News,* April 26, 1969. [exh. *Afro-American Artists since 1950,* sponsored by Brooklyn League of Afro-American Collegians, at Brooklyn College Student Center, New York]

[Statement]. *The Black Experience.* Exh. cat., Lincoln University, Jefferson City, Mo., 1970. [statements by RB, Jay Jacobs.] [*Igoe (1981)]

"The Poetics of Collage." In *Art Now: New York* 2, no. 4 (1970): unpaginated folio.

Artist's Statement. In "Black Art: What Is It?" *The ART Gallery* 13, no. 7 (April 1970): 32–35. [with statements by ten others; RB, p. 33]

[book review: *American Negro Art* by Cedric Dover]. *Leonardo* 3 (April 1970): 241–43.

Bearden, Romare, and Carl Holty. [book review: *Theories of Modern Art: A Source Book by Artists and Critics* by Herschel B. Chipp]. *Leonardo* 3 (July 1970): 361–62.

"Foreword." *Fifteen under Forty: Paintings by Young New York State Black Artists.* Exh. cat., Gallery Museum, Hall of Springs, Saratoga Performing Arts Center, N.Y., July 1–July 31, 1970.

"The 1930's—An Art Reminiscence." *New York Amsterdam News,* September 18, 1971, D24, D26.

Bearden, Romare, and Harry Henderson. *Six Black Masters of American Art.* New York: Doubleday & Co., Inc., 1972.

Bearden, Romare, and Philip S. Foner. Teacher's Guide, *The Black Experience.* Stamford, Conn.: Sandak, [1973?] [with set of 60 slides of works in exh. *The Black Experience in Prints,* Pratt Graphic Art Center (February 1972)]

Bearden, Romare, and Harry Henderson. "Letters to the Editor: Black Art." *Art in America* 61 (March–April 1973): 117. [response to Henri Ghent's reviews of *Six Black Masters*]

"Historical Notes." In *The Barnett-Aden Collection.* Washington, D.C.: Smithsonian Institution Press, 1974. Published for Anacostia Neighborhood Museum, in cooperation with Barnett-Aden Gallery. [catalogue for exh. at Anacostia Neighborhood Museum, Smithsonian Institution, Washington, D.C., January 20–May 6, 1974; Corcoran Gallery of Art, Washington, D.C., January 10–February 9, 1975] [note: RB and thirteen others contributed tributes to founders of Gallery]

"A Painter in the Fifties." *Arts Magazine* 48, no. 7 (April 1974): 36–37. [discusses Carl Holty]

"Letters: More on Edmonia Lewis." *Art in America* 62 (November–December 1974): 168. [letter to editor in response to article by Eleanor M. Tufts, *Art in America* 62 (July–August 1974)]

"Humility." *NYT,* Saturday, June 21, 1975, 27. [from a graduation speech given at Carnegie Mellon University, Pittsburgh]

"A Master Looks Back." *Black Enterprise* 6 (December 1975): 64–65, 69.

[book review: *The Afro-American Artist: A Search for Identity* by Elsa Honig Fine]. *Leonardo* 8 (Winter 1975): 82–83.

[comments] In *Dana Chandler (Akin Duro): "If the Show Fits, Hear It!"—Paintings and Drawings, 1967–1976.* Exh. cat., Northeastern University Art Gallery, Boston, March 8–April 2, 1976. [not paginated] [RB comments dated March 4, 1974]

Statement. In "View from the Top: The Pluses and Minuses of Being an Only Child." *Buffalo Courier-Express,* August 15, 1976. [RB as "Romard" Bearden] [*clipping AAA/RB]

"The Black Man in the Arts." *New York Amsterdam News. Special Black Bicentennial Edition* (Summer 1976): C7.

"Horace Pippin." In *Horace Pippin.* Exh. cat., Phillips Collection, Washington, D.C., February 25–March 27, 1977, n. p. Circulated: Terry Dintenfass Gallery, New York, April 5–30, 1977; Brandywine River Museum, Chadds Ford, Pa., June 4–September 5, 1977.

"Horace Pippin." *Art/World* (April 1977): 10.

"A Tribute to 'Spinky' Alston—By Romare Bearden." *New York Amsterdam News,* June 18, 1977, A1, A6.

"An Artist's Plea for Harmony." *School Arts* 77 (September 1977): 72–73.

"Foreword." In Elton C. Fax. *Black Artists of the New Generation.* New York: Dodd, Mead, and Company, 1977.

"Eating at Ma Chance's." *Essence* 9 (April 1979): 112–14.

"Kosta Alex." *Art/World* 2, no. 9 (May 10/June 10, 1978): 10. [exh. review, Lee Ault Gallery, New York]

"A Final Farewell to Aaron Douglas." *New York Amsterdam News,* February 24, 1979, 65. [reprinted as "Farewell to Aaron Douglas." *Crisis* 86 (May 1979): 164–65]

"Sharing Yesterdays with Norman Lewis (1909–1979)." *New York Amsterdam News,* December 15, 1979, 27. [reminiscences; part 1 of 2; see next citation]

"Norman Lewis Remembered." *New York Amsterdam News,* January 5, 1980, 22. [part 2 of 2; see above citation]

Bearden, Romare, et. al. "To Our Colleague." *Freedomways* 20, no. 3 (1980): 179–83. [six artists; RB p. 179, on Charles White (1918–79)]

"Hale Woodruff: Tribute from Friends." *New York Amsterdam News,* November 22, 1980, 35. [reprinted in *Harlem Cultural Review,* April 1981, 8] [remarks at Community Church memorial to Hale Woodruff]

"Herbert Gentry." In *An Ocean Apart: American Artists Abroad.* Exh. cat., SMIH, October 8, 1982–January 9, 1983, 9–10.

"An Artist's Renewal in the Sun." *NYT Magazine* 133 (October 2, 1983): section 6: 46–48, 52.

[statement]. *Celebration: Eight Afro-American Artists Selected by Romare Bearden.* Exh. cat., Henry Street Settlement, Louis Abron Arts for Living Center, New York, February 17–April 1, 1984. [artists: Emma Amos, Toyce Anderson, Ellsworth Ausby, Vivian Browne, Nanette Carter, Melvin Edwards, Sharon Sutton, Richard Yarde] [statements by RB, Susan Fleminger; artists commentaries].

"Scale." In Donald Canty, ed. "Artists on Architecture." *Architecture* 73 (May 1984): 230–41, 335. [RB, p. 240]

"A Tribute to Robert Blackburn." In *Art in Print: A Tribute to Robert Blackburn.* Exh. cat., NYPL/SC, November 30, 1984–January 19, 1985. Text: Emma Amos; RB; Julia Hotton.

"Clouds in the Living Room." *NYT Magazine,* part 2 (October 6, 1985): SMA80–81.

Artist's Statement. In *Romare Bearden: Origins and Progressions.* Exh. cat., Detroit Institute of Arts, September 16–November 16, 1986. Text: Lowery S. Sims. [excerpts from RB's 1947 and 1949 journals, edited by Davira S. Taragin]

Artist's Statement. In *Artists Observed.* Photographs by Harvey Stein. Text: Cornell Capa; Elaine A. King. New York, 1986.

"Artists in Focus: Photographs of and Statements by Contemporary Artists: Romare Bearden." *American Artist* 50 (June 1986): 12. [photo; excerpt from Harvey Stein's *Artists Observed;* commentary by RB on approach to art]

Perspectives: Angles on African Art. Exh. cat., Center for African Art, New York, and Harry N. Abrams, Inc., 1987. Text (based on interviews by Michael John Weber): James Baldwin; RB; Ekpo Eyo; Nancy Graves; Ivan Karp; Lela Kouakou; Iba N'Diaye; David Rockefeller; William Rubin; Robert Farris Thompson. Introduction by Susan Vogel.

Artist's Statement. In "1988: Previews from 36 Artists." *New York Times,* January 3, 1988, H1, H30, H31. [Bearden, H31]

"Reminiscences." In *Riffs and Takes: Music in the Art of Romare Bearden.* Exh. cat., North Carolina Museum of Art, Raleigh, January 23–April 3, 1988.

Poems ["Andre's Dream," "Eugene," "Have We Played Enough?" "Hungry Morning," "Sometimes I Remember My Grandfather's House"] and journal entries [September 5, 1947 and December 19, 1947], from the collection of Nanette Rohan Bearden. In *Romare Bearden: A Memorial Exhibition.* Exh. cat., ACA Galleries, New York, May 11–June 10, 1989. [reprinted in *Romare Bearden in Black-and-White: Photomontage Projections 1964.* Exh. cat., Whitney/Philip Morris, January 17–March 20, 1997]

Bearden, Romare, and Harry Henderson. *A History of African-American Artists: From 1792 to the Present.* New York: Pantheon Books, 1993.

Bearden, Romare. *Li'l Dan, the Drummer Boy: A Civil War Story.* New York: Simon & Schuster, 2003. Foreword by Henry Louis Gates [children].

PUBLISHED AND RECORDED MUSIC

(Arranged alphabetically by title.)

"Cello on the Rhine." Words and music by Larry Douglas and Romare Bearden. Published by Laerteas Music Company, New York. [*http://.com database record]

Dry Is My Cup. [printed]. Words and music by Larry Douglas, Nelson Glover, Rommie Bearden. New York: Citation Music, 1953. [one score, two leaves; melody and bass line; chord symbols] [OCLC: 30508344] [Library of Congress call no: M1630.2.D]

"Early Times." (recorded by Doryce Brown; Joe Lipman and His Orchestra) Words and music by [Larry] Douglas, [Fred] Norman, and [Romare] Bearden. [*LC recording: M-G-M 12014 (78A); sound disc, 78 rpm, mono; 10 inch, standard (shellac); and MGM K12014; sound disc, 45 rpm, 7 inch]

"Kay (Meet Me at the Lido Snack)." Words and music by Larry Douglas and Romare Bearden. Published by Laerteas Music Company, New York. [*http://.com database record]

Larry Douglas à Paris. [record album] [Barclay (record label)] [Larry Douglas and His Orchestra] [recorded April 1960 at "Comédie Champs-Élysées," Paris, France. Arrangements: Jean-Pierre Landreau and Pierre Delvincourt. Sound engineer: Gilbert Preneron. Assistant sound engineer: Claude Pascaud] [jacket notes (in French) by Pierre Hiegel. A Larry Douglas Production] [includes: "A New Tomorrow" (L. Douglas, F. Norman, R. Bearden); "Early Times" (L. Douglas, F. Norman, R. Bearden); "Kay, Meet Me at the Lido Snack" (L. Douglas, R. Bearden); "Cello on the Rhine (Cello ma Chérie)" (L. Douglas–R. Bearden); "Sea Breeze" (L. Douglas, F. Norman, R. Bearden); "Blackberry Blue & Rose Blossom Pink" (L Douglas, F. Norman, R. Bearden)] [*private archive]

"Missus Santa Claus." (recorded by Leslie "Uggams" Crayne) Words and music by Larry Douglas, A.S.C.A.P., Fred Norman, A.S.C.A.P., and Rommie Bearden. © 1953 by Laerteas Music Pub. Co., New York.

"My Candy Apple." (recorded by Leslie "Uggams" Crayne) Words and music by [Larry] Douglas, [Fred] Norman, and [Romare] Bearden. Fred Norman, orchestra conductor. [*Library of Congress recording: M-G-M 11676 (78A); sound disc, 78 rpm, mono; 10 inch, standard (shellac)]

"My Love for Dorothy." (dedicated to Dorothy Dandridge; recorded by Fred Norman and His Orchestra) Words and music by Larry Douglas, A.S.C.A.P., Fred Norman, A.S.C.A.P., and Rommie Bearden. © 1954 by Laerteas Music Pub. Co., New York.

"My Stocking Is Empty." (recorded by Leslie "Uggams" Crayne) Words by Larry Douglas, Fred Norman, and Rommie Bearden; music by Larry Douglas and Fred Norman. © 1953 by Mills Music, Inc., New York.

"New Tomorrow." Words and music by Larry Douglas, Fred Norman, and Romare Bearden. Published by Laerteas Music Company, New York. [*http://.com database record]

"Quicksand." Words and music by Larry Douglas, Fred Norman, and Romare Bearden. Published by Laerteas Music Company, New York. [*http://.com database record]

"Seabreeze." (recorded by Billy Eckstine) Words and music by Larry Douglas, A.S.C.A.P., Fred Norman, A.S.C.A.P., and Rommie Bearden. © 1954 by Laerteas Music Pub. Co., New York.

"So Much More." (recorded by Mitzi Mason) Words and music by Larry Douglas, A.S.C.A.P., Fred Norman, A.S.C.A.P., and Rommie Bearden. © 1954 by Laerteas Music Pub. Co., New York.

"Who Can Say." (recorded by Mitzi Mason) Words and music by Larry Douglas, A.S.C.A.P., Fred Norman, A.S.C.A.P., and Rommie Bearden. © 1954 by Laerteas Music Pub. Co., New York.

POLITICAL CARTOONS AND OTHER ORIGINAL IMAGES

(Arranged chronologically. It has not always been possible to determine from the source whether an image was created for a book, article, or product such as a calendar or poster, or if it is in fact a reproduction of an existing work of art. Unless otherwise specified, only images thought to have been created specifically for the publications listed are included.)

Cover illustration. *The Beanpot* 12, no. 3 (November 1931).

"Gimme de 'Ballyhoo'!" *The Beanpot* 12, no. 3 (November 1931): 12.

"Rosita, in View of Present Economic Conditions You Are to Have One Less Biscuit a Day." *The Beanpot* 12, no. 3 (November 1931): 13.

"Dis Mob Was O.K.! But Den Youse Began Going to dem Gangster Pictures!" *The Beanpot* 12, no. 4 (December 1931): 4.

"Knocked out in de Fust Round Ugin, Eh! You Is YELLOW, Dat's What!" *The Beanpot* 12, no. 4 (December 1931): 7.

"Musclin' in on Me Territory, Huh!" *The Beanpot* 12, no. 4 (December 1931): 7.

Cover illustration. *The Beanpot* 12, no. 5 (January 1932).

"Nope,—We're All out of Ham!" *The Beanpot* 12, no. 5 (January 1932): 4.

Cover illustration. *The Beanpot* 12, no. 6 (February 1932).

"It Ain't Hygenic!" *The Beanpot* 12, no. 6 (February 1932): 2.

"I Am Writing My Memoirs for the News." *The Beanpot* 12, no. 7 (March 1932): 2.

Cover illustration, *The Beanpot* 12, no. 7 (March 1932).

Cover illustration, *Opportunity* 10 (March 1932).

"So! You're Gettin' Temperamental Again, Eh?" *Medley* [New York University] 21 (December 1933): 19.

"8:30, and My Secretary Is Late Again!" *Medley* 21 (January 1934): 6.

"So I Says, 'Do I Look Like from Cooney Island?'" *Medley* 21 (January 1934): 14.

"Two Thousand, Five Hundred, Right! Now, Can I Have That Electric Cigarette Lighter?" *Collier's* (February 24, 1934): 41.

"If We Keep Going at This Rate, We'll Be on Broadway in No Time." *Medley* 21 (March 1934): 13.

"This Is the 'Lady Patricia' Model—Our Very Latest Creation." *Medley* 21 (March 1934): 12.

"Dis Razor Ain't Been a Bit of Good... Since Dat Time I Shaved wid It." *Medley* 21 (April 1934): 8.

"No Help Wanted." *The Crisis* 41 (April 1934): 105.

"Giving Him Some Fresh Ideas." *The Crisis* 41 (June 1934): 158.

"The Picket Line." *The Crisis* 41 (July 1934): 205.

"Little Man, What Now?" *The Crisis* 41 (August 1934): 237.

"A Few Days Ago, in Germany, Events Occurred Which... Made Me... Physically Sick." *The Crisis* 41 (September 1934): 257.

"For the Children!" *The Crisis* 41 (October 1934): 294.

"They Voted for Judge Parker 'Of All Their Titles, the Best Is "*Ex*-Senator"!' (Apologies to Heywood Brown)." *The Crisis* 41 (December 1934): 362.

"This Is Professor Smithers—He's Doing Wonders with Fruit Flies." *Medley* 22 (December 1934): 6.

"Eighth Avenue Market, New York City, Sketches from an Art Student's Notebook." *Opportunity* 13 (January 1935): 22.

"The Guardian Angel." *Medley* 22 (March 1935): 9.

"Marching along Together (Popular National Recovery 'Pep' Song)." *The Crisis* 42 (March 1935): 144.

"Morris Is Becoming Very Conservative Lately." *Medley* 22 (March 1935): 8.

"We're Sure Lucky Getting This Bus All to Ourselves Aren't We Dear?" *Medley* 22 (March 1935): 16.

"Italy Takes 'Precautionary Measures.'" *The Crisis* 42 (April 1935): 111.

"Under Fire!" *The Crisis* 42 (May 1935): 144.

"I Wish To Report a Leak, Sir." *Medley* 22 (May 1935): 12. [unsigned]

"My, Your Spelling Is Atrocious Lately." *Medley* 22 (May 1935): 15.

"Of Course, Rivera's Approach Is Different." *Medley* 22 (May 1935): 9.

"Found—The Forgotten Man. ('Oxford, Miss.—None of the mob which lynched Elwood Higginbotham here, on September 17, has been identified')." *Baltimore Afro-American*, September 28, 1935, 6.

Cover illustration. *Medley* 23 (October 1935).

"He Says His Name Is Smith, Sir." *Medley* 23 (October 1935): 9.

"Peace Pacts." *Baltimore Afro-American*, October 5, 1935, 6.

"Italian Civilization? Passes By!" *Baltimore Afro-American*, October 12, 1935, 6.

"About Time to Wake Up." *Baltimore Afro-American*, October 19, 1935, 6.

"Into the Web..." *Baltimore Afro-American*, October 26, 1935, 6.

"His Master's Voice." *Baltimore Afro-American*, November 2, 1935, 6.

"The Conflagration." *Baltimore Afro-American*, November 9, 1935, 6.

"A Trail Blazen in Blood." *Baltimore Afro-American*, November 16, 1935, 6. [unsigned]

"The Real Judge at Scottsboro." *Baltimore Afro-American*, November 23, 1935, 6.

"The Handwriting on the Wall." *Baltimore Afro-American*, November 30, 1935, 6.

"Civilization on the Run." *Baltimore Afro-American*, December 7, 1935, 4.

"The Watchman. ('News Items—Share croppers in South robbed of federal funds intended for them. One million colored persons still jobless. Thousands dropped from relief rolls. Vital problem of poor is to obtain good housing. All surveys show high death and crime rate')." *Baltimore Afro-American*, December 14, 1935, 6.

"A Giant amongst the Pygmies." *Baltimore Afro-American*, December 21, 1935, 6.

"...And Goodwill toward ALL Men?" *Baltimore Afro-American*, December 28, 1935, 6.

"The Handwriting on the Wall." *The Crisis* 42 (January 1936): 16. [courtesy *Afro-American*]

"Traveler, the Road Leads On and On." *Baltimore Afro-American*, January 4, 1936, 6.

"The Question before Congress." *Baltimore Afro-American*, January 11, 1936, 6.

"Is Your Name on the Lists?" *Baltimore Afro-American*, January 18, 1936, 6.

"The Music Goes Round and 'Round." *Baltimore Afro-American*, January 25, 1936, 6.

"The Aftermath of Scottsboro." *Baltimore Afro-American*, February 7, 1936, 4.

"Alabama Attempts a Little Whitewashing—." *Baltimore Afro-American*, February 8, 1936, 4.

"Going Over with a Bang!" *Baltimore Afro-American*, February 15, 1936, 4.

"The Last One Up—." *Baltimore Afro-American*, February 22, 1936, 4.

"A Grim Monument to Man's Greed." *Baltimore Afro-American*, February 29, 1936, 4.

"Still on the Outside." *Baltimore Afro-American*, March 7, 1936, 4.

"Sire—You Can Do Anything with Bayonets but Sit on Them ... (Tallyrand to Napoleon)." *Baltimore Afro-American*, March 14, 1936, 4.

"News Item—'Another War Imminent.'" *Baltimore Afro-American*, March 21, 1936, 4.

"Why Not Flood Control Legislation to Stop This?" *Baltimore Afro-American*, March 28, 1936, 4.

"Near the End of a Long, Long Trail." *Baltimore Afro-American*, April 4, 1936, 4.

"Another Cross to Bear." *Baltimore Afro-American*, April 11, 1936, 4.

"The Rain (of Death) in Ethiopia—." *Baltimore Afro-American*, May 2, 1936, 4.

"Civilization Has Reached Addis Ababa—." *Baltimore Afro-American*, May 9, 1936, 4.

"Do You Call That Religion? ('Remember! Your church voted for segregation back on earth—')." *Baltimore Afro-American*, May 16, 1936, 4.

"Do You Call That Religion? ('Come on out—and let's see who you are')." *Baltimore Afro-American*, May 23, 1936, 4.

"A Beacon Light." *Baltimore Afro-American*, May 30, 1936, 4.

"The Ghost Walks." *Baltimore Afro-American*, June 6, 1936, 4.

"The Black Cat in the Path." *Baltimore Afro-American*, June 13, 1936, 4.

"Why Stay in Dixie? ('The Watch Dog')." *Baltimore Afro-American*, June 20, 1936, 4.

"The Championship ('If you can keep your head when all about you Are losing theirs and blaming it on you.'—Kipling)." *Baltimore Afro-American*, June 27, 1936, 4.

"Sure, we'll promise 'em anything to get their votes." *Baltimore Afro-American*, July 4, 1936, 4.

"I Wonder Where My Colored Supports Are ('X represents spot where colored voters always used to be found in G.O.P. lineup')." *Baltimore Afro-American*, July 18, 1936, 4.

"Putting the Finger on It!" *Baltimore Afro-American*, July 25, 1936, 4.

"Murder Will Out." *Baltimore Afro-American*, August 1, 1936, 4.

"Look Who's in Landon's Camp Already!" *Baltimore Afro-American*, August 8, 1936, 4.

"Look Up, World!" *Baltimore Afro-American*, August 15, 1936, 4.

"Goes 'Round and 'Round. ('Do you suppose Landon can get the beast to quit running around in circles?')." *Baltimore Afro-American*, August 22, 1936, 4.

"The Aftermath of a Kentucky Holiday." *Baltimore Afro-American*, August 29, 1936, 4.

"All Together on the Old Camp Ground ('News Item—The subject of Secretary Harold Ickes's was "Hearst Over Topeka"')." *Baltimore Afro-American*, September 5, 1936, 4.

"Caught in the Tentacles Again—." *Baltimore Afro-American*, September 12, 1936, 4.

"While Down Below—." *Baltimore Afro-American*, September 19, 1936, 4.

"Swept Out by a Real Political Hurricane." *Baltimore Afro-American*, September 26, 1936, 4.

"The Great Barrier to Equality. ('In 1875 Congress passed a Civil Rights Act which guaranteed equal rights to colored people in theatres, hotels, public conveyances and forbade our exclusion from juries. Except that it was a war measure and Presidential proclamation affecting the rebel States only, the Supreme Court would undoubtedly have declared the Emancipation Proclamation unconstitutional')." *Baltimore Afro-American*, October 3, 1936, 4.

"—And The Greatest of These Is Charity." *Baltimore Afro-American*, October 10, 1936, 4.

"About Time to Break This Chain—." *Baltimore Afro-American*, October 17, 1936, 4.

"Haven't We Always Had Our Own Way?" *Baltimore Afro-American*, October 24, 1936, 4.

"The Question—To Whom Will He Swing His Support?" *Baltimore Afro-American*, October 31, 1936, 4.

"America, Look—." *Baltimore Afro-American*, November 7, 1936, 4.

"—Lest We Forget—." *Baltimore Afro-American*, November 14, 1936, 4.

"Together—In the Supreme Court Junk Pile." *Baltimore Afro-American*, November 21, 1936, 4.

"Above—The Promise of Better Thanksgiving to Come—." *Baltimore Afro-American*, November 28, 1936, 4.

"The Rising Tide of College Youth—." *Baltimore Afro-American*, December 5, 1936, 4.

"The Witness—." *Baltimore Afro-American*, December 12, 1936, 4.

"Lincoln Freed the Slaves in 1863?" *Baltimore Afro-American*, December 19, 1936, 4.

"Strange Words in This Day." *Baltimore Afro-American*, December 26, 1936, 4.

"Over and above All the Shouting—." *Baltimore Afro-American*, January 2, 1937, 4.

"Beginning to Loom Larger and Larger on the Horizon." *Baltimore Afro-American*, January 9, 1937, 4.

"A Mandate from the Colored Citizens." *Baltimore Afro-American*, January 16, 1937, 4.

"Trail-Blazers towards a Better Era—." *Baltimore Afro-American*, January 23, 1937, 4.

"The Battle Ahead for Colored America." *Baltimore Afro-American*, January 30, 1937, 4.

"The Troubled Father of Waters—." *Baltimore Afro-American*, February 6, 1937, 4.

"Colored Labor Still Bears the Brunt of the Burden—." *Baltimore Afro-American*, February 13, 1937, 4.

"Rumblings before a Complete Eruption." *Baltimore Afro-American*, February 20, 1937, 4.

"Tossed out of the Window." *Baltimore Afro-American*, February 27, 1937, 4.

"No Wonder—Look Who's Behind It." *Baltimore Afro-American*, March 6, 1937, 4.

"The Iron Heel of Fascism. ('News Item—Hundreds of Ethiopians Massacred in Bombing Reprisals')." *Baltimore Afro-American*, March 13, 1937, 4.

"Another Sit-Down Strike Begins in Real Earnest." *Baltimore Afro-American*, March 20, 1937, 4.

"Labor Presents a New Front." *Baltimore Afro-American*, March 27, 1937, 4.

"Shall This Continue to Be the Plight of Colored Labor?" *Baltimore Afro-American*, April 3, 1937, 4.

"The Shadow Becomes Longer and Longer." *Baltimore Afro-American*, April 10, 1937, 4.

"Still out on the Limb." *Baltimore Afro-American*, April 17, 1937, 4.

"Shall Mob Rule Continue as the Expression of Southern Justice?" *Baltimore Afro-American*, April 24, 1937, 4.

"Shall the Tail Wag the Dog?" *Baltimore Afro-American*, May 1, 1937, 4.

"Freed through United Effort." *Baltimore Afro-American*, May 8, 1937, 4.

Department of Industrial Relations, National Urban League. *They Crashed the Color Line!* New York, April 1937. Illustrations by Romare Bearden. [reprint (fiche), Alexandria, Va.: Chadwyck-Healey, 1987] [includes five essays (one on E. Simms Campbell) by Elmer A. Carter, and one by Ishmael P. Flory]

Frontispiece illustration (p. 76) for "The Negro's War." *Fortune* 25 (June 1942): 76–80, 157–58, 160, 162, 164. [biographical note on Bearden, p. 77]

Cover illustration. *Fortune* 77 (January 1968). [note, p. 2]

Cover illustration. [*John Lindsay*, photo collage, 1968] *Time*, November 1, 1968. [see also biographical notes and remarks re: cover collage on p. 7, in James R. Shepley, "A Letter from the Publishers"] [Cover story: "John Lindsay's Ten Plagues," pp. 20–24, 29]

Cover illustration. *Afro-American Artists: Since 1950*. Exh. cat., Brooklyn College, New York, April 15–May 18, 1969. [organized by Henri Ghent] Text: Albert Bowker; Louis Breglio; Brooklyn League of Afro-American Collegians (BLAC); Henri Ghent; George A. Peck. [RB not exhibitor; cover commissioned by BLAC and Brooklyn College]

Cover illustration. [*Soul History*, collage] *NYT Magazine*, April 20, 1969. [related article: "American History (White Man's Version) Needs an Infusion of Soul" by C. Vann Woodward, pp. 32–33, 108–14] [note, p. 22] [see also Henri Ghent, "Letters to the Editor: Soulful," *NYT Magazine*, May 11, 1969, 132]

Cover illustration. *Crisis* 77 (March 1970).

Cover illustration. [*Justice*, collage] *Contact* 3 (July 1972). [note, contents page (3)]

Cover illustration. *Black Enterprise* 3 (December 1972).

Book jacket. Oritz Walton. *Music: Black, White & Blue. A Social Survey of the Use and Misuse of Afro-American Music.* New York: William Morrow, 1972. [*Mint Museum (1980), 121]

Line drawings by Bearden. In Samuel W. Allen, ed. *Poems from Africa.* New York: Cromwell, 1973.

Album cover. *Billie Holiday: The Original Recordings.* Columbia Records/CBS, Inc., New York, 1973. Produced by John Hammond. [*Mint Museum (1980), 120]

Book jacket. Lofton Mitchell. *The Stubborn Old Lady Who Resisted Change.* New York: Emerson Hall Publishers, 1973. [*Mint Museum (1980), 121]

Cover illustration. *Freedomways* 14, no. 3 (1974). [*Mint Museum (1980), 121]

Cover illustration. *The Harvard Advocate* 107, no. 4 (1974). [Special issue: *Black Odyssey: A Search for Home*]

Book jacket. Albert Murray. *Train Whistle Guitar.* New York: McGraw Hill Book Company, 1974.

Cover illustration. *TV Guide* 25, no. 4 (January 22, 1977). [cover story: Alex Haley, "'Roots': The Story behind the Search"]

Unidentified drawing [*The Street (Composition for Richard Wright)*] used as illustration for Richard Wright, "What Sets Storms to Rolling in His Soul." *NYT,* April 8, 1977, A27. [in the collection of the National Gallery of Art, Gift of Werner H. and Sarah-Ann Kramarsky and Collectors Committee Fund, 2001.58.1]

Album cover. *Tribute to Charlie Parker,* Vol. 6. Warner Brothers Records, Burbank, Calif., 1977. [*Mint Museum (1980), 120]

Cover illustration. *TV Guide* 25, no. 38 (September 17, 1977). [image: Football]

Album cover. *Thank you... for F.U.M.L.* Elektra/Asylum Records, Los Angeles, Calif., 1978. Produced by Donald Byrd for Bluebyrd Productions, Inc.

Cover illustration. *Black Enterprise* 8 (June 1978).

Book jacket. Dizzy Gillespie, with Al Fraser. *To Be, Or Not... To BOP: Memoirs.* Garden City, N.Y.: Doubleday, 1979 [1978?] [*Mint Museum (1980), 121]

Untitled illustration. *The Poets' Encyclopedia.* New York: Unmuzzled Ox Foundation Ltd., 1979, 272–73.

Du Bois, W. E. B. *Dusk of Dawn: An Essay Toward an Autobiography of a Race Concept.* Franklin Center, Pa.: Franklin Library, 1980. Illustrated with ten works by RB, selected by the artist.

Approximately 30 watercolors for opening sequence of motion picture *Gloria.* Directed by John Cassavetes. Produced by Sam Shaw. United States: Columbia Pictures Home Entertainment, 1980.

Unidentified collage used as illustration for Robert I. Rotberg, "Zimbabwe Needs Aid." In *NYT,* December 8, 1981, A31.

Album cover for *Strong Men.* Music by Saxophonist/pianist Kamau Kenyatta. Album dedicated to writer Sterling Brown; liner notes by Kofi Natambu; produced by Walter O. Evans (1982).

Unidentified collage used as illustration for Jesse L. Jackson, "It's Not the Bus. It's Us." *NYT,* March 8, 1982, A19.

Walcott, Derek. *The Caribbean Poetry of Derek Walcott and the Art of Romare Bearden.* New York: Limited Editions Club, c. 1983; Portland, Maine: Anthoensen Press. [colophon title: *Poems of the Caribbean.*] [Poems selected by RB from published collections] [each book contains original lithograph (one of eight created for this purpose) by Bearden, who also designed cover]

Dust jacket illustration. [*Under Morning Skies,* collage, 1982] Virginia Hamilton, *The Magical Adventures of Pretty Pearl.* New York: Harper and Row, 1983. [children]

The Nanette Bearden Contemporary Dance Theatre, New York. Program for performance at Manhattan Community College Performing Arts Center, Inc., December 14 and 16, 1983. [RB created cover design; program notes he designed costumes for *Clowns Carnival* and set projection "Street Scene" for *The Duece*] [RBF archives]

Chance, Jeanne Louise Duzant. *Ma Chance's French Caribbean Creole Cooking.* New York: Putnam, c. 1985. Art by RB. Edited and compiled by June Kelly.

Untitled drawing/illustration with article, "A South African Fights from Exile" (interview with Oliver Tambo by Anthony Heard), *NYT,* December 6, 1985, A35.

Cover illustration. Lasana M. Sekou. *Born Here.* Philipsburg, St. Maarten, Caribbean: House of Nehesi Publishers, 1986. [original painting was for this publication, per correspondence with publisher, February 23, 2003]

Johnson, Herschel. *A Visit to the Country.* New York: Harper & Row, 1989. Paintings by RB. [children]

Cover illustration. Lasana M. Sekou. *Love Songs Make You Cry.* Philipsburg, St. Maarten, Caribbean: House of Nehesi Publishers, 1989. [original painting was for this publication, per correspondence with publisher, February 23, 2003]

Sekou, Lasana M. *Mothernation: Poems from 1984 to 1987.* Philipsburg, St. Maarten, Caribbean: House of Nehesi Publishers, 1991. Commentary by Armando Lampe, cover illustration by Ras Mosera, illustrations by Romare Bearden, Brenda Williams. [According to the publisher, Bearden contributed two drawings specifically for use in this publication prior to his death. One was a study related to *Mysteries* (1964; collage on board). The second may also be a study related to a previous work, although this has not been confirmed (per correspondence with the publisher, February 23, 2003).]

Section 4 About Bearden

(Arranged alphabetically. Published material produced in conjunction with an exhibition—including, but not limited to, pamphlets, brochures, catalogues, and checklists, but excluding exhibition announcements, invitations, or other such mailings—are identified as "exh. cat." in this bibliography. A distinction between a brochure and a catalogue is noted only when both items were produced for the same exhibition.)

MONOGRAPHS AND SOLO EXHIBITION CATALOGUES

The Archetypal Image: Myth and Ritual in the Art of Romare Bearden. Exh. cat., Pinnacle Gallery, Savannah College of Art and Design, January 15–March 7, 1999. Text: Cynda L. Benson.

The Art of Romare Bearden. Exh. cat., Grand Rapids Art Museum, Mich., 1984. Organized by Sheldon Ross Gallery, Birmingham, Mich. Text: Myron Schwartzman. Brochure also.

The Art of Romare Bearden: Recollections of Mecklenburg County. Exh. cat., Staten Island Institute of Arts & Sciences, New York, September 20, 2001–February 28, 2002. Text: Peggy Hammerle-McGuire.

Ascendancy: The Art of Romare Bearden. Exh. cat., Spelman College Museum of Fine Art, Camille Olivia Hanks Cosby Academic Center, Atlanta, March 7–May 22, 2000. M. Akua McDaniel, curator. Text: Tuliza K. Fleming.

Bearden. [Exh. cat.?], Daniel Cordier & Michel Warren, Inc., New York, 1961. [*exh. cat. (no. 24) on list: "Romare Bearden Album Vol. II Exhibition Catalogues (filed chronologically)," MoMA Scrapbooks (fiche 1.81), microfiche, Alexandria, Va.: Chadwyck-Healey, 1986; image on fiche 1.82 inconclusively identifiable as catalogue]

Bearden. [Exh. cat.?], Michel Warren Gallery, New York, [1960]. [*exh. cat. (no. 23) on list entitled "Romare Bearden Album Vol. II Exhibition Catalogues (filed chronologically)," MoMA Scrapbooks (fiche 1.81), microfiche, Alexandria, Va.: Chadwyck-Healey, 1986; image on fiche no. 1.82 inconclusively identifiable as catalogue]

Bearden: Paintings and Water Colors Inspired by Garcia Lorca's "Lament for a Bullfighter." Exh. cat., Kootz, New York, 1946. Text: Garcia Lorca, *Lament for Ignacio Sanchez Mejias.*

Bearden, Romare, and Langston Hughes. *The Block.* New York: Metropolitan Museum of Art and Viking, 1995. Collage by RB, poems by Hughes. Selected by Lowery S. Sims and Daisy Murray Voigt. Introduction by Bill Cosby.

Brown, Kevin. *Romare Bearden.* Black Americans of Achievement series. New York: Chelsea House, 1995. [children]

Campbell, Mary Schmidt. "Romare Bearden: A Creative Mythology." Ph.D. dissertation, Syracuse University, N.Y., 1982.

A Celebration of the Life of Romare H. Bearden, 1912–1988: The Cathedral of St. John the Divine. New York, 1988. [folded sheet; tributes by the White House, Fabian Badejo, Mary Schmidt Campbell, Ralph Ellison, Derek Walcott; musical works: one co-composed by RB and one by Merton Simpson; loan exhibition from collections of Richard V. Clarke, Bernice and Jack Fein, June Kelly, NYPL/SC, and others]

Collages: Romare Bearden. Profile/Part II: The Thirties. Exh. cat., C&E, New York, 1981. ["Picture titles and text reviewed and edited by Albert Murray"]

"Exactitude Ain't Interesting": Romare Bearden. Exh. cat., Louis Stern Galleries (in association with ACA Galleries, New York), Beverly Hills, January 14–March 6, 1992.

An Exhibition of Prints by Romare Bearden. Typewritten handout, Filderman Gallery, Hofstra University, Hempstead, N.Y., May 1982. Text: Milton Gardner; James M. Shuart. [6 pp., including title page; produced for RB receipt of Doctor of Fine Arts degree, *Honoris Causa,* commencement exercises, May 17, 1982; RB gave commencement address]

Finding the Tone: Romare Bearden's Monotypes and Robert Blackburn's Printmaking Workshop. Exh. cat., Lori Bookstein Fine Art, New York, February 10–March 25, 2000. Text: Deborah Cullen.

First New York Exhibition: Romare Bearden. Exh. cat., Kootz, New York, 1945. [folded sheet; statement by RB]

A Graphic Odyssey: Romare Bearden as Printmaker. Exh. cat., organized and circulated [1992 to 1997] by Council for Creative Projects, Inc., New York; distributed by University of Pennsylvania Press, Philadelphia, 1992. Text: Nanette Rohan Bearden; Gail Gelburd; June Kelly; Alex Rosenberg.

Hallowell, Bay. *Let's Look! The Art of Romare Bearden.* Pittsburgh: Carnegie Museum of Art, Carnegie Institute, 1992.

Harlem Culture & Southern Memories: Selected Works by Romare Bearden. Exh. cat., Springfield Art Museum, Mo., January 31–March 14, 1993. Text: Jerry A. Berger; Greg G. Thielen.

Hartfield, Claire. *Happy Birthday, Uncle Romie.* New York: Dial Books for Young Readers, 2001. [children] [includes biographical sketch and collage-making instructions; illustrated by Jerome Lagarrigue]

Igoe, Lynn. *Artis, Bearden, and Burke: A Bibliography and Illustrations List.* Durham: Museum of Art/North Carolina Central University, 1977.

"The Iliad": 16 Variations by Romare Bearden. Exh. cat., Niveau Gallery, New York, 1948.

Joy of Living: Romare Bearden's Late Work. Exh. cat., North Carolina Central University, Durham, October 17–December 3, 1993. Circulated. Text: Lynn Moody Igoe; Norman E. Pendergraft.

The Lamp. New York: NAACP Legal Defense and Educational Fund, Inc., 1984. [brochure announcing publication of lithograph *The Lamp* (1984) for benefit of Legal Defense Fund; commissioned to commemorate 30th anniversary of the U.S. Supreme Court decision *Brown v. Board of Education.* [*RBF archive]

A Look at Romare Bearden. Exh. cat., Albright Knox Art Gallery, Buffalo, N.Y., May 11–July 28, 2002. Text: Claire Schneider.

Memory and Metaphor: The Art of Romare Bearden 1940–1987. Exh. cat., Studio Museum in Harlem, New York, April 14–August 11, 1991. Published by Oxford University Press, New York. Circulated. Text: Mary Schmidt Campbell; Kinshasha Holman Conwill; Sharon F. Patton. Brochure also.

Mysteries: Women in the Art of Romare Bearden. Exh. cat., Everson Museum of Art of Syracuse and Onondaga County, Syracuse, N.Y., 1975. Text: Mary Schmidt Campbell.

New Paintings by Bearden. Exh. cat., Kootz, New York, 1947. Text: Barrie Stavis.

Of the Blues: Romare Bearden. Exh. cat., C&E, New York, 1975. Text: Albert Murray.

The Painted Sounds of Romare Bearden. Exh. cat., organized by Council for Creative Projects, New York, 1994. Circulated. [Tour arranged and funded in part by Arts America Program, Bureau of Education and Cultural Affairs, United States Information Agency] Text: Gail Gelburd; Richard A. Long.

The Passion of Christ. [Exh. cat.?], G Place Gallery, Washington, D.C., June 1945. [single sheet with printed statement by RB, dated June 1945] [*exh. cat. (no. 2) on list "Romare Bearden Albums Vol. II: Statements by Bearden," MoMA Scrapbooks (fiche 1.81), microfiche, Alexandria, Va.: Chadwyck-Healey, 1986. [no additional materials from catalogue located]

Recollections of Charlotte's Own Romare Bearden. Exh. cat., Mint Museum, August 24–October 27, 2002. [interviews with David C. Driskell, Herb Jackson and Laura Grosch, and Jerald L. Melberg]

Riffs and Takes: Music in the Art of Romare Bearden. Exh. cat., North Carolina Museum of Art, Raleigh, 1988. Artist's statement. Text: Huston Paschal.

Romare Bearden. [Exh. cat.?], Barone Gallery, New York, 1955. [*exh. cat. (no. 20) on list "Romare Bearden Album Vol. II Exhibition Catalogues (filed chronologically)," MoMA Scrapbooks (fiche 1.81), microfiche, Alexandria, Va.: Chadwyck-Healey, 1986. Image on fiche 1.82 inconclusively identifiable as catalogue]

Romare Bearden. Exh. cat., C&E, New York, [1973]. [included subjects: Prevalence of Ritual, Martinique, Rain Forest]

Romare Bearden. Exh. cat., C&E, New York, 1967. [folder] [*MoMA (1971)]

Romare Bearden. Exh. cat., Firehouse Gallery, Nassau Community College, Garden City, N.Y., 1976. Presented by Art Department and Afro-American Studies Department, Nassau Community College, in honor of Bicentennial of American Revolution. Text: Hale Woodruff.

Romare Bearden. Exh. cat., Morgan State University Gallery of Art, Carl Murphy Fine Arts Center, Baltimore, 1981. Text: James E. Lewis; Richard A. Long.

Romare Bearden. Exh. cat., National Academy of Sciences, Washington, D.C., April 11–June 9, 1989. Text: unidentified author.

Romare Bearden. Exh. cat., Neighborhood Arts Center, Inc., Atlanta, 1978. Text: Jim Alexander; Richard A. Long.

Romare Bearden. Invitation/leaflet produced for RB lecture on Henry Ossawa Tanner and inaugural presentation (by James Van Der Zee to Bearden) of "James Van Der Zee Award" at Philadelphia Museum of Art, September 30, 1976, sponsored by Brandywine Graphic Workshop. Text: Allan L. Edmunds.

Romare Bearden: Collages. Exh. cat., J. L. Hudson Gallery, Detroit, 1967. Text: John Canaday (reprinted from *NYT,* October 14, 1967); RB statement.

Romare Bearden: Collages. Exh. cat., Malcolm Brown Gallery, Shaker Heights, Ohio, 1982. Text: Lowery S. Sims.

Romare Bearden: Collages. Profile/Part 1: The Twenties. Exh. cat., C&E, New York, 1978. ["Picture titles and text reviewed and edited by Albert Murray."]

Romare Bearden: Drawing, Collage, Printing and Watercolor. Exh. cat., Bacardi Art Gallery, Miami, 1985. Text: Juan Espinosa.

Romare Bearden: Finding the Rhythm. Exh. cat., University of Oklahoma, Museum of Art, Norman, September 20–October 27, 1991. Circulated. Text: Albert Murray (interviewed by Thomas Toperzer); reprint of Murray, "Bearden Plays Bearden: The Visual Equivalent of Blues Composition," originally in Mint Museum (1980).

Romare Bearden: Jazz. Exh. cat., Birmingham Museum of Art, Ala., 1982. Circulated. Text: Edward F. Weeks. [smaller version shown at McIntosh Gallery, Atlanta, 1982; same catalogue used, plus checklist on Gallery letterhead]

Romare Bearden: Jazz Collages. Exh. cat., Sheldon Ross Gallery, Birmingham, Mich., 1980.

Romare Bearden/Matrix 7. Exh. cat., Wadsworth Atheneum, Hartford, 1975. Text: Andrea Miller-Keller.

Romare Bearden: Mecklenburg Autumn. Exh. cat., C&E, New York, 1983. Text: Calvin Tomkins.

Romare Bearden: Mecklenburg, Morning & Evening. Exh. cat., C&E, New York, 1986.

Romare Bearden: 1911–1988: A Memorial Exhibition. Exh. cat., ACA Galleries, New York, May 11–June 10, 1989. Organized by Jonathan Bergen. Text: Mary Schmidt Campbell; Jonathan Bergen and Diana Dimodica Sweet, eds.

Romare Bearden: 1970–1980. Exh. cat., Mint Museum [of Art], (Department of Art), Charlotte, N.C., 1980. Text: Dore Ashton; Albert Murray; Jerald L. Melberg and Milton J. Bloch, eds. Circulated. Brochure also.

Romare Bearden: Narrations. Exh. cat., Neuberger Museum of Art, Purchase College, State University of New York, Purchase, September 22–December [illegible], 2002. Circulated. Text: Sharon F. Patton.

Romare Bearden: Odysseus. Collages. Exh. cat., C&E, New York, 1977. Text: Calvin Tomkins. [reprinted in "Odysseus. Collages by Romare Bearden," *Massachusetts Review* 18, no. 4 (Winter 1977): 681–88, with photograph of RB by Niki Ekstrom]

Romare Bearden: Oils, Gouaches, Water Colors, Drawings 1937–1940. Exh. cat., 306 West 141st Street, New York, [1940]. RB statement. [folded sheet]

Romare Bearden: Origins and Progressions. Exh. cat., Detroit Institute of Arts, 1986. Text: Lowery S. Sims; Davira S. Taragin. RB statement. [excerpts from RB's 1947 and 1949 journals, edited by Davira S. Taragin]

Romare Bearden: Paintings and Projections. Exh. cat., Art Gallery, State University of New York, Albany, 1968. Text: Ralph Ellison.

Romare Bearden: Paper Icons. Exh. cat., Exhibit A Gallery, Savannah College of Art and Design, February 5–March 10, 1996. Text: Cynda L. Benson; Carroll Greene (interviewed by Darrell Johnson: "Interview with Carroll Greene: Reminiscences of Romare Bearden").

Romare Bearden: Personal Memories and Blues Reveries. Exh. cat., Albany Museum of Art, Ga., November 7, 1996–January 12, 1997. Text: Cory Micots.

Romare Bearden: Projections. Exh. cat., Corcoran Gallery of Art, Washington, D.C., 1965. RB statement.

Romare Bearden: Projections. Exh. cat., C&E, New York, 1964. [folder] [MoMA (1971) indicates cat. includes "Statement by the artist," not located]

Romare Bearden: Rituals of the Obeah. Exh. cat., C&E, New York, 1984. Text: Derek Walcott (poem, "To Romare Bearden").

Romare Bearden: Six Panels on a Southern Theme. Exh. cat., Bundy Art Gallery, Waitsfield, Vt., 1967. RB statement.

Romare Bearden: The Human Condition. Exh. cat., ACA Galleries, New York, October 3–26, 1991. Text: Alexandra Anderson-Spivy (English and German)

Romare Bearden: The Prevalence of Ritual. Exh. cat., MoMA, New York, 1971. Circulated. Text: Judy Goldman; Carroll Greene; April Kingsley.

Romare Bearden: Work with Paper. Exh. cat., Baruch College Gallery, City University of New York, February 8–March 6, 1991. Text: Julia Hotton; Myron Schwartzman.

Romare Bearden: Working with Juxtaposition. Jefferson City, Mo.: Scholastic Inc., 1996. Cover title of *Scholastic Art* [journal] 26, no. 4 (February 1996). [Formerly *Art & Man.* Published in cooperation with National Gallery of Art, Washington, D.C.; 16 pp.]

Romare Bearden: Works on Paper. Exh. cat., Forbes Magazine Galleries, New York, January 25–April 27, 2002.

Romare Bearden in Black-and-White: Photomontage Projections 1964. Exh. cat. Whitney/Philip Morris, January 17–March 20, 1997. Circulated. Text: Gail Gelburd; Thelma Golden; Albert Murray (interview). Also poetry by RB, reprinted from *Romare Bearden: A Memorial Exhibition,* exh. cat., ACA Galleries, New York, 1989. [The Mint Museum produced brochure for its venue (1998).]

Schwartzman, Myron. *Romare Bearden: Celebrating the Victory.* New York: Franklin Watts, 1999. [children]

Schwartzman, Myron. *Romare Bearden: His Life and Art.* New York: Harry N. Abrams, Inc., 1990.

Selected Works, 1964–1987. Romare Bearden. Exh. cat., Sheldon Ross Gallery, Birmingham, Mich., November 17–December 29, 1990.

Shange, Ntozake. *I Live in Music.* New York: Welcome Enterprises, Inc., 1994. Illustrated with paintings by RB. Linda Sunshine, ed. [children]

Sims, Lowery Stokes. *Romare Bearden.* New York: Rizzoli International Publications, Inc., 1993.

Sound Collages and Visual Improvisations. [Exh. cat. and/or brochure for performance?], Artworks Gallery and Real Art Ways, Hartford, 1986.

Such Sweet Thunder: African Elements in the Art of Romare Bearden. Exh. cat., Kent State University School of Art Gallery, Ohio, April 9–May 9, 1997. Text: Fred T. Smith; Lyneise Williams.

Ten Hierographic Paintings by Sgt. Romare Bearden. Exh. cat., G Place Gallery, Washington, D.C., [1944]. Text: James A. Porter.

A Tribute to Romare Bearden. Exh. cat., Newark Museum, N.J., 1993. [for "A Gala Celebration in Tribute to Romare Bearden in commemoration of his contributions to Art, Poetry, Jazz, Friday, June 18, 1993," published in conjunction with exh. *A Tribute to Romare Bearden,* Newark Museum, Traphagen Promenade, June 16–August 1, 1993; includes exh. checklist, biography]

Washington, M. Bunch. *The Art of Romare Bearden: The Prevalence of Ritual.* New York: Harry N. Abrams, Inc., 1973. Introduction: John A. Williams. [various dates have been used for publication: NYPL has copies catalogued as 1973 and 1974; *Books in Print* gives publication date as Dec. 1973; a press release for the book gives publication date as November 28, 1973]

Williams, Lyneise. "Such Sweet Thunder: African Elements in the Art of Romare Bearden." Master's thesis, Kent State University (School of Art), Ohio, 1996.

ARTICLES AND REVIEWS

Abelman, Lester. "Black Artist Moonlights Way to Star Billing." *New York Sunday News*, March 28, 1971, 1. [exh. MoMA] [slightly revised version of article (reprinted in another edition) titled, "Black Artist at Top after Span of Years." *Sunday News*, March 28, 1971, B32]

"Abstract Artist, 46, Loses to Firemen on Studio in a Loft." *NYT*, March 24, 1961, 27.

"Actualités: Baltimore: Les collages de Bearden." *Connaissance des arts* 351 (May 1981): 41. [exh. *Romare Bearden: 1970–1980*, Baltimore Museum of Art]

Aehl, John. "Dissonance—Romare Bearden's Jumble of People, Places and Things Either Repulses or Enthralls." *Wisconsin State Journal*, September 14, 1997, 1F. [exh. *Romare Bearden in Black and White: Photomontage Projections 1964*, Madison Art Center]

Agovino, Michael. "'90s Are Witness to a Boom in the Works of Bearden." *Charlotte Observer*, December 11, 1994, 4F.

Albright, Thomas. "Berkeley's Life Style: Impressive New Mural." *San Francisco Chronicle*, January 3, 1974, 40.

Aldridge, Cathy. "Bearden's Collages Sold Though Exhibit Goes On." *New York Amsterdam News*, November 4, 1967, 23.

Alexander, Elizabeth. "Romare Bearden: An African-American Theory of Collage." In "Collage: An Approach to Reading African-American Women's Literature (Cooper, Anna Julia; Shange, Ntozake; Lorde, Audre)." Ph.D. dissertation, University of Pennsylvania, Philadelphia, 1992.

———. "Two Poems: Van Der Zee and Bearden." *American Poetry Review* 17, no. 2 (March–April 1988): 39.

Allen, Charles. "Have the Walls Come Tumbling Down?" *NYT*, April 11, 1971, sec. 2: 27, 28. [exh. *Prevalance of Ritual*, MoMA]

Allman, Paul. "Art Who?" *Berkeley Gazette* [?], November 1_ [?], 1971. [exh. *The Prevalence of Ritual*, University Art Museum, Berkeley] [*clipping from AAA/RB]

"Along the Color Line: Music, Art, and the Drama: *Crisis* Cartoon." *Crisis* 41 (June 1934): 169. [RB won first prize for cartoon in April 1934 *Crisis*.]

Alter-Muri, Simone, and Gail E. Gelburd. "Romare Bearden: More Than Collages in February." *School Arts* 101 (February 2002): 26–27.

Anderson, Jack. "Dance: Concert Features 'Museum' and a 'Puzzle'; 'Romare Bearden Day' in South." *NYT*, January 12, 1980, 12.

André, Michael. "New York Reviews: Romare Bearden." *Art News* 75 (March 1976): 131–32, 134. [exh. *Of the Blues (Second Chorus)*, C&E]

———. "Romare Bearden." *Art News* 74 (May 1975): 95. [exh. *Of the Blues*, C&E]

Andreae, Christopher. "The Home Forum: Romare Bearden." *Christian Science Monitor*, December 30, 1969, 8. [repr. *Interior with Profile*; ref. to RB's inclusion in Whitney Annual]

Andrews, Laura. "Links to Honor Romare Bearden at Newark Museum." *New York Amsterdam News*, June 12, 1993, 27.

Appelhof, Ruth Ann. "Art in the Area: The Nature of Woman." *Syracuse New Times*, October 5, 1975, 22, 23. [exh. *Mysteries: Women in the Art of Romare Bearden*, Everson Museum of Art, Syracuse]

"Art." *Newport News (Va.) Press*, October 28, 1945. [exh. *Passion of Christ*, Kootz, New York] [*AAA/RB, frame 0513, reel N/68-87; same text as clipping marked Savannah, Ga., *News*, October 28, 1945, from Romeike press clipping service, in AAA/RB, box 2/3] [*clipping also in MoMA Scrapbooks, fiche 1.79]

"Art: New Bearden Collages." *Bostonia* (Boston University) (September–October 1987): 10. [photo of RB and assistant Andrew Teabo; caption announces exh. Thomas Segal Gallery, November]

"Art and Dance to Benefit from Painter's Will." *NYT*, May 9, 1988, C14.

"Art in New York: Romare Bearden." *Time* (October 23, 1964): NY5. [exh. C&E; RB quoted]

"Art Spotlight: American Scenes." *Scholastic Art* 32 (February 2002): 10–11. [discussion of *Liza in High Cotton*]

"Art Spotlight: Rooms with a View." *Scholastic Art* 28 (November 1997): 10–11. [discussion of *Morning of the Rooster*]

"Art Talk: Bellevue to the Rescue." *Art News* 98 (Summer 1999): 36. [*CityScape: Scenes from Life in Harlem*, Bellevue Hospital]

"Art Work of Writer's Son on N.Y. Exhibit." *Washington Afro-American*, October 27, 1945. [*AAA/RB, box 2/3] [full text: "Romare Bearden, young artist son of Bessye Bearden, newspaper writer, is having his first one-man show at the Samuel B. Kootz gallery. Leading art critics have reported favorably on most of his work."]

"Artist Wants Cavanaugh to Attend His Showing." *New York Amsterdam News*, April 1, 1961, 30. [*MoMA (1971)]

A[shton], D[ore] (?). "About Art and Artists: Exhibitions at Two Galleries Here Show Painters Profited by Their Absence." *NYT*, November 3, 1955, 28L. [exh. at Barone Gallery, New York]

Ashton, Dore. "Romare Bearden: Projections" (with French summary). *Quadrum* 17 (1964): 99–110, 185.

A[tirnomis]. "In the Galleries: Bearden at Cordier and Ekstrom." *Arts Magazine* 44 (March 1970): 57. [exh. *Romare Bearden: Recent Collages*]

Auer, James. "Bearden Show Illuminates Black Experience." *Milwaukee Journal Sentinel*, October 21, 1997, *Cue*, 1. [exh. *Romare Bearden in Black-and-White*, Madison Art Center]

———. "December Exhibit Planned. Bearden Works Join Museum: Artist Worked Wonders with Collages, Elevating Them to an Art Form." *Milwaukee Journal Sentinel*, November 13, 1996, 10. [exh. of two new acquisitions]

Badejo, Fabian. "Art Gallery Opens with Bearden's 'Magical Expressionism.'" *St. Maarten/St. Martin Newsday* 9, no. 971 (February 6, 1985): 1–2A, 6A. [exh. *Rituals of the Obeah*, Nanette Bearden Fine Arts Gallery]

———. "Bearden, the Magic Language of Form and Colour." *St. Maarten/St. Martin Newsday* 9, no. 975 (February 15, 1985): 1B, 4B, 5B. [exh. *Rituals of the Obeah*, Nanette Bearden Fine Arts Gallery]

———. "Romare Bearden, Oh What A Blessing!" *St. Maarten/St. Martin Newsday* 12, no. 1315 (February 10, 1988): 2, 10. [exh. Nanette Bearden Fine Arts Gallery]

———. "Romare Bearden's Rhapsody in Green." *St. Maarten/St. Martin Newsday* 11, no. 1181 (January 28, 1987): 1, 15. [exh. Nanette Bearden Fine Arts Gallery]

Baker, Kenneth. "Feasts for the Eyes: Art Books Offer Delicious Works by the Masters." *San Francisco Chronicle*, November 28, 1993, Sunday Review, 1. [book reviews: includes RB and Henderson, *A History of African-American Artists* (1993)]

Bartlett, Andrew Walsh. "Representation, Aesthetics, and 'Maximum Multiplicity': Romare Bearden's Collages." In "The Free Place: Literary, Visual, and Jazz Creations of Space in the 1960s." Ph.D. dissertation, University of Washington, 1999.

Baxter, Paula. "Growing the Collection: A Bumper Crop of Beauty: The Fifty Best Recent Art Books." *Wilson Library Bulletin* 68 (June 1994): 30–34. [RB and Henderson, *A History of African-American Artists* (1993): 32]

Beals, Kathie. "Two Opportunities to See Bearden Works." *Weekend* [Gannett Westchester Newspapers?], November 6, 1981, 13. [exh. *Romare Bearden: 1970–1980,* Brooklyn Museum, and exh. at Paper Work Gallery, Larchmont, N.Y.]

"Bearden: Beauty from Discord." *[Charlotte?] Observer,* December 27, 1975. [brief discussion based on *Ebony* magazine article (November 1975)] [*Biography files, Carolina Room, Public Library of Charlotte and Mecklenburg County, N.C.]

"Bearden, a Master of Collage." *The (San Francisco/Oakland?) Post,* October 2, 1980, 6. [exh. Parsons-Barnett Gallery, Oakland] [*RBF archive]

"Bearden Back Home." *Horizon* (October 1980): 5. [exh. Mint Museum]

"Bearden Collage a Perfect Fit: 'Before Dawn' Scene Is Bold, Vital, Optimistic and Local." *Charlotte Observer,* August 17, 1988. [editorial]

"Bearden Exhibition." *NYT,* February 1, 1985, C3. [exh. *Black Roots, Jazz Music, Universal Myth,* Lehman College Art Gallery, Bronx]

"Bearden Gala." *News: New Jersey State Museum* (September–October 1983). [benefit performance by Contemporary Dance Theatre (Nanette Bearden's company); RB is honored guest] [*private archive]

"Bearden Honored at Wadsworth Atheneum." *Hartford Inquirer,* May 5, 1986, 3. [brief article on Bearden/McLean performance; receives Proclamation from mayoral executive]

"Bearden Painting in Presidential Suite." *New York Amsterdam News,* January 7, 1961, [7?] [*Golden Dawn* in John F. Kennedy's preinaugural suite at Carlyle Hotel] [*AAA/RB, frame 0518, reel N/68-87]

"Bearden's Legacy." *Charlotte Observer,* December 26, 1993, 1F. [reference to exh. *A Graphic Odyssey,* South Carolina State Museum; repr. *Mother and Child;* biographical caption]

"Bearden's Work Comes Alive at Baltimore Museum Reception." *African American News and World Report,* May 3, 1981. [exh. *Romare Bearden: 1970–1980,* Baltimore Museum of Art; report on reception with biographical notes and upcoming related events] [*RBF archive]

"Beardon [sic] Show a 2nd Homecoming." *Staten Island Advance,* September 25, 1981, D8. [exh. *Romare Bearden: 1970–1980,* Brooklyn Museum]

Beauregard, Sue-Ellen. "Adult Books for Young Adults: Nonfiction—*A History of African-American Artists: From 1792 to the Present* by Romare Bearden and Harry Henderson." *The Booklist* (Chicago) 90 (October 15, 1993): 424.

Bell, Jane. "Arts Reviews: Romare Bearden." *Arts* 49 (April 1975): 5. [exh. *Of the Blues,* C&E]

Berkley, Gail. "Romare Bearden Speaks on Art." *The (Oakland/Berkeley?) Post,* November 8–9, 1980, 6. [exh. Parsons-Barnett Gallery, Oakland] [*RBF archive]

Berman, Avis. "Color Me Blues: The Collages of Romare Bearden." *Eastern (Airlines) Review* (October 1980): 44–49. [exh. *Romare Bearden: 1970–1980,* Mint Museum]

———. "Romare Bearden: 'I Paint out of the Tradition of the Blues.'" *Art News* 79 (December 1980): 60–67. [profile; substantial quotations]

Bishop, Don. "Bearden Is Rising as Modern Artist." *Charlotte Observer,* August 3, 1952, 2D.

———. "Dixie All Over: Modern Art Has Unique Place, Says Bearden." [*Charlotte Observer*?], August 3, 1952 [*AAA/RB, frame 0516, reel N/68-87; also in MoMA Scrapbooks, fiche 1.79]

"Black Art: Romare Bearden." *The Black Collegian (Tenth Anniversary Commemorative Book)* 11, no. 2 (October–November 1980): 88–89. [profile; exh. *Romare Bearden 1970–1980,* Mint Museum]

Bolden, Tonya. "Building a Black Library: Part II." *YSB* 4 (October 31, 1994): 52. [very brief mention of RB and Henderson, *A History of African-American Artists* (1993)]

Bonetti, David. "Mostly off the Street: Where Do All the Galleries Meet." *Boston Phoenix,* December 18, 1987, 3: 8. [exh. Thomas Segal Gallery]

Borelli, Carol. "Neighborhood Collages." *Arts and Activities* 117 (April 1995): 41. [classroom project based on *The Block*]

Bostick, Alan. "Collage Master: Belmont Displays Works of Avant-Garde Romare Bearden." *Tennessean,* February 27, 2000, 1F. [exh. Leu Art Gallery, Belmont University, Nashville]

Bourdon, David. "Music to the Eyes." *Village Voice,* March 10, 1975, 84. [exh. C&E]

———. "Romare Bearden: 1970–1980." *Vogue* 171 (February 1981): 38. [exh. Mississippi Museum of Art, Jackson]

Braff, Phyllis. "Romare Bearden's Images of the Black Experience, in Prints." *NYT,* February 11, 1996, LI22. [exh. *Romare Bearden as Printmaker,* University Center, Adelphi University, Garden City, N.Y.]

Brenson, Michael. "The All-Including Works of Romare Bearden." *NYT,* April 19, 1991, C26 (L). [exh. *Memory and Metaphor,* SMIH]

———. "Art: Romare Bearden, 'Rituals of the Obeah.'" *NYT,* November 30, 1984, C23. [exh. *Rituals of the Obeah,* C&E]

———. "Art: The Tightrope Helen Frankenthaler Walks." *NYT,* December 9, 1983, C30. [embedded review of exh. *Romare Bearden—Mecklenburg Autumn,* C&E]

———. "A Collagist's Mosaic of God, Literature and His People." *NYT,* January 11, 1987, H33–34. [exh. *Romare Bearden: Origins and Progressions,* Bronx Museum of the Arts]

———. "A Look at Romare Bearden's Long Life Journey." *NYT (Current Events Edition),* June 9, 1989, C24. [exh. *Romare Bearden (1911–1988): A Memorial Exhibition,* ACA Galleries]

———. "Romare Bearden: Jazz." *NYT,* June 1, 1990, C26. [exh. ACA Galleries]

———. "Romare Bearden's Work: Its Complexity and Sweep." *NYT,* April 19, 1991, B6 (N). [exh. *Memory and Metaphor,* SMIH] [same as "The All-Including Works of Romare Bearden," *NYT,* April 19, 1991, C26 (L)]

"Brilliant Artist's Work Appears in European Art Magazine." *The African* (New York) (April–May 1948): 14, 19. [*Igoe (1981)]

Brockington, Horace. "Romare Bearden's Photomontages at the Whitney/Philip Morris." *Review* (February 1, 1997): 5.

Brooks, Helene. "Romare Bearden, Icons and More." *McCall's* 108 (March 1981): V8. [exh. *Romare Bearden: 1970–1980,* Mississippi Museum of Art, Jackson; profile]

Brown, Joe. "Color & Collage from Bearden." *Washington Post,* October 9, 1992, Weekend: N53. [mural by Howard University students inspired by RB in conjunction with exh. *Memory and Metaphor,* National Museum of American Art, Washington, D.C.]

Brown, Johanne. "MTA Unveils Bearden Mosaics." *Baltimore Afro-American,* March 26, 1983, 1, 2. [*private archive]

Brown, Karlene. "Entertainment Best Bets." *New York Newsday,* June 18, 1995, 58. [exh. *A Graphic Odyssey,* Brooklyn Museum]

Brown, Linda Luise. "Art: Romare Bearden, Again." *Creative Loafing* (Charlotte, N.C.), December 30, 1995, 23. [exh. Jerald Melberg Gallery, Charlotte]

Brown, Tony. "Collages by Renowned Artist Bearden Focus of Complex Art Case, FBI Probe." *Charlotte Observer,* March 28, 1992, 1C, 5C.

Buckham, Tom. "A Collage of Events Shape a Lasting Friendship." *Buffalo News,* May 5, 2002, F1, F6. [exh. *A Look at Romare Bearden,* Albright-Knox Art Gallery, Buffalo; biographical]

Budick, Ariella. "The Sensuous Collages of Romare Bearden." *Newsday,* April 21, 2000, B31. [exh. *Dr. Dorothy Cohen: The Bearden Years,* Great Neck Arts Center, N.Y.]

Bundy, Ora Brinkley. "'Bearden and Bearden' Cultural Event Planned." *Philadelphia Tribune,* August 21, 1987. [exh. Lucien Crump Art Gallery, Nanette Bearden Contemporary Dance Company performance, "Citation of Merit" awarded to both Beardens] [*RBF archive]

B[urckhardt, E[dith]. "Reviews and Previews: Romare Bearden." *Art News* 58 (February 1960): 16. [exh. Michel Warren Gallery]

Burnett, W.C. "Art Goes to the Heart of Black America." *Atlanta Journal,* March 29, 1978, 4B. [exh. Neighborhood Art Center]

Burnett, W.C., Jr. "Black Artist Made Honorary Citizen: Atlanta Claims Bearden as Her Own." *Atlanta Journal and Constitution,* November 21, 1976, 4C.

Burnside, Madeleine. "Romare Bearden." *Art News* 78 (February 1979): 172–73. [exh. *Profile/Part 1: The Twenties,* C&E]

Burrows, Carlyle. "Bearden's Return." *New York Herald Tribune,* January 24, 1960, 6. [exh. Michel Warren Gallery]

Caldwell, Bill. "Romare Bearden." *Essence* 6, no. 1 (May 1975): 70–73.

"California: Los Angeles Museum of Art. A Graphic Odyssey: Romare Bearden as Printmaker." *American Art Review* 6 (June–July 1994): 170. [exh. review]

C[ampbell], L[awrence]. "Reviews and Previews: Romare Bearden." *Art News* 68 (February 1970): 10. [exh. *Romare Bearden: Recent Collages,* C&E]

Campbell, Mary Schmidt. "Romare Bearden: Rites and Riffs." *Art in America* 69 (December 1981): 134–41.

Canaday, John, "The Art of Romare Bearden." *Contact* 5 (Spring 1974): 33. [review of Washington (1973), followed by a repr. *Train Whistle Blues, Number One* and one-page biographical sketch by Booker Williams]

———. "Bearden, Graffiti, and Life All over the Place." *NYT,* August 13, 1972, 2: 18. [exh. *Prevalence of Ritual,* SMIH]

———. "Romare Bearden Focuses on the Negro: Treatment Is Poignant but Not Mawkish." *NYT,* October 14, 1967, 23. [exh. C&E]

"Capture Paris." *New York Amsterdam News,* June 25, 1975, D12. [announces RB and Alvin Ailey openings (Bearden exh. *Black Experience in America,* Albert Loeb Galleries, Paris); photo of RB and Ailey]

"Carnegie Exhibit Spotlights Subway Station Artist." *Pittsburgh Post-Gazette,* June 19, 1992, B1. [exh. *Memory and Metaphor,* Carnegie Museum of Art]

Carrington, Karlynn. "Two Collages Installed at Center Coliseum." *Hartford Courant,* October 3, 1980, A17.

Chalfant, Arnold R. "A Black Man's Truth." *Prism* (July 1974). [*partial clipping RBF archive]

Chambers, Veronica. "An Artist's Life Is Hard Enough." *Los Angeles Times,* January 2, 1994, Book Review section, 2. [book review: RB and Henderson, *A History of African-American Artists* (1993)] [reprinted: "From Bearden, a Complete Picture of African-American Artists." *Baltimore Sun,* January 23, 1994, 6E; "Two Centuries of Black Creativity." *Chicago Sun-Times,* January 23, 1994, Show: 12]

Chandler, Mary Voelz. "Bearden's Variety Creates Artistic Melting Pot." *Denver Rocky Mountain News,* April 26, 1996, 8D. [exh. *A Graphic Odyssey,* Metropolitan State College]

Chapin, Louis. "The Medium Is the Message." *Christian Science Monitor,* July 28, 1973, 15. [RB's collage methods; repr. *April Green, Reunion*]

Chase-Riboud, Barbara. "A History of African American Artists from 1792 to the Present." *African American Review* 30 (Spring 1996): 115–16. [book review: RB and Henderson, *A History of African-American Artists* (1993)]

Childs, Charles. "Bearden: Identification and Identity." *Art News* 63 (October 1964): 24–25, 54, 61.

Churchill, Peg. "Brush Marks." *Schenectady Gazette,* December 12, 1968, 46. [exh. Art Gallery of the State University of New York at Albany]

Clement, Russell T. "Book Reviews: Arts and Humanities. *A History of African-American Artists: From 1792 to the Present.*" *Library Journal* 118, no. 16 (October 1, 1993): 91. [RB and Henderson, *A History of African-American Artists* (1993)]

Coker, Gylbert. "Romare Bearden's Sentimental Journey." *New York Amsterdam News,* January 6, 1979, D6. [exh. *Profile/Part 1: The Twenties,* C&E]

Colby, Joy. "Memories, Missions, Mosaics: A Dia Exhibit Showcases Romare Bearden's Varied Career." *Detroit News,* September 14, 1986, 7B, 10B. [exh. *Origins and Progressions;* also *Quilting Time* mural; exh. Sheldon Ross Gallery, Birmingham, Mich.]

Colby, Joy Hakanson. "Bearden's Nightscapes: Hot, Wet and Jazzy." *Detroit News,* March 13, 1983, 3H. [exh. *New York at Night: Recent Watercolors,* Sheldon Ross Gallery, Birmingham, Mich.]

———. "A Collage Named Romare Bearden." *Detroit News,* September 2, 1984, 1, 4D. [profile; exh. *Romare Bearden: Watercolors from St. Maarten,* Sheldon Ross Gallery, Birmingham, Mich.]

———. "A Double Helping of Bearden's Bounty." *Detroit News,* May 1, 1984, B1. [exh. Grand Rapids Art Museum, Mich.]

———. "Jazz in Shapes and Colors: Harlem-Born Artist Has a Trained Eye and a Feel for Intervals." *Detroit News,* April 13, 1980, 4G. [exh. Sheldon Ross Gallery, Birmingham, Mich.]

Coleman, A.D. "Depth of Field: A Patchwork Mythology: Romare Bearden's Photocollage." *Camera & Darkroom* 14 (August 1992): 12–13. [photocollage process; exh. *Memory and Metaphor* (touring)]

"The Collage Art of Romare Bearden: Fragmented Images of Black Life." *NYT,* January 3, 1987, 1: 15. [exh. *Origins and Progressions,* Bronx Museum of the Arts; photo of RB by Frank Stewart]

"Colorful Harmonies (Analysis of Musical Influences in Four of Romare Bearden's Collages)." *Scholastic Art* 26 (February 1996): 6–9. [teacher's guide/reference; see also *Romare Bearden: Working with Juxtaposition* (Jefferson City, Mo., 1996)]

"Comprehensive Portraits of Black Talent." *USA Today,* December 13, 1993, 4D. [book review: RB and Henderson, *A History of African-American Artists* (1993)]

Conheim, Maryanne. "A Magical Master Who Is Thriving on 'Painting the Blues.'" *Philadelphia Inquirer,* May 6, 1982, 1D, 7D. [profile; exh. *The Worlds of Romare Bearden,* Jenkintown Fine Arts Gallery, Pa.]

Conroy, Sarah Booth. "Black Life in Collage: Art from Things Found on the Street." *Washington Post,* July 11, 1971, K1, K3. [biographical; exh. *The Prevalence of Ritual,* National Collection of Fine Arts, Washington, D.C.]

Cook, Ande. "Hand Out: Making a Collage." *School Arts* 96 (February 1997): 28. [lesson plan for collage-making, with RB as inspiration]

Cotter, Holland. "The Many Styles and Inspirations of Romare Bearden." *NYT,* June 16, 1995, C5. [exh. *A Graphic Odyssey,* Brooklyn Museum]

Craig, Charlotte W. "Party Line: Dedication of 'Quilting Time.'" *Detroit Free Press,* September 15, 1986, 3C.

Cram, Ronald H. "Memory and Metaphor." *Religious Education* 93, no. 3 (1998): 332–38. [Cram's visit to exh. *Memory and Metaphor,* High Museum of Art, Atlanta]

Crenshaw, Holly. "Around Town: Parks Workers Hope for Laurels." *Atlanta Journal and Constitution,* May 28, 1998, JN1. [exh. *Romare Bearden: 'In the Garden,'* Modern Primitive Gallery]

Cullinan, Helen. "Promenade Kicks off Two Shows." *Cleveland Plain Dealer,* September 18, 1986, E11. [exh. Malcolm Brown Gallery, Shaker Heights, Ohio]

———. "The Romare Bearden Mystique." *Cleveland Plain Dealer,* November 14, 1982, 31C. [exh. Malcolm Brown Gallery, Shaker Heights, Ohio]

Cummings, Judith, and Albin Krebs. "Notes on People: A Carolinian Insists He Can Go Home Again." *NYT,* October 10, 1980, B5. [exh. *Romare Bearden: 1970–1980,* Mint Museum; *Bearden Plays Bearden* film]

Cutajar, Mario. "Precious Memory: Romare Bearden at UCLA and Louis Stern Galleries." *Artweek* 23 (January 30, 1992): 1, 12. [exh. Frederick S. Wight Gallery, University of California; Louis Stern Galleries, Los Angeles]

Daly, Ann. "2 N.Y. Artists Ready to Dig in to Projects for PAT Subway." *Pittsburgh Press,* January 28, 1984, B6. [primarily about RB]

Davis, Douglas. "Putting Things Together." *Newsweek* 77 (April 5, 1971): 52–53. [exh. *Prevalence of Ritual,* MoMA]

Davis, Kaiser Gregson. "Reflections on Omeros." *South Atlantic Quarterly* 96 (Spring 1997): 229–46. [RB and Derek Walcott's poem "Omeros"?] [*Project MUSE, Johns Hopkins University, online database; *http://muse.jhu.edu*]

Dawson, Bob. "Bearden Collages on Display at Mint Museum." *Charlotte Weekly—East,* October 16, 1980, 12.

Devree, Howard. "In Various Ways. Five Contemporaries Reveal Diversity of Themes and Styles Today." *NYT,* November 6, 1955, X17. [exh. Barone Gallery, New York]

———. "Work by Europeans, Americans: Contemporary Americans." *NYT,* March 31, 1946, 6X [Art]. [exh. *Lorca,* Kootz]

Diaz, Sonia G. "Bearden and Baldwin."*BAND (Black Arts National Diaspora Magazine):* 3, nos. 1–2 (March–June 1989): 27.

Doar, Harriet. *Charlotte Observer,* October 19, 1969, 5F. [book review: RB and Holty, *The Painter's Mind* (1969)]

———. "Artist's 'Carolina Shout' Comes Back to Its Roots." *Charlotte Observer,* April 20, 1975, 1B, 9B.

———. "Charlotte Native Is in New York Art World Spotlight." *Charlotte Observer,* November 12, 1967, 2G. [profile; exh. *The Evolution of Afro-American Artists*]

Donohoe, Victoria. "Art: Romare Bearden's Show Celebrates the Joy of Living." *Philadelphia Inquirer,* March 12, 1982, E42. [exh. Rodger LaPelle Galleries]

Dorsey, John. "At Baltimore Museum, Bearden Prints Are a Beautiful Symphony for the Eye." *Baltimore Sun,* June 17, 1993, 5E. [exh. *A Graphic Odyssey*]

———. "Bearden Welds a Whole from the Many Cultures in American Experience." *Baltimore Sun,* December 6, 1992, 1L. [exh. *Memory and Metaphor*]

———. "Bearden's Artwork Rich, Complex Exhibit Focuses on Charlotte Native's View of Life in America." *Charlotte Observer,* December 13, 1992, 6F. [exh. *Memory and Metaphor,* National Museum of American Art, Washington, D.C.]

———. "Bearden's 'Memory' Captures Americana." *Chicago Sun-Times,* January 3, 1993, Show: 11. [exh. *Memory and Metaphor,* National Museum of American Art, Washington, D.C.]

Douglas, Carlyle C. "Romare Bearden: Fame and Fortune Finally Come to One of America's Most Distinguished Black Artists." *Ebony* 31 (November 1975): 116–18, 120–22.

Douglas, Robert L. "From Blues to Protest/Assertiveness: The Art of Romare Bearden and John Coltrane." *International Review of African American Art* 8, no. 2 (1988): 28–43.

Driskell, David. "A History of African-American Artists (book review)." *International Review of African American Art* 12, no. 3 (1995): 50–52.

Driskell, David C. "Romare Bearden (1914–1988)." *Art Papers* (special issue on contemporary black artists) 12, no. 4 (July–August 1988): 43. Atlanta: Atlanta Art Papers, 1988.

"Ebony Book Shelf." *Ebony* 27 (October 1972): 34. [announcement: RB and Henderson, *Six Black Masters* (1972)]

Ellis, Edward. "Welfare Worker Arrives in Art: Romare Bearden's Job Provides Him with Inspiration." *New York World-Telegram,* October 21, 1949, 31.

Ellison, Ralph. "The Art of Romare Bearden." In *Writers on Artists,* Daniel Halpern, ed. San Francisco: North Point Press, 1988, 309–16. [originally catalogue introduction for exh. *Paintings and Projections,* Art Gallery of the State University of New York, Albany, November 25–December 22, 1968; also in RB and Holty, *The Painter's Mind* (1969); reprinted in *Massachusetts Review* 18, no. 4 (1977): 673–80; in Ralph Ellison, *Going to the Territory,* New York: Random House, 1986; and in *The Collected Essays of Ralph Ellison,* ed. John F. Callahan, New York: Modern Library, 1995]

———. "Bearden." In "In Memoriam: Romare H. Bearden, 1912–1988." *Callaloo* 11 (Summer 1988): 416–19.

———. "Romare Bearden: Paintings and Projections." *Crisis* 77, no. 3 (March 1970): 80–86. [reprint of introduction to exh. cat. *Paintings and Projections,* Art Gallery of the State University of New York, Albany, 1968]

Emerling, John Anthony. "The Politics of the Fragment: A Theory of Romare Bearden's Black-and-White Photomontages." Master's thesis, University of California, Los Angeles, 2000. [OCLC: 46966824]

Engler, Sam. "Romare Bearden: A Top Artist Returns Home to Charlotte." *Charlotte* 13, no. 4 (September–October 1980): 53–54. [exh. *Romare Bearden: 1970–1980,* Mint Museum]

"Etcetera: Miscellany." *Art Gallery* 15 (May 1972): 32. [RB and Henderson, *Six Black Masters* (1972)]

"Etcetera: Miscellany." *Art Gallery* 15 (Summer 1972): W16. [RB's mural and collage commission from New York City Parks, Recreation and Cultural Affairs Administration, on view in Times Square]

"Exhibitions." *North Carolina Museum of Art Bulletin* 12 (December 1973): 81–90. [listing for *The Prevalence of Ritual,* 81; installation shot, 88]

"Exhibits on Tour." *American Artist* 44 (October 1980): 89. [exh. *Romare Bearden: 1970–1980,* Mint Museum]

F., C. L. "In the Galleries: Romare Bearden." *Arts Magazine* 30 (November 1955): 50. [exh. Barone Gallery, New York]

"Famous Black Artist Exhibits in Toronto." *Contrast,* January 23, 1976, 8. [exh. Graphis Gallery]

ffrench-frazier, Nina. "Romare Bearden." *Art News* 76 (October 1977): 141–42. [exh. *Odysseus,* C&E]

F[ischer], J[ohn]. "In the Galleries: Romare Bearden." *Arts Magazine* 42, no. 3 (December 1967–January 1968): 62. [exh. C&E]

FitzHugh, Donald. "Romare Bearden: Negro Culture Depicted Here." *Washington Sunday Star,* October 4, 1965, A23. [exh. *Projections,* Corcoran Gallery of Art, Washington, D.C.]

Fox, Catherine. "Critic's Notebook: Bearden's Metaphor, Legacy Continue to Inspire Local Artists." *Atlanta Journal and Constitution,* March 22, 1992, N2.

———. "Exhibit Preview: 'Memory and Metaphor: The Art of Romare Bearden, 1940–1987.'" *Atlanta Journal and Constitution,* February 23, 1992, N1–2. [profile]

———. "Visual Arts: Joyous Use of Color and Form Show the Artist's Lighter, Lyrical Side." *Atlanta Journal and Constitution,* June 19, 1998, Q4. [exh. *Romare Bearden: "In the Garden,"* Modern Primitive Gallery]

———. "Visual Arts: One Master Echoing Another in the Ascendancy: Artists' Works Suffused with a Rich Eclecticism." *Atlanta Journal and Constitution,* May 12, 2000, Q8. [exh. *Ascendancy: The Art of Romare Bearden,* Spelman College]

———. "Visual Arts: Two Faces of Bearden: Photomontages Have Power, Directness of a Documentary." *Atlanta Journal and Constitution,* June 19, 1998, Q4.

"Fragments of the Past." *Scholastic Art* 26 (February 1996): 4–5. [profile; see *Romare Bearden: Working with Juxtaposition,* Jefferson City, Mo.: Scholastic Inc., 1996]

Frankenstein, Alfred. "The Epic of Black Life: Berkeley Exhibit of Bearden." *San Francisco Chronicle,* November 8, 1971, 43. [exh. *Prevalence of Ritual,* University of California Art Museum, Berkeley]

Fressola, Michael. "Bearden Turned Art into Adventure." *Staten Island Sunday Advance, Punch,* June 4, 1989, F1. [exh. *Romare Bearden: A Memorial Exhibition,* ACA Galleries, New York]

Fry, W. Logan. "Swatches: A Look at Romare Bearden and the Textile Metaphor." *Fiberarts* 19 (September–October 1992): 22–23.

Gaither, Edmund Barry. "Romare Bearden: Carolina Interior." *Art Education* 43 (November 1990): 39–40. [lesson plan based on RB's collage]

"Gallery Previews in New York: Bearden." *Pictures on Exhibit* 23 (February 1960): 12. [exh. Michel Warren Gallery; repr., p. 7]

"Gallery Previews. Romare Bearden." *Pictures on Exhibit* 8 (April 1946): 34. [exh. *Lorca,* Kootz]

García-Herraiz, Enrique. "Crónica de Nueva New York: Romare Beardem [sic]: Tardio reconocimiento." *Goya* 104 (September–October 1971): 131–34. [exh. MoMA, p. 133]

Genauer, Emily. "Art and the Artist." *New York Post,* April 3, 1971, 34 (magazine p. 14). [exh. MoMA]

———. "Art & the Artist." *New York Post,* March 6, 1976. [exh. *Of the Blues (Second Chorus),* C&E] [*private archive]

———. "Art and Artist." *New York Post,* August 5, 1972, 32 (magazine page 14). [Times Square mural]

Getlein, Frank. "An Official Institution Celebrates Black 'Counter Culture.'" *Washington Sunday Star,* July 18, 1971, C5. [exh. *The Prevalence of Ritual,* National Collection of Fine Arts, Washington, D.C.]

———. "Art and Artists: Confrontation at Corcoran." *Evening Washington [Sunday] Star,* October 3, 1965, F6, F7. [exh. *Projections,* Corcoran Gallery of Art, Washington, D.C.]

Ghent, Henri. "And So It Is." *School Arts* 68 (April 1969): 21–26. [profile pp. 22–23; illus.]

———. "Art Mailbag: Gide's Words." *NYT,* April 19, 1970, 2: 22. [response to Hilton Kramer, "Black Experience and Modernist Art: Romare Bearden Uses Photos in Collages," *NYT,* February 14, 1970, review of RB and Barbara Chase-Riboud exhibitions]

———. "Black Art." *Art in America* 60 (November–December 1972): 34–35. [book review: RB and Henderson, *Six Black Masters* (1972)]

———. "Letters to the Editor: Soulful." *NYT Magazine,* May 11, 1969, 132. [comment on *Soul History* cover for *NYT Magazine,* Sunday, April 20, 1969]

Gibson, Eric. "Exhibit Gives Bearden His Due—Sort Of." *Washington Times,* October 4, 1992, D2. [exh. *Memory and Metaphor,* National Museum of American Art, Washington, D.C.]

———. "New York: Romare Bearden." *Art International* 22 (February 1979): 24. [exh. *Profile/Part 1: The Twenties,* C&E]

———. "Remaking Bearden." *New Criterion* 10 (November 1991): 62–65. [profile; exh. *Memory and Metaphor,* Museum of Contemporary Art, Chicago]

———. "Romare Bearden: In Tune with Jazz." *Art News* 94 (September 1995): 102. [exh. *A Graphic Odyssey,* Hampton University, Va.]

Glazer, Lee Stephens. "Signifying Identity: Art and Race in Romare Bearden's Projections." *Art Bulletin* 76 (September 1994): 411–26.

Glueck, Grace. "A Brueghel from Harlem." *NYT,* February 22, 1970, 2: 29. [exh. C&E]

———. "Minority Artists Find a Welcome in a New Showcase." *NYT,* December 23, 1969, 22. [Cinque Gallery; RB quoted]

———. "New York: Big Thump on the Bass Drum." *Art in America* 59 (May–June 1971): 128–33. [exh. *Prevalence of Ritual,* MoMA, 130–31]

———. "Think Up a New Brand Name: New York Gallery Notes." *Art in America* 55 (September–October 1967): 108–11. [exh. C&E, p. 111]

———. "Works of Bearden and Hunt Are Displayed: Scenes of Negro Life Depicted by Painter." *NYT,* March 24, 1971, 50. [exh. *Prevalence of Ritual,* MoMA]

Goodstein, Barbara. *Art and Antiques* 9 (January 1992): 87. [exh. ACA Galleries, New York]

Graham, Gladys. P. "Intercultural Events and Gifted Communicative Arts and Artist Awaken Sleeping Giants." *The Voice,* April 2, 1971. [exh. *Prevalence of Ritual,* MoMA] [*private archive]

Grau, Jane. "Bearden's Madonna's Celebrate Real Maternity." *Charlotte Observer,* May 3, 1998, 1F, 2F. [exh. Jerald Melberg Gallery, Charlotte]

Gruen, John. "Galleries and Museums: The Rhythms of Life." *New York* 4 (April 12, 1971): 61. [exh. *Prevalence of Ritual,* MoMA] [*Igoe (1993)]

H., R. "Romare Bearden Opening." *Crisis* 88, no. 6 (July 1981): 302. [exh. C&E]

H[ope], H[enry] R. "Public Art Museum Notes." *Art Journal* 30 (Summer 1971): 406, 408. [exh. *Prevalence of Ritual,* MoMA, 408]

Hale, Christy. "Masterpiece of the Month: Romare Bearden." *Scholastic Instructor* 112 (August 2002): 38–39.

Hall, Jacqueline. "Collages, Woodcarvings Define Black Artists." *Columbus Dispatch,* January 28, 2001, 8F. [exh. *Romare Bearden: Selected Collages and Watercolors,* Keny Galleries]

———. "Independent Venues Prepare Diverse Lineup." *Columbus Dispatch,* September 3, 2000, 12. [exh. Keny Galleries]

Hall, James C. "The Prevalence of Ritual in an Age of Change: Romare Bearden." In *Mercy, Mercy Me: African American Culture and the American Sixties.* New York: Oxford University Press, 2001. [compare Hall's chapter in "'There Is No Deed But Memory': African-American Antimodernism and the American Sixties," Ph.D. dissertation, University of Iowa, 1992, 286–331]

Hammond, Leslie King. "Romare Bearden: A Black Artist for Our Times." *Metropolitan* (April 1981): 10–11. [exh. *Romare Bearden: 1970–1980,* Baltimore Museum of Art]

Hammond, Sally. [or Helen Dudar?] "Close Up: Of Form and Color." [*Post* (New York) ?] [profile; exh. *The Evolution of Afro-American Artists: 1800–1950,* City University of New York] [*clipping with Dudar byline, *New York Post,* undated, from AAA/RB; also from MoMA Scrapbooks, fiche 1.80, hand-annotated: October, 1967. A second clipping with Hammond byline, otherwise unannotated, in RBF archives; title and text of the two clippings is identical, with photo of RB] [Washington (1973) cites Hammond, *New York Post,* October 23, 1967]

Hamrick, Grace. "Artist Romare Bearden to Be Honored at 2 Events." *Charlotte Observer,* May 16, 1985, 7C. [social events related to exh. Jerald Melberg Gallery]

Hanson, Bernard. "In Innovative Exhibit, Bearden Executes Jazz on Canvas." *Hartford Courant,* June 15, 1986, G7.

Hartman, Ronald J. "MTA's Romare Bearden." *Baltimore Sun,* December 31, 1990, 6A. [Letters to the Editor. Writer, manager of Baltimore Metro, calling attention to subway mural]

Hartranft, Ann. "Everson Exhibits Bearden's Powerful Imagery." *Syracuse Herald-American,* September 28, 1975, 4. [exh. *Mysteries: Women in the Art of Romare Bearden,* Everson Museum of Art, Syracuse, N.Y.]

H[ayes], R[ichard]. "Reviews and Previews: Romare Bearden." *Art News* 60 (April 1961): 61. [exh. Cordier & Warren]

Henry, Gerrit. "Reviews and Previews: Romare Bearden." *Art News* 72 (May 1973): 87. [exh. C&E]

Herbert, Bob. "Where Spirit Still Triumphs." *New York Daily News,* February 26, 1987, 37. [exh. *Origins and Progressions,* Bronx Museum of the Arts]

Herbert, Gayle. "Romaire [sic] Bearden, Renaissance Man from Harlem, U.S.A." *Philadelphia New Observer,* May 6, 1982, 4, 12. [exh. Jenkintown Fine Arts Gallery, Pa.]

Heron, W. Kim. "One Jacket Covers a Collage of Artistry." *Detroit Free Press,* March 14, 1983, 9A. [RB collage, record jacket design for jazz musician Kamau Kenyatta]

Hertzog, Joan. "At Mississippi Museum of Art: Romare Beardon [sic] Patches Art and Culture." *Jackson Capital Reporter,* February 12, 1981, 5. [exh. *Romare Bearden 1970–1980,* Mississippi Museum of Art]

Herzog, Melanie. "The Art of Collage (Artist Romare Bearden)." *School Arts* 89 (January 1990): 23–26.

Hines, Diane Casella. "Art Books and Videos: A History of African-American Artists from 1792 to the Present, by Romare Bearden and Harry Henderson." *American Artist* 59 (September 1995): 77–78. [review]

Holt, Nora. "Romare Bearden Wins High Praise for Exhibition, 'The Passions of Christ.'" *Amsterdam News,* October 27, 1945, 6. [debut exh. Kootz]

Hooton, Bruce Duff. "Odyssey of an Artist." *Horizon* 22, no. 8 (August 1979): 16–24. [excerpted in *Art/World* 6, no. 1 (September 26–October 17, 1981): 1, 7]

Hope, Andrew. "Bearden's Collages." *Jamaica Sunday Gleaner,* May 10, 1987, 2C. [*RBF archives]

Houchens, Douglas. "Romare Bearden: Davidson Had Him First." *Charlotte Observer,* October 14, 1980, 19A.

Howe, Susan. "Romare Bearden at Cordier & Ekstrom." *Art in America* 64 (November–December 1976): 122. [exh. *Of the Blues (Second Chorus)*]

Howell, Camille. "Arts: Bearden's Multilevel Genius." *Springfield News-Leader,* Weekend, February 5–7, 1993, 12. [exh. *Harlem Culture and Southern Memories,* Springfield Art Museum, Mo.]

H[ubbard], G[uy]. "Clip & Save: Art Notes." *Arts and Activities* 117 (April 1995): 40. [biographical notes with featured reproduction, *The Prevalence of Ritual: Baptism* (1964), 34]

Hubbard, Guy. "Clip & Save: Classroom Use." *Arts and Activities* 117 (April 1995): 33. [notes and classroom suggestions for featured reproduction ("Clip & Save Art Print"), *The Prevalence of Ritual: Baptism* (1964), 34]

Hughes, Robert. "Visual Jazz from a Sharp Eye." *Time,* June 10, 1991, 72–73. [exh. *Memory and Metaphor,* SMIH; biographical notes]

Humphries, Dedria. "Successful Black Artist Paving Road for Others." *Michigan Chronicle,* December 8, 1979, A3.

H[unter], S[am] (?). "Bearden, Gerard Display Paintings." *NYT,* November 12, 1948, 21. [exh. *Iliad,* Niveau Gallery, New York]

Huntington, Richard. "This Week: Art: Worlds Together." *Buffalo News,* February 14, 1993, Entertainment: 1. [exh. *Romare Bearden: A Cultural Hero,* Memorial Art Gallery, Rochester]

Ianco-Starrels, Josine. "Art News." *Los Angeles Times* [home edition], May 4, 1986, 110. [exh. Brockman Gallery] [citation: *http://www.latimes.com* and Lexis/Nexis]

"Important Notes: Black Artists to Be Shown at the Modern." *ABA: A Journal of the Affairs of Black Artists* 1, no. 1 (1971): 19. [exh. *Prevalence of Ritual,* MoMA]

Ingle, Tom. "Books." *Art Gallery* 13 (October 1969): 15. [book review: RB and Holty, *The Painter's Mind* (1969)]

Jacobs, Jay. "Past and Future." *Art in America* 57 (November–December 1969): 56–59. [book review: RB and Holty, *The Painter's Mind* (1969), 59]

James, Curtia. "Bearden Art Illuminates Program Text." *Richmond Times-Dispatch,* January 11, 1998, H1, H2.

———. "Reviews: Washington, D.C.: Romare Bearden." *Art News* 92 (March 1993): 118, 120. [exh. *Memory and Metaphor,* National Museum of American Art, Washington, D.C.]

———. "Romare Bearden: National Academy of Sciences." *New Art Examiner* 17 (September 1989): 56–57. [exh.]

J[ewell], E[dward] A[lden]. "Among the Local Shows." *NYT,* October 14, 1945, X7. [debut exh. Kootz]

Jewell, Edward Alden. "In Abstract Vein: Exhibitions Range from Nonobjective to Expressionist and Surrealist. Sharp Contrasts." *NYT,* March 2, 1947, X7. [exh. Kootz]

Jodidio, Philip. "Romare Bearden: Les expériences d'un peintre noir américain." *Connaissance des arts* 321 (November 1978): 114–19.

Johnson, Herschel. "Romare Bearden Rediscovers Himself." *Soho Weekly News,* December 7, 1978, 73–74. [exh. *Profile/Part I: The Twenties,* C&E] [*RBF]

Johnson, Mark M. "Arts & Activities Clip & Save Art Print." *Arts & Activities* 104 (September 1988): 26. [biographical; commentary about *Noah, Third Day* (1972), featured repr., 25]

J[udd], D[onald]. "In the Galleries: Romare Bearden." *Arts Magazine* 39 (November 1964): 60. [exh. C&E]

Judson, Bay. "Romare Bearden: Pittsburgh Memories." *Art Education* 39 (March 1986): 25–26. [lesson plan based on RB's collage, grades K–3]

Julian, Bea. "Artist Romare Bearden Speaks Out." *Ebony Jr.!* (November 1980): 20–21. [exh. *Romare Bearden: 1970–1980,* Mint Museum] [children]

Kaiser, Ernest. "Recent Books." *Freedomways* 12 (2nd quarter, 1972): 166–67. [RB and Henderson, *Six Black Masters* (1972)]

———. "Recent Books." *Freedomways* 14 (4th quarter, 1974): 365–82. [*Igoe (1981): reference (in review of Milton Brown, *Jacob Lawrence*) to RB and Harry Henderson, *Six Black Masters* (1972), 367]

Kalfas, Caroline. "'Romare Bearden: Collages and Prints,' African-American Artist Pushes Medium to New Heights." *East Weekend,* October 16, 1998, 6. [exh. *Romare Bearden: Collages and Prints,* Greenville Museum of Art, N.C.]

Kampen, Michael E. "Art and Artists: Bearden Combines Fragments of Life into a New Whole." *Charlotte Observer,* October 5, 1980, F11. [exh. *Romare Bearden: 1970–1980,* Mint Museum]

———. "Art and Artists: Richness, Poetry, Power in Bearden's Work." *Charlotte Observer,* October 19, 1980, 8F. [exh. *Romare Bearden: 1970–1980,* Mint Museum]

Kelly, June. "Romare Bearden." *International Review of African-American Art* 9, no. 4 (1991): 19–27.

Kendrick, Gerald, Dilys Winegrad, and Allan L. Edmunds. "The Bearden Project: An Educational Collaboration." *Hot Topics* newspaper supplement, 1996. [commissioned from the Hollister Publication Services, Inc., by Newspaper in Education (NIE) department of the *Philadelphia Inquirer,* in conjunction with exh. *A Graphic Odyssey: Romare Bearden as Printmaker* and part of citywide educational effort coordinated by the Arthur Ross Gallery, University of Pennsylvania (September 7–October 26, 1996) and Brandywine Workshop (opening September 9)]

Kenner, Hugh. "Cut and Paste: Romare Bearden's Collages Reflect His Life in Many Worlds." *Art and Antiques* 9 (May 1992): 96.

Kimmelman, Michael. "Art in Review: Bearden's Epic Intimacy." *NYT,* December 13, 1996, C30. [exh. ACA Galleries, New York]

Kimzey, Ann. "Bearden: Society's Impatience Influences Artist." *Charlotte Leader,* June 12, 1985, 8, 12.

Klein, Ellen Lee. "Romare Bearden." *Arts Magazine* 61 (December 1986): 119–20. [exh. C&E, September 23–November 1]

Kohen, Helen L. "Bearden's Backdrops Augment Ailey." *Miami Herald,* November 13, 1983, L1.

Kozik, K.K. "Romare Bearden: ACA Galleries." *Cover* (March 1992): 15. [exh. *The Human Condition,* SMIH]

Kramer, Hilton. "Art: Drawings with Graphic Subtlety. Romare Bearden." *NYT,* March 31, 1973, 31. [embedded review exh. C&E]

———. "Art: Intimacy and the 'Infinite.'" *NYT,* June 22, 1974, 18. [exh. *Prevalence of Ritual* screenprints, C&E]

———. "Bearden's 'Patchwork Cubism.'" *NYT,* December 3, 1978, 2: 35, 36. [exh. C&E]

———. "Black Experience and Modernist Art: Romare Bearden Uses Photos in Collages." *NYT,* February 14, 1970, 23. [exh. *Romare Bearden: Recent Collages,* C&E] [see also Ghent (1970) and Smith (1970), (Letters to the Editor)]

———. "The Critic's Eye: The Art of Romare Bearden." *MD* 35, no. 12 (December 1991): 12–17. [exh. *Memory and Metaphor,* Wight Art Gallery, University of California, Los Angeles]

———. "Marden Art at the Guggenheim: Painter Points Way for Color-Field Abstraction." *NYT,* March 15, 1975, 15. [embedded review exh. *Of the Blues,* C&E]

Krebs, Patrica [sic]. "At Last, a Homecoming for Charlotte's Bearden." *Charlotte Observer,* April 9, 1978, F1, F4. [exh. Davidson College Art Gallery, N.C.]

Krebs, Patricia, and Gloria Anderson. "Artist Seeks Childhood Scenes in Charlotte." *Charlotte Observer,* May 7, 1976, 1C.

Kuspit, Donald B. "New York: Romare Bearden." *Artforum International* 30 (November 1991): 137–38. [exh. *Memory and Metaphor,* SMIH]

La Badie, Donald. "'Jazz' Comes out of the South to Prelude Fall Show." *Memphis Commercial Appeal,* August 8, 1982, Fanfare: 18. [exh. University Gallery of Memphis State University]

Lake, Edwin B. "A Voice of the People (Mural by Romare Bearden)." *Black Enterprise* 13 (June 1983): 42.

Lanese, Sandra. "Romare Bearden: A Soul on Canvas." *Art Review* (June–July 1984): 20–21, 28–29.

Lanese, Sandra M. "Romare Bearden's Pieces of a Life." *Metropolitan Detroit* (September 1986): 84–86, 145–46. [profile; exh. *Romare Bearden: Origins and Progressions,* Detroit Institute of Arts]

Langdon, Ann R. "The Sounds of Romare Bearden." *Hartford Advocate,* June 16, 1986, 22. [exh. *Sound Collages and Visual Improvisations,* Real Art Ways Gallery]

Larrubia, Evelyn. "Romare Bearden Abstracts Shown." *St. Petersburg Times,* April 7, 1991, 10F. [exh. Museum of African American Art, Tampa; profile]

Larson, Kay. "Talking about Life." *New York* 24 (May 13, 1991): 99–100. [exh. *Memory and Metaphor,* SMIH]

"A Leading Black Artist Drawing Crowds in Raleigh." *Charlotte Observer,* May 4, 1972, B14. [exh. *Prevalence of Ritual,* North Carolina Museum of Art, Raleigh]

Leimbach, Dulcie. "Luminous Art That Softens a Subway." *NYT,* January 20, 1994, C3. [*City of Glass* mural, East Tremont subway station, Bronx]

Levine, Eleanor. "Romare Bearden Exhibit at the Whitney and Tribute to Marian Anderson at Carnegie Hall." *New York Amsterdam News,* January 25, 1997, 29. [exh. *Romare Bearden in Black and White: Photomontage Projects 1964,* Whitney/Philip Morris]

Lipson, Karin. "Bearden: From Uptown to the Islands." *New York Newsday,* February 24, 1986, 2: 17. [exh. Flushing Gallery, Queens, New York]

———. "Jazz and Mysticism by Romare Bearden." *New York Newsday,* February 12, 1987, 12. [exh. *Romare Bearden: Selections from the Jazz Series and Obeah Series,* University Center Gallery, Adelphi University, Garden City, N.Y.]

Litt, Steven. "Exhibitions Celebrate Decades of Black Art." *Cleveland Plain Dealer,* May 2, 1997, 1E. [exh. *Graphic Odyssey,* Cleveland Museum of Art]

———. "Reflecting a Joyful Spirit: Romare Bearden's Works Demonstrate Big-Hearted Outlook." *Cleveland Plain Dealer,* June 20, 1997, 1E, 4E. [exh. *Romare Bearden: Collages, Watercolors, Graphics,* Malcolm Brown Gallery, Shaker Heights, Ohio]

Logan, Betti. "Black Artist Captures a Cultural Synthesis." *New York Newsday,* April 1, 1976, 2: 11A.

"A Look at Romare Bearden." *Albright-Knox Art Gallery Calendar* (May–June 2002): 1. [exh.]

Lynch, Kevin. "Cutting and Pasting for Art." *Madison Capital Times,* September 3, 1997, 1D. [exh. *Romare Bearden in Black and White,* Madison Art Center, Wis.]

MacAdam, Barbara. "Culture and Context." *Art News* 93 (May 1994): 110. [book review: RB and Henderson, *A History of African-American Artists* (1993)]

MacDonald, Ruth K. "A Visit to the Country." *School Library Journal* 35 (December 1989): 82. [book review: Herschel Johnson and RB, *A Visit to the Country*]

"Major Bearden Show Set." *First World* 2, no. 4 (1980): 34. [exh. *Romare Bearden: 1970–1980,* Mint Museum] [*private archive]

Marger, Mary Ann. "Bearden's Works Go on Display." *St. Petersburg Times,* November 8, 1996, Weekend: 30. [exh. *Romare Bearden: An Homage to Paper,* Museum of African American Art, Tampa]

Markus, Julia. "Romare Bearden's Art Does Go Home Again—to Conquer." *Smithsonian* 11, no. 12 (1981): 70–77. [profile; exh. *Romare Bearden: 1970–1980* (touring)]

Maschal, Richard. "The Art of Music: Charlotte-Born Artist Captures the Essence of Jazz in Paintings." *Charlotte Observer,* February 27, 1988, 1D, 2D. [exh. *Riffs and Takes: Music in the Art of Romare Bearden,* North Carolina Museum of Art, Raleigh]

———. "Arts Commission Approves Bearden Mural for Library." *Charlotte Observer,* February 26, 1988, C1, C3.

———. "ArtsWatch: Visual Arts: Mural, Mural on the Wall." *Charlotte Observer,* June 14, 1989, 1D. [*Before Dawn* unveiled]

———. "Bearden Elevated Collage to a New Level of Creativity." *Charlotte Observer,* August 23, 2002, 22E.

———. "Bearden, Viewed Afresh, Brims with Vitality." *Charlotte Observer,* October 13, 2002, 6H. [concurrent exhs. Mint Museum; Jerald Melberg Gallery, Charlotte]

———. "Bearden Works: New Home in Hometown (BofA [Bank of America] Presents 6 Collages by Noted Artist to Mint)." *Charlotte Observer,* August, 24, 2002, 1A, 10A.

———. "Bearden's Breaking out All over Town." *Charlotte Observer,* August 25, 2002, 1H, 8H. [exh. *Charlotte's Own—Romare Bearden,* Mint Museum, plus ancillary shows: Christa Faut Gallery, Cornelius, N.C.; Jerald Melberg Gallery, Charlotte]

———. "Bearden's Charlotte Gone, but in His Art." *Charlotte Observer,* January 14, 2001, 10F.

———. "Bearden's Death Puts Sales of His Artworks on Hold." *Charlotte Observer,* March 15, 1988, 2B.

———. "Bearden's Mastery Sparkles." *Charlotte Observer,* November 9, 2001, 17E. [exh. *Romare Bearden: Collages, Prints, and Watercolors,* Christa Faut Gallery, Cornelius, N.C.]

———. "Bearden's Mecklenberg: Artist's View Lives on in 'Dawn' at New Library." *Charlotte Observer,* June 14, 1989, 1A.

———. "A Brush with Fame: Charlotte Native Romare Bearden's Gift for Painting Is Kept Alive in a Book about His Life." *Charlotte Observer,* December 23, 1990, 1F, 2F.

———. "Commission Should Consider a Bearden Work." *Charlotte Observer,* December 21, 1986, 1E.

———. "Commissioners to Vote on Bearden Mural." *Charlotte Observer,* April 5, 1988, B1, B2.

———. "Honor City's Greatest Artist, Romare Bearden." *Charlotte Observer,* February 16, 2002, 19A.

———. "Honor for a Native Son: Artist Romare Bearden, Revered Elsewhere, Deserves Better Treatment in His Home Town." *Charlotte Observer,* January 14, 2001, 1F.

———. "Name Uptown Park after Artist Bearden." *Charlotte Observer,* July 1, 2001, 1F–2F.

———. "National Gallery Will Showcase Bearden's City Scenes." *Charlotte Observer,* January 14, 2001, 1A.

———. "New Bearden Works Leaner, Richer." *Charlotte Observer,* June 2, 1985, 3F. [exh. Jerald Melberg Gallery, Charlotte]

———. "Romare Bearden: Acclaimed Artist Celebrates Charlotte Roots." *Charlotte Observer,* October 5, 1980, F1, F4, F5. [profile; exh. Mint Museum]

———. "Romare Bearden: Artist's Early Years in Charlotte Inspired Collages." *Charlotte Observer,* May 18, 1985. D1, D2. [profile; exh. Jerald Melberg Gallery, Charlotte]

———. "Romare Bearden Found His Roots under the City's Concrete." *Charlotte Observer,* October 12, 1980, C1, C6.

———. "Romare Bearden's Jazz Collages Exhibited at Melberg Gallery." *Charlotte Observer,* October 19, 1986, 4F.

———. "Scholarship Named for Bearden: Award Established at Davidson for Black Art Students." *Charlotte Observer,* December 10, 1993, 2B.

———. "Uptown Library Chosen to House Bearden Collage." *Charlotte Observer,* August 12, 1988, 1C, 2C. [article also published with headline variant: "Bearden's 'Before Dawn' Chosen for Charlotte's Uptown Library"]

Mason, Marilynne S. "Black Artists Conquer Indifference." *Christian Science Monitor,* February 28, 1994, Home Forum: 16. [book review: RB and Henderson, *A History of African-American Artists* (1993)]

Masters, Leslie. "Black Artist Captures Life." *The Eccentric,* December 16, 1976, 13C. [exh. Sheldon Ross Gallery, Birmingham, Mich.]

McB[ride]., H[enry]. "Attractions in the Galleries." *New York Sun,* March 30, 1946, 9. [exh. *Lorca,* Kootz]

McCoy, Frank. "Bearden's Final Gift—A History of African American Artists: From 1792 to the Present." *Black Enterprise* 24 (March 1994): 93. [book review: RB and Henderson, *A History of African-American Artists* (1993)]

McKenna, Kristine. "Art Review: Brockman Offers Bearden Works." *Los Angeles Times* [Home Edition], May 21, 1986, pt. 6: 6. [exh. Brockman Gallery]

McKenzie, Barbara. "Collage Paintings Are Magical, Mysterious." *Atlanta Journal and Constitution,* June 16, 1986, B2. [exh. McIntosh Gallery]

McNally, Owen. "Jazz, Art Combine Cleverly." *Hartford Courant,* May 5, 1986, D5. [Bearden/McLean performance]

Meilgaard, Manon. "Bearden Collages—Intimate Gems." *The Eccentric,* September 25, 1986, 1E. [exh. Sheldon Ross Gallery, Birmingham, Mich.]

M[ellow], J[ames]. R. "In the Galleries: Bearden." *Arts Magazine* 34 (February 1960): 65. [exh. Michel Warren, New York]

"Memory and Metaphor." *American Visions* 6 (April 1991): 12. [exh. *Memory and Metaphor,* SMIH]

"Memory and Metaphor: The Art of Romare Bearden, 1940–1987. Wight Gallery, UCLA." *Journal of the Print World* (Fall 1991): 3. [exh. review]

Mercer, Kobena. "Romare Bearden: African American Modernism at Mid-Century." In *Art History, Aesthetics, Visual Studies,* ed. Michael Ann Holly and Keith Moxey. Williamstown, Mass.: Sterling and Francine Clark Art Institute, 2002.

Mercer, Valerie. "In Short: Non-Fiction: Black Perspectives." *NYT Book Review,* February 20, 1994, sec. 7: 22. [book review: RB and Henderson, *A History of African-American Artists* (1993)]

Merritt, Robert. "Bearden Show Opens Tuesday at Museum." *Richmond Times Dispatch,* June 28, 1981, J1, J4. [exh. *Romare Bearden: 1970–1980,* Virginia Museum of Fine Arts]

Mesch, Claudia. "Romare Bearden at Museum of Contemporary Art, Chicago." *New Art Examiner* 19 (January 1992): 37. [exh. review]

"Michel Warren Gallery." *Visitor's Report* [?] [exh. at Michel Warren Gallery, New York, January 20–February 19, 1960 (?)] [undated (1960?)] [*AAA/RB, frame 0517, reel N68-87; also MoMA Scrapbooks, fiche 1.79]

Milani, Joanne. "Exhibit Celebrates Art of Romare Bearden." *Tampa Tribune,* November 7, 1996, BayLife: 1. [exh. *Romare Bearden: An Homage to Paper,* Museum of African-American Art, Tampa]

Miro, Marsha. "Bearden's Collages Transcend Time to Speak about Black Realities." *Detroit Free Press,* November 30, 1990, 5C. [exh. Sheldon Ross Gallery, Birmingham, Mich.]

———. "Eye on Art: Birmingham Bloomfield Art Association." *Detroit Free Press,* May 27, 1986, 10D. [exh. juried by RB]

———. "Eye on Art: Sheldon Ross Gallery." *Detroit Free Press,* October 7, 1986, 5B. [exh. at Sheldon Ross Gallery, Birmingham, Mich.]

———. "Making Ethnic Art Work with Symbolic Images." *Detroit Free Press,* December 5, 1976, 11F. [exh. Sheldon Ross Gallery, Birmingham, Mich.]

———. "'Quilting Time' Collagist Bearden Captures the Black Experience." *Detroit Free Press,* September 12, 1986, C1, C7.

———. "Recreating the Feelings of His People and Their Places." *Detroit Free Press,* December 20, 1979, 1C, 4C.

———. "Sky-High Inspiration." *Detroit Free Press,* March 11, 1983, 6C. [exh. Sheldon Ross Gallery, Birmingham, Mich.]

Mixon, Veronica. "Bearden Featured in Exhibit." *Philadelphia Tribune,* June 6, 1995. [exh. *A Graphic Odyssey,* Brooklyn Museum] [*private archive]

"Monitor: Charlotte, N.C." *New National Black Monitor,* June 1980, 8. [exh. Mint Museum]

Montgomery, Carleton English. "Jerald Melberg Gallery: New Collages by Romare Bearden." *Arts Journal* (May 1985): 5. [exh. Jerald Melberg Gallery, Charlotte]

Moser, Rex. "Black Icons." *Daily Californian,* November 19, 1971. [exh. *Prevalence of Ritual,* University Art Museum, Berkeley] [*AAA/RB]

Moses, Wilson J. "Untold Stories, Unseen Pictures—*A History of African-American Artists from 1792 to the Present,* by Romare Bearden & Harry Henderson." *Commonweal* 121, no. 4 (February 25, 1994): 20–21. [book review: RB and Henderson, *A History of African-American Artists* (1993)]

Muchnic, Suzanne. "An Artist's Garden of Memories." *Los Angeles Times,* May 28, 1980, pt. 6: 1, 2, 3. [exh. Swope Gallery, Venice, Calif.; profile]

Mullarkey, Maureen. "Finding the Tone: Romare Bearden's Monotypes and Robert Blackburn's Printmaking Workshop: Lori Bookstein Fine Art." *Review* (March 1, 2000): 13–14.

M[unro], E[leanor]. C. "Reviews and Previews: Romare Bearden." *Art News* 54 (December 1955): 58. [exh. Barone Gallery, New York]

"Mural to Plug Fun City Fun." *New York Daily News,* June 14, 1972, A31. [Times Square mural]

"Museum Acquires Work by Romare Bearden." *North Carolina Museum of Art* (supplement to *Durham Herald-Sun*), (Summer 1995): 3. [*New Orleans Ragging Home*]

"Museum Buys Bearden's Work." *Charlotte Observer,* July 26, 1970, 4F.

Nathan, Jean. "The Transom: Tribute." *New York Observer,* August 27, 1990, 3. [column, "The Transom," includes discussion (with excerpts) of August Wilson's introduction to Schwartzman (1990)]

Naves, Mario. "Romare Bearden at the Whitney." *New Criterion* 15 (March 1997): 57–59. [exh. *Romare Bearden in Black and White: Photomontage Projections 1964,* Whitney]

"NCMA Buys Collage." *North Carolina Museum of Art Calendar of Art Events* 14 (October 1970): 2. [*Carolina Blue;* RB quoted]

Ne'matt, Salameh. "Artistic Links via Electronic Dialogue." *Jordan Times* (Amman), April 4, 1985. [RB discusses experiences as artist with panel of Jordanian artists and journalists via telecommunications link] [*private archive]

Neugass, Fritz. "Foto-Montagen und Collagen erzielen hohe Preise." *Foto Magazine* (Munich) (February 1964): 42. [*Mint Museum (1980). Note: Washington (1973) gives 1965 date]

"A New History of African-American Artists." *Los Angeles Sentinel,* February 10, 1994, C4. [book review: RB and Henderson, *A History of African-American Artists* (1993)]

"Newark Museum Opens 'Tribute to Bearden.'" *(New Jersey) Star-Ledger,* June 16, 1993, 61. [exh.]

"News and Notes of Art." *NYT,* April 26, 1940, 19 (L). [exh. at 305 (sic) West 141st Street]

Nicholson, David. "Book World: The Art of Being Black in America." *Washington Post,* December 21, 1993, B2. [book review: Henderson and Bearden, *A History of African-American Artists* (1993)]

"The 1977 'Business in the Arts' Awards: About the Artist." *BCA News* [publication of Business Committee for the Arts, Inc.] 41 (April 1978): 1, 4. [profile of RB, as creator of award print] [*private archive]

Nixon, Bruce. "Rhythm-a-ning." *Artweek* 22 (January 17, 1991): 15–16. [exh. Bomani Gallery, San Francisco]

"Notes on People: A Carolinian Insists He Can Go Home Again." *NYT,* October 10, 1980, B5. [RB quoted]

"Notes on Twelve Former League Students: Romare Bearden." In *Centennial Decade 1968–1969. 93rd Regular Session, September 16, 1968–May 28, 1969. The Art Students League of New York.* New York, 1968, 94.

"NY/AEA Members in the Limelight: Romare Bearden Stars in Two Exhibitions." *New York/Artists Equity Association* (October 1981): 5. [exhs. C&E (*In 4/4 Time*); Brooklyn Museum]

O'Doherty, Brian. "Art: O'Keeffe Exhibition. Her Pictures Displayed at the Downtown—Bearden and Resnick Works on View." *NYT,* April 11, 1961, 75. [exh. at Cordier and Warren]

———. "Art: Year-End Review. Shahn's Exhibition on The Bomb and Gaudnek's House Were Highlights." *NYT,* December 16, 1961, 23. [exh. Cordier and Warren in April]

O[ffin], C[harles] Z. "Gallery Previews in New York: Romare Bearden." *Pictures on Exhibit* 28 (October 1964), 10. [exh. *Romare Bearden: Projections,* C&E]

"1,043 Attend Bearden Exhibition's Last Day." *Charlotte Observer,* January 6, 1981, 12A.

Oppel, Richard. "Honored Guest Nearly Canceled." *Charlotte Observer,* October 19, 1980, 2B.

"Other Exhibitions Seen about Town." *New York Sun,* October 13, 1945, 9. [exh. *Passion of Christ,* Kootz]

"Painter Combines Concert with Sax." *Imprint Papers,* April 25, 1986. [RB–Jackie McLean collaboration for Artworks Gallery] [*private archive]

"Painting: Touching at the Core." *Time* 90 (October 27, 1967): 64. [exh. C&E]

Pajewski, Steven. "'All Painting Is a Kind of Talking about Life': The Pittsburgh Memories of Romare Bearden." *Carnegie Magazine* 61, no. 3 (May–June 1992): 14–21.

Paris, Jeanne. "Romare Bearden." *Long Island [Sunday] Press,* March 7, 1976. [exh. Firehouse Gallery, Nassau Community College, Garden City, N.Y.] [*private archive]

Parker, Evelyn. "Romare Bearden: Collage Master to Visit Oakland." *The Post* [Oakland, Calif.?], October 14, 1980, 4. [profile] [*private archive]

Parrent, Mark. "Bearden Artwork Debuts in Metro." *Evening Sun* [Baltimore?], March 23, 1983, F18. [*RBF archive]

"Patchwork Nostalgia." *Time* 90 (October 27, 1967): 65. [repr. *Summertime; Tomorrow I May Be Far Away*]

Patterson, Ben. "Civil Rites." *Wired* 5 (September 1997): 138. [*Uncover (online database) summary: "In *The Dove,* artist Romare Bearden captured the day-to-day of African-American life against the backdrop of the civil rights movement. 2 pages"]

Patterson, Tom. "Abrupt Turn by Bearden: 'Black-and-White' at Mint Captures the Sharpening of Artist's Style." *Charlotte Observer,* April 10, 1998, 20E. [exh. *Romare Bearden in Black and White,* Mint Museum]

———. A Clear Vision: Romare Bearden's Career Celebrated in Two Exhibits." *Winston-Salem Journal,* December 17, 1995, E1, E3. [Charlotte exhs. *Graphic Odyssey,* Spirit Square Center for Arts and Education; *The Print—The Source,* Jerald Melberg Gallery]

———. "Evans Show Displays Range of Self-Taught Artist's Work." *Charlotte Observer,* May 15, 1994, 1F. [exh. *Joy of Living,* Hickory Museum of Art, N.C.]

———. "2 Exhibits Show Growth of Homegrown Charlotte Artist Romare Bearden." *Charlotte Observer,* December 17, 1995, 1F, 4F. [Charlotte exhs. *Graphic Odyssey,* Spirit Square Center for Arts and Education; *The Print—The Source,* Jerald Melberg Gallery]

Patton, Sharon F. "A Divine Presence in the Art of Romare Bearden." *Prism/Yale Institute of Sacred Music, Worship, and the Arts* (New Haven, Conn.) 15 (1992): 29–32. [theme of issue: "The African American Experience in Worship and the Arts"]

Payne, Les. "America's Greatest (Overlooked) Artist." *New York Newsday,* January 17, 1988, cover, 6–11, 18–20.

———. "Jazz Came Alive on His Canvas." *New York Newsday,* December 9, 1990, Currents: 6.

Paysour, LaFleur. "Bearden Wins Award." *Charlotte Observer,* August 6, 1986, 18B. [Carolina Prize]

Peery, Richard M. "Artist Bearden to Show Works." *Cleveland Plain Dealer,* November 12, 1982, Friday sec.: 49. [exh. Malcolm Brown Gallery, Shaker Heights, Ohio]

Pennella, Florence. "Romare Bearden: 1912–1988: Local Artist Shares Fond Memories of His Friend and Mentor." *Poughkeepsie Journal,* March 18, 1988, 1D.

"People Are Talking About…" *Vogue* (November 15, 1964): 111. [briefly notes RB's collages as subject of interest; mentions exh. C&E] [*MoMA Scrapbooks, fiche 1.80; Washington (1973) citation: November 12, 1967]

Perry, Mary Ellen. "Exciting City Mural Envisioned." *San Francisco Post,* May 4, 1972, 4. [*RBF archive]

"Personal Glimpses." *Reader's Digest* 107 (September 1975): 103. [RB's story of winning first prize in poster contest as child, told upon acceptance of honorary degree at Carnegie-Mellon University; quotations]

Pincus, Robert L. "Bearden Finally Getting His Due." *San Diego Union-Tribune,* May 5, 1991, E1. [exh. *Memory and Metaphor,* SMIH]

"Pittsburgh's Black Artist Son." *Pittsburgh Post-Gazette,* March 17, 1988. [editorial] [*RBF archive]

Plagens, Peter. "Holiday Books: Art: The Untold Story." *New York Newsday,* December 5, 1993, 46. [book review: RB and Henderson, *A History of African-American Artists* (1993)]

———. "Unsentimental Journey (the Studio Museum in Harlem Kicks Off a Retrospective of the Collagist Romare Bearden)." *Newsweek* 117 (April 29, 1991): 58–59. [exh. *Memory and Metaphor,* SMIH]

Pogue, Kim, and Roger James. "Romare Bearden." *Artistic Pedigree* [Preston Jenkins Artists Agency, Inc.], 2, no. 1 (February 18–March 4, 1993): 6–7. [exh. *Memory and Metaphor,* National Museum of American Art, Washington, D.C.]

Pokroy, Laurian Janis. "Romare Bearden: Defining a Personal Aesthetic through the Rhythms of African American Life." Senior honors thesis, Brandeis University, Waltham, Mass., 1992. [OCLC: 26001237] [*WorldCat online database citation]

Pomeroy, Ralph. "Black Persephone." *Art News* 66 (October 1967): 44–45, 73–75. [exh. C&E]

"Portrait of an Artist (*Newsday* color photo by Bill Davis)." *New York Newsday,* April 28, 1991, *Fanfare:* 15. [biographical caption]

Powell, Richard J. "What Becomes a Legend Most? Reflections on Romare Bearden." *Transition* 55 (1992): 63–72.

"A Powerful 'Spokesman' for the Negro—with His Brush." *Elegant* 3, no. 4 (March 1967): 28–31, 64. [profile; no byline, but Henri Ghent was staff writer for periodical]

P[reston], S[tuart]. "Around the Galleries: Romare Bearden." *NYT,* April 16, 1961, X11. [exh. Cordier and Warren]

Preston, Stuart. "Art: Decorative Action. Explosive Works of Reva on Display—Other Exhibitions Offer Variety." *NYT,* January 23, 1960, 19. [exh. Michel Warren, New York]

———. "Art: Summary of the Weeks' Events. Romare Bearden." *NYT,* October 10, 1964, 26(L). [exh. C&E]

Princenthal, Nancy. "Romare Bearden at Cordier & Ekstrom." *Art in America* 75 (February 1987): 149.

Purdie, James. "Bearden: Humanism amid Oppression." *Toronto Globe and Mail,* February 4, 1976, 13. [first Canadian solo exh. Graphis Gallery]

Quirk, Bea. "Romancing Romare." *Charlotte* 1, no. 2 (November–December 1995): 20–22. [exhs. *Graphic Odyssey,* Spirit Square Center for Arts and Education; *The Print—The Source,* Jerald Melberg Gallery, Charlotte]

"Radicals—Redicals: Berkeley Mural." *BCU* [Berkeley Citizens United] *Bulletin* 13, no. 8 (September 1972) [2-page newsletter] [RB mural commission for city council chambers]

Raven, Arlene. "Like Opening a Door." *VillageVoice* 36 (July 30, 1991): 89. [exh. *Memory and Metaphor,* SMIH]

Ray-Jones, Anna. "A History of African-American Artists." *Art and Design* 9 (July–August 1994): xxii. [book review: RB and Henderson, *A History of African-American Artists* (1993)]

R[aynor], V[ivien]. "In the Galleries: Romare Bearden." *Arts Magazine* 35 (April 1961): 64. [exh. Daniel Cordier & Michel Warren, Inc., New York]

Raynor, Vivien. "Art: Brooklyn Show, 'Monumental Drawing.'" *NYT,* October 3, 1986, C24. [exh. C&E]

———. "Constructive Art at Purchase, Bearden's Fantasy at Lehman." *NYT,* February 10, 1985, 24 WC. [exh. *Black Roots, Jazz Music, Universal Myth,* Lehman College, Bronx]

———. "A Glance at Romare Bearden at the Bronx Museum of the Arts." *NYT,* January 4, 1987, sec. 11: 24 WC [exh. *Origins and Progressions,* Bronx Museum of the Arts]

Reasoner, Dina. "Works of Art." *Columbus Dispatch,* March 21, 1993, 9D. [exh. *Soul of a People: Romare Bearden's The Family Dinner,* Toledo Museum of Art, Ohio]

"Recommended Books—*A History of African-American Artists from 1792 to the Present* by Romare Bearden and Harry Henderson." *American Artist* 58 (May 1994): 75.

Reid, Maya M. "Romare Bearden at the Baltimore Museum of Art." *Aura* [a Maryland, Washington, D.C., and Virginia arts publication], May–June 1981, 11. [exh.]

"Remembering Bearden." *Charlotte Observer,* January 17, 2001, 12A. [editorial]

"Remembering Bearden: Gift, Exhibit Should Spur City to Honor Renowned Artist." *Charlotte Observer,* August 25, 2002, 2D. [editorial] [exh. *Charlotte's Own,* Mint Museum]

"Remembering Romare Bearden: Artist Captured Black Experience." *Denver Post,* April 25, 1996, E8. [exh. *A Graphic Odyssey,* Metropolitan State College, Denver]

"Reviews & Previews: Romare Bearden." *Art News* 45 (February 1947): 42. [exh. Kootz]

"Reviews and Previews. Romare Bearden: Bull-Fight Inspiration." *Art News* 45 (April 1946): 53. [repr., 54]. [exh. Kootz]

"Reviews and Previews: Romare Bearden." *Art News* 47 (December 1948): 52. [exh. *Iliad,* Niveau Gallery, New York]

Rhodes, Lisa R. "Romare Bearden: A Memorial Exhibition at ACA Gallery." *Manhattan Arts* 6, no. 4 (June 1989): 6. [exh. ACA Galleries, New York]

Rhodes, Lolita M. "Vivid Pictures of Black Lives: Romare Bearden's Collages 'Almost Unmanageably Rich.'" *Greensboro News & Record,* August 17, 1986, G1, G4. [RB chosen for North Carolina Prize; exh. at Jerald Melberg Gallery, Charlotte, in October]

Richard, Paul. "The Integrated Art of Romare Bearden." *Washington Post,* April 26, 1981, H1, H5. [exh. *Romare Bearden: 1970–1980,* Baltimore Museum of Art]

———. "Romare Bearden: Integrating Scholarship and Soul." *Washington Post*, October 4, 1992, G1, G7. [exh. *Memory and Metaphor,* National Museum of American Art, Washington, D.C.]

Rickey, Carrie. "Reviews: New York." *Artforum* 17, no. 6 (February 1979): 60–63. [exh. *Profile/ Part I: The Twenties,* C&E, 61–62]

———. "Romare Bearden: Few Easy Pieces." *Voice* (October 15, 1979): 100. [*Artists File, Whitney]

Riley, Clayton. "Romare Bearden —'Of the Blues.'" *Contact* 5 (Spring 1975): 31–33. [exh. C&E]

Roberts, Colette. "L'oeuvre de Bearden en sa gravité sereine." *Le Courrier des Etats-Unis,* February 19, 1970. [exh. at C&E] [*private archive]

Rogers, Paul. "Ralph Ellison, the Collage of Romare Bearden and Race: Some Speculations." *International Review of African American Art* 11, no. 3 (1994): 7–10.

"Romare Bearden." *Arts Magazine* 53, no. 6 (February 1979): 21. [exh. *Profiles/Part I: The Twenties,* C&E]

"Romare Bearden." *Art News* 44 (October 15, 1945): 28. [debut exh. Kootz]

"Romare Bearden." *New York Herald Tribune,* October 10, 1964. [exh. C&E] [*AAA/RB, frame 0383, reel N/68-87; also RBF archive]

"Romare Bearden." *Pictures on Exhibit* 9 (February 1947): 20, 22. [exh. Kootz]

"Romare Bearden: A Color Portfolio of the Artist's Works." *Contact* 3 (July 1972): 40–41. [biography, several illustrations including cover]

"Romare Bearden: 1970–1980." *Mint Museum Newsletter/Calendar.* September–October 1980. [notes by Milton J. Bloch; Jerald L. Melberg]

"Romare Bearden: A 1970–1980 Retrospective." *Crisis* 88, no. 2 (1981): 75–82. [*ABC-Clio Inc. (America: History and Life) online database citation]

"Romare Bearden: The Odysseus Collages." *Massachusetts Review* 18, no. 4 (Winter 1977): 681–88. [photo of RB by Niki Ekstrom, 681; reprint of C&E catalogue essay by Calvin Tomkins, 682; six illustrations]

"Romare Bearden as Printmaker: Baltimore Museum of Art." *Journal of the Print World* (Summer 1993): 16. [exh. *A Graphic Odyssey*]

"Romare Bearden at the Studio Museum." *Black Shades: A Black Art Newsletter* 2, no. 8, (1972): n. p. [exh. *The Prevalence of Ritual,* SMIH]

"Romare Bearden Exhibition." *Black Art* 4, no. 2 (1980): 62. [exh. *Romare Bearden: 1970–1980,* Mint Museum]

"Romare Bearden Exhibition: Mint Museum of Art, Charlotte." *Black Art* (Jamaica, N.Y.) 4, no. 2 (1980): 62.

"Romare Bearden to Display His Paintings." *New York Amsterdam News,* May 4, 1940, 8. [exh. 306 West 141 St., New York]

"Romare Bearden to Have One-Man Show of Paintings." *New York Amsterdam News.* [solo exh. at 306 West 141st St., 1940] [*AAA/RB, frame 0499, reel N68-87] [*MoMA Scrapbooks, fiche 1.79; appears wrongly hand-annotated, 1941]

"Romare Bearden Wins North Carolina Prize." *NYT,* August 13, 1986, 21(N).

"Romare Beardon [sic]." *Time* 84 (October 16, 1964): [NY 2] 10. [exh. C&E]

"Romare H. Beardon [sic]." *Weekly Reader* (New York) 9 (1969): 11–12. [children: biographical; discussion of art; activities] [*MoMA Scrapbooks, fiche 1.80]

Rosen, Janet. "NYU Grad Romare Bearden: He Sees Life through Bursts of Color." *Washington Square News*, October 7, 1981, 5. [exh. *Romare Bearden: 1970–1980,* Brooklyn Museum]

———. "Romare Bearden's Artistic Career Began as NYU Cartoonist in 1930s." *Washington Square News*, October 7, 1981, 5.

Rosenberger, Jack. "Art: The Fake Bearden Files." *New York* 28 (August 28, 1995): 32–36.

Roucher, Nancy. "Instructor Gallery: Roles Come to Life in Collage." *Instructor and Teacher* 99 (September 1989): 46–47. [collage, related projects, reference to RB; poster insert of *She-Ba*]

Russell, John. "Art: Alex Katz's Idyllic and Simplified World." *NYT,* February 28, 1976, 22L. [embedded review, exh. *Of the Blues (Second Chorus),* C&E]

———. "Art: Bearden from Homer to Henri." *NYT,* April 29, 1977, C22. [exh. C&E; repr. *Battle with Cicones*]

———. "Jazzy Collages by Romare Bearden at The Brooklyn." *NYT*, October 2, 1981, C1, C28. [exh. *Romare Bearden, 1970–1980,* Brooklyn Museum]

Sartorius, Tara Cady. "Art across the Curriculum: A Plot in Paradise." *Arts & Activities* 131 (February 2002): 42–44.

Scarborough, Ellen. "Bearden Exhibit Will Put Mint on Cultural Map." *Charlotte Observer* (March 16, 1980), 1F, 10F. [exh. *Romare Bearden: 1970–1980,* Mint Museum]

———. "Mint Museum Basking in Glow of Successful Exhibit." *Charlotte Observer,* January 3, 1981, 4A. [exh. *Romare Bearden: 1970–1980,* Mint Museum]

Schramm, Susan L., and Rhonda B. Jeffries. "African American Trickster Representations in the Work of Romare Bearden." *Art Education* 53 (September 2000): 19–24.

Schwartz, Sanford. "New York Letter." *Art International* 17 (Summer 1973): 83–85, 99–100. [exh. C&E, 84]

Schwartzman, Myron. "Of Mecklenburg, Memory and the Blues: Romare Bearden's Collaboration with Albert Murray." *Bulletin of Research in the Humanities* 86, no. 2 (Summer 1983): 140–61.

———. "Romare Bearden Sees in a Memory." *Artforum International* 22 (May 1984): 64–70.

Scott, Nathan A., Jr. "Romare Bearden." In "In Memoriam: Romare H. Bearden, 1912–1988." *Callaloo* 11 (Summer 1988): 420–22.

Seaman, Donna. "The Arts: *History of African-American Artists: From 1792 to the Present* by Romare Bearden and Harry Henderson." *Booklist* 90 (October 15, 1993): 405. [book review]

Seremet, Patricia. "Show's Audience Creates Its Own Collage." *Hartford Courant,* May 5, 1986, D5. [report on party following Bearden/McLean collaboration]

"Sgt. Romare Bearden et Pietro Lazzari." [*Arts?*] October 24, 1945. [text in French] [*AAA/RB, frame 0513, reel N/68-87]

"A Shared Museum Experience." *Baltimore Sun,* April 29, 1981, A18. [exh. Baltimore Museum of Art]

S[harp], M[arynell]. "Fifty-Seventh Street in Review: Bearden Paints 'The Iliad.'" *Art Digest* 23 (November 15, 1948): 32–33. [exh. Niveau Gallery, New York]

Shepard, Richard F. "Going Out Guide." *NYT,* September 26, 1981, 1: 14. [exh. *Romare Bearden: 1970–1980,* Brooklyn Museum]

Shepley, James R. "A Letter from the Publishers." *Time* 93 (November 1, 1968): 7. [cover: *John Lindsay,* photo collage, 1968]

Shere, Charles. "Berkeley Unveils Portrait of a City and Its People." *Oakland Tribune,* January 13, 1974, 26. [Berkeley mural]

Shirey, David. "The Black World of Romare Bearden." *Dialogue* [date unknown], 57–70. [*AAA/RB]

"Sights and Sounds." *NYT,* May 2, 1986, C8. [RB and saxophonist Jackie McLean performance]

Sims, Lowery S. "The Unknown Romare Bearden." *Art News* 85 (October 1986): 116–20.

Sirmans, M. Franklin. "A History of African-American Artists: From 1792 to the Present." *Quarterly Black Review of Books* 1 (May 31, 1994): 45. [book review: RB and Henderson, *A History of African-American Artists* (1993)]

Smith, Alvin. "Art Mailbag: Not Judicious." *NYT,* April 19, 1970, 2: 22. [response to Hilton Kramer, "Black Experience and Modernist Art: Romare Bearden Uses Photos in Collages," *NYT,* February 14, 1970]

Smith, Miles A. "Bearden Collages Are Special Exhibit Subject." *New Brunswick (N.J.) Sunday Home News,* April 25, 1971. [exh. *Prevalence of Ritual,* MoMA] [*RBF archives]

"Sound Collages and Visual Improvisations." *"Say You Saw It in the Northend Agents Newspaper,"* March 24, 1986, 2[?]. [profiles Bearden and Jackie McLean prior to performance at Wadsworth Atheneum, May 4] [*private archive]

Southgate, M. Therese, M.D. "The Cover. (Return of the Prodigal Son by Romare Bearden)." *JAMA: The Journal of the American Medical Association* 287 (February 6, 2002): cover, 555.

———. "The Cover. Romare Bearden, Still Life." *JAMA: The Journal of the American Medical Association* 265 (February 6, 1991): cover, 573.

Sozanski, Edward J. "Bearden's Work Melds Two Cultures on One Vision. Prints by the African American Artist Are Featured in Exhibits at Two Local Galleries." *Philadelphia Inquirer,* October 10, 1996, C1. [exh. *Graphic Odyssey,* Arthur Ross Gallery and Brandywine Workshop]

———. "He Solved a Predicament of Black Painters: Honor His Culture or Paint Like Whites? Bearden's Answer Is in a D.C. Show." *Philadelphia Inquirer,* October 18, 1992, F1. [exh. *Memory and Metaphor,* National Museum of American Art, Washington, D.C.]

Spears, Dorothy. "Romare Bearden." *Arts Magazine* 66, no. 3 (November 1991): 80. [exh. *Memory and Metaphor,* SMIH; profile]

Steelman, Ben. "Visual Magic and Music on View." *Wilmington (N.C.) Morning Star,* February 6, 1987, 1D. [exh. *Romare Bearden: Collages and Prints,* St. Johns Museum of Art, Wilmington, N.C.]

Stevens, Elisabeth. "Bearden's Art: Myth and Memory Mixed." *Baltimore Sun,* April 26, 1981, Magazine cover, 14–15, 30–32. [exh. *Romare Bearden: 1970–1980,* Baltimore Museum of Art; RB quotes, biography, illustrations]

———. "'Powerful Lyricism' in Two Forms." *Wall Street Journal,* April 13, 1971, 16. [exh. *Prevalence of Ritual,* MoMA]

Stomberg, John. "Colossal Remnants: Romare Bearden." *Bostonia* (Boston University) (Spring 2001): 12–18.

Strickland, Carol. "Looking Past the Hardscrabble Life." *Christian Science Monitor,* May 22, 1995, Arts: 14. [exh. *A Graphic Odyssey,* Brooklyn Museum]

Strickland, Edward. "Regional Reviews: Wendell Street Gallery/Cambridge: Romare Bearden." *Art New England* 15 (October–November 1994): 66. [exh. review]

———. "Romare Bearden Exhibit at Wendell Street Gallery." *Bay State Banner,* November 26, 1987, 14. [exh. Wendell Street Gallery, Cambridge, Mass.]

Sulaiman, Madeline. "Romare Bearden: Master of Ritual Painting and Collage." *About... Time* (September 1980): 12–13. [profile; exh. *Romare Bearden: 1970–1980,* Mint Museum] [*private archive]

Summers, Marion. "ART Today: A Talented Artist in the Picasso Idiom." [unidentified source] [exh. *Lorca,* Kootz] [*AAA/RB, frame 0515, reel N/68-87] [also MoMA Scrapbooks, fiche 1.79]

Taylor, Priscilla. "Romare Bearden: Larger Than Life Collagist." *Big Red* (October 3, 1981). [exh. *Romare Bearden 1970–1980,* Brooklyn Museum] [*private archive]

Temin, Christine. "Auction Benefits Native Americans." *Boston Globe,* November 28, 1987, Arts and Film: 8. [exhs. Thomas Segal Gallery, Boston; Wendell Street Gallery, Cambridge, Mass.]

Thompson, James. "Collage Call and Recall: Bearden's Visual Blues." *Asheville Citizen-Times,* March 15, 1992, 8L. [exh. *Memory and Metaphor,* High Museum of Art, Atlanta]

Thompson, Mary Ann. "Bearden's Artistic Tour of Harlem and the South." *Springfield (Mo.) News-Leader,* January 29–31, 1993, Weekend: 3, 13. [exh. *Harlem Culture and Southern Memories: Selected Works by Romare Bearden,* Springfield Art Museum, Mo.]

"Time Off: Diversions and Excursions/Albuquerque, N.M., A Graphic Odyssey: Romare Bearden as Printmaker." *Wall Street Journal,* November 19, 1996, A20.

"Times Square Billboard Depicts Parks Events." *NYT,* August 31, 1972, 27.

"Times Square Getting Giant Mural." *NYT,* June 14, 1972, 38.

Tomkins, Calvin. "Profiles: Romare Bearden: Putting Something over Something Else." *New Yorker* 53 (November 28, 1977): 53–77.

"Tomorrow in Washington: 'Projections' at Corcoran Features Abstract Collages." *Washington Evening Star,* October 4, 1965, C21. [exh. Corcoran Gallery of Art, Washington, D.C.]

Toppman, Lawrence. "Charlotte Artist Coming Home for Celebration." *Charlotte News,* May 1, 1980, 1D, 5D. [exh. Mint Museum.]

———. "1964 in Black and White." *Charlotte Observer,* March 13, 1998, 20E. [exh. *Romare Bearden in Black and White,* Mint Museum]

———. "Professor Will Talk about Romare Bearden's Place in History." *Charlotte Observer,* November 9, 1995, 1E. [speaker: Richard Powell]

"Tormented Faces." *Newsweek,* October 19, 1964, 105. [profile; exh. *Projections,* C&E]

Trebay, Guy. "Talking Heads: Romare Bearden's Way." *Village Voice,* October 14–20, 1981, 63.

Trescott, Jacqueline. "Skillful Portrait of Beardon [sic]." *Washington Post,* February 4, 1982, C6. ["Bearden Plays Bearden" documentary on PBS]

Turner, Elisa. "Exhibit a Compelling Window into Black Culture." *Miami Herald,* June 6, 1999, 7I [exh. *Romare Bearden in Black and White,* Art and Culture Center of Hollywood, Fla.]

Turner, Norman. "Romare Bearden." *Arts Magazine* 52 (September 1977): 29. [exh. at C&E, April 27–May 28]

Tynes, Harcourt. "Art Tackles Life." *Gannett Westchester Newspapers,* October 18, 1981, F1, F5. [exh. *Romare Bearden, 1970–1980,* Brooklyn Museum]

Tyre, Peg, and Jeannette Walls. "Bearden's Widow: Artistic License?" *New York,* June 12, 1989, 11.

[untitled clipping]. *New York Herald Tribune,* March 31, 1946. [exh. *Lorca,* Kootz; mentions this is RB's second show there in single season] [*AAA/RB, frame 0515, reel N68-87] [also MoMA Scrapbooks, fiche 1.79]

[untitled exh. notice]. *Herald Tribune,* March 21, [1947?]. [exh. *New Paintings by Romare Bearden,* Kootz] [*MoMA Scrapbooks, fiche 1.79 clipping, hand-annotated "March 21 [1946]," but discusses Rabelais subject matter which was exhibited February 24–March 15, 1947]

Verlomme, Hugo. "La Semaine des galeries: L'Art à l'estomac: Free Collages." [*Le Quotidien de Paris*?] (May, 24–25, 1975): 13. [exh. Albert Loeb, Paris] [*private archives]

Verongos, Helen. "Art Reflecting Life's Rhythms." *Jackson (Miss.) Clarion-Ledger,* January 30, 1981, C1, C3. [exh. *Romare Bearden: 1970–1980,* Mississippi Museum of Art]

"Visual Arts." *Charlotte Observer,* October 11, 1992, 5F. [exh. Jerald Melberg Gallery, Charlotte]

Walker, Richard. "Art Market. Romare's Renaissance." *Art News* 91 (February 1992): 21.

Wallach, Amei. "Catching Daily Life in Visual Jazz." *New York Newsday,* October 4, 1981, pt. 2: 17–18. [exh. *Romare Bearden: 1970-1980,* Brooklyn Museum]

———. "Collages in Terms of the Blues." *New York Newsday,* April 20, 1980, pt. 2: 15–16.

———. "He Captures the Universal Experience." *New York Newsday,* January 17, 1988, 11. [*Newsday.com]

———. "A New Light on African Creations Antiquities, New Work in Brooklyn." *New York Newsday,* July 7, 1995, B3. [exh. *A Graphic Odyssey,* Brooklyn Museum]

———. "The Saints Make Room for Romare Bearden." *New York Newsday,* April 28, 1991, 15–16. [exh. *Memory and Metaphor,* SMIH]

Warren, Cathy. "Exhibit Reviews: Romare Bearden 1970–80 at Mint Museum of Art." *Art Voices* 4 (January–February 1981): 116.

Washington, M. Bunch. "Letters: Romare Bearden." *Ebony* 31 (January 1976): 16. [letter to the editor: corrects an error of authorship (John A. Williams' introduction erroneously attributed to Washington) in November 1975 article on RB; lists Bearden's writings]

Watkins, Eileen. "Tribute to an African-American Artist: Romare Bearden." *(New Jersey) Star-Ledger,* July 16, 1993, 41. [exh. *A Tribute to Romare Bearden,* Newark Museum]

Watson, Walter Ray, Jr. "Bearden: An International Artist in Our Basement." *New Pittsburgh Courier,* February 14, 1987, B1.

Welzenbach, Michael. "Romare Bearden, at the National Academy of Sciences." *Washington Post,* May 13, 1989, C2. [exh. National Academy of Sciences, Washington, D.C.]

White, Miles. "An American Odyssey: Romare Bearden's Prints Celebrate Artist's Life." *South Bend (Ind.) Tribune,* July 27, 1997, E2, E3. [exh. *A Graphic Odyssey,* South Bend Regional Museum of Art]

White, Pat. "Control and Vitality Mark Much of Bearden Show." *Charlotte Observer,* May 15, 1988, 1F, 4F. [exh. *Romare Bearden—In Memoriam,* Jerald Melberg Gallery, Charlotte]

Willi, Denise. "A Living Art. (African American Artist Romare Bearden First Began Creating His Collages in the Mid-1960s, during the Civil Rights Movement)." *Scholastic Art* 26 (February 1996): 2. [see also *Romare Bearden: Working with Juxtaposition* (Jefferson City, Mo.: Scholastic Inc., 1996)]

Wills, Garry. "The Real Thing." *New York Review of Books* 41, no. 14 (August 11, 1994): 6. [RB and Henderson, *A History of African-American Artists* (1993)]

"Windward and Leeward." *The Monthly Letter of the Limited Editions Club,* no. 533 (series 46, vol. 10) (May 1983). [*NYPL/SC archive] [profile; discusses *Poems of the Caribbean* (Walcott), edited and illustrated by RB]

Wilson, August. "On Romare Bearden." In *Drawing Us In: How We Experience Visual Art.* Ed. Deborah Chasman and Edna Chiang. Boston: Beacon Press, 2000. [reprint of Foreword in Schwartzman, *Romare Bearden: His Life and Art* (1990)]

Wilson, Judith. "Getting Down to Get Over: Romare Bearden's Use of Pornography and the Problem of the Black Female Body in Afro-U.S. Art." In *Dia Center for the Arts: Discussions in Contemporary Culture, Number 8: Black Popular Culture.* A Project by Michele Wallace. Ed. Gina Dent. Seattle: Bay Press, 1992, 112–22.

Wilson, William. "Art Review: Romare Bearden: Sharing Senses of Life." *Los Angeles Times,* December 10, 1991, F1, F4–5. [exh. Wight Art Galleries, University of California, Los Angeles]

———. "A 'Graphic Odyssey' Reveals an Innovative Spirit of Hope." *Los Angeles Times,* July 20, 1994, F2.

Windell, James. "Lighting Up the Night with Watercolors." *Pontiac (Mich.) Oakland Press,* March 6, 1983, A14. [exh. *New York at Night,* Sheldon Ross Gallery, Birmingham, Mich.]

———. "Spotlight on Art: St. Maarten an Inspiration for This Artist." *Oakland Press* (Mich. [?]), undated. [exh. *Romare Bearden: Watercolors from St. Martin,* Sheldon Ross Gallery, Birmingham, Mich., August 30–September 22, 1984] [*clipping in two private archives, but could not be verified by the paper's copy editor]

Wingate, Jennifer. "Romare Bearden." *Art Criticism* 14, no. 1 (1999): 7–10. [profile]

Witkovsky, Matthew S. "Experience vs. Theory: Romare Bearden and Abstract Expressionism." *Black American Literature Forum* 23, no. 2 (Summer 1989): 257–82.

Wolf, Ben. "Bearden—He Wrestles with Angels." *Art Digest* 20 (October 1, 1945): 16. [debut exh. Kootz]

———. "Bearden Abstracts Drama of the Bull-Ring." *Art Digest* 20 (April 1, 1946): 13. [exh. Kootz]

———. "Bearden Sings of the Cup That Cheers." *Art Digest* 21 (March 1, 1947): 19. [exh. Kootz]

Wood, William R. "Bearden Sets Record Straight on Role of the Black Artist." *The Call and Post,* December 11, 1982, 14B. [exh. Malcolm Brown Gallery, Shaker Heights, Ohio]

Wootten, Dick. "Romare Bearden: America's Jazziest Artist." *Cleveland Plain Dealer Sunday Magazine,* November 14, 1982, 32–34, 36–38. [profile; exh. Malcolm Brown Gallery, Shaker Heights, Ohio]

"Works of Romare Bearden on View at Studio Museum." *New York Amsterdam News,* July 22, 1972, D6.

Worsham, Doris G. "Artist Basks in Glow of New Recognition." *Oakland Tribune,* October 28, 1980, C1, C6. [profile; exh. Parson-Barnett Gallery, Oakland, Calif.]

Wyatt, Hugh. "Hospital Art Wasting Away in Warehouses." *Daily News,* October 22, 1976, 4. [Bearden mural in storage]

Zeaman, John. "A Life's Story, Piece by Piece." *The (Bergen County, N.J.) Record,* May 10, 1991, 13. [exh. SMIH]

Zimmer, William. "Musings on Collage: The Photomontages of Romare Bearden." *NYT,* May 11, 1997, 13CN, 18. [exh. *Romare Bearden in Black and White,* Whitney/Stamford]

———. "Odyssey Is Key to the Printmaking of Romare Bearden." *NYT,* September 26, 1993, CN20. [exh. *A Graphic Odyssey,* Norwalk Community Technical College, Conn.]

———. "The Strong Pull of Romare Bearden." *NYT,* October 20, 2002, sec. 14WC: 10. [exh. *Romare Bearden: Narrations,* Neuberger Museum of Art, Purchase College, State University of New York, Purchase]

Zucker, Helen. "Bearden Goes Back to North Carolina: Recreates His Childhood in Exhibit." [*The Eccentric* (Mich.)?] January 4, 1979, 12C. [exh. Sheldon Ross Gallery, Birmingham, Mich.] [*private archive]

OBITUARIES AND TRIBUTES

"Artist Romare Bearden Succumbs to Bone Cancer." *Jet* 73 (March 28, 1988): 17.

Badejo, Fabian. "Tribute to Romare Bearden, Master Artist (1912–1988)." *St. Maarten/St. Martin Newsday,* March 16, 1988, 1A, 10A.

"Bearden Memorial Service." *NYT,* March 28, 1988, D11.

Becklund, Laurie. "Romare Bearden, Celebrated Black Artist, Dead at 75." *Los Angeles Times,* March 14, 1988, 1: 3, 20.

———. "Romare Bearden, 75, Leading U.S. Artist." *Philadelphia Inquirer,* March 14, 1988, B6.

Brasley, Patrick. "Artist Romare Bearden, 73, Dies." *Newsday,* March 13, 1988, 6.

Brenson, Michael. "Art View: Romare Bearden: Epic Emotion, Intimate Scale." *NYT*, March 27, 1988, H41, H43.

"Dean of Black American Artists, Founding Member and Former President of The Harlem Cultural Council, Inc. Dies." *Black Arts New York* (Newsletter of the Harlem Cultural Council) 1, no. 6 (March 1988): 1. [see also photo of Bearden and reproductions of his work, *Black Arts New York* 1, no. 6 (March 1988): 8]

"Deaths." *USA Today*, March 14, 1988, 2A.

Fox, Catherine. "An Appreciation: Bearden Was Breaker of Art Barriers: Honored Black Artist's Works Speak to Everyone." *Atlanta Journal and Constitution*, March 15, 1988, B3.

Fraser, C. Gerald. "Artist Bearden Dies: Charlotte Native Has Stroke at 75." *Charlotte Observer*, March 13, 1988, 1A.

———. "Romare Bearden, Collagist and Painter, Dies at 75." *NYT*, March 13, 1988, sec. 1, pt. 1: 36.

"House of Representatives: Tribute to Artist Romare Bearden." *Congressional Record* 134, no. 32, March 16, 1988.

"In Memoriam: Romare H. Bearden 1912–1988." *Callaloo. A Journal of Afro-American and African Arts and Letters* 11, no. 3 (Summer 1988): 401–46. Text: Ralph Ellison; Michael S. Harper; Marilyn Richardson; Charles H. Rowell; Myron Schwartzman; Nathan A. Scott, Jr. Includes images by Jacob Lawrence and Ralph Arnold.

"Keep Bearden's Memory Alive." *Charlotte Observer*, March 15, 1988 (editorial).

Litt, Steven. "Romare Bearden: An Appreciation." *Raleigh (N.C.) News and Observer*, March 19, 1988, D1, D2.

Maschal, Richard. "Artist Romare Bearden Dies at 76." *Charlotte Observer*, March 13, 1988, 1A, 12A.

———. "Bearden—A Retrospective: An Artist for the Soul in All of Us." *Charlotte Observer*, March 14, 1988, 6A, 7A.

"Memorial Service for Painter Bearden." *Philadelphia Inquirer*, March 16, 1988, D4.

"Milestones." *Time*, March 28, 1988, 69.

Miro, Marsha. "Romare Bearden Dies, Was Nation's Foremost Collagist." *Detroit Free Press*, March 13, 1988, 7A.

Nash, Dawn J. "The Legacy of Bearden." *Black Enterprise* 18 (June 1988): 49.

"1988 in Review: Obituaries: Romare Bearden." *Art in America* 77 (August 1989): 63.

"N.C. Native Romare Howard Bearden, Prominent Collage Artist, Dies at Age 75." *Raleigh (N.C.) News and Observer*, March 13, 1988, 43A.

Payne, Les. "Artist with an Eclectic Mind Made Great Art from Black Life." *Asbury Park Press*, April 19, 1988, A15.

———. "An Evening with a Painter Who Hated to Work Alone." *New York Newsday*, April 10, 1988, 10.

Perlman, Bennard B. "The Man Who Made Jazz Visible." *Baltimore Sun*, March 18, 1988, 19A.

Richard, Paul. "Appreciation: Romare Bearden's Blues. The Black Artists' Rich Collage of Experience." *Washington Post*, March 14, 1988, B1, B9. [another version published as "Bearden's is a Legacy of Integrated Blues." *Hartford Courant*, undated clipping, RBF archives]

Richardson, Marilyn. "Romare Bearden: Odysseus Returned." In "In Memoriam: Romare H. Bearden, 1912–1988." *Callaloo* 11 (Summer 1988): 423–26.

"Romare Bearden (Obituary)." *Art in America* 76 (May 1988): 202.

"Romare Bearden Dies, Was Nation's Foremost Collagist." *Detroit Free Press*, March 13, 1988, 7A.

"Romare Bearden Memorial Held; Trust Funds Set Up in Will to Aid Artists (Obituary)." *Jet* 74 (April 25, 1988): 60.

"Romare Bearden, Master of Collage." *New York Newsday*, March 14, 1988, 33.

"Romare Bearden, Painter and Collage Artist, Dies at 75." *Washington Post*, March 14, 1988, D6.

"Romare Bearden, 75, Noted Artist." *The Hackensack (N.J.) Record*, March 14, 1988, A8.

Schaer, Sidney C. "Passings 1988: A Remembrance of the People Whose Lives Touched Ours." *New York Newsday*, December 30, 1988, 2.

Stavis, Barrie. "Bearden's Enduring Contribution." *Charlotte Observer*, October 16, 1988, 1B. [excerpt from eulogy, *Art News* (Summer 1988)]

———. "Intimations of Immortality." *Art News* 87 (Summer 1988): 40, 42.

Tapley, Mel. "Art Community Mourns Death of Romare Bearden, Master Collagist. (Obituary)." *New York Amsterdam News*, March 19, 1988, 27.

"Topics of the Times: Romare Bearden's Adventure." *NYT*, March 16, 1988, A26.

Wallach, Amei. "An Appreciation: Romare Bearden's Homey Genius." *New York Newsday*, March 14, 1988, 2: 3.

Weatherby, W. J. "Romare Bearden: 'Black by Choice.'" *Manchester Guardian*, March 15, 1988, 37.

"Widely Known Artist Romare Bearden." *Charlotte Observer*, January 3, 1989, 3B.

Woldemariam, Metasebia. "Artist Romare Bearden Dies." *The Black American* 28, no. 12 [1988]: 28.

Yarrow, Andrew L. "The Life and Works of Romare Bearden Recalled in a Tribute." *NYT*, April 7, 1988, D21.

Section 5
General Reference

(Arranged alphabetically. All citations include some reference to Bearden. All works of art listed are by Bearden. Only catalogues for exhibitions in which Bearden's work was included are listed in the Group Exhibition Catalogues section. Exhibition catalogues are included in the Books section when Bearden is mentioned in the text but not included in the exhibition. With rare exceptions, the exhibition reviews included here are limited to those that mention Bearden specifically and were written prior to the artist's death in 1988. One such exception is citations for Charlotte Observer *reporter Richard Maschal, who has made a study of Bearden's career over many years, and who is the author of more than twenty-five articles, including exhibition reviews written since the artist's death.)*

BOOKS

African Americans in Art: Selections from the Art Institute of Chicago. The Art Institute of Chicago Museum Studies. Chicago: Art Institute of Chicago, with the University of Washington Press, 1999.

African-American Artists—III. New York: Bill Hodges Gallery, 2002. Text: Bill Hodges; Susan Inniss; Sonia Silva.

The Afro-American Collection. Nashville, Tenn.: Fisk University, Carl Van Vechten Gallery, 1976. Text: David C. Driskell; Earl J. Hooks.

Anderson, Jervis. *This Was Harlem: A Cultural Portrait, 1900–1950.* New York: Farrar Straus Giroux, c. 1982. [*Igoe (1993)]

Andrews, Benny. *Between the Lines.* New York: Pella Publishing Co. Inc., 1978. [seven reprints of articles; some with ref. to RB]

———, and Rudolf Baranik, eds. *Attica Book/by the Black Emergency Cultural Coalition and Artists and Writers Protest against the War in Vietnam.* South Hackensack, N.J.: Custom Communications Systems, 1971. [*Holmes (1978)]

Barnwell, Andrea D. *The Walter O. Evans Collection of African American Art.* Seattle and London: The Walter O. Evans Foundation for Art and Literature, with the University of Washington Press, 1999. Text: Tritobia Hayes Benjamin; Kirsten P. Buick; Walter O. Evans; Amy M. Mooney.

Beyond Adversity: African-Americans' Struggle for Equality in Western Pennsylvania, 1750–1990. Pittsburgh: Museum Programs Division, Historical Society of Western Pennsylvania, 1993.

Black Arts Festival. Program brochure, Lincoln University, Lincoln, Pa., October 19–26, 1969. [*Prevalence of Ritual: Tidings,* front cover. RB a participant, October 26] [program in archives of Langston Hughes Memorial Library, Lincoln University; MoMA Scrapbooks, fiche 1.83, reproduces mailer with 10 artists photos, including RB]

Britton, Crystal A. *African American Art: The Long Struggle.* New York: Smithmark Publishers, 1996.

Brommer, Gerald F. *The Art of Collage.* Worcester, Mass.: Davis Publications, 1978.

Brown, Milton W., Sam Hunter, John Jacobus, Naomi Rosenblum, and David M. Sokol. *American Art. Painting, Sculpture, Architecture, Decorative Arts, Photography.* Englewood Cliffs, N.J.: Prentice-Hall, Inc., and New York: Abrams, 1979.

Butcher, Margaret Just. *The Negro in American Culture: Based on Materials Left by Alain Locke.* New York: Alfred A. Knopf, 1968. [6th printing; first published September 17, 1956]

Callicot, Burton, Grace M. McKay, and Gary Witt, eds. *The Art Today Collection.* Memphis: Brooks Memorial Art Gallery, 1977.

Castleman, Riva. *American Impressions: Prints since Pollock.* New York: Alfred A. Knopf, 1985.

Catalog of 117 Oil and Water Color Originals by Leading American Artists. New York: War Assets Administration, 1948.

Cederholm, Theresa Dickason. *Afro-American Artists: A Bio-bibliographical Directory.* Boston: Trustees of the Boston Public Library, 1973.

Chase, Judith Wragg. *Afro-American Art and Craft.* New York: Van Nostrand, 1971. [*Igoe (1981)]

Contemporary Black Artists in America. Exh. cat., Whitney, New York, April 6–May 16, 1971. Text: Robert M. Doty. [reprinted, "The Introduction in the Catalog of the 'Contemporary Black Artists in America' Exhibition at the Whitney Museum, April 1971," in *Black Art Notes,* ed. Tom Lloyd (New York, 1971), 31–36]

Craven, Wayne. *American Art: History and Culture.* New York: Harry N. Abrams, 1994. [LC records McGraw-Hill (New York) to publish a 2003 edition]

Davis, Lenwood G., and Janet L. Sims. *Black Artists in the United States: An Annotated Bibliography of Books, Articles, and Dissertations on Black Artists, 1779–1979.* Westport, Conn.: Greenwood Press, 1980.

Donaldson, Jeff Richardson. "Generation '306'—Harlem, New York." Ph.D. dissertation, Northwestern University, Evanston, Ill., 1974.

Dover, Cedric. *American Negro Art.* London and Greenwich, Conn.: New York Graphic Society, 1960.

Driskell, David C. *The Other Side of Color: African American Art in the Collection of Camille O. and William H. Cosby Jr.* San Francisco: Pomegranate, 2001.

———, ed. *African American Visual Aesthetics: A Postmodernist View.* Washington, D.C.: Smithsonian Institution Press, 1995.

Emory, Frank, Doris Lucas, Tom Parramore, and Earlie Thorpe, eds. *Paths toward Freedom.* Raleigh: Center for Urban Affairs, North Carolina State University at Raleigh, 1976. [*Igoe (1981)]

Fax, Elton C. *Black Artists of the New Generation.* New York: Dodd, Mead, & Company, 1977. Foreword by RB.

———. *Seventeen Black Artists.* New York: Dodd, Mead, & Company, 1971.

Fine, Elsa Honig. *The Afro-American Artist: A Search for Identity.* New York: Holt, Rinehart and Winston, Inc., 1973.

Fineberg, Jonathan David. *Art since 1940: Strategies of Being.* New York: Harry N. Abrams, Inc., 1995.

Fleming, Robert, ed. *The Wisdom of the Elders.* New York: Ballantine Books, 1996. [excerpt from RB, "The Negro Artist and Modern Art." (1934)]

Franklin, John Hope. *From Slavery to Freedom: A History of Negro Americans.* 4th ed. New York: Knopf, 1974. [*Igoe (1981)]

Freedgood, Lillian. *An Enduring Image: American Painting from 1665.* New York: Thomas Y. Crowell Company, 1970.

Gates, Henry Louis, Jr. *Thirteen Ways of Looking at a Black Man.* New York: Random House, 1997. [profile of Albert Murray, with RB refs.]

———, and Cornel West. *The African-American Century: How Black Americans Have Shaped Our Country.* New York: Free Press, 2000.

Gill, Brendan. *Late Bloomers.* New York: Artisan, 1996. [children] [*CATNYP call no.: JFC 98-1028] [ISBN: 1885183488] [OCLC: 33817703]

Greenberg, Jan, and Sandra Jordan. *The American Eye: Artists of the Twentieth Century.* New York: Delacorte Press, c. 1995. [children]

Guilbaut, Serge. *How New York Stole the Idea of Modern Art: Abstract Expressionism, Freedom, and the Cold War.* Chicago: University of Chicago Press, 1983. [refs. Kootz Gallery]

Harlem Renaissance: Art of Black America. Exh. cat., Studio Museum in Harlem, N.Y. [Harry N. Abrams, New York], 1987. Text: Mary Schmidt Campbell; David C. Driskell; David Levering Lewis; Richard Powell; Deborah Willis Ryan; Jeffrey Stewart. [LC records cat. was republished, New York: SMIH: Abradale Press, 1994 (LC: N6538.N5 H286 1994)]

Harrison, Paul Carter. *Black Light: The African American Hero.* New York: Thunder's Mouth Press; Emeryville, Calif.: Distributed by Publishers Group West, 1993. [created by Bill Duke; introduction by Danny Glover] [children] [*Baltimore (Md.) County Public Library online catalogue, call no.: J973.0496 H]

Haskins, James. *One More River to Cross: The Stories of Twelve Black Americans.* New York: Scholastic Inc., 1992. [children]

Hatch-Billops Collection, Inc., Archives of Black Cultural History. New York: Hatch-Billops Collection, 1979. [*Igoe (1981)]

Holmes, Oakley N., Jr. *The Complete Annotated Resource Guide to Black American Art.* Spring Valley, N.Y.: Black Artists in America, 1978.

Holmes, Oakley Norman. "Black Artists in America: An Introduction to Seven Internationally Recognized Black Visual Artists." Ed.D. dissertation, Columbia University, New York, 1973.

hooks, bell. *Art on My Mind: Visual Politics.* New York: The New Press, 1995.

Igoe, Lynn Moody, with James Igoe. *250 Years of Afro-American Art: An Annotated Bibliography.* New York: Bowker, 1981. Updated: Lynn Igoe, *African-*

American Artists on Disc. New York: G.K. Hall & Co., c. 1999. [*laser optical disk, plus guide, University of Virginia Libraries (VIRGO) online catalogue; call no. XX(3527037.1); ISBN: 0783885393]

Irvine, Betty Jo, and Jane A. McCabe, compilers. *Fine Arts and the Black American/Music and the Black American.* Focus: Black America Bibliography Series. Bloomington, Ind.: Indiana University Libraries, 1969. [*Cederholm (1973)]

Jefferson, Louise, E. *Contemporary Art by Afro-Americans.* New York: Friendship Press, n.d. Introduction by Carroll Greene, Jr. Portfolio of prints with pamphlet of artists' biographies. [*Igoe (1981)]

Johnson, Una E. *American Prints and Printmakers: A Chronicle of over 400 Artists and Their Prints from 1900 to the Present.* Garden City, N.Y.: Doubleday & Co., Inc., 1980.

Jordan, June. *Who Look at Me.* New York: Crowell, 1969. [*Igoe (1981)] [poetry; illustrated with art by RB, others; artists' biographies]

Klotman, Phyllis Rauch, ed. *Humanities through the Black Experience.* Dubuque, Iowa: Kendall/Hunt, 1977. [*Igoe (1993)]

Larkin, Oliver W. *Art and Life in America.* New York: Rinehart and Company, Inc., 1949. [revised, enlarged edition: New York: Holt, Rinehart and Winston, 1960]

Lewis, David Levering, ed. *The Portable Harlem Renaissance Reader.* New York: Viking Penguin, 1994. [reprint of RB, "The Negro Artist and Modern Art" (1934)]

Lewis, Samella. *African American Art and Artists.* Berkeley and Los Angeles: University of California Press, 1990.

———. *Art: African American.* New York: Harcourt Brace Jovanovich, Inc., 1978.

Lewis, Samella Saunders, and Ruth G. Waddy, eds. *Black Artists on Art.* Rev. ed. Los Angeles: Contemporary Crafts, 1976.

Littleton, Taylor D., and Maltby Sykes. *Advancing American Art: Painting, Politics, and Cultural Confrontation at Mid-Century.* Introduction by Leon F. Litwack. Tuscaloosa and London: University of Alabama Press, 1989.

Locke, Alain. *The Negro in Art. A Pictorial Record of the Negro Artist and of the Negro Theme in Art.* New York: Hacker Art Books, 1968. [first printing: Washington, D.C.: Associates in Negro Folk Education, 1940]

Maguire, Roberta S., ed. *Conversations with Albert Murray.* Jackson: University Press of Mississippi, 1997.

McKay, Claude. *Harlem: Negro Metropolis.* New York: E.P. Dutton & Company, 1940. [*Igoe (1981)]

Meilach, Dona Z., and Elvis Ten Hoor. *Collage and Assemblage: Trends and Techniques.* New York: Crown Publishers, 1973. [*Mint Museum (1980)]

Memorial Tribute in Honor of Romare H. Bearden. Cultural Center (Backstreet), April 16, 1988. [program]

Murray, Albert. *The Blue Devils of Nada: A Contemporary American Approach to Aesthetic Statement.* New York: Pantheon Books, 1996. ["Bearden Plays Bearden: The Visual Equivalent to Blues Composition" (revision of essay in Mint Museum (1980)]

Murray, Alma, and Robert Thomas, eds. *Black Perspectives.* Scholastic Black Literature Services. New York: Scholastic Book Services, 1971. [*Mint Museum (1980)]

Murray, Florence, comp. and ed. *The Negro Handbook.* 3rd ed. New York: Current Reference Publications, 1946–47. [*Igoe (1981)]

New Black Artists. Exh. cat., Brooklyn Museum, New York, October 7–November 9, 1969; Columbia University, November 20–December 12, 1969. Text: Edward K Taylor. [organized by Harlem Cultural Council, New York, with School of the Arts and the Urban Center, Columbia University, New York]

Patterson, Lindsay, ed. *The Negro in Music and Art.* Vol. 2, International Library of Negro Life and History. New York: Publishers Co., 1967. [*Igoe (1981)]

Patton, Sharon F. *African-American Art.* Oxford and New York: Oxford University Press, 1998.

Port Authority of Allegheny County: Public Art Program for the Light Rail Transit System. [Pittsburgh, n.d.] [*Pittsburgh Recollections* (1984)]

Porter, Horace A. *Jazz Country: Ralph Ellison in America.* Iowa City: University of Iowa Press, 2001. [chapter on Ralph Ellison, RB, Albert Murray]

Porter, James A. *Modern Negro Art.* New York: Dryden Press, 1943. [republished by Arno Press and NYT, New York, 1969; Howard University Press, Washington, D.C., 1992, new introduction by David C. Driskell]

Powell, Richard J. *Black Art and Culture in the 20th Century.* London and New York: Thames and Hudson, 1997.

Prigoff, James, and Robin J. Dunitz. *Walls of Heritage, Walls of Pride: African American Murals.* San Francisco: Pomegranate Communications, Inc., 2000.

Pugliano, Carol, and Julianna Dunham. "Romare Bearden: An Artist's Life for Him." In *African-Americans Who Made a Difference: 15 Plays for the Classroom.* New York: Scholastic Professional Books, 1996. Grades 4–8. [children] [*Worldcat (OCLC) FirstSearch online database] [OCLC: 36707490]

Rathburn, Mary Chalmers, and Bartlett H. Hayes, Jr. *Layman's Guide to Modern Art.* New York: Oxford University Press, 1949. [*MoMA (1971); LC records book based on exh. *Seeing the Unseeable,* Addison Gallery of American Art, Phillips Academy, Andover, Mass., January 3–March 10, 1947] [LC:ND1265.R38]

Reynolds, Gary A., and Beryl J. Wright. *Against the Odds: African-American Artists and the Harmon Foundation.* Exh. cat., Newark Museum, N.J., January 15–April 15, 1990. [© 1989]. Circulated. Text: David Driskell; Clement Alexander Price; Richard J. Powell; Deborah Willis.

Rigg, Margaret R., ed. *Survivor's Box: To the Family of Man & Woman Kind: The Network.* Saint Petersburg, Fla.: Possum Press, 1977. [reprints of Susan Howe, "Romare Bearden at Cordier & Ekstrom," *Art in America* 64 (November–December 1976), 122; and RB, "Humility," *NYT,* Saturday, June 21, 1975, 27; photos, illustrations]

Roalf, Peggy. *Musicians.* Looking at Paintings series. New York: Hyperion Books for Children, 1993. [repr., discussion of *Three Folk Musicians* (1967)] [children]

Rogers, Paul A. "Race and the Discourse of Nature in the Art of the Americas, 1850–1965." Ph.D. dissertation, Yale University, 1993. [WC: OCLC: 40726380; UMI order number: AAT 9433720: Photocopy. Ann Arbor, Mich.: University Microfilms International, 1998]

Rollock, Barbara. *The Black Experience in Children's Books.* New York: New York Public Library, 1974.

Rosenberg, Bernard, and Norris Fliegel. *The Vanguard Artists: Portrait and Self Portrait.* Chicago: Quadrangle Books, 1965. [LC records book reprinted by Arno Press, New York, 1979; and by New Amsterdam, New York, 1990]

Roucek, Joseph S., and Thomas Kiernan, eds. *The Negro Impact on Western Civilization.* New York: Philosophical Library, 1970. [*Cederholm (1973)]

Russell, Dick. *Black Genius and the American Experience.* New York: Carroll & Graf, 1998. Foreword by Alvin F. Poussaint.

Schwartz, Barry. *The New Humanism: Art in a Time of Change.* New York: Praeger, 1974. [*Igoe (1981)]

Seventy-Five Years of Freedom: Commemoration of the 75th Anniversary of the Proclamation of the 13th Amendment to the Constitution of the United States. Washington, D.C.: Government Printing Office, United States Library of Congress, 1943. [*Igoe (1981)]

A Shared Heritage: Art by Four African Americans. Exh. cat., Indianapolis Museum of Art, 1996. Text: Margaret T.G. Burroughs; Floyd Coleman; Edmund Barry Gaither; Corrine Jennings; William E. Taylor; Harriet G. Warkel. [artists: William E. Scott, John W. Hardrick, Hale A. Woodruff, William Majors]

Siegel, Jeanne. *Artwords: Discourse on the 60s and 70s.* New York: Da Capo Press, 1992. [first published, Ann Arbor, Mich.: UMI Research Press, c. 1985]

———. "Four American Negro Painters: 1940–1965, Their Choice and Treatment of Themes." [Horace Pippin, Eldzier Cortor, RB, Robert Thompson] Unpublished M.A. thesis, Columbia University, New York, 1966. [*Igoe (1981)]

Simpson, George Eaton, and John Milton Yinger. *Racial and Cultural Minorities: An Analysis of Prejudice and Discrimination.* 4th ed. New York: Harper and Row, 1972. [*Igoe (1981)]

Smith, Jessie Carney, ed. *Black Heroes of the 20th Century.* Detroit: Visible Ink Press, 1998. Foreword by Nikki Giovanni.

Spradling, Mary Mace. *In Black and White: Afro-Americans in Print—A Guide to Afro-Americans Who Have Made Contributions to the United States of America from 1619–1969.* Kalamazoo, Mich.: Kalamazoo Library System, 1971. [*Igoe (1981)]

Stovall, Tyler. *Paris Noir: African Americans in the City of Light.* New York: Houghton Mifflin Company, 1996.

Sullivan, Charles, ed. *Children of Promise: African-American Literature and Art for Young People.* New York: Harry N. Abrams, Inc., 1991. [children]

Sylvester, Melvin R. *African-Americans in the Visual Arts: A Historical Perspective.* Brookville, N.Y.: Long Island University, C. W. Post Campus, 1996. [computer file: text/html *http://www.cwpost.liunet.edu/cwis/cwp/library/aafaahp.htm*]

Taha, Halima. *Collecting African American Art: Works on Paper and Canvas.* New York: Crown Publishers, 1998. Forewords by Deidre Bibby and Samella Lewis. Introduction by Ntozake Shange. Afterword by June Kelly.

The Thirtieth Anniversary Convocation of Founder's Day. Program. B.N. Duke Auditorium, North Carolina Central University, Durham, November 4, 1977. [brief biography]

Unseld, Teresa S. *Portfolios: Africa-American Artists.* Palo Alto, Calif.: Dale Seymour Publications, 1994. [teacher resource, grades 4–12]

Waldman, Diane. *Collage, Assemblage, and the Found Object.* New York: Harry N. Abrams, 1992.

Wilmerding, John. *American Art.* Pelican History of Art. Harmondsworth, England; New York: Penguin Books, 1976.

Wilson, Charles Reagan, and William Ferris, eds. *Encyclopedia of Southern Culture.* Chapel Hill: University of North Carolina Press, 1989. [*Igoe (1993)]

Yancy, Roberta J., ed. *The New York Black 100: A Tribute.* New York: New York Public Library; Astor, Lenox and Tilden Foundations, 1998. [presented by NYPL/SC, with the Black New Yorkers/Black New York Consortium] [CATNYP call no.: Sc F 98-1124]

GROUP EXHIBITION CATALOGUES

Abstract and Surrealist American Art. Exh. cat., Fifty-Eighth Annual Exhibition of American Paintings and Sculpture. Art Institute of Chicago, 1947. Text: Katherine Kuh; Daniel Catton Rich; Frederick A. Sweet.

Advancing American Art. Exh. cat., Met., New York, 1946. [*MoMA (1971)]

Advancing American Art: Politics and Aesthetics in the State Department Exhibition, 1946–1948. Exh. cat., Montgomery Museum of Fine Arts, Ala., 1984. Circulated. Text: Ross C. Anderson; Margaret Lynne Ausfeld; Virginia M. Mecklenburg.

Africa in Diaspora. Exh. cat., Rockland Center for the Arts, West Nyack, N.Y., 1974. [*Igoe (1981); Holmes (1978)]

African-American Art: 20th Century Masterworks. Exh. cat., Michael Rosenfeld Gallery, New York, November 18, 1993–February 12, 1994. Text: Beryl J. Wright; halley k. harrisburg, ed.

African-American Art: 20th Century Masterworks, II. Exh. cat., Michael Rosenfeld Gallery, New York, February 1–April 8, 1995. Circulated. Text: Harold B. Nelson; Richard J. Powell.

African-American Art: 20th Century Masterworks, III. Exh. cat., Michael Rosenfeld Gallery, New York, February 1–April 6, 1996.

African-American Art: 20th Century Masterworks, IV. Exh. cat., Michael Rosenfeld Gallery, New York, January 24–March 26, 1997. Circulated. Text: Kevin Grogan; Michael Rosenfeld.

African-American Art: 20th Century Masterworks, V. Exh. cat., Michael Rosenfeld Gallery, New York, January 22–March 21, 1998. Circulated. Text: Nancy A. Corwin; Leslie King-Hammond; Michael Rosenfeld.

African-American Art: 20th Century Masterworks, VI. Exh. cat., Michael Rosenfeld Gallery, New York, January 14–March 6, 1999. Circulated.

African-American Art: 20th Century Masterworks, VII: Educating Our Children. Exh. cat., Michael Rosenfeld Gallery, New York, January 13–March 4, 2000. Circulated.

African-American Art: 20th Century Masterworks, VIII. Exh. cat., Michael Rosenfeld Gallery, New York, January 18–March 10, 2001. Circulated. Text: Alvia J. Wardlaw. Statements by Benny Andrews; Eldzier Cortor; Herbert Gentry; Betye Saar.

African-American Art: 20th Century Masterworks, IX. Exh. cat., Michael Rosenfeld Gallery, New York, January 17–March 9, 2002. Circulated. Text: Leslie King-Hammond; Carey Picard.

African-American Artists (Bannister to Mitchell). Exh. cat., Bill Hodges Gallery, New York, February 6–April 3, 1999.

African-American Artists 1880–1987: Selections from the Evans-Tibbs Collection. Exh. cat., SITES, Washington, D.C., with the University of Washington Press, Seattle and London, 1989. Text: David C. Driskell; Guy C. McElroy; Sharon F. Patton; Richard J. Powell.

African-American Artists—II. Exh. cat., Bill Hodges Gallery, New York, February 12–March 18, 2000.

African American Works on Paper from the Cochran Collection. Exh. cat., The Collection, La Grange, Ga., 1991 [Atlanta, Ga.: Double Density]. Circulated. Text: Camille Billops; Robert Blackburn; Richard A. Long; Judith Wilson.

Afro-American Artists, 1800–1969. Exh. cat., Philadelphia, The School District, Division of Art Education, in cooperation with the Museum of the Philadelphia Civic Center, [1969]. Text: Randall J. Craig.

Afro-American Artists, New York and Boston. Exh. cat., Museum of the National Center of Afro-American Artists, School of the Museum of Fine Arts, and Museum of Fine Arts, Boston, 1970. Text: Edmund B. Gaither.

Afro-American Artists: North Carolina, USA. Exh. cat., North Carolina Museum of Art, Raleigh, 1980. Text: Eva Hamlin Miller.

Afro-American Painting, Sculpture, Works on Paper, 1864–1980. Exh. cat., Goucher College, Kraushaar Auditorium, Towson, Md., 1981.

The Afro-American Presence in the Arts, Past and Present, from North Carolina Collections. Exh. cat., Hickory Museum of Art, N.C., 1982. Text: Lynn Moody Igoe.

American Masters of the Twentieth Century. Exh. cat., Oklahoma Art Center, Oklahoma City, 1982. Traveled to Terra Museum of American Art, Evanston, Ill., 1982. Text: John I.H. Baur.

American Negro Art, 19th and 20th Centuries. Exh. cat., Downtown Gallery, New York, [1941].

American Negro Art: Contemporary Painting and Sculpture. Exh. cat., Newark Museum, N.J., 1944.

American Painting Today—1950. Exh. cat., Met., New York, 1951. Text: Francis Henry Taylor.

An American Portrait, 1776–1976: 33 Contemporary Masters Join in a Trilogy Celebrating the Bicentennial. [Exh. cat.?] New York: Transworld Art Corp., 1975. [*Igoe (1981): "Catalog promoting 3-vol. set of prints accompanied by readings"; repr. *The Family,* with comments; circulating exh.]

The Americans: The Collage. Exh. cat., Contemporary Arts Museum, Houston, 1982. Text: Linda L. Cathcart; Emily L. Todd.

Amistad II: Afro-American Art. Exh. cat., Fisk University, Nashville, 1975. Edward Grady, curator. Text: David C. Driskell; Allan M. Gordon; Clifton Johnson; Grant Spradling.

Art/America: An Exhibition of More Than Fifty Significant Paintings and Sculptures. Exh. cat., Bamberger's, N.J. [a division of R.H. Macy & Co., Inc.], [n.d.]. [Dore Ashton, director of exhibition]

Art by African Americans in the Collection of the New Jersey State Museum. Exh. cat., New Jersey State Museum, Trenton, September 19–December 31, 1998. Text: Tritobia Hayes Benjamin; David C. Driskell; Ronne Hartfield; Carl. E. Hazlewood; Lisa Farrington-Kent; Sharon Patton; Calvin Reid; James Smalls; Margaret Rose Vendryes; Alison Weld.

Art en Route: MTA Arts for Transit. Exh. cat., PaineWebber Art Gallery, with Metropolitan Transit Authority, New York, July 14, 1994–September 23, 1994. Circulated. William Ayres and Sandra Bloodworth, curators. Text: Suzanne Gyorgy; Wendy Feuer; Donald Marron; Peter E. Stangl.

Art Inc.: American Paintings from Corporate Collections. Exh. cat., Montgomery Museum of Fine Arts, Ala., 1979. Circulated. Text: Mitchell Douglas Kahan.

Art in Print: A Tribute to Robert Blackburn. Exh. cat., NYPL/SC, New York, 1984. Text: Emma Amos; RB; Julia Hotton.

The Art of the American Negro: Exhibition of Painting. Exh. cat., 144 West 125th Street, New York, 1966. [sponsored by Harlem Cultural Council]

The Art of Collage: Romare Bearden, David Driskell, Kenneth Falana, Sam Gilliam, Ulysses Marshall, Barbara Mosley, Betye Saar, Sharon Sutton. Exh. cat., Evans-Tibbs Collection, Washington, D.C., 1985. Text: Thurlow E. Tibbs, Jr.

The Art of Jazz. Exh. cat., NYPL/SC, New York, 1982. Text: Julia Hotton; James Briggs Murray; Ron Welburn.

Art on Paper 1972. Exh. cat., Weatherspoon Art Gallery, University of North Carolina at Greensboro, 1972. Text: Henry Geldzahler; James E. Tucker. [annual juried exhibition]

Art Students League of New York, 1875–1976: Druckgraphik. Exh. cat., Berliner Festwochen 1976, Kunstamt Wedding, Walther-Rathenau-Saal, Rathaus Wedding (Altbau), Berlin, 1976.

Artists for Core. Third Annual Art Exhibition and Sale. Exh. cat., Gallery of American Federation of Arts, New York, 1964. [see also: combined listing, *Artists for Core: Fourth and Fifth Annual Catalogs* (1965 and 1966) in Holmes (1978)]

Aspects of Collage. Exh. cat., Guild Hall Museum, East Hampton, N.Y., May 5–June 9, 1991. Text: Christina Mossaides Strassfield.

Augusta Savage and the Art Schools of Harlem. Exh. cat., NYPL/SC, New York, October 9, 1988–January 28, 1989. Text: Deidre L. Bibby; Howard Dodson; Juanita Marie Holland.

The Barnett-Aden Collection. Washington, D.C.: Smithsonian Institution Press, 1974. [for Anacostia Neighborhood Museum, Smithsonian Institution, with the Barnett-Aden Gallery (selected works shown at the Anacostia Neighborhood Museum, 1974, and the Corcoran Gallery of Art, Washington, D.C., 1975)] [RB contributed essay and tribute to gallery founders]

Biennale Internationale de l'Affiche. Exh. cat., Warsaw, 1968. Text: Jerzy Wasniewski. [*MoMA (1971)]

The Big Top. Exh. cat., Kootz, New York, 1946. Text: Samuel M. Kootz.

Black Achievement in the Arts. Exh. cat., The Equitable Gallery, New York, 1982. Text: Robert H. Browning.

Black American Artist Seminar. Program and exh. cat., Reynolda House Museum of American Art, Winston-Salem, N.C., 1972. [seminar, March 9 and 10]

Black American Artists/71, Exh. cat., Illinois Bell Telephone, Chicago, 1971. Circulated. Text: Robert H. Glauber. Statements by Ralph Arnold; Sam Gilliam; Russell T. Gordon; Joseph B. Ross, Jr.; Vincent Smith; Edward K. Taylor.

Black American Artists of the 19th and 20th Century (Visual Arts Exhibition Series). Exh. cat., Afro-American Cultural Center, Charlotte, N.C., 1980.

Black Artist in Graphic Communication. Exh. cat., Gallery 303, New York, 1970. [*MoMA (1971)]

Black Artists in America: 19th and 20th Centuries. Exh. cat., Wilcox Gallery, Swarthmore College, Pa., 1968. Text: Dorine Keith. [typescript]

Black Artists in Historical Perspective, Part 2. Exh. cat., Schenectady Museum, Schenectady, N.Y., 1978. [Black Dimensions in Art, Inc.] [*Igoe (1981)]

Black Artists in the New York Scene. Exh. cat., Acts of Art Gallery, New York, [1974]. Text: Nigel Jackson. [*Igoe (1981)]

Black Artists/South. Exh. cat., Huntsville Museum of Art, Ala., 1979. Text: Ralph M. Hudson; Clifton Pearson.

Black Artists: Two Generations. Exh. cat., Newark Museum, N.J., 1971.

Blocked Metaphors. Exh. cat., C&E, New York, 1969. [*MoMA (1971)]

A Blossoming of New Promises: Art In the Spirit of the Harlem Renaissance. Exh. cat., Emily Lowe Gallery, Hofstra University, Hempstead, N.Y., February 5–March 18, 1984. Text: Gail Gelburd; Richard Long.

The Blues Aesthetic: Black Culture and Modernism. Exh. cat., Washington Project for the Arts, Washington, D.C., September 14–December 9, 1989. Circulated. Text: Dwight D. Andrews; Sherrill Berryman-Miller; Joseph A. Brown; S.J, John Cephas; Kellie Jones; E. Ethelbert Miller; Richard J. Powell; Jock Reynolds; Jeffrey Stewart; Eleanor W. Traylor; John Michael Vlach.

Building a Modern Collection. Exh. cat., Kootz, New York, 1946. Text: Samuel M. Kootz.

Celebration and Vision: The Hewitt Collection of African-American Art. Exh. cat., Bank of America Corp., Charlotte, N.C., 1999. Circulated. Text: Hugh McColl, Jr.; Regenia Perry; Todd D. Smith. [purchased by Bank of America for Afro-American Cultural Center]

Center Ring: The Artist. Two Centuries of Circus Art. Exh. cat., Milwaukee Art Museum, 1981. Circulated. Text: Dean Jensen; Gerald Nordland; Susanne-Christine Voeltz; Robert H. Wills.

Coalition 70. Exh. cat., Staten Island Museum, New York, 1970. Text: Barry Leo Delaney.

Collage: Beardon [sic], Bultman, Motherwell, Nickle, Roeber. Exh. cat., Purdue University, Department of Creative Arts Gallery, Lafayette, Ind., 1969. Text: Tony Vevers.

Collage: The State of the Art. Exh. cat., Bergen Museum of Art and Science, Paramus, N.J., 1985. Text: Regina DeRosa; Elaine Hyman.

Collages: Selections from the Hirshhorn Museum and Sculpture Garden. Exh. cat., SITES, Washington, D.C., 1981. Text: Howard N. Fox.

Contemporary Black Art: A Selected Sampling. Exh. cat., Florida International University, North Miami and Tamiami Campuses, 1977.

Contemporary Collage. Exh. cat., Vassar College Art Gallery, Poughkeepsie, N.Y., 1974.

Contemporary Graphic Art on Contemporary Law and Justice. Exh. cat., The House of the Association, New York, 1970. Text. Franklin Feldman; Andrew Stasik. [organized by Pratt Graphics Center, New York, for Centennial of Association of the Bar of the City of New York]

Contemporary Religious Paintings. Exh. cat., Barnett Aden Gallery, Washington, D.C., 1948. Text: J[ames] W. L[ane]. [fifth anniversary exhibition of Gallery; sponsored by Catholic Interracial Council of Washington]

Contemporary Tapestries. Exh. cat., Ringling Museum of Art, Sarasota, Fla., 1978. [announcement with checklist]

Contemporary Urban Visions. Exh. cat., New School Art Center, Wollman Hall, New York, 1966. Text: Paul Mocsanyi. RB statement.

Creativity: The Human Resource. Exh. cat., published by Chevron/ Standard Oil Company of California, San Francisco, n.d. [c. 1979?]. [brochure] Circulated. [Franklin Institute Science Museum, Philadelphia, also produced a brochure]

Creativity and the Negro. Festival cat., Rockford College, Festival of the Arts, Ill., 1965. [festival, March 3–7, included exh. *Contemporary Negro Art,* March 3–12]

Dimensions of Black. Exh. cat., La Jolla Museum of Art, Calif., 1970. Text: Jehanne Teilhet, ed. [student project, University of California, San Diego]

Directions in Afro-American Art. Exh. cat., Herbert F. Johnson Museum of Art, Cornell University, Ithaca, N.Y., 1974. [cosponsored by Africana Studies and Research Center] Text: Rosalind R. Jeffries; Thomas W. Leavitt; James E. Turner.

Drawing and Collage: Selections from the New York University Art Collection. Exh. cat., Grey Art Gallery and Study Center, New York University, New York, 1977. Text: Bonnie Janowsky; Amalia Hoffman; Peggy Pine; Ann Troise.

Drawings by Contemporary American Artists. Exh. cat., Cranbrook Academy of Art, Museum, Bloomfield Hills, Mich., 1975.

Durham Chatauqua: The Black Man in Art. Exh. cat., Stanford L. Warren Branch Library, Durham County, Durham, N.C., 1974. [mimeographed brochure]. Text: Norman Elvis Pendergraft. [RB cited as Beardon]

East/West: Contemporary American Art. Exh. cat., California Afro-American Museum, Los Angeles, 1984. Text: Sharon F. Patton.

Eight New York Painters: "Patterns of American Culture, Contributions of the Negro." Exh. cat., University of Michigan Museum of Art, Ann Arbor, 1956. Text: Hale Woodruff.

Encounters: An Exhibit in Celebration of the Charlotte-Mecklenburg Bi-Centennial. Exh. cat., Johnson C. Smith University, James B. Duke Library, Charlotte, N.C., 1968. Text: Eugene Grigsby. Poem by RB.

The Evolution of Afro-American Artists, 1800–1950. Exh. cat., City University of New York, in cooperation with Harlem Cultural Council and National Urban League, 1967. Organized by RB and Carroll Greene, Jr. Text: Carroll Greene, Jr.

Exhibit of Selected Paintings by Contemporary Negro Artists. Exh. cat., Stanford L. Warren Public Library, Durham County, N.C., 1944. [from 1944 Atlanta University competitive exhibition]

Exhibition of the Art of the American Negro (1851 to 1940). Exh. cat., Tanner Art Galleries, Chicago, 1940. Text: Alain Locke. [organized by the American Negro Exposition]

Exhibition of Contemporary American Painting. Seventh Annual Southeastern Circuit, 1945–'46. Exh. cat., Clearwater Art Museum, Fla., 1946. Text: E. R. Hunter.

An Exhibition of Contemporary Painting, Sculpture and Graphic Art. Exh. cat., Academy Art Gallery, National Institute of Arts and Letters, New York, 1965.

An Exhibition of Contemporary Painting, Sculpture and Graphic Art. Exh. cat., National Institute of Arts and Letters, Academy Art Gallery, New York, 1966.

Exhibition of Liturgical Arts. Exh. cat., Philadelphia Civic Center, 1976. Organized by 41st International Eucharistic Congress. Text: Victoria Donohoe; John Cardinal Krol; John Miller.

Exhibition of Paintings and Sculpture by Negro Artists. [Exh. cat.?], Artists of Today, Newark, N.J., 1945. [*MoMA (1971); Igoe (1981)] [single sheet, "Purchasing Information" (artists, works, prices), in MoMA Scrapbook, fiche 1.81]

Exhibition of Sculpture and Painting Presented by the Labor Club. Exh. cat., [New York], 1939. Checklist. [RB as Beardon]

Exhibition of Work by Newly Elected Members and Recipients of Honors and Awards. Exh. cat., Academy Art Gallery, American Academy of Arts and Letters and National Institute of Arts and Letters, New York, 1966.

Exhibition of Work by Newly Elected Members and Recipients of Honors and Awards. Exh. cat., Art Gallery and the Museum, American Academy of Arts and Letters and National Institute of Arts and Letters, New York, 1972.

Faces of Time: 75 Years of Time Magazine Cover Portraits. Exh. cat., National Portrait Gallery, Smithsonian Institution, Washington, D.C., March 20–August 2, 1998. [Bullfinch Press Book: Little, Brown and Company, Boston, New York, Toronto, London] Circulated. Text: Jay Leno; Henry Muller; Frederick S. Voss.

The Festival of Arts. Exh. cat., Temple Emanu-el, Yonkers, N.Y., [1965]. Text: Abraham J. Klausner. [*MoMA Scrapbook, fiche 1.82]

Figural Art of the New York School: Selections from the CIBA-GEIGY Art Collection. Exh. cat., Baruch College Gallery, City University of New York, 1985. Circulated. Text: Katherine B. Crum.

The Figurative Tradition and the Whitney Museum of American Art: Paintings and Sculpture from the Permanent Collection. Exh. cat., Whitney, New York, with University of Delaware Press (Newark), Associated University Presses (London and Toronto), 1980. Text: Patricia Hills; Roberta K. Tarbell.

Five Famous Black Artists. Museum of the National Center of Afro-American Artists, Roxbury, Mass., 1970. Text: Carroll Greene, Jr.

Four African-American Artists: The Freedom Place Collection. Exh. cat., Lowe Art Museum, University of Miami, Coral Gables, Fla., September 18–November 16, 1997.

14 Afro-American Artists. Exh. cat., Pratt Institute Gallery, Brooklyn, N.Y., 1976. Text: Norma McMichael. [poster/ announcement] [biographies, photos (except RB's drawn self-portrait)]

Fourth Annual Exhibition of Paintings, Sculpture and Prints by Negro Artists. Exh. cat., Atlanta University, Ga., 1945.

Fragments of American Life: An Exhibition of Paintings. Exh. cat., The Art Museum, Princeton, N.J., 1976. Text: Anne Jones Willis; John Ralph Willis.

Free within Ourselves: African American Artists in the Collection of the National Museum of American Art. Exh. cat., National Museum of American Art, Smithsonian Institution, Washington, D.C., with Pomegranate Artbooks, San Francisco, 1992. Circulated. Text: Kinshasha Holman Conwill; Regenia A. Perry.

Killens, John Oliver. "Another Time When Black Was Beautiful." *Black World* 20 (November 1970): 20–36. [*Igoe (1981): on Harlem Renaissance]

Kimmelman, Michael. "Review/ Art: Views of American Life In 'Urban and Suburban.'" *NYT*, April 8, 1988, C30. [exh. *Urban and Suburban*, Sid Deutsch Gallery, New York]

Kinzer, Stephen. "Arts in America: Charlotte Acclaims Romare Bearden as a Native Son." *NYT*, October 2, 2002, B2. [exh. *Charlotte's Own: Romare Bearden*, Mint Museum of Art]

Kisselgoff, Anna. "Dance: Gala at the Ailey with Premiere to Match." *NYT*, December 4, 1982, 17. [set for Talley Beatty's *The Stack-Up*]

———. "Dance: Three Season Premieres by Ailey Troupe." *NYT*, July 15, 1984, 48. [set for Talley Beatty's *The Stack-Up*]

"Koch Honors 6 in the Arts with Awards." *NYT*, November 28, 1984, C21. [Mayor's Awards of Honor for Arts and Culture]

Kramer, Hilton. "Art View: Black Art or Merely Social History?" *NYT*, June 26, 1977, 2: 25. [exh. *Two Centuries of Black American Art*, Brooklyn Museum]

———. "'Black Art' and Expedient Politics." *NYT*, June 7, 1970, 2: 19. [exh. *Afro-American Artists: New York and Boston*, Museum of Fine Arts, Boston]

———. "Is Politics Submerging Black Art?" *Louisville Courier Journal & Times*, June 7, 1970. [*Cederholm (1973)]

Krause, Betsy. "Visions of a Turbulent Time." *Columbia (Mo.) Daily Tribune*, November 23, 1986, 47. [exh. *Tradition and Conflict: Images of a Turbulent Decade, 1963–1973*, Museum of Art and Archaeology, University of Missouri-Columbia]

Kriegsman, Alan M. "Dance: Ailey's Classic Sizzle." *Washington Post*, August 15, 1985, B2. [set for Talley Beatty's *The Stack-Up*]

Lane, James W. "Afro-American Art on Both Continents." *Art News* 40 (October 15–31, 1941): 25. [exh. at McMillan, Inc., New York; RB as Romery Bearden]

Langrall, Peggy. "Romare Bearden's Paintings Emphasize Subjects Derived from African-American Genre and Myth." *St. Louis Journalism Review* 22 (April 1993): 18–19. [book review: *Free within Ourselves*]

L[ansford], A[lonzo]. "Eight Who Share the Modern Approach." *Art Digest* 22 (October 1, 1947): 19. [exh. *Eight Paintings*, Kootz]

———. "Kootz Anniversary." *Art Digest* 22 (April 1, 1948): 13.

Lansford, Alonzo. "Sic Transit." *Art Digest* 22 (July 1, 1948): 13, 21. [sale of State Department collection; lists *At Five in the Afternoon* and *Mad Carousel*]

Larsen, Susan C. "*Ms.* on the Arts: Art—Discovery: Two Centuries of Black American Art." *Ms.* 5 (January 1977): 24, 26, 27.

"Leading Negro Artists: Talent Breaks Bias Bond." *Ebony* 18 (September 1963): 131–32, 134, 136, 138, 140.

"Leading Young Artists." *Ebony* 13 (April 1958): 33–38. [RB named among established artists]

LeBrun, Caron. "Comprehensive Exhibit at Museum: Blacks' Art on Display." *Boston Herald Traveler*, May 26, 1970, 29. [exh. *Afro-American Artists, New York and Boston*]

Lenson, Michael. "Notable Art Show in Bayonne." *Newark Sunday News*, May 10, 1970, E20. [exh. *GEIGY Art Collection*, Bayonne Public Library, N.J.]

Lindsley, Lorna. "American, Other Art Here." *Paris Post* [October 1945?]. [Pietro Lazarri/ Bearden exh. organized by Caresse Crosby at Galerie John Devoluy, Paris] [*AAA/RB, frame 0513, reel N/68-87]

Lipson, Karin. "Black Artists of the Civil-Rights Era." *Newsday*, April 11, 1986, Weekend: 21 (Nassau and Suffolk Ed.). [exh. *Tradition and Conflict: Images of a Turbulent Decade, 1963–1973*, Heckscher Museum, Huntington, N.Y.]

———. "Creativity with the Public's Blessing." *Newsday*, February 27, 1987, 27 (Nassau and Suffolk Ed.). [exh. *Second Annual Invitational Show*, Studio K, Long Island City, Queens, New York]

———. "Faces in Disguise and Metamorphosis." *Newsday*, May 8, 1987, 29 (Nassau and Suffolk Ed.). [exh. *An American Portrait*, Hofstra University Library, Hempstead, N.Y.]

———. "A History of New York's Black Artists." *Newsday*, January 9, 1987, 23 (Nassau and Suffolk Ed.). [exh. *Master and Pupils: The Education of the Black Artist in New York, 1900–1980*, Jamaica Arts Center, New York]

Littleton, Taylor D. "'The Life of Our Design': Advancing American Art." *National Forum* 76 (April 1, 1996): 24 (2 pp.). [exh. *Advancing American Art* and sale by War Assets Administration] [online citation (ProQuest) gives number of total pages, plus starting page number only]

"Living Negro Art Popular." *Art Digest* 16 (December 15, 1941): 11. [permanent exh. at McMillen, Inc., New York]

Lorber, Richard. "Arts Reviews: Group Show." *Arts Magazine* 50 (December 1975): 25. [exh. C&E]

———. "Art Reviews: Group Show/Tapestries." *Arts Magazine* 50 (December 1975): 24. [exh. Pace Editions, New York]

Loring, John. "American Portrait." *Arts Magazine* 50 (November 1975): 58–59. [Transworld Art Bicentennial portfolio]

———. "American Prints from Fuses to Fizzles." *Art in America* 65 (January–February 1977): 31–34.

"Mammoth Art Show Now at City College Great Hall." *New York Amsterdam News*, October 21, 1967, 10. [exh. *The Evolution of Afro-American Artists, 1800–1950*, City University of New York]

McCausland, Elizabeth. "American Negro Art of 19th and 20th Centuries." *Springfield (Mass.) Union and Republican*, December 21, 1941. [*MoMA Scrapbooks, fiche 1.79]

McCoy, Garnett, ed. "The Art Students League, Part II." *Archives of American Art Journal* 13, no. 2 (1973): 1–18. [excerpts Henri Ghent interview with RB (1968)]

McDonagh, Don. "Hats Off!" *Financial Times*, February 27, 1970. [exh. *Blocked Metaphors*, C&E, repr. *Mauritius*] [*private archive]

McLean, Deckle. "What Blacks Say Is Missing in Met Show: 'Harlem on My Mind' Hit for Lack of Art, Dignity." *Boston Globe*, March 9, 1969, A17. [RB quoted]

Marein, Shirley. "Exhibitions: New York/Fiber." *Craft Horizons* 36 (August 1976): 48. [exh. *Printed Quilts/Quilted Prints*, Pratt Graphics Center Gallery, New York, April 9–May 20]

Margolies, Beth Anne. "Bibliographic Essay on Three African American Artists: William H. Johnson, Romare Bearden, and Jacob Lawrence." *Art Documentation* 13, no. 1 (1994): 13–17.

Marr, Warren, II. "A Second Renaissance?" *Crisis* 79 (June–July 1972): 198–203. [on expanded interest in black culture; RB mentioned, exh. *Evolution of the Afro-American Artist*, City University of New York]

"The Martin Luther King Art Exhibit." *Sepia* 18 (March 1969): 48–51. [exh. sponsored by Southern Christian Leadership Conference at MoMA; photo of visitor with *Soul Three* (as *Soul Tree*)]

Marvel, Bill. "In Art World, Too, the Word Is 'Soul': Accepted at Last, Some Blacks Spurn Museums." *National Observer*, May 11, 1970, 22. [RB quoted]

Maschal, Richard. "African-American Artists Exhibited." *Charlotte Observer*, June 21, 1989, 1D. [exh. *African American Artists, 1880–1987*, Afro-American Cultural Center; focus on RB and Charles Alston]

———. "Mint Keeps Longtime Link Alive: Old Pals David Driskell and the Late Romare Bearden Reunited through Art Exhibit." *Charlotte Observer,* August 23, 2002, 22E. [opening of two exhs., *Narratives of African American Art and Identity* and *Charlotte's Own—Romare Bearden,* at the Mint Museum]

Masheck [sic], Joseph. "New York: John Ferren, A.M. Sachs Gallery; The Bestiary, Cordier and Ekstrom Gallery; Le Corbusier, Denise René Gallery." *Artforum* 10 (April 1972): 87–90. [exh. *The Bestiary,* C&E, pp. 87–88]

Mashek, Joseph. "New York: Morris Louis, Rubin Gallery; Michael Steiner, Marlborough Gallery; Black Artists, Visual Arts Gallery." *Artforum* 9 (September 1970): 79–80. [exh. *Black Artists 1970,* Visual Arts Gallery, New York]

Master-Karnik, Paul. "South Shore Exhibit 'Comfortable'... While Black Artists Need Unifying Theme." *Staten Island Advance,* March 16, 1979, C7. [exh. of work by black artists, sponsored by Black Educators United of Staten Island, at Newhouse Gallery-North, Snug Harbor Cultural Center]

"A Matter of State." *Art Digest* 20 (July 1, 1946): 15. [exh. of watercolors sponsored by U.S. State Department]

"Medals for Artistic Mettle." *USA Today,* June 18, 1987, 2D. [National Medal of the Arts]

"A Million Visitors." *Art Digest* 21 (September 15, 1947): 16. [group exh. Minnesota State Fair, St. Paul]

Miro, Marsha. "Eye on Art." *Detroit Free Press,* May 27, 1986, 10D. [RB juries Fifth Annual Michigan Fine Arts Competition]

———. "Master of Mosaic: Ancient Art Lives on in New Mural at DIA." *Detroit Free Press,* September 16, 1986, C1–C2. [about mosaicist Costante Crovatto]

Mizell, Don. "The Evolution of a Collector: Don Mizell Talks with Alitash Kebede." *International Review of African American Art* 16, no. 2 (1999): 40–46.

Molotsky, Irvin. "National Medal of Arts Awarded to 11 by Reagan." *NYT,* June 11, 1987, C25.

Muchnic, Suzanne. "Art Review: Collecting Black Art for Its Own Sake in 'Collects.'" *Los Angeles Times,* November 7, 1987, Calendar: 1, 10. [exh. *Los Angeles Collects,* Museum of African American Art]

Murphy, Carolyn Shafer. "Dothan, Alabama: The Blount Corporate Collection." *American Art Review* 11, no. 3 (1999): 142–47. [*Back Home from up the Country* repr., discussed]

"Nanette Bearden Contemporary Dance Theatre." *BAND (Black Arts National Diaspora) Magazine* 3, nos. 1–2 (March–June 1989): 12.

"National Conference of Artists. Remarks at a White House Reception, April 2, 1980." *Weekly Compilation of Presidential Documents* 16 (April 7, 1980): 600–603. [*Igoe (1993)]

Neal, Larry. "Any Day Now: Black Art and Black Liberation." *Ebony* 24 (August 1969): 54–58, 62.

"Negro Art Awards." *Art Digest* 18 (May 1, 1944): 26. [exh. *Third Annual Exhibition,* Atlanta University, Ga.; Bearden receives honorable mention]

"The Negro Artist Comes of Age." *Art News* 43 (February 1–14, 1945): 16, 29–30. [exh. Albany Institute of History and Art; *Factory Workers* repr.]

"The Negro Artist Comes of Age." *Rhode Island School of Design Museum Notes* 4 (January 1946): (2) [not paginated]. [exh. organized by Albany Institute of History and Art, circulates]

"Negro Artists: Their Works Win Top Honors." *Life* 21 (July 22, 1946): 62–65.

"Negro Contributions." *Art Digest* 18 (April 15, 1944): 20. [exh. *American Negro Art,* Newark Museum, N.J.]

"News and Notes of Art." *NYT,* September 26, 1941, 21. [exh. McMillen, Inc., New York]

"News and Notes of Art." *NYT,* December 4, 1941, 30. [exh. McMillen, Inc., New York]

"Newsbriefs: National Medal of Arts Winners Announced." *New Art Examiner* 14 (Summer 1987): 11.

"Newsmakers: Fitzgerald, Bearden get President's Medal of Arts." *Jet* 72 (July 6, 1987): 52.

Newton, James E. "Slave Artisans and Craftsmen: The Roots of Afro-American Art." *Black Scholar* 9 (November 1977): 35–42. [*Igoe (1981)]

"Obituaries: Mrs. B.J. Bearden, Negro Leader, 52." *NYT,* September 17, 1943, 21.

O'Doherty, Brian. "Public Art and the Government: A Progress Report." *Art in America* 62 (May–June 1974): 44–49. [Works of Art in Public Places program, National Endowment for the Arts; City Council Chambers mural, City Hall, Berkeley, Calif.]

O'Meally, Robert G. "Jazz Albums as Art: Some Reflections." *International Review of African American Art* 14, no. 3 (1997): 38–47. [RB art on Wynton Marsalis covers]

O'Neill, Ann W. "The Court Files: But Does It Match the Sofa?" *Los Angeles Times,* August 23, 1998, B7. [questionable Beardens]

"On the Cover: Bicentennial Banners at Chuck Levitan, Inc." *Art Now: Gallery Guide* 6, no. 10 (Summer 1976): cover, 2. [*Prince Cinque* banner repr. on cover; commentary on banner project and exhibition]

"Painting in the South." *USA Today* 113 (November 1984), 26–31. [exh. at J. B. Speed Art Museum, Louisville, Ky.] [*Periodical Index/1983–93 (online database): citation and abstract]

Paul, April J. "Introduction à la Peinture Moderne Américaine: Six Young American Painters of the Samuel Kootz Gallery: An Inferiority Complex in Paris." *Arts Magazine* 60 (February 1986): 65–71.

"People in the News." *Encore American,* December 4, 1978, 42–43. [*Igoe (1981): RB recipient at 21st annual Freedom Fund awards dinner, Atlanta]

"Perspective in Black." *[IPS] Photo Bulletin* 70 (November 1969): 386–93. [RB, pp. 386–87]

Pierre-Noel, Lois Jones. "American Negro Art in Progress." *Negro History Bulletin* 30 (October 1967): 6–9.

Pincus-Witten, Robert. "New York: William Zorach (Paintings), Brooklyn Museum; Zorach (Sculpture), Danenberg Galleries; Black Artists of the 1930s, Studio Museum in Harlem; Joe Baer, Al Leslie, Goldowsky Gallery; June Leaf, Frumkin Gallery." *Artforum* 7 (February 1969): 64–67. [exh. *Invisible Americans, Black Artists of the '30s,* SMIH]

Pinder, Kymberly N. "'Our Father, God; Our Brother, Christ; or Are We Bastard Kin?': Images of Christ in African American Painting." *African American Review* 31 (Summer 1997): 223–33.

Pinson, Hermine D. "Geography and Identity in Melvin Dixon's 'Change of Territory.'" *Melus* 2, no. 1 (1996): 99–111.

Porter, James A. "L'art afro-américain contemporain." In *1er Festival mondial des Arts nègres. Dakar, 1–24 Avril 1966. Colloque sur l'Art nègre. Fonction et signification de l'art nègre dans la vie du peuple et pour le peuple [30 mars–8 avril]. Rapports:* Tome 1. Paris: Editions Présence Africaine, 1967, 451–68. [Organisé par la S.A.C. (Société Africaine de Culture) avec le concours de l'U.N.E.S.C.O. sous le patronage du Gouvernement du Sénégal] [RB cited as Beardon] [revised for *The Negro in American Art,* exh. cat., University of California, Dickson Art Center, Los Angeles, September 11–October 16, 1966]

———. "Contemporary Black Art." In *The Negro Impact on Western Civilization,* ed. Joseph S. Roucek and Thomas Kiernan. New York: Philosophical Library, 1970: 489–503. [*Igoe (1981)]

Powell, Richard J. "Art History and Black Memory: Toward a 'Blues Aesthetic.'" In *History and Memory in African-American Culture,* ed. Geneviève Fabre and Robert O'Meally. New York: Oxford University Press, 1994.

"Pratt Institute Gallery Exhibits 14 Afram Artists." *New York Amsterdam News,* December 4, 1976, D12. [exh. *14 Afro-American Artists*]

Raynor, Vivien. "The Church as Art Patron—Why It Doesn't Work." *NYT,* August 1, 1976, 24D. [exh. *Exhibition of Liturgical Arts,* Civic Center, Philadelphia]

———. "Contemporary Collages." *NYT,* December 19, 1986, C38. [exh. Forum Gallery]

———. "State Museum Shows Work of 'Six Black Americans.'" *NYT,* March 2, 1980, NJ24. [exh. *Six Black Americans,* State Museum, Trenton, N.J.]

Reed, Judith Kaye. "Art at Christmas along Fifty-Seventh Street: In Abstract Idiom." *Art Digest* 20 (December 1, 1945): 15. [exh. Kootz]

———. "Moderns at Kootz." *Art Digest* 20 (September 15, 1946): 11. [exh. *In the Sun,* Kootz]

Reichardt, Jasia. "Public Art Museum Notes: Museum of Fine Arts, Boston." *Art Journal* 29 (Summer 1970): 464. [exh. *Afro-American Artists: New York and Boston*]

Reinhardt, Ad. "Tree of American Art, 1946: How to Look at Modern Art in America [cartoon]." *Art News* 60 (Summer 1961): 36. [reprinted from *P.M.* (New York), 1946] [Bearden named on "tree"]

"Reviews and Previews: Congolese, Afro-American Surveys." *Art News* 66 (November 1967): 67. [exh. *Evolution of the Afro-American Artist,* City College, New York]

"Reviews and Previews: 'Homage to Jazz.'" *Art News* 45 (December 1946): 45. [exh. Kootz]

"Reviews and Previews: 'In the Sun.'" *Art News* 45 (September 1946): 43. [exh. Kootz]

"Reviews and Previews: 'Women.'" *Art News* 46 (September 1947): 39. [exh. Kootz]

"Reviews and Previews: Two Group Exhibits." *Art News* 45 (June 1946): 68. [exhs. *Building a Modern Collection* and *Modern Paintings for a Country Estate,* Kootz]

Richard, Paul. "Image Old and New in 2 Centuries of Art." *Washington Post,* June 25, 1977, B1. [exh. *Two Centuries of Black American Art,* Brooklyn Museum, New York]

Richie, Mary. "The Art of Black America." *Eastern Review* 2 (January 1977): 18–23. [*Igoe (1981)] [exh. *Two Centuries of Black American Art,* High Museum, Atlanta]

Riley, Clayton. "The Creative Black Man: Artists Struggle to Overcome Limiting Concepts of Art." *Ebony* 27 (August 1972): 134–39.

Robbins, Eugenia S., ed. "College Museum Notes: Exhibitions: Afro-American." *Art Journal* 32 (Fall 1972): 53. [RB, consultant for exh. *Roots of Afro-American Art,* Cornell University]

———. "People and Programs." *CAA Newsletter* 2 (December 1977): 6–9. [honorary doctorate, North Carolina Central University, Durham; symposium conducted by RB and Selma Burke]

Roberts, Lucille. "The Gallery of Eight." *Topic* (Washington, D.C.) 5 (1966): 21–25. [*Igoe (1981); MoMA Scrapbooks, fiche 1.80 (copy is difficult to read)] [*Topic* published by Press and Publications Service, U.S. Information Agency, for distribution in Africa]

Roberts, Sally. "Twelve Americans: Masters of Collage." *Arts* 52 (February 1978): 37. [exh. Andrew Crispo Gallery, New York]

Robinson, Louie. "Two Centuries of Black American Art." *Ebony* 32 (February 1977): 33–36, 38, 40, 42. [circulating exh.]

"Romare Bearden: 1914–1988." In *Modern Arts Criticism: A Biographical and Critical Guide to Painters, Sculptors, Photographers and Architects from the Beginning of the Modern Era to the Present,* vol. 1, ed. Joann Prosyniuk, Thomas Ligotti, Sean R. Pollock, and Laurie Sherman. Detroit: Gale Research, Inc., 1991, 107–21.

Rose, Barbara. "Black Art in America." *Art in America* 58 (September–October 1970): 54–67.

Rosenberg, Harold. "The Art World: Being Outside." *New Yorker* 53 (August 22, 1977): 83–86. [exh. *Two Centuries of Black American Art,* Brooklyn Museum]

Rosenblum, Robert. "Art: Contemporary Collage. Masterful Arrangements of Mixed Media." *Architectural Digest* 52 (May 1995): 162–67.

Rosenwald, Peter J. "An All-American Company Dances for Joy." *Wall Street Journal,* December 28, 1983, 10. [set for Talley Beatty's *The Stack-Up,* adaptation of RB's *Under the Bridge;* Beatty's *Blueshift* uses RB's "wonderful decor"]

Russell, John. "Art: Masters of Collage." *NYT,* November 25, 1977, C18. [exh. *Twelve American Masters of Collage,* Andrew Crispo Gallery, New York]

———. "Art: On Display at the Studio Museum in Harlem." *NYT,* August 30, 1985, C23. [exh. SMIH]

———. "Art: Through Dubuffet's Eyes." *NYT,* April 8, 1977, C10. [embedded review of Horace Pippin show at Dintenfass Gallery; quote from RB's cat. essay]

"Salvation Army and Art." *Today's Art* 19 (July 1971): 23. [Salvation Army annual report, published as supplement to *NYT,* with art by Bearden, others]

Schacter, Erica. "The Fine Art of Diplomacy." *Wall Street Journal,* August 27, 1998, A12. [Arts in Embassies Program]

Scheier, Rachel. "Art Interrupts Grit and Grime in N.Y. Subways." *Christian Science Monitor,* September 23, 1994, Arts: 10. [mural at Westchester Square station]

Schjeldahl, Peter. "New York Letter." *Art International* 13 (October 1969): 74–78. [concept of "black art"]

Schwartz, Therese. "The Political Scene." *Arts* 45 (March 1971): 15–16. [RB as Beardon, on Art Students League panel on Art and Politics]

Seltz, Johanna. "Black Artists Open Museum at NCCU." *Raleigh News and Observer,* November 13, 1977, V6. [*Igoe (1981): exh. *Heralds of Life: Artis, Bearden, and Burke,* North Carolina Central University]

Seltzer, Ruth. "Citing Creativity—At the Logical Place." *Philadelphia Inquirer,* November 14, 1980, 2C. ["City of Philadelphia" awards for special achievement to RB, and others, at Franklin Institute; exh. *Creativity—the Human Resource,* Franklin Institute]

S[hapiro], D[avid]. "Reviews and Previews: Group Shows: Cordier and Ekstrom's 'Bestiary.'" *Art News* 70 (February 1972): 20B.

Shepard, Richard F. "Going Out Guide: People Watching." *NYT,* July 16, 1985, C12. [exh. *The Figure in Twentieth Century Art: Selections from the Metropolitan Museum of Art,* National Academy of Design, New York]

———. "10 Painters Quit Negro Festival in Dispute with U.S. Committee." *NYT,* March 10, 1966, 29. [artists withdraw in protest from World Festival of Negro Art, Dakar, Senegal]

Shirey, David. "Art in Geneva: Afro-American Artists: A Misnomer for a Show." *International Herald Tribune,* August 3, 1971, 5. [exh. *Eight Afro-American Artists,* Rath Museum, Geneva, Switzerland] [see Henri Ghent's response: "Comment." *International Herald Tribune,* August 28–29, 1971, 7]

Shirey, David L. "An 'Afro-American' Show That Isn't." *NYT*, August 1, 1971, D17. [exh. *Eight Afro-American Artists*, Rath Museum, Geneva, Switzerland] [see Henri Ghent's response: "Art Mailbag: Protesting the Instant Experts and Their 'Black Art.'" Letter to the Editor, *NYT*, August 15, 1971, D17]

Simon, Leonard. "The American Presence of the Black Artist." *American Art Review* 3 (November–December 1976): 104–19. [exh. *Two Centuries of Black American Art*, Los Angeles County Museum of Art]

Sims, Lowery S. "African American Artists and Postmodernism: Reconsidering the Careers of Wifredo Lam, Romare Bearden, Norman Lewis, and Robert Colescott." In *African American Visual Aesthetics: A Postmodernist View*, ed. David C. Driskell. Washington: Smithsonian Institution Press, 1995, 101–20.

———. "African-American Artists' Passionate Visions: Generations Rediscovering Authenticity." *American Visions* 9 (April–May 1994): 20–26.

———. "Black Americans in the Visual Arts: A Survey of Bibliographic Material and Research Sources." *Artforum* 11 (November 1973): 66–79.

Sisson, Frederic R. "Exhibition of Negro Art Provides and Opportunity." *Providence Journal* [1942]. [exh. at Faunce House Gallery, Brown University (smaller version of show originally at Downtown Gallery, New York)] [*MoMA Scrapbooks, fiche 1.79]

Smith, Helen C. "Ailey's Bird: Dance Company Flies High in Charlie Parker Tribute." *Atlanta Journal-Constitution*, March 9, 1986, J1. [sets for Talley Beatty's *The Stack-Up*]

Smith, Marie. "Hoping to See Rusk: French Invading State Department." *Washington Post*, September 13, 1962, B8. [*Silent Valley of Sunrise* in Secretary of State Dean Rusk's office]

Smith, Roberta. "Reviews: Sol LeWitt, John Weber Gallery; Elliott Lloyd, Gary Smith, Jack Whitten, Carol Engelson, Stuart Hitch, Gary Tenenbaum, Soho Center for Visual Artists; Brice Marden, Bykert Gallery; Léger, Gerner-Heller Gallery; 'Directions in Afro-American Art,' Herbert F. Johnson Museum of Art Cornell University." *Artforum* 13 (January 1975): 60–65. [exh. *Directions in Afro-American Art* (pp. 64–65)]

Sozanski, Edward J. "4 Centuries of Southern Art." *Philadelphia Inquirer*, May 10, 1984, 4C. [exh. *Painting in the South: 1564–1980*, National Academy of Design, New York]

———. "Reflecting on Two Centuries of Black Art in America." *Philadelphia Inquirer*, August 23, 1987, G14. [exh. *Hidden Heritage: Afro-American Art, 1800–1950*, Pennsylvania Academy of Fine Arts]

Steele, Mike. "The Black Artist—At Last, Whites Are Looking." *Minneapolis Tribune* (October 13, 1968), 4. [*Igoe 1981: RB as Beardon]

"Story of Negro Art Fills the Great Hall." *The Campus* [City College (New York) student newspaper], October 19, 1967. [exh. *The Evolution of Afro-American Artists: 1800–1950*, City College] [*AAA/RB]

Stretch, Bonnie Barrett. "Art Market. New York: A Pent-Up Demand." *Art News* 93 (March 1994): 29–30. [mention RB and Henderson, *A History of African-American Artists* (1993); RB named in context of recognition of Elizabeth Catlett]

Strickland, Edward. "NY's Premier Black Gallery Marks 25th." *Bay State Banner*, April 14, 1994, 15. [Cinque Gallery 25th anniversary exhibition; brief discussion of gallery history]

Sutherland, Jane. "The Art of Cutting and Pasting." *American Artist* 61 (August 1997): 10–11.

Tallmer, Jerry. "The Writer's 'Lunch Bucket.'" *New York Post*, March 23, 1988, 31. [August Wilson's *Joe Turner's Come and Gone*, inspired by *The Millhand's Lunch Bucket*]

Tannenbaum, Judith. "U.S. Olympic Editions 1976 at Kennedy Graphics." *Arts* 49 (January 1975): 20–21.

Tapley, Mel. "About the Arts." *New York Amsterdam News*, October 6, 1973, D7. [exh. *Blacks: USA: 1973*, New York Cultural Center]

———. "About the Arts." *New York Amsterdam News*, September 14, 1974, B6. [exh. *Black Artists in the New York Scene*, Acts of Art Gallery, New York]

———. "About the Arts." *New York Amsterdam News*, March 29, 1975, D8. [exh., *Black Enterprise* Magazine offices, New York]

———. "Artists Give Our History Other Dimensions." *New York Amsterdam News*, February 12, 1994, 21, 34.

———. "Cinque Gallery: Harlem's Downtown Exposure." *New York Amsterdam News*, June 25, 1977, D2.

Taragin, Davira Spiro. "From Vienna to the Studio Craft Movement." *Apollo* n. s. 124 (December 1986): 539–44. [*Quilting Time* (p. 544)]

"Ten Black Artists Honored at White House." *NYT*, April 3, 1980, C22. [reception for National Conference of Artists]

"39 Artists to Cook for Benefit." *NYT*, June 23, 1982, C18. [Cinque Gallery]

Thomas, Barbara. "The Building, Bearden, and All That Jazz." *Arts and Activities* 117 (April 1995): 32, 68. [elementary school student project inspired by RB collages]

Thomas, Lorenzo. "Black Art/Handbills." *Callaloo* 4 (October 1978): 73–76. [reproduces handbills from Black Arts Repertory Theatre/School, including one from exh. *Black Painting: Directions* (May 30–June 30, 1965)]

"Traveling Exhibits." *Ocular* 1 (September 1976): 61–93. [RB in two circulating exhs.: *The List Art Poster Program, 1963–1973*, American Federation of Arts; *Twenty Bicentennial Banners*, SITES]

Turner, Norman. "Arts Reviews: Heads and Tails." *Arts* 52 (December 1977): 25. [exh. C&E]

[untitled clipping] *Herald Tribune*, September 8, 1946. [exh. *In the Sun*, Kootz] [AAA/RB, frame 0509, reel N/68-87]

[untitled clipping] *Herald Tribune*, December 8, 1946. [exh. *Homage to Jazz*, Kootz] [AAA/RB, frame 0509, reel N/68-87]

"The 'Vasari' Diary: Straphanger Art." *Art News* 76 (February 1977): 30. [poetry on buses project, Pittsburgh and Philadelphia; RB quoted; repr. RB illustration for poem by Kristan Hunter]

Walker, Hudson D. "Artists Equity." *Magazine of Art* 40 (May 1947): 188. [RB on board of governors]

Wallach, Amei. "Debating the Color Line. Which Comes First: Art or Identity?" *Newsday*, February 8, 1995, B4. [discusses "black" subject matter]

Walters, Beth Resler. "Charlotte: The Queen City's New Crown." *USAir Magazine* (July 1992): 53–57, 96. [*Before Dawn* mural; repr. (detail)]

Wasserman, Isabelle. "Museum of Art Plans Summer Exhibition of African Artifacts." *San Diego Union-Tribune*, May 10, 1987, E6. [RB co-curator *Perspectives: Angles on African Art*, San Diego Museum of Art, organized by Center for African Art, New York]

Weathers, Diane. "Artists and the 'Fine Art' of Survival." *Black Enterprise* 6 (December 1975): 18–24.

———. "Black Artists 'Taking Care of Business.'" *NYT*, August 19, 1973, 2: 19–20. [criticism of John Canaday's comparison of work of Vincent Smith to Romare Bearden (see Canaday, "Art: Vincent Smith's Expressive Style," *NYT*, April 21, 1973, 23)]

———. "Kaleidoscope: News Briefs on the Arts: Visuals 1974." *Black Creation* 6 (Annual 1974–75): 19–20. [RB's MoMA retrospective (1971), p. 19; exh. *Directions in Afro-American Art,* Cornell; Cinque Gallery; benefit for New York-New Jersey region of the National Conference of Artists]

Wechsler, Pat, and Ruth G. Davis. "Intelligencer: The FBI Yanks Christie's Bearden." *New York,* May 16, 1994, 11. [questionable Beardens]

Wehrwein, Austin C. "College Festival Honors Negroes." *NYT,* March 7, 1965, 80. [arts festival "Creativity and the Negro" at Rockford College, Ill.]

Werner, Alfred. "Black Is Not a Colour." *Art and Artists* 4, no. 2 (May 1969): 14–17.

———. "Letters to the Editor of the Times: Racialism in Art." *NYT,* November 23, 1968, 46. [in response to picketing at the Whitney, argues against charge of racism in the arts]

Wesley, Charles H. [?] "Editorial: The American Negro Academy, 1897–1916, and the Black Academy of Arts and Letters, 1967–1970." *Negro History Bulletin* 33 (November 1970): 156–57. [RB a founding member of Black Academy of Arts and Letters]

Whatley, JoAnn. "Bob Blackburn's Print Workshop." *ABA: A Journal of the Affairs of Black Artists* 1, no. 1 (1971): 11–13.

Willig, Nancy Tobin. "Ithaca: Anger and Heritage." *Art News* 73 (December 1974): 62–63. [exh. *Directions in Afro-American Art,* Herbert F. Johnson Museum of Art, Cornell University, Ithaca, N.Y.]

Windeler, Robert. "Modern Museum Protest Target." *NYT,* March 31, 1969, 33. [article notes a protester's sign at MoMA demanded an RB retrospective]

Winsten, Archer. "'Gloria' Fights the Mob Scene." *New York Post,* October 1, 1980, 33. [John Cassavetes film]

Wolf, Ben. "Abstract Artists Pay Homage to Jazz." *Art Digest* 21 (December 1, 1946): 15. [exh. *Homage to Jazz,* Kootz; repr. *A Blue Note*]

———. "Modern Religious Paintings Provide Exciting Charity Show." *Art Digest* 20 (January 1, 1946): 5, 31. [exh. Durand-Ruel Galleries, New York]

———. "Roy Neuberger Collection on Exhibition." *Art Digest* 20 (May 1, 1946): 14. [exh. Kootz]

———. "With Modern Accent." *Art Digest* (May 15, 1946): 17. [exh. *Building a Modern Collection,* Kootz]

Wolff, Theodore F. "Choice Art from Africa—Handsome, Fascinating." *Christian Science Monitor,* October 14, 1987, Arts and Leisure: 22. [RB as co-curator of exh. *Perspectives: Angles on African Art,* Center for African Art, New York]

———. "Rare Exhibit of Afro-American Works of Art." *Christian Science Monitor,* July 8, 1985, Arts and Leisure: 23. [exh. *20th-Century Afro-American Artists,* Newark Museum, N.J.]

———. "Traveling Afro-American Art." *Christian Science Monitor,* February 14, 1986, Arts and Leisure: 26. [exh. *Hidden Heritage: Afro-American Art, 1800–1950,* Bronx Museum, New York]

Woodson, Carter Godwin. *Journal of Negro History* 30 (April 1945): 227–28. [book review: *The Negro Artist Comes of Age,* exh. cat., Albany Institute of History and Art; RB among artists gaining recognition]

"Writers and Artists to Speak at Library." *NYT,* October 6, 1986, C15. [upcoming RB lecture at NYPL]

Yarrow, Andrew L. "Cherishing a Black Past." *NYT,* February 2, 1990, C1, C16. [survey of institutions that champion black art]

Zimmer, William. "2 Ways of Looking at the Subways." *NYT,* April 7, 1985, 14. [exh. *The Subway Show,* Lehman College Art Gallery, Bronx] [proposal for Westchester Square station mural]

PHOTOGRAPHY CREDITS

Every effort has been made to locate copyright holders for the photographs used in this book. Any omissions will be corrected in subsequent editions.

EXHIBITION PLATES

nos. 1, 5–8, 15, 19, 20, 33, 37, 42, 46, 54, 58, 68–70, 76, 81, 84, 91, 96, 110, 116, 118, 120, 124, 129, 130, 132a–c, 141: Becket Logan

no. 10: Thomas DuBrock

nos. 11, 16, 51, 59, 72, 77, 94, 103, 113: Lyle Peterzell

no. 22: Erik Gould

no. 23: ACA Galleries, New York

nos. 24, 25, 142: Lee Stalsworth

nos. 35, 111, 112, 139: Michael McKelvey

nos. 2, 36, 61, 79, 85, 102, 105: Ricardo Blanc

nos. 39, 86–90, 133, 134, 135a–p: Lorene Emerson

no. 50: © 2003 Board of Trustees, National Gallery of Art, Washington, photography by Lorene Emerson

no. 62: Ben Blackwell

nos. 65, 66, 138: Dirk Bakker

nos. 67, 140: © 2003 Board of Trustees, National Gallery of Art, Washington, photography by Ricardo Blanc

no. 75: Michael Pilla

nos. 78, 95, 123: Will Brown

nos. 83, 98: Hadley Fruits

no. 107: Courtesy Winston Wächter Mayer Fine Art, Inc., New York

nos. 99, 114, 125, 126, 128: David Ramsey

no. 121: Charles Mayer

no. 131: Steven Oliver

no. 137: Courtesy Deborah Ronnan Fine Art

FINE / *The Spaces Between*

pages 2–3: Paul Waters; figs. 1, 21, 43: David H. Ramsey; figs. 2, 42: Frank Stewart; fig. 3: Sean Busher; figs. 8, 10–16, 19, 20, 26, 29, 30, 32, 33, 34–38, 41a, b, 44, 50: Becket Logan; figs. 9, 17, 18, 23, 25: Kristin Holder; fig. 24: courtesy of Albright-Knox Art Gallery; fig. 28: courtesy of Reginald Gammon; figs. 31, 39, 40: Ricardo Blanc; figs. 45, 47: Charles Mayer; figs. 49, 51: Lorene Emerson

KENNEL / *Bearden's Musée Imaginaire*

pages 138–139: Frank Stewart; figs. 1, 4: Becket Logan; fig. 2: © Scala / Art Resource, NY; fig. 9: digital image © 2003 The Museum of Modern Art, New York; fig. 10: © Erich Lessing / Art Resource, NY; fig. 14: photograph © reproduced with the permission of The Barnes Foundation. All Rights Reserved; fig. 16: All Rights Reserved, The Metropolitan Museum of Art; fig. 18: © Erich Lessing / Art Resource, NY

ELLEH / *Bearden's Dialogue with Africa and the Avant-Garde*

pages 156–157: Frank Stewart; fig. 3: © Werner Forman / Art Resource, NY; figs. 4, 11: Becket Logan; fig. 5: Lorene Emerson; fig. 6: Sobhi al-Sharuni; fig. 10: digital image © 2003 The Museum of Modern Art, New York

FRANCIS / *Reading Bearden*

pages 172–173: Blaine Waller; copy photograph by Becket Logan; figs. 1–9, 15, 16: Becket Logan; fig. 10: Lorene Emerson

GOLER / *A Refracted Image*

pages 190–191: Frank Stewart; fig. 3: courtesy of Whitney Museum of American Art, NY; fig. 10: James Rudin

CHRONOLOGY

pages 212–213: Frank Stewart; fig. 7: All photographs by Morgan Smith; fig. 8: photographer unknown, copy photograph by Becket Logan; fig. 9: Becket Logan; figs. 10, 11, 14, 15, 20: Lorene Emerson; fig. 13: Chuck Wiese; fig. 16: digital image © 2003 The Museum of Modern Art, New York; fig. 17: copyright Chester Higgins, Jr., All Rights Reserved; fig. 19: Mary Ellen Andrews; figs. 22a, b: David Stansbury; fig. 23: © 1982, Charles Storer; fig. 24: David H. Ramsey; fig. 25: Frank Stewart, fig. 27: copyright DavidLubarsky.com

INDEX

Page numbers in *italic* type refer to illustrations. Titles of Romare Bearden's (RB) works are followed by the date of execution if given in text. Exhibitions mentioned in the essays are listed by title and venue; the chronology is selectively indexed.

C

D

K

L

M

N

U

V

W

Y

Z